Second Edition

A Comprehensive Guide to Child Psychotherapy

CHRISTIANE BREMS
University of Alaska Anchorage

WAVELAND PRESS, INC.
Long Grove, Illinois

For information about this book, contact:
Waveland Press, Inc.
4180 IL Route 83, Suite 101
Long Grove, IL 60047-9580
(847) 634-0081
info@waveland.com
www.waveland.com

This book is dedicated to Jan Strubel
and his graceful transition to adulthood.

CONTENTS

FIGURES AND TABLES

PREFACE

Welcome to the second edition of the *Comprehensive Guide to Child Psychotherapy*. If you are holding this book in your hands to decide whether to buy it, please read on; the information in this preface should help you make up your mind. If you have already purchased it, thank you and enjoy! The preparation of this text was a pleasure, and I hope that the readers of the book not only will learn, but will also discover within themselves an enthusiasm for the work described that will translate into a happy and fulfilling career.

Why I Wrote This Book

This book represents the culmination of my personal experiences as a psychotherapist for children, a supervisor of individuals who wish to learn this skill, and a teacher who has introduced graduate students to the principles and concepts of conducting child psychotherapy. It presents a comprehensive metatheoretical approach to psychotherapy with children age 3 years to approximately 12 years. It discusses psychotherapy with children for novices and advanced professionals in the mental health field; thus, it provides thorough introductions, definitions of key concepts, and outlines to clarify material.

A *Comprehensive Guide to Child Psychotherapy* was developed to address several concerns I had developed over the years about existing books written about child therapy. The most important features are as follows:

■ The book differs from others in its pragmatic approach to psychotherapy with children. It is a down-to-earth reference that can be helpful not only to students, but also to seasoned professionals. It does not get lost in the intricate details of research but is nevertheless research-based. It provides tables and figures that quickly summarize material that is important enough to be at a clinician's fingertips.

■ The book differs from others in its applied nature. It was written as a companion to the actual process of treatment with a child. The sequencing of chapters mirrors the sequence of events in an actual treatment situation, making it possible for clinicians to read along in the book as the therapy of a child evolves.

■ The book differs from others in its theoretical complexity. It does not (or at least tries very hard not to) push any single approach to psychotherapy. Instead, it provides a thorough metatheoretical foundation for assessment and conceptualization that is conducive to tailored and individualized treatment that is not specific to the clinician, but rather to the child who is being treated.

■ The book differs from others in its diversity of presented techniques. Because it is not founded in a single theoretical system or based on a single therapeutic approach, the book can be broad and creative in its presentation of techniques, helping clinicians to recognize the great variety of possibilities that can be explored to help children and their families grow in treatment.

■ The book differs from others in its ease of presentation. Given that it was conceived as a reference for novices and experts alike, the book was written in a clear and jargon-free style that makes it easy to read and understand. There are no pretensions, and all aspects of the book were developed to make learning as easy as possible.

For Whom I Wrote This Book

The book is written for students and professionals alike. It has a certain level of sophistication that requires some prior exposure to mental health training. Thus, in an academic setting, it is not likely appropriate for undergraduate students, but rather for graduate students with prior courses in basic psychotherapy or counseling skills. Despite its advanced nature, the text makes ample use of features that facilitate learning, as well as summarizations and illustrations that appeal not only to the novice but also to practicing professionals. Case examples are provided to bring the material alive and to help the reader better understand the more complex points that are being made in the text.

The book targets any professional or budding professional in a mental health discipline that concerns itself with the mental health of children and their families. Thus, students and practitioners in the following fields should find the *Comprehensive Guide* useful:

■ Clinical or counseling psychology
■ Counseling or counselor education
■ Clinical social work
■ Marriage and family counseling
■ Child psychiatry
■ Psychiatric nursing

What I Cover in the Book

The book, written as a companion to an actual therapy with a child, is laid out in such a way as to reflect the normal sequencing of events that a clinician encounters over the course of treatment. The book walks its reader through all preliminary and crucial steps of therapy in four distinct sections of the text:

■ In the first section, the *Comprehensive Guide* prepares the clinician to make decisions about the actual environment in which she or he will work with children, ranging from discussions of the physical layout of a clinic to specific objects in the therapy room. The book then provides thorough overviews of relevant issues in ethics, development, and multicultural psychotherapy.

■ In the second section, the *Comprehensive Guide* walks the child therapist through the initial stages of intake, assessment, and conceptualization before moving on to therapeutic issues.

■ In the third section, the *Comprehensive Guide* focuses on the therapeutic process and specific techniques in the middle stages of psychotherapy.

■ In the fourth section, the *Comprehensive Guide* ends with a thorough discussion of termination issues.

The conceptual system underlying the book is theoretically complex while being utterly applied and pragmatic. The *Comprehensive Guide* draws heavily on developmental, interpersonal, family systems, and self-psychological schools of thought. It integrates the core components of all of these approaches in a clear and concise manner that results in a conceptualization for child treatment that is both complex and practical. Not surprisingly, the book emphasizes the need for intensive assessment to precede conceptualization and treatment planning, which will lead to the use of a variety of techniques as dictated by the needs of each individual child and family. The techniques covered in the text include everything from simple play to art, storytelling, behavior modification, and parent education. Although combining strategies of these diverse approaches may sound incompatible upon first reading, it is actually a preferable way of conducting child psychotherapy. Literature exists that is supportive of psychodynamic and behavioral approaches, and clinical experience has demonstrated that a combination of the two schools of thought is highly successful in creating change in children. Specifically, a comprehensive and integrating approach will avoid the mistake of disregarding important features in a child's life. Strict adherence to one approach of looking at children is simplistic and disregards the realities of modern life. Children rarely grow up in the vacuum of a nuclear family anymore, nor is the family an easily understood system. Children are profoundly affected by their larger environments and culture, and all of these factors must be considered. Similarly, children are not merely the product of cause-and-effect or reinforcement contingencies. Human interactions are much more complex than such a strict behavioral approach would suggest. Nevertheless, behavioral strategies are a critical piece in the treatment of children.

What I Chose Not to Do

This book is not to be mistaken as a text on child psychotherapy research. It does not cover specifics about matching diagnoses with treatment approaches. Although such considerations are beginning to appear in the child psychotherapy literature and are no doubt important and valuable, they are beyond the scope of this book. Here, the reader is merely introduced to the basic and practical principles of direct clinical work with children. Once these basic principles have been mastered, the clinician is encouraged to move on to research-focused texts that cover specific findings with regard to evaluating the appropriateness of various family or child interventions in relation to specific presenting concerns or diagnoses.

Old and New Features of the Second Edition

It is as important to talk about what is the same in the second edition of *A Comprehensive Guide to Child Psychotherapy* as it is to talk about what has changed. The second edition has not changed the format of the book; it continues to speak to both the student and the practicing professional; it is still an excellent companion over the course of a therapy for children; it still has many tables and figures for easy reference; and it still remains theoretically complex, suggesting an individualized approach to the treatment of each child with whom a clinician works. Thus, all the features that made the first edition of the *Comprehensive Guide* popular among its readers have been maintained.

To address the fact that the *Comprehensive Guide* was aging rapidly at a time of many changes and advances in the field of child therapy, changes were needed as well. The revisions for the second edition involved several major alterations that were chosen carefully to bring the book into the new millennium. As such, the following primary modifications were accomplished:

- All diagnostic information was updated to be consistent with DSM-IV-TR, and several new descriptions of disorders not previously included were added.

- The section on assessment instruments was brought up to date. If revisions had been made to an instrument, this information was added; if new instruments emerged that met one of the purposes deemed essential to child treatment, they were included; if tests had become obsolete or outdated, they were deleted; websites for publishing companies were added.

- More information was added about how best to prepare parents, and through them their children, for an intake interview and course of therapy. The importance of working positively with parents alongside the child who is being seen in individual treatment is stressed.

- Legal and ethical issues were updated as needed, and a new template for an informed consent was included to reflect the enormous changes in the field secondary to managed care and other third party reimbursement issues.

- All references were updated as relevant and needed. New editions of books previously cited were incorporated and referenced, new research findings as gleaned from professional journals were perused and presented as appropriate, and obsolete material was deleted.

- A new index was prepared, separating subject and author key words.

- Lists of tables and figures were added to help the reader move around the text more easily.

I hope these changes will please instructors who have been loyal to the first edition of the *Comprehensive Guide* and will serve to entice those who have never seen the book before to pick it up and read it. I would love to hear from you, both good and bad, as it is my goal to make this book better and better as it grows and evolves over the years. The book has now moved from its childhood to its adolescence—a happy evolution indeed, with hopes for an even more sophisticated adulthood in the future.

Happy reading!

Acknowledgments

I wish to express my gratitude

to my life partner, best friend, and valued colleague, Mark Johnson, who not only contributed valuable chapters to this book, but also patiently endured my preoccupations and busy schedule and lovingly supported my every effort as I wrote this text;

to my students who were willing to read portions of this book as it was being developed, who listened to and expressed appreciation about my lectures, and who challenged me with their cases as I supervised their work;

to my small clients, who often opened new worlds for me in my attempts to help them, who trusted me and allowed me into their lives, and who helped me crystalize many of the ideas expressed in this volume;

to my own teachers and supervisors over the years who have contributed to my growth, my love for my profession, and my enthusiasm about my work;

to the reviewer of this edition, Thomas M. Krapu;

to my family, Rosemarie and Bernherd Brems; Gabriele, Fish, and Jan Strubel; and Lina, Carol, and Rudi Hilsheimer, who provided a nurturing and safe home for me in which to grow and mature, build the self-confidence to become a psychologist, and form the strengths to become a teacher;

and to my friends Mike Mills and Rose Catalanotti, who offered their technical assistance during the final days of this revision.

Thank you all.

CHAPTER

1

The Environment and the Materials of Child Therapy

By choosing this book, the reader clearly has made a decision to work with child clients. As such a decision is difficult and has many implications, this book was written to help the reader in the process of becoming a child therapist. Children are a unique therapy population in that all therapists who choose to work with children have childhood as an experience in their own background. It is often claimed that therapists are most successful and empathic in working with clients who have concerns that the therapist herself or himself has encountered at some point in life. The only population of which it can easily be said that all therapists have experienced life from its perspective is that of children. All therapists have been there; however, having been a child, or even having children of one's own, does not suffice to qualify a therapist to work with children in psychotherapy. There are too many issues to be aware of, too many blind spots unknown about, and too many preconceived notions that may interfere. To think that having been a child will help a therapist to understand all children better is just as unrealistic as believing that being a woman automatically makes one a better therapist to work with women or being a man makes one a better therapist for men. In fact, it is often with exactly the population with which the therapist feels a special affinity or understanding that preexisting beliefs, values, and attitudes enter the treatment processes in an uncontrolled, unmonitored manner.

Further, even the best training and experience in working with adults will not prepare the therapist for interventions with children. Children are unique and different from adults in a variety of ways that can prove to be a challenge to the therapist. They are at a different developmental level and thus have different tasks to master and take different approaches to problem solving, living, and setting priorities. Their language is not as well developed, nor are their cognition or emotional expression and perception. A child therapist not only has to understand these differences from an intellectual, or knowledge, point of view, but also has to realize that these differences alter the type of therapist-client relationship that will develop. Special sensitivities are necessary, and verbal interchanges are no longer primary in the therapy process, as they are in the treatment of adults. Often the therapist has to rely on nonverbal exchanges to understand the child, to communicate understanding back to the child, to help the child process difficult issues, and to work through difficult transferences and countertransferences. This use of nonverbal communication is often a significant challenge to adults, especially bright and highly educated adults, who have been taught for many years that verbal communication is the panacea for most problems that arise.

Consequently, it is extremely important for all therapists who work with children to do so only after they have informed themselves about the process of child therapy as much as possible. This book is designed to help with this process by outlining a number of preliminary issues involved in the work with children before moving on to the discussion of assessment and treatment. The first, and perhaps most important, consideration in treating children has to do with the physical plant in which therapy is conducted. Although a simple office suffices for most work with adults, children have special needs that are directly related to their uniqueness as less verbal and more exploratory human beings. Hence, it is important to assess whether the environment that is available to the therapist is one that can be rendered conducive to the conduct of child therapy.

For clients, entering a clinic is much like entering the house of a new friend. Clients will look at furnishings, artwork, cleanliness, and layout to glean information about the people working and living in this environment. Judgments may be made on the basis of these first impressions, and it is certainly worthwhile for the enhancement of rapport to keep the clinic as inviting as possible. It is not important that the furnishings and equipment be shiny, brand-new, or even expensive. They merely must be arranged in such a way as to communicate privacy, safety, and caring to the children and their families. The environment is best if it is clean and warm and obviously designed with children in mind. Entering a psychotherapy center that is disheveled, dirty, or dark may communicate a lack of caring and concern that could leave the child frightened and the parent concerned. Of course, excellent work can potentially be done in such an environment, but if disarray and negative atmospheres can be avoided, it is preferable to do so to set the best stage for beginning the work with children and their families.

There are a number of considerations with regard to clinic design and equipment. None is written in stone, but all are to be carefully weighed before making the decision to begin seeing children. These considerations include the general physical layout and design of the clinic, the arrangement of the waiting area, decisions about appropriate places and cleanup arrangements for child therapy, and the play therapy room itself with all its necessary play or activity materials and furnishings. In pondering each of these facets of child therapy, there are four factors that appear to have been agreed upon by child therapists (e.g., Coppolillo, 1987; Landreth, 1991, 2000; Simmons, 1987; Spiegel, 1996) that are foremost on the clinician's mind: the atmosphere and safety of the setting, the child's and family's privacy, the child's and therapist's comfort, and the convenience of all individuals involved. All four will be addressed here for each of the considerations that go into successful clinic design. For all of the considerations, optimal design and solutions are discussed. These optimal conditions are not supposed to keep committed clinicians from attempting to make less optimal conditions work. It is surprising how well clinics can function under less than the best conditions. Optimal conditions merely give the clinician something to strive for if the flexibility for change in the physical environment should arise. Less than optimal conditions are also described below to illustrate how with some ingenuity and tenacity, even difficult situations can be mastered. However, as the examples will show, there is always the danger that something will go wrong at the wrong time in treatment when the conditions are not as good as they could be.

The Physical Layout and Design of the Clinic

The optimal layout of a clinic will address foremost safety and privacy, but also comfort and convenience. If sacrifices have to be made, they should be made in descending order, safety being most important and convenience least important. Safety is an extremely important feature in working with children. It has many therapeutic implications and plays strongly into the psychotherapeutic process and relationship. Safety is often something that children who present for treatment do not experience in their everyday lives. Therefore, to provide a corrective experience, safety must be ascertained as completely as possible in the therapy setting. If a child does not feel safe in her or his therapy room and clinic, uninhibited unfolding of the child's necessary therapy work might not occur.

Safety is important inside the therapy room itself, but also with regard to where the therapy room is placed in the clinic. Clinics are often located within office buildings, rather than being a building in and of themselves. This provides an excellent extra safety feature that can be used in choosing which room will serve as the children's therapy room. Specifically, the therapy room proper is safest if it does not have a door that opens to the outside of the clinic itself. The door should always face into the clinic and even then should be chosen in such a manner as to maximize the distance that must be traveled from the play therapy room door to the exit door of the agency. On the way to the exit door, the child should have to pass the reception area.

Although play therapy is generally confined to the play therapy room, it does happen that children "escape" because of the overwhelming psychological tasks and emotions that often face them, especially early in the therapeutic work before the relationship with the therapist has solidified and presents safety in and of itself. In such an instance, it is a relief for the therapist to know that the child not only will have to travel quite a distance to get to the exit door, but also will have to pass by the reception area, so that she or he cannot leave the clinic undetected. For instance, one child, who had been brought for treatment upon the recommendation of a teacher because of suicidal ideation and severe social withdrawal, managed to escape the therapy room of a clinic that was less than optimally designed. Not only was the therapy room located next to the exit door, but it also allowed leaving without being seen by the receptionist, and the exit door faced into a busy street. This child's escape presented a major problem to his safety and certainly was dramatized further by the fact that one of his prior suicide attempts had consisted of running in front of a moving car. This example demonstrates that even the most careful of therapists must consider physical clinic layout, as a desperate child can manage to do what appears to be the impossible.

In considering floor plans, placement of the waiting area must be addressed as well. In working with children, there is almost always an adult who will be waiting for the duration of the session. Placement of a waiting room next to the therapy room may result in the child's questioning of her or his privacy, especially if soundproofing is poor. For example, in the therapy of one 12-year-old girl, the poor design of the center resulted in great hesitation on her part to open up to her therapist. Several sessions were spent dealing with issues of privacy and confidentiality. It was very difficult for the therapist to deal with the child on these issues, as the therapist herself had doubts about the appropriateness of the center's design.

Of course, there are always exceptions to rules. For instance, one 3-year-old child, who was referred because of severe abandonment fears secondary to her custody and visitation arrangements, had such a hard time separating from her parents during the first few sessions that she had to peek out of the therapy room door when particularly difficult themes emerged in her play. For her, the faulty design of the clinic, where the waiting area was placed immediately adjacent to the therapy room, presented a saving grace that ultimately resulted in this child's ability to tolerate being apart from her parents, as she knew that they were always just outside the door.

Placement of the therapy room must also consider where the noise that is unavoidable in the treatment of children is least intrusive or disruptive for others. In one university clinic, the play therapy room was located directly next to a classroom that was not actually a part of the center. This therapy room was used for a children's play therapy group every Monday afternoon. As the children began to feel safe and comfortable in the therapy environment, noise levels often escalated, especially around ending time. Complaints from students in the adjacent classroom quickly began being registered by the clinic supervisor. Finally, during one particularly noisy group session, the instructor of the class that was held at the same time as the group opened the therapy room door and intruded into the safety of the therapy process. She had waited as long as she could and had reached her own limit of what she could tolerate for her students. Needless to say, her decision to intrude had definite repercussions for the therapy of these children.

The previous example also points toward a larger issue of privacy. Often, clinics are located in larger office buildings, university buildings, or other larger structures. Although this arrangement increases safety, it may compromise privacy and confidentiality. Certainly, no clinic should operate in such a manner that a complete stranger can proceed through an entire clinic and into a therapy room without being stopped. But on a lesser scale, clinic designers must also be aware that glass doors into a clinic that allow an easy look into the clinic's waiting room are a violation of privacy for the individuals who are waiting for their therapist. The absence of bathrooms or water fountains inside the clinic present equal challenges to privacy, as clients should be able to access these facilities without having to leave the center itself. It is not uncommon for people to cry during treatment and to search for a bathroom where they may put themselves together again physically before they reenter the outside world. The repercussions of the absence of a bathroom inside the clinic are obvious.

Further, although children should not generally have to use the bathroom during their session, occasionally this cannot be avoided. Therefore, a bathroom should not require the crossing of the waiting area, should be easily accessible, and should be designed with children in mind. In all of these design features, the first one is the most important. As was mentioned earlier, usually a parent is waiting for the child in the waiting area. The crossing of this area and the contact with the parent in the middle of a session may interfere with the therapy process. Similarly, although there is little need for a child to ever leave the therapy room for a drink of water, preferably there would be more than one water fountain so that one can be used by people in the waiting room and a different one by those in the therapy rooms. If there is only one water fountain, it should be most easily accessible from the waiting area.

The size of the therapy room needs to be considered as well. It appears that a 120 to 150 square foot area works very well for most individual therapies with children. A room that will also be used for group therapy with children might need to be slightly larger, perhaps up to 250 or even 300 square feet, without being so large that individual treatment is hampered. A very large room can be just as difficult to manage as a very small room. Although children, especially in groups, might need personal space to diffuse emotions, there should not be so much space that the child has to be chased around during treatment. If the choice is between a room that is slightly too large and one that is slightly too small, it may be preferable to use the smaller room. It is easier to contain a child in a smaller room, and the atmosphere is generally warmer and more conducive to self-disclosure. However, children do need space to be active, so a room that is too confining or claustrophobic could inhibit the child.

Some thought needs to be given to windows. Windows can help to make a very small room appear larger, yet they may present a source of distraction. A room without windows will minimize distractions from the external environment but may appear closed-in and threatening. A good compromise appears to be to have a few windows equipped with blinds that can be drawn if necessary. Blinds are important not only to screen out distractions, but also to maintain privacy and confidentiality, especially if the clinic is on a first floor or if children are being seen when it is dark outside. Activities in a lighted room will easily be visible when it is dark outside. Windows in a therapy room should either not open at all or open only so far that no child could fall out.

Beyond the general layout of the clinic and its rooms, there is the consideration of design and furnishings. These two features of the environment will greatly influence the atmosphere of the clinic. A clinic where children are seen must be furnished and designed in such a way that children feel safe and welcome. Breakable knickknacks, inaccessible bookshelves, and lack of children's reading or activity materials in the waiting area all communicate that the clinic is not truly responsive to the special needs of children. Furniture must be sturdy enough to survive being climbed on, water fountains low enough to be reached even by the occasional 3-year-old, and carpets sufficiently water resistant and stainproof to endure spills and dirty shoes without problems. Artwork must be tasteful and versatile enough for a clientele of a large age range. A separate children's area can solve the problem of appropriate artwork selection and entertainment while waiting.

The Waiting Area

Design and furnishing are most obvious in the waiting area, and it is here that the tone of welcome for children is set. Child-size furniture, children's activity materials, and children's books and magazines should be provided. In choosing children's books, therapists may include some of the many existing picture books that have specific therapeutic value (e.g., Blomquist and Blomquist, 1990; Cain, 2000; Crary, Katayama, and Steelsmith, 1996; Marcus and Marcus, 1990). The area has to be safe and sturdy, as well as relatively soundproof so that waiting children will not disrupt therapy in adjacent therapy rooms. There is some controversy about what materials should be available in a waiting area for children. Some therapists endorse televisions or radios, because the noise generated from these devices will mask any sounds emanating from therapy rooms (see Coppolillo, 1987). Others believe that televisions are strictly off limits. This has to be an individual decision of each clinic's staff. Any clinic rules are best posted in the waiting room, clearly visible to all individuals using it. The only such rule that appears quite universally enforced in an environment serving children is that of no smoking.

In addition to designing the waiting area with children's use of the area in mind, clinic personnel also must remember that the waiting area will be used by parents waiting for their children. Privacy must be guaranteed for the waiting parent, as well as for the working child. A waiting area that is too close to the therapy room may interfere with the child's therapy or may result in a very concerned parent. For instance, the 3-year-old child with abandonment fears mentioned above became very spontaneous and uninhibited in her doll play during one session. She pretended to cry and be sad in her play, doing an excellent job of mimicking these feelings. In fact, she did such an excellent job, that her mother, who was waiting in the adjacent, too closely located waiting room, became very concerned and knocked on the therapy room door to ascertain that her child was fine.

Appropriate Places and Clean-Up Arrangements

Before moving on to a discussion of the therapy room itself, it is necessary to detour to some related topics, namely, the decisions about where treatment with children is conducted and who cleans up once a session is completed. The most common approach to the former, is to restrict therapy to the therapy room. However, there are clinicians who have presented arguments for the opposite (see Landreth, 2000; Simmons, 1987). They believe that there may be occasions when therapy with children can be conducted in cafeterias, basements, attics, or even outside (Landreth, 2000). Such decisions may be driven by therapeutic goals, such as generalization of treatment progress, or by limitations of the clinic, which might not be equipped with a play therapy room per se. Low-income clinics are likely to have to strike compromises that result in the use of creative and unconventional therapy spaces. Good work can still be done in less than optimal spaces. However, in using such spaces, the clinician has to pay attention to the safety and privacy issues discussed previously. The decision to move the therapy out of the therapy room has to be one that is made only after careful consideration of the potential advantages and disadvantages. It is important to discuss liability issues with parents and insurance carriers before moving therapy out of a safely confined and defined space.

Beyond the privacy and safety issues, there are also treatment issues that must be pondered. Specifically, it is questionable whether a public place, such as a playground, will allow for the development of a therapeutic relationship wherein the child will be fully uninhibited and spontaneously self-disclosing. The possibilities of escaping difficult emotions and topics in public places or wide-open spaces are almost endless, allowing for the possibility of a dilution of treatment that may present too large a trade-off for the advantages inherent in the choice of such alternative settings. Finally, the use of a well-defined and circumscribed space will allow for the development of a special feeling or atmosphere that may never be created if the setting varies and has undefined and unclear boundaries. One rule of thumb may be to avoid the use of alternative spaces except if there is an overriding therapeutic need for a child to develop gross motor skills, if generalization of treatment progress calls for it, or if a child tends to be so highly agitated around the ending of a session that she or he needs to run or act out physically in some way other than what can be managed safely in the therapy room to calm herself or himself before being able to return to the parent in the waiting room. However, even then, it is prudent to stay within parameters that the therapist can manage comfortably and safely. In fact, even therapists who do use settings other than the therapy room can be firm about setting physical boundaries and limits in these alternative environments.

Sometimes the decision is not one of using the play therapy room or an alternative larger environment, but one of using a general therapy office because of lack of a designated play therapy room. The absence of space reserved for children's work does not have to be entirely prohibitive of doing play therapy with children. Although it may be challenging to approximate the atmosphere of a play therapy room in a regular office or alternative space, this can be done. If the use of a regular office is necessary, it is best to designate a particular area in that office as the play therapy area and to inform the child of the (somewhat imaginary) boundary that runs through the room. The equipment placed in this section of the room will be quite comparable to the equipment that is stocked in a regular therapy room, though there may be somewhat fewer materials and perhaps more limitations in how some materials may be used. For instance, whereas Play-Doh may be used quite freely in a special therapy room with plastic tile floors or washable carpet, the same material may be present in the general office, but its use might be restricted to the tabletop.

With regard to design and furnishing, the cautions that were applicable to the waiting area in a children's clinic apply to the therapist's office or other alternative space that doubles as a child therapy area. Specifically, breakable objects are best avoided, carpets must be easily cleanable, wallpaper washable, and furniture sturdy. Personal items are generally kept to a minimum to avoid the confounding of transferences that tend to arise in child clients. Photographs of family members and pictures of or by other children should especially be avoided. Artwork in the children's area is best if appropriate to children, and materials need to be easily accessible for them.

Regardless of where the treatment takes place, a decision must be made about who is responsible for cleaning the therapy room or area after its use. There are differing philosophies about this issue. Some therapists believe that a person should be hired specifically for that purpose so that neither the therapist nor the child has to become preoccupied during the session about cleanup (Ginott, 1964). This approach appears to bear at least two obvious problems. First and therapeutically, it might not be realistic to suggest to a child that she or he can create messes or disarray without having to take some responsibility for cleanup. Second and pragmatically, such an approach would suggest either that a cleanup person has to be available immediately after each session with a child or that the room is cleaned only once a day, making it impossible for more than one child to be seen per day.

The second approach asks for the therapist to clean after the child client has left. This practice can present problems in several ways. First, again the child is not asked to take responsibility for her or his actions in the therapy room. Second, the therapist might become preoccupied with having to clean messes that are being created, thus possibly inhibiting the spontaneous unfolding of play activity in the child. Third, the therapist might resent having to do this task for the child and might feel rushed if cleaning has to take place in the brief ten minutes between two consecutive sessions.

The third approach is one in which child and therapist cooperate in the cleanup of the room during the last few minutes of each session. This approach is recommended because it represents the highest level of realism in that the child is held responsible for her or his actions by having to help deal with their consequences. Further, it allows for an additional act of cooperation and positive interchange between the child and the therapist as they engage in the activity together. It is often quite a new experience for a child to be helped freely by an adult. Finally, in this approach, the room is in order when a session is over, and the therapist does not have to be concerned about the readiness of the room for her or his next appointment. If this approach is chosen, it must be introduced to the child during the first session to clearly delineate what is expected of the child and prepare the child for responsible interaction.

The Therapy Room

Once a therapist has chosen to do therapy with children, has determined the best location of a therapy room within a clinic, and has decided upon a space for the work with children, decisions must be made about furnishings and equipment to be used in this space. Furnishings are quite straightforward and generally agreed upon. Guidelines for the types of toys and materials are equally clear and straightforward.

Furnishings

Preferably, the room will contain a child-size table with at least two chairs: one for the child and one for the therapist. If children's groups will be conducted in the room as well, extra chairs need to be available to create space for all group members. Cabinets along the bottom third of the walls of the room are very useful for the storage of toys. Some of these cabinets may be lockable for materials to which the therapist wants to have access if necessary but may want to reserve only for a few children. Some of the cabinets should not have any doors at all, displaying the materials contained within them for easy surveying of the available toys. Such open spaces in a cabinet can also serve as an excellent hiding place for the child, who needs to withdraw during the course of a session. If shelves are placed sufficiently low, this can be quite safe. Shelves that are high up, yet accessible to the child, can be quite dangerous, as a child may decide to climb into them; therefore, such shelves should be avoided. The main characteristic of cabinets and shelves is their accessibility for all ages of children. To truly give the child a choice of materials so that the choice may be used for interpretive purposes, the child must have free access to all materials. Such unlimited access also encourages autonomy, creativity, and trust on the child's part.

Floor coverings in children's therapy rooms should be safe but easily cleanable. Stain-resistant carpet or soft vinyl tile is best. Hard tile can present problems and tends to give the room a cold atmosphere. Walls should be washable, and the color should be cheerful yet relatively neutral. It is important to remember that it is the child who should set the mood for the session, not the environment. Light paints, such as ivory or peach, are sufficiently bright yet neutral to allow for this. Wallpapers are generally not recommended, for the same reasons that artwork should not be displayed. Both introduce content that is unnecessary and that may affect the child's mood externally.

Some play rooms have a sink. If this is so, hot water should be avoided to prevent burns. Clinics without running water in the play room can easily deal with this problem by having a plastic tub with a secure lid that contains fresh cold water. This will accommodate children who want to play in the water or who want to be sure to wash their hands or faces in the course of or after a particular play activity. For instance, one young child was very hesitant to use the sandtray for several sessions. She would stick part of her hand or foot into the tray, then withdraw it and inspect it for dirt. She became much more at ease with the use of sand when she was made aware that a tub of water and a towel were available if she needed them. Ultimately, this led to her willingness to use the sand freely and creatively—and, after a while, even without cleaning herself so meticulously after each use. This ability represented significant progress in her therapy as it showed that some of her inhibitions that had been overcome to make her affect more appropriate for the 4 years of age that she was. A water tub in a room without sink need not be large; in fact, it should not be too large so that spills can be managed easily. One size that has been found successful is a tub that is approximately 5 inches deep and 10 inches square.

Sandtrays or sandboxes are another common feature in play therapy rooms. Again, not all clinics come equipped with this, and a very large plastic tub with a tight-fitting lid can easily be substituted. One size that has been found very useful is approximately 7 inches deep, 2 feet wide, and 3 feet long. This tub holds enough sand or rice that it is too heavy for most children to overturn and that spills stay small. If a sandtray or sandbox is available, so should be a small broom and dust pan for the child to be able to clean up spills. Further, a water sprayer must be handy to be able to wet sand to avoid dust that can irritate children's eyes or other mucous membranes. An assortment of toys should be available for use in the sandtray; this will be addressed in detail later. Finally, a free-standing or mounted easel and chalkboard will facilitate drawing activities and should be easily accessible and fully equipped with paints and chalks.

General Guidelines for the Selection of Materials

A foremost consideration in the selection of toys is safety. Often, children come to therapy from very unsafe and disorderly environments. It is hoped that the therapy can be used at least in part as a corrective experience in which the child can learn that there are safe and orderly places that can be used to put a life back in order. Safety and orderliness can be expressed through the equipment of the therapy room. Specifically, all materials that are freely accessible should be safe for children of all ages who might choose to use them. All materials should be as sturdy as possible and should be in good working order; damaged toys should be removed, repaired, or replaced. Toys should be such that a child does not have to worry about breaking them through regular use. In other words, very fragile or meticulous toys will defeat the purpose of the therapy room. There are some materials, such as paper and crayons, that need to be replenished from time to time, and it is best to keep a supply handy so that this can be done immediately when the need arises. Paper can be easily obtained in large rolls from local newspaper companies. They are generally willing to make tax-deductible donations to clinics of unused newsprint that is too short to be of use in the printing of papers. Other materials, such as Play-Doh, clay, and paints, will spoil over time and must be replaced. Again a supply should be kept handy.

Toys and materials need to be chosen carefully. As Landreth (1991) points out, "toys and materials should be selected, not collected" (p. 117). In other words, therapists should not accumulate toys randomly, but rather should choose toys according to a meaningful, therapeutically relevant rationale. Toys and play are a child's language and primary means of communication. They represent the tools and work of a child and thus are serious business for children. They can be used to facilitate interaction or to encourage solitary play.

They can be used to communicate encouragement or inhibition, and they can be presented in such a manner as to stimulate or squelch creativity. All of these features must be on the therapist's mind while equipping the room.

Although it is still true that there are few researched guidelines for the selection of therapy room materials (Ginott, 1960), child clinicians have developed several guidelines and lists of materials that have proven quite useful in the selection of toys. First, Ginott (1960) presented an approach wherein toys are selected for one of several purposes. Specifically, he suggested that a therapy room have toys that facilitate the therapeutic relationship, toys that allow for catharsis of affects and needs, toys that can enhance the development of insight, and materials that allow for defense, especially sublimation. Landreth (2000) suggests that toys should be chosen to facilitate emotional and creative expression and play, to stimulate exploration and interest in a child in a nonverbal manner, to allow for nonstructured activity, and to allow for their use without having to worry about breakage or damage. Coppolillo (1987) suggests keeping toys to a minimum to be sure that "toys are [merely] for the purpose of offering vehicles for expression of the child, not dazzling or seducing him [sic]" (p. 25). Thus, the final choices will reflect very personal decisions of the therapist. But the overriding consensus appears to be that the toys have to facilitate the unfolding of therapeutic process, not the entertainment of the child. The diversity, yet convergence of opinions, about the selection of play room materials results in several points of consensus that a therapist might want to consider in selecting materials.

Self-Expression.   First, there appears to be a consensus in the literature that toys must facilitate a child's self-expression. This self-expression is to be as unstructured as possible. Thus, generally, toys that have a prescribed use, such as board games or theme toys (e.g., Star Wars figures or Power Rangers figures) tend to be avoided. Instead, toys that allow for a free flow of self-expression without being limited by prescribed rules are preferred. For instance, Play-Doh can be used for in successful self-expression in a nonverbal manner that is very easily understood by the therapist. One 8-year-old boy who had presented to treatment as a very angry and aggressive child quickly chose Play-Doh as his primary mode of therapeutic self-expression. He used the medium to create exploding volcanoes when he was angry, biting "wiener dogs" when he felt he had to defend himself against external intrusions from his family, or airplanes when he wanted to escape difficult situations. He found a literally unlimited number of uses for Play-Doh and very successfully expressed his needs and affects through this medium.

Creativity.   The second consensus that appears to emerge from the literature is that the materials need to stimulate creativity. Self-expression and creativity are difficult to differentiate and often go hand in hand. It is possible for a child to be self-expressive without being creative; however, it does not appear possible for a child to be creative without also being self-expressive. Thus, materials that enhance creativity also tend to work well in the area of self-expression. Further, creativity and the development thereof are likely to affect self-esteem and self-confidence positively and may therefore be desirable in that sense as well. The creative use of several wooden toy trucks that were available in the therapy room was demonstrated by one 10-year-old girl. She used them as barricades as well as missiles, showing creativity and functional flexibility in the use of the toy, in addition to expressing her feelings of having been violated and hurt. Pride in her accomplishments in the use of the toys also appeared to be a strong factor in her repeated choice of these materials.

Societal Consensus.   A third consensus emerges with regard to toys that carry a societal consensus about their appropriate use. Toys in this category are theme toys that are patterned after TV shows or movies, athletic gear such as baseball bats and balls, and board games. Any toy that has a rigidly prescribed use tends not to work very well in the therapy setting, as it provides the child with an opportunity to play without working, that is, without being creative or self-expressive. The presence of a Snoopy doll in one therapy room resulted in the acting out of a Charlie Brown Christmas television special by a child who was very hesitant to use the materials in the room to self-disclose. He quickly found the toys that should not have been in the therapy room to begin with and easily used them to hide himself from the therapist. Similarly, the often-used "bobo doll" appears to be of little interpretive value because it is very much equated with a punching bag. Thus, if a child hits a bobo doll, what is really communicated? Probably not much beyond the fact that the child can correctly identify a toy that has a definite and predetermined societal use. Pillows, on the other hand, can serve the same function as the bobo doll without that purpose being immediately obvious to the child (though it appears to become more and more obvious to some adult clients!).

Variety of Uses.   A fourth consensus deals with the variety of uses presented by a particular toy. Paper, glue, and crayons can be used for a multitude of activities by the creative and self-expressive child. They can be used to draw, fold, construct, build, tear, shred, throw, cover, mend, or repair. Further, within each of these uses, many subthemes can emerge that are directly related to what the child is attempting to communicate. This will help the therapists to understand the child better and ultimately will facilitate the child's self-understanding. For instance, one 5-year-old child used the pencil and paper for drawing only. He repeated the same drawing over and over. This drawing depicted a poisonous mushroom that was large enough to serve as the house for a large family, yet with doors that were out of proportion to other features of the drawing. This child expressed several things through his rigid use of pencil and paper. First, he exhibited functional fixedness in that he could not think of alternative uses for paper and pencil. Second, he was very constricted in his affect and need expression, as evidenced by the monotony of the drawings and the repetitiveness of the task. Third, he demonstrated where his problem originated: in a poisoned environment in his own home!

The same materials were used by another child, a 5-year-old girl, in a much different way. She used the paper to build airplanes and to tear into little pieces, depending on affects she needed to express. She was much less inhibited in her emotional expression and had freer access to her needs than the little boy who had chosen the same materials. These examples demonstrate that materials with multiple uses can add several interpretive dimensions to their specifically chosen use by a particular child client.

Safety.   A fifth consensus relates to the safety of the items that are available in the play therapy room to the children of the various ages that may use the room. It is important to differentiate safety from appropriateness. Although optimally, all items would be equally appropriate for all ages, this is not practically feasible. A baby doll and baby bottle are often found in play therapy rooms but are not often used by 11- or 12-year-old children. However, their presence is appropriate in the room, as they are clearly not unsafe for any of the children. However, a pair of regular scissors, while perhaps appropriate for an 11- or 12-year-old child, is clearly not only inappropriate for the 3-year-old who does not know how to use them, but also unsafe and should therefore be avoided. Safe toys are those that are soft, do not break, and have no sharp edges. Sand and water are generally considered safe, though their use can be rendered unsafe if not monitored closely by the therapist. Their potential for unsafe use is greatly outweighed by their therapeutic potential and excellent potential for creativity and self-expression.

Therapeutic Value.   The requirement for therapeutic value is the sixth area of consensus about therapy materials. This requirement clearly is more subjectively evaluated by each individual therapist and may even differ from child to child. Thus, occasionally a therapist may introduce and have available a particular toy for one child only. This happens rarely but is possible and should be kept in mind. *Therapeutic value* refers to the potential of the toy to be used by the child in a meaningful way that enhances her or his working through of problems and expression of needs and affects. Dolls and dollhouses have great therapeutic value because of what children can project upon them. They tend to result in more meaningful verbal expressions and self-talk than toys such as puzzles or books (Lodhi and Greer, 1989), thus being much more facilitative of actual therapeutic work and exchanges.

The therapeutic value of dolls and a dollhouse was demonstrated by one 6-year-old child who used these materials to reflect upon her parents' divorce situation. She chose the dollhouse and then indicated that she also had to build a second house with the available blocks, as she needed two houses. She proceeded to place the mother doll in the dollhouse and the father doll in the newly created house. Three children were placed in the mother's house first, then in the father's house, and ultimately between the two houses. This child clearly expressed her ambivalence about living with her mother, who had failed to meet all of her affective needs. However, she also did not feel entirely comfortable with her father, who only since the divorce had begun to show significant interest in his children.

Symbolic Value.   The seventh consensus regarding toys and materials has to do with their symbolic value. Almost any toy that is not clearly defined as a theme toy (e.g., a movie or TV character) can have symbolic value. Symbolism is an excellent and safe medium for children to share their life story without having to do so through words. The symbolic value of a toy is determined by the child and is generally guided by the child's real-life experiences. The same toy can have completely different meanings for two different children—or for the therapist, for that matter. Thus, to be able to understand the symbolism of a toy or an activity, the therapist must thoroughly understand the child and her or his situation. It might require several uses of a toy by one child before the therapist can be sure to have correctly understood the meaning or symbolism expressed by a child. The more nondescript and ill-defined an object is, the more symbolic value can be endowed upon it by a child. In fact, in many cases, but especially with abused children, less obvious toys might be more appropriate in helping them to reenact traumata or to express emotions than more explicit toys. For instance, in one study, abused children tended to prefer larger, softer dolls and teddy bears to the standard human-shaped family figurines that come with dollhouses (Sinason, 1988). Although the larger teddy bears were less humanlike, they were also less threatening to the children and more easily endowed with the symbolism or projections children had to express to reenact their trauma and the associated feelings.

Therapist Needs.   The final consensus refers to whether toys are chosen for the therapist's or the client's benefit. Toys should not be bought because the therapist always wanted one like it when she or he was a child, just as parents need to avoid this pitfall in selecting gifts for their children. Toys that have symbolic or therapeutic value for the therapist, may not at all speak to the child or facilitate a projection or self-expression. Thus, a toy that is laden with emotion for the therapist is best avoided in equipping a room.

Addressing these points of consensus about child therapy room equipment (which are summarized as questions in Table 1.1) will prove to be very helpful when materials are being selected. If all questions in Table 1.1 can be answered affirmatively, the toys or materials are probably appropriate for use. Certainly, not all materials will be equally appropriate for all children that will pass through a therapy room. However, children will make their own selections and are generally very capable of recognizing materials that will be useful to them in their therapeutic work. They will become more creative and self-expressive as they become more familiar with the therapist and the therapy process and once they have figured out the uniqueness of the therapy environment. If a child does not immediately make use of a wide variety of toys, this does not mean that the therapist has to buy more materials. It may merely indicate that the child needs some time to get accustomed to the new environment and nothing but patience must be added to the equipment list. Again, the room merely sets the stage for successful therapy work, and the materials within it are merely props that can be used in a variety of ways. It is the child who determines how the stage and props will be used, what type of play will be performed, and what purpose will be expressed (Goldstein, 1994).

Specific Toys and Materials Commonly Used

There are a number of toys that meet most, if not all of the requirements expressed by child clinicians as outlined above and the use of which is documented consistently throughout

TABLE 1.1   Points to Ponder in the Selection of Therapy Room Materials

1. Does this toy promote a wide range of nonstructured self-expression of feelings and needs?
2. Does this toy encourage meaningful creativity that enhances the child's self-esteem and self-confidence?
3. Is this toy free of societal connotations for its use?
4. Does this toy have multiple uses to encourage self-exploration and enhance self-understanding?
5. Is this toy safe for use by children of all ages?
6. Does this toy have potential therapeutic value to allow the working through of problems and the development of self-esteem and skills?
7. Does this toy have potential symbolic value to allow for expression of the child's real-life experiences?
8. Is this toy free of the therapist's own unfulfilled desires?

the child therapy literature (see Coppolillo, 1987; Dodds, 1985; Landreth, 2000). Empirical investigation has confirmed the usefulness of these toys and has provided a ranked listing of materials (Lebo, 1979). These toys represent the basics or essentials of a well-equipped therapy room and will be discussed here briefly with regard to their therapeutic usefulness and an example of their use will be provided. An overview of the essential toys and materials is provided in Table 1.2. A few extras will also be discussed, pointing out potential benefits and pitfalls.

TABLE 1.2   Essential Therapy Room Toys and Materials Checklist

_____	Puppets (predator, prey, humanlike, nondescript)
_____	Large dolls of ethnic variety
_____	Family of anatomically correct dolls
_____	Doll families of ethnic variety sized for a dollhouse
_____	Two dollhouses
_____	Nondescript, humanlike figures or dolls
_____	Schoolhouse (e.g., Fisher-Price) and schoolbus
_____	School figures
_____	Baby bottle
_____	Pretend food
_____	Cookware, dishes, and silverware
_____	Construction and drawing paper (large newsprint rolls)
_____	Easel and/or chalkboard
_____	Paints, finger paints, pencils, markers, and glitter glue
_____	Glue and children's scissors
_____	Clay and/or Play-Doh
_____	Blocks and/or Tinker Toys
_____	Two sandboxes or sandtrays (one with sand, one with rice)
_____	Sandbox figurines (humans, animals, houses, vehicles)
_____	Plastic animals (farm, zoo, prehistoric)
_____	Dress-up clothes, shoes, and accessories
_____	Telephones
_____	Cash register with play money
_____	Soft pillows and a blanket
_____	Stuffed animals

Puppets.   Puppets are perhaps the single most important piece of child therapy room equipment. They provide excellent means for the child to act out fantasy material and to express needs and feelings in indirect, nonthreatening ways. They come in a variety of shapes and symbolic values and should be selected carefully. As a rule of thumb, four to five puppets are enough. However, if a children's group is conducted in the room, there should be enough puppets for each child to have access to at least one. Of the available puppets, there should be at least one animal of prey and one predator. In the former category, sheep, lambs, and rabbits are popular. In the latter category, lions, tigers, and bulls work well. One additional neutral animal is also generally helpful to allow for completely symbolism-free projection on the child's part. Pigs, dogs (especially puppies), and bears (despite being predators, bears appear to have neutral value to children because of their use as teddy bears) fall into this category. A couple of fairly nondescript humanlike puppets are also useful. These may come in the form of a fairy-tale character or an anthropomorphic animal. Some therapists (e.g., Spiegel, 1961) also use more traditional puppets, including Casper, that are used in actual puppet shows. These therapists may have a puppet show per se in addition to the free use of puppets by the child. Sometimes these therapists will ask the child to put on a puppet show first and then have a puppet show of their own wherein they highlight the themes expressed in the child's play (Hawkes, 1979). Although there is no definitive correct or incorrect way of using puppets, the puppet show approach appears to be losing its adherents, with more therapists using free puppet play with nondefined puppets.

Puppets are very useful because they allow for direct expression of feelings and needs, as well as for opportunities for problem solving and skill development, without the child having to own directly any of the material that is being expressed. Thus, they can be used for very direct diagnostic and intervention work without the child or therapist ever having to acknowledge or openly interpret this directness. For example, one 11-year-old boy who had a chronic sense of failure and overall lack of self-esteem had begun to clearly favor one of the humanlike puppets that was available in the therapy room. Whenever he chose to play with this puppet, he also chose a second puppet for the therapist to handle. Early in the treatment, the two puppets would have long conversations about safe topics that were basically designed to get to know one another. As therapy progressed, so did the depth of the topics for the puppet play. Often, the boy's puppet would ask for advice from the therapist's puppet, and slowly, the boy's puppet was encouraged to find its own solutions. In a much later therapy session, after a several-week hiatus in the use of puppet play, the boy was observed during a particularly anxiety-provoking activity in the session to pick up his favorite puppet and a second puppet. Here is the conversation they had, both parts being played by the boy, some time after the boy had drawn a picture of his science project that he had worked on with his dad (a very judgmental man with high expectations for his three sons):

SECOND PUPPET: You are so stupid! Why did you do that?

FAVORITE PUPPET: I am not... (meekly)

SECOND PUPPET: Yes you are. You always do it that way even though you know it's wrong, Stupid!

> **FAVORITE PUPPET:**   Do not! (quite forcefully)
>
> **SECOND PUPPET:**   Stupid!
>
> **FAVORITE PUPPET:**   Stop it. Don't call me stupid. I am sick of it. I did what you told me to do. Leave me alone!

The child then returned to another activity in the play room and within 3 minutes returned to the incomplete drawing of his science project, indicating that even though he had not gotten it to work yet, he would finish it today because he thought he had finally figured out what had gone wrong! Although this is not the most profound example of puppet play, it illustrates very well how a child can use puppets without being directly aware of what she or he is working on. Further, it demonstrates that puppet play is quite conducive to letting the child do the questioning and the answering both, without the therapist getting trapped into giving advice. Finally, the sense of accomplishment felt by the child can be real, despite the imaginary scenario of play.

Dolls and Doll Families of Ethnic Variety.   Four types of dolls should be available in a therapy room: anatomically correct dolls, ethnically varied large dolls, ethnically varied dollhouse-size dolls, and humanlike figures. Dolls, much like puppets, present an excellent medium for realistic self-expression of needs, affects, and desires. They allow the child to project as much of her or his own conscious and unconscious material as she or he can tolerate and yet keep the child often safely unaware of her or his own metacommunication. Obviously, the added use of a dollhouse that is scaled to the dollhouse dolls is highly recommended. However, children are often quite ingenious in their ability to make do with available materials, so the absence of a dollhouse might not necessarily be seriously detrimental to the therapy work that can be done. If possible, two dollhouses are optimal, given the reality that most child clients spend their lives in split homes and more than one household.

One of the most important considerations in purchasing dolls for a therapy room is that of ethnic and gender stereotyping perpetuated by doll manufacturers. Many dolls—family dolls and professional dolls alike—are still utterly stereotypic in how they are depicted. They tend to be white, and the males are depicted in professions of high responsibility, such as physician, engineer, police officer, or fire fighter, whereas the females are depicted in stereotypic low-power positions, such as nurse, secretary, or homemaker. Buying such dolls is irresponsible and delivers a sad message to the nonwhite or female child. Similarly, this may put unnecessary strain on the male child, who receives a clear message of a strong need on his part to become a high achiever. Lack of availability of ethnically varied dolls is a disservice to ethnic children, who then have to use one additional level of abstraction in their use of dolls, as identification with white dolls may be much more difficult for them. Further, it is a disservice to all children, ethnic minority or white, not to have ethnically correct dolls, because children need to have role models from their own ethnic group available for use and need to learn that their ethnic identity is an important and proud aspect of their self-identity. There are more and more sources for ethnically varied dollhouse-size dolls; however, ethnically varied large dolls are still relatively difficult to find. It is best to have a set of white dolls, African American dolls, Hispanic dolls, and Native or Asian American dolls. Fortunately, more and more mail-order distributors of play therapy materials are selling professional dolls as well as grandparents and babies to complement the nuclear family dollhouse doll set. These additional dolls add reality to the doll assortment and can serve to expand the repertoire of the child's play.

Anatomically correct dolls do not have to be specifically identified as such and can actually often serve the dual purpose of being used as the large human dolls as well. When dressed, there is really no difference. The anatomical doll or large human doll set should include an adult male and adult female doll, a child male and female doll, as well as a baby doll. Extra clothing for all dolls will stimulate exploration of the dolls and will be more likely to result in the discovery of the anatomical doll's "private parts." Although some clinicians believe that sexually correct dolls may be frightening to some small children (e.g., Spiegel, 1996), this is generally not the case if the dolls are tastefully designed. Further, the presence of anatomically correct dolls is becoming more and more important as the reported incidence of child sexual abuse continues to escalate. Children should, of course, never be forced to use any particular toy, including the anatomical doll, in the course of therapy. Although such prescribed play may have its place in an assessment of a child, it is inappropriate in the context of actual psychotherapeutic work.

For some children, the use of human dolls is too threatening, as it is too directly or obviously related to their actual trauma or problem. They may prefer humanlike dolls, such as anthropomorphic animals, fairy-tale figures, or Gumby dolls. Even then, attention must be paid to gender and race stereotyping, and a good variety of dolls should be available. Sometimes children will use dolls of a different ethnic group to gain additional distance from their real-life experience. In this instance, the use of the ethnically different dolls should be interpreted not as a rejection of the child's own ethnic background, but rather as the child's need to distance from reality, much in the same way that use of humanlike figures would imply. For instance, one 10-year-old African American boy refused to use the black family that was available for the dollhouse for several weeks early in his therapy. Instead, he chose the white family and played with it extensively and aggressively, killing various family members and burying them in the sandbox. As his anger began to be worked through, he slowly and one by one began introducing African American dolls into his play activity. Ultimately, he shifted completely to the use of black dolls. This shift did not represent acceptance of ethnic identification, but rather a working through of familial conflict.

School Figures. A useful set of toys includes a schoolhouse, schoolbus, schoolchildren, teachers, and playground equipment scaled to match the dollhouse and its families. Again, preferably, the human figures should be available in both genders and from a variety of ethnic backgrounds. School figures are important especially if a referral was initiated by a teacher or if the social/interpersonal adjustment of the child is in question. School is a large part of a child's life and therefore is likely to be the setting of conflicts and problems. The schoolbus can often double as a regular bus, thus adding more variety to the repertoire of available toys.

Nurturance Toys and Materials. Nurturance materials include baby bottles, pretend food, and kitchen equipment. All of these materials share their ability to evoke themes of nurturance, as well as the expression of emotional neediness or dependence. They are extremely useful in assessing and working through problems related to being overwhelmed by a parent who is not sufficiently nurturing, can be used in the context of working through abandonment fears, and can be used by the child to calm or soothe herself or himself when faced with difficult therapeutic or real-life situations. For example, one very young boy who was seen in treatment because of his biological mother's concerns over the joint custody situation with the biological father made extremely good use of food and cooking materials. This child would spend one week with his father, then three weeks with his mother. After each week with his father, he returned quite emotionally depleted and overwhelmed. During his therapy session, these feelings and needs were expressed through increased use of pretend food. Although he always used food and cooking activities in his sessions, upon the return from his father, he would often sneak food and would refuse to share it with the therapist. He would often ask the therapist to prepare the food for him and serve him. This behavior was very unlike the behavior that he displayed once he had been with his mother for a week. Then, he would freely share food with the therapist and cook for himself and her.

Some clinicians endorse the use of actual foods (e.g., Haworth and Keller, 1964; Straus, 1999). This practice should be well thought through before engaging in it. Therapy is not a real-life situation, and the actual nurturance is quite a different way of approaching therapy from the symbolic psychological nurturance or the understanding of the need for nurturance. The decision to use real food versus pretend food will thus be driven largely by the therapist's theoretical orientation. A therapist who does not know which way to decide is best advised to use pretend food. The use of real food can result in very strong emotions on the child's part and is often driven by countertransference reactions on the therapist's part. Too often, food is provided by the therapist who would like to give the child something or who desires to take care of the child. However, the temporary provision of food to a child will not help the child learn how to nurture herself or himself psychologically.

Creativity Materials.   Creativity materials include anything from paper products to paints and crayons to glue and paper clips, as well as clay and Play-Doh. In terms of paper, an excellent possibility is rolls of leftover newsprint, which can generally be obtained at no cost from the local newspaper. Creativity materials are some of the least structured toys that leave the most up to the child's imagination and creativity. They are excellent and varied tools of self-expression that are often very appealing to older children, who might find the rest of the play room materials too immature or demeaning. In fact, clay and drawing materials are often very useful in the treatment even of adolescents. The definite advantage of these types of materials is that there is not only a process of creation and expression that is to be observed, but also a final product that can be explored for its symbolic value. How a drawing is created will tell one important story. However, the end product will add another essential component.

For example, in a group therapy session, the children decided to make a group drawing. The group drawing ended up being much of an individual activity for each child and then became a group process once again when each child spoke about her or his drawing. In the course of this process, a 7-year-old girl who had recently been faced with a painful parental divorce drew a colorful rainbow, clouds, sunshine, and two houses. The process of her drawing was interesting to watch, as she had begun the drawing with the rainbow. As she added the houses and then the unique features of each house, she also added the clouds. This process helped the therapist to understand that although this girl wanted her life to be happy and full of rainbows, there were some intrusions (the separation of the parents as symbolized by the separate houses) that literally clouded her life. As the girl explained her drawing to the other children in the group, she took a black marker and slowly marked across her drawing until the entire rainbow had been covered in black. The end product of her drawing left no doubt that she felt strongly affected by her parents' divorce and that she was still struggling to come to terms with the brighter side of this process.

The use of three-dimensional materials such as clay can be equally telling. One 14-year-old adolescent who had been extremely reluctant to open himself up to treatment was finally able to commit himself to the process when he discovered the availability of clay in the therapy room (this was a regular office, not a play therapy room; the latter would be quite inappropriate for a child of this age). He began by merely using the clay for the sensory experience, molding it into nonspecific shapes of various sizes. Slowly, he began using the clay to underscore the stories he told the therapist, giving significant clues as to which parts of his tales were most important to him. Thus, once while telling of how he had wrecked his brother's car, he shaped a human figure. Although his verbal account of the incident stressed the car (he described it in great detail), his clay figure gave away the true concern, namely, the strain that had been placed by the incident on the relationship with his brother.

Construction Materials.   Construction materials simply consist of blocks of various sizes and shapes or Tinker Toys. Although more complex and expensive building sets exist, for instance, Lego's Technic Series, these are rarely necessary. Children often use building blocks to represent their daily life experience of having to create things, accomplish things, and master tasks. The construction of a tower can tell a lot about a child's ability to delay gratification, to deal with frustration, to persevere under difficult circumstances, and to work independently and consistently. The construction of sophisticated buildings or even creatures will give hints as to the things that are important to a child's life, as well as being proof of the child's creativity and level of determination. Constructing with building blocks can give a child a new sense of mastery and accomplishment that can greatly enhance self-esteem. For example, a 5-year-old boy whose father had died from a drug overdose came to therapy because he appeared quite depressed and withdrawn. He was a very quiet child who was afraid of new activities and environments and who had difficulty separating from his mother for his sessions. When he discovered a wooden block set in the therapist's office, he became animated for the first time. He asked for much help building his first tower but, across several sessions, developed and honed his skills to the degree of being able to build a tower reaching all the way to his elbow by himself. Upon this accomplishment, he felt and expressed pride for the first time in his sessions. His activities in the therapy room became much more spontaneous after this experience, and he appeared more self-assured.

Sandtray Materials.   Two sandtrays or sandboxes are great assets to a therapy room, as they provide the opportunity for a completely unstructured activity that most children have not been allowed to encounter indoors or around an adult. Two trays are best so that one may be filled with sand and one with rice. This not only provides two different media, but also accommodates children who cannot use sand because of dust allergies. They generally present a very new experience for the child and one that allows for the free flow of affective expression and catharsis. Children of all ages will enjoy sand activities, once they have overcome their initial shyness about making a mess or doing something that often results in reprimand from an adult. Sand is a wonderful medium for constricted children who have not been allowed to get dirty physically or psychologically, that is, who are not allowed the free expression of affects in their home. Sand activity is productive in and of itself but can be greatly enhanced by the presence of figurines that can be used in the sand. These figurines can simply be in the form of inexpensive plastic zoo, farm, and prehistoric animals; tiny plastic humans; tiny plastic houses and cars; and many other humanlike figures. The possibilities of what can be used in a sandbox are endless. The figures for the sandbox are easily stored in a plastic fishing gear chest with drawers and small compartments. This renders them easily accessible and makes cleanup easy.

Children use the sandtray both to manipulate the sand or rice itself, for the tactile stimulation this provides, and for the playing out of familiar scenes using the figurines. An example of a therapeutic use of the sandtray with figurines is that of an 11-year-old boy who had been severely physically abused by his father, felt very insecure, and had a poor self-image. He created an entire city in the sandtray with homes, trees, people, and animals. In the midst of this scene, he buried a treasure, not allowing the therapist to see the exact placement of the treasure. In his play with the sand and the figures, he actively involved the therapist, whose task it was to find and exhume the treasure. This activity was repeated several times upon the request of this child. Each time the therapist found the treasure, this usually somber and serious child was delighted. It quickly became evident to the therapist that the hidden treasure was representative of the child's own strength and positiveness that he was about to discover in his therapy. The fact that the therapist could find it for him delighted and strengthened him. The success of this therapeutic activity, however, became most obvious when the child asked the therapist to bury the treasure so that he could find it himself. When he did so, he was truly excited and also very relieved. He left this session with a newly discovered sense of security and self-confidence.

An example of a child who used the sand without figurines for the tactile experience of it is that of a 9-year-old parentified child who had been the caretaker of her 4-year-old sister ever since the latter's birth. She was very afraid of getting herself dirty during her therapy sessions and avoided the sand, as well as the water activities that were available. She often referred to the fact that sand was dirty and should not be played with in the house. However, it was also noted that she appeared quite torn about her own statement, apparently very much wanting to feel and use the sand. After many sessions of being encouraged to use the sandtray, she finally did. Once she began, she was quickly taken in by the experience, to the degree of asking to take off her shoes and socks to step in the sand. Once she began to use the sand in this manner, she opened herself to new challenges and more childlike behaviors in many ways. She had finally found within herself permission to be a child.

Pretend Play Materials.   Materials in the pretend category include dress-up clothes, shoes, and accessories, as well as telephones and play money. These items allow the child to try on various roles and to act out fantasies or real-life scenarios. Pretend clothing with accessories allows the child to become an adult who is capable of dealing with a difficult situation or a baby who needs to be taken care of and nurtured, merely by choosing what to wear. Thus, both ends of the spectrum of adaptation can be enacted: the healthy end of self-care and self-soothing as well as the less developmentally advanced end of physical and psychological dependence. One young child often chose red dress-up shoes in the therapy room when she was faced with a situation that caused her insurmountable anxiety and then referred to herself as Dorothy. In her pretend world, she had found a way to escape difficult situations.

Play money can be useful for a child who does not know how nurturance and control are given and accepted. This child can experiment by either controlling the money or letting the therapist control it. In one example, a 6-year-old boy was quite thrilled upon the discovery of a cash register and play money in the therapy room. He immediately fetched the pretend food and set up a store, then asked the therapist to come shopping at his store. However, although the therapist was supposed to do the shopping, the child controlled the money and gave the clinician only as much money as he found fit. His delight over being in control of the dispensing of food was great and was understood in the context of his family, in which he generally had little control over his own life, being almost ruled by a very controlling father who did not allow him to make his own decisions. The fact that the male clinician allowed the child to have control over psychological nurturance represented an important corrective experience for this boy.

Pretend telephones are yet another means for a child to communicate with the therapist without having to do so directly. Children often surprise therapists with what they are willing to disclose over the toy telephone that they would not otherwise be able to say. One 5-year-old boy managed to disclose physical abuse by his biological mother using the telephone, whereas he had repeatedly refused to talk about his visits with his mother in direct face-to-face contact with his therapist.

Soothing Materials.   Although they are not truly therapeutic materials, pillows and one or two stuffed animals do have their place in a therapy room. Children do occasionally overwhelm themselves with their own self-disclosures, whether these be direct or through metacommunications. At these times, they may seek nurturance and soothing from an external object that reminds them of a safe place. Such a transitional object is best represented by a huggable stuffed animal, a pillow, or a soft blanket. One 4-year-old girl, after having worked very hard in her session, indicated that now she needed a nap. She grabbed a blanket and teddy bear and lay down to rest, asking the therapist to tuck her in. After no more than 45 to 50 seconds of thus soothing herself, she was ready to continue her session.

Extras.   Extras are toys or materials that might not be routinely available in a well-equipped therapy room but that might occasionally have their place in a particular child's therapy. Often their use is more serendipitous than properly planned. For instance, one 8-year-old boy had evidenced significant difficulty in accepting his therapist as trustworthy and sufficiently strong for his needs. During one session, a checkers game, not usually available in the therapy room, had been left behind by another therapist. The child, much to the therapist's chagrin, immediately spotted the game and asked to play. The therapist, somewhat unprepared for the request, agreed. He was not sure of his role in the game and decided to let the child win. The child became increasingly agitated as the therapist's mistakes became obvious and ultimately made several moves for the therapist to ascertain that the therapist would not lose the game. Finally, the therapist realized that this was his chance to demonstrate to the child that he would indeed be able to be strong and capable for the child, thus becoming more trustworthy in the child's mind. He realized that he had to win the game. Once he had noticed the child's need for his strength, he was able to use the checkers game for a definite therapeutic advantage that had many positive future implications for the child-therapist relationship. This example serves to demonstrate not only the serendipitous therapeutic use of a structured board game, but also the falseness of adults' assumptions that children always want to win a game lest their self-esteem be destroyed. Clearly, this child needed a strong therapist, and a strong therapist cannot lose a simple game of checkers!

Other extras may consist of materials that are more useful for assessment than for therapy. For instance, large floor puzzles can be an excellent means of assessing a young child's independent problem-solving ability. However, their use in therapy is questionable. The *Talking, Feeling, Doing Game* (Gardner, 1973) can be very useful in assessment, as well as in the early phases of treatment. Various sizes and shapes of toy cars can be useful for some children, as they may be used to present the child and her or his family. Balls or other athletic equipment may be used to assess a child's physical prowess or to help a child develop a sense of physical self-confidence in the therapy.

The use of Dictaphones or tape recorders has also been documented as a valuable way of helping children express themselves in therapy (Durfee, 1979). For instance, one severely psychotic 3-year-old boy had been seen in daily psychotherapy at an inpatient facility for over a month with little change and little attachment to the therapist. One day, he discovered the therapist's tape recorder on the windowsill. He was very curious about this machine, as he had never encountered anything like it in his home. The therapist decided to show him the recorder, as the child had never displayed this amount of interest or affect in a session before. She played back the last few minutes of the session, and the child became elated when he recognized his own voice. For the remainder of the session, he recorded his voice, then listened to it, over and over again. He had for the first time recognized his continued existence across time, and this presented a major breakthrough in his treatment. It should be evident by now that most extras are to be used with specific children for a specific purpose. They should not be routinely kept in the therapy room, or at least not out in the open, as they may be too structured or too specific for most therapy clients.

A word must also be said about the use of games in the therapy of children. There is some controversy about the use of games. Some therapists argue that games are too structured and specific to be considered useful therapeutic tools (see Ginott, 1999). Proponents of the use of games, on the other hand, point toward their usefulness in addressing specific topics in a therapy or making assessment decisions about a child who is being seen for an intake or early in treatment (Schaefer and Reid, 2000). These therapists argue that games are an important day-to-day activity in the latency period of childhood (ages 6 to 12) and thus can play an important role in the therapy. They tend to group games into three categories: games of chance, games of strategy, and games of skill. Schaefer and Reid (2000) have discussed games in these three categories and have placed them in the context of therapeutic usefulness. As such, they demonstrate how games can be used to enhance the therapeutic alliance between child and therapist, to facilitate self-expression, socialization, communication, and ego enhancement, and can be introduced merely to add a component of pleasure or enjoyment to the early stages of treatment. They discuss a number of games, and it is notable that many of these are chosen for their lack of competitiveness and free-dom from structure. Thus, some excellent games that are compatible with the rules out-lined in Table 1.1 do exist and can be considered even by the therapist who believes in little structure or direction in her or his interaction with the child. These include, but are not nec-essarily limited to, the *Imagine!* game (Burks, 1978), the *Talking, Feeling, Doing Game* (Gardner, 1973), the *Ungame* (Zakich, 1975), the *Reunion* game (Zakich and Monroe, 1979), and the *Talking/Listening Game* (Shadle and Graham, 1981).

Summary and Concluding Thoughts

In summary, the furnishings, design, and equipment of a mental health center that serves children must be carefully planned and implemented. Children as clients have special needs that must be acknowledged and addressed through the general layout of the center, as well as through the materials that are available for the child's and therapist's use. The more thought can be put into the design of a clinic before children are first seen, the more likely it is that the work with them will be successful. Just as the beginning child therapist has to take inventory of herself or himself, so does she or he have to take inventory of the clinical environment to assess its potential for successful work with children. Just as the therapist must dress appropriately for the down-to-earth activity with children, so must she or he design the environment in a similarly indestructible and pragmatic manner. Once the therapist and the setting have been prepared for the child, the therapist is ready to seriously consider treatment of her or his first child client.

CHAPTER

2 Legal and Ethical Issues in Child Therapy

The years 1989 and 1990 marked a significant worldwide advance in children's rights that are bound to have a profound effect on children's mental health laws and public policy. In 1989, the 159 member states of the United Nations adopted the U.N. Convention on the Rights of the Child, a treaty that went into effect after being ratified by twenty U.N. nations less than one year later, in September 1990. Since then, all but two U.N. nations have ratified the convention, the two exceptions being Somalia and the United States. In the United States, President Clinton signed the U.N. Convention on February 16, 1995, but its ratification in the Congress is still pending (Walker, Brooks, and Wrightsman, 1999). Ratification of the treaty means that its articles became legally binding for those nations that adopted it.

The ratification of the U.N. Convention on the Rights of the Child is the culmination of efforts to change the attitudes of literally centuries that denied children basic rights that were enjoyed by adults and even basic protections that were granted to animals! Before the eighteenth century, children had no protection under the law. Both in England and in the United States, the courts granted all rights of control to the parents, even sanctioning capital punishment for children who disobeyed (Hart, 1991). In fact, parents could abandon, abuse, and exile their children without retribution or consequences.

Only in the eighteenth century did attitudes toward children change somewhat. They began to be treated as valuable property. The nineteenth century saw a primarily societal attitudinal shift in that children were now considered pure and malleable, therefore worthy of protection by the state and church. At this time, child labor laws were enacted, and school attendance became compulsory. However, it was not until the twentieth century that children were regarded as persons, and not until the middle of that century did the courts recognize children as persons under the law. In this context, nurturance and protection rights were emphasized. The U.N. Convention is a significant document because, in addition to granting nurturance and protection rights, it balances them with self-determination and autonomy rights that were previously not viewed as in the purview of children at all. It is important to note in this context that the U.N. Convention granted these rights to the children as individuals, not as family members. Thus, the rights of the child were placed ahead of the rights of the family (Cohen and Naimark, 1991; Walker, Brooks, and Wrightsman, 1999).

Several of the rights of children spelled out in the U.N. Convention can have a potentially strong impact on mental health practitioners' attitudes and behaviors toward children. One of the most applicable articles is the granting of the right to privacy to children.

Further, children are granted the right to live with their parents, to express an opinion, to be protected from any form of abuse or neglect, to receive protection if no adequate family environment is available, to receive special help and training to aid in the achievement of self-reliance and an active life, to receive a high standard of health care, to be educated in and enjoy their own culture, to be protected from economic exploitation or hardship, and to receive all necessary physical and psychological help to recover from victimization of any kind (as summarized by Wilcox and Naimark, 1991).

Thus, the U.N. Convention recognizes the dignity of the child, the child's right to protection and treatment, and the child's rights to self-determination. It also placed the child into a developmental context, advocating treatment of the child that is developmentally relevant and appropriate. These privileges and rights clearly have implications for the mental health practitioner. Melton (1991) has summarized the major implications into six principles, which he suggests as relevant to future public policy regarding children's mental health.

In his first principle, Melton (1991) suggests that "the provision of high-quality services for children should be a matter of the highest priority for public mental health authorities" (p. 68). This implies that children should have free access to medical and mental health care—that is, that many more resources need to be allocated for such social services in the future.

Second, "children should be viewed as active partners in child mental health services with heavy weight placed on protection of their liberty and privacy" (p. 69). This implies not only that the child should be free to express opinions, but also that the child should be involved in treatment planning and should not be subjected to treatments that she or he could now or later perceive as demeaning or belittling.

Third, "mental health services for children should be respectful of parents and supportive of family integrity" (p. 69). This principle implies shared decision making and respect, not blame, for all parties involved. It is clearly aimed at ascertaining that the family be made the best place to foster the child's continued health and growth.

Fourth, "states should apply a strong presumption against residential placement of children for the purpose of treatment, with due procedural care in decision making about treatment and with provision of community-based alternatives. When out-of-home placement is necessary for the protection of the child, it should be in the most family-like setting consistent with those objectives" (p. 69). This principle has already gained widespread acceptance among mental health practitioners who have for years attempted to provide least restrictive environments. It protects the integrity of the child's family, as well as the child's dignity.

Fifth, "when the state does undertake the care and custody of emotionally disturbed children, it also assumes an especially weighty obligation to protect them from harm" (p. 69). In other words, it is not enough to place a child; the placement must provide care and safety.

Finally, "prevention should be the cornerstone of child mental health policy" (p. 69). Although this is yet again a principle that has been widely promoted (though not necessarily always practiced) among mental health practitioners, it has found little financial support among social policymakers. The U.N. convention would suggest that such social policy is not only prudent, but also required of any state that wishes to respect and honor its children.

These six principles, as well as the entire U.N. Convention, which the reader is urged to read in its entirety (United Nations General Assembly, 1989) or in its summarized form (Walker, Brooks, and Wrightsman, 1999; Wilcox and Naimark, 1991), will need to be kept in mind as current mental health laws and ethics are reviewed. It is quite likely that the reality of current mental health law will remain in conflict with some of the U.N. Convention articles or with Melton's (1991) principles for some time, especially since the United States remains one of only two nations not to have ratified the convention for itself. However, it is unlikely that conflicts between the convention and current law are great or that they will impact a clinician's work too profoundly. It may be necessary for individual clinicians to find their own viable and morally acceptable compromises. Most important, children's rights to protection and nurturance will need to continue to be weighed against their rights to self-determination and autonomy. There are not always easy answers to ethical questions around the work with children, but keeping the child's best interest at heart will help to give the clinician the guidance to make the best choice possible in each individual case.

Technical Summary of Relevant Legal and Ethical Issues

In the current court system of the United States, individual actions of all citizens can be prosecuted under either criminal or civil law. Criminal law covers crimes such as assault, murder, and robbery and is always prosecuted by the government. Even the aiding and abetting of such crimes can result in a criminal trial. Civil law, on the other hand, is reserved for noncriminal offenses and is generally prosecuted by individuals. Most mental health laws or statutes that govern the behaviors and actions of mental health service providers fall into this category.

Further, professional affiliations' ethical guidelines or principles, such as the American Psychological Association (APA) Ethical Principles for Psychologists (1992), the American Counseling Association (ACA; 1995) Ethical Standards, the Ethical Standards of the American School Counselors Association (ASCA; 1998), and the Principles for Professional Practice of the National Association of School Psychologists (NSAP; 1997) provide necessary guidance for the mental health practitioner. Although these ethical guidelines are not laws or legally binding, they are generally enforced by the professional organizations that developed them. Thus, breaches of ethics by a psychologist may be reported to the American Psychological Association, which may choose to expel the psychologist from the organization if the behavior was indeed found to conflict with APA principles. Further, and perhaps more important, "courts may also look to the self-imposed standards of the profession to determine liability" of a practitioner if there is no applicable law or precedent to guide the court in its decision-making process (Anderson, 1996, p. 9). Thus, familiarity with the professional ethical standards is paramount to the work of a clinician. The therapist's primary professional self-definition will determine which code of ethics is to be followed.

All codes of ethics that are relevant to mental health service provision share certain commonalities: All guarantee confidentiality, subscribe to appropriate mental health laws such as the duty to warn and the duty to protect, and have behavior codes for therapists regulating the nature of the therapist-client relationship. In the work with children, four topics emerge that are of particular relevance: informed consent, confidentiality, duty to warn and to protect, and duty to report.

Informed Consent

Informed consent "applies to client decisions regarding whether to engage in therapy, what happens during the course of therapy, and what information to allow the therapist to disclose to others" (DeKraii, Sales, and Hall, 1998, pp. 540–541). No one can force an individual to be in therapy against her or his will or without a signed informed consent. The signing of the consent document itself must be done voluntarily, knowingly, and competently. These three aspects of informed consent pose a challenge to the work with children, as will become clear. Voluntariness refers to the fact that a signature may not be obtained under duress, but rather must be provided of free will. Knowledge refers to the fact that the client must have been informed of all relevant information that may affect the therapy process in any way. Thus, information about taping, observation, risks and benefits of treatment, and confidentiality and its limits must be provided to the client and must be understood. This latter issue of understanding leads to the problem of competence, which refers to the ability of the client to make an intelligent and informed decision about treatment. Competence is defined in the United States arbitrarily via the age of the client, and the age that determines competence can vary from state to state. Given the focus of this book on children up to age 11 to 12, it can be safely assumed that these children will not qualify in any state to be competent to render informed consent.

When informed consent cannot be obtained from a client because of legal incompetence, as defined by age or disability, the parents, legal guardians, or any agent in loco parentis is required to provide the informed consent in lieu of the client (see DeKraii, Sales, and Hall, 1998). Because states differ somewhat in their definitions of competence, it behooves each practitioner to investigate her or his state laws and statutes so as to avoid breaking them. APA Ethical Principles generally agree with the legal definitions of competence and imply that minors cannot give voluntary and competent informed consent. They urge clinicians to use their judgment of what is in the best interest of the child when tricky issues arise. Further, some writers have suggested that developmental, as opposed to legal, information and guidelines should be used to make decisions about informed consent issues. For instance, Gustafson and McNamara (1987) agree that children from approximately age 14 on are cognitively capable of and should be involved in making informed consent decisions; children under the age of 11 do not have sufficient cognitive complexity to do so. Regardless of these opinions, all states do require parental consent for treatment of minors with only few exceptions that are relevant to adolescents only, such as birth control counseling and services, abortions, substance abuse treatment, and crisis or emergency intervention (Corey, Corey, and Callanan, 1998). Parental consent always has to be provided by the parent identified as the legal custodian of the child in the case of divorce or separation.

Clearly, the U.N. Convention may restimulate the debate about informed consent as it guarantees privacy to the child, as well as free or unlimited access to health (including mental health) care. It will be interesting to see whether the U.N. articles will affect the age at which parental informed consent is required. Perhaps, given the sensitivity to developmental issues of the U.N. Convention, it will serve to redefine competency age in developmental, as opposed to strict chronological, age terms.

Confidentiality

It is generally believed among therapists that confidentiality not only protects the interests of clients, but also facilitates the development of trust and rapport. Without confidentiality, clients are thought to be more hesitant to initiate treatment, more likely to end treatment prematurely, and less likely to disclose all therapeutically relevant and necessary information (see DeKraii, Sales, and Hall, 1998). Although children hardly ever initiate treatment on their own, and thus, although their decision to begin treatment might not be affected by confidentiality rules, the other two advantages presented by maintaining confidentiality are still applicable.

Confidentiality with children is a difficult topic. Although all clinicians certainly agree that there is to be strict confidentiality as far as other agencies and nonparental figures are concerned, the approach to the disclosure to children's parents varies greatly, from complete disclosure to none (Gustafson and McNamara, 1987). Generally, release of information to parents is based upon the clinician's judgment about what is in the best interest of the child. Legally, however, parents who provide consent are to be granted access to records and information upon their request (DeKraii, Sales, and Hall, 1998), as parental rights to information have to be honored (Gustafson and McNamara, 1987). However, most clinicians attempt to reach a compromise by getting the child's informed assent before making disclosures, by inviting the child to participate in feedback sessions with parents, and by providing access only if it is in the best interest of the child. Refusal by the child, however, would not be sufficient to deny a parent access to records if she or he insisted upon it.

Although parents have the right to access information about their child's treatment, they do not necessarily have the right to release such information (Melton, Ehrenreich, and Lyons, 2001). It does not appear to be usual clinical practice to receive permission of the child to release records. However, legally speaking, additional consent by the child may actually need to be obtained to be able to release information to other agencies and individuals, especially if the child has sufficient cognitive complexity to give such consent (Melton, Ehrenreich, and Lyons, 2001). Local state laws may need to be investigated by the individual practitioner on this topic if a conflict between the child's and parents' wishes should arise.

Finally, although parents have the legal right to access, children do not have this right in all but three states. In other words, although parents are allowed to view a child's records, the child does not have this right in most states (Melton, Ehrenreich, and Lyons, 2001). This differential treatment of child and parents certainly should be discussed with the child before treatment begins.

Hardly any rights are absolute; the right to confidentiality is not either. There are circumstances in which the right to confidentiality has to be forfeited for the sake of securing the safety of a client or others. The Model Act for State Licensure of Psychologists (APA, 1987a), which serves as a model for most state licensing agencies and laws, outlines eight reasons why confidentiality may be breached in an individual case:

1. Where abuse or harmful neglect of children, the elderly, or disabled or incompetent individuals is known or reasonably suspected;
2. Where the validity of a will of a former patient or client is contested;
3. Where such information is necessary for the psychologist to defend a malpractice action brought by the client;
4. Where an immediate threat of physical violence against a readily identifiable victim is disclosed to the psychologist;
5. In the context of civil commitment proceedings, where an immediate threat of self-inflicted damage is disclosed to the psychologist;
6. Where the patient or client, by alleging mental or emotional damages in litigation, puts his or her mental state at issue;
7. Where the patient or client is examined pursuant to court order or,
8. In the context of investigations and hearings brought by the patient or client and conducted by the board, where violations of this act are at issue (APA, 1987a, p. 703).

Despite this widely accepted standard, states vary a great deal in how they have integrated these reasons into their own laws and statutes. Although it is best for each clinician to familiarize herself or himself in detail with the laws and statutes of the state of residency and licensure, a quick summary is provided with state-by-state information by Howell and Ogles (1989). From this summary, it can be noted that the only reason that is agreed upon by all states for sharing information with other agencies or individuals is that of having obtained a written release of information by the client or, in the case of a child, the client and the parent or legal guardian who signed the informed consent for treatment. Other reasons have various precedents in U.S. courts. Most important, the duty to warn and the duty to report have been well-established reasons for releasing privileged communication without the client's (and/or parents') consent.

Duty to Warn and Duty to Protect

The duty to warn and duty to protect as covered in the Model Act (APA, 1987a; item 4) dates back to the *Tarasoff* v. *Regents of the University of California* case in 1976 (Brems, 2000). In this case, the California Supreme Court set a precedent for holding liable any mental health practitioner who fails to warn a victim who is identified as such, even potentially, in privileged communication by a client. In other words, if a client discloses the desire to hurt or kill an identifiable victim and the clinician deems the threat to be serious and likely to be carried out, she or he has the responsibility to warn the victim directly about the client's intent. In the Tarasoff case, the court implied that the confidentiality of the communication remains such, as long as the threat is vague and not directed against one identifiable person.

Since 1976, the duty to warn has been expanded by various court decisions (Swenson, 1997). For instance, in 1985, the duty to warn was extended to being applicable to identifiable groups, not just individuals, by the Vermont Supreme Court in the *Peck* v. *Counseling Services of Addison County, Inc.* case. In 1989, the Arizona Supreme Court further extended the duty to include any general threat to a general group of people in the *Hamman* v. *County of Maricopa* case, as did the Colorado Supreme Court in the *Perreira* v. *Colorado* case (Anderson, 1996).

The expanded version of the Tarasoff decision, now called the unidentifiable but foreseeable standard, thus refers to a generic risk for others posed by a client and indicates that if the client refuses hospitalization or confinement, and if commitment is not deemed appropriate, the clinician has the duty to warn family members of the client, police, and any other likely person the client may contact (Pietrofesa, Pietrofesa, and Pietrofesa, 1990). This is a vague standard and leaves much room for error. However, the clinician is released from the duty to warn once she or he has warned all relevant individuals and/or has been successful in arranging hospitalization for the client (Pietrofesa, Pietrofesa, and Pietrofesa, 1990). The duty to warn is likely to be applied by the courts in future cases to clients who have HIV/AIDS and are threatening to spread the infection (Swenson, 1997).

The duty to warn or protect is also applied if the threat is against the self, that is, if suicide is the violence planned by the client (Corey, Corey, and Callanan, 1998). In this case, parents or police must be warned of the client's threat, or the client must be hospitalized, perhaps even committed involuntarily or by a parent. This ethical and legal issue has caused much controversy, since some clinicians, as well as a good number of clients, believe that suicide is a personal right (Firestone, 1997). However, the legal responsibility is clear, and the failure by a therapist to report suicidal ideation and planning is currently the number one reason for lawsuits against mental health practitioners (Corey, Corey, and Callanan, 1998).

The duty to warn might not need to be invoked often by child clinicians; however, even children occasionally express the desire to hurt or kill someone else or themselves. If this desire is expressed in a therapy session, the clinician must be prepared to make a report. The report is to the potential victim, if there is a clearly identifiable one, as well as to the child's parents. If a vague victim or group of victims is specified, the police must be notified (Ahia and Martin, 1993).

Duty to Report

The duty to report refers to the mandated report of child abuse and neglect. Most U.S. states have specific statutes requiring mental health professionals to report in good faith any suspicion of abuse or neglect (Barnett, Miller-Perrin, and Perrin, 1997). In fact, by 1967, all states had some type of relevant law in this regard (Zellman, 1990). The states with reporting statutes usually include an article that gives the mental health care provider immunity from liability for such reports; that is, despite the breach of confidentiality, the clinician cannot be prosecuted for her or his disclosure of privileged communication (Bulkley, Feller, Stern, and Roe, 1996; DeKraii, Sales, and Hall, 1998).

Although different states define abuse and neglect in slightly different terms, the definitions provided by Walker, Bonner, and Kaufman (1988) capture the essence of most legal definitions. They define physical abuse "as inflicting injury such as bruises, burns, head injuries, fractures, internal injuries, lacerations, or any other form of physical harm lasting at least 48 hours.... [This] may also include excessive corporal punishment and close confinement... (Walker, Bonner, and Kaufman, 1988, p. 8). Emotional abuse is defined as "the use of excessive verbal threats, ridicule, personally demeaning comments, derogatory statements, and threats...to the extent that the child's emotional and mental well-being is jeopardized" (p. 8). Sexual abuse has been defined as "the involvement of dependent, developmentally immature children and adolescents in sexual activities they do not fully comprehend, are unable to give informed consent to and that violate the social taboos of family roles" (Helfer and Kempe as quoted in Walker, Bonner, and Kaufman, 1988, p. 8). Finally, neglect is defined through "acts of omission in which the child is not properly cared for physically (nutrition, safety, education, medical care, etc.) or emotionally (failure to bond, lack of affection, love, support, nurturing, or concern)" (Walker, Bonner, and Kaufman, 1988, p. 8).

It is important for the child therapist to recognize that almost all state statutes written to protect children from abuse or neglect require the mental health provider to report not only actual proven incidents of abuse and neglect, but also the mere suspicion thereof (Azar, 1992). Thus, even indirect evidence that emerges in the treatment with a particular child needs to be reported. Most states have provisions for criminal prosecution of clinicians who fail to make a good-faith report. As is the case with the duty to warn, the duty to report supersedes confidentiality laws and holds the clinician harmless. Although practical suggestions about how to best make reports will be covered later, it should be pointed out here that if the therapist believes that the reporting of abuse to the appropriate state agency would result in the family's fleeing or other behavior to avoid prosecution, she or he is obligated to keep the child on the premises of the clinic while the report is being made—in fact, until a child protection worker arrives (Walker, Bonner, and Kaufman, 1988).

The consequences of a report of child abuse can vary widely. If the reported offense is the first reported perpetration and is relatively minor, often nothing happens to the family. Investigations tend to result only after more than one report about the same offender or if the child's life appears to be endangered. At the other extreme, if the reported offense represents a repeated incident or if it is considered severe, the child may be removed from the home and placed in foster care immediately. Often, treatment rather than prosecution is ordered after few or mild offenses. Child abuse can be prosecuted in court as a criminal offense if the perpetrator is not a family member or as a civil action if the offender is a family member. Child sexual abuse may be tried twice—once in civil court if perpetrated by a family member, and again in criminal court (Bulkley, 1988; Swenson, 1997).

Miscellaneous Other Issues

There are many other legal issues that a clinician may encounter, though perhaps none as disheartening as the necessity to report abuse of a child. Search and seizure is a problem that can have a profound impact on client-therapist relationships even if the warrant was not for the particular child (DeKraii, Sales, and Hall, 1998). In search and seizure cases, law enforcement officers may go through all of a therapist's client files, thus breaching confidentiality for the clinician's entire caseload. When such a court order was obtained for an Anchorage, Alaska, school counselor because of a case of suspected sexual abuse of a student by a teacher, police ransacked all of the counselor's confidential files in the attempt to gather evidence about the case in question. When the information about police officers reading confidential files became known among students, they felt extremely violated, and trust became a difficult issue in student-counselor and student-teacher relationships.

Dual relationships, an extraordinarily important issue in the practice with adults, may also become of issue in the work with children. Dual relationships are defined as relationships wherein the clinician and the client have a relationship other than that contained within the therapy room. Such other relationships may include, but are not limited to, sexual relationships, friendships, instructor-student relationships, and employer-employee relationships (Brems, 2000, 2001). They are not only ethical transgressions, but also inhibit the development of a healthy, therapeutically valuable relationship. Dual relationships are less likely to occur between a clinician and a child client than between a therapist and an adult. However, some dual relationships with children may not involve the child directly. For instance, a therapist's friendship or familial relationship with a child's parent precludes this child from ever seeking therapy from that particular clinician. If the clinician is the parent of the potential child client's friend, the child should be referred to another therapist. If the clinician already sees another member of the child's nuclear family, the child is probably best not taken on as a client. Thus, although dual relationships with children may not be as straightforward as those with adults, they do exist, are unethical, and must be avoided. The American Psychological Association (1992) has strong guidelines against dual relationships with psychotherapy clients, and violations result in a report to local licensing boards or the APA ethics committee.

Another ethical issue is that of adequate training of the clinician (Corey, Corey, and Callanan, 1998), as well as continuing education of already seasoned child therapists. It is important for therapists to treat only those clients whom they are qualified to treat. The American Psychological Association has specified this requirement clearly, and, as is the case with other ethical violations, noncompliance may result in a report to a local licensing board or the APA ethics committee.

Despite the coverage of this technical legal and ethical information, questions probably remain about the practical implementation and application of these principles. Exact legal language, and hence implementation, may vary slightly from state to state as laws differ and as procedures vary from agency to agency. For instance, in some states, the office to be notified in the case of suspected abuse is housed in the Department of Health and Human Services (e.g., Oklahoma), in others the Department of Family and Youth Services (e.g., Alaska). Each clinician will need to take the responsibility to review local laws and statutes, to familiarize herself or himself with relevant professional ethical codes, and to learn about specific reporting procedures for the state in which she or he practices. Nevertheless, some general guidelines and practical tips are available and will be shared here.

Practical Implications and Applications of Relevant Legal and Ethical Issues

The practical implementation of legal and ethical issues in the treatment of children is critical but much easier than may be anticipated. In fact, much of what needs to be done is part and parcel of a clinician's normal repertoire of intake and therapeutic skills. The first face-to-face contact with clients is used to introduce all legal and ethical concepts, though a lot of detail might not be provided until a particular issue is called into question. For instance, the actual procedure of a report about child abuse might not be discussed with a family until the need for it arises. However, the information about the possibility of such a report must be disclosed in the first session.

Informed Consent

Most prudently, a signature on the written informed consent form is collected from a family before the intake interview begins. This informed consent is a critical piece of paperwork that must include information about confidentiality, limits of confidentiality, duty to warn, duty to protect, duty to report, clinic procedures, observation and recording policies, and possibly even fee schedules. Any tape recording practices and observation provisions must be shared with the family. If the therapist has a supervisor, the family must be told, preferably with a disclosure of the supervisor's name. The informed consent is a written document, and care must be taken to ascertain that there is one literate, legally competent (i.e., above the state's legal age of competence and capable of sufficient cognitive complexity) member in the family group, who not only is an identified legal guardian or can respond in loco parentis, but also can comprehend and respond to the document. If no one in the family can read it, a clinic staff must be available to read and explain the form to the family and to collect signatures from the appropriate guardian as defined above. If the identified child client is above age 11 or 12 and the clinician so chooses, the child's signature may be collected as well. A suggested format of a generic informed consent is provided in Figure 2.1. An informed consent that could be read by the child is presented in Figure 2.2.

Despite having obtained written informed consent, it behooves the clinician to cover the informed consent information again verbally at the beginning of the initial session. This coverage should be such that it is comprehensible even to the youngest child in the group (unless that child is below approximately 3 to 4 years of age). In this discussion, the clinician should reiterate all of the issues and should take care to define them well and in a therapeutic context. Thus, confidentiality may be introduced as a privacy issue, the duty to warn or protect as a safety issue, and the duty to report as a protection issue.

Confidentiality

While going over informed consent information verbally, limits and parameters of confidentiality are particularly important to note. Parents and children should be informed about the therapist's rules regarding disclosure to the parents of information provided by the child and vice versa. Although, as was noted above, legal guidelines are not clear on this issue, and individual practices vary widely, each clinician must adopt a uniform stance that is carried out with all clients consistently. Using one approach with one client and another with a different client is bound to cause confusion and mistakes. If a clinician has decided to disclose all information to everybody, regardless of when and how it was obtained, the family must be informed of this procedure. However, if the therapist has a policy of sharing only progress reports without specific details, then this approach must be explained and justified. Explanations and procedures may need to be repeated with the child or children individually, in addition to having been covered at the beginning of the intake session to make them more understandable at the appropriate developmental level.

It is often critical to inform children, especially older children, of disclosure policies vis-à-vis parents. Many children will feel much more at ease with a progress report policy than a detail-by-detail disclosure policy. It is possible to negotiate with the child what information can and cannot be shared with the parents within the appropriate confines of

FIGURE 2.1 Informed Consent Form—Adult

[*Clinic Name*]   Date:

[*Clinic Address*]   Name:

Welcome to the [*Clinic Name*]. This document contains important information about our center's professional services and business policies. Please read it carefully and note any questions you might have so you can discuss them with the clinician conducting your screening appointment. Once you sign this consent form, it will constitute an agreement between you, you on behalf of your minor child (if applicable), your therapist(s), and the [*Clinic Name*]. In this document, the term "client" is used for the individual or individuals seeking services. Thus, "client" may refer to an individual adult client, a family, or a part of a family (e.g., a child, or a parent).

Nature of Psychological Services

Psychotherapy is not easily described because it varies greatly depending on the therapist, the client (whether an individual, a family, or a part of a family), and the particular problems a client presents. There are often a variety of approaches that can be utilized to deal with the problem(s) that brought a client to therapy. These services are generally unlike any services you may receive from a physician in that they require your active participation and cooperation.

Psychotherapy has both benefits and risks. Possible risks may include the experience of uncomfortable feelings (such as sadness, guilt, anxiety, anger, frustration, loneliness, or helplessness) or the recall of unpleasant events in your life. Potential benefits include significant reduction in feelings of distress, better relationships, better problem-solving and coping skills, and resolutions of specific problems. Given the nature of psychotherapy, it is difficult to predict what exactly will happen but your therapist will do her or his best to make sure that you will be able to handle the risks and experience at least some of the benefits. However, psychotherapy remains an inexact science and no guarantees can be made regarding outcomes.

Procedures

Therapy usually starts with an evaluation. It is our practice at the [*Clinic Name*] to conduct an evaluation that lasts from 2 to 4 sessions. This evaluation begins with a screening appointment and is followed up with an intake interview (that may last 1 to 3 sessions). During the evaluation, several decisions have to be made: the therapist has to decide if the [*Clinic Name*] has the services needed to treat your presenting problem(s), you as the client (whether an individual, a family, or a part of a family) have to decide if you are comfortable with the therapist(s) that has(ve) been assigned to you, and you and your assigned therapist(s) have to decide on your goals for therapy and how best to achieve them.

In other words, by the end of the evaluation, your therapist will offer you initial impressions of what therapy will involve, if you (as an individual, a family, or a part of a family) decide to continue. Therapy generally involves a significant commitment of time, money, and energy, so it is your right to be careful about the therapist you select. If you have questions about any of the [*Clinic Name*] procedures or the therapist(s) who was (were) assigned to you, feel free to discuss these openly with the therapist. If you have doubts about the [*Clinic Name*] or your assigned therapist(s), we will be happy to help you to make an appointment with another mental health professional.

If you decide to seek services at the [*Clinic Name*], your therapist(s) will usually schedule one fifty-minute session per week at a mutually agreed time (under some special circumstances sessions may be longer or more frequent). This appointment will be reserved for you on a regular basis and is considered a standing appointment (i.e., if you miss one week, you will still have the same appointment time next week). The overall length of psychotherapy (in weeks or months) is generally difficult to predict but is something your therapist(s) will discuss with you as the initial treatment plan is shared with you after completion of the evaluation.

Fee-Related Issues

The [*Clinic Name*] works on a sliding fee schedule that will be discussed with you during your initial appointment. Screening appointments always cost $[*insert clinic fee*]. Fees for therapy range from $[*insert range of fees*], depending on income and therapist. In addition to charging for weekly appointments, the [*Clinic Name*] also charges special fees for other professional services you may require (such as telephone conversations which last longer than 10 minutes, meetings or consultations with other professionals that you have requested, etc.). In unusual circumstances, you may become involved in litigation wherein you request or require your therapist's (and her or his supervisor's, if applicable) participation. You will be expected to pay for such professional time required even if your therapist is compelled to testify by another party.

You will be expected to pay for each session at the time it is held, unless you and your therapist agreed otherwise. Payment schedules for other professional services will be agreed to at the time that these services are requested. In circumstances of unusual financial hardship, you may negotiate a fee adjustment or installment payment plan with your assigned therapist(s). Once your standing appointment hour is scheduled, you will be expected to pay for it (even if you missed it) unless you provide 24 hours' advance notice of cancellation.

To enable you and your therapist(s) to set realistic treatment goals and priorities, it is important to evaluate what resources are available to pay for your treatment. If you have a health benefits policy, it will usually provide some coverage for mental health treatment if such treatment is provided by a licensed professional. Your therapist will provide you with whatever assistance possible to facilitate your receipt of the benefits to which you are entitled, including completing insurance forms as appropriate. However, you (*not* your insurance company) are responsible for full payment of the fee. If your therapist is a trainee, you will not be able to use your insurance benefits.

Carefully read the section in your insurance coverage booklet that describes mental health services and call your insurer if you have any questions. Your therapist will provide you with whatever information she or he has based on her or his experience and will be happy to try to help you understand the information you receive from your carrier. The escalation of the cost of health care has resulted in an increasing level of complexity about insurance benefits that often makes it difficult to determine exactly how much mental heath coverage is available. "Managed Health Care Plans" such as HMOs and PPOs often require advance authorization before they will provide reimbursement for mental health services. These

(continued)

FIGURE 2.1   *Continued*

plans are often oriented towards a short-term treatment approach designed to resolve specific problems that are interfering with level of functioning. It may be necessary to seek additional approval after a certain number of sessions. Although a lot can be accomplished in short-term therapy, many clients feel that more services are necessary after the insurance benefits expire. Some managed care plans will not allow your therapist to provide reimbursed services to you once your benefits are no longer available. If this is the case, [*Clinic Name*] staff will do their best to find another provider who will help you continue your psychotherapy.

Please be aware that most insurance agreements require you to authorize your therapist to provide a clinical diagnosis, and sometimes additional clinical information such as treatment plans or summaries, or in rare cases, a copy of the entire record. This information will become part of the insurance company's files, and, in all likelihood, some of it will be computerized. All insurance companies claim to keep such information confidential, but once it is in their hands, your therapist has no control over what your insurer will do with the information. In some cases, the insurer may share the information with a national medical information data bank.

It is best to discuss all the information about your insurance coverage with your therapist, so you can decide what can be accomplished within the parameters of the benefits available to you and what will happen if the insurance benefits run out before you are ready to end treatment. It is important to remember that you always have the right to pay for psychological services yourself if you prefer to avoid involving your insurer.

Contact Hours

The [*Clinic Name*] is open from 9 a.m. to 5 p.m. daily but some evening and weekend appointments may be available. Your therapist is generally not available for telephone services but you can cancel and reschedule sessions with the assistance of the receptionist or through leaving messages on the confidential answering machine. If you need to reschedule an appointment, your therapist will make every effort to return your call on the same day, with the exception of calls made after hours or on weekends and holidays. If you are difficult to reach, please leave some times when you will be available. If you have an emergency but are unable to reach your therapist, call your family physician, emergency services at [*insert name of local crisis line*], or the emergency room at [*insert name of local hospitals*]. Please note that the [*Clinic Name*] itself does not have emergency services or facilities.

Videotaping and Record-Keeping Procedures

All client sessions are videotaped. These tapes are made for supervision or consultation purposes only and are kept in a confidential locked placed until the therapist has reviewed them with a supervisor or consultant as needed. Once tapes have been reviewed, they are erased. Most tapes are erased within less than one week; no tapes are kept for more than two weeks. In addition to videotapes, therapists also keep case notes. These notes are also kept under lock and key and are strictly confidential. The case notes are reviewed by the therapist, by his or her supervisor or consultant (if applicable), and then are filed permanently in a client's record. All records are locked and kept confidential. Information in the client records may be used for evaluation, research, and service planning purposes. Such use is entirely anonymous, and no individual client data will ever be used. No client names are ever associated with data extracted from records for research or evaluation purposes, and all data will merely be presented in group data format, a format that preserves anonymity and never reveals individual client data.

Both law and the standards of the profession of psychology require that therapists keep treatment records. You are entitled to receive a copy of these records, unless your therapist believes that seeing them would be emotionally damaging to you. If this is the case, your therapist will be happy to provide your records to an appropriate mental health professional of your choice. Although you are entitled to receive a copy of your records if you wish to see them, your therapist may prefer to prepare an appropriate summary instead. Because client records are professional documents, they can be misinterpreted and can be upsetting. If you insist on seeing your records, it is best to review them with your therapist so that the two of you can discuss what they contain. Clients will be charged an appropriate fee for any preparation time that is required to comply with an informal request for record review.

If a client is under eighteen years of age, the law may provide parents with the right to examine the minor child's treatment records. It is [*Clinic Name*] policy to request an agreement from parents that they consent to give up access to the child's records. If they agree, the therapist will provide the parents only with general information on how the child's treatment is proceeding unless there is a high risk that the minor client will seriously harm herself or himself or another person. In such instances, the therapist may be required by law to notify the parents of her or his concern. Parents of minors also can request to be provided with a summary of their child's treatment when it is complete. Before giving parents any information, the therapist will discuss this matter with the minor client and will do the best she or he can to resolve any objections the child client may have about what will be discussed. Please note that the [*Clinic Name*] does not provide treatment to minors without their parents' consent.

Confidentiality

In general, the confidentiality of all communications between a client and a psychologist is protected by law, and your therapist can release information to others about your therapy only with your written permission. However, there are a number of exceptions:

- In most judicial proceedings, you have the right to prevent your therapist from providing any information about your treatment. However, in some circumstances (such as child custody proceedings and proceedings in which your emotional condition is an important element), a judge may require your therapist's testimony if the judge determines that resolution of the issues before her or him demands it.
- There are times when it may be helpful for other professionals to gain access to all or parts of your treatment records. Under such circumstances, data can be released from your [*Clinic Name*] record if you give your therapist written permission (in the form of a Release of Information) to do so. Such release cannot take place unless you consent in writing.
- There are some situations in which your therapist is legally required to take action to protect others from harm, even if such action requires revealing some information about your treatment:
  - If your therapist believes that a child, an elderly person, or a disabled person is being abused, she or he is required by law to file a report with the appropriate state agency (in Alaska this is the Department of Family and Youth Services).

(continued)

FIGURE 2.1 *Continued*

- If your therapist believes that you are threatening serious bodily harm to another person, she or he is required by law to take protective actions, which may include notifying the potential victim, notifying the police, or seeking appropriate hospitalization.

  - If you threaten to harm yourself (e.g., suicide), your therapist is required to make all necessary arrangements to protect your safety, a process that may include seeking hospitalization for you or contacting family members or others who can help provide protection.

- At the [*Clinic Name*], some therapists are working under the supervision of licensed psychologists who meet with the therapists on a weekly basis in a one-on-one meeting to review client cases. If your assigned therapist is one of these, you will be told so. Your case will be then discussed during the weekly meetings between your therapist and her or his supervisor. The supervisor is a part of the [*Clinic Name*] staff and is bound by the same confidentiality laws as your therapist. The supervisor and therapist will also review therapy tapes as necessary to the therapist's education.

- At the [*Clinic Name*], some therapists occasionally seek consultation to assist with treatment decisions. Such consultation occurs only as needed and is done in such a manner as not to identify the client in any way. Additionally, consultants are bound by the same confidentiality laws as therapists and hence are prohibited by law to disclose any of the information they receive from the therapist about clients.

- At the [*Clinic Name*], all therapists participate in weekly staff meetings. These meetings are used as opportunities for consultation, and each week a client case is presented. Your case may be one of the cases that will be presented during these meetings. The meetings are confidential and only [*Clinic Name*] staff participate. Only first names of clients are used and all members of the [*Clinic Name*] staff are bound by the same confidentiality laws as your therapist.

Signatures Verifying Agreement

Your signature below indicates that you have read the information in this document, that you have understood it, and that you agree to abide by its terms as long as you are a [*Clinic Name*] client.

_____   _____
Client/Parent/Guardian Signature and Date   Witness Signature and Date

Special Note: *This informed consent was developed on the basis of a sample provided by Drs. Bruce Bennett and Eric Harris of the American Psychological Association during a workshop on Risk Management in Psychology in Anchorage, Alaska, in November 1995. The original sample (called an* Outpatient Service Contract) *can be requested from the APA Insurance Trust at 750 First Street NE, Suite 605, Washington, DC 20002-4242.*

Informed Consent

I understand that I am about to start therapy at this clinic. That means that I will sit down with a therapist and talk about myself and about my family and any problems or fights we might be having. I know that my therapist has a video camera and uses it to record us when we talk or play. I also know that these tapes are secret and are erased every week.

I know that I don't have to talk about anything I don't want to talk about. My therapist can't make me do anything I don't want to do. I also know that I have the right to say that I don't want to come back.

I understand that what I tell my therapist is between me and the therapist, and my therapist only tells my parents if I am feeling better or worse. My therapist does not tell my parents what I say about them or my family.

The only time my therapist has to talk to other people about what I told is if I tell the therapist that somebody is hurting me badly in some way. For instance, if somebody beats me so hard that I have bruises, my therapist would have to tell. If I told my therapist that I wanted to hurt myself, then my therapist would have to tell.

If my therapist wants to talk to anybody else besides my parents about me, my parents and I first have to say in writing that this is okay to do.

I agree to talk to my therapist now that I know all these things about therapy. I have put my name on this paper to show that I agree to start therapy.

_____

Child's Name (written by the child)

_____   _____

Child's Name (written by the therapist)   Date

FIGURE 2.2   Informed Consent Form—Child

legal requirements. Regardless of how disclosure is made to parents, ethical guidelines for clinicians do require that parents be informed of progress; in fact, they have the right to be informed objectively and caringly (Brems, 1996; Lampe and Johnson, 1988). Just as confidentiality in the work with adults facilitates the adult's decision to seek therapy, a well-established parental disclosure policy for children facilitates the establishment of therapeutic rapport and trust. Further, children need to be informed that they themselves do not have to share information about their sessions with their parents. Sometimes, parents do pry and ask many questions of their children. It is acceptable for the clinician to inform parents that this is inappropriate and that it is the child's choice when and what to disclose about an individual session (Brems, 1996; Dodds, 1985).

A therapist also needs to decide how to handle information obtained between sessions. It does occur that parents or child protection workers may contact the clinician between a child's session with critical information. One way of handling such data gathering is to let the child know at the beginning of the next session what new information was obtained and how. This sharing of information and information sources can avoid suspicion and lack of trust on the child's part and discourages parents from calling the clinician without a very serious reason. Taking phone calls from parents between sessions about minor issues may lead the child to feel that the clinician cannot be trusted and is working in cahoots with the parents.

Also related to confidentiality are release of information procedures involving other agencies and schools. Given the legal guidelines, clinicians are required to collect signatures from the legal guardian or parent if communication with schools or other agencies is necessary. Only if a child is considered "competent" would her or his permission also need to be secured. Competent children, and obviously most adolescents, should be involved in this decision-making process, not merely because of legal requirements, but also for therapeutic reasons. The more the child is involved in her or his own treatment decisions, the more likely that she or he will feel that this treatment is helpful and growth-promoting. This approach is also in line with the recommendations put forth by the U.N. Convention, which stress privacy rights of children and children's involvement in treatment planning.

When releases of information have been obtained, it is important to outline for the family and child the exact nature of the information that can be communicated among the various agencies and individuals. This issue holds particular importance in interactions with schools, in which the flow of information must be carefully controlled so as not to result in stigmatization or prejudice. If teachers need to be involved in treatment implementation, such as developing a behavior modification program in the classroom, the parents and child may need to be involved in the meeting between clinician and teacher to ensure that everyone knows how much information was exchanged. Even when teachers are asked to implement treatment plans in the classroom, they generally do not need to find out everything the clinician knows about the child client. Thus, a verbal information exchange is often more appropriate than a release of clinical paperwork, such as intake reports or treatment plans to the school. If paperwork is released from a clinic, it is best to clearly mark "Not for rerelease" to prevent a report reaching undesired targets.

Duty to Warn and Duty to Protect

In the context of discussing informed consents and, more specifically, the limits of confidentiality, the clinician also has to inform the clients of her or his duty to warn and protect. This issue is generally only shared in a matter-of-fact manner and not discussed in detail unless it has to be invoked owing to a concrete threat made by the child or the parent. If a parent threatens to harm the child, the clinician is legally responsible to inform the police. However, in this case, it is best also to involve the appropriate child protection agency to ascertain that alternative care can be arranged for the child. If the parent is considered a significant danger, commitment procedures might need to be initiated. This generally involves contacting a local psychiatric institution and getting help from a physician and the court system, because few states allow psychologists to make involuntary commitments.

If a child threatens to harm a parent or sibling, it may be sufficient to notify the parents of the intent if the clinician is confident that the parent will be able to protect herself or himself or the sibling sufficiently. If there is doubt about the parent's ability to protect, the police must be involved. Threats of suicide from children must be shared with their parents, who also need to be involved if the clinician believes that hospitalization is necessary. Each therapist, when she or he begins to work with children, needs to identify a hospital to which children can be referred if they are considered a threat to themselves or others. It is important for the clinician to familiarize herself or himself with that clinic's intake and emergency procedures so that when a referral has to be made, she or he knows what to do and can help the parents deal with the stresses of that situation. Having to help parents and trying to find out procedures at the same time does not tend to instill much confidence in the parents and leaves them feeling unsure and vulnerable.

Although therapists must keep progress notes and records of all interactions with clients at any time, particular care should be taken to document any situation that may involve the limits of confidentiality (Brems, 2000; Pietrofesa, Pietrofesa, and Pietrofesa, 1990). Good record keeping is critical to the documentation of situations that involve the possibility for a duty to warn or protect, to safeguard the clinician from legal liability. This liability may involve the disclosure of privileged information if the therapist does not document that the duty to warn or protect was invoked, or may involve the failure to report. Whenever a client makes a threat, the exact nature of the threat must be recorded along with the procedure followed by the clinician either to rule out the threat and maintain confidentiality or to validate the threat and warn. Similarly, careful record keeping is necessary in the context of the duty to report.

Duty to Report

When a clinician has suspicion or evidence of child abuse or neglect, a report must be made to the local child protection agency. Obviously, to be able to conform to this law, a clinician must be prepared to identify children who have been abused or neglected. Although there are no foolproof ways of so doing, there are some guidelines upon which the therapist may rely. Physical neglect is relatively easy to identify by inspecting the child's relative height and weight, her or his grooming and hygiene, and the cleanliness of clothing. There may also be a decrease in intellectual functioning, as well as overall developmental delays. Common symptoms include repression of feelings, violence, and inability to empathize (Gil, 1991; Helfer, Kempe, and Krugman, 1997). Emotional neglect is not only difficult to identify with tangible signs, but also difficult to prove to a child protection worker. Nevertheless, emotional neglect is extremely harmful and must be reported. An emotionally neglected child may be identified by looking for signs of insecurity, overly anxious relating, inability to trust, caretaking behavior toward younger siblings, or denial of obvious family problems. Common symptoms include behavior problems, low self-esteem, parentified role in the family, and attachment problems (Gil, 1991; Iwaniec, 1995). Although all of these signs and symptoms can have other reasons, they warrant further investigation of the child-parent relationship to assess whether the child receives the emotional support and nurturance necessary to facilitate her or his growth and maturation.

Physical abuse, if it is ongoing, is obviously easier to identify than sexual abuse, which rarely leaves physically visible marks. The clinician must be aware of bruises, cuts, and other unusual marks or evidence of physical trauma on the child's body. Reports of frequent accidents, unusual injuries, and frequent trips to the emergency room for serious injuries should alert the clinician to the possibility of physical abuse. Common presenting problems include oppositionality or withdrawal, hypervigilance, pseudomaturity, elimination disorders, behavior problems, and low self-esteem (Gil, 1991; Oates, 1996). Obviously, none of these factors by itself can be considered evidence of abuse. However, frequent occurrence or joint occurrence implies that the therapist must begin to ask questions of the child and the family regarding abuse. If these inquiries lead to further suspicions in the clinician, as opposed to alleviating her or his concerns, a report is warranted.

Sexual abuse victims are difficult to spot. However, reported sudden changes in the child's academic performance or daily routines, such as appetite, sleeping, or behavior, may hint at added stress in a child's life (Barnett, Miller-Perrin, and Perrin, 1997). If these signals are accompanied by increased aggressiveness or fearfulness, sexual preoccupations, above-normal levels of sexual play and sexual exploration, above-expected level of sexual knowledge or interest, or overly sexualized behavior in the company of adults, the clinician must investigate further. Common presenting symptoms include, but are not limited to, depression, fears, anger, school problems, and runaway behavior (Burkhardt and Rotatari, 1995; Gil, 1991). Again, as with physical abuse, none of these indicators in and of itself is sufficient. However, it must be stressed that in most states, a suspicion suffices for a report to be made.

Once a child has been assessed and the clinician believes that the child has been victimized in some form, a report must be made. The best preparation for having to make such a report is to have investigated the procedures beforehand. Just as was discussed in relation to the duty to protect, the clinician should familiarize herself or himself with local agencies and procedures of reporting abuse and neglect. It is good practice to phone the local agency and make an appointment to discuss procedures and to glean a sense of how families are treated once a report has been made. This helps the family to anticipate more exactly what will happen to them and leaves them feeling more trusting of the clinician. There is some controversy among clinicians as to whether reporting laws interfere with therapeutic rapport with parents and families and significant noncompliance with the law has been reported (e.g., Kalichman, Craig, and Follingstad, 1990; Sedlak, 1990). Although the question about the impact of reporting on the therapeutic relationship is an important one, it remains somewhat academic, as the laws are completely clear: There is no leeway. If there is a suspicion or evidence of neglect or abuse, a report must be made! Once the report has been made, the therapeutic relationship can once again be attended to.

It does appear that there is some consensus in the clinical literature that getting the abuser to make the report herself or himself in the clinician's presence is preferable to the therapist making the report (Brems, 2000; Dodds, 1985; Walker, Bonner, and Kaufman, 1988). These therapists indicate that when a suspicion or evidence has been discovered, the abuser is reminded of the clinician's duty to report. The client is then asked to make the report herself or himself from the clinician's office in the clinician's presence. Then the clinician always follows up with her or his own phone call. Generally, the client can be reassured that this procedure will result in more leniency from the child protection agency toward the perpetrator. Further, it places the responsibility for the behavior squarely in the perpetrator's lap and often serves to preserve a relationship between the therapist and abuser. If the abuser refuses to make the call herself or himself, the therapist should make

TABLE 2.1   Information Critical to the Duty to Report

- Biographical data of the victim
- Location of the victim
- Current location and addresses of the family of the victim
- Current location and addresses of the perpetrator
- Current location and address of the reporter
- Nature, severity, and chronicity of the situation
- Current status of the victim (e.g., extent and description of bruises or injuries)
- Dates of recent incidents
- Names of witnesses
- Immediate safety issues concerning the victim

the call in the abuser's presence at this time. Once the agency has been informed, the clinician should ask about the agency's immediate plan so that she or he can notify the family of what is likely to happen before they leave the office.

If a report is to be made, there are certain pieces of information that the child protection worker is likely to request. It is best to be prepared by having the child's chart available during the conversation and to have ascertained that it contains sufficient detail that very specific questions can be answered. The therapist must be prepared to identify the child, the perpetrator, the child's family, potential witnesses, and herself or himself, as well as the exact circumstances of instances of abuse and neglect and the child's current state of health and safety. Critical information is summarized in Table 2.1.

Once a report has been made, it may be advisable to schedule a quick follow-up appointment with the family to enhance the chances of keeping them in treatment. The follow-up appointment would serve to help them deal with the investigation by the child protection agency and, more important, to address issues of trust and rapport between the family and the therapist. The therapist must be very sensitive to hurt feelings and feelings of rejection and betrayal by the family and each individual member. The individual child, on the basis of whose disclosure the report was made, must also be seen individually to explore issues of trust, rejection, and guilt. Dealing with a family in the wake of a report of abuse or neglect is not easy. However, not dealing with them is even more detrimental to everyone involved.

Summary and Concluding Thoughts

A number of ethical and legal issues emerge in the work with children. However, none is insurmountable and, in most cases, the duty to warn, protect, or report never has to be invoked. Further, being prepared for having to move beyond any of these limits to confidentiality protects the clinician from legal liability and makes it more likely that treatment success can still be achieved. Finally, familiarity with the U.N. Convention on children's rights will give child clinicians an appreciation of the special issues involved in the treatment of children and places this work in the proper context of balancing children's rights to self-determination and independence with needs for protection and nurturance.

3 A Developmental Context for Child Psychotherapy

No discussion of children can be complete without giving some thought to development. Not too many years ago, childhood and development were treated synonymously, with many clinicians disregarding the impact of development on, and its continuation throughout, adult life. Nevertheless, there is general agreement that developmental events are at their peak during childhood and that development progresses more rapidly during this part of life than any other (Eliot, 1999; Spiegel, 1996). This rapid development brings with it rapid changes and influences the lives of children profoundly. Any adult who works with children in any capacity must have a genuine appreciation of these changes and of the milestones children must reach in their early years (Schroeder and Gordon, 1991). Only then will adults remember never to treat children like miniature adults, as used to be the case (Russ and Freedheim, 2001), but rather to keep aware and abreast of the special needs and behaviors that development brings for children. Only then will adults remember that children constantly evolve and that the perception of them has to change to follow their development. In other words, the adults in a child's life must have the flexibility to revise their view of and approach to the child with each new developmental task that has been mastered to maintain a realistic and respectful relationship with the child. It is often the very lack of this flexibility on parents' parts that brings families to treatment. Many therapists have encountered parents who were not able to allow an adolescent daughter to separate when she was ready to do so or parents who did not think their 10-year-old son would understand why they were divorcing because they had lost track of his ever-advancing cognitive complexity. Thus, a thorough appreciation of development is essential for the therapist to keep up with her or his child client and to set realistic therapeutic goals.

Development: Definition, Influences, and Types

Definition of Development

Although there are several models of development, only one is quite comprehensive in its look at the interaction between the individual and the environment. This dialectic model stresses that development occurs and is not only guided by physical or biological factors that occur within the individual, but also affected by psychological, cultural, and external factors (Lerner, Skinner, and Sorrell, 1980). Given this complex interaction, development is viewed as a never-ending process that is shaped by the individual's experiences in her or his environment. It emphasizes that development resembles evolution, and results not only in the acquisition of behavior, but also, perhaps even more important, in "the maintenance and transformation of useful skills and the extinction of formerly adaptive behaviors" (Wimbarti and Self, 1992, p. 37). Thus, the focus of this model is on change, rather than on a predetermined end state.

This dialectic model of development harmonizes extremely well with the focus of psychotherapeutic work with children. In both developmental psychology and psychotherapy, children are observed and encouraged to change and grow. In the former, this observation and encouragement occur within the normal or healthy context of self-perpetuating evolution of behavior, self, and relationships; in the latter, observation and encouragement occur in the context of helping children to return to their healthy developmental trajectories after they had been derailed for one reason or another. However, both watch children grow, and both make the attempt to understand each individual child from her or his unique developmental perspective at any given time in the child's life.

Influences on Development

When attempting to determine a child's developmental maturity and adjustment, the dialectic developmental perspective takes a look not merely at the child's age, but also at the biological, psychological, cultural, and "outerphysical" (Wimbarti and Self, 1992, p. 33) factors that have occurred or are occurring in the child's life. For instance, a dialectic developmentalist would not assume that a child who is referred for aggressive behavior evidences "normal" manifestations of an autonomy struggle just because the child is 3 years old but would also explore whether the child has been subjected to any psychological, biological, cultural, or outerphysical events that may have contributed to this behavior. Perhaps the child is aggressive, not because of an age-determined milestone (i.e., Erikson's autonomy versus shame and doubt conflict), but because of the death of a parent (psychological factor), frequent severe headaches (biological factor), or having survived a recent earthquake (outerphysical factor). Considering all of these influences on development, as well as when and how they occur, helps the professional to understand the child much better and can help to place the child's actions, needs, and affects in a developmental context that is unique to this child.

Biological Factors.   Biological factors that may affect a child's development are often easy to spot. Some are related to age-specific bodily changes, such as the onset of puberty. Others are related to larger historical changes, such as malnutrition due to a long-term drought-related food shortage or low socioeconomic status. Who has not seen pictures of African children whose development was delayed because of their starvation diets? Finally, some biological factors occur out of the blue, completely unexpectedly, such as a head injury after a bicycling accident. Such an injury is likely to affect the child's development, especially if it is severe.

Psychological Factors.   Psychological factors, like biological factors, can occur at expected age-related times, can be products of historical occurrences, or can arrive unpredictably. The sudden and unexpected death of a parent can affect a child's development just as profoundly as the historically driven equal rights movement of women. Finally, the age-specific development of peer group relationships will affect the child's maturation and behavioral evolution.

Cultural Factors.   Age-relevant cultural factors impact a child's development. For example, children's lives are greatly altered when they begin school at age 6. Historical cultural events will also affect children's maturation. Early contact with alcoholic beverages in a community that endorses their free and unlimited use may have serious effects upon a child's cognitive and behavioral development. Finally, cultural events, such as being born and raised in an inner city, may have significant impact on a child.

Outerphysical Factors.   Outerphysical factors include events such as earthquakes, storms, pollution, and threats of nuclear war over which the individual has virtually no direct control. They can affect development significantly. For instance, lead poisoning can retard cognitive maturation, and living through a tornado may result in phobias about wind.

Types of Development.   The child psychotherapist who is sensitive to developmental issues in children and who attempts to see their symptoms within the developmental framework of the child will pay attention to these influencing factors and have an appreciation of age-normed expectations within various realms of development. However, these age-normed factors are never to be used in isolation, but rather are always to be explored within the dialectic framework of the child's whole experience. Thus, while hundreds of books exist that outline tables for normal motor development, emotional development, cognitive development, language development, and so on, none of these guidelines should ever be abused by attempting to determine where a child should be on the developmental continuum merely because of her or his age. To expect a 3-year-old boy to deal with autonomy issues when he has just survived an earthquake is irresponsible. More than likely, this outerphysical event has affected the child to such a degree that he may once again be grappling with simple trust in his world. Helping him to deal with the experience of the environmental event will be the better course of action. Nevertheless, all child therapists must have some awareness of the stages of development.

Although discussing them individually would be beyond the scope of this book, there are several arenas of development in which expected (or "normal") behaviors have been plotted against normative age ranges. These have been alluded to above and include motor development (Gallahue and Ozmun, 2002; Haywood and Getchell, 2001), language development (Owens, 2001), cognitive development (Bjorklund, 1999; Piaget, 1967), moral development (Killen and Hart, 2000; Kagan and Lamb, 1990), self development (Stern, 1977, 1985, 1989), emotional development (Kail, 2001; Lane and Schwartz, 1986), psychosocial development (Erikson, 1950), and psychosexual development (Freud, 1952). A thorough overview of these therapeutically relevant arenas, grouped according to children's expected age ranges, is provided in Tables 3.1 to 3.7. To be able to appreciate the developmental needs and milestones of the children she or he treats, the responsible child therapist must have familiarity with all of these developmental models in much more detail than is provided in these tables; the therapist is referred to developmental texts for that purpose (Gesell, Ilg, and Ames, 1995; Newman and Newman 1998; Shaffer, 2000; Thomas, 2000).

TABLE 3.1   A Model of Cognitive Development in Childhood as Developed by Jean Piaget

Type of Thought Subphases	Characteristics	Age
Sensorimotor	preverbal; growth is estimated via infant's vision, taste, smell, hearing, and tactile perception	Birth to 2 years
Reflex Activity	exercising inherited reflexes tracking objects without reaction to their disappearance imitation of facial expressions	0 to 1 month
Primary Circular Reactions	repetitious act to practice skills staring reaction to disappearing objects repetition of behavior that was responded to	1 to 4 months
Secondary Circular Reactions	repetition of purposeful acts searching reaction to disappearing objects	4 to 8 months
Secondary Schemata	searching for concealed object crude attempts at imitation	8 to 12 months
Tertiary Circular Reactions	experimenting with new situations searching and finding concealed objects sophisticated imitation of action	12 to 18 months
Mental Combinations	symbolic thought; cognitive representations object concept and permanence deferred imitation	18 to 24 months
Preoperational Thought	language development has strong impact on cognitive development progression from perception-bound to symbolic thought	2 to 7 years
Preconceptual Period	inability to consider more than one aspect of a situation egocentric social communication	2 to 4 years
Intuitive Period	increasingly decentrated (more than one aspect) intuitive impressions of social situations (not purely perception-bound)	4 to 7 years
Concrete Operations	increased ability to deal with hypotheticals progression from concrete logic to sophisticated logic and abstraction mastery of conservation and compensation ability to carry out action in thoughts only (internalization) recognizes reversibility and reciprocity	7 to 11 years
Formal Operations	thought no longer bound by time and immediate perception progression from already logical and abstract thought to higher levels of sophistication and flexibility; creativity recognition of transitivity thought completely independent of action hypothetico-deductive reasoning	11 to 15 years

TABLE 3.2   **Emotional Development across the Life Span Adapted from Lane and Schwartz**

Period	Experience of Affect	Expression of Affect	Differentiation of Affect
Early Sensorimotor Period	bodily sensation only; no cognitive experience or understanding	inability to express affect either for self or other	undifferentiated arousal
Late Sensorimotor Period	global arousal and tendency to act upon it	specific actions are now associated with specific emotions	global perception specific actions associated with specific emotions recognizable by others
Pre-Operational Thought	limited range of experience only either-or experience (no "mixed" feelings)	stereotypic and unidimensional expression of limited repertoire	can identify only one affect at a time can only tie one affect to one distinct situation
Concrete Operations	awareness of blends of feelings	complex, modulated, and well-differentiated expression	recognition of concurring as well as opposing emotions recognition of subtle change with specific times or situations
Formal Operations	peak differentiation and blending experience of nuances	rich expression of quality and intensity	simultaneous recognition of blends in self and others recognition of novel feelings and patterns

Source: This table was adapted from "Levels of emotional awareness: A cognitive-developmental theory and its applications to psychopathology" by R. D. Lane and G. E. Schwartz, 1986, *American Journal of Psychiatry, 144,* pp. 133–143, 1987. Copyright 1987, the American Psychiatric Association. Reprinted by permission.

Development Made Relevant to the Child Therapist

In addition to the use of the dialectic developmental viewpoint by the child psychotherapist to better understand the factors affecting her or his overall level of development, consideration and knowledge of development are also important because of the "overriding importance of interaction among developmental dimensions in determining functioning during any developmental period" (Wimbarti and Self, 1992, p. 48). In other words, the overall developmental level of a child, as assessed dialectically through exploration of her or his psychological, biological, cultural, and outerphysical determinants, does indeed have profound effects on expectations about that child's behavior, cognition, emotion, language, activity level, types of activities, and needs. Further, these distinct subareas of a child's overall development interact to present an even more complex picture that must be appreciated by the clinician. Achievement or lack of achievement in one developmental arena

TABLE 3.3   Psychosocial Development across the Life Span as Established by Erik Erikson

Age	Conflict	Characteristics of Success	Outcome
Birth to 1	Basic Trust vs. Mistrust	learning to trust others and to see them as dependable and trustworthy; becoming trustworthy oneself	Hope
2 to 3	Autonomy vs. Shame and Doubt	learning self-assertion and rudimentary independence; taking pride in one's actions and exercising judgment	Will
4 to 5	Initiative vs. Guilt	becoming curious and participating purposefully in the environment; exploring and asking questions	Purpose
6 to 12	Industry vs. Inferiority	learning how to do and complete tasks; trying out new skills and discovering interests	Competence
13 to 19	Identity vs. Role Confusion	sense of independence and personal efficacy; integrating interests and skills into a whole that is identity	Fidelity
20 to 24	Intimacy vs. Isolation	entering relationships and learning to compromise and sacrifice; caring for others outside the self	Love
25 to 64	Generativity vs. Stagnation	establishing careers and meaningful life; guidance of the next generation; creation of ideas, works, or children	Care
65 to Death	Ego Integrity vs. Despair	reviewing life and feeling satisfied and successful; continuing to contribute to society or family	Wisdom

can strongly affect reaching a milestone in another. For instance, a child cannot be expected to master separation-differentiation from her or his primary caretaker (psychological arena) if she or he has not yet mastered object constancy (cognitive arena).

Further, knowledge of developmental stages, milestones, and tasks is useful in determining whether therapy is successful in helping a particular child return to the healthy developmental trajectory that she or he had left before the referral to the clinician was made. Knowing what to expect from children of certain ages or developmental stages will help the therapist to evaluate whether the child is back on track, is making satisfactory progress, or needs to continue to stay in treatment (Johnson, Christie, and Yawkey, 1998).

As development continues across the life span and is clearly influenced by a number of factors, the clinician who is aware of dialectic approaches to development will remember that the environment has not only influenced development up to the time when the child is seen in treatment, but will also continue to affect the child beyond the termination

TABLE 3.4 Psychosexual Development across the Life Span as Proposed by Sigmund Freud

Age	Stage	Desire	Purpose	Characteristic	Outcome
0 to 1	Oral	pleasure from activity of the mouth—sucking	taking in food for physical survival; rudimentary ego development	primary narcissism pleasure principle immediate gratification	identification accept other's beliefs object cathexis
1 to 3	Anal	pleasure from activity of the anus—defecating	delay gratification develop reality principle ego differentiation	autonomy struggles control issues clash with objects in way of wish fulfillment	enhanced frustration tolerance
3 to 6	Phallic	pleasure from the genital area	superego acquisition ego development self-identification	object cathexis focus on sexuality Oedipal/Electra Complex external prohibitions	healthy superego parental cathexis
6 to 13	Latency	dormant—focus on peer relationships	skill development discovery of interests	nonsexual play activity	competence in skills academic achievement
13 →	Genital	gratification in sexual love-making	mature love to satisfy instincts affection	marriage aim-inhibited lust and affection empathy and caring	maturity in self maturity in relationships

TABLE 3.5   A Model of Self Development as Proposed by Daniel Stern: The Five Senses of Self

Age	Sense of Self	Critical Developments	Critical Contributions from Others
Birth	Sense of Emergent Self	emergence of organization around invariants (e.g., first around physiological regulation)	strong need for an object that helps the child regulate physiological needs and helps meet them appropriately
2 to 7 months	Sense of Core Self	awareness of self-agency, self-coherence, self-history, and self-affectivity self and other are sensed as separate entities	strong need for an object that helps the child self-regulate affects and need states need for another who facilitates repetition which is critical to the child's need to order her or his world
7 to 18 months	Sense of Subjective Self	recognition of shareability of self and affect development of intersubjectivity through shared attention, shared intentions, and shared affective states	critical need for another who is willing to share her or his own affects, intentions, and attention with the infant critical need for another who is capable of affect attunement
15 to 18 months	Sense of Verbal Self	objective (or conceptual) as opposed to experiential self-experience deferred imitation symbolic play language	need for models who can be imitated in play and day-to-day activities need for another who facilitates language development and who listens and shares personal knowledge
3 to 4 years	Sense of Narrative Self	placing of self and others into historical contexts consideration of past and future	need for other who will listen to and show interest in child's life story

of the therapy. It thus helps the clinician focus on environmental factors and modifications that can contribute to change in the child. Similarly, the knowledge of developmental milestones sensitizes the clinician to the presence of vulnerabilities in the child (or the adult for that matter), thus recognizing when stressors may have more of an impact and when problems are merely an issue of failed adaptation, as opposed to disease (Johnson, Rasbury, and Siegel, 1997).

Not unlike the dialectic approach to a definition of development, recent research on infants has pointed toward the importance of the context and the many contributing and shaping factors that affect a child in the interpersonal matrix in which she or he matures (Brems, 1998a; Chess and Hertzig, 1990; Zeanah, Anders, Seifers, and Stern, 1991). Research is beginning to provide evidence that the infant is indeed very active from the

TABLE 3.6   Milestones of Motor Development in Early Childhood

Age	Motor Movement Milestones
Infants and Toddlers	
1 to 2 weeks	sucking response; fetal position
1 month	lifts head
2 months	holds head up; lifts chest
3 months	reaches by swiping at objects
4 months	rolls over; sits with support
5 months	reaches and grasps; sits on laps
6 months	sits on high chair
7 months	sits up alone
8 months	stands with help
9 months	stands holding on to furniture; develops pincer grasp
10 months	crawls or creeps on hands and knees
11 months	walks when led
12 months	pulls self up to stand; plays with large objects; gains control of grasping and letting go of objects
13 months	climbs stairs on all fours
14 months	stands alone
15 months	walks alone with a waddle; controlled and intentional placement of objects
18 months	runs alone; steps off low heights
24 months	climbs alone; strings beads on stiff string; puts together simple two- to four-piece puzzles; waves and points; jumps off low heights; walks using arms for balance; throws with awkward, jerky movements
30 months	runs stiffly; walks upstairs; jumps up with both feet; climbs up, but not down; throws ball with rigid arm movement unsupported by other body movement
Preschool Children	
36 to 48 months	rides tricycle; alternates feet while climbing; gallops; hops on one foot for a few steps; walks downstairs two feet on a step; runs smoothly; exerts control over stopping quickly from running; leaps over obstacle with one foot at a time; maintains basic balance; works large zippers and snaps; brushes teeth; dresses self; skips on one foot; cuts and pastes; draws; begins to learn how to throw a ball
48 to 60 months	leaps over obstacle with both feet simultaneously; broad-jumps; hops 8 to 10 steps; catches objects while balancing self effectively by assuming a wide-legged stance; walks and runs a curved line with good control over stopping and starting; changes direction while running; walks stairs with alternating steps; climbs up and down obstacles; balanced jumping up and off; roller skates, ice skates, and kicks balls; throws with overhand motion from the elbow; walks balance beams; skips with one foot

TABLE 3.6   Continued

Age	Motor Movement Milestones
60 to 72 months	walks like an adult; bicycles; skips, alternating feet; runs faster and with fewer falls; jumps rope; jumps high and far; perfects the skill of throwing a ball; throws using coordinated whole-body movements

Early School-Age Children

72 months and older	plays games involving gross motor skills (e.g., baseball, football, soccer, tennis); engages in physical activity that challenges gross-motor coordination (e.g., swimming, gymnastics, skiing); engages in activities that develop fine motor control (e.g., knitting, sewing, arts and crafts); develops special skills (e.g., playing a musical instrument, singing); learns excellent fine motor control to write and draw; achieves excellent balance and coordination

Source: Based on Schickedanz, Schickedanz, Forsyth, and Forsyth, 2000.

moment of birth, interacting with and affecting her or his environment and the people within it (Lichtenberg, 1990, 1991). Further, these developments are continuous and present across the life span, indicating that development moves forward regardless of context but may be altered by it significantly. This model suggests that regression or fixation is not the best way of approaching psychopathology (Westen, Klepser, Ruffins, Silverman, Lifton, and Boekamp, 1991) and that clinical issues such as dependence, trust, autonomy, and industry are not tied to a particular period of development, but rather are continuously relevant throughout the life span.

"Shifts in the social 'presence' or 'feel' of the infant…[are thus not] attributed to the departure from one specific developmental-task-phase and the entrance into the next" (Stern, 1985, p. 10), but rather to the changes in the infant's self-experience and interaction with important people in her or his environment. Such self-experience and interaction must be understood by the child therapist to appreciate the needs of each individual client and to be capable of developmentally sensitive assessment and treatment planning. In addition to plotting such normal development, the beginning child therapist must also have some familiarity with literature outlining particular problem behaviors or disorders as associated with when in a child's life they are likely to occur in a nonpathological manner (e.g., Crowther, Bond, and Rolf, 1981). For instance, stubbornness has been attributed to the 1- to 2-year-old child (Brooks, 1999), disobedience to the 2- to 5-year-old child (Rothbaum and Weisz, 1989), lying to the 5- to 6-year-old child (Johnson, Rasbury, and Siegel, 1997), and self-consciousness to the adolescent (Harter, 1990). Similarly, disorders such as phobias have been reported more commonly among 2- to 5-year-olds (Kronenberger and Meyer, 1989), whereas eating disorders appear commonly among adolescents (Garner and Garfinkel, 1997).

Although such figures can be helpful to the child therapist, they are counterproductive if used in isolation or to make diagnostic decisions. Instead, responsible use of this information results in nonpathologizing developmentally appropriate behaviors or affects

TABLE 3.7   Receptive, Expressive, and Pragmatic Language Development in Childhood

Age	Receptive	Expressive	Pragmatic
Birth to 1 month	differentiates, turns to, and prefers voices	differentiated cries (e.g., pain, hunger)	nonverbal expression of needs
1 month to 4 months	uses eyes to search for speaker	cooing all vowels and some consonants (s, k, g)	nonverbal expression of needs collection of information
4 months to 8 months	responds to own name and familiar tones of voice	babbling four distinct syllables	expression of needs nonverbal requests (e.g., raises arms to be picked up)
9 months to 12 months	listens selectively responds to "no" and verbal requests understands new words	first real words symbolic gestures words with idiosyncratic meaning	expression of needs nonverbal requests protestations
12 months to 18 months	points to named body parts can identify objects understands commands	many single words: average of ten words by 18 months; echoes words heard	verbal expression of comments protestations verbal requests
18 months to 24 months	follows series of two to three commands points in response	telegraphic speech (i.e., two-word sentences)	can report to someone else enters into dialogue
36 months and upward	increasing ability to follow commands increasing ability to understand spoken language	some complex sentences grammatical mistakes (e.g., "goed")	skilled conversation maintenance of topic role playing indirect requests
60 months and upward	acknowledges listener takes listener into consideration	better grammar complex syntax increasing vocabulary	good conversational skills (to be refined into adulthood)

Source: Based on Bjorklund, 1999; Whitehurst, 1982.

and recognition of nondevelopmentally appropriate symptoms. One framework for such assessment has been provided by Wenar (1982), who suggests that behavior and affects be evaluated as to whether they are developmentally expected, regressed, or fixated. In other words, the child therapist assesses whether a given problem is common among children of the developmental level presented by the current child client (Wenar and Kerig, 1999). If the answer to this question is negative, the clinician follows up by assessing whether the behavior or affect reflects a regression or a fixation. If the behavior began at an expected age, then disappeared developmentally appropriately but recurred, a regression has taken place. However, if the behavior never disappeared once the child progressed developmentally, a fixation has occurred. In either case, intervention is recommended (Wenar, 1982). Johnson, Rasbury, and Siegel (1997) also suggest that behaviors and affects be evaluated according to their severity and effect on day-to-day functioning. Thus, whereas high activity levels are reportedly common and generally not treated among 5-year-old children, this behavior might not be considered normal in a 5-year-old whose general functioning (e.g., concentration and new learning) is interfered with by her or his excessive activity.

Given the critical need of a child clinician to be knowledgeable about expected maturation in the areas of emotional expression, cognition, language, motor activity, psychosocial crises, and self development, following will be descriptions of healthy development among children grouped into three categories: early, middle, and late childhood.

Common symptoms are included in the descriptions to sensitize the beginning therapist to the fact that children at different ages may manifest some behaviors or affects that, while considered indicative of psychopathology at some ages, are considered perfectly normal or nonpathological at others. These descriptions are rendered to provide the beginning child therapist a framework against which to compare children who are referred for treatment. It is important to recognize that not all children, in fact only very few, will evidence delays in all arenas of development. Instead, it may be noted that only one or no developmental deficit exists. Any deficits that are noted invariably become part of the child's treatment plan and must be considered when the child's presenting problem is conceptualized. Obvious deficits in language, motor, and cognitive development are addressed most completely by involving a pediatrician and/or developmental psychologist to rule out physical or neurological deficits as causative factors. Deficits in psychosocial, emotional, and self development can generally be addressed sufficiently by the child therapist.

Early Childhood

Early childhood for the purposes of this book is defined as the period of life between birth and 5 years of age, that is, the time of life most children spend with their families before they enter the school system. Early childhood is a time of rapid and intriguing change, as it includes infants, toddlers, and preschool children. Infants are never and toddlers are rarely seen in psychotherapy. Hence, although infants and toddlers are fascinating human beings, here descriptions will be provided only of healthy 4- and 5-year olds.

Four- and 5-year-old children are motorically quite sophisticated. They have advanced to an age at which they are quite capable of walking, running, and generally moving very independently of adult help. They have become mobile also through their ability to ride a tricycle or bicycle, to make their way past obstacles, and to climb stairs effectively. Five-year-old children master these tasks more effectively and easily than 4-year-olds, who still fight for balance and full control of their bodies. For instance, although both can run very well, only the 5-year-old has the full ability to change direction while running and to start and stop easily and quickly. Some 4-year-olds, although able to climb to the top of obstacles, may find themselves unable to climb down and need the help of verbal instructions rendered by a nearby adult to master this task. Five-year-olds, on the other hand, generally are able to climb up and down obstacles freely and without help.

Four-year-olds have developed sufficient motor control to dress themselves, working large zippers and snaps easily and independently. They are generally able to brush their own teeth, feed themselves, help themselves to tools and utensils, and help with small chores. Five-year-olds become more sophisticated and are able to tie their own shoes and work buttons easily. Fine motor control continues to improve, readying the child for school. Large motor movements are easily mastered by 5-year-olds, who learn to skate, kick balls, walk on balance beams, and skip with one foot. These children enjoy being creative and love to learn new tasks that challenge their motor development. They enjoy drawing, cutting and pasting, and simple arts and crafts. However, they also continue to be very fond of unstructured activities that stimulate them kinesthetically. They love to play in mud and water, feel gooey materials, and create nondistinct shapes from Play-Doh. These activities are gratifying not because of the creation of products, but rather because of the process and kinesthetic stimulation they provide.

The independence brought on by the young child's motor development is supplemented by her or his sophisticated use of language. By this age, children can communicate extremely well through language while still being very much attuned to nonverbal communication. They still prefer to model after others, rather than following verbal instructions but, if necessary, are able to do the latter if it is kept simple and direct. Much of their play remains symbolic and nonverbal, and some 4-year-olds may be quite sparse in their use of language while playing intently. Nevertheless, language is sophisticated by this age. These children use complex sentences, have an ever-increasing vocabulary, and understand simple instructions. They have become skilled conversationalists who can stick with a topic at hand and can focus in on their communication partner. Many 4-year-olds continue to struggle with the pronunciation of some consonants and various grammatical rules. They are aware of global language rules and apply them indiscriminately, which results in the overgeneralization of rules that leads to common grammatical mistakes, such as "go-ed" instead of "went" or "do-ed" instead of "did." Such mistakes are best not corrected by adults around the child. Instead, adults are better off striving to model appropriate language by obeying grammatical rules and exceptions in their own speech (Schickedanz, Schickedanz, Forsyth, and Forsyth, 2000). Grammar improves among 5-year-olds, who also are more skilled at engaging their conversation partner. They can begin to take the listener into account and acknowledge her or his communication and response. Children at this age have become excellent listeners who understand language well, even if it is not directed at them. They can follow clear instructions, as long as only one or two steps are involved. They listen to conversations, and much incidental language learning takes place through this activity. However, recent findings from a longitudinal study tracking children over several decades revealed that only communication that is directed specifically toward the child actually enhances the child's ultimate cognitive performance (Hart and Risley, 1995, 1999).

It is not surprising that as language skills develop, children's cognitive development also grows by leaps and bounds. Although children below the age of 4 were unable to consider others or to understand complex tasks, 4- and 5-year-olds begin to recognize relationships and to consider the perspective of others. Nevertheless, the 4-year-old still might not understand that her or his mother can also be the sister of an aunt. Mother can only be one thing: mother; additional relationships are difficult to fathom given this child's preoperational thought. Children at this age are very inquisitive and curious. They are beginning to understand that there are rules and generalities and are exploring these eagerly. This process is related not only to their increasing cognitive sophistication, but also to their need for structure and rules as they learn to differentiate right from wrong. These children desire cognitive stimulation, and they love to listen to stories and leaf through picture books.

Their thinking is becoming decreasingly perception-bound; as their ability for symbolic thought increases, they are more and more capable of symbolic play and make-believe. These children's ability to think can be mistaken as a level of cognitive complexity that allows logic and reasoning. However, this is not so. Children at 4 and 5 years of age cannot yet transfer the knowledge they have accumulated from one situation to another, in other words, they cannot yet generalize and reason logically. Thus, while their cognition has moved beyond being perception-bound in the sense that these children can engage in symbolic thought, in fact, can even engage in simple imagery, their logic remains largely bound to perception, as it does not yet formally contain the crucial elements of thought underlying conservation and perspective, as defined by Piaget (1967).

Conservation refers to the ability to realize that although a quantity of material may appear in different shapes, it ultimately remains the same or, inversely, that although the appearance of a container may be identical, the contents may vary in quantity. For instance, 4- and 5-year-olds are unable to realize that two rows of objects that are laid out so that the rows are of equal lengths may actually contain different numbers of objects because the spacing between objects may be different in each row. Similarly, they cannot yet understand that a cup of water poured from a large round container into a skinny square container is still a cup of water. They will claim that there is more water in the second container because the water level reaches higher than it did in the first container. They are unable to compensate (the example of the number of objects in a row), nor can they reverse (the example of the water in two different containers). This inability is related to the same reason that mom can only be a mother, not a sister: These children only focus in on one dimension—the length of a row, the tallness of a container. Conservation requires a person to manipulate a minimum of two dimensions at a time (e.g., the tallness of the container and the circumference of the container), thus remaining theoretically out of the 4- and 5-year-old child's cognitive range. Recent findings, however, have challenged that 4- and 5-year-olds are unable to conserve, and clever experiments (Donaldson, 1987) have indicated that if children are challenged with conservation tasks in practical settings, they are more likely to be able to solve them. Hence, although it appears that preschoolers have difficulties with tasks involving more than one dimension, these tasks are not impossible for them. They may merely require more practice, patience, and some guiding help by an adult (Schickedanz, Schickedanz, Forsyth, and Forsyth, 2000).

Similarly, 4- and 5-year-olds were once thought to be exclusively egocentric, that is, capable only of taking their own physical perspective. However, research (e.g., Flavell, Shipstead, and Croft, 1978) has revealed that even preschoolers are able to see the world from another person's perspective if they are encouraged to do so. They merely prefer to view things from their egocentric perspective, perhaps because this task is less cognitively challenging. The egocentric perspective of the child was originally also explained by the fact that the child can view only one dimension at a time (as noted above in the discussion of conservation). However, this dimension does not have to be the child's perspective. It could be the other person's perspective, enabling the child to view the world from a different focal point than her or his own. This cognitive concept has also been supported by research focusing on interpersonal situations, that is, emotional perspective, which has demonstrated that children are indeed capable of empathic attunement even at this very young age (Stern, 1989).

Four- and 5-year-olds are also becoming aware of and able to differentiate between reality and appearance. For instance, if they are shown a bogus spider or snake, they can recognize that it is not real. This ability was not present in the 3-year-old and hence is tenuous in the 4-year-old child. Because this is a new skill, it can be the source of great excitement and approach-avoidance for children. They may waver in their amount of certainty about their estimation of an object or activity as real versus fake, approaching it with some hesitancy, then delighting in it when they have convinced themselves that what is presented is really only make-believe. Children use their ability to pretend in their symbolic play and to gratify needs. They may recognize when they cannot do something or accomplish a task but can pretend that they have completed it.

Emotionally, children become more sophisticated at this time. They can identify how they feel and begin to relate specific emotions to specific situations. They are now able to communicate their feelings to others, providing an excellent example of the interaction between language and cognition. Specifically, the child would not be able to understand emotion without her or his increasing cognitive complexity and would not be able to communicate it verbally without the acquisition of necessary language skills. Nevertheless, 4- and 5-year-old children can express and experience only one emotion at a time, being incapable of feeling nuances of feelings or mixed emotions. They remain clear-cut in their emotional expression, dealing with one affect at a time. This singular experience of affect may result in the quick changes in emotion that can be observed in 4- and 5-year-olds. A young child who might have just been observed playing contently and happily might suddenly break into tears when another child destroys her or his creation or attempts to take away a toy. Children at this age will not verbally express emotions easily, but will talk about their feelings if they are encouraged to do so. Pressing a 4- or 5-year-old for subtle description and sophisticated explanation, however, is inappropriate and taxes her or his ability. Similarly, these children cannot yet understand that situations which evoke a strong and specific type of emotion for them may result in an entirely different feeling for another person. Hence, pressing a child to take the emotional perspective of another person in a highly emotionally laden situation is equivalent to requesting the impossible.

Children at this age feel that they are now individuals in their own right. They can initiate actions, are aware of their past and present, recognize consequences of actions, and desire to share themselves with others and for others to share themselves with them. Children become curious about what they can and cannot do and, in their attempts to find out what kind of people they are, begin to take initiative in their own lives (Erikson, 1950). They become curious about their parents, friends, and environment, always asking questions, engaging in play, experimenting, and role-playing new situations. If parents act in an understanding manner and guide the child's motives and behaviors into socially acceptable avenues, there is a sense of purpose that ultimately leads to the child's setting of life goals and identification with parents. If initiative of the child is punished by parents, she or he will feel guilty about her or his attempts to find out about self and others and may be stunted in development. Preschoolers are very much concerned with what their family members think of them and have a strong desire to fit in and be appreciated. They model after parents, friends, and preschool teachers, thus becoming socialized to the rules and regulations of their culture and community.

In summary, 4- and 5-year-old children are complex and enjoyable human beings with whom it is easy to interact. Their language skills have grown to an extent that results in easy conversation with adults, even adults who are exceedingly verbally focused. Although preschooler's cognitive complexity is growing rapidly, their thought remains somewhat illogical, and their increasing facility with language is not to be mistaken for logic and reasoning. The child's emotional expressiveness becomes more sophisticated and is more easily shared with adults, though it still lacks the complexity of mixed emotions and recognition of nuances. Socially, they become curious as they discover their own mission and interests. They like to take charge of their actions but generally evidence very socialized behavior due to their desire to be loved and to fit into their community of family and friends. Nevertheless, 4- and 5-year-olds may show some stubbornness and have occasional temper tantrums. They demand much attention from the adults in their lives and may easily become jealous. Fears are common among 4- and 5-year-olds, but tend to resolve themselves as the child's cognitive skills mature.

Middle Childhood

Middle childhood for the purposes of this book is defined as the period of life between 6 and 10 years of age, that is, a time of life when children adjust to and become comfortable in the school environment and learn to interact with adults and children outside of their families. Middle childhood involves great strides in motor development and skills learning, with particular emphases placed on cognitive and fine and gross motor skills in the schools.

By 6 years of age, children have achieved excellent balance and coordination. They walk like adults, can ride bicycles easily, run faster and with fewer falls, and are working on perfecting their fine motor skills. These children love games that challenge their gross motor skills, and it is of no surprise that this is the age when children begin to play team sports. Baseball, soccer, volleyball, and similar physical activities serve to enhance the child's large motor control and overall physical mastery. Fine motor tasks gain in importance and are slowly honed in many academically related activities. It makes developmental sense that children at this age enter school, as their fine motor control is only now sufficiently sophisticated to allow for the practice of neat handwriting, careful drawing, and other fine motor skills, such as sophisticated arts and craft. Younger children would have faced these tasks with too much frustration, and learning may have been hindered by physical or emotional, rather than cognitive, factors and limitations. Special skills often emerge at the age of 7 or 8 when children may begin to play musical instruments or choose a particular sport over others. Tennis, skiing, and similar physical activities can now be attended to with an eye on technique and a goal of improvement. Motor skills clearly continue to develop through the ages, and a lot of growth takes place between the ages of 6 and 10. However, the major milestones of physical development—namely, balance and coordination—were attained by age 6 and continued development from this age forward reflects refinement of skills, a quantitative rather than qualitative shift.

Similarly, language skills continue to be refined at this age. Children become aware of exceptions to grammar rules, thus becoming more correct in their use of language. Vocabulary explodes, especially as children add reading to their activities. They continue to be excellent listeners and now are able to track conversations easily. They can follow instructions and can remember several steps at a time that may be involved in following directions. However, young school-age children still have some difficulty with syntax of language as they remain very focused on context. Toddlers spoke only through grammatical morphemes that were understood in the context of their speech. For instance, a toddler's statement "mommy look" could be interpreted in two different ways, depending on context. If the child was playing and attempting to draw the mother's attention to a tower she or he had constructed, the utterance can be understood as a request for mother to take a look. However, if the child entered the room and noticed mother looking out the window, the utterance may be a mere reflection of the mother's current activity. This focus on content remains intact even among children of early school age. Much of their understanding of language still is created on the basis of context. However, it is at school age that reading activity and more complex instructions require that the child begin to analyze language on the basis of syntax, not content. For instance, an early school-age child still may have difficulty recognizing that the sentence "the doll is hard to see" does not indicate that the doll has difficulty seeing, but rather that it is difficult for another person to see the doll. The child's focus on context makes it difficult for her or him to focus on syntax, that is, to recognize that a different rule applies to analyzing the phrase "hard to see" than to the phrase "can see." These fine syntax-related rules of language begin to develop slowly as the 6-year-old child matures. By age 10, subtle rules have been learned and are used with ease.

On the way to learning sophisticated language and syntax rules, children discover that language can be used to surprise and play as they hit upon language-based jokes, such as riddles and puns. Third- and fourth-graders love to play word games in which they use unexpected meanings of words (also called lexically based ambiguity), alike pronunciation (also called phonologically based ambiguity), and unexpected interpretations (also called syntactically based ambiguity). The latter is the most difficult type of joke or riddle and generally is not acquired until the child is about 10 years old. Some easy phonologically based jokes, on the other hand, can even be understood by bright 6- and young 7-year-olds. A favorite lexically based joke for school-age children might go like this:

> *Why did the robot eat electric light bulbs at noontime?*
> *I don't know, why?*
> *Because she wanted a light lunch!*

Or like this:

> *You can't park your car here!*
> *Why not??? The sign said: "Fine for Parking!!"*

A phonologically based joke might go like this:

> *I saw the robber running down the road!*
> *Did the police catch him?*
> *No, he stepped on a scale and got a weigh.*

Additional easy phonologically based jokes that even young school-age children enjoy are the famous knock-knock jokes:

Knock, knock
Who's there? Boo.
Boo who?
Oh, don't cry!

Knock, knock
Who's there?
Ida.
Ida who?
Ida baked a cake if Ida known you were coming!

A more difficult syntactically based joke for older school-age children goes as follows:

Did you hear about the stick-up on the barn?
No! What happened?
Some kid threw it up there!

Or like this:

The police are looking for a man with one leg named Smith...
Oh? What's the other leg called??

School-age children's ability to grasp jokes and riddles also reflects their increased cognitive complexity. Unlike preschoolers, 6- to 10-year-olds develop increasingly sophisticated reasoning skills and logic. They can easily consider more than two dimensions or perspectives at a time, thus mastering tasks involving conservation. They can also explain conservation concepts, being able to point out that quantity did not change because nothing was added or taken away (i.e., identity was preserved), that quantity did not change because while one is taller, the other is fatter (i.e., one dimension was compensated for by another), or that quantity remained the same because the new arrangement could be turned back into the previous one (i.e., reversibility). As was pointed out previously, post-Piagetian research has indicated that even younger children can conserve if they are given time and advice. Hence, the qualitative cognitive change that takes place in the school-age child discussed here is that she or he is not only able to conserve, but can explain why this process works! These reasoning skills, however, are still tied to what the child can see or experience directly and cannot yet be carried out abstractly, that is, the child cannot yet develop new hypotheses or advance her or his own logic. Children's logic remains relatively concrete, and they continue to interpret meanings directly and concretely. For instance, sayings such as "The grass is always greener on the other side of the fence" might prompt this child to look over a fence to observe this phenomenon. Children have not yet learned to abstract that meanings might not be concrete, but rather symbolic. Symbolic thought and abstract interpretation do not emerge until late childhood or even adolescence (around age 12 or 13).

However, by age 8, children are beginning to think more and more logically and become able to analyze thinking itself. They can plan strategy and begin to play games such as chess wherein they have to anticipate moves and think through the consequences of their own actions analytically and indirectly. They become more capable of responding to complex directions or instruction in the absence of a model. Before this age, most instructions either were simple commands or were accompanied by the modeling of a skill if new task learning was involved. By age 8 or 9, children can listen to taped instruction of activities and figure out how to engage in the task by themselves. These children are also able to recognize if instructions are incomplete or do not make sense. If instructions contain unfamiliar words or skip important steps, children are left confused or attempt to make up their own meaning. This can lead to mislearning and misconceptualization of problems and procedures. Clear instructions in children's language hence remain important even at this age.

Children's emotional expressiveness and understanding becomes more complex at this time. Just as they are able to consider two dimensions to explain conservation, so too are they now becoming increasingly aware of two emotions at a time. Mixed emotions were impossible for the 5-year-old, remain difficult for the 6- and 7-year-old, and become increasingly possible for the 8- to 10-year-old. Seven-year-old children can be aware of two emotions at the same time if these do not appear incompatible, that is, two positive emotions such as happiness and excitement, and are directed toward the same situation. Eight-year-olds are aware that two compatible emotions can be felt at the same time and about two different situations. However, not until 10 years of age can children acknowledge two incompatible emotions, such as excitement and fear, and even then only if the two emotions are evoked by two different situations, such as excitement about going to the fair and fear about the train ride to get there.

In addition to recognizing more than one emotion, school-age children also become more aware of nuances in their affects. They can recognize that certain situations may result in more intense emotions than others. Their expression of emotions is becoming more complex and differentiated. They are able to share the nuances with others, in part because they are developing the language skills to communicate fine differentiation. Further, they are able to express emotion in a modulated manner much more than the preschooler, for whom emotion was still an all-or-none phenomenon. The school-age child, especially with increasing age, can feel very angry but might not express her or his anger violently. This development is both good and bad, as this is also the age when children may recognize that certain emotions are not well tolerated by their environment and may begin to repress or deny certain affects within themselves.

Social development for these children is highly correlated with the fact that school, teachers, and peers have developed great salience for the child. Teachers become important role models for these children, who work diligently toward becoming competent and industrious individuals. Children learn how to create things and complete tasks and feel satisfaction through their accomplishments. Continuous failure or critical adults may lead the child to feel uncertain about herself or himself and may result in feelings of inferiority. To maintain a positive sense of self and to accept feelings of competence and the associated willingness to attempt new tasks, the child needs responsive and supportive adults in her or his environment. Although for the 6-year-old child, adults have more salience than children, this changes quickly, and as the child ages, peers gain in importance until adolescence, when adults are not uncommonly rejected as role models and significant persons.

Popularity becomes important to children at this age, and they strive to meet many peers and attempt to initiate interactions. Almost all 6- to 10-year-olds are outgoing, but only the friendly and positively outgoing children tend to be considered popular by their peers. Aggressively outgoing children tend to be rejected by peer groups. As the school-age child matures, groups become increasingly important. Whereas the 6-year-old might prefer a few special friends, the 10-year-old seeks to belong to a larger group. Children in this age group tend to favor children of their own gender for interactions and play. Further, they model more after adults of their own gender. Given these social interaction patterns, it is not surprising that this is a critical period in children's lives with regard to gender role socialization. Certainly, even younger children (in fact, even infants) experience external gender-bound socialization, but it is at this age that patterns of gender-specific behaviors tend to be established. Finally, children's understanding of right and wrong is internalized by the age of 10, and moral reasoning, not unlike cognitive development, is becoming more complex at this time. Much like gender role socialization, endorsed morality for children this age tends to reflect the rules and beliefs of her or his family, community, and culture.

In summary, the time period between ages 6 and 10 is one replete with major changes in the child's cognitive and social functioning. Although motor and language development have seen the last of their major qualitative changes at this time in life, cognition and socialization continue to undergo major qualitative shifts as these children enter late childhood. Middle childhood is a time of great sensitivity to environmental factors as social and moral aspects of the self are internalized. Any biases that are expressed and reinforced by the child's environment are likely to be perpetuated from here on out in the child's development. Important patterns of behavior and judgments are set at this time. Common developmentally tied problems encountered among middle childhood children may include arguments, bragging, showing off, and self-consciousness. These issues tend to resolve themselves as the child continues through her or his healthy developmental trajectory.

Late Childhood

For the purposes of this book, late childhood is defined as the period of life between 11 and 12 years of age, that is, a time of life when children begin to grapple with social interaction issues that will follow them into adolescence, when largely hormonally driven physical changes become of great importance. The differentiation between 12- and 13- to 15-year-olds can be quite arbitrary as many children in Western, i.e., industrialized countries are beginning to enter puberty at earlier and earlier ages (see Schickedanz, Schickedanz, Forsyth, and Forsyth, 2000). Nevertheless, the distinction will be made here, but with the provision that the child clinician must remember its arbitrariness.

As was mentioned previously, motor and language development do not undergo any further qualitative shifts once a child enters late childhood. However, this is not to imply that development in these arenas is complete. Nothing could be farther from the truth. In fact, late-childhood children increase their vocabulary and improve their grammatical skills by leaps and bounds. Their language skills receive a great boost from the increase that is in reading and writing required through schoolwork or motivated by individual children's interests and hobbies. Similarly, motor skills become more and more refined and sophisticated as children develop interests in certain sports and practice to improve their fine and gross motor skills. However, in both areas, the critical aspect of development is refinement and sophistication, not qualitative shifts.

Qualitative shifts, on the other hand, are still necessary to move along the child's cognitive complexity to a level whence continued development would imply mere refinement and increasing sophistication. Specifically, the child has to master the task of moving to formal operations as defined by Piaget (1967). Such thinking involves complex logic, symbolic thought, independent generation of hypothesis and new learning, and abstract reasoning. Although children as young as age 11 may enter the phase in which such qualitative shifts are noted in thought, it is not guaranteed that all children or even adults will ever have equal abilities to think abstractly and symbolically. Nevertheless, most late-childhood children begin to be capable of pure thought that is not tied to current experience or independent action, are able to reason deductively, and form hypotheses about their world. These cognitive skills are supported by school curricula that stress science and mathematics, that is, abstract thought and hypothesis testing and generation.

Closely tied to cognitive sophistication and language skills, emotional shifts take place at this time of life as well. The child is now able to experience and acknowledge two incompatible or competing emotions about a single event. She or he can begin to recognize novel affects that she or he never experienced before and begins to make sense of feelings, tying them to specific events. Children are now fully aware of blends and nuances not only in their own affects, but also in the feelings of the adults and children around them. Expression of emotion continues to take place in a modulated manner and verbal communication about feelings becomes increasingly sophisticated. Late childhood children are willing to discuss their feelings and can analyze them carefully. They recognize that the same situation can evoke different feelings at different times and for different people. These children's ability to perceive and accept their own widely varied affects greatly facilitates empathy for and understanding of others' feelings as well.

Socially, no great qualitative shifts are noted between middle and late childhood. The next large social shift does not take place until adolescence, at which time children begin to struggle with clear future planning, self-identity, budding sexuality, and sexual relationships. Until adolescence, late childhood children remain greatly concerned about their same-gender peer group, internalize moral standards, seek popularity, and develop interests and gender-specific behaviors.

In summary, the primary marker of late childhood is the continued refinement and increasing sophistication of motor, language, and social skills acquired in middle childhood. Cognitively and emotionally, late-childhood children evidence qualitative shifts that ready them for the greater complexities of adolescent life. Adolescents will continue the pattern of refinement in skills and, while faced with different psychosocial challenges, will continue development not through qualitative, but through quantitative changes. It is the lack of qualitative shifts in motor, language, cognitive, and emotional development that may have contributed to the old notion that the developmental phase of life ends at age 18. However, development is clearly not dependent upon qualitative shifts alone, but also upon the refinement of "old" skills and talents. Social tasks continue to change throughout the life span, and new challenges face people in different ways at any age. These new tasks challenge people to continue to grow regardless of age and result in lifelong development in psychosocial terms.

Summary and Concluding Thoughts

This chapter presented a developmental framework for the child therapist to emphasize the importance of developmental knowledge when working with children. The dialectic approach to development endorsed in this chapter is considered very useful to the work of the child therapist because of its integrative and thorough nature. It challenges the therapist to recognize that development is not merely the acquisition of new or qualitatively different tasks and behaviors, but instead is an evolution that reflects increasing refinement and sophistication across many arenas of development. Child therapists who have not had a lot of contact with young children, and hence have not observed firsthand the rapid developmental changes (both qualitatively and quantitatively) that occur between birth and adolescence, might want to consider seeking out opportunities for additional learning. Such opportunities may include the reading of some of the many references provided in this chapter; observations in nurseries, preschools, or schools; volunteer work with healthy children; and the viewing of tapes about childhood and development.

It is essential for a child therapist to be knowledgeable about developmental milestones and sequences to be able to engage in appropriate diagnosis, case conceptualization, and treatment planning. The child therapist must also remember that all age norms must be taken with a grain of salt, as they merely represent an average at which to expect certain development to take place. Individual children, different cultures, and all the factors (e.g., psychological, biological, outerphysical) discussed in the dialectic approach to development remain important variables in determining whether a given child remains on a healthy developmental trajectory.

4 A Culturally Sensitive Approach to Therapy with Children

BY MARK E. JOHNSON*

It is virtually inevitable that the child therapist will work with a client who has a racial, ethnic, or cultural background different from her or his own. This will be true whether the therapist is of African, Asian, European, or Native American descent and whether she or he is working in a private practice, community mental health center, or hospital setting. Gaining the skills and knowledge necessary to deal with a racially, ethnically, and culturally diverse child clientele is as important to a trainee's education as gaining the basic skills and knowledge of child therapy itself.

Before a discussion of culturally sensitive treatment approaches to child therapy can commence, a clear understanding of several critical terms has to be developed. Specifically, the labels *race, ethnicity,* and *culture* are often mentioned in the literature that concerns itself with cross-cultural therapy approaches and need to be defined briefly. The term *race* refers to a biological classification that is based on physical and genetic characteristics, with only three primary races identified: Caucasoid, Mongoloid, and Negroid. *Ethnicity,* by contrast, refers to a classification that is based on shared social and cultural heritage, such as, for example, Native or Asian Americans. Finally, *culture* refers to learned behavior that is shared and transmitted within a group across generations or with new members, for instance, as occurs in gay and lesbian cultures. To elaborate further, although members of the Jewish ethnic group have a shared social, cultural, and religious heritage, they do not constitute a race. Similarly, within the white ethnic group in the United States, there are a number of cultures, such as Irish Americans, Italian Americans, and German Americans, each of which has a learned set of values, attitudes, beliefs, and behaviors.

In other words, race breaks down further to ethnicity, which, in turn, may cross racial boundaries (e.g., a Native American individual who has a biological race combining Mongoloid and Negroid). Similarly, ethnicity breaks down further into cultures, which in turn may cross ethnic boundaries (e.g., a gay individual who has an African American and Alaska Native ethnic identification). Individuals can belong to several cultural groups at once (e.g.,

*Dr. Johnson is Professor of Psychology at the University of Alaska Anchorage.

may be upper middle class, Caribbean African American, and physically challenged), they may have varied ethnic backgrounds and identify with more than one ethnic group (e.g., may be Italian American and Navajo, identifying primarily with their Navajo upbringing but also incorporating Italian American values), and they may be biologically racially mixed (e.g., may have one Caucasoid and one Negroid parent). In fact, in modern society, most clients will have such multiple identifications and diverse backgrounds. Clearly, race, ethnicity, and culture are not identifiable by looking at the outside of a person or even easily observed behaviors, an assumption that is often made in day-to-day life. To understand a client's racial, ethnic, and cultural identity, careful questioning is needed to assess that person's identification and perception. The group with which the client identifies most (in which the client claims heritage) becomes that individual's reference group and will have the strongest impact with regard to having shaped behaviors, attitudes, and values (Phinney, 1990, 1996).

In addition to differences accounted for by ethnic or cultural backgrounds of children, there are also differences based on minority status. Although ethnic or cultural status often overlaps with minority status of a group of people, this is not always so. A comprehensive approach to multigroup or multicultural sensitivity therefore must encompass not only ethnicity and culture, but also minority status. Minority status as relevant in the therapy context has nothing to do with actual number of people within a specific group. Instead, a minority group is best defined as

> A group of people who, because of physical or cultural characteristics, are singled out from others in the society in which they live for differential and unequal treatment, and who therefore regard themselves as objects of collective discrimination…. Minority status carries with it the exclusion from full participation in the life of the society (Wirth, 1945, p. 347).

Given this definition, it is evident that the term *minority* characterizes a number of groups in American society that experience oppression and, as a result, are not able to participate fully in society as a whole. This definition also makes the conceptual identification of a minority separate from the numerical concept. For example, in the United States, as in most countries, women suffer oppression at the hands of males, rendering them a cultural minority, despite being a numerical majority in the United States. Using this definition, other minorities include physically disabled individuals, elderly, gays and lesbians, and individuals who are economically disadvantaged. Thus, the child therapist in a culturally diverse society works with individuals who vary not only in terms of ethnic or cultural background, but also in terms of other avenues of oppression. Given these definitions, the remainder of this chapter is written to be relevant to children of different ethnic groups, cultural backgrounds, and minorities.

Ethnic and Cultural Diversity of the United States

Throughout its history, the United States has been a pluralistic society. Even in the centuries before the European conquest of the continent, there were scores of different Native American tribes, each with its own unique heritage and culture. Since the mass immigration of Europeans, the United States has attracted individuals of various ethnicities and from different cultures around the world. Some of these people were brought here as slaves to serve the white settlers; some flocked to the new country to avoid economic and religious persecution; others came in hopes of attaining a new life. Over the years, immigration to the United States of America has continued and resulted in a society that is defined largely by its cultural diversity.

This diverse society is often referred to as a "melting pot," implying that the United States is a conglomeration of different elements that leaves the final product different from the parts that constitute it. One adverse implication of this term is that by using a concept of merging cultures, it is implied that as different cultures are integrated into mainstream society, they lose their unique identity. This further implies that to become part of society, individuals from different cultural backgrounds must forsake their unique cultural heritage and background to be accepted into the mainstream. A more accurate and realistic depiction of the United States would be as a "pluralistic quilt." In this characterization, the uniqueness of each culture is recognized and each culture adds to and strengthens society as a whole. The members of diverse groups are able to maintain their cultural background while being embraced by and functioning within society as a whole. It is within this framework of a pluralistic quilt that child therapy interventions and therapist attitudes and behaviors will be placed in this chapter.

The nature and extent of the pluralistic quilt that is the United States become evident when demographic data of its population are examined. In 1980, approximately 80 percent of the population were White and 20 percent were nonwhite, primarily of African, Asian, Hispanic, and Native American descent (U.S. Bureau of the Census, 1980). By 1990, the White population comprised 75.6 percent of the total population, and by 2000, 69.1 percent. In contrast, the Hispanic population grew to 9 percent in 1990 and 12.5 percent in 2000; the African American population grew to 11.7 percent in 1990 and 12.1 percent in 2000; the Asian American population grew to 2.7% in 1990 and 3.6 percent in 2000; the Native populations (including Native Americans, Alaska Natives, and Native Hawaiians) remained at less than 1 percent of the total population throughout this time period (U.S. Census Bureau, 2001). By 2060, it is projected the Whites will be in the minority, making up 49.6 percent of the total population. By contrast, Hispanics will make up 26.6 percent, African Americans 13.3 percent, Asian Americans 9.8 percent, and Native populations 0.8 percent.

Breaking down these population numbers by age further reinforces the need for child therapists in particular to be culturally sensitive and prepared to deal with culturally diverse clients. In 2000, approximately 22 percent of the Whites in the United States were under the age of 18 years. This percentage contrasts with the approximately 31 percent of African Americans, 35 percent of Hispanics, 24 percent of Asian Americans, and 33 percent of Native Americans under the age of 18 years. Given the higher fertility rate among non-Whites in the United States, the differences in number of members under the age of 18 years between Whites and non-Whites will continue to grow throughout this century, resulting in an increasingly non-White child clientele. Nowhere is this trend toward the increasing presence of nonwhite children in the general population more evident than in the public school system. For example, as of 1985, over 50 percent of California's elementary school population and 46 percent of Texan schoolchildren were ethnic minority members (Hodgkinson, 1985). Across the United States, 33 percent of all elementary school children were non-White, and by the year 2020, this percentage will have increased to 39 percent (One-Third of a Nation, 1988). Clearly, the need for increased cultural sensitivity is not a fad or trend that will dissipate with time, but rather a realistic and necessary movement for all child therapists.

In recognition of the diversity of the population inside and outside of the United States and the need to adequately and appropriately provide mental health services to all ethnic, cultural, and minority members of a given society, the American Psychological Association, the American Counseling Association, the National Association for Social Workers, and other professional mental health organizations have expressed strong support of the need for therapists to be culturally sensitive and for training programs to help meet this need. For example, the APA's ethical guidelines clearly state that "psychologists are aware of cultural, individual, and role differences, including those due to age, gender, race, ethnicity, national origin, religion, sexual orientation, disability, language, and socioeconomic status" (American Psychological Association, 1992, p. 1599). Similarly, the need for inclusion of cultural issues in all therapists' training was advanced by the National Conference on Graduate Education in Psychology (American Psychological Association, 1987b) when this committee stated that "psychologists must be educated to realize that all training, practice, and research in psychology are profoundly affected by the cultural, subcultural, and national contexts within which they occur" (p. 1079). Obviously, then, there is a growing press from professional organizations, as well as from individual practitioners, for therapists to become culturally sensitive to meet the needs of a culturally diverse population and clientele (cf. Iijima Hall, 1997; Ponterotto, Casas, Suzuki, and Alexander, 2001).

The challenge presented to the child therapist by these statistics, definitions, and ethical dictates is one of becoming culturally sensitive to the wide diversity of clientele that may present for treatment. In the following sections of this chapter, practical guidelines will be provided that a therapist can use to become more culturally sensitive herself or himself. Finally, general issues that may arise in cross-cultural therapy situations are reviewed.

Becoming a Culturally Sensitive Child Therapist

Although becoming a truly culturally sensitive child therapist can be a difficult, arduous, and challenging task, it is well worth the effort, both on a professional and a personal level. A large aspect of the difficulty of some individuals to become culturally sensitive is due to the fact that growing up in the United States has exposed them to a long history fraught with biases, stereotypes, and prejudices. Although it may be argued that prejudices have lessened considerably over the years and now exist only in isolated situations, it can also be asserted that prejudice is as pervasive as ever, though more covert than before. Regardless of the position taken, it is very difficult to deny the definitive presence of prejudice in our society toward many minorities. The ongoing presence of prejudice in the United States is easily exemplified by the growing incidence of racially inspired violence on college campuses, the increasing membership in and visibility of white supremist groups, and the relatively low numbers of women and other minorities on corporate executive boards and in elected positions.

Perhaps more damaging than overt prejudice, however, is the pervasive presence of covert discrimination and prejudice. This form of prejudice can be most damaging because it is insidious and difficult to recognize and challenge immediately. Covert discrimination is present throughout the public media through their negative depiction of minorities. Women are either given the roles of helpless victims who need to be saved by a strong male or depicted in stereotypically female positions such as homemaker, nurse, secretary, and so on; Americans of African, Hispanic, or Asian descent are cast either as criminals or in roles in which they serve whites in the main roles, such as in the role of waiter, cook, or janitor; gays or lesbians are characterized in stereotypical manners that are very inaccurate and demeaning. Although the media have become more sensitive to these issues in recent years and have made some progress in eliminating stereotypic roles, pervasive prejudice remains.

Another very covert manner in which prejudice is maintained and propagated in the United States is through the language that is used to describe various situations. A few very obvious examples of this type of prejudice and derogation are terms such as *jew one down* to depict bargaining over a price, *nigger rigged* to characterize expeditiously repairing an item, and *Indian giver* to illustrate someone who gives something only to take it back later. Obviously, once examined, these examples emerge as clearly and overtly prejudicial and yet they are commonly used. Less overt, but equally prejudicial are depictions of goodness, purity, and virginity as white and evil and corruption as black. Other subtle linguistic examples of prejudice are contained in terms such as chairman, serviceman, and councilman, words which seem to exclude women from holding these positions. Similar damage is done by referring to all people with masculine pronouns such as *he, his,* or *him* and the generic use of the word *man*, as in *mankind.*

Growing up amidst overt and covert prejudices invariably has an impact on every child, leaving lasting impressions that, without some intervention, may carry forward into adulthood. This can be particularly difficult for minority children who are not able to find positive role models in public media and may begin to hold stereotypic prejudices toward (or against) their own peoples. Although it is not the individual's fault that she or he grew up in a racist, sexist, and heterosexist society, it is every individual person's responsibility to cast out as many personal remnants of prejudice as possible. Eliminating prejudices is not always an easy task, but it is a critical step in the journey toward becoming a culturally sensitive child therapist.

Cultural sensitivity and competence are developed through introspective work and require a great deal of self-exploration and personal openness on the part of the developing mental health care professional (Singelis, 1998). This effort is not only worthwhile, but also meets the spirit of contemporary professional ethical codes for the mental health professions. It is best applied toward the development of cultural competence that has three major components: cultural awareness, cultural knowledge, and cultural skills (Pedersen, 2000). Simply put, cultural awareness is gained through self-reflection and respect for others, as well as through the strong recognition of and belief in the notion that difference does not equal deviance (Namyniuk, 1996). Cultural knowledge can be accumulated via familiarization with cultural, anthropological, historical, and related events involving or affecting all cultural and ethnic groups with whom a clinician anticipates working (Ponterotto, Casas, Suzuki, and Alexander, 2001); and cultural skill is developed through learning about alternative approaches to intervention, reduction in prejudicial or stereotyped use of language, and political activism (Ivey, 1995). Clinicians who strive to be culturally sensitive and competent need to be able to claim that all three of these traits are a part of their repertoire of skills and beliefs. Entire books have been written to assist mental health care providers develop these sensitivities (e.g., Hogan-Garcia, 1999; McGrath and

Axelson, 1993; Singelis, 1998). Each of the three categories deserves further exploration, and an overview is provided in Table 4.1. After a discussion of each of these three areas, information is provided on self-monitoring to maintain and continue to enhance cultural sensitivity.

TABLE 4.1   Characteristics of a Culturally Sensitive Child Therapist

Awareness
- Aware of and sensitive to own cultural heritage
- Aware of personal reactions to and behaviors with members of differing cultures
- Conscious and embracing of all minority groups of which she or he is a member
- Values and respects cultural differences
- Seeks out experiences involving members of differing cultural backgrounds
- Aware of own values and biases and their effect on therapy
- Sensitive to neither overemphasizing or underemphasizing therapist-child cultural differences
- Aware of personal language use
- Aware of personal cultural identity and level of acculturation
- Comfortable with cultural differences between self and client
- Sensitive to situations that may require referral of a minority client to a member of the same cultural heritage
- Aware of within-group differences and respects individuality of all people

Knowledge
- Understanding of how the sociopolitical system in the United States treats minorities
- Knowledgeable about the presence of racism, sexism, and heterosexism and their effects on minorities
- Knowledgeable about U.S. history, especially as relevant to various cultural groups
- Familiar with history of mental health treatment for minorities and potential biases of traditional psychotherapy theories
- Aware of cultural definitions of mental illness and perspectives on mental health services
- Knowledgeable about cultural and minority groups in the United States
- Knowledgeable about political, social, and economic pressures that come to bear on various cultural groups
- Possesses specific knowledge about particular groups with whom she or he is working
- Has clear and explicit knowledge and understanding of the generic characteristics of therapy
- Familiar with cross-cultural applications of psychotherapy skills
- Recognizes potential biases inherent in traditional psychotherapy theories
- Knowledgeable about clients' native language
- Aware of effects that therapy setting and office can have on minority clients
- Knowledgeable about institutional barriers that prevent minorities from using mental health services

Skills
- Adept at adjusting communication and therapeutic style to match individual clients' needs
- Able to pay appropriate amount of attention to role of culture
- Skillful at appropriate use of nonverbal communication and silence
- Skillful at not categorizing individuals
- Flexible in providing services to meet needs of clients
- Able to exercise, when appropriate, institutional intervention skills
- Able to select and implement treatment strategies as appropriate for a given client
- Acts as a social change agent to help reduce or eliminate racism, sexism, and heterosexism
- Able to use language that is devoid of prejudice and bias

It is worth noting that cultural sensitivity cannot only be learned, it can also be measured (Ponterotto and Alexander, 1996). This measurement is based in the belief that regardless of how well trained a counselor is in certain multicultural skills or how well she or he chooses techniques or tests on the basis of the client's cultural and ethnic background, ultimately any tool is only as good (i.e., as multiculturally competent) as the person using it; in other words, "what is of paramount importance is the clinician's multicultural awareness, knowledge, and interpretive skill" (Ponterotto and Alexander, 1996, p. 651). A number of instruments—for example, the Cross-Cultural Counseling Inventory-R (LaFramboise, Coleman, and Hernandez, 1991), the Multicultural Awareness-Knowledge-and-Skills Survey (D'Andrea and Daniels, 1991; D'Andrea, Daniels, and Heck, 1991), and the Multicultural Counseling Inventory (Sodowsky, Taffe, Gutkin, and Wise, 1994)—exist for this purpose. The interested reader is referred to Suzuki, Meller, and Ponterotto (2000) and McGrath and Axelson (1993) for more detail as well as exercises and self-report measures.

Awareness

Cultural awareness refers to the process of recognizing personal biases, prejudicial beliefs, and stereotypic attitudes or reactions. Gaining awareness has to precede modification of behavior and attitudes and can be a painful effort as clinicians begin to recognize that they are not free of recalcitrant prejudicial behaviors and beliefs.

A good first step toward gaining awareness involves the novice child therapist examining her or his own cultural background, cultural assumptions, and cultural stereotypes. This is best begun by taking a look at the cultures and minority groups of which the therapist is a member. Using the definition provided above—that a minority is a group that is a victim of oppression—the therapist-in-training needs to consider what aspects of his- or herself have been subject to oppression. Beginning with the novice therapist's cultural heritage, she or he has to take into account various aspects such as country of origin, language, skin color, and cultural practices. In so doing, it has to be kept in mind that, although there have been some consistent recipients of oppression over the years, the focus of prejudice has shifted from culture to culture. Further, the degree of bias against a given culture may have waxed and waned but has always remained present in one form or another. There are numerous other considerations in identifying the minority groups of which a new therapist may have been, or may currently be, a member. Gender is a consideration; despite being a numerical majority in the United States, women have experienced considerable oppression. Physical limitations are to be considered; physically disabled individuals have been the target of much bias. Another possible minority group is based on sexual preference; gays, lesbians, and bisexuals have been the focus of much prejudice. As a trainee begins to identify the minority groups of which she or he is a member, she or he must contemplate the experiences that were the result of being a member in that group.

Once identification of personal backgrounds has taken place, new mental health care providers can shift to assessing their day-to-day reactions to different situations and different people to determine their biases and prejudices. As such, as trainees go through their day, they may begin to make an effort to become aware of personal reactions to people from different cultures and minority groups. Most people do not routinely assess such reactions. However, it is an important process on the road to becoming culturally aware. There are various ways in which the therapist may be able to work on issues regarding other cultures. Internal reactions to ethnic jokes, for example, may provide valuable information to help the therapist develop self-awareness. Behavior while interacting with someone who is culturally different from the self can be attended to with new awareness. Many new therapists recognize for the first time that they truly react differently with people from other ethnic, cultural, or minority groups, a realization that sometimes causes concern or embarrassment. However, shaming the clinician is not the point of assessing daily reactions. Rather, the point is to help trainees realize that everyone, even the most open-minded individual, has been influenced by societal and familial training. It is highly unlikely that anyone exists who is completely free of biases and differential reactions. The point of assessment is to begin to become conscious of these reactions, not to chastise oneself for them. It can be helpful to attend to any undue generalizations from one member of a group to all members of that group; to take stock of the cultural heritage or ethnic backgrounds of people with whom the therapist in training spends personal time; and to evaluate honestly whether friends and acquaintances are primarily of the same culture, and, if so, how this pattern came to pass.

The next step in developing increasing awareness involves the seeking out of experiences with different cultural, ethnic, or minority groups and to begin to identify stereotypic beliefs and biases. In so doing, it is helpful to keep in mind that stereotypes can be both positive and negative but that both can be equally destructive because they move the clinician away from interacting with a client as an individual. Once stereotypes have been identified, they must be evaluated for accuracy, because for many stereotypes, there is a kernel of truth that renders them quite compelling. Testing stereotypes can be particularly difficult because it is always possible to think of at least one example to verify a preconceived notion. Therefore, it is important to look at the bigger picture of reality in evaluating stereotypes. For example, there is a prevalent stereotype that minority members in the United States exploit the welfare system. Although some minority members may be identified for whom this may hold true, the reality is that the majority of welfare recipients are white, as are the majority of individuals who commit welfare fraud!

As the therapist striving to become culturally sensitive begins to monitor personal reactions to different situations and people, awareness of personal language will add an important component to self-exploration. Words selected often are representative of thought processes used. In addition to tracking the use of blatant ethnic epithets, attention must also be paid to more subtle indicators of bias and prejudice (Sharma and Lucero-Miller, 1998). For example, the frequency with which terms are used that are derogatory or prejudicial must be assessed. For instance, does the therapist use terms to describe an occupation that imply that women are incapable of holding the position, such as *chairman, journeyman,* or *congressman*? When referring generically to any professional, is the word *he* used? Is the assumption made when referring to clients that they are female whereas therapists are male? Are phrases used in which there is an ethnic bias present, for example, *jew me down, being gypped, Indian giver, welsh on a deal,* or *Irish temper?* The use of racist and sexist terms is not permissible even if the child herself or himself uses the terms. That is, if a child in therapy uses offensive language, the therapist may reflect the child's feelings, but must substitute the appropriate term. In other words, the child's use of words such as *Jap, nigger,* or *wetback never* justifies the use of such expressions by the therapist.

Although some of these examples might seem subtle and innocuous, consider the potential negative effects of using words that incorporate *man* as the generic designation for both women and men. By using such terms, not only does the therapist run the risk of offending the adult women in a family and possibly the men, but it will also send subtle messages to the young children in treatment. That is, if a therapist is working with a young girl who is quite withdrawn or unsure of herself, use of sexist language by the therapist will no doubt contribute to the girl's view of herself as passive, as unable to reach many goals in life because they are reserved for men, and as not in control of her own destiny. Such sexism is not limited to the words that the therapist selects, but may also be contained in her or his actions. For example, sexism can occur in the choice of activities, toys, or rules set in the therapy room. The culturally sensitive therapist needs to recognize her or his own stereotypes about what is deemed appropriate for girls versus boys. In actuality, every activity available in the room, every rule ever made in treatment, and every statement uttered by the therapist should be applicable to girls and boys alike. Even the most subtle influences over the child's behavior that are sex-role stereotyped can have long-lasting effects.

Are inappropriate behaviors, such as laziness, seductiveness, anger, untrustworthiness, or excessive thriftiness, explained away or identified on the basis of a person's ethnicity? Another common prejudicial form of communication that is commonly used is to refer to members of a culture different from one's own as *they* or *them*. This depersonalizes and segregates members of that culture, further perpetuating the separation of groups. As the child therapist in training becomes aware of such linguistic choices that reveal prejudice or bias (whether intentional or inadvertent), she or he is ready to to select alternatives and to eliminate language that conveys prejudice and bias, no matter how subtle. As a therapist, one is looked up to and serves as a role model for many children and their parents. A therapist's behavior will be scrutinized, and even subtle and covert prejudice may be modeled and thus perpetuated. Therefore, it is critical that a therapist, especially a child clinician, present as a nonbiased professional. If all therapists are conscious of their own behavior and are in the process of becoming culturally sensitive, this will help to make psychotherapy a considerably more valuable service for children of any ethnic or cultural heritage.

Given the focus on general respect for individuals, regardless of cultural or ethnic background, it is important for the child clinician to become aware that there are great differences among people within the same culture or ethnic group. These differences within a group are often greater than those between cultures. One major within-group difference of which a therapist must be aware is the level of cultural identity development attained by an individual and the relative importance placed on an individual's own culture versus other cultures. Cultural identity development requires each individual member to go through a process involving a number of stages. There are several models to describe this developmental process, including the Minority Identity Model (Atkinson, Morten, and Sue, 2002), the Black Identity Development Model (Jackson, 1975), and Negro-to-Black Conversion Experience (Cross, 1971). As an example, Cross's (1971) model views the development of an African American's cultural identity as passing through four stages: *preencounter, encounter, immersion,* and *internalization.* In the preencounter stage, the individual holds disdain and hatred for being black; in the encounter stage, the person begins to value herself or himself for being black; in the immersion stage, the individual rejects and hates all that is not black; and in the internalization stage, the person gains a sense of self-confidence and security in who she or he is and is able to embrace all cultures. Although all models have been developed to describe the process encountered by minority group members, there are parallels to these models in white ethnic identity development (Carter and Helms, 1993; Helms and Carter, 1993). Further, this process does not hold true only for clients, but is present also among therapists. In recognition of this, to become culturally sensitive, the child therapist must explore her or his own level of cultural identity. To do so, she or he will need to examine deeply the sentiments that are held about her or his own and other cultures. This process will be important for the therapist in becoming culturally sensitive, and it will be an important consideration in assessing and working with child clients.

Related to the issue of cultural identity development, the child clinician needs to be aware that individuals within a given culture will vary considerably with regard to their level of acculturation. Acculturation is defined as the degree to which an individual adopts the dominant society's social and cultural norms to the exclusion of her or his own culture's social and cultural norms (Dillard, 1983). Acculturation is typically not a matter of endorsing one set of cultural norms versus another, but rather refers to the degree of incorporation of values or attitudes derived from both cultures. There are many factors that may affect a child's or family's level of acculturation, including socioeconomic status, number of generations that have been in the United States, educational and employment opportunities, and geographical location. Gauging a person's level of acculturation is an important part of getting to know her or him and involves an evaluation of several factors, including the degree to which traditional cultural practices are followed and the native language that is used in thinking and speaking (Gibbs and Huang, 1998).

Four levels of acculturation have been identified (e.g., Dana, 1993): *traditional* (adherence to the birth culture), *assimilated* or nontraditional (adherence to majority culture), *bicultural* (adherence to birth and majority culture), and *marginal* (lack of adherence to either culture). A child's level of acculturation will affect how she or he interacts with members of both cultures and may have an influence on the therapeutic approach chosen to help the child. For example, if a Native American client appears very committed to her or his Native culture, then therapy might make more use of storytelling, a commonly used technique in Native culture, to resolve problems. It is also important for the child therapist on her or his path to cultural sensitivity to examine her or his own level of acculturation, to further clarify her or his own cultural identity.

The previous paragraphs have presented but a few steps toward increasing a clinician's awareness on the road toward cultural sensitivity. In most major communities, workshops and courses are offered that will aid and enhance this process of self-discovery and awareness. Further, there are a number of valuable books that may help the child therapist to increase her or his cultural sensitivity (e.g., Pedersen, 2000; Weeks, Pedersen, and Brislin, 1986). Novice therapists are encouraged to take advantage of as many of these opportunities and resources as possible.

Knowledge

While awareness is being established, the clinician also strives to become more knowledgeable about cultural issues. The definition of cultural knowledge is broad and multidisciplinary, requiring individuals to utilize many resources. Courses, workshops, and seminars are obvious avenues for gaining accurate knowledge about the many issues related to culture. A number of additional possibilities are presented below. Cultural knowledge is critical for many reasons, including the fact that accurate information may help to dissolve any stereotypes of which mental health care providers have become aware about a group and will lead to better appreciation and understanding of different cultures. In general, if used appropriately, knowledge will assist counselors to be better able to interact effectively with members of other cultures. However, caution must be exercised so that newly acquired knowledge is not represented as the truth about all members of any given group. Such stereotypic or overgeneralized use of knowledge can be destructive and can get in the way of being truly effective and empathic (Namyniuk, 1996).

Knowledge gathered from books is best not limited to one discipline and optimally starts with a firm and accurate understanding of the history of the United States in general and the history of different ethnic and cultural groups within the United States in particular (e.g., Tataki, 1993; Zinn, 1995). This acquisition of knowledge may include an investigation of the history of immigration; the introduction, role, and history of slavery; and the conquest of the continent. It is important to remember that history books can be very biased and selective in their reporting. As a result, it is often difficult to find books that provide a balanced perspective on history, making it important to read a variety of books and accounts written by numerous authors. Although not a panacea to the problem of biased reporting of historical events, it may be helpful to focus on recently published books. Through this reading, the therapist will gain a better appreciation of what certain groups had to endure over the years and a better understanding of the contemporary issues with which they are faced.

Although it is important to have a historical perspective on the role of racism in the United States, this knowledge would be incomplete without the information about the role of racism, sexism, and heterosexism in society today. In this context, the therapist must learn about the role of racism, sexism, and heterosexism in the development of minority children's self-identity. She or he needs to become knowledgeable about the processes of internalization and the adverse effects it can have on the minority member who adopts the biases about her or his own group, as well as other groups within society. The skilled therapist is able to use this knowledge to help her or his clients deal with prejudice in such a way that it does not adversely affect self-esteem and self-definition. Integrating this information with current statistics and data on poverty may provide added insights into the lives of many members of minority groups. Further, much has been written about economic political pressures that come to bear on minorities within the United States. Gaining this knowledge will help to put many aspects of child clients' behavior into a more comprehensive and sensitive perspective.

The path toward cultural sensitivity includes the reading of books within the discipline of psychology, not just psychotherapy, but also such topics as the psychology of racism. These readings also must include a review of empirical information about cross-cultural differences within the United States. However, a word of caution about much of this literature is in order. Some of this research, particularly projects that were completed before the 1980s, focused on comparing different cultural groups with European Americans, implicitly establishing White Americans as the cultural norm against which other cultures have to be compared to identify differences and similarities. Consequently, the results are frequently (mis)interpreted within a context of Whites as the ideal norm. Clearly, this is an inherent bias against cultural groups other than Whites that must be considered and compensated for when reading such research reports. Readers interested in more information about cultural biases in research are referred to Ponterotto and Casas (1991), Matsumoto (1994), and Walker, Noble, and Self (2000).

More specific to the field of child therapy, the road to cultural sensitivity must include a perusal of various books written on cross-cultural therapies. There are a number of books that offer specific information about providing therapy to members of various cultures. Of particular interest to child therapists are *Children of Color*, edited by Gibbs and Huang (1998), and *Ethnicity and Family Therapy*, edited by McGoldrick, Pearce, and Giordano (1996). Other books that provide separate chapters on providing therapy to members of various cultural groups (but not necessarily with a child-related focus) include those written by Atkinson, Morten, and Sue (2002), Lee (1997), Pedersen, Lonner, Draguns, and Sue (1999), Ponterotto, Casas, Suzuki, and Alexander (2001), and Sue and Sue (1999). In reading these texts, the novice child therapist must take caution to remember that within-group differences are often greater than the between-group differences, which are the primary foci of these texts. Therefore, the information provided in these books should be considered as general guidelines or possibilities rather than established facts that will hold true for every individual member of a given ethnic group or culture. That is, the therapist is encouraged to read these materials but to remain aware that not every member of a given culture will fit the information that is provided.

Further, the child therapist needs to become knowledgeable about the often nonflattering history of mental health treatment for minorities. For instance, much has been written about the inherent biases that exist in many of the assessment tools (especially intelligence tests) that are commonly used in therapy settings (Dana, 1993; Samuda, 1998; Suzuki, Meller, and Ponterotto, 2000). Most of these instruments were normed on a primarily White population that did not include many, if any, individuals from other cultures. These instruments have been used historically in a very discriminatory manner. For example, Hispanic and African American children were often placed in special education classes solely on the basis of their scores on intelligence tests that were normed on White children. These placement decisions led to a disproportionate number of minority children in special education classes, ultimately resulting in a number of successful lawsuits ostensibly intended to eliminate this practice. Similarly, because of biases in norms, many tests tend to overpathologize members of cultures that are different from the White culture for which the instrument was standardized. With this knowledge, it is important that the culturally sensitive child therapist select assessment tools that have the most culturally appropriate norms and, if available, local norms. Even with these norms, the well-trained therapist remains cautious in making clinical judgments based solely on assessment tools and has to consider the possible role of a child's culture in making interpretations and decisions.

In the process of becoming culturally sensitive, the child therapist will learn that the dominant theories of therapy in the United States were developed by White Europeans (predominantly male) and might not have universal application. Traditional personality theories as they are currently taught in most mental health programs emphasize values and worldviews that are ethnocentric in nature; specifically, they tend to be Eurocentric, reflecting European cultural heritage of majority culture. Personality theories were developed to provide a context in which to explore individuals with regard to their behaviors, values, beliefs, attitudes, language, relationship, and so forth. All of these aspects of what it means to be human are entirely culture-bound (Armour-Thomas and Gopaul-McNicol, 1998; Barnouw, 1985). To look at these variables in clients or oneself without knowing the cultural context in which they developed is likely to distort what is expressed.

For instance, most primary personality theories focus on the individual and state as a basic premise that it is important for a child to individuate and separate from her or his family. From this perspective, the indicators for a child's progress toward health would be lessened reliance on family and others along with increased independence. Continued dependence or reliance would be viewed as a sign of pathology and perhaps resistance to therapy. Such a viewpoint would clearly not be compatible with cultures, such as that of Asian Americans, that emphasize the importance of the family and the role of the individual within it (Singelis, Triandis, Bhawuk, and Gelfand, 1995). The culturally sensitive child therapist knows that the application of any therapeutic approach must be done within the individual client's own family, cultural, and societal world. She or he does not try to impose a standard therapeutic or theoretical approach to all children, regardless of their cultural heritage.

The child therapist trainee must also become aware that there is no one universally accepted definition of "normal" and that it will vary from one culture to another (Lum, 1999). Therefore, she or he needs to learn not to rigidly apply one single standard or definition of mental health across all children. Cultures vary greatly in what they consider a problem or an appropriate strategy for coping within a given situation (cf. Castillo, 1997; Dana, 1993; Iijima Hall, 1997). What constitutes abnormality in one culture may be acceptable, if not mainstream behavior, in another. Different cultures may also express the same type of problem in different ways, choosing different idioms to describe an essentially identical emotional level and type of pain (Matsumoto, 1994). For example, depression among mainstream White clients may conform to the criteria outlined in the DSM-IV, whereas depression among the Chinese manifests itself through a different set of highly somatized symptoms, such as constipation, loss of appetite, and fatigue, with little expressed dysphoric affect (Castillo, 1997; Dana, 1993). Some disorders seem to be culture-bound, appearing only (or predominantly) in some but not all cultures (American Psychiatric Association, 2000; Suzuki, Meller, and Ponterotto, 2000). This latter phenomenon may be explained by the observation that different cultures reinforce different traits and behaviors. As any traits or behavior taken to an extreme may result in pathology, different cultural groups will have different manifestations of pathology based on the types of traits it emphasizes in its healthy population (Alarcon and Foulks, 1995; Iijima Hall, 1997).

Further, it is important for the child therapist to realize that mental health services are not universally held in high regard. Some cultures place greater emphasis on seeking assistance from family members or community elders; other cultures see any sign of mental illness as a disgrace to the family that must be hidden from all (Suzuki, Meller, and Ponterotto, 2000). Some minority members view mental health services either as irrelevant to their everyday struggle for survival or as yet another tool for the white majority to pacify and control minorities.

The child therapist needs to become knowledgeable about the institutional barriers that may prevent minorities from seeking and using mental health services. She or he must learn that, for many reasons, minorities tend to underutilize mental health services (LaFramboise and Foster, 1996; Sue, Allen, and Conaway, 1978). Reasons for this pattern include the possible perception by clients that mental health service providers are insensitive to diverse needs and may try to impose personal values upon clients, the hours and days of operation, and the amount of charges for services. The therapist needs to be aware that minorities are disproportionately represented in lower socioeconomic strata and take this into consideration when setting hours and fees. In further recognition of this reality, each child therapist should provide pro bono or reduced fee therapy as often as fiscally possible.

It is particularly critical to gain extensive knowledge about the primary minority group or groups with whom a therapist anticipates the bulk of her or his work. For example, if a therapist were to conduct child therapy in rural Alaska, it would be in the therapist's and clients' best interest for the therapist to learn about Alaska Native cultures, particularly about the Native groups who live in neighboring areas. If a therapist were to work in a city with a predominantly Hispanic population, such as El Paso, Texas, it would be in everybody's best interest for the therapist to learn about Hispanic culture and, if at all possible, to speak Spanish. Not only does this knowledge enable the therapist to be more effective in her or his work with children from these cultures, but it will grant greater credibility to the therapist. The therapist may not want to overlook one important source for learning about the child's culture: the child herself or himself. The child is an especially valuable source of information, as she or he will provide the therapist with the child's perspective of her or his culture, information that may prove invaluable in the therapist's assessment, case conceptualization, and development of a treatment strategy (Brems, 1998b).

If at all possible, the therapist is encouraged to learn the native language of the children with whom she or he will be conducting treatment. Although this can be a difficult task, it will pay considerable rewards in the increased rapport and respect that will be gained from clients, both children and parents. Certainly, learning a language is a difficult process, and a therapist may never be completely comfortable conducting therapy in her or his second language. However, as a bare minimum, the therapist should begin the process by learning a few common words of greeting and farewell, as well as commonly used terms or phrases. If nothing else, trying to learn a second language will give the therapist a better appreciation of and empathy for those clients who are themselves learning a second language, namely, English!

Beyond reading and taking classes or workshops, one of the most important avenues to gaining knowledge about different cultures is to become involved in firsthand experience (Lum, 1999). There are many different avenues to gain this experience and the trainee is encouraged to take advantage of as many as possible. One possible approach is to attend various cultural events that are offered by or about the culture. These might include dances, plays, movies, and lectures. A word of caution here is for the trainee to remember that these are merely pieces of the culture, not complete reflections of the entire cultural process and heritage. This caution is given because many people will attend these cultural events that highlight the artistic or romantic aspects of the culture to the exclusion of other, perhaps less attractive, aspects. If these were the only contacts with a given culture, the therapist would indeed derive a highly distorted understanding.

Another avenue to gaining specific information about a culture is to seek out opportunities for interaction with members of cultures different from her or his own, preferably including both professional and personal involvements. For instance, professionally speaking, there may be opportunities to volunteer time at a community mental health center that offers special programs for members of a specific culture or that is located in a neighborhood that is predominantly made up of minority members. On a personal level, opportunities need to be sought out that allow for interaction with members of other cultures on a social level. All professional and personal efforts to learn more about a cultural or ethnic group with whose members the therapist anticipates treatment not only will lead to more knowledge and experience, but also will have the added benefit of increasing visibility, and hence added respect, among the people in that group.

It is presumed that all contemporary graduate programs in the mental health professions teach cultural competence and sensitivity. Courses and curriculum infusion of these topics can be further enhanced through practical and internships that involve a culturally diverse clientele. If this cannot be achieved solely through careful selection of practicum or internship sites while in graduate school, seeking additional volunteer experiences can augment graduate training, as can supervised employment attained upon graduation. Counselors need to take responsibility to encourage their supervisors to challenge them with a culturally diverse clientele, given the limitations and parameters of a specific clinical site. If the choice is available to trainees, they can select a practicum or internship site that is located within a culturally diverse neighborhood or city. Throughout all of these experiences, culturally sensitive supervision is a critical component. Within supervision, focus should be placed, as appropriate, on the counselor's experience of different types of clients. Through this use of supervision to monitor reactions to culturally different clients, the therapist will learn to avoid repeating any previously learned biases and stereotypes.

Skills

Clinicians' awareness and knowledge of cultural issues will have to be translated into skills lest they be of no use to clients. The process of becoming culturally sensitive therefore must include both the acquisition of new skills and the possible adaptation of existing skills. Perhaps most important, in recognition of the fact that there are cultural differences in the emphasis placed upon different forms of communication, it is important for the child therapist to become adept at adjusting her or his communication style to meet the needs of each individual child client (Kim, 1994).

Using language skillfully will help the clinician adapt to these differences. Cultures differ in their emphasis in communication. Some individuals are most concerned about the clarity of their message, some about the relationship between speaker and listener, some about the evaluation they will receive on the basis of their expression, some about the impositions made by their remarks, and some about the effectiveness of their communication (Kim, 1994). Clinicians need to learn to recognize their clients' and their own personal preferences in communication and adjust accordingly. For example, a client who tends to express issues in treatment in a manner that is mostly concerned with how the clinician will respond to the client (i.e., is most concerned with being evaluated) may have a tendency to withhold facts that are perceived as potentially leading to negative evaluation. Another client, who is mainly concerned with not hurting the clinician's feelings, might not self-disclose information that is perceived as potentially critical of the clinician. Concern for relationship in communication tends to be correlated with cultures that are more collectivistic; concern for communication of facts and effectiveness with cultures that are more individualistic (Triandis, 1989).

Relatedly, the therapist must learn that some cultures may place greater emphasis on nonverbal communication and that members of these cultures are less likely to view talking therapies as ideal therapeutic modalities. Among these members, silence may need to be understood as a sign of respect, not resistance. Children from such a culture may be even less inclined to verbalize their feelings than other children, but instead will demonstrate them in nonverbal manners.

Knowing that different groups of human beings have different preferences for diverse therapeutic modalities (Sue and Sue, 1999), culturally competent clinicians have to acquire the skills to identify and carry out the techniques that will be most effective with any given client. Rather than approaching each and every child client in the same manner, the therapist recognizes the need to modify her or his therapeutic approach depending on the needs of the individual client (Ponterotto, Casas, Suzuki, and Alexander, 2001). With increased sensitivity to the differences in how children from different cultures may communicate, the therapist will not pathologize a child on the basis of these differences (Brislin, 1993; Singelis and Brown, 1995). However, the therapist is also aware that there are marked differences *within* any given culture and is careful not to make broad generalizations of the types of treatments that will work for all members of that culture. Thus, the therapist needs to have the skills to be flexible in her or his therapeutic approach and use this flexibility in a competent and appropriate manner when dealing with children from different cultures.

Along with having flexibility in the use and choice of therapeutic techniques, in becoming culturally sensitive, the child therapist increases her or his awareness of the many issues that emerge concerning communication between the therapist and the child. First, the therapist becomes cognizant of possible language difficulties that the child client may experience. Care is taken to determine a child's native language and her or his degree of proficiency in the therapist's predominant language. If the therapist is not fluent in the child's native tongue, the therapist will take into consideration any language problems and adapt the therapy accordingly, including making appropriate referrals if necessary.

As was mentioned above, the child therapist needs to have an increased awareness that different cultures may have preferred modes of communication. Some cultures may emphasize nonverbal and indirect communication; others may emphasize a verbal and direct approach. The therapist needs to become aware of and sensitive to these cultural differences. She or he will not only adapt therapeutic approaches to match child clients' communication styles, but also adapt her or his own communication style. That is, the therapist not only becomes aware of how to "hear" the client, but also is aware of how the client "hears" her or him. The therapist knows that a child in therapy may be anxious initially and that this may be further compounded by the recognition that the therapist is culturally different. Given these factors, the therapist knows that she or he will have to work hard to develop rapport and communication with the child. One important avenue to facilitate this process is to choose a style of communication that matches the child's as closely as possible. For example, in many cultures, indirect communication is valued. If a child from such a culture holds many of the traditional cultural values, the therapist might want to deemphasize direct communication and instead focus on using stories or art to communicate information to the child. Conversely, some cultures value direct communication, and for children from these cultures, the use of art or metaphors might not be effective.

Also crucial is the ability to place the appropriate amount of attention on the role of culture in therapy. That is, the therapist must neither overemphasize nor underemphasize the importance of culture in therapy with a given child. Therefore, the therapist needs to have the skills to evaluate a situation effectively and to assess the level of attention that needs to be given to culture with a child at any given time. She or he knows that stereotyping and generalizing are very destructive to the therapy process and that even within a given culture, the members will have varying degrees of commitment to traditional cultural values and behaviors. She or he recognizes that the within-group differences are as great as or greater than those between-group differences. In other words, the skilled therapist recognizes that the differences among the members of a given culture will vary greatly; indeed, these differences may vary as much as or even more than the differences between members of that culture and another. Figure 4.1 provides a graphic representation of this concept. In this figure, two cultures are represented by two normal curves. By using the concept of overlapping normal curves, it is evident that the differences within each culture (dashed line arrows) are greater than the differences between the two cultures (solid line arrows). Finally, the commonalities between the two groups (shaded area) are larger than the differences (white areas). It becomes clear from this representation that the similarities between any of the two cultures can outweigh the differences. The culturally sensitive child therapist recognizes that there are great similarities and is aware that there are likely to be some differences. Adaptation of style is therefore important at an individual child level. Making assumptions about a child based on the child's ethnic or cultural identification is as destructive as ignoring this aspect of the child altogether.

One example of a misguided attempt at being culturally sensitive is that of a child therapist who based his treatment planning on a generalization about a specific culture. After a lengthy intake, this therapist presented the child's case at a staffing. In concluding his presentation, he indicated that this family was completely run and organized by the child's mother, adding that this was to be expected because the child was African Ameri-

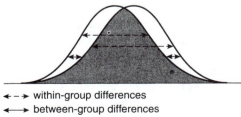

◄– ► within-group differences
◄——► between-group differences
▬▬▬ commonality

FIGURE 4.1   Depiction of Within-Group and Between-Group Differences and Commonality

can. Several clinicians who had listened to his presentation were quite surprised by his conclusions, as in actuality it was the father who had brought the family to treatment, the father who was caring for the children (he was unemployed, the mother worked), and the father whom the children sought out for problem solving! In the therapist's attempt to be culturally sensitive, he imposed his own stereotypes about African American culture onto this family to such a degree that he let it override the evidence that had been presented to him by the family. Thus, the culturally sensitive therapist must juggle her or his desire to know as much as possible about each ethnic group in general with the need to be open-minded and enter each intake interview without preconceived notions about what to expect.

Commensurate with the information reflected in Figure 4.1, the child therapist needs to have the skill not to categorize individuals according to their ethnic or cultural background, that is, not to treat all members of any given group as identical (Richardson and Molinaro, 1999). To help the novice therapist gain an appreciation of the inherent difficulty in attempting to categorize individuals into groups, the demographic information presented earlier in this chapter should be considered. In presenting these data, the population was categorized into five major groups: Whites, African Americans, Hispanic Americans, Asian Americans, and Native Americans. However, within each of these broad categories, a number of subcategories exist. For example, within the broad category of Asian Americans, there are a number of smaller groupings, each with its own unique cultural background and heritage. The group includes individuals whose cultural backgrounds lie in very diverse countries, including China, Japan, Samoa, North and South Korea, Vietnam, and Guam. Further complicating this issue is the fact that even within each of these country-based subgroups, there are further subgroups. For example, within Vietnam, there is a significant proportion of ethnic Chinese who have, over the years, maintained great autonomy from other Vietnamese. Further, even within the Chinese-Vietnamese group, there may be major differences such as rural versus urban, rich versus poor, gay versus straight, and Buddhist versus Christian. This example clarifies that broad categorization of individuals ignores the numerous differences that exist within this larger grouping. The same obviously holds true for other ethnic groups. For instance, among Whites, there are individuals from countries such as Ireland, Germany, or France or who differ according to many other variables such as sexual orientation, physical abilities, socioeconomic status, religion, and age.

With the recognition that some institutional barriers exist that may prevent minorities from utilizing mental health services, the child therapist needs to become flexible in the provision of services (Namyniuk, Brems, and Clarson, 1997). She or he must recognize that some problems reside outside the client and nontraditional steps may need to be taken to help resolve the situation. For example, if a minority child presents for therapy because of feelings of inadequacy or depression, the intake interview may reveal that the child is the only culturally different student in a predominantly White student body and that the White students have been making racist comments. The child, unable to make friends at the new school and subject to ongoing derogation, soon begins to incorporate many of these negative perceptions into her or his self-concept. In this situation, there is an outside force (racism at school) that has had a direct and adverse impact on the child. Hence, focusing solely on the child in an attempt to improve her or his self-concept will most likely not be the most effective intervention. Instead, therapy will be most effective if a three-pronged intervention approach is adopted that involves the child, the family, and the school. By including interventions in the school setting, the therapist may be able to make an impact on the child's environment, which in turn, it is hoped, will have a positive effect on the child's self-esteem.

In becoming culturally sensitive, another important set of skills the child therapist needs to cultivate is that of being a social change agent (Hogan-Garcia, 1999; Monges, 1998). She or he needs to learn how to eliminate any form of discrimination, including that based on ethnicity, sexual preference, age, mental or physical limitations, religion, or gender. Being culturally sensitive, the child therapist acts to ensure that everyone has access to the services and resources that are needed. In so doing, she or he takes a proactive advocacy stance to help victims of discrimination. The trainee needs to recognize that as a therapist, she or he will be granted a great deal of power by child clients, their parents, and other community members. She or he must recognize her or his responsibility to use this power to help eliminate discrimination in our society, both directly and indirectly. Indirectly, the therapist will come to serve as an example of a nonbiased individual. She or he will learn to be careful of chosen words and actions to convey perceptions of equality of all persons and respect for individuals from all walks of life. The therapist comes to recognize that people, particularly impressionable children, will model their behavior after hers or his. With this recognition, the therapist needs to learn to be careful of any interpersonal interactions that might convey prejudice or bias, even of the most subtle kind.

When necessary and appropriate, the child therapist will learn ways in which to take direct actions to prevent or eliminate all forms of discrimination. This direct action can range from not condoning racist or sexist jokes told in her or his company to using the political system to create positive changes in society. In becoming culturally sensitive, therapists recognize that the primary purpose of therapy is to help enhance the quality of clients' lives and that it is equally important to complement this individual approach to improving life with a more general approach to enhancing the quality of our society. Thus, the therapist will come to do everything possible to help create a society that is more respectful and humane in its treatment of all individuals.

Self-Monitoring

Becoming a culturally sensitive child therapist is not a final goal, but rather is an ongoing process. There will be no one point at which a therapist has gained all of the awareness, knowledge, and skills to finish or complete her or his quest for cultural sensitivity. Instead, attaining cultural sensitivity is a continual process in which the therapist not only remains open and responsive to further knowledge and experience, but also actively seeks it out. While gaining additional knowledge and experience, she or he continues to assess her or his reactions to different situations and people in a continuous quest for personal growth. The therapist looks for personal residues of stereotypes or biases that may affect her or his perceptions and seeks out challenges that will broaden her or his cultural horizons. For example, the therapist will endeavor as much as possible to have as diverse a clientele as possible, given the community in which she or he lives. If this is not possible, the therapist could volunteer her or his time at an agency that has a more diverse population. For further challenges, perhaps the therapist will take a sabbatical leave from her or his present position and spend some time living in a different culture or country. These are merely a few examples of how the culturally sensitive child therapist needs to try to challenge herself or himself to continue the process of personal growth.

A major aspect of the journey toward growing cultural sensitivity is the role of consultation and supervision. It is important to realize that bias and prejudice are insidious attributes that are often beyond the awareness of the individual. The therapist who is brought up in a racist or sexist family or society may have incorporated many racist or sexist attitudes without being aware of them. Often, these attitudes are so subtle that they are very difficult for the individual to identify, let alone eliminate. Although self-exploration is a necessary and crucial approach to identifying personal biases and prejudices, there is a limit to the growth it can provide. Often, it is necessary to help promote self-awareness through the presence of an outsider who is interested in the well-being and growth of the therapist and can foster it through ongoing supervision and consultation. Such consultation will give the therapist an objective viewpoint about her or his therapy skills and cultural sensitivity within the therapy setting. In addition to focusing on general psychotherapy skills, the supervision or consultation should pay attention to the therapist's level of cultural sensitivity, and while it can be difficult to do so, it is important for the therapist to remain open and responsive to supervisory feedback. Feedback can be particularly difficult to accept when it involves the identification of biases and prejudices, as these are not commonly considered professional, but rather personal, attributes. Hence, it is important for the supervisee to remember that the supervisor or consultant has the therapist's and the client's best interest in mind, as this perspective may enhance the therapist's receptivity to feedback.

Selecting a supervisor or consultant to help the therapist who is in the process of enhancing cultural sensitivity is an important consideration. The selection of an individual who is culturally insensitive will not help the therapist in her or his quest. Considering that supervision often evokes the presence of parallel process in which the supervisee and supervisor reenact the therapy process that is occurring between the supervisee and client, it may be desirable to have a supervisor or consultant who is culturally different from the therapist. This may enable the therapist to explore cultural issues that might not otherwise be present in supervision or consultation were it done with someone of the same culture as the therapist. Short of this, it would be valuable to receive supervision or consultation from someone who has considerable experience, both personal and professional, with different cultures. This need for supervision and consultation is predicated on the fact that, as was mentioned previously, attaining cultural sensitivity is a process, rather than an end state.

Process Issues in Cross-Cultural Child Therapy

Under the best of circumstances, therapy is a very complex and complicated process, with no two therapy relationships ever being exactly alike. A major contributing factor to this complexity are the numerous and often considerably divergent personal factors that therapist and client bring to the therapy room. These factors include personal characteristics such as the therapist's and client's cognitive styles, self-perceptions, life experiences, behavioral styles, modes of learning, coping strategies, ways of perceiving, family characteristics, social skills, and so forth. They also include expectations that the client brings to the therapy room about the client's and therapist's role, preferences for different therapist characteristics, attitudes toward the therapy process, and personal perceptions of reasons for presenting for therapy, as well as professional aspects of the therapist, including theoretical orientation, level of competence, and therapy style. Even without considering culture, the therapy process is a rich and complex situation. When a therapist's and a client's cultures are added as a consideration, the process becomes even more complicated (Canino and Spurlock, 2000). Some cultural factors that may affect the therapy process include the therapist's and the client's ethnicity, minority status, degree of acculturation, and level of minority identity development, as well as each person's degree of cultural awareness and sensitivity. These cultural factors not only may further complicate the therapy, but also can make the process more rewarding for both individuals. Figure 4.2 identifies just a few of these personal, professional, and cultural factors that

FIGURE 4.2   Personal, Therapy, and Cultural Contributions of Child and Therapist

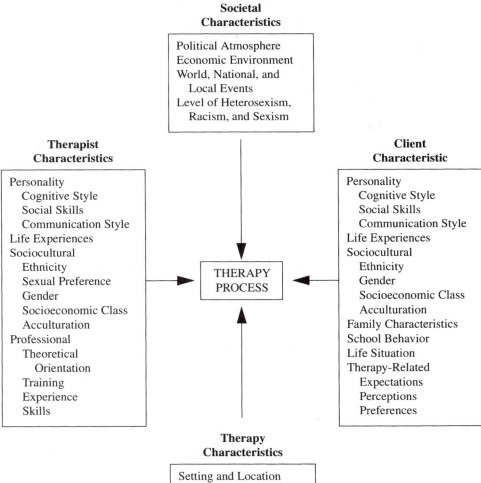

may affect the development and maintenance of the therapy relationship, as well as the outcome of the therapy.

Following is a description of several important, though certainly not all, process issues that are likely to arise in cross-cultural therapy situations. The influence of ethnicity or culture on the therapy process can begin at the moment the therapist meets her or his child client and family. The manner in which the therapist greets the family, the physical appearance of the therapist, and the therapy setting are but a few factors that can affect the therapeutic process and relationship from the outset. Many of these events can occur without the therapist's awareness and may leave her or him wondering what happened. One such event may be the manner in which the therapist chooses to address the child client. Therapists must be careful never to anglicize children's names automatically. For example, a client named Jose or Yosaf should never automatically be called "Joe," even if this practice would be easier and more familiar for the English-speaking therapist, as it would show considerable disrespect for the individual's culture. The therapist should also be aware that different cultures have different uses of names. For example, in Vietnam, an individual will typically have three names, such as Nguyen Duy San. In this case, Nguyen is the family name (similar to Smith or Jones), Duy a middle name, and San the given name (similar to Jim or Jane). For Vietnamese, because the family name is rarely used, this individual would be referred to with their given name, Mr. San, or San for close friends. Thus, being on a first name basis with someone from this culture may have an entirely different connotation than it does with someone from a European heritage. The safest and most respectful approach in both of these situations is to pay attention to how the client addresses herself or himself and to follow suit. Alternatively, or if the client does not reveal her or his preferred address, the child can be asked what she or he would like to be called. The main issue is to be aware not to apply presuppositions across the board to everyone. Failure to take this sensitive and sensible approach may lead to the therapy getting off on the wrong foot.

Conversely, what the therapist expects the child or parents to call her or him has important potential cultural implications as well. Many cultures vary with regard to the level of respect given to professionals. For some cultures (e.g., Hispanic), the professional is seen as deserving of great respect and reverence. For the therapist to prematurely insist that a child from such a culture call her or him by the first name may provoke undue and unnecessary discomfort for the child. This speaks again to a level of cultural sensitivity and understanding on the child therapist's part. Perhaps the safest guideline is for the therapist to refer to herself or himself, at least initially, with formal titles, such as Dr., Ms., or Mr. As the relationship with the client develops and more information is gained about the client's cultural identity, decisions may be made about allowing the child and her or his parents to call the therapist by a first name.

Another issue that may arise in conducting cross-cultural therapy is the potentially divergent meaning of nonverbal communication. That is, although there are some universal nonverbal communications, such as a smile, there are considerable differences across cultures for many other nonverbals. For example, cultures can vary considerably in regard to the amount of personal space that is required to feel comfortable in the presence of another person. Members of some cultures (e.g., English) keep considerable distance from one another, whereas members of other cultures (e.g., many Asian cultures) keep quite close to one another, often continually touching. This difference in personal space can lead to many misunderstandings and miscommunications and may also be present in the child therapy setting. Similarly, cultures often vary in the amount and type of acceptable touching between people.

Members of some cultures (e.g., many Middle Eastern cultures) have no reticence in touching other members of the same gender without any sexual connotation. In other cultures (e.g., White Americans), however, this is deemed unacceptable and inappropriate. Similarly, eye contact may be emphasized by some cultures (e.g., dominant United States society) and viewed as demonstrative of honesty and self-confidence. Other cultures (e.g., Native American cultures) place less emphasis on eye contact and, in fact, may consider it inappropriate in certain situations, such as between male and female strangers. Further, there are cultural differences in the amount of eye contact that is considered acceptable with a professional, such as a child therapist. Some cultures (e.g., Hispanic) encourage their members to avoid eye contact, as it is considered a sign of disrespect. Children from these cultures are often encouraged to be deferential and avoid eye contact with adults, particularly professionals. Not only do other cultures have no such mandates, but such behavior would be interpreted in a considerably different manner. Failure to understand these possible connotations may lead to misinterpretations on the clinician's part. For example, it is foreseeable that a culturally insensitive White child therapist might automatically assume that a culturally different child has low self-esteem just because the child does not make eye contact with the therapist.

Another serious danger in cross-cultural therapy situations is the inappropriate imposition of therapist values and attitudes onto the client. Although the threat of a therapist imposing her or his values onto clients is present in all therapy situations, it is of particular concern when the therapist and the client differ in terms of cultural heritage. As has been mentioned previously, given that there are few universally accepted values, cultures vary relative to the importance and presence of different values. It is crucial that the therapist take these differences into consideration in the therapy situation. One example of differing values is the relative importance different cultures place on the role of the individual versus the group. Whereas traditional psychotherapy places greater emphasis on an individual's independence, many cultures place greater emphasis on the individual's role in the larger group, whether it be the family, the community, or the culture as a whole. For example, traditional Native Americans emphasize the collective interdependence of members of their culture, with complex relationships among extended family members. In working with a child who grew up in a community that holds such an interdependent perspective, it would be a travesty to try to impose a value of independence. This is but one example of many in which cultures differ relative to values. Some other examples include level of self-disclosure, importance of material belongings and success, emotional expressiveness, degree of competitiveness, and importance of education.

As in all therapy situations, another major issue that will come up in cross-cultural work is the presence of transference and countertransference. In cross-cultural therapy situations, these processes may be motivated by cultural differences between the client and the therapist. The child might demonstrate transference by reacting to the therapist in the same way that she or he reacted to other members of the therapist's cultural background. These reactions may be based on prior experiences or on expectations the child has incorporated from her or his parents, family members, or friends. Although this transference might have occurred regardless of the therapist's cultural heritage, it may be particularly strong if the therapist is White. This is likely because the minority child is more likely to have had negative experiences of oppression at the hands of Whites than members of any other ethnic or cultural group and therefore may transfer anger onto the therapist. As with all forms of transference, cultural transference needs to be attended to and resolved within the therapy setting. Of course, transference is not always negative, and there may be instances of positive cultural transference that actually serve to facilitate the therapy process.

Cultural countertransference is also a strong possibility in cross-cultural therapy situations. The therapist might react to a child of different cultural heritage in the same way in which she or he responds to other members of that culture. It is in this type of situation that the therapist's own biases and stereotypes, both positive and negative, begin to interfere with the therapy process. Countertransferences can be based on previous experiences with members of another ethnic or cultural group or from public media representations of that culture. The problem that is presented by cultural countertransferences is the possibility that the therapy might become focused not on the child's presenting issues, but rather on the problems the therapist has projected onto the family. These problems will exist whether the stereotype is positive or negative because the therapist fails to recognize the child as she or he really is. It is the therapist's responsibility to maintain awareness of the presence of both cultural and other forms of countertransference and to take appropriate steps to alleviate the situation. These steps include consultation, supervision, and, if the problem is not immediately resolvable and is detrimental to the client, referral to another therapist.

Another process issue that may emerge in cross-cultural therapy situations is presented by the child or family who is rejecting of her or his cultural heritage. Some children might want to reject the part of themselves that is culturally different, often because of the negative experiences that they have suffered at the hands of other children and adults. The renouncing of the personal heritage thus occurs as the child's attempt to "fit in" more completely and to try to avoid future harassment. This situation presents a potentially difficult ethical dilemma to the therapist. On one hand, the client may have set this as a therapy goal, and it is the therapist's responsibility to at least consider this as a legitimate goal for treatment. On the other hand, the therapist might want to focus attention on helping the child incorporate, not reject, all parts of herself or himself, including those that are a result of the child's ethnic or cultural heritage. There is no easy solution to such a conflict, but it certainly needs to be explored thoroughly with the child, and her or his parents might need to be consulted on this matter before any intervention can take place.

Another situation that may arise for the child therapist is the possibility of a child client's having been subjected to discrimination or abuse by peers because of her or his parents' minority status. For example, children of gays or lesbians are often exposed to verbal and physical insult by other children at school. This can be extremely difficult for the child, as she or he often experiences very mixed emotions about the situation. Such children may incorporate the negative self-perceptions and direct them against themselves or their parents and develop feelings of anger or disgust. They may incorporate a misdirected fear within themselves that they too may be gay or lesbian, and the child's confusion about the situation may be aggravated by society's general lack of acceptance of gays and lesbians. Thus, general societal prejudice can serve to alienate the child from her or his parents. Similarly, children who have a culturally different stepparent might be subjected to verbal and physical abuse by other children.

Children from biracial parental relationships may present another unique situation for a child therapist. These children are often subjected to verbal abuse from and rejection by children of both parental cultures. As a result, the child can become confused about her or his own cultural identity and begin to feel different and separate from both cultures. To reconcile feelings of confusion, the child might reject one of the two cultures and thus push away part of herself or himself as well as the parent of that culture. This withdrawal from or rejection of the parent and self may then generalize to a rejection of all members of that culture. Helping such a child to attain a positive cultural identity can present a considerable challenge to the child therapist.

Even with the most culturally sensitive child therapist, there may be times when cultural differences will necessitate referral of a child to a therapist of her or his own cultural background. Although this may occur under numerous circumstances, perhaps the most common situation is one wherein parents or child resist therapy from a therapist of a differing background. The therapist recognizes that although this may be due to resistance based on other issues, such as the parents' own stage of ethnic identity or the parents' or child's personal biases, the most appropriate solution in this situation might be to refer to a different therapist. However, the sensitive therapist uses discretion in this situation to ensure that the transfer is not done hastily and that it is handled in a therapeutic and educative manner.

Summary and Concluding Thoughts

In the process of becoming a child therapist, there is much that a therapy trainee has to learn. She or he will need to learn about children and their development, various aspects of the therapy process, including assessment and intervention, and application of various therapy techniques. The therapist will go through a process of learning and self-exploration that, it is hoped, will lead to becoming a skilled child therapist. A crucial part of this learning process is the journey toward cultural sensitivity. Such sensitivity is crucial not only for ethical, personal, and humanitarian reasons, but because of the demographic fact that it is most likely that the child therapist will interact with children from a wide variety of cultural heritages and ethnic groups. Indeed, cross-cultural therapy interaction is inevitable, owing to the presence of a plethora of different cultures and minorities within contemporary society.

Gaining cultural sensitivity is an ongoing process for all child clinicians that begins with self-exploration and awareness and is followed by the acquisition of knowledge and skills. Owing to the presence of an overt and covert racist, sexist, and heterosexist atmosphere in which most people grow up, it can be a very challenging and difficult process. To maintain growth in the area, constant self-monitoring is necessary, and occasional supervision and consultation might need to be sought. However, the benefits provided by the cultural sensitizing process in terms of personal growth for the therapist far outweigh any costs that may be incurred along the way.

Providing therapy to a child who is culturally different from the therapist can be a challenging situation. However, cross-cultural therapy can also be extremely rewarding for therapist and child, resulting in considerable growth for both. Some unique situations can arise within the cross-cultural therapy context that present potential obstacles to the child and the therapist. By striving for cultural sensitivity and through seeking additional learning opportunities, experiences, and supervision, the therapist not only will be prepared to deal with these situations, but also will be more prepared to deal with a culturally diverse society in general.

5 The Intake Interview

The intake interview is probably the single most important assessment tool available to a therapist who works with children and their families. In fact, this process is so important that entire books have been dedicated to only this purpose (Bourg et al., 1999; Greenspan and Greenspan, 1991; Simmons, 1987; Zwiers and Morrisette, 1999). It is during the intake interview that a clinician becomes familiar with the child and the family in which the child resides. It is during the intake interview that the clinician interacts if not with all, with most of the important figures in a child's life. It is largely on the basis of the information that is derived during the intake interview that the clinician makes a treatment plan and gives treatment recommendations to the family. The intake interview represents the unique opportunity to view and assess the child within the given dynamics of the child's current interpersonal environment. Hence, much thought needs to be given to this interview. The clinician needs to be extremely clear about what type of information is to be derived from this interview, decide beforehand how the interview is to be structured, and have clear goals in mind before sitting down with a family.

The intake interview is lengthy and might appear overwhelming to the novice. However, given the ample time the clinician can take to collect the necessary information, she or he can rest assured that this task is indeed possible. Further, although this chapter will suggest one 4-hour session with the family, it is certainly possible to break up this session into various parts that are conducted on separate days. Such a structure would perhaps provide the novice with some necessary breaks to collect her or his thoughts, plan additional questions, and consult with a supervisor. The intake interview, regardless of how many sessions the therapist decides to commit to it, will always include several components: sessions with the entire family to assess their family dynamics, individual sessions with the children and the adults in the family, and a feedback session to share findings. Preliminary information can be collected through a thorough intake form that may guide the clinician's work throughout the intake interview.

Preliminary Data Collection

To be optimally prepared for each specific family, the clinician can send child intake forms to the parents before the intake interview is scheduled. Enough of these forms are mailed that a family may complete one form for each child. In other words, specific information needs to be gathered about all the children in the family, not just the identified client. The intake form needs to give the clinician a thorough history of each child's life within the current, and any previous, family. As such, it inquires about a number of details with regard to the child's life that are summarized in Table 5.1.

The use of a formal intake form for the gathering of this information is recommended because much of this information is easily forgotten during the interview when many other present-time features of the child and her or his family are being observed. A sample form is provided in Figure 5.1. Only after the intake forms have been mailed to and received by the family is an appointment for the actual intake interview scheduled. Intake forms are never to be used as substitutes for an actual interview, nor do they give the clinician permission to take shortcuts during the interview. They are merely supplements to a thorough in-person assessment. Intake forms are best not completed during the interview, neither by the family, nor by the therapist. If a family does not have any members who are literate or sufficiently fluent in English, the therapist or family might attempt to find an individual, perhaps a staff person in the clinic, who can sit down with the family before the appointment to complete the form. This needs to be done in a very courteous manner to avoid offending the family!

The Necessary Information to Be Derived from the Intake Interview

Before beginning the intake interview with a family, a clinician needs to know what information needs to be gathered, so as not to be caught off guard. It is often too difficult to try to reconvene families after an initial intake interview has taken place to gather missing information. Thus, the better prepared the clinician, the less difficult follow-up work will need to be done later. There are a number of questions about several topic areas that the clinician wants to be able to answer after the intake interview has been completed. These topic areas are summarized in Table 5.1. Once the clinician knows *what* information needs to be collected, the structure of *how* to collect this information can be addressed.

TABLE 5.1 Topics to Be Assessed in the Intake Form and Intake Interview

Interview Topics	Intake Form Topics
■ presenting problem	■ preferred name or nickname
■ family relationships	■ age and date of birth
■ school or preschool issues	■ mother's pregnancy and delivery
■ social and peer relationships	■ current family
■ sociocultural factors	■ other families (adoptive and foster families)
■ recreation, interests, and hobbies	■ medical history and developmental milestones
■ developmental and health issues	■ legal involvements
■ plans for future, fantasies, and daydreams	■ living arrangements
■ behavioral observations	■ previous treatment

Before you come for your appointment at our clinic, please complete this form. Some of the questions might be difficult to answer, but please give them a try. Try not to use words such as "average" or "normal," instead, describe the situation as it is. This form is confidential and will not be released to others without your written permission.

Parent's Signature   Today's Date

Child's legal name   Nickname

Sex   Ethnicity   Birth date   Age

Grade   School

If this child has ever been known by another last name, please give that name:

Present address   City

State   Zip   Home Phone   Work Phone

Legal custodian

Who is raising the child (circle all that apply)

Biological parents   Parent and step parent   Foster parents
Single parent   Adoptive parents   Relatives
Institution   Other (explain: _____)

Describe the people the child currently lives with:

Name of primary caregiver   Birthdate   Relation to child

Address

Home Phone   Work Phone

Occupation   Employer

Education (circle highest grade)   1 2 3 4 5 6 7 8 9 10 11 12

Years of College: _____   Degree(s) attained: _____

FIGURE 5.1 Sample Child Intake Form

(continued)

Name of second caregiver   Birth date   Relation to child
_____

Address
_____

Home Phone   Work Phone
_____

Occupation   Employer

Education (circle highest grade)   1   2   3   4   5   6   7   8   9   10   11   12

Years of College: _____   Degree(s) attained: _____

Other Children in This Child's Home

    Name   Birth date   Relationship   Grade/School

1. _____

2. _____

3.` _____

4. _____

5. _____

6. _____

Brothers and Sisters out of This Child's Home:

    Name   Birth date   Relationship   Grade/School

1. _____

2. _____

3. _____

4. _____

5. _____

Marital status of biological parents (circle)

married	never married	living together
one parent dead	custodial parent remarried	separated
both parents dead	divorced	other (specify)

_____

Date of Marriage   Date of Separation(s)   Date of Divorce

FIGURE 5.1 _Continued_

Comments: _____

_____

_____

Information on one or both natural parents (*if* child is *not* living with them):

Name of mother   Birthdate   Marriages

_____

Address

_____

Home Phone   Work Phone

_____

Occupation   Employer

Education (circle highest grade)   1   2   3   4   5   6   7   8   9   10   11   12

Years of College: _____   Degree(s) attained: _____

_____

Name of father   Birthdate   Marriages

_____

Address

_____

Home Phone   Work Phone

_____

Occupation   Employer

Education (circle highest grade)   1   2   3   4   5   6   7   8   9   10   11   12

Years of College: _____   Degree(s) attained: _____

Other persons with whom this child has lived:

_____

Name   Relationship   When

_____

Name   Relationship   When

_____

Name   Relationship   When

_____

Name   Relationship   When

_____

(continued)

If the child was adopted:

Adoption agency's name: _____

_____

Age when adopted   Date adopted   Does child know?

Reaction of child to adoption: _____

If the child is a foster child:

Agencies involved: _____

_____

Age when placed into foster care   Age when placed with these foster parents

_____

Age when placed into foster care   Age when placed with these foster parents

Reaction of child to being in foster care: _____

Reason for foster care: _____

Physicians this child has seen (from most to least recent)

Current Physician	Address	Date	Reason
Current Physician	Address	Date	Reason
Past Physician	Address	Date	Reason
Past Physician	Address	Date	Reason

Accidents this child has had

Type of Accident	When	Where	Who Present
Type of Accident	When	Where	Who Present

Hospitalizations

Hospital	Address	Date	Reason
Hospital	Address	Date	Reason

FIGURE 5.1 *Continued*

Medication this child takes (please list all)

Name or Kind	Dose/Strength	How Often	Physician

Condition _____

Name or Kind	Dose/Strength	How Often	Physician

Condition _____

Name or Kind	Dose/Strength	How Often	Physician

Condition _____

Has the child been evaluated previously?   Yes   No

    Psychological Evaluation: _____
                   where   when

    Educational Evaluation: _____
                   where   when

    Neurological Evaluation: _____
                   where   when

    Other: _____: _____
                   where   when

Is child currently involved with legal authorities?

If yes, who? _____

Please explain: _____

_____

_____

Dates of anticipated related court hearings: _____

Family health history

If any family member has or had any of the following illnesses, please indicate with an "X":

	This Child	Father	Mother	Sibling	Grand-parent
Birth Defect	_____	_____	_____	_____	_____
Speech/Hearing Prob.	_____	_____	_____	_____	_____

(continued)

	This Child	Father	Mother	Sibling	Grand-parent
Epilepsy or Seizures	_____	_____	_____	_____	_____
Cancer	_____	_____	_____	_____	_____
Diabetes	_____	_____	_____	_____	_____
Heart Disease	_____	_____	_____	_____	_____
Asthma	_____	_____	_____	_____	_____
Alcoholism	_____	_____	_____	_____	_____
Mental Retardation	_____	_____	_____	_____	_____

If any family member is or has seen any of the following professionals or agencies for treatment, indicate with an "X":

	This Child	Father	Mother	Sibling	Grand-parent
Physical Therapist	_____	_____	_____	_____	_____
Educational Specialist	_____	_____	_____	_____	_____
Psychiatric Hospital	_____	_____	_____	_____	_____
Mental Health Center	_____	_____	_____	_____	_____
Psychologist	_____	_____	_____	_____	_____
Psychiatrist	_____	_____	_____	_____	_____
Social Worker	_____	_____	_____	_____	_____
Marriage Counselor	_____	_____	_____	_____	_____
Pastoral Counselor	_____	_____	_____	_____	_____
Speech or Hearing Specialist	_____	_____	_____	_____	_____

Child's developmental history
Pregnancy:

_____

Where was baby delivered?   Hospital   City

birth weight: _____ lbs. _____ oz.   birth height: _____ inches

_____

drugs used during pregnancy   during delivery

FIGURE 5.1 *Continued*

problem with labor   with delivery

prematurity or other complications? _____

At birth

Did baby cry immediately?   yes   no   explain: _____

Did baby need oxygen?   yes   no   explain: _____

Did baby need incubator?   yes   no   explain: _____

Growth and development
(record the age at which child accomplished the following)

sat alone _____   smiled _____   recognized you _____

crawled _____   stood _____   walked alone _____

said words _____   used sentences _____

at what age did you begin toilet training? _____

when was child finally toilet trained? _____

did wetting or soiling occur once trained? _____

does child wet now?   yes   no   daytime? _____   nighttime? _____

does child soil now?   yes   no   daytime? _____   nighttime? _____

Daycare, preschool, school

Did child attend preschool?   yes   no   when? _____

How did child adjust? _____

Did child attend kindergarten?   yes   no   when? _____

How did child adjust? _____

Does child have school problems?   yes   no

    If yes, please explain: _____

    _____

    _____

Is child taking remedial classes?   yes   no

(continued)

If yes, what subjects and grades?_____

_____

_____

_____

Does child have any other school-related problems?   yes   no

    If yes, please explain: _____

_____

_____

Special concerns

Has child ever abused drugs?   yes   no   not sure   suspect so

Do you have any concerns about child's sexual behavior?   yes   no

    If yes, please explain: _____

Does child have any strong fears?   yes   no

    If yes, list: _____

Has child been subjected to any of the following and how did she or he respond?

Parental separation or divorce: yes   no   _____

Death of a family member: yes   no   _____

Hospitalization of family member: yes   no   _____

Loss or death of pet: yes   no   _____

Discipline

How do you discipline child (circle all that apply):

family sets and enforces rules   discussion   lecture
other physical punishment   spank   isolate
denial of privileges   other _____

Who disciplines child (circle all that apply):

mother   father   others: _____

Parental agreement on discipline?   yes   no

If no, why not? _____

FIGURE 5.1   *Continued*

Child's reaction to discipline (circle all that apply):

pout	cry	tantrum	ignore	walk off
talk back	hit	accept	complain	yell

others: _____

Family life

Number of family moves in child's life _____

Length of residence in the present home _____

Do the siblings get along?   yes   no

    If no, explain: _____

Tell about other children in the household and how the child who is to be seen feels toward her or his sisters and brothers.

_____

_____

_____

Tell about the current parents' home life and living situation. Are there problems that may have affected the child?

_____

_____

_____

Recreation

How does child spend free time? _____

_____

What kind of play does child enjoy? _____

_____

What special interests, hobbies, skills, or sports does child engage in? _____

_____

What type of playmates does child prefer (circle all that apply):

older	younger	own age	all ages
adults	male	female	both genders

(continued)

Is child a loner?   yes   no

   If yes, elaborate: _____

How many friends does child have? _____

Does child have a best friend?   yes   no   age of friend? _____

What are child's strong points, assets, or abilities: _____

_____

_____

_____

Your current reasons for seeking help

What are your main concerns at the present time? _____

_____

_____

_____

Did a specific event lead to this application?   Yes   No

If yes, what and when? _____

_____

_____

How have you prepared child for the evaluation here? _____

_____

_____

Did someone else refer you here? If so, why? _____

_____

_____

_____

Is there anything significant the form did not ask which you would like to add? _____

_____

_____

_____

FIGURE 5.1 *Continued*

Do you have any questions you would like to ask during the first meeting? _____

_____

_____

_____

_____

The Presenting Problem

A lot more than a mere presenting problem needs to be explored here. Specifically, most families present not with one, but rather with a list of problems. Therefore, the first important step is to find out about all the presenting problems in this family, not just with regard to the identified child client, but also with regard to other family members. For each presenting problem, a number of issues need to be attended to.

First of all, the problem itself needs to be defined in detail. Specifically, the clinician needs to know *when* the problem occurs. Are there certain situations that are more likely to result in the problem behavior? Are there certain people who are usually present when the child presents with a specific symptom? The clinician needs to know *where* the presenting problem occurs. Are there certain places that are more likely to elicit the problem than others? Is the problem confined to one specific locality? If so, what are the features of that locality? The clinician needs to know *how* the presenting problem occurs. Is there a certain way in which the problem develops? Does the problem behavior start in a certain manner and then escalate to other symptoms? The clinician needs to know *with whom* the presenting problem occurs. Is the symptom more likely in the company of certain individuals? Is the symptom's occurrence restricted to the company of adults or children? The clinician needs to know *how long* the presenting problem occurs. Is this problem consistently present, or does it occur briefly? Does the problem repeat itself in exactly the same sequence each time, or does it vary slightly? The better the definition of the problem, the easier it is for the clinician to decide whether the problem is a valid concern, a developmental issue, or a normal presentation.

Second, a history of the presenting problem provides important information. It is useful to know when the problem was first noted and who identified it as a problem. It is necessary to find out whether the problem has changed over time and whether it tends to go away for time periods, only to recur later. If the family can pinpoint the exact time of onset, it is important to explore what changes might have been occurring in the child's life at that time. This information helps the therapist to put the problem in perspective and often gives useful information for a conceptualization that explains the presence of the symptoms. This type of information is likely to affect treatment recommendations. For instance, the treatment of depression may vary for two children, despite similarity in actual symptoms, based on the historical information derived. If one child's depression had a clear onset after the death of the child's father who was a primary caretaker and is present at all times, whereas another child's depression began on the first day of classes and is present only during school hours but never at home, then these two children will receive very different treatments.

Finally, the impact of the problem on the child and the family is worthy of exploration. Certain problems may affect only the individual child; others affect the family as a system or individual family members. The presenting problem may also affect the identified client differently in different environments. It may restrict the behavior of the child or the entire family, thus creating additional problems with which the child and the family have to cope. For instance, children who are enuretic or encopretic often are severely affected by the disorder as far as their social lives are concerned. They frequently are less likely than other children to spend the night with friends and to belong to clubs that have overnight outings, such as scouts. Thus, the presenting problem has a variety of impacts on the child's life that can hinder psychological growth in other arenas of development.

Family Relationships

Several components of family relationships are important to inquire about in detail. These include discipline strategies, parental family histories, spousal relationship, sibling relationships, and extended family issues. Thorough data collection about parenting or discipline strategies will reveal the approaches parents take toward their children and, if there is more than one parent, whether they agree on how to discipline and raise children. Specific preferred strategies need to be investigated, as does the degree of consistency with which they are applied. This assessment also needs to consider implicit and explicit family rules, as well as consequences for members who break the rules. Consistency is investigated not only with regard to consistency in the use of particular strategies and the application of rules, but also with regard to consistency across children and situations. For example, it is important to note whether parents use different disciplinary strategies with one of their children (unless there is an age-appropriateness reason) or whether they use different strategies for the same misbehavior depending on whether the family is at home or in public. The family's actual behavior during the interview will give important clues about parenting and disciplinary styles.

Parental histories are taken with regard to all parents' unique backgrounds. Issues to be explored include how the parents themselves were parented when they were children; relationships of the parents with their own parents; parental social, academic, and professional backgrounds; and medical as well as mental health histories for their extended and nuclear families. The more background information can be gleaned from and about each individual parent, the better. It will lend an enormous amount of understanding to the family's presenting problem if the clinician understands the parents' histories. For instance, the presence of child abuse in a family that is being assessed can be better understood if it is revealed that one or more parents were the victims of abuse during their own childhood, as these behaviors do tend to be passed along from generation to generation.

If there is more than one parent in the home and these two individuals are in an exclusive sexual (whether heterosexual or homosexual) relationship, this relationship becomes a crucial component of the family assessment. A thorough dating history is often important, as is an assessment of conflicts, shared and disagreed-upon values, attitudes, common interests, and shared activities. It is not uncommon for tension in the parental dyad to lead to symptoms in the children in the family. If only one parent is currently living in the home, the relationship of that parent to the other biological parent of the child or children in the home becomes the focus of the assessment. Two people need not live together to have an impact on their children. If two biological parents fight frequently, even if they do not share the same residence, their behavior will affect their children. Further, the possibility exists that children become the bearer of messages between the parents, thus being pulled into the middle of arguments and conflicts.

Attention will also need to be paid to the relationships among the siblings who live in the same household. This is true whether the siblings are full, half, adoptive, or foster siblings. It is important to find out how well the various children in the same household get along and how they interact with one another. Further, siblings who do not share the same residence will also need to be inquired about, especially if they come for visits on any regular basis. Sibling relationships often help the clinician to gain some insight into why one child may present with more symptoms than another.

One suggested format for collecting this type of data is the construction of a genogram. In a genogram, the clinician and the clients plot out the family history by creating a family tree showing all family members on both the maternal and paternal side of the child who is presented as the problem person in the family. The tracing goes backward to grandparents, great-grandparents, and aunts and uncles, as well as forward to siblings, and nieces and nephews if applicable. For all mentioned family members, salient information is taken down. An example of a genogram for a child who presented to therapy because of depression is provided in Figure 5.2. A thorough description of the process of constructing a genogram is presented in McGoldrick and Gerson (1999), as well as in Scarf (1987).

School or Preschool Issues

For the identified client, the clinician needs to assess school performance and related school behaviors. Specifically, academic capacity and intellectual/cognitive functioning need to be evaluated. This can be done through interview or through releases of information to obtain school records. Rating forms and behavior rating scales can be very helpful in this process (these assessment tools are discussed in Chapter Six). If there is any question about the cognitive functioning of a child, or about the possibility of learning disabilities or neuropsychological deficits, the evaluation needs to go beyond existing data and interview. A referral to an appropriate professional such as a neuropsychologist or educational/school psychologist might be in order (referrals are discussed in Chapter Six).

In addition to purely academic performance data, the clinician also needs to evaluate the child's performance with regard to relationships with fellow students and teachers. A thorough history of any problems needs to be taken. Just as with the presenting problems, time frames and situational components of the behavior, affect, or attitude need to be assessed. Behavior rating scales can add useful information about school behavior.

Social and Peer Relationships

Information about the child's peer relationships and social involvement is extremely helpful in assessing the degree of pervasiveness of a presenting problem. Often, children who

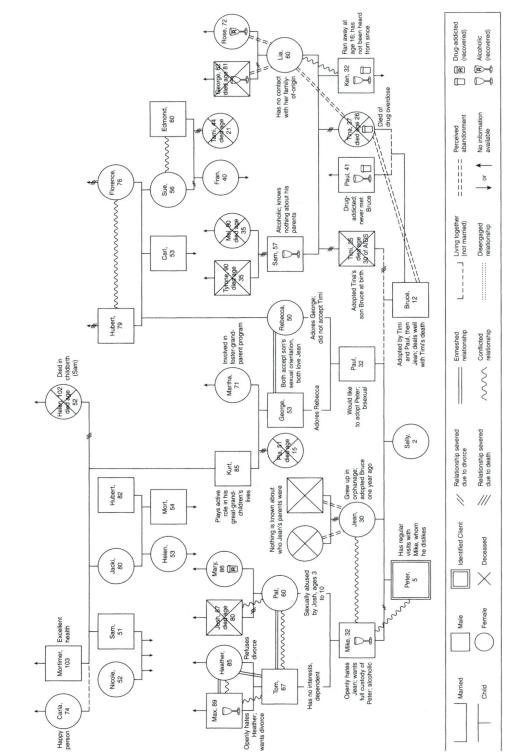

FIGURE 5.2 Genogram for a Depressed Child

106

may experience significant problems in one setting may not have these in another, indicating to the clinician that the problem may be largely a situational one. With regard to this area of information, the therapist needs to investigate whether the child has or ever has had a best friend. The gender of this friend is important, as well as a description of that friend provided by the child. Children often choose friends for characteristics in the friend that are either alien to but desired by the child or very similar to those of the child. Therefore, asking the child to tell the clinician what the child likes and dislikes about this particular friend may have implications about what the child likes and dislikes about herself or himself. The absence of a best friend is reason for concern, more so than the absence of a large number of occasional playmates.

In addition to exploring relationships with best friends, the clinician will also find it helpful to ask about playmates and their ages. Preferred games and activities that are engaged in during play are also important to inquire about. The clinician should not easily accept the child's simple "yes" or "no" about whether she or he has many playmates but should rather inquire about their names, positive traits, common interests, and common shared activities. Only then can the clinician assess whether the child's perception of an adequate social network is realistic. A sociogram collected by the child's teacher can also be considered.

A differentiation may also be made about whether the child's playmates are encountered primarily during school hours or whether the children actually meet outside of school. Questions about sleepovers and after-school activities will be helpful here. Finally, it is important to investigate whether there has been a change in playmate relationships and numbers over time. This information will be helpful in pointing to the possible onset of the child's (i.e., the family's) presenting problem. It is not uncommon for children's friendship patterns to change after a major move, a divorce, or similar experiences. Of course, a change in and of itself does not indicate that there is a problem; rather, how the change is perceived by the child is of importance and clinical value.

In summary, a child's friendship patterns are helpful hints about the child's personality traits and problem behaviors in social settings. They should not be overlooked, nor should they be taken for granted. The parents' perspective on the child's friendship patterns with best friends and playmates is often a useful supplement to the information provided by the child.

Sociocultural Factors

Children are influenced not only by the psychological and emotional climate of a family, but also by its socioeconomic and sociocultural background. It is therefore important for the clinician to have accurate information about these aspects of the child's life. Specific information needs to be collected about the family's financial status, about the neighborhood in which they currently live and where they have lived previously, about the family's general attitudes about money and possessions, and about the family's self-assessed socioeconomic status. This information is very important for follow-up planning as well as for referral decisions. For instance, a family that is unable to pay is very unlikely to follow through with referrals to high-cost private practitioners. Ignoring this information not only may lead to inappropriate referrals, but also may affect treatment recommendations. A family that has a hard time making ends meet financially cannot be expected to adhere to costly treatment recommendations. Similarly, they may be quite unable to come to the clinic if they have no regular means of transportation. Failing to consider true financial needs and limits may set the family up for failure with regard to their ability to follow through on recommendations made by the clinician.

Even more important, the therapist needs to be sensitive to the cultural backgrounds and attitudes of children's families. Children are socialized very early in life, thus carrying forth the cultural beliefs, attitudes, and values of their parents. These values and ideals are utterly important for the clinician to grasp as they have a profound impact upon the harmonious functioning of a family and the children within this family. Specific information needs to be gathered about the ethnic group's attitudes toward mental health, toward normal family functioning with regard to generational attitudes, toward normal affective expression, toward accepted academic functioning, toward self-expression, and many other facets of day to day functioning. All clinicians should have some cultural sensitivity through education and by reading about the values and ideals of various cultural groups and as they relate to mental health issues. However, it is negligent not to assess the degree to which these cultural beliefs fit for a specific family that is being seen for treatment. In other words, the clinician needs to be sensitive not only to the ethnic background, but also to the degree of acculturation or adherence to the traditional ways of a family's ethnic heritage.

The impact of culture or ethnicity on a family's life cannot be underestimated and needs to be strongly considered, in both assessment and treatment planning. For instance, a project in the state of Alaska involved the training of assertiveness skills in high schoolers of Alaska Native cultural backgrounds (Gasta, 1976). This was considered a very worthwhile effort, as teachers had noted that Native high schoolers were less assertive than their White counterparts and therefore often appeared less academically skilled because of less involvement in the classroom. The training program was indeed effective in training students to become more assertive but was found to have profound side effects in these students' home lives. Specifically, given their Alaska Native heritage, assertive skills toward parents did not fit the cultural norm and resulted in increased conflicts between parents and children. This is an excellent example of good intentions about the improvement of children's mental health that failed to consider the children's ethnic backgrounds and values. Imposing White, or majority, values and beliefs on clients of other ethnic backgrounds, and hence values and needs, is not only insensitive, but also possibly iatrogenic!

Within this category of sensitivity to personal or familial belief and value systems, it is also important to explore religious affiliation and involvement. This is another component of family life that can have potentially profound influences on how likely a family is to become involved in the treatment process and has implications for treatment planning. Family lore, family secrets, familial ways of doing things, and similar aspects of a family's functioning are all important components of a thorough assessment that respects the family for who they are and what they have created for themselves over generations.

Recreation, Interests, and Hobbies

Interests, hobbies and recreational activities are an important aspect of family and personal functioning. They should be assessed for each individual family member, as well as for the family as a whole. The absence of any of these is as important as finding out specific preferences. Treatment interventions may be structured in such a way as to make use of existing interests and shared hobbies.

Related to this issue is the family's social involvement. Are there other people in this family's life who can offer a potential social support network? If there are no such external resources, the clinician should assess the reasons for their absence. Again, it is important to investigate whether the children in this family have friends and acquaintances, and how often they interact with them. The existence of friendships needs to be explored with some detail to assess how important and enduring they have been. Sensitivity to the number of family moves, as well as to changes in the family structure (e.g., due to divorce or foster-parenting) is valuable in this regard.

Developmental and Health Issues

Although developmental and health information is most important about the identified client, other family members may need to be assessed in this regard if it appears to be of importance to the family's level of functioning or to the identified client's adjustment. For instance, if there is a sibling with a chronic illness or a parent with a terminal illness, these issues need to be discussed with regard to their relevance to the family and the children within it. Specific developmental and health related information includes, but is not limited to, information about the pregnancy with the identified client, birth/delivery information, postnatal physical state (e.g., APGAR scores), developmental milestones of the identified client, childhood illnesses, accidents, hospitalizations, frequency and circumstances of mild illnesses (e.g., stomachaches, headaches), and frequency and circumstances of minor injuries (e.g., bruises, scratches).

Particular attention should be paid to the potential contribution of abuse or neglect to the state of the child's health. For instance, frequent minor injuries or a series of bone fractures should lead to questions related to the potential of physical abuse. Medical problems involving vaginal infections, bladder infections, or similar symptoms should lead to questions regarding sexual abuse. Similarly, a child who failed to reach developmental milestones within age-appropriate limits should be assessed with the potential for neglect in mind. Previous reports to federal or state agencies need to be inquired about.

Plans for the Future, Fantasies, and Daydreams

On a more positive note, and for prognostic purposes, the clinician also needs to find out information about a family's aspirations, as well as each individual member's daydreams and hopes for the future. Planning and goal setting are important components of a well-functioning family.

Behavioral Observations

Behavioral observations are collected throughout the intake process. They include observations of individuals, as well as of the family system as a whole. Things to look for in all members of the family include cleanliness and appropriateness of dress and appearance, physical characteristics and mannerisms, adjustment to the intake process and the meeting with a stranger (the clinician), affect and mood, communication and general interaction styles, capacity for cooperation and negotiation, willingness to listen and compromise, changes in mood and behavior as the intake session progresses, psychological mindedness and attitudes toward treatment, level of interest and curiosity, and estimates of cognitive ability and verbal skills. Sometimes, behavioral observations can be augmented through the use of mental status examinations (to be discussed in Chapter Six). However, most commonly, all the necessary information about the overall physical and psychological functioning of all family members can be gleaned from good behavioral observations throughout the various sections of the intake interview.

Once the therapist is cognizant of the type of information that needs to be collected, the purpose of the intake interview becomes much clearer. The interview is then much easier to conduct, as the clinician has a clear plan in mind. However, the actual structure of how to see a family is an important consideration that is worthwhile thinking about before beginning the intake interview.

The Structure of the Intake Interview

As the actual intake process is discussed, reference will be made repeatedly to parents, mothers, fathers, spouses, and partners. This is done merely to facilitate writing and reading and has no implications for the actual gender, marital status, or sexual orientation of the adults within the family system. In fact, most of what will be said will apply directly to blended families, foster families, adoptive families, and even single parent families. Thus, as the reader goes through the material, she or he should not assume that what is discussed is applicable only to the "American dream" family. Quite to the contrary, most family interviews that the clinician will conduct will not be with intact biological nuclear families, but rather with blended, single, or other types of families. The intake process as described below will still apply.

Preparing for the Interview

Information about the topic areas outlined in the previous section is gathered through various processes during the intake interview. By the sheer amount of necessary information, it becomes evident that a child therapy intake interview is generally very lengthy. Each individual therapist will need to decide how long an intake ought to take to ascertain sufficient time to collect all necessary data. A recommended time frame is 4 hours. Given this lengthy process, families need to be warned about the length of the appointment at the time of scheduling so that they can arrange to take time off work and to take the children out of school. Clinicians who are willing can accommodate families by scheduling afternoon appointments. Stressing to the family that only the initial appointment will require this much time enhances their cooperation and willingness to commit to the assessment period. Surprisingly, many families are very uncertain about the therapy process and need to be educated about parameters that therapists often take for granted. As such, during their initial phone contact, families should be told about the expectation that therapy involves more than one appointment and in fact may mean weekly appointments for several weeks. Families need to learn that therapy sessions last for a certain amount of time (generally either 50 or 90 minutes) and are scheduled on a regular basis. The better informed and prepared the family is before committing to the intake, the more likely they are to follow through with their commitment not just to the initial appointment, but the therapy process as a whole.

The family also needs to be informed of who is to be included in the family interview. Generally, it is preferable to have all persons who reside in the same home as the child come for the session. However, if there are other primary caretakers who do not live in the home, but who are willing to participate, they would be excellent resources to include. Further, if the child lives in a blended or single parent family, some thought needs to be given to inviting all biological parents. This, of course, needs to be discussed with the custodial parent who legally is the only person who can make the initial contact with the therapist. It is often difficult to get the entire family to cooperate and to appear for the initial intake. However, the therapy is best served by maximizing the number of family members who can be convinced to come for the first session. Some therapists refuse to see a family if not all members are present for the first appointment, whereas others hold the philosophy that one should work with whoever can be attracted to the therapy process. There is no correct approach to this problem, but a therapist is better off being clear about which approach is to be taken. The decision to see only entire families versus subgroupings that are willing to come is best not made on the day of the appointment, but rather is a decision that the therapist makes beforehand and informs her or his clients of. Thus, a therapist who will not conduct a session without all relevant members present must inform the family of this requirement before the family appears for their first appointment. This eliminates confusion and limit-testing on the family's part, as well as arbitrary decision making on the therapist's part.

Building rapport with the parents is critical to the success of the child's treatment and begins at first contact (Kottman, 1995). During the first phone conversation with a parent, the therapist must be aware that she or he needs to build a relationship with the parent that is supportive, empathic, and respectful so as not to jeopardize the parent's willingness to support the child's therapy. The phone contact can be utilized to ensure that the parents know what to expect from therapy and that they are clear that they need to prepare the child for the intake session (cf. Brems, 1994). Parents can be given support by referring them to existing literature that has been designed to facilitate entry into therapy by children, such as Nemiroff and Annunziata's excellent *Child's First Book about Therapy* (1990).

Table 5.2 provides an overview of the topics that are best covered with parents during the initial phone contact to help them prepare themselves and their child(ren) for the assessment interview and possibly for any subsequent therapy. Because this initial phone contact can be very important to ultimate cooperation by the family and may elicit clinically relevant information, it is made by the clinician, not a receptionist or secretary.

Format of the Interview

The actual intake interview can be structured in many different ways. One suggested format is to see the entire family together, then to split the family into various subgroups or holons. The term *holon* is preferred to the term *subgroup* because of its special connotation. Specifically, holons denote subgroupings of a family that are both part of a greater whole, and thus incomplete and autonomous and self-preserving as a whole in and of

TABLE 5.2   **Preparing Parents for the Intake Interview and Subsequent Treatment**

Information to Provide	Additional Details
▪ introduce reason for return phone call	→ provide name, reason for call, other detail as needed
▪ provide opportunity for a brief discussion of presenting concerns	→ limit this interaction to 2–5 minutes as clinical material should not be discussed in detail on the telephone
▪ length of the intake session	→ 3–4 hours
▪ reason for the long intake session	→ to glean a thorough understanding of child and family
▪ who is best present for the intake session	→ all members of household and/or involved caretakers
▪ what will happen if not all invited show up	→ provide clinician's rules about this (e.g., reschedule session, proceed without all members)
▪ how to prepare the child for the intake session	→ recommend a book or explain in clinician's own words
▪ explain the need to prepare the child for the intake session	→ increases cooperation and removes negative expectations
▪ explain that therapy involves more than a single session	→ there will be more sessions after the intake; these sessions will be much shorter; their number cannot be predicted at this time
▪ provide cost information	→ details about fees, charges for additional services, cancellation policy, and so forth
▪ discuss intake form that will be mailed and must be completed before the intake session	→ helps to orient and prepare family and clinician; saves time during the interview
▪ if needed, explain legal and ethical issues	→ if parents inquire, cover issues dealing with confidentiality, dual relationships, duty to report, and so forth
▪ if needed, help parents understand that problems may get worse before getting better	→ prevents later questioning of the clinician's skill and expertise; makes expectations about treatment more realistic
▪ if needed, discuss insurance issues	→ explain clinic policies and, if possible, insurer requirements
▪ if possible, schedule the intake session	→ if parents cannot yet commit to a meeting time, schedule a phone time to follow up
▪ if requested, provide clinician credentials	→ provide information about professional qualifications

themselves (Minuchin, Simon, and Lee, 1996; Nichols, Schwartz, and Minuchin, 1994). Each holon carries its own unique information, process, and communication, as well as containing the whole family's program or integrative energy. From this definition, it becomes clear why it might be important to meet with separate holons individually, as they can all provide a sense of the overall family structure, but additionally, they can give information about the impact of the whole on its parts and of the parts on the whole. This inter-dependence is crucial not only to the overall functioning of the family, but also to the therapist's understanding of the family and each member.

In splitting up the family into appropriate holons, the therapist needs to decide which are the important subgroupings. There is much uniformity in this regard, and a general approach might be as follows. After the family has been seen together, the parents are identified and seen as one holon, the siblings as another, and the identified client as a third; each of the holons requires interviews of varying lengths. Finally, the whole family is reconvened for feedback and recommendations. However, there are other potential options for the intake interview, such as to see the family as a whole only, to see only the child and not insist at all on the presence of other family members, to see only the parental holon to assess their relationship, or to see individual holons without seeing the family as a whole unit. Although there are no hard empirical data that would point toward the superiority of one particular structure for the assessment interview, each of these options has clinical advantages and disadvantages that have to be weighed by the clinician who will decide on how to proceed. Each clinician will have to develop a unique and workable personal style. The format suggested here has the advantage of providing maximal access to all family members, both as a system, and as individuals. Thus, the clinician is exposed to a large number of dynamics that involve intrapsychic, as well as interpersonal processes. Observation of the entire system, as well as its subsystems or holons, becomes possible. Further, this approach may reduce resistance, as family members start out in a conjoint meeting; thus, there is less concern about blame being placed, scapegoating being fostered, or secrecy being encouraged. Having the whole family present for the initial section of the intake may well result in greater trust in the process of psychotherapy, therefore being a great way of addressing one of the most common resistances to treatment (Simmons, 1987). However, there are disadvantages. Specifically, some children may be very concerned about confidentiality, not trusting that the therapist will indeed not discuss the topics that arose between the child and the clinician with the parents. Similarly, parents sometimes attempt to abuse the structure to keep a hidden agenda that they refuse to discuss with the family as a whole, thus perpetuating dysfunctional communication patterns within the family. Each therapist has to consider the risk factors inherent in all the different approaches and then needs to decide which approach has the least disadvantages and the most advantages from the individual clinician's perspective.

The Interviewers

Next, it will be necessary to decide whether a therapist wants to work alone or with a cotherapist. In the structure discussed above, if two clinicians are working together, both would be present during the initial interview with the entire family, then one would see the parents and the other would see the children. After all holons have been assessed by the therapists, the two clinicians need to take some time to evaluate and process together the data that have been gathered so far. A therapist working alone will need to go through this process without the valuable input from a second clinician. A preliminary conceptualization is developed at this time, a treatment plan is made, and then the family is reconvened for a feedback session. The treatment decisions will be discussed with the family in the form of presenting them with treatment choices. It will be up to the family to decide which treatment suggestions to take.

The whole intake process from the initial family session to the feedback session, if conducted according to the model provided above, will take approximately 4 hours. Related to the feedback process are decisions about who will follow through with the various treatment options that are presented to the family. If two clinicians are collaborating, they will decide before they meet the family who will work with the parents (both during the intake and during therapy if that should be one of the recommendations), and who should work with the identified child client. If only one therapist is involved, that individual needs to decide whether it is wise for one clinician to see various holons of the family for therapy (it is necessary to do so during the intake). This decision is important because conflicts can easily arise for the clinician who sees parents in couple's therapy while seeing their child in individual treatment. Parallel therapies such as this often present threats to confidentiality, as it is easy to forget which piece of information about the family was derived from which member. However, parallel therapies may also have the advantage of being aware of everybody's perception of family dynamics and struggles. Again, each clinician will need to decide which process is most efficient and workable within the theoretical perspectives and practical limitations of the therapy that is being conducted.

Final Thoughts about the Interview

The format of the interview with the identified client and with the siblings will be determined largely by their ages and personality styles. It will be more focused on free play without questioning for younger children, whereas more structure is possible, but not always necessary, with older children. The use of the play therapy room needs to be considered for its appropriateness. A general guideline is to use the play therapy room and play as a technique for children under age 10; for children 10 and over, play and conversation may be mixed as determined by the child's spontaneous choices; with adolescents, talking therapy will probably prove most productive and appropriate.

Decisions about confidentiality among family members need to be made before the session starts and need to be shared with the family. The legal and ethical guidelines were discussed in Chapter Two. Families, including young children, have the right to be informed of these legal and ethical issues at the time of the intake interview. As was mentioned before, this takes place during the first section of the intake interview when all family members are present. Once the therapist or therapists have decided the structure of the intake interview, they are ready to begin the intake session. For each subsection, certain goals with regard to data collection emerge and certain purposes are served. These are discussed below and summarized in Table 5.3.

The Intake Interview with the Family

In addition to obtaining information about the presenting problem and its history, a major goal of this initial joint interview with the entire family is to hook the family into treatment and to get away from the concept of there being one identified client. Instead, the clinician attempts to get the family to collaborate in the effort to help the child who was identified as having the problem in the family within the context of the entire system. The joint family

TABLE 5.3   **Outline, Order, and Goals of the Sections of the Initial Interview**

Section	Holon Members	Goals
Family Interview	all members of the household who are willing to come	1. gather information about the presenting problem 2. overcome family resistance 3. build rapport with all family members 4. assess family structure 5. assess family competence 6. assess family process 7. assess family relating
Parent Interview	all adults who function in a parental role	1. collect specifics about the presenting problem 2. gather background information about the identified child 3. assess parenting styles and discipline strategies 4. gather parents' family of origin information 5. gather information about the spousal relationship
Sibling Interview	all siblings who are present for intake	1. get a fresh perspective on the presenting problem 2. assess siblings' roles within the family
Client Interview	identified child	1. establish rapport 2. gather information 3. set the stage for therapeutic intervention
Feedback Session	all members of the household	1. provide feedback 2. make specific treatment recommendations 3. set treatment goals 4. prepare the family for therapy

interview is best used not for the collection of very specific data, but rather for a general assessment of the presenting problem and the overall character and functioning of the family. Thus, observations of family interactions are as important as the asking of specific questions to solicit detailed information, if not more so.

This interview is crucial to overcoming resistance. It is the first time that the clinician meets with this family, and the stage for a working relationship is set at this time. Issues of distrust, resistance, and perceived differences are going to become more evident during this portion of the interview than at any other time during the intake contact. It is very important to pay attention at this time to the family's hesitations about treatment and to their resistance about seeing the presenting problem from a family perspective, as well as an individual perspective. Such resistances are always present; it is only a matter of degree as to whether they will actually interfere with treatment or whether they can be overcome successfully. It is never worth attempting to ignore the resistances; they are best dealt with openly and addressed directly with the parents, though not in the presence of the child (Greenspan and Greenspan, 1991). Resistance should not be labeled as such to the parents, but rather should be addressed from a perspective of the parent trying to protect the child and the family. Most resistances have purposes, at least historically were adaptive or functional, and cannot be overcome by challenging them outright (Kohut, 1984). Instead, it is best to join with the parents, explore their concerns and fear, and then attempt to make them feel understood and respected enough that they are willing at least to give therapy for the child (or the family) a try.

The clinician will also become aware of potential barriers to treatment that are part of this family and will have an opportunity to educate the family about psychotherapy and diagnostic assessment. This interview presents a unique opportunity for the therapist to begin to establish a rapport that may carry through the rest of this family's or its individual members' treatment. Thus, successful joining of the family is of utmost importance in this interaction.

Joining, or rapport building, can be accomplished through a myriad of strategies. Perhaps the easiest and most commonly used strategy that is often not even recognized as joining behavior is that of nonverbal communication (Brems, 1999). A friendly tone of voice that reflects warmness, acceptance, and respect, as well as a smiling face, may go a long way to make a family feel welcome and comfortable in this new situation. Greeting all of them through shaking hands acknowledges every individual as important, and can put people at ease.

Verbal communication is equally important. First of all, the therapist must make every attempt to match a family's vocabulary. Thus, with a very sophisticated family that is psychologically minded, some jargon might be appropriate, whereas with a less sophisticated or less educated family, the use of jargon would alienate and distance. As a rule of thumb, jargon should be avoided, especially for the children's sake. Verbal communication must be adapted so that it is appropriate for the adults as well as the children in the family. This may mean communicating the same message in two different ways. The clinician always avoids talking above children's heads without later turning back to help them understand what was being said.

Another verbal means of building rapport or joining family members is through matching predicates in verbal communication (Grinder and Bandler, 1975). Different people have different sensory modalities that are primary and most commonly relied upon. Thus, information conveyed through the use of predicates of that modality, are more salient to that person and are therefore more likely to be picked up on. For instance, using an "I see" with a visual person may be perceived as much more understanding than an "I hear." On the other hand, "I hear what you are saying" with an auditory individual may communicate powerfully that you understand that person. Kinesthetic people will focus on feeling statements and thus will perceive those as most understanding. A person's orientation is easily recognized by listening to her or his choice of language. Matching can then take place individually with each family member.

Attunement and cross-modal attunement have gained significant importance in the developmental literature (Stern, 1985) and are excellent rapport building strategies. Attunement involves the verbal and nonverbal reflection that the clinician has understood what a person is expressing on a content and process level. A typical example of attunement may be a statement such as "I am hearing you say that you are very unhappy in this situation and that you feel like no one understands quite what you are going through." This statement reflects the person's affect without parroting what she or he said directly. Cross-modal attunement accomplishes the same thing, except that rather than choosing the same medium of communication, the therapist switches to an alternative one. For example, a client who may be rapidly tapping a foot might be responded to verbally with a statement such as "You are feeling quite anxious right now." Similarly, a child who has just started crying, thus revealing sadness, may be responded to with a calming, low voice that matches the affect that is being expressed (as opposed to responding with a cheerful, everything-will-soon-be-better voice). Such attunement is extremely successful in communicating a thorough understanding of people's affective states and often leads to greater levels of trust and self-disclosure.

Finally, there are several joining strategies borrowed from family therapists. Specifically, several behaviors, grouped under the label *confirmation* (Minuchin, Simon, and Lee, 1996; Nichols, Schwartz, and Minuchin, 1994), may be used to make family members feel understood and cared for. For instance, recognizing holons or individuals and rewarding them; responding with sensitivity to what is being said or done; sympathetic responding with statements such as "I understand"; and describing transactions as they occur and are observed by the clinician. Strategies labeled *tracking* (Minuchin, Simon, and Lee, 1996; Nichols, Schwartz, and Minuchin, 1994) ask clarifying questions that help the family to gain some understanding and insight and thus help them feel understood and accepted more deeply. Many more rapport building strategies exist, and entire books have been written on the subject. The novice therapist is referred to those sources for more information.

While rapport is being established, the interview will generally begin with some introductory statements about what the family can expect of their 4 hours with the clinician. Confidentiality and ethical issues (as discussed in Chapter Two) will be presented to the family at this time, in a manner that is sensitive to every member's cognitive capacity. This implies that the same concept may need to be explained in various ways: once for the cognitive level of the parents and once for each of the cognitive capacities of the children. Although this is more cumbersome than speaking to only one holon of the family, it also models for the family appropriate behavior in groups that include both adults and children. It also reaffirms that for the clinician, the inclusion of the adults and children in the therapy is equally important.

Once the stage has been set, it is time to elicit information about the reasons for the family's decision to seek treatment, or referral if this was not a self-motivated process. It is recommended that every family member is permitted, and in fact encouraged, to offer her or his unique perspective on the presenting problems. Ensuring that everybody is heard and respected lays important groundwork for the therapy that might follow. It is during the exploration of the different perspectives on the presenting problem that the clinician has the best opportunity to observe family interaction. In this regard, four major components of family functioning are assessed: family structure, competence, process, and relating.

Family Structure

Family structure deals with family functioning as far as boundaries and alliances are concerned. As such, it addresses the family's stability, cohesiveness, divisiveness, closeness, and distance. All families have to have several sets of boundaries that are acknowledged and respected by all family members. Not always are these boundaries considered healthy or productive from a family therapist's point of view, but they always do exist. Healthy boundaries delineate the holons of a family. For instance, children should not be part of the spousal holon; there should be a clear dividing line which the children in the family are not allowed to traverse. Thus, if there is a conflict in the spousal holon, the boundary would be such that the children are not drawn into this conflict. As becomes evident, in problem families, this healthy boundary often does not exist. Frequently, it is replaced by an unhealthy boundary. For instance, one of the spouses might actually engage in an alliance with a child against the other spouse, thus rearranging the boundaries within the family. Obviously, boundaries and alliances then often go hand in hand in families and can be used to estimate the level of psychological health of the system (Minuchin, Simon, and Lee, 1996; Nichols, Schwartz, and Minuchin, 1994). Boundaries have a direct impact on who is close to whom and on how family members interact. Alliances function in much the same manner.

Family structure and boundary issues also deal with how engaged various members of the family are with others. In some systems there may be overengagement, or enmeshment, between two members, whereas another member is often quite disengaged from the family. An often cited example of the disengaged member is the parent who has withdrawn from the family and has redirected her or his energies to work activities instead. The example of the enmeshed parent is the one who has trouble letting go of a child even once that child is an adult and is attempting to leave home. Finally, family structure also has to do with a family's affective status. Their character or emotional state within their system is often quite obvious. Specifically, just as individuals, families can be angry, anxious, depressed, reluctant, and so forth. It is interesting to note what a family's overall affective state is and then to compare that affect to the affect of the separate holons, particularly to the identified child client. Certainly, much more can be said about family structures and their effects on the mental health of the children in that family (and of the adults, for that matter). The interested reader is referred to the vast family therapy literature for a more in-depth discussion of this topic.

A simple, and by no means conclusive, way of assessing family boundaries and alliances is to pay attention to who is seated where. Do the parents sit together? Is there a child who squeezes between the parents even after they have chosen adjacent chairs? Is a child crawling onto a parent's lap? Are there family members who are turning their backs to the rest of the family? Another simple clue is to pay attention to who speaks and when. Do certain family members speak more than others? Are some family members always interrupted? Is there one spokesperson for the family? All of these patterns are interesting to note and can render some hypotheses about this aspect of family functioning.

Family Competence

Family competence refers to the capacity of a family to carry out the tasks assigned to families. Specifically, a well-functioning family's primary task is that of raising children and providing an environment that fosters growth and mental health for all members. The specific duties or tasks involved in this mission of the family depends on the developmental stage of the family. As family therapists point out, a family begins through the establishment of a spousal holon that decides to have children. When the first child is born, the spousal holon has to reorganize around the new tasks involved in the new role of being parents. Parenting patterns will be set, and the spouses need to rearrange their relationship to include the child or children, without jeopardizing their couple relationship. As children begin school, the family is once again faced with a new developmental task. Children come into contact with the outside world more frequently now, which leads to a reorganization of control and power within the family. Issues of autonomy and self-sufficiency become important as the child or children near adolescence. Finally, as children leave the parental home, whole new sets of relating have to be worked out [see Minuchin, Simon, and Lee (1996) and Nichols, Schwartz, and Minuchin (1994) for more detail].

Family competence has to do with how effectively a family adapts to the new demands of passing to a new developmental stage and to the task of providing a mentally healthy environment for the children. However, it also has to do with smaller issues, such as the family's ability to problem-solve together, to work out compromises, and to weather crises. Their capacity for cooperation is crucial to their everyday functioning, but also has implications for the psychotherapy they are about to embark upon. The more cooperative the family, and the more competent, the more likely that they will be supportive of a child's treatment. Further, their psychological mindedness and the degree of psychological health of the unit and individual members will strongly impact the prognosis for each individual member, the system, and most of all the identified client.

Family Process

Family process refers to characteristic sequences of interaction among members and between the family and its environment. It has to do with the family's capacity for communication and with the potential role the presenting problem plays in the family system. For instance, a family process issue that may affect the presenting problem is that of triangulation. In triangulated families, conflicts between spouses are diverted through the problem behavior of a child. Thus, it may be noticed that as a mother and a father begin to fight more intensely, a child may suddenly begin to act out or complain of various physical symptoms. This family has learned how to avoid facing conflict between the parents by redirecting their attention to a child's symptoms.

Communication patterns are particularly important to observe. Who speaks to whom, who speaks first when the family is asked questions, who interrupts whom, and who listens are all important features of family interaction of which the clinician will need to become aware during the family interview. These dynamics will identify dominant versus submissive individuals in the family and will provide insights into who is in charge of this family. The identification of family patterns or characteristic sequences of interchanges will also give the clinician a better understanding of how conflict and crises develop in this family and how this might affect the functioning of the identified client.

Family Relating

Family relating, the final aspect of family functioning, reaches outside the family system and therefore depends more on verbal interchange than on mere observation of the system in action in the treatment room. Family interaction has to do with how the family relates to the outside world. The clinician will assess whether the family is isolated, distant, or involved with their environment. An isolated family will be likely to spend all their free time only with immediate family members or each alone individually, and interaction with, as well as observation of, the community will be nonexistent. A distant family will behave very similarly in that there is minimal interaction with the outside world, but here the members will actively observe what happens in their community and will stay abreast of environmental developments. An involved family seeks out interaction with the community, is involved in various social activities, and therefore is most likely to have a good support network that can be used therapeutically or for support during crises.

Family relating is often directly tied to family values, which are often strongly influenced by the cultural or social network with which a family identifies. For instance, families who are very involved in a particular religious group are very likely to carry that religion's values into their everyday family life. Active membership in an ethnic group will result in an acceptance of that group's values and traditions. Awareness of these factors assists the clinician in several ways. First, it will provide additional insight into the family's functioning and hence their presenting problem. Second, it will have implications for the compatibility between family and therapist. A clinician should never pretend to understand a family's social, cultural, or religious beliefs. If the therapist is not thoroughly familiar with a family's choice of values and beliefs, she or he needs to ask the family to explain. Although this may seem awkward to the novice, it is actually a wonderful joining strategy if done respectfully and with genuine interest.

In conclusion, the family interview provides a wealth of information that will enhance the clinician's understanding of the identified client, her or his family, and the role of the presenting problem within that system. The interview will have begun to provide the therapist with hypotheses about the contributing, precipitating, and reinforcing factors within the family system that affect the behavior of the child whom the family identifies as having a problem. The importance and implications of these contributing, precipitating, and reinforcing factors will be addressed in depth when conceptualization and treatment planning are discussed in Chapter Seven.

The Intake Interview with the Parents

In addition to the parental interview's usefulness for collecting more specifics about the presenting problem from the unique perspective of the parents, the major goal of this session is fourfold. First, the interview serves to gather background information about the identified client and her or his family. Second, it is used to gain a thorough understanding of the parents' parenting styles and discipline strategies. Third, it serves to obtain a thorough history of the parents' own families of origin. Fourth, is serves to glean a thorough understanding of the parents' spousal relationship. The fourth purpose is relevant primarily in families in which there are indeed two parents (who of course by no means have to be married, heterosexual, or living together for this interview to be useful!). In single-parent households, this information will still be gathered, but the purpose of exploring the spousal relationship will then primarily be one of looking at this aspect of the family from a historical perspective. The four purposes are introduced to the parents at the beginning of the interview by providing them with an overview of the topic areas that will be covered. Then these areas are addressed separately. Generally, it is easiest for parents to begin talking about the child and then their parenting styles, as this material is the least personal and least intrusive of the four. The parenting discussion is followed logically by an exploration of parents' backgrounds, as this is where parents have learned most of the parenting strategies they employ. Finally, it is hoped that the clinician and parents hopefully will have developed a sufficiently trusting relationship for the parents to feel comfortable discussing their relationship.

Throughout this interview, the clinician needs to continue to think about rapport building and joining behaviors. It is not helpful to this interview for the therapist to be blaming. Instead, the parents need to be understood from their own unique perspectives. They are not cold people who consciously want to hurt their child. Instead, they are often people who are in pain and suffer with and for their child. After all, they will no doubt see themselves in their child and will see their child as an extension of themselves that validates their ability as parents. It can be an incredible narcissistic injury to parents to see their child embroiled in emotional or psychological difficulties (Spiegel, 1996). Additionally, many parents have read articles in magazines that have placed the burden of responsibility for children's problems entirely on the shoulders of the parents. Even mental health professionals have played a role in thus adding much guilt to the pain that is often already experienced by the parents through coining phrases such as *schizophrenogenic mothers, disengaged fathers, cold or absent parents,* and many more (Coppolillo, 1987). The more the clinician can be attuned to the pain, guilt, and needs of the parents, the better they will feel understood, and the more they will cooperate with the therapist and their child's treatment.

Background Information about the Identified Client

The need for this information has been explained in detail above. Much of this information will be gleaned from the intake form. Thus, during this section of the parental interview, it might be useful for the clinician to refer to this form to complete any gaps that may have been left by the parents. This interview section is focused primarily on the identified child and her or his developmental milestones, developmental task resolution, relationships with peers, medical history, accidents, and similar issues. It is an information-gathering section and, as such, is largely directed by the clinician. It is best to warn parents that this section of the interview will be very structured, as there are a certain amount and type of information that need to be gleaned. If the intake form was completed thoroughly and was reviewed by the clinician beforehand, this section of the interview can be quite brief.

Parenting Styles and Discipline Strategies

Discipline strategies are an important topic, as most parents have never taken classes in this area and are merely operating on belief systems that stem from their own childhoods. In this regard, it is important to explore not only the types of strategies the parents use, but also how consistently they are applied, who enforces or implements them, and whether both parents agree about the appropriateness of certain strategies. Disagreements between parents about what constitutes adequate disciplinary strategies are not at all uncommon.

When this is the case, it is equally likely that the child is aware of the conflict and uses it to her or his advantage (though generally neither consciously nor maliciously so). Often, it is necessary to ask very specific questions of the parents to gain an understanding of how they discipline their child or children. Also, it is generally worthwhile to investigate whether the same strategies are employed with all children, by both parents, in all situations, and at all times. Some specific questions that may be asked include, but certainly are not limited to, the ones provided in Table 5.4.

These questions demonstrate how specific the clinician needs to be to do an adequate assessment of parents' disciplinary strategies. Whenever the clinician asks about whether the parents know of a certain strategy, she or he should also ascertain that the parents know the correct definition and application of that technique if they answer affirmatively. Knowing about a strategy and using it correctly are often two completely different things. If parents are unfamiliar with a strategy, define it briefly. It could be that they are using it without being aware of its label. Throughout this line of questioning, the therapist needs to be sure to check with both parents. Thus, information about how consistent both parents are will be gained almost automatically. It is often very illuminating to ask parents about their favorite and best parenting strategy, as well as about what they perceive to have been their worst intervention as a parent. Also, a question about what strategies seem to work and not work with the children in this household can be helpful.

TABLE 5.4   Questions about Parental Discipline Strategies

- How do you reward good behaviors of your children?
- How do you discuss disagreements about rules with your coparent?
- Do you think that all strategies work equally well with all of your children regardless of their ages? Explain.
- Can you explain what active listening is and how you use it?
- When do you use active listening with your children?
- How do you encourage your child to solve her or his own problems?
- Would you explain what time out is and when best to use it?
- When and where do you use time-out with your children?
- Would you explain what extinction is and how you use it?
- When and where do you use extinction with your children?
- What are logical and natural consequences?
- How and when do you use logical and natural consequences?
- Do you take into consideration what motivated a child's behavior?
- Do you ever spank your child?
- Where on the child's body do you hit?
- How often do you hit your child?
- Do you ignore or shame your child to punish her or him?
- Do you want your child to feel guilty after a misbehavior?
- Do you react to your child without asking reasons for behavior?
- Do you tell your child you do not love her or him when she or he misbehaves?
- Do you threaten your child? How?
- Do you ground your child for misbehavior?
- Do you think that all strategies work equally well in all situations? Explain.

Finally, it is important to talk with parents about their philosophy of parenting (Brooks, 1999), again exploring the issue for both parents. Parenting styles can take at least three forms: authoritarian, permissive, and authoritative (Baumrind, 1973). Authoritarian parents tend to be extremely restrictive, expecting their children to follow rules without questioning. They are generally strict disciplinarians who have little tolerance for negotiating a compromise or for letting the child work toward her or his own solutions to problems. These parents have strict rules and expect the child to abide by them. Violation is punished without asking about purpose or reason for the transgression.

Permissive parents have very loose rules, and the child is often not clear about what is expected. Whatever rules there are, they are often not consistently enforced, and limits are notoriously unclear. This leaves little room for structure and often has the child guessing about appropriateness of behavior and acceptability of affect. As children are not born with an innate sense of rules, this permissive style can be quite unsettling and anxiety-provoking for the child. Permissive parents are often found not in a parental, but rather a peer relationship with the child. Thus, as children need adults in their environment to figure out what is right and wrong in their society and neighborhood, they are often left guessing and unsure of themselves.

Authoritative parents have developed a compromise between having no rules, like permissive parents, and having too many rigid rules, like authoritarian parents. They generally have several sensible rules that are explained to the child and are often agreed upon and renegotiated as the child develops and matures. Although these parents are still in charge of the family, they are tolerant of input from their children and are more likely to run a fairly democratic household in which every member is perceived as having input about what is appropriate and acceptable and what is not. Authoritative parents are not personally threatened by a child's misbehavior or stubbornness, but rather see it in perspective and can deal with it constructively. Of the three parenting styles, the authoritative is the most psychologically sound approach to parenting. The clinician needs to assess which style is favored by the parents and whether both parents have the same style. Disagreements in styles are a major problem that often results in conflict and arguments for parents.

One additional aspect of parenting is the setting and clarification of rules in a household. As was mentioned above, a well-functioning family has to have rules that are explicitly stated and that have certain predictable consequences associated with their violation. These explicit rules, as well as the consequences of violation or transgression, need to be investigated. Further, most families also have several implicit rules. Although these are more difficult to assess directly, they are still worth pursuing. The origin of all rules needs to be explored, as well as the parents' willingness to renegotiate them according to the developmental needs of their children. For instance, rules about bedtime are very appropriate and common in most families. However, they need to be renegotiated as children grow, and they need to be different for the different children in the same family depending on ages. It is not uncommon for a family to have instituted a 9 P.M. bedtime only to continue to enforce it for all children, despite the fact that the eldest child has reached adolescence.

Finally, if the child spends considerable time with other adults who have parental or disciplinary roles vis-à-vis the child, the clinician needs to inquire about these individuals' parenting or discipline strategies and styles as well. Just as conflict between two parents affects the child, so does conflict between parents and other adult caretakers who are important in the child's life.

Family of Origin Information

A very convenient way to lead into the gathering of family history is the shifting to the exploration of the parenting that the parents received as children within their own families of origin. Specific questions as outlined in the previous section can be asked, now not in terms of the parents endorsing and using these strategies and philosophies, but in terms of having been the recipients thereof. Most parents have some awareness that their own parenting has been affected by the parenting they received from their own parents. Many are quick to point out that they are doing certain things to be different from their parents, whereas they do others because they are modeling after their parents. Nevertheless, much of their interaction with their children remains automatic and unexplored. Careful questioning by the clinician can help parents to recognize that much of what they do is a direct reaction to what they experienced as children. This recognition often leads to the desire to learn more and to change. Thus, this aspect of the interview not only is relevant for assessment purposes, but often provides the basis for therapeutic intervention.

The specifics about and importance of other pieces of information about family history have been described previously. The mechanics are such that it is best to include both parents and gather parallel information from both partners at the same time. There are several advantages to this approach. First, using this approach, the clinician will not inquire about a certain set of circumstances regarding one parent and then forget to explore the same issue with the other parent. Second, the clinician will need to introduce the specific topic only once; thus, time is saved. Third, and most important, through this procedure, the parents gain a new awareness of the similarities and differences in their own family histories and backgrounds. It is not uncommon for parents to have significant therapeutically valuable insights about their bases for conflict and approaches to their children during this interview. They often recognize for the first time how their own background has shaped their behavior and how the partner has a similar experience of being steered by her or his experiences within the family of origin. Again, the construction of a genogram may facilitate the process of collecting family histories.

Of particular importance during this aspect of the parental interview is the assessment of abuse histories in both parents' family backgrounds. Specific questions about sexual, physical, and emotional abuse need to be asked. Neglect, both physical and emotional, needs to be ruled out or ascertained. Similarly, substance abuse histories, as well as current substance use (or abuse) patterns, are important to assess. These topics are often very sensitive, especially as both parents or partners are present. However, their open exploration conveys the message to both parents that this type of information needs to be discussed openly and honestly and should not be kept secret. It is hoped that modeling of this communication style can then generalize to the extent that both parents will feel more comfortable investigating the topic of abuse with their children.

Finally, this section of the interview provides a unique opportunity for the clinician to assess how empathically attuned the two parenting partners are to one another, how respectful they are of one another, and how much they have communicated with each other about themselves. The setting allows the therapist to evaluate the potential of open communication between the two parents and the potential for negotiation of compromise.

Spousal Relationship

Once the parents' family backgrounds have been explored, it is necessary to investigate their intimate relationship. This can often be accomplished in the most nonthreatening way by beginning this section of the interview with an investigation of how the couple met, what they liked about one another, and how long they dated before getting married or beginning to live together. Exploring the relationship in a time sequence manner keeps this discussion focused and less intrusive. Parents feel less need to defend themselves and their relationship if the initial focus is not on what is wrong between them, but rather on what is positive and healthy. If only one parent is in the family at this time, this information will be gathered from a historical perspective. Then the clinician needs to investigate whether there is any contact between the two partners, for instance around visitations of children. The nature of these contacts needs to be explored to assess its impact upon the child. Additionally, the presence of new significant other adults in the respective parents' lives needs to be inquired, and the prominence of that person's presence in the child's life needs to be estimated.

This approach allows the clinician to explore changes in the intimate relationship as a function of the birth of the children that make up this family. Thus, it provides important information about the emotional climate in which the identified client grew up.

Once all of this information has been collected from the parents, the clinician has a wealth of data that can facilitate the understanding of the child. For instance, strict parental discipline may contribute to a child's stubbornness; a parental history of physical abuse may put harsh punishment of the child in a historical context; frequent fights between parents may make somatic concerns without physical basis more understandable in the child.

A final and secondary purpose of the parental interview is to assess how likely the parents will be to support the therapy of their child. There are several parental traits that have been identified as corollary to the facilitation of a child's therapy. These include, but are not limited to, parents' willingness to supply information, to report on the child's behavior between sessions, to encourage the child to trust the therapist, to recognize their role in the child's problem, to trust the therapeutic process even though there is no advice for them, to tolerate confidentiality between child and therapist, and to bring their child to treatment on a regular basis (Adams, 1982). The more of these factors that can be answered positively for the identified client's parents, the more likely that the therapy of the child will actually become reality. Parents who have much ambivalence about these factors often end up undermining the child's treatment by missing sessions, coming late, and dropping out prematurely.

The Intake Interview with the Siblings

The major goal of the interview with the siblings of the identified patient is to get a fresh perspective on the presenting problem from individuals who may be less directly involved or less emotionally invested. Siblings can be interviewed as a group or individually, depending on the clinician's preference and the children's ages. For instance, if there are very young and very old children, it might be more productive to see these two sets of children separately. Occasionally, the clinician might choose to begin the interview with all children present and then move to separate interviews with various subgroupings of this family holon.

Siblings are an important holon to consider during the assessment or intake phase, as they represent the identified client's first peer group. If all siblings are seen together, patterns of negotiation, communication, cooperation, and competition among the siblings can be observed directly during this session. If siblings are seen separately, this information can only be inferred. Roles of various siblings may emerge during this interaction. For instance, it may be observed that an older child has assumed a parental role with the younger children in the family; one child may have assumed the role of clown who distracts when problems emerge; another child may be in charge of decision making. These roles, and their relationship to the presenting problem can provide important information about the dynamics of the identified child's difficulties.

The sibling interview is also helpful in assessing why a specific child member of this family was presented as the identified client. Specifically, the clinician now has the opportunity to observe all the children in the family without the often limiting presence of the parents. The behavior that unfolds will help the clinician to understand whether other children in this family evidence emotional or behavioral difficulties, whether one child is being scapegoated, and whether the children who were not identified as having problems indeed function appropriately. Further, the siblings will also be able to give further information about the family's problems by providing their opinions about the causes and implication of the identified client's behavior or about the effect for the family as a whole.

Strategies that can be used in this interview to solicit information are very similar to those used with the identified client. Again, they are selected on the basis of clinician's preference and client's age. Strategies include, but are not limited to, free play, open-ended questions, projective questions, drawings, and storytelling. All of these strategies will be discussed in detail below. If they are used in the sibling interview, all children who are present need to be given the opportunity to answer or engage in each activity.

The Intake Interview with the Identified Client

The major goals of the interview with the identified child client are the establishment of a meaningful relationship and the gathering of information. For these purposes to be fulfilled, the child must feel trusting, supported, and free to feel emotions while she or he is working with the therapist. The importance of the establishment of such therapeutic rapport cannot be overemphasized in this section of the intake process, as it is during this interview that the stage is set for the therapeutic relationship between the child and therapist if a recommendation for individual treatment of the child is made (Lovinger, 1998). There are many ingredients that are necessary for a therapeutic interaction, and it is impossible to give a firm recipe that will work with all children. In fact, selecting the right approach with a child is a bit like trial-and-error learning. The therapist will need to meet the child with a number of available strategies, but how and when to use them will be determined through the process that unfolds as the clinician and the child interact. Some of the basic ingredients are discussed here. Some of these are therapist characteristics; others are strategies that can be used by the therapist. All can be acquired by the committed therapist, though some will come more naturally than others.

Characteristics and Strategies to Build Rapport and Gather Information

One of the most important characteristics of the therapist that is often instrumental in creating an atmosphere that is conducive to rapport building and information gathering with a child is that of *flexibility.* It is best not to follow a fixed or rigid interview schedule (Brems, 1999), but rather to rely on creativity and spontaneity to guide the interview or interaction with the child.

It is important to be *nondirective,* that is, to follow the child's lead, all along thinking about the symbolism and dynamic implications of the child's choices (verbalization of these issues, however, is reserved for later stages of treatment). However, nondirectiveness is not equal to passivity. The therapist might well choose to comment, reflect, and mirror a child's feelings. Further, the expression of emotionality when reflecting and mirroring for the child can be quite appropriate.

Another important therapist trait is that of *permissiveness.* However, this permissiveness is not to be misunderstood as the absence of rules and structure, but rather has to do with creating an atmosphere in which the child is encouraged to express all feelings openly, even negative ones, and in which the child can do whatever she or he chooses to do (within limits of safety). It implies that the therapist will not try to hurry things along, but rather will allow the process to unfold at the child's speed and ability.

Being *accepting* is another important ingredient for rapport building. This implies that the therapist pays attention to a child's feelings, is empathic, mirrors needs and feelings, and fosters understanding and trust. All of this requires that the clinician be nonjudgmental about the child's feelings, needs, and self-expressions. The clinician needs to be capable of reflecting feelings, as appropriate, through verbal or nonverbal modes of communication.

Further, the use of *simple language* is crucial to communicating with children. In fact, therapists have to learn to adapt their language. Being highly educated individuals, clinicians generally are used to speaking at a high level of sophistication when communicating verbally. Some relearning is in order when the client is a child. Additionally, the clinician needs to be capable of understanding metaphors and idioms. Much communication with children takes place through the use of *symbolism.* In using this mode of communication, it is preferable to use the child's metaphors and idioms.

Another important component of the therapist-child relationship is *respectfulness* of the child and her or his choices. This implies that the therapist must at times be satisfied to follow the child's lead when it comes to choosing activities, must follow the child's exploration of topics, must follow the child's approach to self-expression, and must understand the importance and impact of various topics from the child's perspective. Respectfulness also implies not belittling the child's feelings and not undoing a child's work.

Another good practice is the *avoidance* of questions that begin with "why." All too commonly, *"why" questions* indicate to children that they did something wrong or that their choices are being challenged. Simple rephrasing will lower a child's resistance and will make a meaningful response more likely. For instance, rather than asking a child who is using Play-Doh to build a volcano that then erupts with a sudden burst of energy, "Why did the volcano erupt so suddenly?" the clinician might ask, "What was happening when the volcano erupted?" Open-ended questions are preferable to questions that allow for a simple "yes" or "no" in response.

The clinician can also resort to the use of various projective strategies to elicit additional material from the child. For instance, the use of *projective questions* can be very productive in producing some unconscious material that can be used to corroborate or refute certain hypotheses that are forming in the mind of the therapist as she or he is working with a particular child. Common projective questions include the three wishes, people to take to a desert island, the animal the child would choose to be, the age the child would choose to be, and naming of a favorite color or number. In the *three wishes,* the clinician asks the child what she or he would wish for if the child had three chances to wish for what ever she or he wants. Children's answers are often quite revealing. For instance, the following response was given by a 7-year-old girl who was brought for an intake because of severe sexual abuse by her father during visitations with him in prison: "I wish that my daddy would have a smaller lap." When the girl was asked further questions about this wish, she indicated that if he had a smaller lap, as she had wished for, she could not sit in it during visitations. As it was revealed that her father had been forcing intercourse on this little girl during these visits, her wish was very telling.

The *desert island* question asks the child to indicate whom she or he would want to have with her or him, should the child become stranded on a desert island. Once the child invites one person, the clinician may give two more choices. Again, the responses will indicate important dynamics. For instance, it is interesting to note whether the child chooses a parent to be with her or him, whether the choice involves a sibling, whether the choices all directly exclude any family members, and so forth.

Asking the child what *animal* she or he would like to be can provide useful information. For instance, the children in a family of five (three children, two adults) made the following choices, revealing several of their family dynamics and their impact on the children. The youngest child, the only girl, wished to be a bear because bears were soft and cuddly and always had enough food to eat. Her older brother, the middle child, wished to be a horse because horses were able to run fast and could get away from dangerous situations. The oldest child in the family wished to be a turtle because turtles had a shell that could protect them from harm. These children were being raised in a family with chronic marital strife between the two biological parents. The amount of nurturance was minimal ("not enough food"), and physical abuse of the oldest child was not uncommon ("shell that protects from harm"). The middle child had found that he could have many of his needs met by leaving the family and searching for important adults among his teachers ("run fast and get away").

The question about what *age* a child would be if she or he had the choice can be similarly revealing. For instance, one 8-year-old boy indicated that he would like to be 80 years old and, when asked further, revealed that this age was appealing to him because then his life would be behind him, rather than ahead of him. This desire was understandable in the context of his family, in which constant arguing and conflict contributed to his significant level of depression and occasional suicidal ideation. Similarly, *favorite numbers and colors* can provide information about mood and the number or nature of important individuals in a child's life. Favorite jokes, daydreams, fantasies, dreams, and similar material may also be solicited to gain more information about the child.

Although the purely diagnostic use of projective drawings must be reserved for the appropriately trained and educated psychologist, any counselor or therapist can use *drawings* to corroborate hypotheses. Useful drawings are those of the child's family and those of a person. Both the execution of the task and the finished product can provide the clinician with useful information. Interpretation of drawings, however, is complex and must be done carefully. Excellent books are available on this subject (e.g., Goodenough, 1926; Kestenbaum and Williams, 1992; Malchiodi, 1998).

Another useful tool to extract more information from the interview without direct questioning is the *Talking, Feeling, Doing Game,* distributed by Creative Therapeutics (Gardner, 1973). This game involves the child in the answering of questions that either address the cognitive, affective, or behavioral realm. Many of the questions are similar to projective questions and challenge the child to develop her or his own solutions and responses to difficult situations. The questions range from difficult to relatively nonthreatening, and the clinician may stack the deck before engaging the child in this task. For instance, children may be asked to respond to questions ranging from asking the child about secret wishes about her or his mother to asking the child to hop around the room on one foot.

Storytelling (Gardner, 1986, 1993) is another way of getting children to share information without direct inquiry. The formal technique as developed by Gardner (1986, 1995) will be described in detail later; simple modifications of the strategy can be used even during the intake session. Specifically, the clinician can encourage the child who is unable to play or talk freely to make up a story. These stories can be very meaningful to the assessment process. For instance, a 7-year-old girl told the story of a treasure that was well hidden beneath the sand in her backyard. Only one person knew where the treasure was, and she refused to dig it up to buy food for the starving children in the city. This child had been placed in a foster home after her parents were charged with severe physical neglect of their five malnourished children.

Finally, and perhaps most important, the child's *free play* is used to gain an understanding of her or his presenting problem. The interpretive use of play will be discussed in detail in the chapter about play therapy. Here it must suffice to say that the child's play behavior must be viewed symbolically and metaphorically and that it generally has representative value that gives the clinician new insights into the child's life (Gitlin-Weiner, Sandgrund, and Schaefer, 2000). For instance, an 8-year-old boy very much enjoyed playing hide-and-go-seek with the therapist. He delighted in being found but was threatened when the therapist was hidden too well for the child to find her. It appeared that this child who had been abandoned by his biological mother and was severely abused by his biological father and stepmother, was working on his abandonment fears through this advanced form of peek-a-boo that infants so delight in as they gain object constancy! Play can be viewed as an outline of a child's problem, much like the free association of an adult client.

Limit Setting

Despite the fact that the good child clinician will be permissive and nondirective as defined above, she or he also needs to set limits in the intake session and the therapy. There are three important reasons for setting limits. First, the clinician is responsible for the child's safety, as well as her or his own, in the therapy room. Therefore, there will be certain actions that are not permitted because of their threats to this physical safety. Further, limits anchor therapy to real life, in which the child is also unable to engage in certain behaviors because of their impact on others. Finally, limits serve to make the child aware of her or his responsibility within the therapeutic relationship. Children are not born with an innate sense of right or wrong, but rather need to learn these rules from the adults in their environment. The creation of an environment in which there are neither rules nor limits is artificial and not conducive to the generalization of change. This is not to imply that the intake interview or the therapy for the child will be restricted by rigid rules and regulations. Quite to the contrary, only those rules will be set that are directly necessary for the assurance of the physical safety and integrity of client, therapist, and room. Each clinician will need to decide what rules she or he wants to have and enforce. A few universal rules include no physical aggression (hitting, kicking, etc.) toward self or therapist, no willful destruction of playroom equipment, no removal or taking home of playroom equipment, and no leaving the therapy room.

Setting the stage for limit setting in the intake and therapy process involves providing the child with the information about the existence of the limit. Thus, a clinician might choose to accompany her or his introductory statement about the playroom with a statement of rules, such as "This is the playroom. In here you may do whatever you choose as long as what you do does not hurt you or me. You may play with anything in this room, and everything will stay here when you leave, so it will be here when you come back." Note that the statement of the limits was done in a very positive, rather than restrictive, manner.

If a child attempts to violate a limit that has been set, the therapist needs to address this violation consistently and immediately. However, the first step in this process generally involves a mere comment on the possible meaning of the behavior rather than restricting the behavior, with the expectation that the comment will gratify the child's underlying need and will thus terminate the inappropriate behavior. If the child does not respond to the comment about the behavior, the clinician needs to move to the next step. This involves a statement about the therapist's own feeling or thought in response to the child's violation of the rule. It is only if the child again fails to respond to the clinician's intervention that the clinician will verbalize (i.e., remind the child of) the limit. If the child continues the behavior, a consequence for the behavior must be verbalized. If this does not serve to change the child's actions, the consequence must be enforced as it was stated. Thus, the therapist should never state a consequence that she or he is not willing to enforce and justify in her or his own mind. An example of an instance where a therapist had to move through all stages of limit-setting is provided below:

> A 9-year-old boy who had arrived for his session very anxious and upset after having been teased in school about several bruises on his forehead, became very angry during his therapy session. As was his tendency, he expressed this anger outwardly; however, this time by attempting to attack the therapist by kicking and hitting in the direction from where she was watching. The therapist remained calm and did not speak until the boy began to hit her directly, at which time she said, "It appears to me that you want to fight with me."

Note that according to the first step in the limit-setting procedure, the therapist merely comments on what she perceives the meaning of the behavior to be. Also note that she avoids the labeling of the underlying affect, which was anger that covered abandonment fears. She avoided the labeling of the affect "anger," as she had experienced previously that the child was unable to tolerate the verbal expression of negative affects and that his behavior tended to escalate whenever this occurred.

> As the child continued to hit, the therapist immediately stated, "It makes me uncomfortable and it is not safe when you hit."

Note that the therapist did not wait long before moving to the next step in the limit-setting procedure. It is unnecessary for her to endure the hitting any longer than a few seconds. However, also note that she does not skip any stages in the limit-setting procedures, giving the child a fair chance to stop his behavior before she intervenes behaviorally.

> The child hesitated momentarily, then continued to hit and kick, so the therapist said, "You may want to yell at me to let me know that you want to fight with me, but you may not hit or kick me."

The therapist at this point restates the limit of the restriction of physical acting out in the therapy room. However, even while doing this, she does allow the child his affect and his desire to fight with her; in fact, she provides him with an alternative means of self-expression.

> Because there was no change in the child's behavior, the therapist followed up her previous statement with an immediate outlining of consequences: "If you continue to hit and kick me, we will need to end our session for today because, remember, I must make sure that we are safe as long as we are in this room."

Although this consequence appears quite severe, and perhaps rejecting, this child had a history of physical violence outside of the therapy room that led to the gratification of his needs by motivating his parents to pay him attention by physically holding him down. Therefore, to avoid repeating a pattern of reinforcing physical acting out through making physical contact with this child, the therapist chooses the termination of the session as the consequence for the child's behavior.

> The child hesitated, but this was the first time that therapist and child had been faced with this type of situation, and he was not sure whether she would enforce the limit. When he continued to hit (he did stop kicking), she turned and opened the door of the room. When he refused to leave, she took his shoulders and guided him out of the room to the waiting room, where his mother received him.

Fortunately, it is quite rare that a therapist must go to this length to convince a child client that limits in the therapy room are firm and that her or his behavior does have limits and consequences. More often than not, children will obey the limit once the consequence has been spelled out verbally. Not all consequences have to be as severe as the one in the example. However, they must be of sufficient strength that the gratification derived from the acting out behavior is counterbalanced by the noxiousness of the consequence once it is imposed.

Outline of the Interview

Equipped with strategies, characteristics, and the ability to set limits, the therapist is ready to begin the interview with the identified client. The first task of the interview will be to observe how the child separates from her or his parents. Given that the child interview follows a lengthy interaction between the family and the therapist, most children will separate easily from their parents to follow the therapist. It is notable, however, if the child clings or cries upon the request to leave the parents. It is important to note whether the child clings to both parents, to the mother, or to the father. Further, it may be interesting to observe the parents' reactions as the children leave. Some parents may show no concern; others may feel the need to warn children to behave, to do what they are told, and so on.

Once the therapist and child have entered the play therapy room, the true work begins. As was mentioned previously, there is no firm approach to this interview, unlike the interview with the parents. Instead, it is up to the clinician to allow the process between her or him and the child to unfold. The child may be briefly introduced to the room, but no other structure needs to exist for this interview. Therefore, it is of the utmost importance to observe how the child adjusts to the situation and what the child chooses to do. The succession of different play activities, the child's attention span, and her or his interests are all important components to note. If the child evidences difficulty with this unstructured situation, the therapist might choose to introduce some structure through questioning or through the use of the strategies outlined above. It is important to remember the primary purposes of this interview: information gathering and rapport building in preparation for individual therapy work with the child. Thus, anxiety should not be allowed to build to intolerable levels in the child during the assessment session.

The session may be used by the clinician to define therapy, preferably through play activity that is shared with the child. For instance, the therapist can set the stage, by communicating to the child that this is her or his time to choose what to do with, to assure the child that the clinician is there for her or him, to allow the child to lead while the therapist follows. More about the therapy or intake process may be explained verbally if the child asks, always attempting to address the child's anxieties that might underlie the questions.

Some clinicians may prefer to do a semistructured interview with the child, exploring the presenting problem, family dynamics, friendship patterns, and hobbies or interests, and this choice is also driven somewhat by the age of the child. However, most of this material can be gathered more spontaneously and less intrusively through interaction with the child in her or his initiated play activity. Generally, the child has some awareness of the reasons for the interview and will spontaneously volunteer information. This is a sign for the therapist that additional questioning is appropriate and tolerable for the child. However, if a child signals to the therapist discomfort with direct questioning (e.g., by withdrawing, turning away, occupying herself or himself with various other activities, ignoring the therapist, or refusing to answer questions), that line of approach should be abandoned. This can be done easily if the therapist can remind herself or himself that much of the specific information about behaviors and family dynamics can be gleaned more easily through the intake interview with the parents.

Once enough corroborating information has been gathered and the child appears to feel comfortable with the therapist, the interview can be closed. A fair warning about ending this aspect of the intake meeting should be given, so that the child may complete tasks or finish explorations that remain incomplete. It is important to note how the child anticipates the return and how the child actually does return to the parents. It is not uncommon for children to attempt to stretch out the interview with the clinician as long as possible. Very few children have ever had the experience of having an adult pay attention to and respect their behavior for an extended period of time. Thus, they often do not want to conclude this gratifying and unexpected experience. Other children become notably anxious about the return to their parents. Perhaps they have paint on their hands or clay on their clothing and they are worried about their parents' response to their perceived messiness. Perhaps they have recognized that they do not feel as comfortable in the adult company of their parents, as in the adult company of the therapist. Some children, on the other hand, are quite eager to meet their parents to tell them about their experiences in the playroom. Others may welcome the end of the session as the prolonged contact with an adult proved very anxiety-provoking to them. These patterns provide the clinician with additional material that can be used diagnostically and conceptually.

The identified client interview is often the most lengthy of all the interviews and the most important with regard to establishing rapport and setting the stage for the individual work with a child [for more information, see Greenspan and Greenspan (1991)]. The outline of the session, as well as the discussion of strategies, characteristics, and limits cannot guarantee successful completion of this interview, but it can enhance the new therapist's chances of having a positive first contact with an identified child client. The session with the identified client concludes the interview section of the intake contact with the family. Now that all interviews have been completed, the clinician or clinicians need to take a few minutes to review all the materials, to develop a preliminary conceptualization that is sufficient to develop recommendations, and to set preliminary goals that can be discussed and negotiated with the family. Then it is time to share this information with the family during the feedback and recommendation session.

The Feedback and Recommendations Section of the Intake Interview

Once an intake is complete, the therapist must take time to provide thorough and understandable feedback to the parents about the child and the family. Although such feedback includes providing diagnostic and treatment information, feedback must be free of jargon and labels and must be delivered respectfully and without condescension. It is best presented as a means of enhancing parents' understanding of their child and the situation that brought them to treatment (Greenspan and Greenspan, 1991). As such, it is best to talk about observations and summaries of situations, not conclusions and problems; to start with descriptions of behavior, not labels or diagnostic codes; and to point out patterns within a developmental and systems context, not to wax philosophical about abstract concepts such as interpretations about underlying dynamics.

In giving feedback to parents, it is a primary goal to come to an agreement with them about what is going on with the child and family and about what needs to be done to improve the situation or presenting concern (cf. Brems, 1994, 1996). The failure to communicate feedback in such a manner may be the reason why 50 percent of parents fail to follow through with the recommendations made by child clinicians (Greenspan and Greenspan, 1991). Agreement is reached most easily if the clinician has taken into consideration the parents' expressed resistance, their unique histories and needs, and their emotional and social circumstances. On the basis of such information, the therapist will be able to join with the parents, helping them to see that treatment of the child is a joint venture of the parents and the therapist to promote the child's psychological health, emotional growth, and developmental adjustment, not a threat to the parents or system.

Before discussing the specifics about the feedback session, there is an important clarification that must be attended to. Specifically, although it is important to structure an assessment period, and although this assessment period remains separate from the actual therapy, this distinction is somewhat arbitrary. Much happens during the intake interviews that has a profound therapeutic effect for the family and its various members. Similarly, even once therapy has begun, the clinician will continue to assess and gather new data with each contact with the child or her or his family members. This arbitrariness becomes most noticeable to the therapist during the feedback session with the family. Technically, this section of the interview is still part of the intake session. However, it may also be viewed as the beginning of the therapeutic relationship and process.

The prior establishment of positive rapport with all family members, particularly the child's parents, is crucial to the success of this section of the intake interview. The feedback session includes all family members and clinicians who have been involved with the intake session thus far and it contains four distinct phases. First, the clinician needs to share with the family what she or he has learned about them from the various interviews that have taken place thus far, and what conclusions were drawn. Second, treatment recommendations follow and are a direct outgrowth of what has been shared with the family about the clinician's understanding of the family system and the presenting problem. This is a very important and sensitive task, as it often shatters illusions and dreams that parents and children have built up about their families (Coppolillo, 1987). It may also represent the shattering of explanations that parents and children have produced to explain their interactions and behaviors. Thus, the family may react with guilt, anger, shame, or disappointment. It does happen occasionally that families react with relief upon hearing that their problem is not unsolvable and that, through hard work, they can help themselves change. When this happens, the clinician can feel comfortable in making positive prognostic predictions. Third, once the family has accepted a set of recommendations, they need to set treatment goals with the collaboration of the therapist. Fourth, the family receives preparation for therapy if they have agreed to return for treatment. If the family refuses all recommendations made by the clinician, obviously phases three and four become obsolete. The family will be encouraged to reconsider, and their file will be closed. How the therapist prepares for recommendations and goal setting will be discussed in the next chapter. Here the focus is merely on the mechanics and procedures that are involved.

Sharing the Conceptualization

It is the purpose of this interview to share the understanding the clinician has derived from the interview with the family. Many of the same rules that were discussed relative to the family interview apply with regard to language, to whom to speak, and so forth. However, all of these issues are slightly more complicated now that the therapist faces the task of putting in laypersons' terms complex psychological dynamics of individuals and families. Preparation for a brief statement before the therapist enters this final meeting with the family is of utmost importance so that the therapist will not appear scattered or arbitrary in her or his feedback. A sample of a simple feedback statement developed for the benefit of the adults and the children in the family is provided below. It is presented by one therapist, even though two therapists were involved in the assessment.

> We have spent the last three and a half hours getting to know one another, and you have provided us with a lot of information about each of you individually and about the family as a whole. We feel that we now have a pretty good understanding of what is happening with your family and all its members and would like to share our understanding with you to see if it rings true for you as well. Please stop us any time you have any questions or comments.

This introduction helps everybody to capture the purpose of this section of the interview. It is a standard introduction; that is, it is the same for all families and can be used for a variety of circumstances.

> You came here today because Nancy has been having a lot of stomach problems in the last 9 weeks and was diagnosed last month by Dr. Chad to have a preulcer condition.

It is recommended that before delving into an explanation, the clinicians repeat the presenting problem. The amount of elaboration with which this is done is up to each clinician and often depends on the complexity of the problem. In this example, the presenting problem was very straightforward, and not much time needed to be spent on its summary.

> We think that Nancy's stomachaches have something to do with how the whole family works together. You told us that mom and dad are fighting a lot, that dad is really working too hard, and that mom is upset because she has to do most of the work that has to do with chores around the house and with Nancy and Tom. That has made everyone in the family pretty nervous, and you told us that sometimes it's like walking on eggshells. Well, often when these kinds of things are going on in a family, one of the kids will get stomachaches or headaches because they are reacting to the stress in the family around them.

In this example, a simple systemic explanation was offered as to why the identified client is evidencing certain symptoms. The conceptualization is offered in simple terms so that even the children can understand what is being said, and it is phrased so that no one member in the family is blamed. The explanation is neither detailed nor sophisticated but reflects the essence of the conceptualization derived for this case by the two therapists.

If a family cannot relate to or agree with the conceptualization at all, the therapist will try to explain it in more detail or will try to investigate why they are resisting. She or he needs to ask the family whether they have an alternative explanation for their problems and then search for common threads between the therapist's and the family's explanation. It is never worthwhile to force the family to accept the therapist's explanation. Instead, it is hoped that the clinician and family can arrive at an understanding that is mutually acceptable. It might not be as thorough as the initial conceptualization offered by the therapist, but the family will have more ownership of it, and therefore it will be more meaningful to them.

Sharing the Recommendations

Once the feedback has been received—that is, heard, understood, and more or less accepted—by the family, the therapist's next task becomes the outlining of treatment recommendations. These recommendations are based upon the clinician's assessment or conceptualization of the presenting problem, the goals set for treatment, and an assessment of the family's level of cooperation. How the therapist arrives at conceptualizations and treatment goals will be discussed in detail in Chapter Seven. Therefore, reading that chapter is crucial to being able to do a skillful feedback session with a family. Generally, the therapist will have come to certain conclusions about what will be best for an identified client with regard to future treatment contacts. This understanding needs to be conveyed to the family. The context for this has been set through the feedback about how the clinician understands the family and its presenting problem.

Outlining treatment options for a family is preferable to providing only one solution, especially if the therapist expects some resistance to her or his recommendations. Thus, if it is the therapist's opinion that the underlying dynamic of the presenting problem of the identified child in actuality is one of marital conflict between the parents, the treatment of choice that is offered first to this family will be marital therapy for the parents. However, if the parents refuse, possibly because they are not yet capable of openly admitting to their conflicts with one another, a second option of family therapy may be offered to this family. This would still be an appropriate treatment of choice as the children in this family obviously have become entangled in the parental conflict, but the focus would be less directly on the parents, thus perhaps making them more willing to comply with treatment. If the family refuses again, a third alternative of parenting education may be offered. This is a viable alternative, as the conflict between the parents in the spousal relationship doubtlessly interferes with their parental relationship and results in unfortunate parenting choices. Finally, if this treatment modality is also refused, some individual intervention might be appropriate with the children in this family. This intervention would then focus primarily on helping the children adjust to and deal with the conflict evidenced in the spousal relationship of their parents.

It becomes obvious from this example that the therapist needs to have some flexibility yet needs to remain within the therapeutic boundaries and implications of the treatment strategies that are being offered. Before the therapist agrees to move to less preferred treatment strategies, it behooves her or him to explore the family's resistance and to attempt to overcome it. It is in this role that the feedback and recommendation session clearly leaves the boundaries of an assessment session and enters the boundaries of a therapeutic intervention.

Setting Goals

In every therapy with any client, three sets of goals will probably emerge: goals that the therapist and client agree upon, goals that the client has that are of lesser or no importance to the therapist, and goals that are important to the therapist but not shared by the client. It is the purpose of this section of the feedback and recommendation session to define all of these goals, although focusing primarily on the first category. Once everyone has articulated goals for the therapy, it is crucial that the family or the individuals who will be seen in treatment agree on some goals that can become the direct and overt focus of treatment. Parents' agreement is very important in this regard, as they are more likely to follow through with treatment if they agree with the hoped-for outcome. Specifics about goal setting and prioritization will be discussed in another chapter.

Preparation for Treatment

If the family agrees to return for therapy, preparation for therapy should be ascertained by reiterating the parameters of therapy. Although issues of confidentiality were already discussed when the parents rendered informed consent, it is good practice to reiterate the limits of confidentiality at this time. Care must be taken to inform parents about reporting laws, the duty to warn, and the duty to protect (Brems, 1996). The boundaries of treatment need to be explained thoroughly, as much of the success of the child's therapy will hinge on the parents' cooperation. As such, the clinician points out her or his rules about cancellations (e.g., no more than three in a given period of time), no-shows (e.g., no more than two), being on time, payment (i.e., how much, when it is expected), and commitment to therapy in general (i.e., not undermining the work of the therapist). The frequency and length of future sessions need to be decided, as well as an estimated overall length of treatment. It is often helpful to settle on a certain number of sessions, after which time the family will meet again as a whole to renegotiate and reevaluate treatment and their progress so far. The importance of consistency and timeliness in coming to scheduled appointments needs to be stressed and explained. Policies about fees, payment schedules, cancellations, and no-shows need to be reemphasized.

Also important is the acknowledgment that though the parent has the legal right to the child's records and to be updated on treatment progress, the clinician will generally not disclose specific contents of what the child talks about or does while in the therapy room. Finally, the therapist must reiterate that she or he will not be able to serve as the parents' therapist but will be available to the parent in other capacities (as outlined below; see also Kottman, 1995). To maximize the likelihood of consistent and conscientious follow-through, the clinician may highlight the potential effects on the child in case the parents chose to undermine treatment. Thus, when the family leaves, they will have no unanswered questions about procedures, policies, ethics, and legal issues that could be used to sabotage their return to treatment.

Summary and Concluding Thoughts

The intake interview is a lengthy process that serves several purposes. First, it is used to glean as much information about the identified client and her or his family as possible. Second, it serves to build rapport and to interest the family in treatment. Third, it sets the stage for therapy by informing and educating the family about their presenting concern from a professional perspective; by providing the family with a thorough set of recommendations for treatment procedures and goals; and by thoroughly preparing them for the therapeutic process that is yet to come. A well-executed and prepared intake interview will provide the family with a feeling of trust and safety that makes them more likely to return for therapy. It will have answered their questions and alleviated their anxieties about the treatment process. Nevertheless, the ultimate decision about whether to return for therapy will rest solely with the family, and needs to be accepted and respected by the clinician.

Once therapy with the child has begun, it is important to keep in close touch with the parents to keep them interested in treatment. This is best accomplished through regular session updates of the therapist with the parents. The frequency of updates will vary depending on the type of case. More complex cases might require that updates occur every two weeks; for many cases, monthly updates suffice. The session updates have a twofold focus. First, they serve as a means for the therapist to assess whether the child is making changes at home and at school by soliciting this information from the parents. Second, session updates serve as a means for the therapist to keep the parents interested in the child's treatment by filling them in on noted progress and explaining the therapeutic process that is taking place. What is not done is discussion of specific content or play activity (Brems, 1994). For some parents, session updates do not suffice. They may be quite emotionally needy themselves, or they may be faced with social circumstances that are overwhelming. With these parents, the clinician will take on the additional and perhaps more active roles, such as providing emotional and logistical support.

"Given the importance of parents in the lives of children, it seems vital that any kind of professional intervention in relation to the child should be concerned with supporting and strengthening the parents" (Fine and Gardner, 1991, p. 33). By listening to the parents' needs (Chethnik, 2000) and reflecting their feelings (Kottman, 1995), the child's clinician can become such an important emotional support. This is true especially for those parents for whom session updates do not suffice to maintain enough motivation to keep bringing a child to therapy. Although a child therapist should not be enticed into becoming the parent's therapist as well, she or he can nevertheless help the parents through making appropriate referrals to a therapist of their own, hooking them up with social support networks, assessing them for eligibility for social services (e.g., WIC, respite care for children) and helping them to apply for these, and being generally supportive and understanding. Often, just being willing to listen to the parents' concerns about themselves and their child(ren) is sufficient to help the parents feel supported and understood.

The approach the clinician takes with parents in such supportive work does not come from a deficit perspective, even if the family is in crisis (Fine and Gardner, 1991). Instead, it focuses on empowering the parents—that is, helping them to recognize that they can bring about change and can influence their own and their children's fate and adjustment to difficult circumstances (cf. Fine and Gardner, 1991). It is best in such work to recognize the interconnectedness of family roles, functions, relationships, and behavioral patterns and to be sensitive to each family's unique needs and requirements. Families are not a group of independent individuals; rather, they are a system and have to be dealt with from that perspective (Fine and Gardner, 1991). Further, families are not an independent unit; rather they are thoroughly tied into a culture and environment that again represents an interdependent context that must be considered for the family and parents to feel understood, represented, and supported (Brems, 1996).

6 Supplementary Assessment Strategies

WITH MARK E. JOHNSON

Once the intake interview has been completed, the clinician is left with a wealth of information that needs to be organized, understood, and utilized to develop the best possible treatment program for the child client. However, it is not uncommon that although many questions were answered during this interview, many remain. These are often best addressed through supplementary assessment strategies, such as obtaining school records and previous treatment records, consulting with other professionals, and conducting psychological evaluations. Clinicians should not hesitate to receive permission from the child's legal guardians for these types of assessments, as they can fill in information gaps that might prove crucial to the successful treatment of the child. A summary of relevant sources of additional information is provided in Table 6.1. It is evident from inspection of this table that there are basically two modes of additional data collection. First, the clinician can gain access to records that already exist for the child, either from the child's school(s) or from the child's previous service provider(s). Second, the clinician can gain additional information by asking the child to submit to further evaluation, either in the form of consultation with and treatment by other professionals or through additional psychological assessment.

School Records

School records are the most accessible records and are often of great value in that they may validate the information gathered during the intake interview. School records can only be obtained if appropriate releases of information were obtained from the child's legal guardians. These releases can serve not only to obtain records, but also to obtain permission to communicate with the child's teacher(s). School records are particularly helpful when presenting problems include issues of attention or concentration, peer relationships, learning difficulties, developmental concerns, separation anxiety, deterioration of grades, frequent parental meetings with teachers or principals, behavior problems at school, or referral of the child by school personnel. However, as children spend a large part of their lives within the school setting, obtaining records from the educational environment—be that preschool, Head Start, kindergarten, or grade school—may be indicated for all children who present for psychotherapy.

TABLE 6.1   Sources of Additional Information

Type of Record or Service	Type of Professional or Test
Obtaining Existing Information	
School Records	■ educational/academic tests ■ psychological evaluations ■ teachers' observations ■ teachers' ratings ■ sociograms
Previous Treatment Records	■ psychology/therapy ■ hospitalization ■ medicine ■ hearing ■ speech
Creating Additional Information	
Referral Sources/Consultations	■ medicine ■ pediatrics ■ neurology ■ speech ■ audiology ■ developmental psychology ■ classroom observation
Psychological Assessment	■ mental status examination ■ behavior rating forms ■ personality assessment ■ projective testing ■ achievement testing ■ intelligence testing ■ neuropsychological testing

The most obvious components of school records are the child's grades and test scores on standardized educational or academic achievement tests. This information provides data about the child's intellectual potential and correlated achievement. However, these scores can also be used to investigate whether there was a significant change in a child's performance, when this change occurred, and the external factors to which it might be tied. For instance, a sudden drop in grades after a change to a new school or teacher might reveal that the child is having difficulties adjusting to a new environment. A drop in performance after a hospitalization that resulted from a severe injury to the head during an episode of physical abuse toward the child may indicate either that the child missed much material while hospitalized or that the child's neurological system was damaged. Vast differences in academic achievement versus actual cognitive capacity can give clues about the child's emotional state or about the possibility of a specific developmental disability. Although many of these hypotheses will certainly need to be investigated further through additional testing or consultation, school records may be the crucial documents that point the way for the clinician to even consider these factors.

In addition to academic testing and grades, school records will also contain any psychological evaluations that may have been conducted for a particular child. Access to these types of assessments can save the clinician from repeating them unnecessarily and may provide new insights and pieces of information that did not emerge in the intake interview. Further, the very existence of such evaluations in a child's school records indicates that there have been concerns about this child in the school setting as well.

Communication with the child's teachers often provides much insight. Teachers, especially in the lower grades, tend to know their students very well, have an appreciation of changes in their pupils, and can compare the child to peers in the same classroom. They are generally very willing to share their observations about the child in question and tend to be able to verify or dispute information obtained from parents. Although not entirely objective, teachers are less subjective than parents in their evaluation of children and tend to have a standard against which to compare a child. It is also possible to ask teachers to evaluate the child formally through the use of behavior rating scales and checklists (covered in the assessment section below). There is also a Student Referral Checklist (Schinka, 1988) that was developed specifically to be completed by teachers. Further, teachers sometimes are able to provide sociograms of the child's classroom. It is important to remember not only to talk to current teachers, but to also interview previous teachers. This is especially important when the behavior of the child appears to have changed significantly or a current teacher is the person raising complaints about a child.

Teachers are best involved when the presenting problem is relevant to the child's school performance, such as in cases of attention deficit hyperactivity disorder, learning disability, or developmental disability. In these situations, a phone interview with a teacher can be an unobtrusive yet very valuable source of information that will neither stigmatize the child nor take much time for the clinician. Such a contact can even take the place of a time-consuming classroom observation (see the section on referrals/consultations). Getting information from more than one teacher also provides additional corroboration or validation of information collected from all individuals. One final reason to contact schools and teachers has to do with treatment implementation. Teachers tend to be more cooperative with treatment recommendations that involve them or their classroom if they were part of the assessment period and feel that they had some input.

Despite all of these advantages of obtaining school records, the discussion of this assessment procedure can not be complete without also mentioning some of its disadvantages. Contacting schools for records and especially communicating directly with teachers makes them very aware of the fact that a child has been identified as having a problem. The risk thus becomes one of creating a self-fulfilling prophecy, especially if the teacher never perceived the child as a problematic one to begin with. In instances in which the presenting problem of the child appears clearly contained outside of the classroom, a release of school records should be weighed carefully against the potential risk of marking the child. If there appears to be some question about the child's academic performance but no concern about peer relationships and classroom behavior, the least intrusive approach might be to obtain simply a release of records, without communication with teachers or agency-school communication exchange.

Previous Treatment Records

Although it appears obvious that a clinician would obtain previous treatment records for a child presenting for treatment, this is probably one of the most neglected sources of information available. The reticence to obtain previous treatment records is partly due to long waiting periods, as many agencies take a long time to respond to requests for information. In fact, it is not unusual to have to follow up written requests with a telephone call to receive any records at all. Nevertheless, this source of data is very important, and utilizing it can save much time and expense for the child, the family, and the service provider. In considering this type of release, the clinician must be aware of the wide number of sources of information when working with children. It is not sufficient to obtain releases merely if the child previously has had mental health services. It is very common for adults to take children who evidence some problematic behavior or affect to physicians or pediatricians. Therefore, the investigation of medical records can often be quite illuminating. Further, speech problems or hearing deficits can contribute to problems or behavior that appear psychological or emotional in nature. For instance, it is not uncommon for very young children who appear slightly developmentally delayed with regard to psychosocial development to have ear infections that have prevented the children from hearing well enough. Because of this hearing deficit, these children develop more slowly, not because of an emotional or psychological problem, but rather because of a physiological problem. Obtaining records from physicians can clarify these types of etiologies.

Obtaining records from hospitals where the child may have been hospitalized is also important. Not only is it possible that the emotional trauma of being separated from parents has contributed to the child's current difficulties, but it is possible that hospital personnel have noticed certain behaviors that are still present or even exacerbated. The trauma of hospitalization at a young age should never be underestimated, and hospital records may help the mental health professional to assess how traumatic the experience was for the child. For instance, one child who presented for treatment had a prolonged hospital stay at age 5. He was an inpatient for 6 weeks and, during that time, had no contact whatsoever with his family. Upon his return to the family home, extended family members frequently commented on the personality change that he had undergone. Whereas before, he was a fun-loving, outgoing child, he was now shy, reserved, and afraid to seek out others for simple interactions. He tended to play by himself and was most comfortable alone or around adults. Clearly, the experience of being hospitalized had a great effect on this child's psychological adjustment and must be considered in the understanding of the etiology of his current presenting problem and in treatment planning.

Referral Sources/Consultation

Just as it is important to realize that past treatment records, whether they be medical, psychological, academic, or otherwise, provide a wealth of information that might otherwise be missed, it is crucial to recognize when a presenting problem might be beyond a clinician's expertise and requires a referral to another professional. There are several common childhood presenting problems that a mental health professional should never encounter without making a medical contact. This contact may merely consist of a release of information if the family had previously sought medical consultation for the same problem; it may involve a consultation with a medical professional; or it may necessitate a referral to a physician, pediatrician, psychiatrist, or neurologist. Examples of disorders requiring such action include, but are not necessarily limited to, enuresis, encopresis, tic disorders, attention deficit hyperactivity disorder, eating disorders, severe depression, and psychosis. The rationales for involving a medical practitioner are slightly different from disorder to disorder. For instance, with regard to enuresis and encopresis, a referral to a physician is important to rule out a physiological reason, as opposed to a psychological one, for the child's inability to exercise control over bladder or sphincter. Children with symptoms of anorexia, bulimia, overeating, or rumination often need to be evaluated for weight issues, nutrition issues, and blood analyses to ascertain that they have no severe vitamin or mineral deficiencies and that their electrolytes are properly balanced. Thus, while the reason in the first set of disorders (elimination disorders) is to rule out a functional or physiological cause, the reason in the second set of disorders (eating disorders) is one of ruling out negative consequences of the disorder as far as physical well-being is concerned. For disorders of attention or psychoses, the primary reason for referral has to do with assessing the need for medication to relieve the negative side effects of the severe symptomatology that is often involved. Tic disorders may have neurological bases and therefore should never be treated without a thorough examination by a neurologist.

It behooves the mental health practitioner who works with children to identify a few physicians in the community to whom referrals can be made. A good working relationship between the therapist and the medical professional will facilitate the referral, will be easier for the child and her or his family, and will not result in the lack of cooperation or the problem of losing the client to the other professional. These types of professional relationships can often be started successfully by asking other mental health service providers for references for physicians who appear most capable of forming such a liaison. Then a letter, followed by a phone contact, can pave the way for a good working relationship. It is best to have such a relationship with a child psychiatrist. Unfortunately, these professionals are rare. Pediatricians and family practitioners are next in order of preference, with general practitioners after that. Once a relationship has been forged with one of these types of physicians, they will be able to make more specialized referral recommendations, such as for neurology or surgery.

Medical referrals are not the only sources of consultation in the work with children. As was previously pointed out, speech and hearing deficits can significantly affect children's psychological well-being. Therefore, if there is any concern about a child's speech or hearing, a referral is absolutely crucial. Many child guidance centers across the country can provide these services. Also, many schools are equipped with speech therapy services. Thus, these referrals can often be made at low cost to the family. The relative payoff if an actual speech or hearing problem is detected is worthwhile indeed. If developmental delays appear to be present but speech and hearing evaluations were negative, it is often a good idea to involve a developmental psychologist. Although mental health service providers have some understanding of human, and especially child, development, this is not their area of expertise. Developmental psychologists, on the other hand, are specifically trained to assess a child's developmental appropriateness. They are trained to assess children's developmental levels across several domains, such as language, social adjustment, fine and gross motor movement, cognition, emotional expression, and others. Whenever a question about developmental appropriateness arises, a developmental psychologist should be consulted.

Finally, one easy consultation that is often neglected is direct observation of the child in the classroom. This observation involves a conference with the teacher as well and can generally be conducted by the mental health professional herself or himself. Thus, it is not a referral in the usual sense, but it does move the assessment of the child beyond the therapy room. In conducting mental health observations in the classroom, the clinician receives firsthand information about the child's peer relationships, involvement in the classroom, learning capacity, interactions with teachers, and general behaviors in a structured and challenging setting. Further, it can corroborate information obtained from the child or the family. This is similar to obtaining releases of information for school records or conversations with teachers but is somewhat preferable, as the information is obtained firsthand and is independent of another individual's assessment or interpretation. Details about how to do classroom observations are beyond the scope of this book; however, many sources of information are available (e.g., Shapiro and Kratochwill, 2000).

Psychological Assessment

A final excellent source of creating additional information about a child for etiological understanding and treatment planning is that of psychological assessment. Literally hundreds of tools have been developed to help clinicians learn more about a child and her or his family in an objective manner. These tests can be grouped into several large categories:

- mental status examination
- behavior rating forms
- achievement testing
- intelligence testing
- objective personality testing
- projective personality testing
- neuropsychological testing

These categories are ordered according to the amount of specialized training that is necessary to utilize the tests contained within each. In other words, the farther down on the list the strategy is that is desired for further assessment, the more critical it is to identify a professional who is appropriately qualified through specialized intensive training to render the service. Specifically, mental status exams and behavior rating scales can be administered by any conscientious mental health service provider who has thoroughly familiarized herself or himself with the procedure of the task and the interpretation of the scores. On the other hand, the use of projective tools is restricted to professionals who have taken several courses covering tests such as the Children's Apperception Test, the Rorschach Inkblot Test, or the Kinetic House-Tree-Person Test. Finally, neuropsychological testing can be conducted only by neuropsychologists whose entire graduate (or postdoctoral) training was devoted to the study of neuropsychology. Table 6.2 provides an overview of the minimum qualifications necessary for the various categories of psychological testing. The approach taken in Table 6.2 could be

TABLE 6.2   Minimum Qualifications Required for Various Types of Psychological Assessment

Category of Testing	Minimum Qualification
Mental Status Examination	Master's degree in a mental health service profession *and* thorough familiarity with mental status procedures
Behavior Rating Forms	Master's degree in a mental health service profession *and* thorough familiarity with the chosen instruments
Achievement Testing	Master's degree in an applied branch of psychology (i.e., clinical, counseling, or school) *and* formal training in the use of the chosen test
Intelligence Testing	Doctoral degree in an applied branch of psychology (i.e., clinical, counseling, or school) *and* formal training in the use of the chosen test
Objective Personality Assessment	Doctoral degree in an applied branch of psychology (i.e., clinical, counseling, or school) *and* formal training in the use of the chosen test
Projective Personality Testing	Doctoral degree in clinical or counseling psychology *and* formal training in the use of the chosen test
Neuropsychological Testing	Doctoral degree in neuropsychology *or* doctoral degree in clinical or counseling psychology *with* postdoctoral training in neuropsychology

perceived as very conservative. However, in considering that important treatment decisions can be based on the findings derived from such instruments, it will become clear that such conservatism is more than justified.

Inspection of Table 6.2 reveals that the only mental health professionals who are qualified to administer psychological testing beyond the level of mental status exams or behavior rating forms are those trained within the field of psychology. Although clinical social workers and psychiatrists are capable of providing excellent psychotherapeutic services for children, they are not qualified to do psychological testing. Much specialized and formal classroom training is necessary for this purpose, and neither social work nor psychiatry provides such training. Nevertheless, a broad understanding of the categories of psychological assessment tools is important for any mental health professional, if only because it is helpful when it comes to reading an assessment report that was written for a child who was assessed in response to a referral made by the clinician. What follows is a brief discussion of some of the major instruments broken down by category to provide the reader with such a broad understanding of commonly used assessment tools for children. In this discussion, more emphasis will be placed on the categories of tests called "Mental Status Examination" and "Behavior Rating Scales," as these two categories are amenable for use by most mental health professionals who are willing to read more about these procedures. Table 6.3 provides an overview of current assessment tools that will be discussed in some detail in the pages that follow.

TABLE 6.3   Assessment Instruments

Behavior Rating Forms

Achenbach System of Empirically Based
Assessment (ASEBA)
  Youth Self-Report (Achenbach, 1991a)
  Child Behavior Checklist for Ages 1½ to 5
    (Achenbach and Rescorla, 2000)
  Child Behavior Checklist for Ages 4 to 18
    (CBCL; Achenbach, 1991b).
  Teacher's Report Form (TRF; Achenbach, 1991c)
  Caregiver-Teacher Report Form for Ages 1½ to 5
    (C-TRF; Achenbach and Rescorla, 2000).
  Direct Observation Form for Ages 5 to 14 (DOF;
    Achenbach, 1991d)
  Semistructured Clinical Interview for Children
    and Adolescents Aged 6–18 (SCICA;
    McConaughy and Achenbach, 1994)

Behavior Assessment System for Children
  (Reynolds and Kamphaus, 1992)
  Parent Rating Scales (BASC-PRS)
  Teacher Rating Scales (BASC-TRS)
  Self-Report of Personality (BASC-SRP)
  Structured Developmental History (BASC-SDH)
  Student Observation System (BASC-SOS)

Conners' Rating Scales (Conners, 1997)
  Parent Rating Scale-Revised
  Teacher Rating Scale-Revised

Vineland Adaptive Behavior Scale (VABS; Sparrow,
  Balla, and Cicchetti, 1984)

Achievement Testing

Kaufman Test of Educational Achievement (K-TEA;
  Kaufman and Kaufman, 1985)

Peabody Individual Achievement Test-Revised
  (PIAT-R; Markwardt, 1989)

Wechsler Individual Achievement Test, Second
  Edition (WIAT-II; Wechsler, 2001)

Wide Range Achievement Test—3 (WRAT-3;
  Wilkinson, 1993)

Woodcock-Johnson III Complete Battery (W-J III;
  Woodcock, McGrew, and Mather, 2000).

Intelligence Testing

Kaufman Assessment Battery for Children (K-ABC;
  Kaufman and Kaufman, 1983)

Kaufman Brief Intelligence Test (K-BIT; Kaufman
  and Kaufman, 1990)

Peabody Picture Vocabulary Test—Third Edition
  (PPVT-III; Dunn and Dunn, 1997)

Stanford Binet Intelligence Scale, Fourth Edition
  (SBIS-IV; Thorndike, Hagan, and Sattler, 1986)

Wechsler Abbreviated Scale of Intelligence (WASI;
  Wechsler, 1999)

Wechsler Intelligence Scale for Children, Third
  Edition (WISC-3; Wechsler, 1991)

Wechsler Preschool and Primary Scale of
  Intelligence—Revised (WPPSI-R; Wechsler,
  1989)

Objective Personality Assessment

Beck Youth Inventories of Emotional and Social
  Impairment (Beck, Beck, and Jolly, 2001)

Children's Personality Questionnaire (CPQ; Porter
  and Cattell, 1985)

Personality Inventory for Children Family of Tests
  Personality Inventory for Children (PIC-2;
    Lachar and Gruber, 2001)
  Personality Inventory for Youth (PIY; Lachar and
    Gruber, 1995)

Piers-Harris Children's Self-Concept Scale
  (PHCSCS; Piers, 1984)
  Student Behavior Survey (SBS; Lachar,
    Wingenfeld, Kline, and Gruber, 2000).

Reynolds Child Depression Scale (RCDS; Reynolds,
  1989)

Revised Children's Manifest Anxiety Scale
  (RCMAS; Reynolds and Richmond, 1978)

Self Perception Profile for Children (SPPC; Harter,
  1985)

State-Trait Anxiety Inventory for Children (STAIC;
  Spielberger, 1973)

Projective Personality Assessment

Children's Apperception Test-Animal (CAT-A;
  Bellak and Bellak, 1949)

Children's Apperception Test-Human (CAT-H;
  Bellak and Bellak, 1965)

Draw-A-Person (Goodenough, 1926)

Kinetic House-Tree-Person Drawing Test (K-HTP;
  Burns, 1987)

Rorschach Inkblot Test (Rorschach, 1942)

Thematic Apperception Test (TAT; Bellak, 1943)

Mental Status Examination

A mental status examination is not a psychological assessment tool in the true sense. It actually tends to fall more in the realm of assessment tools utilized by physicians or psychiatrists. Nevertheless, conducting a mental status examination with children is a skill every mental health service provider who works with children needs to have. The mental status exam provides a context in which to gather certain types of information. It structures for the clinician what type of behavior, affect, cognition, etcetera to look for when working with a child. Because there are several well-accepted components of a mental status exam, its conduct also facilitates communication among professionals, as it provides a focus for questioning and a structure for reporting (Morrison and Anders, 1999).

Although the mental status exam has distinct categories of information, it is an interview that nevertheless can be conducted in a very structured or a very informal manner, depending largely upon the style of the individual clinician and the needs and age of the child that is being assessed (Shaffer, Lucas, and Richters, 1999). Entire books have been written on the subject and should be referred to for specific details if the clinician plans to use this strategy (Simmons, 1987). In fact, formal checklists exist that can be used for the purposes of conducting and recording this type of interview (Dougherty and Schinka, 1989). A brief outline of the crucial components of mental status interviews is provided here. The primary categories of a children's mental status exam always include, not necessarily in this order, appearance and level of physical activity, mood and affect, sensorium and perception, cognitive functioning, health and development, behavior, interpersonal relations, self-concept, and coping strategies and psychological defenses. For each of these broad categories several subsections of exploration and assessment exist. A sampling of these is outlined in Table 6.4.

Appearance and Level of Physical Activity. This category involves information that need not be inquired about, but rather is gleaned from behavioral observations. It directs the clinician's attention to factors such as a child's height and weight, grooming and hygiene, manner and style of dress, eye and hair color, posture, gait, psychomotor movement, and physical characteristics such as scars, bruises, physical handicaps, and prosthetic devices. Several of these characteristics are simply descriptive, whereas others can be evaluated with regard to their appropriateness or can be rated and further defined. Specifically, traits such as eye and hair color are simply described. Hygiene and grooming can be rated as to whether they are appropriate given societal health standards and grooming habits. Size, weight, and height can be judged according to their developmental and health appropriateness. Motor movement must be further defined as agitated, fidgety, unusual, normal, or as including tics, tremors, or motor abnormalities.

Overall, the assessment of appearance and physical activity of children can give many clues about them. For instance, physical characteristics such as dirty clothing, unkempt appearance, or emaciation can be overt signs of parental neglect. Unusual scars, large numbers of bruises, and seductive or cowering body postures can be the first evidence of abuse. Particularly small size, abnormal height and weight can point toward health problems or developmental problems that can affect the child's psychological adjustment.

TABLE 6.4   Components of Mental Status Examinations for Children

Main Components of Exam	Subcomponents
Appearance and Physical Activity	■ size, height, and weight ■ mannerisms and habits ■ type and cleanliness of dress ■ body, hair style, and hygiene ■ notable physical characteristics ■ psychomotor movement
Mood and Affect	■ predominant emotion ■ range and appropriateness of affect ■ variation in mood or affect ■ fluctuation of moods
Sensorium and Perception	■ orientation (time, place, person) ■ reality appraisal ■ functioning of senses ■ hallucinations
Cognitive Functioning	■ intelligence ■ complexity and type of thought ■ academic performance ■ speech and verbalization ■ reality of thought and delusions
Health and Development	■ physical well-being ■ medical history ■ developmental appropriateness
Behavior	■ general patterns of conduct ■ self-destructive behavior ■ hobbies and interests
Interpersonal Relations	■ family relationships ■ peer relationships ■ adult relationships
Self-Concept	■ esteem and confidence ■ self-identity and appraisal ■ values, ideals, and goals
Coping Strategies and Psychological Defenses	■ capacity for coping ■ types of strategies ■ behavioral manifestations of coping and defense

Mood and Affect.   This information can often be solicited through observation as well as some cautious questioning of the child. It assesses a child's primary emotions, paying attention to clinical signs of depression, anxiety, fears, and phobias, but also simply assessing how cheerful, optimistic, angry, irritable, hostile, friendly, or antagonistic a child is during the interaction with the clinician. The stability of these moods needs to be described, especially if the clinician notes that moods appear to fluctuate widely and change quickly. Affect needs to be rated with regard to its range and its appropriateness to the topic of conversation or the theme of play activity and should be described with regard to its most outstanding features. As such, judgments need to be made about whether affect is blunted or restricted, labile or rigid, dramatized or constricted. It is also important to note whether the child is comfortable in the expression of affect. It is not uncommon for some families to have unwritten rules about the appropriateness of some affects over others. Thus, a child may be quite at ease with affects that are positive and may show appropriate expression in that realm. However, as the same child encounters negative affects, expression may be inhibited and clearly uncomfortable for the child.

Sensorium and Perception.   This realm of functioning has to do with a child's contact with reality and orientation to her or his surroundings and can be observed, as well as directly questioned. With regard to orientation and awareness, even very young children (3 to 5 or 6) need to have awareness of where they are in time and space, as well as of who they are. They should be able to provide their name and age, tell the clinician where they are or where their family lives, and say during what part of the day (morning, afternoon, evening) the interview is taking place. Older children should be much more sophisticated about this information and should be able to name the current date and the approximate time (within about 30 minutes to one hour), know the name of the clinic where the interview takes place, state their full address, identify by name their primary caretakers and teachers, and share information about themselves that goes beyond mere name and age.

With regard to reality contact, the functioning of the child's senses must be assessed. This is important, as was pointed out previously, in that malfunctioning of certain senses can result in severe developmental delays that, in turn, may affect psychological adjustment. Thus, the child's ability to hear, see, feel, speak, and taste can be inquired about. It is also interesting to note any obvious preferences of certain senses. Some preferences are developmentally driven. Infants, for instance, prefer to utilize their sense of taste in the exploration of new surroundings. Clearly, such a preference in a 4-year-old would be somewhat disturbing. Similarly, whereas the sense of touch is an important one for the 8-year-old who explores the new therapy environment, an adolescent is more likely to explore simply through the use of the sense of vision.

Further, and perhaps more important, it must be ascertained that the child can differentiate fantasy from reality and that there is no hallucinatory process in any of the realms of sensing. Fantasy can be differentiated from reality to some degree already by age 3; however, full separation may occur as late as age 8. Hallucinations are important to rule out through direct questioning whether the presenting problems include concerns by parents and teachers such as excessive fantasy life, distractedness that appears and disappears suddenly, nightmares or night terrors, and physical concerns or strange physical sensations. Finally, the child's level of consciousness must be assessed through questions about loss of consciousness, such as fainting or blacking out. The intrusiveness of certain environmental stimuli into the child's consciousness must be assessed and gives clues about the child's level of distractibility and ability to pay attention. Dissociations or similar lapses in consciousness need to be recorded, and the presence of seizure disorders must be inquired about.

Cognitive Functioning. The first category of information within the realm of cognitive functioning concerns itself with intelligence, cognitive complexity, and memory. The amount of formality that is used to make these assessments can range from using formal intelligence testing to making judgments based on the child's verbalizations, grammatical correctness, and logic of thought. The clinician can ask the child to perform simple tasks such as counting backwards from 10 to 0 (or from 100 to 0 by intervals of three, depending on the child's age), can ask the child to interpret simple proverbs such as those included in the Wechsler Intelligence Scale for Children (see below), and can assess memory by asking for recall of birthdays, breakfast food on the day of the interview, and similar questions. Much information can be assessed through simple conversation that challenges the child to converse in different topic areas. Abstracting ability can generally best be evaluated by observing the child's problem-solving skills and problem awareness.

The exploration of speech and verbalizations also falls into this category. The mental health professional should pay attention to the spontaneity of the child's speech, the adequacy of word choice and word finding, and the age appropriateness of the child's language. Academic performance is an important topic to inquire about and must be seen in relation to the child's estimated (or formally assessed) level of intelligence. Academic performance can simply be inquired about with the child and/or parents or can be formally reviewed through a release of information to obtain school records.

Once the normal cognitive processes of the child have thus been assessed, it is also necessary to evaluate the presence of cognitive features that may be more pathological in nature, such as delusions, preoccupations, and obsessions. These thought contents need to be further specified with regard to the topic that is prevalent. Common themes that emerge in children include guilt, violence, religion, spirits (demons, ghosts, devils), worthlessness, persecution by peers, and physical complaints. Additionally, the child's thought processes must be evaluated in terms of coherence, circumstantiality, tangentiality, neologisms, unusual associations, and blocking or evasiveness; distortions such as overgeneralization, catastrophizing, black-white thinking, perfectionism, and mind reading should be noted. Finally, the effects of the child's cognitive processes on her or his judgment and level of insight must be estimated.

Health and Development. This category of information relies on observation, releases of information to receive medical records and conversation with the child and/or parents. The child's current and past level of health must be assessed through inquiry about past illness. Accidents and hospitalizations are to be included. The child must be observed to make judgments about developmental appropriateness in the areas of cognition, emotional differentiation and expression, interpersonal relationships, self development, language, fine and gross motor movement, and morality. Health and development in combination may also be used to obtain important information about the possibility of fetal alcohol syndrome. Suspicions about this based on the child's health, appearance, and developmental delays should be corroborated through an interview with the child's (preferably biological) mother and father. General health and developmental information were discussed in detail in Chapter Three and will not be repeated here.

Behavior. Information about a child's behavior can best be gathered through careful observation and through talking to parents and teachers. In this category, general patterns of conduct are the primary focus. The mental health professional should note information about how involved a child can become in activities, how well a child can manipulate toys and execute tasks, how a child responds to frustration, how well a child can delay gratification, whether a child withdraws or seeks to be the center of attention, and whether the child behaves aggressively or meekly. Behavioral tones can include apathy, distractibility, unresponsiveness, demandingness, withdrawal, histrionics, manipulation, and so on. Also in the realm of behavior are patterns such as overeating, bingeing and purging, refusing food, and other self-destructive acts. Acting out behaviors and involvement with legal authorities are behavioral issues, as are school truancy and suspension. If these are of concern, their exact nature and the setting in which they occur must be noted. Their history needs to be inquired about, and the nature of the actions should be described in detail (e.g., assaultiveness toward peers, fire setting, lying, stealing, cruelty to animals). Leadership ability versus follower characteristics are included as well, and hobbies and interests should be noted in detail.

Interpersonal Relations.   This category includes a thorough assessment of peer, adult, and family relationships. As this aspect of the mental status exam is redundant with the type of information that should already have been collected during the intake interview, it will not be discussed in further detail at this time.

Self-Concept.   Information in this category often becomes obvious simply through carefully observing the child with this aspect of personality adjustment in mind. Two important components of self-concept—self-esteem and self-confidence—are often clearly expressed in play and in the interaction with the examiner. A self-confident child will explore the therapy room and will make some spontaneous verbalizations that are directed toward the examiner, whereas a child with little confidence may remain reticent, withdrawn, and unable to exhibit spontaneous behavior or speech. Sometimes children with low levels of confidence also overcompensate by being destructively exploratory and overly garrulous without maintaining safe boundaries and limits. Similarly, self-esteem will help the child to regulate her or his actions in the therapy room and toward the examiner. It will emerge in the child's play, especially when play becomes self-revealing. A child with healthy self-esteem will be much more willing to try a new task or play with an unfamiliar toy than will a child with little self-esteem, who might be afraid of revealing her or his inability to handle the materials correctly.

Self-identity, also an important aspect of self-concept, is often directly expressed through play and conversation. A child who has established some preferences and who has a sense of identity will be assertive in her or his choice of materials and conversation topics. The child who lacks identity has no preferences and will take cues from the environment to determine behavior and selection of toys or activities. This latter child will try to please the adult by performing in line with what she or he perceives the examiner to desire. Realistic self-appraisal is an important characteristic that children must develop early in life. It is demonstrated by the realistic choice of materials that reflects that the child has a certain knowledge of what she or he can and cannot do, without shying away unnecessarily from new situations. Thus, a 4-year-old who has developed appropriate self-appraisal within her or his developmental capacity, will not choose to play (beyond some time of exploration!) with a 1,000-piece puzzle or a game that necessitates reading skills. A 4-year-old who has not developed realistic self-appraisal and has negative self-esteem will not even explore the puzzle or the game and might shy away even from small blocks that require manual dexterity. She or he will be unwilling to try new things for fear of failure. On the other hand, another 4-year-old who has not developed a realistic sense of self-appraisal might be unaware of the inappropriateness of certain toys and will attempt to use them over and over, will fail, and then will feel devastated.

Finally, self-concept also includes the establishment of values, goals, and ideals. Absence of any of these features points toward lack of self-identity that would be appropriate to the child's developmental level and may indicate that the child has not experienced an environment that has helped her or him learn about consistency, boundaries, and limits. Care must, of course, be taken to assess these aspects of self in a developmental context. Thus, a 3-year-old may have the goal of establishing some autonomy in the choice of play materials while interacting with the examiner by refusing what is offered. A 10-year-old, on the other hand, may be more interested in using toys that can be manipulated to simulate interaction among peers, such as puppets or dolls in schoolhouses. An adolescent will choose activities and materials that help to establish direction and sophisticated skill building, such as the use of clay or paints.

Coping Strategies and Psychological Defenses. The information in this category refers to the child's capacity and means to deal with a number of circumstances that might evoke anxiety or feelings of threat or danger. Such circumstances may involve placing the child in a new, uncommon situation; asking the child to meet a stranger; taking the child out of a familiar environment; or placing the child in situations that facilitate or evoke needs or desires that the child may consider inappropriate or impossible to have met. A final coping situation is that which stimulates or encourages strong affect. The mental status situation may fit any of these descriptions, as it involves a new situation, a stranger, a conversation, questioning of the child that may stimulate material that is difficult or painful for the child, and interactions that may evoke strong affects. Observation of the child in any of these circumstances will give the examiner clues not only to whether the child is capable of coping, but also to the types of preferred strategies the child utilizes. Capacity for coping is evidenced by the child's ability to tolerate and adapt to new situations and strangers, to express difficult needs and desires and accept them as important, and to express even strong or difficult affects as they emerge and to deal with them (e.g., diffuse them) successfully. Examples of positive coping within each of these circumstances are provided below.

> A 7-year-old boy was asked to go with the examiner to the play therapy room for a mental status exam. He was hesitant to go with the stranger and asked his mother whether it was okay to go. When she indicated that she knew the person and that she was safe to go with, he accompanied the examiner to the room. Once in the room, he was quiet and withdrawn for a few moments. When he was encouraged to explore the room, he cautiously picked up toys, looked at materials, and put his hands in some of the puppets. He occasionally glanced at the examiner to ascertain that his behavior was acceptable, and as he realized that it was, he became more active and engaged in some puppet play and conversation. Finally, he was able to engage the examiner in his play and was open to being questioned.

This is an example of a child who evidenced good coping skills in a new situation. He first ascertained that the situation was safe by checking with his mother. He then separated from the familiar adult and entered the new setting. Once he had established that the stranger was safe and that the environment was stimulating, he relaxed and opened up.

> A 6-year-old girl who had been seen in therapy for some time often felt very needy and emotionally depleted. During one particular session, immediately after her father had been suddenly and dishonorably discharged from the military, she was overwhelmed by her fear of abandonment and her need for nurturance. She spontaneously began telling a story of a mouse who woke up one morning and was all alone. The mouse was very frightened because it was breakfast time and she was hungry, but no one was around to make her breakfast. After some affective discharge of fear and need, the girl finally indicated that the mouse must now be strong and find her own food. She related that the little animal got out of bed and went to a neighbor's house to tell them that she was home alone and hungry. The neighbor invited her in for breakfast, and the little mouse felt better.

This is an example of a child coping effectively with the emergence of strong needs (need for nurturance and being taken care of). Although the resolution is not one of complete autonomy (the mouse did not find her own food, after all, but rather received it from a helper), it nevertheless indicated that the child had accepted the necessity for the need (the mouse had to find the food because it could not survive without it) and was aware of the need for her to take some part in ascertaining that the need would be met (the mouse got out of bed and went to a neighbor's house).

> A 12-year-old boy was seen for an initial interview and had engaged in exploration for some time. He was now attempting unsuccessfully to work a crane set in the playroom. It was obvious that he was becoming very frustrated because he could not figure out how to work the crane. As his frustration mounted, he appeared tempted to smash the crane. He then talked loudly to himself, saying, "Okay, maybe this thing is broken. Why do they have broken toys in here? It's not nice to make kids play with broken stuff. Maybe it's not broken, maybe there is a trick to how it works." At that point, he turned to the examiner and asked whether there was a trick and whether he could get some help.

This is an example of a child who is coping successfully with a strong affect that was about to get out of control. As he was about to break the crane set in anger, he calmed himself by using a strong voice and self-talk to vent his frustration. As soon as he began to talk, he visibly relaxed. He talked himself through the height of his affect and then was able to ask for help.

Children do not always cope this successfully, and sometimes, rather than coping, they use defenses to deal with difficult situations. Kohut (1984) has reconceptualized defenses as protective mechanisms that are used by people to protect vulnerabilities within themselves. In the work with children, this conceptualization of the defensive process appears extremely appropriate. Children are very vulnerable in the sense that they still depend on adults in their environment to help them care for their physical and psychological needs. If the availability of adults for such purposes is sparse, children have to learn to protect themselves through various mechanisms. These self-protective mechanisms are commonly called defenses. A large number of defenses have been identified in the work with both adults and children, and it is impossible to define and mention all of them here.

The reader is referred to works by Anna Freud (1946) and Laughlin (1983) for details. However, a few defensive strategies are common enough to warrant some discussion and examples, as the mental status examiner must note not only whether a child has the capacity to cope, but also the types of self-protective, or defensive, strategies a child employs in coping situations.

Many children will try to use avoidance, evasion, or diversion when difficult coping situations arise. For instance, a 9-year-old girl was playing interactively with the examiner with the dollhouse family. She placed the mother and father figures in their large bed and removed their clothing. When the examiner asked what the adults were doing, the girl began to cough and said that her throat was hurting. She asked for a glass of water and moved away from the dollhouse. This child's behavior in response to the (somewhat unfortunate) question of the examiner was one of diversion ("my throat hurts") and avoidance (moving away from the dollhouse). Similar maneuvers may include the child's failure to respond to a question, the sudden changing of topics, or the attempt to direct the interaction or questioning to avoid certain subject matter. Somatization was also involved in this example of diversion, in that the chosen diversion was one of physical complaining. This is not uncommonly noted in family interviews, when children suddenly develop stomachaches or headaches as their parents or siblings begin to discuss sensitive information or are fighting loudly.

Withdrawal is a common defense in children and may range from quite severe manifestations to lesser forms of contact shunning. For instance, a child might hide in a closet when a difficult affect emerges. Often, children engage in a defense called undoing. In the following instance, the child had allowed a piece of information to emerge that she or he would then like to make go away. An 11-year-old girl was painting at the easel, indicating that she was drawing her family. She proceeded to draw her father and her brother. Her father had no hands and was placed in the bottom left corner of the page. Her brother was prominently placed in the middle of the page with big muscles and a smirk on his face. She drew her mother and herself only as an afterthought. She then stated that her brother always got all the attention in the family and that he was big and fat. Suddenly, she blushed and stopped talking. She turned away from the examiner, back to her painting, and covered the entire page in black paint. This child had revealed some information that was too difficult for her to deal with at this time. She undid her action by literally covering it up.

Acting out is another common defense among children. If the boy in the crane example had not been able to calm himself through self-talk and asking for help, but had actually kicked the crane, he would have evidenced acting out. However, acting out does not always occur in the context of angry affect, but might also be used to relieve anxiety or fear. For instance, one 6-year-old girl who suffered from severe abandonment anxiety frequently kicked toys and furniture in the play room when this fear emerged through play activity. Other defenses that are frequently used by children but will not be elaborated upon here include denial, rationalization, internalization, projection, and projective identification. The reader is referred to Anna Freud (1946) for a thorough discussion of defense mechanisms in children.

This discussion of the mental status exam is likely to have let the reader note that there is some degree of overlap between a mental status exam and an initial interview in terms of the type of information included. The mental status exam, however, is more evaluative in the sense of making actual judgments about appropriateness of cognition, perception, behavior, and so forth, whereas the initial interview merely collects information. There is also some overlap between the mental status exam and a good conceptualization. However, the mental status exam merely lists the findings and judgments from each area, whereas the conceptualization goes beyond mere listing of data into making sense of how these data fit together to explain the presenting problem of the child and to determine a useful treatment process. This difference is crucial and must be understood. A mental status exam is a tool for obtaining and organizing information. A conceptualization, on the other hand (as will be discussed in Chapter Seven), is a tool to integrate information and understand a child and her or his family system.

Behavior Rating Forms

Behavior rating scales, forms, or checklists provide an easy means of obtaining a somewhat more objective database about a child's behavior than mere interviewing and observation. They are focused on expanding the clinician's pool of information about the child's behavior in various types of settings from the perspective of the adults in the child's environment. They do not provide information about personality, intelligence, or ability but are strictly focused on assessment of overt behavior. A variety of such scales exists, and most were developed in such a manner that they are best cross-validated by administering them to all primary caregivers involved with the child, including parents, baby-sitters, and teachers. A brief overview of some of the most commonly used behavior rating scales will be provided here, with a discussion of each instrument's purpose, psychometric properties, and special features and information about purchasing sources and restrictions.

Achenbach System of Empirically Based Assessment.   The Achenbach System of Empirically Based Assessment (ASEBA; Achenbach and McConaughy, 1996) is a set of integrated scales that were developed to assess children's behavioral problems and social competencies by having their behaviors and actions rated by a variety of informants. Separate forms are available to be completed by parents (Child Behavior Checklist), teachers (Teacher's Report Form, Caregiver-Teacher Report Form), and clinicians (Direct Observation Form, Semistructured Clinical Interview for Children and Adolescents). A Youth Self-Report (YSR; Achenbach, 1991a) is also available for older children aged 11 to 18 years, and a Young Adult Self Report Form (YASR; Achenbach, 1997) is available for clients aged 18 to 30 years.

Depending upon the age of the child, either the Child Behavior Checklist for Ages 1½ to 5 (CBCL/1½–5; Achenbach and Rescorla, 2000) or the Child Behavior Checklist for Ages 4 to 18 (CBCL/4–18; Achenbach, 1991b; 1991d) is to be completed by adults who know the child well. The CBCL/1½–5 consists of ninety-nine problems, descriptions of problems, disabilities, concerns about the child, and best things about the child. Item ratings are summed to yield scores representing seven syndromes: Emotionally Reactive, Anxious/Depressed, Somatic Complaints, Withdrawn, Attention Problems, Aggressive Behavior, and Sleep Problems. Further, two second-order scales, Internalizing and Externalizing, and a global scale, Total Problems, are calculated. This form also yields five scales that are related to the DSM-IV diagnostic categories of Affective Problems, Anxiety

Problems, Pervasive Developmental Problems, Attention Deficit/Hyperactivity Problems, and Oppositional Defiant Problems. Finally, the CBCL/1½–5 incorporates items that to help identify possible language delays.

The CBCL/4–18 consists of twenty competence items within the realms of activities, social relations, and school performance; 118 specific behavioral and emotional problems; and two open-ended questions for reporting additional problems. The competence areas are based on the competence demonstrated as compared to other children in activities in which the child participates. The problem areas are rated on a three-point scale ranging from 0 (not true) to 2 (very true or often true), based on their presence. Nine areas of problem behaviors and three areas of social competence are derived from the responses. The problem behavior areas are descriptively labeled Aggressive Behavior, Anxious/Depressed, Attention Problems, Delinquent Behavior, Sex Problems, Social Problems, Somatic Complaints, Thought Problems, and Withdrawn. Some of these problem areas are combined into two second-order subscales: Internalizing (Anxious/Depressed, Somatic Complaints, and Withdrawn) and Externalizing (Aggressive Behavior and Delinquent Behavior). Finally, a Total Problems score is obtained by summing most of the problem behaviors. The three competence areas are Activities, Social, and School, and a global scale, Total Competence, can be calculated. For both versions of the CBCL, a profile is plotted that provides percentile ranks and T-scores for the child's performance in each area. Thus, a comparison of relative problem areas is easily accomplished by analyzing the profile obtained.

Additional forms can be used to supplement the data obtained through the CBCL. The Teacher's Report Form (TRF; Achenbach, 1991c) is appropriate for use with children aged 5 to 18. It consists of 118 items, 93 of which correspond with items on the CBCL/4–18 and 25 of which are related specifically to school behaviors. Using the same rating scale as on the CBCL, teachers rate the child for the presence of the behavior within the last two months. In addition to the same syndromes obtained on the CBCL (with the exception of Sex Problems) and the Internalizing, Externalizing, and Total Problems scales, the TRF yields scores for Academic Performance, Total Adaptive Functioning, Inattention, and Hyperactivity-Impulsivity. As with the CBCL, raw scores, percentiles, and T-scores are plotted on a profile for easy comparison of problem areas within the child and between the child and the normative sample. Similarly, a Caregiver-Teacher Report Form can be used with children aged 1½ to 5 years that parallels the CBCL/1½–5. To gain further information about the child, the Direct Observation Form (DOF; Achenbach, 1991b) can be used for children aged 5 to 14 years. The DOF consists of ninety-six problem items scored on a four-item scale and allows for an objective observer to observe the child in her or his natural setting to rate the child on the same dimensions as the CBCL. Finally, the Semistructured Clinical Interview for Children and Adolescents Aged 6–18 (SCICA; McConaughy and Achenbach, 1994) provides questions and probes that guide the interviewer to rate the child on eight syndrome scales (Aggressive Behavior, Anxious, Anxious/Depressed, Attention Problems, Family Problems, Resistant, Strange, and Withdrawn) as well as on the Internalizing, Externalizing, and Total Problems scales. These additional forms can greatly enhance the confidence a clinician may have in the results obtained through the CBCL. They can also be invaluable in evaluating a child's behavior across several settings, information that may prove useful in determining a treatment plan. The ASEBA forms can be obtained through the University of Vermont, Department of Psychiatry, Burlington, VT 05401-3456; *http://aseba.uvm.edu.*

Behavior Assessment System for Children.   The Behavior Assessment System for Children (BASC; Reynolds and Kamphaus, 1992) consists of a set of rating scales and self-report forms that were developed to assess the behaviors and emotions of children and adolescents: Parent Rating Scales (BASC-PRS), Teacher Rating Scales (BASC-TRS), Self-Report of Personality (BASC-SRP), Structured Developmental History (BASC-SDH), and Student Observation System (BASC-SOS). Three versions of the Parent and Teacher Rating Scales are available depending upon the child's age (2½ to 6, 6 to 11, and 12 to 18); they comprise 109 to 148 items and take 10 to 20 minutes to complete. Each item is a brief description of behavior, which the respondent rates on a four-point scale from "never" to "almost always." Depending upon the form used, the PRS provides scores on the following twelve scales: Aggression, Hyperactivity, Conduct Problems, Anxiety, Depression, Somatization, Attention Problems, Atypicality, Withdrawal, Adaptability, Leadership, and Social Skills. The TRS forms yield scores on these same scales, as well as information about Learning Problems and Study Skills. For both versions, second-order scales can be calculated, including Externalizing Problems, Internalizing Problems, Adaptive Skills, and Behavior Symptoms Index; a School Problems factor can be calculated on the basis of TRS responses.

The BASC Self-Report of Personality has two versions, one for children (ages 6 to 11) the other for adolescents (ages 12 to 18). The children's form consists of 152 items and provides scores on five composite measures and twelve subscales as follows: Clinical Maladjustment (Anxiety, Atypicality, Locus of Control, Social Stress); School Maladjustment (Attitude to School, Attitudes to Teachers); Other Problems (Depression, Sense of Inadequacy); Personal Adjustment (Relations with Parents, Interpersonal Relations, Self-Esteem, Self-Reliance) and Emotional Symptoms Index. The adolescent form has 186 items and yields the same scores as the children's form, as well as scores on Somatization and Sensation Seeking. Both forms have validity scales; both have an F validity scale (equivalent to that found in the MMPI-2) and a V scale (measuring lack of attention to the items, random responding, or poor reading ability); the adolescent form has an additional fake good scale.

To supplement these forms, the Student Observation System (SOS) provides a system for recording observations of a child's behavior in both timed and untimed situations. The SOS assesses both adaptive and maladaptive behaviors and can be used by a variety of trained individuals. Information gathered from this form can help to fine-tune the assessment process by helping identify behaviors in different settings. Finally, the Structured Developmental History (SDH) provides the equivalent of a thorough intake form, asking detailed questions about various areas in the child's life, including social, psychological, educational, and medical history. It can be completed in a structured interview with the parent or caregiver or can be sent home with the adult to be completed and returned at the next session. The BASC is available from American Guidance Service; *http://www.agsnet.com.*

Conners Rating Scales.   The Conners Rating Scales (Conners, 1997) have seen their greatest use in evaluating and screening children for disruptive behaviors and in tracking these children's progress in treatment. For use with children aged 3 to 17, three different forms are available for gaining data from different informants: Conners's Parent Rating Scale–Revisited (CPRS-R), Conners's Teaching Rating Scale–Revised (CTRS-R), and the Conners-Wells' Adolescent Self-Report Scale (CASS; only for children 12 to 17 years). Long and short versions exist for both the CPRS-R (the long version with eighty items and the short with twenty-seven) and CTRS-R (the long version with fifty-nine items and the short with twenty-eight). Each of the items represents a problem behavior that is rated on a 0 to 3 scale on the basis of the degree to which the target child has demonstrated it within the last month. The long CPRS-R yields scores on the following subscales: Oppositional, Social Problems, Cognitive Problems/Inattention, Psychosomatic, Hyperactivity, DSM-IV Symptom Subscales, Anxious-Shy, ADHD Index, Perfectionism, and Conners's Global Index; the short form provides scores on Oppositional, Hyperactivity, Cognitive Problems/ Inattention, and ADHD Index. The long CTRS-R form provides scores on Oppositional, Social Problems, Cognitive Problems/Inattention, DSM-IV™ Symptom Subscales, Hyperactivity, Conners's ADHD Index, Anxious-Shy, Conners's Global Index, and Perfectionism; the short form yields scores on Oppositional, Hyperactivity, Cognitive Problems/ Inattention, and ADHD Index. T-scores are calculated for all subscales, scores of 61 to 65 being regarded as mildly atypical, 66 to 70 as moderately atypical, and 70 or greater as markedly atypical. The Conners Rating Scales are available from Multi-Health Systems; *http://www.mhs.com.*

Vineland Adaptive Behavior Scale.   The Vineland Adaptive Behavior Scale (VABS; Sparrow, Balla, and Cicchetti, 1984) represents the reorganization and revision of the Vineland Social Maturity Scale (Doll, 1953). It is a measure of adaptive behavior that is administered to an adult who is very familiar with the child's behavior in various settings. There are two versions, which vary greatly in length and time of administration. The survey form with 297 items requires 30 to 40 minutes, and the expanded version, with an additional 280 items, requires approximately one and a half hours of time (a 244-item classroom version also exists, focused on classroom behavior and to be completed by a teacher). Adaptive behavior for the purposes of this instrument is defined as the child's assessed ability to perform the types of daily activities that would make her or him self-sufficient with regard to social interaction and personal care.

Within this context, the VABS assesses the child's behavior in five domains: Communication, Daily Living Skills, Socialization, Motor Skills, and Maladaptive Behavior. The Communication Domain asks the respondent to rate the child's expressive, receptive, and written communication skills; Daily Living rates the child's ability to execute important personal care and domestic duty tasks; Socialization rates the child's ability to relate to others, to play independently, to use free time, and to take responsibility and show sensitivity; Motor Skills rates the child's gross and fine motor development and coordination; and Maladaptive Behavior rates the presence of actions that may interfere with day-to-day functioning and interpersonal interaction.

At the time of this writing, the VABS is undergoing a much-needed revision; the test publishers anticipate that initial field testing will begin in 2001 but have no additional information as of early 2001. The VABS Manual and Kit may be obtained from American Guidance Service; *http://www.agsnet.com.*

Achievement Testing

Achievement tests are highly standardized and well-normed tests that are administered in a highly structured and well-prescribed manner. Their purpose is the assessment of a child's achievements in various academic or vocational skills that are a result of instruction or training. Most commonly, skills such as reading, comprehension, spelling, and mathematics are evaluated; however, literally hundreds of other specialized achievement tests exist to measure a child's accomplishment in a particular area of instruction (e.g., foreign language, science, logical thinking, geography, problem solving). Achievement test administration must be conducted by a well-trained examiner, as it has to be exactly identical from child to child. Only under such highly standardized, structured conditions can information be obtained in such a manner that a child's scores can be confidently compared to those of other children of the same age to make judgments about delayed or accelerated performance. Achievement tests are often administered when there are questions about the possibility of specific developmental disabilities, such as dyslexia. Further, their administration is warranted if a child has to participate in remedial instruction to evaluate the effectiveness of instruction (Anastasi, 1997). Achievement tests cannot provide information about personality or behavior, nor should they be misunderstood as evaluating a child's aptitude, such as for instance, intellectual functioning. Much controversy exists about the cultural fairness of these tests, and this must be considered when a child of an ethnic background other than white American is tested. Specifically, achievement tests are structured in such a way that they tap information and achievement that are most relevant in the dominant white culture, neglecting important aspects of minority cultures (see Sattler, 1992). A brief overview of some of the most commonly used achievement tests is provided here, with discussions of their purpose, psychometric properties, and special features and information about purchasing sources and restrictions.

Kaufman Test of Educational Achievement.   The Kaufman Test of Educational Achievement (K-TEA; Kaufman and Kaufman, 1985) is an achievement test for children aged 6 through 22 that is individually administered and takes approximately 20 to 60 minutes, depending upon the form that is used. Two versions of the K-TEA are available: a Comprehensive Form and a Brief Form. The Comprehensive Form yields norm-referenced scores on Reading, Spelling, and Mathematics, as well as separate scores for five subareas: Reading Decoding, Reading Comprehension, Mathematics Application, Mathematics Computation, and Spelling. The subtests are descriptively labeled and have excellent scoring criteria associated with them. For instance, spelling is not merely scored as correct or incorrect, as for instance on the WRAT-3, but rather is evaluated with regard to phonemic, morphemic, and syllabic components of each word. Thus, scoring takes into consideration not only error or actual performance, but also evaluates the process through which the child arrived at a given response (Kaufman and Kaufman, 1985). The Brief Form is used for quick screening and yields norm-referenced standard scores on Reading, Spelling, and Mathematics. It does not provide the in-depth analysis that is available through the use of the comprehensive version of the K-TEA.

Scoring results in standard scores for each subscale, as well as a composite score, all of which have a mean of 100 and a standard deviation of 15. Raw scores can also be converted into age and grade equivalents to investigate the child's relative grade placement or age performance. A normative update was conducted in 1998 and is included in the current manual. The K-TEA Manual and Kit are available to appropriately credentialed professionals from American Guidance Services; *http://www.agsnet.com.*

Peabody Individual Achievement Test—Revised/Normative Update. The Peabody Individual Achievement Test—Revised/Normative Update (PIAT-R/NU; Markwardt, 1989) is an individually administered scale for children enrolled in kindergarten to high school that requires approximately 60 minutes' time. It consists of six subscales which assess Reading Recognition, Reading Comprehension, Spelling, Mathematics, General Information, and Written Expression. Administration is facilitated by the use of an easel format and by the fact that three of the six subtests are arranged in multiple-choice format. Only the Reading Recognition task requires the child to read out loud, and the General Information task requires the child to give spoken answers, as opposed to pointing. Reading Recognition assesses the child's ability to use letters and read aloud; Reading Comprehension, the ability to make sense of what is read by the child; Spelling assesses the ability to identify letters of the alphabet and spell words; Mathematics assesses the ability to do simple computation, recognize numbers, and use simple geometry and trigonometry principles; General Information assesses the general fund of knowledge acquired by the child in areas such as arts, sports, science, and social studies; and Written Expression assesses written language skills for two levels: prewriting skills (grades K to 1) and ability to write a story (grades 2 to 12) (Markwardt, 1989). The PIAT-R/NU also provides a Written Language Composite (combining Spelling and Written Expression subtests) and a Total Reading score (Reading Recognition and Reading Comprehension subtests). A normative update was conducted in 1998 and is included in the current manual.

Administration of the PIAT renders grade equivalents, age equivalents, standard scores with a mean of 100 and a standard deviation of 15, and percentile ranks. Scores can be calculated for each of the five subtests, as well as for overall achievement performance. The PIAT-R/NU Manual and Kit are available to appropriately credentialed professionals from American Guidance Services; *http://www.agsnet.com*

Wechsler Individual Achievement Test, Second Edition. The Wechsler Individual Achievement Test, Second Edition (WIAT-II; Wechsler, 2001) is an individually administered test that assesses achievement of individuals aged 4 to 89 in nine areas: Word Reading, Pseudoword Decoding, Mathematics Reasoning, Spelling, Reading Comprehension, Numerical Operation, Listening Comprehension, Oral Language, and Written Expression. Word Reading assesses sight-reading ability; Pseudoword Decoding involves ability to decode words; Mathematics Reasoning evaluates problem-solving strategies and skills and includes items from geometry, measurement, and statistics; Spelling assesses encoding and spelling ability; Reading Comprehension measures skills that include comprehension of detail, sequence, cause-and-effect relationships, and inference; Numerical Operations assesses ability to write dictated numerals and solve basic addition, subtraction, multiplication, and division problems and problems with whole numbers, fractions, decimals, and algebraic equations; Listening Comprehension incorporates reception of sounds and words, as well as comprehension as demonstrated by understanding details to draw inferential conclusions; Oral Language gauges the ability to name targeted words, describe scenes, give directions, and explain steps in a sequential task; and Written Expression addresses idea development and organization, as well as writing mechanics. The scales also provide four composite scores for Mathematics, Reading, Language, and Writing. These scales meet the regulatory requirements of the Individuals with Disabilities Education Act

(IDEA) and can be useful for learning disabilities screening, special education placement, and curriculum planning. The items are structured in such a way that they provide information about not only test takers' achievement, but also their problem-solving strategies. The WIAT-II is directly linked with the WISC-II and WPSSI-R, allowing for more precise comparisons between achievement and ability scores when both instruments are administered. Such comparisons provide more in-depth analysis of the tested child, leading to more individualized treatment plans. Administration time is 30 to 60 minutes, depending upon the age and abilities of the child. Standard scores are derived (mean = 100, standard deviation = 15), and normative data are provided for fall, winter, and spring grades for more precise comparisons. The WIAT-II is available from the Psychological Corporation; *http://www.psychcorp.com.*

Wide Range Achievement Test—3. The Wide Range Achievement Test—3 (WRAT—3; Wilkinson, 1993) is a very popular achievement test because its administration time is brief and the procedure is relatively easy, especially considering that it is an individually administered instrument. Overall administration time is approximately 15 to 30 minutes. The test is considered most useful for quick screenings, as it renders only three subtest scores: Reading, Spelling, and Arithmetic. The Reading subtest assesses a child's ability to pronounce or recognize words and letters; the Spelling subtest focuses on the child's ability to write from dictation; the Arithmetic subtest evaluates the child's knowledge of simple counting and computation. None of the subtests provide detailed or sophisticated information about the examinee, and the use of the test appears inappropriate for clinical assessment beyond mere screening.

Items on the WRAT—3 are arranged in ascending order of difficulty. Scores obtained for each subscale can be expressed as stanines, normal curve equivalents, scaled scores, age equivalents, grade equivalents, percentiles, and standard scores. The latter four types of scores are most commonly used and interpreted. Age and grade equivalents indicate what chronological age or grade the examinee would be expected to be, based on the score that was obtained on a given subtest. Standard scores compare the child's performance to that of other children the same age and have a mean of 100 and a standard deviation of 15. Percentiles indicate how many percent of all children in that age range perform worse than the examinee.

Unlike the previous version of the WRAT, in which the test had two separate levels, one for younger children and one for older individuals, the current version consists of only one form that can be used with individuals aged 5 to 75. Two alternative forms of the WRAT—3 are available for instances in which multiple testing is needed. Results from these two forms can be combined to provide more detailed information about an individual's performance. The WRAT—3 Manual and Kit are available to psychologists and psychological associates from Psychological Assessment Resources; *http://www.parinc.com.*

Woodcock-Johnson Complete Battery. The Woodcock-Johnson Complete Battery (WJ-III; Woodcock, McGrew, and Mather, 2000) represents a revision of the commonly used Woodcock-Johnson Psycho-Educational Battery (Woodcock and Johnson, 1989) and consists of two co-normed but distinct tests: the WJ-III Tests of Achievement and the WJ-III

Tests of Cognitive Abilities. These tests are designed to evaluate an individual's general intellectual ability, specific cognitive abilities, scholastic aptitude, oral language, and academic achievement. The Complete Battery can be used with individuals aged 2 to 90, with administration time varying depending on the form used and the age of the individual; the average time is about 5 minutes for each subtest administered. The Tests of Cognitive Abilities consist of twenty-one subtests that assess the following eight cognitive abilities: Long-Term Retrieval (Memory for Names, Visual-Auditory Learning, Delayed Recall-Memory for Names, and Delayed Recall-Visual-Auditory Learning); Short-Term Memory (Memory for Sentences, Memory for Words, and Numbers Reversed); Processing Speed (Visual Matching and Cross Out); Auditory Processing (Incomplete Words, Sound Blending, and Sound Patterns); Visual Processing (Visual Closure, Picture Recognition, and Spatial Relations); Comprehension-Knowledge (Picture Vocabulary, Oral Vocabulary, Listening Comprehension, and Verbal Analogies); Fluid Reasoning (Analysis-Synthesis, Concept Formation, Spatial Relations, and Verbal Analogies); and Quantitative Ability (Calculation and Applied Problems). The Tests of Achievement consist of fourteen subtests that assess achievement within the four domains of Reading (Letter Word Identification, Passage Comprehension, Word Attack, and Reading Vocabulary), Mathematics (Calculation, Reasoning, Quantitative Concepts, Applied Problems), Written Language (Dictation, Writing Samples, Proofing, and Writing Fluency), and Knowledge (Science, Social Studies, and Humanities). The battery can be completed in two forms: standard or comprehensive. The standard form includes seven cognitive tests and eleven achievement tests; the comprehensive form includes administration of all subtests and yields more detailed information about strengths and weaknesses of the examinee. The Tests of Achievement have two alternative forms, allowing for repeated testing of the individual.

Cluster scores can be calculated on the basis of combinations of different subtests. For each cluster, standard scores with a mean of 100 and a standard deviation of 15 can be obtained and converted into percentile ranks. Grade-level scores are provided for the clusters, as well as for the individual subtest scores. In addition to inter-individual comparisons, intra-individual comparisons are available. For example, within the individual's achievement scores, comparisons are made to identify relative strengths and weaknesses. Further, the achievement subtests can be used in connection with the cognitive ability subtests to construct an ability-achievement profile that compares relative ability with actual achievement. The WJ-III is available from Riverside Publishing; *http://www.riverpub.com.*

Intelligence Testing

Intelligence tests are literally used for the purpose their name suggests: the evaluation of a child's intellectual performance. Originally, intelligence tests provided a global score of intelligence that did not assess or emphasize differential skills in various subcategories of intellectual functioning. In more recent decades, however, a more commonly accepted approach has been to differentiate at least verbal versus performance functioning. Intelligence as tested by these tools is supposedly an aptitude, not an achievement, and hence is independent of instruction or training. Intelligence can theoretically be measured before any instruction has taken place in a child's life (of course, there are some obvious practical limitations to this theoretical idea). They are often used as screening instruments before other aptitude or achievement tests are administered. They are also used to identify or classify mental retardation. They share many features of achievement tests. For instance, their administration is equally rigidly standardized and to be followed exactly, they are lengthy, there is a question about their culture fairness, and they are used in the assessment of learning disabilities. One of the most recent uses of intelligence tests is in the area of neuropsychological assessment (along with a number of other tests). Like achievement tests, IQ tests cannot be used to assess personality or behavior. There are only a few intelligence tests, and the most common ones will be outlined briefly, with a discussion of their psychometric properties and special features and information about purchasing sources and restrictions. It is important to note that the intelligence tests that are described here are those used with populations of children that have no physical or sensory handicaps. Nevertheless, a number of intelligence tests have been developed over the years for use with children who have physical disabilities; who are blind, mute, or similarly specially abled; and who have special needs or concerns (Sattler, 1992).

Kaufman Assessment Battery for Children.   The Kaufman Assessment Battery for Children (K-ABC; Kaufman and Kaufman, 1983) was developed as a response to traditional testing for intelligence and achievement for children aged 2½ to 12½. Up to this time, children whose intelligence and achievement needed to be assessed (as for instance is required for the assessment of learning disabilities) had to submit to two separate exams. The K-ABC was developed to provide this information on the basis of the administration of one assessment tool only. Thus, in addition to receiving intellectual assessment scores, the K-ABC provides achievement scores as well. The battery provides one overall IQ score, which is labeled the Mental Processing Composite. This overall score is derived from the scores obtained by the child on four scales, labeled Sequential Processing, Simultaneous Processing, Achievement, and Nonverbal Processing. These four scales are equivalent to the second-level processing of the SBIS—R, or the Verbal and Performance level processing of the Wechsler scales. Sequential Processing refers to the child's ability to solve problems when the component parts that lead to the solution are provided sequentially or in a series, as opposed to simultaneously. It assesses whether the child can process sequence information. Simultaneous Processing, logically, refers to the child's ability to solve problems where all component parts are given at the same time, such as in spatial or organizational problems. It assesses whether a child can process Gestalt information. Achievement refers to the child's performance on subtests that are strongly influenced by academic and other learning situations, such as factual knowledge and skills. Finally, Nonverbal Processing comprises all subtests that require no use of words, either on the examiner's or the child's part.

The three mental processing and the achievement scales are made up of a number of subtests each. There is a total of 16 subscales on the K-ABC, but only three of these are administered to children of all ages (Hand Movements, Gestalt Closure, and Faces and Places). Other tests have age cutoffs that result in the administration of no more than 13 subtests to any one child. The subtests contained in the Simultaneous Processing Scale are Magic Window, Face Recognition, Gestalt Closure, Triangles, Matrix Analogies, Spatial Memory, and Photo Series. The Sequential Processing Scale is derived from the subtests labeled Hand Movements, Number Recall, and Word Order. Achievement is assessed via subtests Expressive Vocabulary, Faces and Places, Arithmetic, Riddles, Reading/Decoding, and Reading/Understanding. Finally, the Nonverbal Processing Scale consists of all subtests administered as part of the other scales for which no words were necessary: Face Recognition, Hand Movements, Triangles, Matrix Analogies, Spatial Memory, and Photo Series.

All of the 16 K-ABC subscales have means of 10 and standard deviations of 3. The three mental processing scores and the achievement scale have means of 100 and standard deviations of 15. The Mental Composite, or IQ equivalent score, also has a mean of 100 and a standard deviation of 15. Administration is highly standardized but facilitated through a convenient easel format. Nevertheless, it requires thorough training and practice on the examiner's part. Not only do children not have to take all subtests, but they also do not have to take all items within each subtest, with entry points determined by chronological age or test performance on previous subtests. Ending points are determined by consecutive failures on preceding items. Administration of the achievement subtests allows for practice items, giving the child a chance to get used to and learn the task before actual scored performance begins. Instructions on the instrument are minimally verbal, thus proving to be an advantage for less verbal children.

Scores on the K-ABC provide a wide range of information. In addition to profile information as is obtained on the SBIS—R and the Wechsler scales, the K-ABC also provides achievement information that can be used for educational purposes. This makes the K-ABC particularly useful for assessment of learning-related difficulties. Further, scores on the three processing scales provide information about the child's preferences, as well as strengths and weaknesses with regard to the type of mental processing that is utilized in problem solving, again with educational implications. The overall Mental Composite renders an IQ equivalent that can be compared to the IQ scores obtained via the SBIS—R and the Wechsler scales. Finally, the overall achievement score allows for immediate comparison of intellectual functioning and actual educational achievement. The K-ABC Manual and Kit are sold to appropriately credentialed psychologists by the American Guidance Service; *http://www.agsnet.com.*

Kaufman Brief Intelligence Test. The Kaufman Brief Intelligence Test (K-BIT; Kaufman and Kaufman, 1990) serves as a brief screening instrument to obtain quick information about a child's intelligence and can be used with individuals aged 4 to 90. It takes 15 to 30 minutes to administer and provides measures of verbal and nonverbal intelligence. Verbal intelligence is measured through a Vocabulary subtest that contains both Expressive Vocabulary and Definitions; nonverbal intelligence is measured through the Matrices subtest, which consists of pictures and abstract designs. Similar to other recent intelligence tests, all items are contained on an easel. Results are provided in the familiar format of a mean of 100 and standard deviation of 15; percentile ranks are provided as well. Comparisons between verbal and nonverbal scores can provide the basis for further assessment for learning disabilities. As with other quick screening tools, this instrument can provide the basis for further assessment, can answer secondary questions, and can be used to verify previous test results. The K-BIT can be obtained from American Guidance Service; *http://www.agsnet.com.*

Peabody Picture Vocabulary Test, Third Edition. The Peabody Picture Vocabulary Test-III (PPVT—III; Dunn and Dunn, 1997) is a quick way to measure an individual's receptive vocabulary and to screen for verbal ability. It is normed for ages 2½ to 90, consists of 204 sets of four pictures, and takes approximately 10 minutes to administer. In administering the test, the child is shown four pictures while the tester says a single word; the child then indicates which picture best represents the word stated by the tester. Arranged on an easel, test administration is straightforward and easy. Two alternative forms are available for situations in which retesting is needed to assess changes or in which the child has previously taken the test. Standard scores (mean = 100; standard deviation = 15), NCEs, stanines, and age equivalents are available. The PPVT-III can be obtained from the American Guidance Service; *http://www.agsnet.com.*

Stanford Binet Intelligence Scale—Revised.   The Stanford Binet Intelligence Scale—Revised (SBIS—R; Thorndike, Hagan, and Sattler, 1986) represents the fourth edition of the original Binet Intelligence Scale, which was the first test of this nature ever to be developed and used in the history of intellectual assessment. The SBIS—R is appropriate for use with individuals from age 2 to adult, and its authors outline four purposes for its use (Thorndike, Hagan, and Sattler, 1986). First, the test is designed to help the clinician differentiate between actual mental retardation versus special learning disability. Second, it can be used to help the examiner understand a child's learning difficulties. Third, the instrument can be utilized to identify gifted students. Fourth, it can have usefulness in the area of research as it can assist in the study of cognitive development through the life span.

Conceptually, the SBIS—R is based on a three-level hierarchical model of intelligence. In this model, an overall Intelligence Quotient is obtained at the first level. This score supposedly measures *g,* or general ability, which comprises an individual's general cognitive makeup and cognitive complexity that is involved in problem solving. On the second level, the overall Intelligence Quotient is divided into crystallized ability, fluid-analytic ability, and short-term memory. Crystallized abilities are those that require quantitative and verbal reasoning processes that are impacted by external factors such as schooling, environmental conditions, and academic abilities. Fluid-analytic abilities, on the other hand, are those that are less influenced by general experience and are made up of nonverbal, flexible cognitive strategies that can be used for problem solving. All three second-level areas of functioning are assessed by a number of different subtests to which the child is subjected on administration of the test. These subtests represent the third level of the hierarchical model. Specifically, crystallized ability is measured through four subtests in the verbal reasoning area, namely, Vocabulary, Comprehension, Absurdities, and Verbal Relations, and via three subtests in the Quantitative reasoning areas, namely, Quantitative, Number Series, and Equation Building. Fluid-analytic ability is assessed via four subtests, namely, Pattern Analysis, Copying, Matrices, and Paper Folding and Cutting. Finally, short-term memory is assessed via four subtests, namely, Bead Memory, Memory for Sentences, Memory for Digits, and Memory for Objects.

Parallel to the three-level hierarchical model, three levels of scores can be obtained from the testing with the SBIS—R. For each subtest, a subtest score is derived which has a mean of 50 and a standard deviation of 8. These scores can be combined according to second-level membership as outlined above to make up the four area scores of Verbal Reasoning, Quantitative Reasoning, Abstract/Visual Reasoning, and Short-Term Memory. The four area scores have means of 100 and standard deviations of 16. Combined, they result in the Test Composite, which is equivalent to the overall IQ score and also has a mean of 100 and a standard deviation of 16. Given these three levels of scores, there are three levels of interpretation. At the third level, the child's strengths and weaknesses can be assessed based on differential subscale performance. Second, analyzing the second-level scores, the child's relative strengths in larger subareas of cognitive functioning can be assessed. At the highest level, an appreciation of the child's overall cognitive functioning is gleaned.

Testing with the SBIS—R is highly standardized and requires thorough training of the examiner. It follows a multistage testing model, in which performance on one of the subtests (namely, Vocabulary) is used to determine at which level to enter subsequent tests. Then, administration of subtests proceeds by establishing ceiling performance (i.e., determining a point within each test beyond which the subject can no longer correctly respond to subtest items) and then moving to the next subtest. This procedure of testing prevents frustration as it does not require children to move through all items of each subtest. Total testing time is approximately 60 to 90 minutes depending on the child's speed of work and cognitive performance.

The Stanford Binet Guide for Administering and Scoring and the Test Kit itself are distributed with strict restrictions (psychologists only) by Riverside Publishing; *http:// www.riverpub.com.*

Wechsler Abbreviated Scale of Intelligence.   The Weschsler Abbreviated Scale of Intelligence (WASI; Wechsler, 1999) provides a quick screening tool for estimating an individual's verbal and nonverbal intelligence and can be used with individuals aged 6 to 89. The WASI can be administered with either four subtests (Vocabulary, Similarities, Block Design, and Matrix Reasoning) or two subtests (Vocabulary and Matrix Reasoning). Taking approximately 30 minutes to administer, the four-subtest form yields Verbal, Performance, and Full Scale IQ scores in the same manner as the WISC-3 and WPPSI-R. The two-subtest form takes about 15 minutes and yields only a Full Scale IQ score. Although the content is different, the format of these subtests is the same as their counterparts in the other Wechsler scales. Indeed, the WASI can be used to estimate Full Scale IQ scores on the more comprehensive Wechsler Scales. Results are provided in standard score format analogous to other Wechsler scales (mean = 100, standard deviation = 15). The WASI can be obtained from the Psychological Corporation; *http://www.psychcorp.com.*

Wechsler Intelligence Scale for Children—Three.   The Wechsler Intelligence Scale for Children—Three (WISC—3; Wechsler, 1991) represents the second revised version (first revision in 1974; WISC—R; Wechsler, 1974) of the original WISC developed in 1949 as a downward extension for children ages 6 to 16 of the original Wechsler-Bellevue Intelligence Scale. The WISC—3 was developed to provide a more visually stimulating and pictorially realistic alternative to the WISC—R. Further, the revision resulted in updated language and removal of most sexist and racist biases. The WISC—3 is based on the concept of global intelligence defined by Wechsler as the overall capacity to cope with and understand the world. As such, the concept of intelligence assessed through the use of the WISC—3 is one of a multifaceted, multidetermined global entity, as opposed to one well-defined and unique trait (Wechsler, 1991). The scale is broken into two component scores: Verbal and Performance. These two areas of functioning are assessed as distinct categories because they are considered to represent the two primary modes of functioning through which human beings express themselves overtly. A total of thirteen subscales is used to assess a child's intelligence. Six fall within the domain of verbal skills, seven in the domain of performance skills. Specifically, Information, Similarities, Arithmetic, Vocabulary, Comprehension, and Digit Span are the verbal subtests; Picture Completion, Picture Arrangement, Block Design, Object Assembly, Coding, Symbol Search, and Mazes are the Performance subtests. Only ten of the thirteen scales are used to compute the overall Intelligence Quotient. (Digit Span, Symbol Search, and Mazes, while scored and administered, are not included in this calculation; Symbol Search may be substituted for Coding.)

Despite the development of the WISC—3 as an intelligence test with two subsets of subscales and one overall intelligence quotient, recent factor analyses have identified the existence of four, as opposed to two, subfactors. These four factors are now commonly accepted among clinicians and generally are reported along with the Verbal, Performance, and Intelligence Quotient derived from the WISC—3 (Wechsler, 1991). The first factor is labeled Verbal Comprehension and includes the Information, Similarities, Vocabulary, and Comprehension subtests. The second factor is labeled Perceptual Organization and includes the Picture Completion, Picture Arrangement, Block Design, and Object Assembly subtests. The third factor is labeled Freedom from Distractibility and includes the Arithmetic and Digit Span subtests. Finally, the fourth factor is labeled Processing Speed and includes the Coding and Symbol Search subtests. All four factors are self-explanatory with regard to the type of information and functioning that they tap in the child.

The information derived from the Wechsler scale is multifold. Most obvious is the overall interpretation of the child's Full Scale IQ that provides an estimate of the child's intellectual functioning as defined by Wechsler. Next, the child's performance can be divided into Verbal and Performance with information being derived not only about the child's skills in each area, but also about any discrepancies between these two subareas of intellectual functioning. Finally, inspection of the subtest scores results in a profile of strengths and weaknesses that the child's performance expressed. This profile analysis can be particularly helpful in assessing where the child evidences signs of problems in an academic or learning setting, versus where the child may be capable of adequate performance. If the factor scores are also calculated, additional information is derived about the child's ability to concentrate and pay attention by analyzing her or his Freedom from Distractibility score.

The WISC—3 is administered according to a strictly standardized procedure wherein all children receive all subtests. Entry level for each subtest is determined by the child's age. Ending of each subtest is determined by a cut-off criterion of a certain number of consecutively failed items. As in the SBIS—R, the testing procedure is such that administration of items clearly beyond the cognitive capacity of the child are not administered, thus minimizing stress levels for the child who is taking the test. Verbal and Performance subtests are alternated in the administration. Thus, frustration levels are minimized in children who may have particular difficulties in one of these two areas of cognitive functioning. Total testing time is approximately 60 to 90 minutes and can vary widely depending on the number of items administered within each subtest, and partially depending on the speed of the work.

Administration of the Wechsler scale results in scaled scores for each subtest, each of which has a mean of 10 and a standard deviation of 3. They are combined to result in two IQ scores, one a Verbal IQ, which is the composite of all verbal subtests (except Digit Span), and one a Performance IQ, which is a composite of all performance subtests (except

Symbol Search and Mazes). These IQs have a mean of 100 and a standard deviation of 15. They are combined into one overall IQ score that reflects the global intelligence concept as originally defined by Wechsler (1974) and is labeled the Full Scale IQ. This IQ has a mean of 100 and a standard deviation of 15. To assess functioning on the four research factors of Verbal Comprehension, Perceptual Organization, Freedom from Distractibility, and Processing Speed, subscale scores are added and converted to standard scores with a mean of 100 and a standard deviation of 15. The WISC—3 Manual and Test Kit are available to only psychologists from the Psychological Corporation; *http://www.psychcorp.com.*

Wechsler Preschool and Primary Scale of Intelligence—Revised. The Wechsler Preschool and Primary Scale of Intelligence—Revised (WPPSI—R; Wechsler, 1989) is the revision of the original scale that was developed by Wechsler in 1967 as a downward extension of the 1949 Wechsler Intelligence Scale for Children. It can be used with children aged 3 to 7. Its format is strikingly similar to the WISC—3. The two scales share the same conceptualization of intelligence, provide three types of IQ scores (Full Scale, Verbal, Performance), and share several of the twelve subtests that can be found on the WPPSI—R. Subscale means are 10 with standard deviations of 3, and IQ means are 100 with standard deviations of 15. The subtests on the WPPSI in the Verbal area are labeled Information, Vocabulary, Arithmetic, Similarities, Comprehension, and Sentences. Sentences is equivalent to Digit Span in the WISC—3. In the Performance area, the subtests are Object Assembly, Animal Pegs, Picture Completion, Mazes, Geometric Design, and Block Design. Interpretation follows the model of the WISC—3, with analysis of overall performance, Verbal and Performance skills, and strengths and weaknesses as demonstrated through scores obtained on the various subtests. The WPPSI—R was developed in such a way as to eliminate gender, ethnic, and socioeconomic biases presented by the original instrument. Further, it was revised to be easier to use and more aesthetically appealing to young children.

Testing procedure is standardized, requires thorough training on the examiner's part, and is highly similar to that of the WISC—3. Failure to abide by the standardized procedure makes scores less interpretable, as it is not clear how they compare to the scores obtained from children in the original sample who were tested under the standardized conditions. Total testing time is approximately 90 minutes. The WPPSI—R Manual and Test Kit are available only to psychologists from Psychological Corporation; *http://www. psychcorp.com.*

Objective Personality Assessment

Objective personality assessment tools are standardized tests that provide the clinician with information about a child's general level of functioning or about a specific subset of the individual's personality, such as mood, motivation, attitudes, self-concept, and so forth. Although individual items may be focused on some facets of the child's overt behavior, the instruments generally are not used to assess behavior per se. They are also not helpful in assessing ability or intelligence. Their primary purpose is to help the clinician understand the personality makeup of the child with regard to her or his emotional, motivational, attitudinal, and interpersonal styles and functioning. These tools are usually normed, and thus provide a means of comparing the child's scores to population scores so that the clinician can make a judgment about the child's personality traits as compared to other children her or his age. Administration of these tests varies, some relying on parental reports and others relying on the child's self-report. An excellent and thorough discussion and overview of child self-report measures is provided by LaGreca (1990). A brief overview of some of the most commonly used personality measures for children is provided here, with a discussion of each instrument's purpose, psychometric properties, and special features and information on purchasing sources and restrictions.

Beck Youth Inventories of Emotional and Social Impairment.   The Beck Youth Inventories of Emotional and Social Impairment (Beck, Beck, and Jolly, 2001) consist of five separate self-report inventories for use with children aged 7 to 14. The five measures are the Beck Depression Inventory for Youth, Beck Disruptive Behavior Inventory for Youth, and Beck Self-Concept Inventory for Youth. Each of the inventories consists of twenty statements about the respondent's thoughts, feelings, and behaviors and takes about 5 to 10 minutes to complete. The child taking the inventory answers how true each statement has been for her or him in the past two weeks. These scales are intended for screening of children for emotional and social difficulties and can be used for monitoring treatment outcome. For each of the five inventories, norms allow for comparisons with similarly aged children, and profiles can be developed to compare the child across all five affective domains to determine particular problem areas. The Beck Youth Inventories are available from Psychological Corporation; *http://www.psychcorp.com.*

Children's Personality Questionnaire.   The Children's Personality Questionnaire (CPQ; Porter and Cattell, 1985) was developed because of the need for a personality assessment tool that could be used for clinical purposes, developmental tracking purposes, and purposes of identification of problem children in the educational system. Its item selection was based on research data that provided the important measurable dimensions of personality that are now tapped by the questionnaire. Specifically, the test has fourteen factors, or source traits, and four second-order factors can also be scored as an optional additional source of information. The instrument is appropriate for children aged 8 to 13. It can be administered in groups of children or individually. Oral administration is possible for children with inadequate reading skills. The fourteen factors obtained through the child's self-report responses to the seventy items are described by the interpretation of their high and low scores, rather than having any one label. Factor A has a high-score definition called Reserved, and a low-score definition called Warm Hearted. Similarly, Factor B is defined by Dull versus Bright. Factor C is anchored by Affected by Feelings versus Emotionally Stable. Factor D is called Phlegmatic versus Excitable. Factor E is defined by Obedient versus Dominant. Factor F is named Sober versus Enthusiastic. Factor G is anchored by Expedient versus Conscientious. Factor H includes Shy versus Venturesome. Factor I is defined by Tough-Minded versus Tender-Minded. Factor J is called Zestful versus Circumspect. Factor N is named Forthright versus Shrewd. Factor O is named Self-Assured versus Guilt-Prone. Factor Q3 is defined as Undisciplined Self-Conflict versus Controlled. Factor Q4 is anchored by Relaxed versus Tense. The four second-order factors are called Extraversion, Anxiety, Tough Poise, and Independence. An excellent guide to interpretation of these dichotomies is provided in the CPQ Manual (Porter and Cattell, 1985).

All first-order factor scores are based on raw scores obtained from the two subsections of the questionnaire. They are entered onto a profile sheet, which in turn provides age-corrected Sten scores (a standardized score with a mean of 0 and a standard deviation of 1) and percentile ranks. Second-factor scores are obtained by combining specific first-order factor scores within each second-order factor in a prescribed manner (e.g., for Extraversion Factors A, E, F, and H are added, and Factor Q3 is subtracted to obtain a total score for this second-order factor). For these scores, Stens (standard scores with a mean of 5.5 and a standard deviation of 2.0) and percentile ranks can be obtained. Through the age-corrected Stens and percentile ranks, a child can be compared to other children her or his age on the first- and second-order factors. This procedure also enables the clinician to track a child's changing performance across time. The CPQ Manual and Kit can be ordered from the Institute for Personality and Ability Testing; *http://www.ipat.com.*

Personality Inventory for Children Family of Tests. The Personality Inventory for Children Family of Tests includes the namesake instrument, Personality Inventory for Children—2 (PIC-2; Lachar and Gruber, 2001); Personality Inventory for Youth (PIY; Lachar and Gruber, 1995); and the Student Behavior Survey (SBS; Lachar, Wingenfeld, Kline, and Gruber, 2000). Each of the three instruments is an independently designed and validated instrument that can be used separately or combined to provide a multisource assessment of a child. Specifically, a parent or other adult completes the PIC-2; the child completes the PIY; and a teacher or other adult completes the SBS on the basis of the child's school behavior.

The Personality Inventory for Children (PIC-2; Lachar & Gruber, 2001) is the first complete revision of the PIC, an instrument with a research history that stretches back more than 40 years and through two previous forms of the test (Wirt, Lachar, Klinedinst, and Seat, 1977; Lachar, 1982). It is appropriately completed by a parent or other adult who is thoroughly familiar with the child for children aged 5 to 18 years (or older if they are still secondary school students living at home). The PIC-2 provides a thorough assessment of a child's behavior, affect, and cognitive status, as well as the child's family climate.

Two formats exist for administration of the PIC-2, Standard Format or Behavioral Summary. The Standard Format is completed in about 40 minutes, includes 275 test items, and is scored for nine adjustment scales: Cognitive Impairment, Impulsivity and Distractibility, Delinquency, Family Dysfunction, Reality Distortion, Somatic Concern, Psychological Discomfort, Social Withdrawal, and Social Skill Deficits. Each adjustment scale consists of two or three nonoverlapping subscales that can be scored for more content specificity. This format also includes three response validity scales: Inconsistency, to verify accurate reading of, and response to, test items; Dissimulation, to assess the tendency to exaggerate or endorse extreme behavioral characteristics; and Defensiveness, to measure the tendency to ascribe perfection and to deny minor problems that even the parents of well-adjusted children will admit in their children. The PIC-2 Behavioral Summary is completed in about 15 minutes and includes the first ninety-six items of the longer format. The items selected for this format present content voiced in the present tense that describes conditions and behaviors that are often the focus of treatment and modification efforts. The Behavioral Summary short adjustment scales correspond to eight of the nine adjustment scales from the Standard Format (all except Cognitive Impairment). In addition, three longer composite scales are derived for more sensitive measurement of change, namely, Externalizing, Internalizing, and Social Adjustment, and there is a Total Score. Hand-scoring of both formats is conducted with scoring templates and profiles that convert raw scores to T-scores for interpretation. The Behavioral Summary can also be administered and scored with an AutoScore form that incorporates both the template and the T-score conversion information. Computer scoring and administration is also available for both formats.

The Personality Inventory for Youth (PIY; Lachar and Gruber, 1995) was designed to assess the emotional and behavioral adjustment of children and adolescents aged 9 to 18. Whereas the PIC is completed by an adult, the PIY is designed to be completed by the child. It consists of 270 items written approximately at a third-grade reading level to which responding children answer either true or false; it takes approximately 30 to 45 minutes to complete. The PIY provides scores on three validity scales and nine clinical scales. The validity scales measure inconsistent or random responding, faking bad, and defensiveness. The clinical scales measure Cognitive Impairment, Impulsivity and Distractibility, Delinquency, Family Dysfunction, Reality Distortion, Somatic Concern, Psychological Discomfort, Social Withdrawal, and Social Skill Deficits. Each of these clinical scales also has two or three nonoverlapping subscales, for a total of twenty-four subscales. Each subscale measures a more narrowly defined content dimension associated with the overall scale and thus provides more detailed information about the respondent. A screening short form is incorporated within the first eighty items. T-scores are calculated for each scale and subscale on the basis of gender norms but not age norms. For the clinical scales, T-scores of 60 and higher are interpreted, while more varied interpretation limits are provided for the subscales and scales of response validity.

The Student Behavior Survey (SBS; Lachar, Wingenfeld, Kline, and Gruber, 2000) is a brief, multidimensional assessment of student adjustment for use in the evaluation of children and adolescents from grades K through 12 (5 through 18 years of age). It consists of 102 statements rated on a 1 to 4 scale (Never, Seldom, Sometimes, and Usually), and it takes approximately 15 minutes to complete. The SBS provides fourteen scales: four scores assess a student's Academic Resources (Academic Performance, Academic Habits, Social Skills, and Parental Participation); seven others address Adjustment Problems (Health Concerns, Emotional Distress, Unusual Behavior, Social Problems, Verbal Aggression, Physical Aggression, and Behavior Problems); and the final three address Disruptive Behavior of clinical concern (Attention Deficit Hyperactivity, Oppositional Defiant, and Conduct Problems). Conventional, age- and gender-based T-scores are calculated, with T-scores of 60 and higher being interpreted and explicit interpretive language provided for the clinically significant T-score ranges on all scales. A carbon form test protocol provides all the materials needed to administer, score, and profile T-scores on the test. The Manuals and Kits for the PIC-2, PIY, and SBS can be obtained from Western Psychological Services; *http://www.wpspublish.com.*

Piers-Harris Children's Self-Concept Scale.

Piers-Harris Children's Self-Concept Scale.   The Piers-Harris Children's Self-Concept Scale (PHCSCS; Piers, 1984) was developed as a measure of children's self-esteem. It was originally designed to assess self-esteem as a unidimensional concept, that is, as a trait a child either did or did not possess, but then was recognized as having six subdomains of self-esteem. These domains are referred to as Physical Appearance and Attributes, Anxiety, Intellectual and School Status, Behavior, Happiness and Satisfaction, and Popularity. The 80-item scale is completed by the child herself or himself and is appropriate for children in fourth to twelfth grades with at least a third-grade reading level. The instrument can be administered to individuals or groups and is an excellent screening tool that can be used with an entire classroom.

Factor analytic studies have called into question the presence of six subscales but have confirmed three: Behavior, Intellectual Status, and Physical Appearance. Overall, the instrument receives heavy clinical use and has been recommended for this purpose over other self-concept measures such as the Coopersmith Self-Esteem Inventory (e.g., Hughes, 1984). The PHCSCS Manual and Kit can be obtained from Western Psychological Services; *http://www.wpspublish.com.*

Reynolds Child Depression Scale.   The Reynolds Child Depression Scale (RCDS; Reynolds, 1989) is a 30-item instrument that is used primarily to assess the level, or severity, of depression evidenced by a child. The scale can be used as a screening instrument in the classroom to identify children who may have depressive symptoms. The test can be self-administered by children with appropriate reading levels or can be orally administered. Group and individual administration is possible for children aged 8 to 12. The scale provides one overall score that can be compared to the normative data collected from the original sample to assess the presence or absence of clinical depression. Further, there are several items that are considered critical items, endorsement of which must be noted and taken seriously by the examiner as added evidence for a depressive process regardless of the overall score that was obtained. The RCDS Manual and Kit can be obtained from Psychological Assessment Resources; *http://www.parinc.com.*

Revised Children's Manifest Anxiety Scale.   The Revised Children's Manifest Anxiety Scale (RCMAS; Reynolds and Richmond, 1978) was developed to assess levels of anxiety in first- to twelfth-graders through self-report which can take place in group administration settings. Reading levels were successfully adapted to make self-report possible even for first-graders. The scale has thirty-seven items, nine of which are used merely to ascertain that the child did not lie in completing the questionnaire and did not attempt to answer the scale in a way that she or he considered socially desirable. Although one overall anxiety score can be obtained from the instrument, three subscale, or factor, scores are also calculated. These are labeled descriptively Physiological Anxiety, Worry/Oversensitivity, and Social Concerns/Concentration. The overall purpose of the instrument is the identification of scope, or severity, as well as type of anxiety in children who may or may not already be manifesting symptoms.

The Lie scale is pointed out as particularly helpful in assessing the usefulness of a child's scores, as it gives an indication of the willingness to respond truthfully. The RCMAS Manual and Kit can be obtained from Western Psychological Services; *http://www.wpspublish.com.*

Self Perception Profile for Children.   The Self Perception Profile for Children (SPPC; Harter, 1985) was developed to measure children's self-esteem, recognizing this trait as a multidimensional construct that has various components rather than reflecting one overall trait. Thus, the instrument emphasizes the assessment of a child's self-concept as situation specific. This approach has resulted in five subscales in addition to providing a global measure of self-worth. Specifically, the test taps self-esteem with regard to Scholastic Competence, Athletic Competence, Social Acceptance, Physical Appearance, and Behavioral Conduct. The 36-item instrument was designed for children aged 8 to 15 and is completed by the children themselves.

The instrument also has two additional versions for use with younger and older children. The version for younger children relies upon pictures as opposed to written materials and is called the Scale of Perceived Competence and Social Acceptance for Young Children (Harter and Pike, 1984). The adolescent version, the Self Perception Profile for Adolescents (Harter, 1988), is very similar to the child version but appears more sophisticated in language and is adapted to adolescent issues. Further, this version of the instrument contains three additional domains of self-worth. Administration is done in groups for the scales for the older children and adolescents but individually for the younger children. All three versions of the Self Perception Profiles, including manuals and materials, may be obtained from Susan Harter, Department of Psychology, University of Denver, Denver, Colorado, 80208; email: *sharter@du.edu.*

State-Trait Anxiety Inventory for Children.   The State-Trait Anxiety Inventory for Children (STAIC; Spielberger, 1973) was developed to assess anxiety feelings in children which are either situationally focused (state anxiety), or which are generally present in the child across situations (trait anxiety). The forty-item scale was designed for children enrolled in fifth or sixth grade but has been found appropriate for children as young as kindergarten age (Papay and Spielberger, 1986). It relies upon the child's self-report and can be group administered at higher grade levels, but must be individually administered at lower grade levels. The STAIC Manual and Kit can be obtained from Consulting Psychologists Press; *http://www.cpp-db.com.*

Projective Testing

Projective testing provides a global approach to the assessment of personality that emphasizes a composite picture of the child's personality, as opposed to being trait-focused as are objective personality assessment techniques (Anastasi, 1997). Projective testing situations are highly unstructured because of the hypothesis that the lack of structure will provide the child with the opportunity to project her or his own needs, affects, thought processes, conflicts, and characteristics onto the test situation. These features of the child's global personality will be reflected in her or his test performance so that the projective test is basically viewed as a screen upon which the child projects her or his salient personality characteristics. Projective tests require a highly trained examiner who is familiar with personality theory, as well as detailed scoring procedures and theories of interpretation. Test administration always has to involve the child herself or himself and is often quite lengthy. Projective instruments have wide clinical use despite the fact that reliability and validity data are often very dissatisfying or discrepant, depending upon the source. Projectives are extremely useful testing tools; however, they are also the most commonly abused psychological instruments. This is so because they appear easy to use to the layperson but actually involve a high level of experience and sophistication in scoring and interpretation. The sole use of projective tools is rarely warranted. Rather, projectives are best used in conjunction with other personality assessment procedures, behavior rating scales, and personal interviews. Although some clinicians hire psychological technicians to conduct the actual test administration, this is not recommended, owing to the wealth of information obtained through the actual testing interaction with the child. Many excellent books have been written about various projective assessment tools (e.g., Burns, 1987). A brief overview of some of the major projective tests is provided here, with a discussion of their purpose and special features and information about purchasing sources and restrictions.

Draw-A-Person Test.   The Draw-A-Person test (DAP; Goodenough, 1926) was originally developed as a quick screening measure of intelligence that did not require verbal interaction. However, upon repeated use, Goodenough noted that the picture drawn by the child often reflected important aspects of the child's personality style and functioning. Today, the DAP is used almost exclusively in the latter context and, in fact, is used very widely, being considered one of the top five projective instruments in use (Hammer, 1997; Handler, 1996). As the title implies, the DAP involves asking the child to draw a person. No more guidance beyond these instructions is provided, to ascertain that the drawing situation remains ambiguous and unstructured so that the child can embellish it according to personal interpretations, needs, and desires. It is believed that the artwork created through this process will reflect not only the child's overt approach and style, but also unconscious material such as intrapsychic conflict, psychological defense, interpersonal adjustment, and similar personality features.

These characteristics are assessed through exploration and interpretation of various components of the child's completed drawing. Specifically, the placement of the drawing on the page, its orthographic features (e.g., pencil pressure, shading), its elaborateness, and its completeness are analyzed and used for interpretation. Much research has been done in all four of these areas and has resulted in many commonly accepted hypotheses about the meaning of various features expressed in a drawing. This body of literature provides an important backdrop for interpretation and must be updated constantly as new findings and understandings emerge. Further, the validity of these general symbolisms and meanings still has to be corroborated for each individual child through other tests and information obtained about and from the individual. Several well-accepted features that can be confidently assessed through the use of the DAP are self-concept, self-identity, coping styles, affect, and presence of psychopathology (Rabin, 1974). The test is an excellent tool for reticent or shy children who cannot be easily approached verbally. It is often used as a starting point for discussions of conflicts and has utility in tracking treatment progress and outcome. Again, as with other projectives, care has to be taken to refer to a properly credentialed, trained, and experienced examiner. This warning is even more appropriate about the DAP, as this is the single most commonly abused tool in terms of being used by individuals without adequate training. No ordered materials are necessary for the administration of the DAP, as all that is required is a clean white sheet of 8½ by 11 inch paper.

Kinetic House-Tree-Person Drawing Test.   The Kinetic House-Tree-Person Drawing test (K-HTP; Burns, 1987) was developed to expand upon the DAP as used by clinicians today. Specifically, Burns developed this instrument to make the drawing technique that had found wide acceptance among mental health professionals through the DAP more amenable to additional interpretations that had to do with the child's or examinee's interactions with the environment, with other people, and with their own image of themselves. Thus, while the DAP is focused primarily on intrapsychic dimensions of personality, as discussed above, the K-HTP is more concerned about interpersonal dimensions (while also lending itself extremely well to intrapsychic interpretations). In being administered the K-HTP, a child is asked to draw a house, tree, and person in the same picture while introducing some activity or action into the drawing. Burns suggests that the artwork derived from these instructions lends itself not only to all interpretations that have been discussed here with regard to the DAP, but also to interpretations that have to do with the story line depicted in the picture, the type of action that is suggested, the placement of all objects on the page, and the relative distances of the objects from one another. Also, spontaneously introduced objects (e.g., a sun or clouds that are added to the picture though the instructions did not mention them) can be of symbolic and interactive value. The K-HTP represents a more dynamic assessment of the child's personality and considers more dimensions. However, it is a relatively new technique and therefore does not enjoy the research base that has been generated for other drawing techniques. Until more research is available on the topic, interpretation rendered from the K-HTP must be viewed with caution and within a wider context of information. Nevertheless, its conceptualization promises that this will become a major assessment tool for children.

An additional note is warranted about the fact that the K-HTP represents the merging of two other techniques that have found wide acceptance among clinicians, the House-Tree-Person Drawing Test (Buck and Hammer, 1969) and the Kinetic Family Drawing Test (Burns, 1982; Burns and Kaufman, 1970, 1972). The K-HTP combines these two established techniques in that it borrows the objects (house, tree, person) from one and the concept of introducing kinesthesis from the other. The merging of the two techniques allows the K-HTP to rely somewhat upon the research that has been accumulated for these assessment procedures to date, providing additional support for its use. No ordered materials are necessary for the administration of the K-HTP, as all that is required is a clean white sheet of 8½ by 11 inch paper.

Rorschach Inkblot Test.   The Rorschach Inkblot Test (Rorschach, 1942) is a personality assessment technique that consists of ten inkblots printed onto one cardboard card each. The cards are presented, one at a time, to the examinee with the very unstructured instructions to tell what she or he sees in each card. The task can be rendered to children as young as age 5, as well as to adults of any age. The inkblots that are still being utilized today were chosen from a large number of blots for their ability to differentiate various clinical groups. They were developed by Hermann Rorschach in 1921, and originally were conceived of as a measure of perception or imagination. However, Rorschach quickly recognized that his examinees varied greatly in their approach to the task of describing what they saw in the inkblots and began to explore the instrument as a psychological assessment tool of personality functioning. As such, the Rorschach is said to have utility in personality description, identification of type and severity of pathology, evaluation of coping ability, and general interpersonal and intrapsychic style.

In completing the Rorschach task, children are first asked to describe what they see in each card without any prompting. Once they have described their percepts for each ink-blot, they are asked to elaborate upon their original response, providing information about why they chose a particular percept, and defining its location and boundaries. Some clinicians, in an attempt for additional data collection, then ask the child to choose a favorite and a worst card. The information gleaned from this administration process is complex and very difficult to interpret. It cannot be understood by the layperson, but rather relies on a well-trained and experienced examiner. There are several ways of approaching the information, and four types of analyses are always included. These are called structural analyses, location analyses, content analyses, and sequence analyses. Norms have been developed for the first two approaches by various researchers and clinicians, including Rapaport, Klopfer, Beck, and Exner. Of these, Exner (1993, 1994) has been particularly successful in developing norms and standards for comparison across ages, genders, and diagnostic groupings that are now widely accepted and used by clinicians. All four types of analyses will be described here briefly.

In a sequence analysis the examiner explores the child's responses in terms of when they occurred and how one percept may have affected another. Thus, if a child had a very disturbing association to one area of a particular inkblot, the clinician may evaluate the next response with regard to how the child dealt with that disturbance—specifically whether the child is withdrawing, becoming aggressive, getting depressed, and so forth. An example of such a sequence follows:

A 7-year-old boy who was referred because of suspected abuse by an uncle who lived with the family, was presented with the father card of the Rorschach (Card IV). His immediate response was a frightened sigh, followed by this description: "This is the big bad monster that walks around in my dreams every night. He has a big tail and is very strong. He makes me scared and I do what he tells me." The child paused for a moment (10 sec.), and then said: "and this little thing over here looks like the neck of a duck, no a swan—a pretty little swan that is swimming to me on the water."

In addition to much other information that is contained in this response, the child's reaction from a sequence analysis perspective tells us that he is having difficulty with the negative image of the monster and undoes it by the positive image of the swan. However, even this undoing is not quite successful in that the child also is looking for some protection (the swan is swimming to *him*). This example demonstrates that sequencing of responses is an important component of Rorschach analysis.

Content analysis refers to the symbolism or latent meaning of the percepts, especially in the context of the specific inkblot for which it was rendered. Examiners' overgeneralizations and abuses abound in the area of content analysis (i.e., it must be done cautiously and with care not to let the clinician's own associations intrude). An example of an attempt to understand a child's response on the basis of the content of the percept follows:

A 5-year-old boy who was diagnosed with schizophrenia was presented with Card 3 of the Rorschach. He looked at the card for nearly a minute (a very long time, especially for such a young child) and then gave the following response: "There is a bone in the middle and it still has the blood on it. They ate it up." After that response, he rejected further exploration of the blot.

Content analysis of this response is influenced by our knowledge that people often see two human beings in this inkblot (children may see animals or humanlike figures). This child, however, not only avoided the areas of the blot that tend to resemble a person, but also chose a very dysphoric content that clearly expressed his depressive affect, as well as his withdrawal from human contact.

Location analysis refers to where in a blot a child sees something and whether the child has a well-balanced selection of responses that include either whole blots or parts of the blot. In the example of the 5-year-old boy, for instance, it was very interesting to note that he avoided those places of the card that are commonly associated with human content. Further, this particular child failed to see any whole-blot percepts in his entire protocol but always picked very small areas of each inkblot to which to respond. In this case, this tendency appeared quite reflective of his preoccupation with details in his day-to-day functioning—for instance, insisting on having his hair perfectly combed and his toys lined up in a very orderly manner in his room.

Finally, structural analysis of Rorschach responses involves the most complex process of interpretation. It first involves the use of an objective scoring system to which every single response rendered by the child is subjected. As such, each verbalization is scored with regard to certain characteristics that are projected onto the card by the child (e.g., use of color, movement, texture). Not only can the particular scores be interpreted, but they can also be combined to provide ratio scores that have been associated with various personality traits. For instance, a depression index has been developed that can be scored for each child and can then be compared to other children's norms to indicate level of depression for this examinee.

Clearly, the analysis and interpretation of a Rorschach protocol are very complex and easily abused. No mental health professionals should attempt to make interpretations without training, nor should they neglect their responsibility in making appropriate referrals. In other words, before referring a child for projective testing with the Rorschach, the clinician should investigate the credentials and training background of the referral source (Brems, 2000). After all, it will be the clinician who will utilize the report rendered by that examiner, and therefore she or he must be able to have confidence in the examiner's performance. The Rorschach Inkblot Test is available from Psychological Assessment Resources (*http://www.parinc.com*), one of the U.S. distributor of the cards that are manufactured in Switzerland. Sale is restricted to properly credentialed professionals.

Thematic Apperception Test, Children's Apperception Test-Animal, and Children's Apperception Test-Human.   The Thematic Apperception Test and its successors (TAT; Bellak, 1943; CAT-A; Bellak and Bellak, 1949; CAT-H; Bellak and Bellak, 1965) that were developed specifically with children in mind, was developed to assess personality style and to help with differential diagnosis. The TAT consists of a total of 31 cards depicting a variety of scenes that are thought to have differing stimulus values. Generally, clinicians choose a subset of ten cards, the stimulus values of which appear particularly relevant to the history and/or identified pathology of the examinee. The CAT-H and CAT-A consist of 10 cards each, which depict various family or interpersonal scenes that are considered relevant to children. They are identical in terms of picture and stimulus value, but the actual characters depicted in the drawings are humans in the CAT-H and animals in the CAT-A. The rationale behind this difference is that younger children are more likely to be able to respond to the animal cards, whereas older children relate better to human content. However, not all clinicians use either of the CAT versions with children, as subsets of the TAT are quite useful with young examinees. While the stimuli (i.e., the pictures on the cards) are very different across the TAT and the CAT versions, the basic administration and interpretation processes are identical, making a joint discussion of the three tests possible.

Administration of an apperception test requires the child to tell a story about each picture that she or he is shown. This story is supposed to include current happenings, antecedents, consequences, and thoughts and feelings of the story's characters. As with all projectives, the apperception test user assumes that the child will project unconscious material upon the card and that her or his responses will provide insight into personality functioning and style. Whereas the Rorschach, for instance, has formal scoring criteria and systems that have found wide acceptance and use, the apperception tests do not. Although attempts have been made at such systems (Bellak, 1997), they have not been widely adopted by clinicians. Instead, most clinicians use their own informal system to evaluate the stories that are provided by the children about the pictures (Dana, 1996). Interpretation generally focuses on manifest content, types of characters, thoughts and feelings that are expressed, conflict resolution and coping patterns, latent contents and symbolisms, interpersonal styles, intrapsychic conflicts, and similar issues. Themes, styles, and patterns that emerge across several stories are explored and given more credence than those that occur only once in an entire protocol. Because of the lack of accepted scoring criteria, the potential for abuse of the apperception tests is great. However, a very vast literature exists about these instruments that suggests their clinical utility, and they are generally identified as frequently used by clinicians (Dana, 1996). This reality makes careful consideration of the clinician to whom one refers children very important. As with referrals for Rorschach testing, care needs to be taken to ascertain that the examiner has training and experience in using the tool. Only then can faith be placed in the report that is subsequently issued about a child's performance. The TAT and CAT cards are available from a number of test publishers, including Psychological Corporation; *http://psychcorp.com*. Sale is restricted to properly credentialed professionals.

Neuropsychological Testing

Neuropsychological assessment is the youngest testing discipline in psychology. Its characteristic feature is the establishment of a relationship between brain functioning and behavior. Although Freud himself was extremely interested in this connection, it had received very little attention and study in the field of psychology until the last three decades. Only then did the discipline catch up with tendencies in the neurosciences and medicine, and now neuropsychology represents the primary link between these disciplines and psychology. Neuropsychological testing is perhaps the most sophisticated and well-standardized type of assessment in psychology today. It was well founded in research from its inception and continues to generate hard data. Neuropsychological testing is concerned primarily with the assessment of pathological, neurological, and brain processes and their effects on behavior and personality. It is not only a diagnostic discipline, but also a necessity to treatment planning and intervention. It assesses the cognitive, psychological, and behavioral strengths and deficits of individuals and relates them to brain functioning. Thus, this type of assessment requires great amounts of training not only in the traditional areas of clinical or counseling psychology, but also in the areas of neuroanatomy, neurochemistry, and neurophysiology. It requires the examiner to be extremely familiar with the standardized testing procedures of the various instruments and with the need to adapt the testing procedure appropriately to individual clients. Neuropsychology was developed originally with and for adult clients. However, child versions of most of the major instruments have now been developed. Further, neuropsychological testing always includes an intelligence scale (of which there are many specifically designed for children), and the use of the Bender Gestalt Visual Motor Test, a tool that was originally developed for children.

The most commonly used neuropsychological test instruments for children include the Halstead Reitan Neuropsychological Test Battery for Children (age 9 to 15) and the Reitan-Indiana Neuropsychological Test for Young Children (age 5 to 9). Both are modifications of the adult version of the battery and include child versions of the Category Test, the Tactile Performance Test, and the age-appropriate Wechsler Scale. In addition, the Halstead Reitan includes the Trail-Making Test and the Speech Sounds Perception Test, while the Reitan-Indiana includes the Aphasia Screening Test and the Sensory Perceptual Exam (all in age-appropriate modified versions). All of these materials were conceived of, developed, and/or organized by Ward Halstead (adult versions only), Ralph Reitan, and Charles Matthews. Materials can be obtained from Dr. Ralph Reitan, Department of Psychology, University of Arizona, Tucson, Arizona, or from Charles Matthews, Department of Neurology, University of Wisconsin, Madison, Wisconsin if the proper credentials can be demonstrated.

Neuropsychological testing is used to assess the child's level and pattern of performance, left-right differences, and pathognomic (signs of a disease process) neurological indicators. This information is then used to answer specific questions regarding a child's severity and type of dysfunction (lesion, tumor, trauma, etc.), type of pathological process (e.g., progressive), cognitive and behavioral strengths and deficits, day-to-day functioning, and implications for treatment and prognosis (Macciocchi and Barth, 1996). Given the extreme need for specialization of training, no specific neuropsychological tests will be discussed here. The reader is referred to primary references such as Lezak (1995).

Summary and Concluding Thoughts

This chapter has provided an overview of various procedures a mental health professional can utilize to expand upon the information gathered about a child in the intake report. Primary sources of previously gathered data include school records and teachers, as well as medical and other treatment records and corresponding professionals. Primary sources for creating new information are referrals to other professionals for consultation and specialized data gathering, as well as psychological testing. With regard to psychological testing, a wealth of data can be obtained from a variety of sources in a variety of contexts, ranging from mental status to behavior to personality, both general and specific, to achievement and intelligence, as well as neuropsychological processes.

7 Conceptualization and Treatment Planning

WITH MARK E. JOHNSON

Once the clinician arrives at the point at which a conceptualization and treatment plan must be formulated, much information has been gathered from the child and her or his family, environment, teachers, and other sources. This information must now be combined in such a way as to make sense of the symptoms with which the child and family are presenting. It is crucial to formulate a conceptualization and related treatment plan before proceeding with treatment. All the work with the child and the family up to this time has been considered assessment, though some therapeutic work may have been initiated on the sidelines of the interaction with the clients. All too often, clinicians proceed from the assessment phase to the therapy phase before clarifying in their mind a thorough conceptualization and a treatment plan that is determined by this understanding of the client. This failure to conceptualize and put on paper a treatment strategy results in treatment without direction, based strictly on trial and error, and only serves to perpetuate the problems in the child's life, in which the lack of direction or organization is often an integral part of the presenting problem. A thorough understanding of what is involved in conceptualization and treatment planning is therefore crucial to the success of the treatment. Only then can the clinician use all the tools that she or he has *effectively* without wasting her or his potential.

→ directive bias

Conceptualization

A conceptualization is the means of pulling together all of the information gathered about the child to make sense of what is happening to the client and the family. It involves reiteration of the problems that have been identified through the assessment phase, formulation of these problems into a diagnosis using DSM-IV, and understanding of the dynamics that have contributed to the development of the problem, as well as to its maintenance. Each of these components of a conceptualization will be discussed in detail.

Problem List

Although creating a problem list might appear unnecessary and redundant with the assessment of the presenting problems, this is not so. Often, as the assessment phase progresses, the clinician will make note of a number of problems that are not mentioned by the family as part of the reason for their presentation to treatment. Further, the problem list focuses the clinician's attention on all potential areas of impact in the child's life, rather than re-stricting the view merely to the psychological. As such, there are several problem areas that need to be addressed individually: psychological, medical/physiological, social, aca-demic, familial, and other problems. Although not all problems that the clinician has become aware of will be obviously related to the presenting problem, all should be listed.

Psychological Problems.   Psychological problems are those which involve the child's emotional, psychological, intrapsychic, and interpersonal adjustment. Emotional adjustment involves the child's affect and mood, including fears, moodiness, depression, and variability in affect. Psychological adjustment refers to the child's functioning with regard to pathology in perception, cognition, awareness, or development, including hallucinations, delusions, lapses in consciousness, delays in development, functional elimination difficulties, and so on. Intrapsychic adjustment refers to issues of self-perception, self-understanding, conflict with self, and life direction, including low self-esteem, lack of interests or hobbies, nightmares, obsessive handwashing, conflicted expression of affect, indecisiveness, and similar prob-lems. Interpersonal adjustment refers to problems that manifest in the context of relating to others, such as family and friends, including difficulties in peer relationships, fighting with parents, ambivalence about attachment and trust, or school anxiety.

Social Problems.   Social problems are those which refer to the child's social situation, hence are focused on environmental, socioeconomic, cultural, religious, and similar issues. Environmental problems may include issues such as inappropriate shelter or nourishment, whereas living in a deprived neighborhood represents an example of a socioeconomic issue. Clearly, the two are often directly and inextricably related. However, sometimes en-vironmental problems may not be as obvious. For instance, exposure to lead-based paint is an environmental issue that can have psychological implications but must not at all be tied to socioeconomic status. Cultural problems may include such issues as lack of appropriate role models of the child's culture in the mass media or the living environment or unfamil-iarity with the cultural context in which the child is educated or cared for, such as might be true for immigrant children. Religious problems may involve concerns such as school prayer, ostracizing because of religious affiliation, and forced church attendance by the family. Other social problems may include concerns over school curricula by parents.

Medical/Physiological Problems.   Medical or physiological problems obviously refer to the child's general level of health and accident proneness. Medical problems can vary from severe (e.g., frequent hospitalizations for a chronic illness) to mild (e.g., allergies). Regard-less of severity, they should be listed here. Developmental deficits and delays (although occa-sionally not physical or physiological in nature) are placed into this category, as are family history of mental or other illness. It is also wise to note obvious medical problems of other family members here because of their potential impact on the child. Neurological and neu-ropsychological problems can be listed here if they were formally assessed.

Academic Problems.   Academic problems refer to issues that emerge in the school set-ting, but primarily focus on actual academic performance, such as grades, changes in func-tioning, exceptional performance, learning disabilities, and so on. There may be some overlap with psychological problems, in that there may be some interpersonal problems, such as peer or teacher relationships that are confined to the academic setting. It is an arbitrary decision as to where to list these types of problems, as long as they are included somewhere.

Familial Problems.   Familial problems refer to conflicts that arise in the family setting. As with academic problems, there is some overlap with psychological problems. This category should be focused on a detailed description of the family problems, not merely a statement of conflict among family members. For instance, triangulation, crossing of generational boundaries, frequent fighting in the marital dyad, lack of trust, history of divorce, and similar issues are appropriate problems to include.

Other Problems.   Other problems simply refer to any other concerns the clinician has at this time that do not appear to fit in any other category or that are not very clearly defined. This category may also include speculations about problems that are suspected, but have not been substantiated. An example of such a problem may be the suspicion of child abuse in a case in which members of the family are denying the allegation. If the listed problem is merely a hypothesis, it must be identified as such.

In writing down all of these concerns and issues, it is best to literally make a list of problems within each of these areas, rather than trying to deal with them in the form of a narrative. To help put identified problems into a context of time and a time-referenced relationship to one another, it helps to note onset or nature in terms of chronicity or acuteness. As such, timing issues can be noted by indicating the number of weeks since a problem or behavior has been noted, by noting a problem or behavior as chronic if it has a long history and is still occurring, and by noting an issue as acute if the onset is recent and of particular importance or salience in the present. Problems that wax and wane should also be noted in some form, as should problems that occurred recently but are currently resolved. An example of a problem list contained in the conceptualization for a child who came to treatment after the divorce of her parents is presented in Table 7.1.

DSM-IV Diagnosis

Diagnosis is the second aspect of a thorough, all-inclusive conceptualization. Diagnosis is generally made based on the nosology provided by the Diagnostic and Statistical Manual of Mental Disorders (Fourth Edition; DSM-IV; American Psychiatric Association; 1994, 2000). This manual provides a symptomatology-based, checklist-type nosology that is used to classify problems in a manner that is as standardized, research-based, and objective as possible. It has become the most commonly accepted diagnostic system among mental health professionals, thus facilitating communication and identification. Further, DSM-IV coding is accepted by all insurance companies and Medicaid for third-party reimbursement purposes. A brief discussion of the DSM-IV multiaxial system is presented here, followed by some of the most commonly used Axis I and Axis II diagnoses available for children.

Multiaxial System.   The DSM-IV uses a multiaxial system of diagnosis that classifies problems along five dimensions, or axes, for purposes of ensuring that clinicians make the

TABLE 7.1   Problem List for a Child Presenting after Parental Divorce

Problem Area	Onset	Specific Problem
Psychological	20 wks	pervasive sadness and mood swings
	12 wks	weight loss and refusal to eat
	12 wks	frequent crying and complaining
	10 wks	decreased interest in play and hobby
	20 wks	decreased self-esteem
	10 wks	nightmares and initial insomnia
	1 year	refusal to sleep at friends' homes
	1 year	isolation from play with peers
Social	12 wks	decreased income in the primary home
	12 wks	move to new inner-city neighborhood
	8 yrs	conflicting religious values in father's (Asian American) and mother's (white) home
	12 wks	lack of Asian cultural role models
Medical/Physical	10 wks	frequent stomachaches (2x daily)
	chronic	maternal history of alcoholism
	10 wks	many recent accidents (burned hand, fell off bike, ran into a wall)
	20 wks	occasional nighttime bed-wetting
	1 year	delay in emotional development
Academic	20 wks	deterioration of grades (As to Cs)
	10 wks	difficulty concentrating
	1 year	withdrawal from schoolmates
	12 wks	pending school initiated assessment of developmental reading disorder
Familial	12 wks	parental divorce
	acute	continued custody battle
	chronic	different values in parental homes
	chronic	attempted triangulation
	chronic	overinvolved maternal grandmother
	10 wks	significant decrease in paternal contacts
Other	12 wks	suspected neglect in maternal home
	4 wks	recent death of only younger sister (severe abuse as possible cause)
	chronic	suspected substance abuse by mother
	10 wks	possible suicidal ideation (e.g., accident proneness)

broadest assessment possible of each client. The five dimensions represent evaluation along the lines of clinical syndromes (Axis I), personality disorders and mental retardation (Axis II), physical disorders (Axis III), psychosocial stressors (Axis IV), and overall level of functioning (Axis V). Once the problem list has been prepared, diagnosis of the child and her or his family using the DSM-IV axis system should be relatively easy, as diagnosis with the DSM-IV is symptom driven and structured somewhat like a checklist, and the problem list provides all the information necessary to make diagnostic decisions. Nevertheless, very thorough familiarity with the manual (American Psychiatric Association, 2000) and related resources (Reid, 1997; Spitzer, Gibbon, Skodol, Williams, and First, 1994) is required for its successful and responsible use. In fact, formal classroom training in its use is preferable to mere studying of the manual and related books (Morrison and Anders, 1999).

Axis I—Clinical Syndromes.   Axis I of the DSM-IV is focused on the identification of major mental disorders such as depression, anxiety, and schizophrenia that generally have periods of florid symptomatology and do not necessarily begin in childhood nor necessarily continue in stable form across the life span. More likely, these disorders have later onsets and fluctuations in the severity of their symptoms across time. This fluctuation is not to be mistaken as the absence of chronicity. It merely indicates that although the disorder itself may be chronic, its actual manifestation through obvious symptoms may wax and wane. Despite this definition of Axis I disorders, there is one category of mental illnesses (Disorders Usually First Evident in Infancy, Childhood, or Adolescence) that is coded on this axis that has its onset during the developmental period of life. Further, even disorders in the other categories may begin early in life. As will be evident, the definition of Axis I disorder is written in such a manner as to accommodate its differentiation from Axis II. It is possible for a child to warrant more than one diagnosis on Axis I. For instance, it is common to have a pairing of Adjustment Disorder with Mixed Anxiety and Depressed Mood and Enuresis. Finally, sometimes a child may meet most of the criteria necessary for a given diagnosis, but does not fulfill all. It is then possible to note this diagnosis as a "Rule Out" category, implying that this diagnosis is a possibility but that more information must be gathered before it can be established for certain.

Axis II—Personality Disorder and Mental Retardation.   In contrast to Axis I disorders, Axis II disorders always have to have their onset during the developmental period of life (birth to age 18). They are always called either Personality Disorders or Mental Retardation, are considered chronic, and their symptoms are stable. The fluctuations in symptomatology that are characteristic of Axis I disorders are not present in Axis II disorders. The Axis I versus Axis II differentiation was made by the authors of the DSM-IV to ascertain that clinicians will never be satisfied looking only at the most florid, or obvious, symptomatology, but will also look at less obvious but more stable and chronic symptomatology of long-term disorders that have their onset in childhood. It is not uncommon to have diagnoses on Axis I and Axis II for the same individual. If this is the case, the clinician is urged to make a judgment with regard to which diagnosis is the primary one or is seen as chiefly responsible for the referral of the client. This diagnosis is then labeled clearly as Principal Diagnosis. Finally, as is true for Axis I, more than one diagnosis can be made on Axis II, and a "Rule Out" category can be provided.

Axis III—Physical Disorders.   Axis III allows for the formal coding of any physical condition or disorder that is seen as relevant to the diagnoses on Axis I and/or Axis II. In other words, the physical condition is relevant either etiologically or in terms of its impact on the person's mental health. Sometimes the condition is a result of the mental disorder, and sometimes it is only loosely or potentially associated. Technically, Axis III *diagnosis* is only in the purview of physicians; however, all clinicians have the responsibility to note already identified disorders or symptoms on this axis. Obviously, whenever there is a notation on Axis III, there must have been some involvement of a physician in the assessment phase of a case (either through study of previous treatment records or through referral).

Axis IV—Psychosocial and Environmental Problems.   Axis IV requires notation regarding the presence of psychosocial or environmental problems in a client's life that may affect the etiology, diagnosis, prognosis, or treatment of disorders noted on Axes I or II. The manual provides a listing of psychosocial problem categories that need to be attended to for each client. These categories are as follows: problems with a primary support group (e.g., death of a parent, parental divorce), problems related to the social environment (e.g., stigmatization of a child because of cultural differences, social isolation), educational problems (e.g., academic performance difficulties, problems with a teacher), occupational problems (e.g., unemployment of a parent), housing problems (e.g., a child living in a shelter, homelessness), economic problems (e.g., poverty), problems with access to health care services (e.g., lack of health insurance, lack of transportation), and problems related to interaction with the legal system/crime (e.g., victim of a crime, incarcerated parent). Each category is best assessed for the absence or presence of a problem; multiple problems may be present and all should be listed on Axis IV. Problems noted on Axis IV are often contributory either to the development, maintenance, or recurrence of a disorder. Occasionally, however, they may actually be the consequence of a disorder; for instance, enuresis may lead to a disturbance of peer relationships, resulting in social isolation.

Axis V—Global Assessment of Functioning.   Ratings on this axis are accomplished via the Global Assessment of Functioning Scale (GAF), which ranges from 0 to 100 and indicates a child's overall level of functioning, considering social, academic, and psychological aspects of the client's life. A rating of zero is used only for inadequate information; in other words, it is equivalent to the absence of a functionality rating. The higher the GAF index, the better a child's functioning. For example, a rating of 90 indicates minimal symptoms of a disorder and good functioning in all three areas mentioned above; a rating of 100 refers to exceptional functioning. A rating of 1, on the other hand, indicates extremely severe pathology with persistent danger of suicide, severe disruption in communication, or gross inability to care for oneself. Examples of ratings are provided in the manual (American Psychiatric Association, 1994, 2000). Ratings are made by using a four-step process that leads the clinician to the most objective evaluation possible of a child's functioning. Step 1 involves reviewing all ranges from functioning from the top down; Step 2 directs the clinician to identify the range of functioning most indicative of the client's symptoms or level of functioning, whichever is worse; Step 3 involves a process of double-checking the correctness of the chosen range; Step 4 helps the clinician to choose a specific index in the chosen range of functioning.

An example of a DSM-IV diagnosis is provided in Table 7.2, for the same child whose problem list was presented in Table 7.1. This example shows the usefulness of the careful preparation of the problem list in making a DSM-IV diagnosis. The example in

TABLE 7.2   DSM-IV Diagnosis for a Child Presenting after Parental Divorce

Diagnosis	Symptoms Present
Axis I:	
296.22 Major Depression, Single Episode, Moderate	depressed mood for more than 1 week decreased interest in activities weight loss (failure to make expected weight gains) loss of energy insomnia difficulty concentrating
307.60 Enuresis, nocturnal only	nighttime bed-wetting frequency of ~2/week
309.0 Rule Out Adjustment Disorder with Depressed Mood	stressor within 3 months (divorce) impairment in academic functioning R/O: above and beyond what would be expected for the circumstances
Axis II:	
315.0 Rule Out Reading Disorder	reading level is markedly below expected level (standardized test is pending) academic achievement is affected
Axis III:	
No formal diagnosis	physical was completed and ruled out physical causes for bed-wetting and headaches
Axis IV:	
Chronic parental arguments Recent parental divorce Sister's death	
Axis V:	
Current Functioning—45	moderate impairment in school and social functioning, severe impairment in psychological functioning
Highest Level of Functioning in Past Year—80	only slight impairment in all areas

Table 7.2 goes somewhat beyond the information that would be included in a child's actual conceptualization, in that for purposes of demonstration, the actual symptoms that matched the DSM-IV checklist used for diagnosis, are provided ("Symptoms Present"). This reiteration of symptoms would not be necessary in the actual case because of its redundancy with the problem list.

Once the clinician is familiar with the DSM-IV diagnostic system, actual differential diagnosis must be made. This process can be aided by the use of decision trees provided in the DSM-IV manual (American Psychiatric Association, 1994, 2000). However, thorough familiarity with the individual disorders is crucial. Here, the most common disorders that are relevant to the work with children are presented briefly.

The first nine broad categories—Mental Retardation, Attention-Deficit and Disruptive Behavior Disorders, Learning Disorders, Motor Skills Disorders, Communication Disorders, Pervasive Developmental Disorders, Feeding and Eating Disorders of Infancy or Childhood, Tic Disorders, Elimination Disorders, and Other Disorders of Infancy, Childhood, or Adolescence—are all Disorders Usually First Diagnosed in Infancy, Childhood, or Adolescence. The last few—Schizophrenia and other Psychotic Disorders, Mood Disorders, Anxiety Disorders, Sexual and Gender Identity Disorders, Sleep Disorders, Adjustment Disorders, and Other Conditions That May Be a Focus of Clinical Attention—can have their onset at any time during a person's life.

This presentation can in no way be substituted for the use of the actual manual! It focuses merely on listing symptoms within each category, and makes no attempt at providing etiological or prevalence data. The reader is referred to child psychopathology books such as Mash and Barkley (1996, 1998), Ollendick and Hersen (1997), Wicks-Nelson and Israel (1999), and Netherton, Holmes, and Walker (1999) for this type of information.

Mental Retardation.   Mental Retardation is characterized by significantly subaverage levels of intellectual functioning, significant deficits in adaptive behavior skills, and onset of symptoms before age 18 (Jacobson and Mulick, 1996). There are several levels of severity, which are determined by the level of impairment in cognitive functioning as determined by the intelligence quotient (IQ) obtained on a standardized intelligence test (Handen, 1998). Levels range from mild (IQ of 50–55 to 70) to moderate (35–40 to 50–55) to severe (20–25 to 35–40) to profound (below 20–25). Unlike all of the other diagnoses noted in this chapter, the diagnosis of Mental Retardation is coded on Axis II.

Attention-Deficit and Disruptive Behavior Disorders.   This class of disorders is well described by Barkley (1997; 1998) and consists of three major diagnostic categories: namely Attention-Deficit Hyperactivity Disorder, Oppositional Defiant Disorder, and Conduct Disorders. These diagnoses "comprise a spectrum of disruptive behaviors that exist along the dual continua of age and severity" (Morrison and Anders, 1999, p. 214). Attention-Deficit/Hyperactivity Disorder is diagnosed when for at least six months, a child evidences either six distinct symptoms of inattention (e.g., is easily distracted, does not follow through on instructions, has difficulty sustaining attention, is forgetful, has difficulty organizing activities) or at least six symptoms of hyperactivity-impulsivity (e.g., fidgets with hands or feet, talks excessively, acts as if "driven by a motor," blurts out answers, interrupts others). Three types of this disorder are differentiated: If only the inattention symptoms are present, Predominately Inattentive Type; if only the hyperactive-impulsive symptoms are present, Predominately Hyperactive-Impulsive Type; if both sets of symptoms are present, Combined Type. Oppositional Defiant Disorder is characterized by at least four distinct symptoms of negativity, hostility, and defiance that are above and beyond what might be expected given a child's age, such as argumentativeness, externalization of blame, loss of temper, vindictiveness, annoying or bratty behavior, and so on. Finally, Conduct Disorders are characterized by at least three distinct symptoms that indicate lack of respect for others' rights and for social norms or rules in a number of settings. Such symptoms include stealing, fire-setting, lying, truancy, cruelty to animals or people, physical fighting with or without weapons, destruction of property, and other even more severe behaviors. Conduct Disorders can be differentiated according to whether the behavior first occurs before 10 years of age (Childhood-Onset Type) or after age 10 (Adolescent-Onset Type).

Learning Disorders.   Learning Disorders are characterized by a child's performance on a standardized achievement test that is substantially below what would be expected given her or his age, education, and intellectual level (Rothstein, Benjamin, Crosby, and Eisenstadt, 1999). The primary subcategories of Learning Disorders are Reading Disorder, Mathematics Disorder, and Disorder of Written Expression, and each requires specific diagnosis and management (Whitmore, Willems, and Hart, 2000).

Motor Skills Disorders.   The only diagnosis in this category is Developmental Coordination Disorder (Elbert, 1999). This diagnosis is given when a child evidences marked impairment in the development of motor coordination, such as dropping things, delays in achieving motor milestones (such as walking, crawling, sitting), and clumsiness. To diagnose this disorder, impairment must interfere with daily life and not be due to a physiological disorder.

Communication Disorders.   This class of disorders consists of four major diagnostic categories: Expressive Language Disorder, Mixed Receptive-Expressive Language Disorder, Phonological Disorder, and Stuttering. All of the disorders interfere with the child's ability to communicate with others (Richman and Wood, 1999). Expressive Language Disorder is indicated when scores on standardized tests of expressive language are considerably lower than both nonverbal intellectual capacity and receptive language. The disorder can manifest as limited vocabulary, errors in tense, or difficulty in producing sentences with developmentally appropriate complexity. Another criterion for this diagnosis is that these problems interfere with the child's academic or social life. In Mixed Receptive-Expressive Language Disorder, the child must have lower test scores on both receptive and expressive language when compared to nonverbal intellectual ability. In addition to symptoms of Expressive Language Disorder, the child has difficulties in understanding words. Phonological Disorder involves difficulties in using developmentally appropriate speech sounds. In Stuttering, the fluency of speech is affected, resulting in elongation or repetition of sounds or syllables.

Pervasive Developmental Disorders.   The primary diagnoses within this category are Autistic Disorder, Rett's Disorder, Childhood Disintegrative Disorder, and Asperger's Disorder. All of these disorders are marked by "severe and pervasive impairment in several areas of development: reciprocal social interaction skills, communication skills, or the presence of stereotyped behaviors, interests, and activities" (American Psychiatric Association, 2000, p. 69). Autistic Disorder is characterized by impairment in social interaction, verbal and nonverbal communication, and repetitive and stereotyped patterns of behavior and activities.

Impairment of social interactions may manifest in the form of lack of empathy for or awareness of others' feelings, inability to form relationships with other children or adult caretakers, absence of comfort-seeking behavior even in situations of clear distress, absence or
impairment of nonverbal cues used in social interactions, lack of social play, or lack of spontaneous seeking out of others. Communication impairment may manifest through delay in or
lack of spoken language, inability to sustain conversations, lack of imaginative play activity,
unusual usage of speech (e.g., echolalia), and similar disturbances. Finally, restriction of behavioral repertoire may manifest as stereotypy, distress over minor environmental changes,
insistence on precise routines, and preoccupation with parts of objects. Autistic Disorder is
very poorly understood and is perhaps the most profound of the developmental disorders
(Cohen and Volkmar, 1997). In Rett's Disorder, following an apparently normal first five
months of development, a marked change in physical and behavioral development begins to
manifest. This change includes a deceleration of head growth, loss of hand skills previously
demonstrated, loss of social interests, loss of coordination, and severely impaired expressive
and receptive language development. Onset of this disorder occurs prior to 4 years of age and
usually in the first or second year of life. Childhood Disintegrative Disorder is marked by
substantial regression in several areas of functioning after a period of at least two years of
normal development. Such regression must occur in at least two areas of language, social
skills, bowel or bladder control, play, or motor skills, resulting in significant impairments in
at least two areas of social interaction, communication, and repetitive or stereotyped patterns
of behaviors and activities. Finally, Asperger's Disorder is characterized by significantly impaired social interaction and some demonstration of repetitive and stereotyped behaviors
(Klin, Volkmar, and Sparrow, 2000). In contrast to Autistic Disorder, these problems manifest in the absence of significantly delayed cognitive and language development. Further, in
Autistic Disorder, the repetitive and stereotyped behavior and activities are varied and usually involve motor mannerisms; in Asperger's Disorder, repetitive and stereotyped behavior
usually centers on a "topic to which the individual devotes inordinate amounts of time
amassing information and facts" (American Psychiatric Association, 2000, p. 82).

Feeding and Eating Disorders of Infancy or Early Childhood.   This class of disorders consists of three major diagnostic categories: Pica, Rumination Disorder, and Feeding
Disorder of Infancy or Early Childhood (Kedesdy and Budd, 1998). All three are marked
by "persistent feeding and eating disturbances in eating behavior" (American Psychiatric
Association, 2000, p. 103). Pica is marked by the eating of substances that are not considered food, such as soil, paint, and cigarette butts. Pica is not uncommonly associated with
Mental Retardation. In Rumination Disorder, the child regurgitates and rechews food without associated nausea or stomach upset, a process that can result in weight loss or failure to
gain weight. Feeding Disorder of Infancy or Early Childhood is characterized by a persistent failure to eat adequately, resulting in either weight loss or the failure to gain developmentally appropriate weight. This disorder is diagnosed when such problems exist in the
absence of a physiological reason.

    In the DSM-III-R (American Psychiatric Association, 1987), Anorexia Nervosa and
Bulimia Nervosa were categorized as disorders usually first diagnosed in infancy, child-
hood, or adolescence and included with the previously noted feeding and eating disorders.
In the DSM-IV, these two eating disorders form a category of their own and are no longer

listed as disorders first diagnosed in childhood. Anorexia Nervosa is defined as weight loss or failure to gain weight that results in at least 15 percent underweight, along with a refusal to eat for fear of being fat. It is generally accompanied by a distorted body image and, in adolescent (or adult) females, by the absence of at least three menstrual cycles. Bulimia Nervosa is a similarly self-destructive disorder that manifests as episodes of binge-eating, during which the person feels an utter loss of control over her or his eating behavior. Bingeing is followed by behaviors designed to prevent weight gain, such as purging, using laxatives, vigorous exercising, or fasting. As in Anorexia Nervosa, there is great concern over body shape and weight. Both diagnoses are unlikely to occur in children, instead usually first manifesting in adolescence; however, child clinicians need to be aware of them nevertheless as they can be present among children as well.

Tic Disorders. This class of disorders consists of three major diagnostic categories: Tourette's Disorder, Chronic Motor or Vocal Tic Disorder, and Transient Tic Disorder. All three are marked by rapid, stereotyped, and recurrent motor movements or vocalizations that are not under the child's voluntary control (Kurlan, 1993). In Tourette's Disorder, these tics involve multiple motor and one or more vocal movements that occur several times per day. Symptoms are identical in Chronic Motor or Vocal Tic Disorder, except that there is either a motor or a vocal tic (never both). In a Transient Tic Disorder, multiple motor and/or vocal tics occur nearly every day; however, the disorder is time-limited to 12 months, at which time it either becomes a Tourette's Disorder or disappears.

Elimination Disorders. This class of disorders consists of two major diagnostic categories, namely, Enuresis and Encopresis [also well described by Christophersen and Purvis, 2001; Luxem and Christophersen, 1999; Schaefer, 1998a]. Both are marked by the child accidentally or purposefully not maintaining control over either bladder or sphincter. Two types of these disorders have been described: Primary, in which the child has never established continence, and Secondary, in which the disorder manifests after a period of continence. In enuresis, urine is voided in an inappropriate place at least twice per week after age 5. In assigning this diagnosis, Enuresis is further coded as Nocturnal Only, Diurnal Only, or Nocturnal and Diurnal. In Encopresis, feces are passed at inappropriate places at least once a month for at least three months after age 4. Functionality always has to be ascertained by a physician and should never be assumed even if the child at one time had complete bladder or bowel control.

Other Disorders of Infancy, Childhood, or Adolescence. Four other disorders that usually first manifest in Childhood or Adolescence are Separation Anxiety Disorder, Selective Mutism, Reactive Attachment Disorder of Infancy or Early Childhood, and Stereotypic Movement Disorder. These disorders do not share any specific traits or symptoms other than their childhood onset. Separation Anxiety is characterized by at least three distinct symptoms of anxiety about being separated from a major attachment figure, such as refusal to go to school, distress upon separation, refusal to go to sleep alone, worries about harm befalling the attachment figure, or fear of being kidnapped or otherwise separated from the person (Bowlby, 1999). For this diagnosis to be made, the duration of the disturbance must be at least four weeks and must cause significant impairment in the child's life. Selective Mutism manifests as a child's refusal to talk in some or all social situations despite the ability to use and comprehend language (Kronenberger and Meyer, 2001). Reactive Attachment Disorder is primarily characterized by disturbances in a child's social relationships that manifest either as failure to initiate social interaction or as inappropriate sociability, in the absence of other severe disorders that might explain this behavior (e.g., mental retardation). It is accompanied by pathogenic care, which may be evidenced as a complete disregard for the child's basic emotional or physical needs by the caretaker or as repeated changes in caretakers that serve to hinder stable attachment (Levy and Orlans, 1998). Finally, Stereotypic Movement Disorder is diagnosed in the presence of intentional, repetitive, and nonfunctional behavior that interferes with normal activities or results in injury to the child. Such behaviors include body rocking, headbanging, self-biting, hand-waving, and so forth, and are not accounted for by other diagnoses (such as Obsessive-Compulsive Disorder or a Tic Disorder).

In addition to the previous nine categories of disorders that are usually first evidenced in childhood, other diagnostic categories of which a child clinician must be aware include Schizophrenia and other Psychotic Disorders, Mood Disorders, Anxiety Disorders, Sexual and Gender Identity Disorders, Sleep Disorders, Adjustment Disorders, and Other Conditions That May Be a Focus of Clinical Attention. These categories include disorders that can have their onset at any time during a person's life, making it possible for a child clinician to encounter them in the practice with children.

Schizophrenia and Other Psychotic Disorders.   Although disorders in this category are most likely to manifest for first time in early adulthood, some occasionally begin during adolescence or (even more rarely) during childhood. The disorders in this category that are most likely to be evidenced in childhood are Schizophrenia, Schizophreniform Disorder, Schizoaffective Disorder, and Shared Psychotic Disorder. Additional disorders in this category that manifest almost exclusively in adulthood, and thus are not reviewed here, are Delusional Disorder and Brief Psychotic Disorder (Volkmar, 1996). Schizophrenia is characterized by a marked decrease in functioning over a minimum period of six months, along with psychotic symptoms such as delusions or hallucinations, incoherence or loose association, catatonia, or inappropriate affect. Schizophrenia is subdivided into more specific manifestations based on specific symptoms evidenced by the individual (e.g., Paranoid Type, Disorganized Type, Catatonic Type, Undifferentiated Type, Residual Type). In Schizophreniform Disorder, the child meets the criteria for Schizophrenia, but the disorder has not necessarily resulted in severe impairment in life functioning and has occurred for less than six months. Schizoaffective Disorder is marked by the presence of a mood disorder (i.e., Major Depressive Episode, Manic Episode, or Mixed Episode) in conjunction with psychotic symptoms, such as delusions or hallucinations, incoherence or loose association, catatonia, or inappropriate affect, as well as the presence of delusions or hallucinations in the absence of the mood symptoms. Shared Psychotic Disorder (also called Folie a Deux) is characterized by the development of a delusion similar in content to the delusion held by someone to whom the child is close. The diagnosis of psychosis in childhood must be made cautiously because of the many stigmas and negative connotations attached to the label. Nevertheless, they exist and must be identified as such when they are present to ascertain correct treatment.

Mood Disorders. The primary disorders in this category are organized into Depressive Disorders (Major Depressive Disorder and Dysthymic Disorder) and Bipolar Disorders (Bipolar I Disorder, Bipolar II Disorder, and Cyclothymic Disorder). All are marked by a disturbance in the child's mood, such as either depression, irritability, or elation (see Kazdin and Marciano, 1998). Major Depressive Disorder involves a constellation of symptoms that are commonly associated with depression, including depressed mood, irritability, diminished interest in previously rewarding activities, insomnia or hypersomnia, fatigue, lack of concentration, significant weight loss or gain, suicidal ideation, and so on. These symptoms represent a change in level of functioning for the child and are present for at least two weeks. Dysthymic Disorder can be considered a milder version of Major Depressive Disorder in that the child manifests depressed mood or irritability with symptoms of poor appetite or overeating, insomnia or hypersomnia, fatigue, poor concentration, and feelings of hopelessness. The difference is that with Major Depressive Disorder, there are discrete episodes of severe depression that represent a change from previous functioning, whereas with Dysthymic Disorder, there is an ongoing presence of less severe symptomatology with few, if any, breaks from the depressed symptoms.

Bipolar disorders, marked by mood swings cycling from depression to elation (or mania), primarily manifest for the first time in late adolescence and early adulthood (American Academy of Child and Adolescent Psychiatry, 1997). The exception to this general rule of age of onset is Cyclothymic Disorder, which may occur among children. Cyclothymic Disorder is characterized by mild depression or irritability that takes turns with mildly elevated mood for at least one year (two years if the client is an adult) without major interruptions. In other words, the child's mood is rarely at a normal level, but rather cycles through symptoms of mild depression versus mild elation (hypomania). Full-blown manic episodes, required for the diagnosis of Bipolar Disorder I, are rare among children.

Anxiety Disorders. Included in this broad diagnostic category are Specific Phobia, Social Phobia, Obsessive-Compulsive Disorder, Posttraumatic Stress Disorder, Acute Stress Disorder, and Generalized Anxiety Disorder. Other diagnoses in this category, generally only applicable to adolescents and adults and therefore not discussed here, include Panic Attack, Agoraphobia, and Substance-Induced Anxiety Disorder. Specific Phobia (formerly called Simple Phobia) is characterized by a persistent fear of an identifiable object or situation and a manifestation of anxiety in its presence (Barrios and O'Dell, 1998). Subtypes of this diagnosis are Animal Type, Natural Environment Type, Blood-Injection-Injury Type, Situational Type, and Other Type. In diagnosing specific phobias in children, care must be taken not to confuse a diagnosable phobia with a normal age-appropriate and transient phobia. In Social Phobia, the child experiences a persistent fear of a social or performance situation in which the child fears that she or he will act in an embarrassing manner. This fear leads to an avoidance of the situation and results in significant interference with the child's life. If the fears include most social situations, the disorder is further specified as Generalized. Obsessive-Compulsive Disorder is diagnosed in the presence of obsessions or compulsions that interfere with the child's life (Francis and Gragg, 1996). Obsessions are recurrent and persistent thoughts, impulses, or images that cause anxiety and are not simple worries about real problems and which the child recognizes are within her or his own mind and attempts to ignore or suppress. Compulsions are repetitive behaviors that the child feels driven to perform and that are intended to prevent or reduce distress or prevent a negative event to occur. Posttraumatic Stress Disorder and Acute Stress Disorder are both reactions to traumatic events, in which the person was confronted with actual or threatened death or serious injury and to which the person responded with intense fear, helplessness, or horror. Both disorders involve the re-experience of the traumatic event through dreams, recollections, flashbacks, or similar occurrences; persistent avoidance of stimuli associated with the event; and anxiety symptoms, such as poor concentration, irritability, hypervigilance, and motor restlessness. Acute Stress Disorder is diagnosed when the symptoms occur within one month of the traumatic event, whereas Posttraumatic Stress Syndrome is diagnosed when symptoms persist for more than one month. Finally, Generalized Anxiety Disorder (which incorporates what was previously referred to as Overanxious Disorder) is characterized by at least three distinct symptoms of excessive and unrealistic worrying, such as irritability, muscle tension, sleep disturbance, difficulty concentrating, easy fatigue, and restlessness (March, 1995). Such anxiety must have occurred for at least six months, caused significant interference in the child's life, and is not confined to features of another disorder.

Sexual and Gender Identity Disorders.   Most of the diagnoses in this category are only applicable to adolescents or adults; the exception is Gender Identity Disorder in Children (Zucker and Bradley, 1999). To be diagnosed with this disorder, the child must demonstrate both a strong cross-gender identification and discomfort over her or his assigned sex. Cross-gender identification is marked by the desire to be, or insistence that she or he is, the other sex, preference for wearing stereotypical clothing of the other sex, preference for taking the role of the other sex in make-believe play, desire to participate in stereotypical activities of the other sex, and preference for playmates of the other sex. Discomfort over assigned sex is demonstrated in a boy through expressed disgust toward his genitalia, rejection of stereotypical male activities, and aversion to rough-and-tumble play; in a girl, it is demonstrated through the assertion that she will grow a penis, rejection of urinating in a sitting position, stating that she does not want to grow breasts or to menstruate, and aversion to stereotypical feminine clothing.

Sleep Disorders.   Sleep disorders are organized into the four categories of Primary Sleep Disorder, Sleep Disorder Related to Another Mental Disorder, Sleep Disorder Due to a General Medical Disorder, and Substance-Induced Sleep Disorder (Schaefer, 1995). The category that is most applicable for children and therefore is reviewed in this chapter is that of Primary Sleep Disorders. Primary Sleep Disorders are broken down into Dyssomnias (marked by disturbances in quality, quantity or timing of sleep) and Parasomnias (marked by abnormal events occurring in association with sleep). Dyssomnias can manifest as Primary Insomnia, Primary Hypersomnia, Narcolepsy, Breathing-Related Sleep Disorder, and Circadian Rhythm Sleep Disorder. Primary Insomnia is characterized by difficulty initiating or maintaining sleep, which in turn causes difficulties in life functioning, lasts for at least one month, and is not related to another mental or physical disorder. In Primary Hypersomnia, the child exhibits excessive sleepiness for at least one month, experiences impairment in life functioning due to this sleepiness, and has no other mental or physical disorder that explains the disorder. Narcolepsy involves attacks of sleep that refresh the child but are invariably followed by renewed sleepiness after a brief period of time. Additionally, the child evidences either cataplexy (brief loss of muscle tone, often in association with intense emotion) or recurrent rapid-eye-movement sleep during the transition between sleep and wakefulness, which can result in hypnagogic hallucinations or sleep paralysis. Breathing-Related Sleep Disorder refers to sleep disruptions caused by difficulties or abnormalities in breathing, resulting in excessive sleepiness during the day or insomnia during the night. Circadian Rhythm Sleep Disorder manifests as excessive sleeping and insomnia that results from a repeated disruption in sleep patterns due to a mismatch in the child's sleeping schedule and her or his circadian sleep pattern. Four types of this disorder are coded: Delayed Sleep Phase Type, Jet Lag Type, Shift Work Type, and Unspecified Type.

The category of Parasomnias includes Nightmare Disorder, Sleep Terror Disorder, and Sleepwalking Disorder. In Nightmare Disorder, the child experiences repeated awakenings with detailed memory of very frightening dreams. Upon awakening, the child becomes rapidly alert. The dreams cause significant impairment in the child's life functioning and are not associated with another mental or physiological disorder. Similarly, Sleep Terror Disorder involves recurrent awakenings from sleep. However, in this disorder, the child awakens with intense fear and arousal, has difficulty getting oriented, and cannot recall the dream. Finally, Sleepwalking Disorder involves the child getting up while asleep and walking about. During the sleepwalking episode, the child has a blank and staring face, is difficult to awaken, and is unresponsive to others; upon awakening, the child has no recollection of the event.

Adjustment Disorders. This class of disorders consists of numerous diagnostic manifestations of the same disorder that are not unique to children: Adjustment Disorders with various emotional and/or behavioral features (Overstreet, Nelson, and Holden, 1999). Adjustment Disorders always involve a major known stressor that has occurred in the child's life within the past three months and must be noted on Axis IV (e.g., a parental divorce). The child evidences a maladaptive pattern of affect or behavior in response to this stressor that goes above and beyond any reaction that would normally be expected. Although this maladaptive reaction involves more than one overreaction, it never lasts longer than six months beyond the moment when the stressor ends. If the stressor has been eliminated but symptoms persist after six months, another diagnosis must be given; on the other hand, if the stressor persists, symptoms may persist, and the diagnosis of adjustment disorder remains appropriate. The type of impairment that characterizes the maladaptive response defines the type of Adjustment Disorder that is diagnosed. Notably, there are Adjustment Disorders With Depressed Mood, With Anxiety, With Mixed Anxiety and Depressed Mood, With Disturbance of Conduct, With Mixed Disturbance of Emotions and Conduct.

Other Conditions That May Be a Focus of Clinical Attention. The DSM-IV includes a number of other disorders that may be relevant to the child clinician. These diagnoses are problems, not mental disorders, though they may coexist with a diagnosable mental disorder; however, the problems are sufficiently severe in and of themselves to require intervention. Many of these are called *V codes* because the diagnostic number starts with a V. Parenthetically, this is important to note because insurance companies often do not reimburse for V code diagnoses. Briefly, some of the diagnoses within this broad category are as follows: Relational Problems (including Parent-Child Relational Problem and Sibling Relational Problem); Problems Related to Abuse or Neglect (including Physical Abuse of a Child, Sexual Abuse of a Child, and Neglect of a Child); and Additional Conditions That May Be a Focus of Clinical Attention (including Child or Adolescent Antisocial Behavior, Borderline Intellectual Functioning, Bereavement, Academic Problem, Identity Problem, and Acculturation Problem).

Although only those categories of disorders as outlined in the DSM-IV that appear most relevant to the work with children are covered here, others exist and can manifest in children. They are discussed in detail elsewhere (e.g., Mash and Barkley, 1998; Ollendick and Hersen, 1997), and the reader is referred to these references for more information. Thus, before attempting to diagnose a child, the mental health professional must familiarize herself or himself more thoroughly with this manual (Morrison and Anders, 1999; Rapoport and Ismond, 1996).

Case Dynamics

Once the problem list has been prepared and is used to aid in the diagnostic process, the clinician must attempt to understand why these problems, or symptoms, exist. This attempt at understanding the etiology of the child's disorder is crucial to treatment planning and involves taking a look at several components or factors surrounding the child and her or his family. Specifically, the mental health professional needs to explore the possibility of factors in the child's environment that may have predisposed her or him to the development of symptoms. Precipitants for the current symptoms as well as for the timing of presentation to the clinic need to be explored. Further, the clinician must look at the environment to assess what is perpetuating the symptom. These factors, in combination with observed conflicts in the child, as well as the family, will give the clinician a sense of direction for the child's treatment, as well as a sense of understanding and empathy for the development of the disorder (Brems, 1999).

Predisposing Factors. A variety of factors predisposing children to mental illness or emotional conflicts have been identified over the years. They have been explored in general, as well as related to particular disorders. Although some generalizations can be made (for instance, the genetic predisposition for mental retardation), it is also important to assess the particular predisposing factors that appear to function in a child's life who is presenting for treatment. Predisposing factors can be societal, environmental, social, familial, personal, biological, and genetic. For each area, the clinician must look at the possibility of influences on the child's mental health and current presenting problems. Often such factors are quite obvious, but rarely can all be assessed accurately. A comprehensive listing of all possibilities will ascertain that no possible component that has contributed to the child's psychological development and adjustment is missed. Rarely will one of these factors alone account for the symptoms that are presented at intake.

Societal Factors. Societal factors can include issues such as Zeitgeist and moral attitudes, prejudice, ostracism of certain population subgroupings, or media-induced societal values. Eating disorders can be said to have a strong societal predisposing component because of the strong focus on certain body types as acceptable in our society. As such, even children as young as 10 or 11 years of age are aware of the strong societal preference for slim, muscular bodies. In an attempt to conform to such body typing, children may fall into unhealthy eating habits or patterns (Gordon, 2000). Adolescent suicide behavior among Alaska Native children may have a strong societal predisposing factor, as the Native culture currently is nearly devoid of heroes or role models from within the children's own culture. This absence of positive role models or ideals leaves children wonting for self-esteem and a sense of life direction, resulting in depression and hopelessness that not uncommonly culminates in suicide (Sullivan and Brems, 1997).

Environmental Factors.   Environmental factors can range from issues such as moving to a new neighborhood or a new school to surviving a traumatic environmental event such as an earthquake or a tornado. Absence of stimulation in the environment, such as might occur in an institutional setting, can be a grave environmental factor that may predispose children for maladjustments of numerous types, including depression, selective mutism, or pervasive developmental disorders (Americn Psychiatric Association, 1994, 2000). Separation anxiety is thought to have an environmental predisposing component, as children who are affected by this disorder often have a history of loss, such as death of a friend, moving to a new neighborhood, or similar experiences (Bowlby, 1999). Adjustment disorders by definition have a strong environmental predisposing component, in which the child is responding very strongly to an environmental stressor. Finally, environmental factors are crucial to the development of posttraumatic stress disorder, in which a major environmental stressor is a required part of the diagnostic picture of the disorder (Putnam, 1996).

Social Factors.   Social factors are often closely related to environmental issues. They include malnutrition, neglect, influences due to a child's living situation (such as growing up in a rural versus inner-urban area), socioeconomic status, acculturation problems, stress levels in their daily living situation, and similar influences. These social concerns are considered important predisposing factors in the development of disorders such as drug or substance abuse (Reinherz, Giaconia, Paradis, Wasserman, and Hauf, 2000), even in children. Further, aggressive behavior disorders and juvenile delinquency are correlated with socioeconomic status, suggesting a potential predisposing link between this social factor and subsequent pathology (Brems, 1995, 2000). Malnutrition may be involved in pica behaviors, as well as being related to developmental disorders. The possibility of these factors as important influences on a child's behavior or affects should never be underestimated.

Familial Factors.   Familial factors include issues such as parental divorce or discord, parental inconsistency in parenting, birth order of siblings, intergenerational conflicts, emotional absence of one parent, abuse of the child by a family member, mental illness of a parent, and other family processes. Obviously, these factors can have a variety of effects on a child, ranging from phobic reactions (Ollendick and Hersen, 1997) to depression (Beckham and Leber, 1995; Brems, 1995), to conduct disorders (Kazdin, 1990), to reactive attachment disorders (Levy and Orlans, 1998, American Psychiatric Association, 1994, 2000).

Personal Factors.   Personal factors are often difficult to differentiate from familial patterns, but may include such unique factors as temperament (Seifer, 2000). They may account for the particular style a child evidences in adapting to a situation or stressor; thus, they may be involved in the development of an adjustment disorder. They may also consist of relatively stable personality patterns that are potentially related to the development of personality disorders (Brems, 1999).

Biological Factors.   Biological factors include a variety of possibilities, such as neurological deficits, biochemical disturbances, handicaps of various types (e.g, physical, sensory), a range of severe or chronic illnesses (e.g., temporal lobe epilepsy, encephalitis), psychoactive substance use or abuse by the mother during pregnancy (e.g., alcohol, caffeine, sleeping pills), and frequent illness or allergies. Fetal alcohol syndrome is considered a primary predisposing factor of a number of behavioral disorders in children, including but not limited to mental retardation, attention-deficit hyperactivity disorder, and learning disabilities (Autti-Raemoe, 2000). A large number of childhood disorders may have other biological predisposing components, including stereotypic movement disorder (American Psychiatric Association, 1994, 2000), autism (e.g., Cohen and Volkmar, 1997), attention-deficit hyperactivity disorder (Ollendick and Hersen, 1997), mental retardation (e.g., Jacobson and Mulick, 1996), and depression (Birmaher et al., 1996). Genetic factors have been found similarly important and may play a role in schizophrenia (McKenna, Gordon, and Rapoport, 1994), mood disorders (Speier, Sherak, Hersch, and Cantwell, 1995) and others. They are best traced through family histories of mental illnesses and psychological disturbances.

Predisposing factors are not noted to determine a definite cause of the child's problems, but rather to obtain a better overview of all the possible components of the child's life that may have contributed to the development of the current symptoms. It is not yet possible to trace definite causes for specific disorders, only high correlations or indications are known at this time. Nevertheless, the possibility of predisposing factors must be considered and noted for each child who presents for treatment.

Precipitating Factors.   Similarly important are precipitating factors. These are factors that triggered either the child's symptoms or the presentation of the family to treatment. Thus, sometimes precipitants may be as simple as a big family fight that made everyone aware that the family needs to seek help to deal with their problems. Sometimes, the precipitant is the complaint of a teacher about a child's behavior. Perhaps the parents had not even noted the child's particular behavior until it was pointed out as problematic by another adult. Precipitants are often most helpful in understanding why a family presents for treatment when they do, especially when it appears that a problem has existed for quite some time. However, sometimes the precipitant is responsible not only for triggering the referral of the family, but also for the manifestation of a particular symptom. Thus, certain factors may be precipitants as well as predisposers. For instance, the sudden divorce of two parents may result in extreme withdrawal behavior in the child. It is likely that although the divorce precipitated the child's symptoms, chronic parental conflict may have predisposed her or him for the development of such symptoms.

Reinforcing Factors.   Just as the mental health professional considers what might have predisposed a child for the development of a mental illness or behavior disturbance and what may have precipitated a symptom, so does she or he need to look at why the symptom is maintained. Not uncommonly, the symptom serves a purpose that perpetuates its display. For instance, if somatic concerns such as frequent headaches in a child distract from parental fighting, the symptom may be maintained because it is less painful for the child than its alternative. Similarly, although enuresis may keep the child from being able to participate in sleepovers, this may be a small price to pay for the reward, which might be nightly attention that helps the child deal with separation anxiety. Perhaps the development of night terrors has convinced a single parent to allow the child to share the same bed. Many more examples are possible. Thus, a symptom, although being reported as uncomfortable or even painful, may have a larger purpose that can be described as secondary gain derived from the disorder. The clinician needs to assess what potential rewards may be inherent in a symptom to evaluate the possible reinforcing factors that maintain it. This provides information with regard to understanding the problem and has implications for treatment planning.

Exploration of reinforcing factors must not be mistaken as an attempt to blame the child for her or his symptoms or as the belief that the child is aware of the reinforcing nature of the symptoms. Secondary gain is generally an unconscious process, and there is hardly ever purposeful (or conscious) production of symptoms on a child's part. Further, not all reinforcing, or maintaining, factors are of a secondary gain nature. Sometimes, the failure of a parent to recognize the impact of her or his own behavior on the child may maintain a problem that would not be as severe if the parent were to change her or his behavior. For instance, use of inappropriate parenting strategies may result in the escalation of a child's acting out or may result in the inadvertent rewarding of misbehavior. An excellent example is that of a father who chooses to buy a tantruming child a treat at the grocery store to get the child to stop screaming. His inappropriate choice or timing of intervention has reinforced the child's misbehavior and has made it more likely to recur in the future.

Examples of predisposing, precipitating, and reinforcing factors are presented in Table 7.3, using the same child who was presented in Tables 7.1 and 7.2. Once the various factors that may have contributed to the development and maintenance of a presenting problem have been explored, this information needs to be combined with all other aspects of this case to arrive at a thorough understanding of the child with regard to her or his intrapsychic dynamics, family dynamics, and interpersonal matrix dynamics. Defenses that are used must be reiterated and understood in the context of the child's intrapsychic adjustment, familial context, and interpersonal matrix. This integration of materials represents the heart of the child's case conceptualization and should be done thoroughly and with care. Often, it is only this section of the conceptualization (in addition to the diagnosis) that is included in the child's intake report.

Intrapsychic Dynamics. Not all clinicians will emphasize the same contents, nor perhaps this entire aspect of a conceptualization, in the same manner. Of all parts of the case conceptualization, it is perhaps this one that will most strongly reflect the mental health professional's primary theoretical approach to the work with children, and therefore may vary greatly depending upon the use of psychoanalytic, psychodynamic, person-centered, cognitive-behavioral, or other systems of psychotherapy. However, all therapies take a look at the individual child and her or his personal adjustment (though behaviorally oriented therapists may take offense to the label "intrapsychic"), making this an integral part of the

TABLE 7.3   Predisposing, Precipitating, and Reinforcing Factors in the Case of a Child Presenting after Parental Divorce

Factor Type	Specific Example
Predisposing Factors	■ chronic parental fighting that often involved the children ■ history of substance abuse by mother and suspected current abuse ■ cultural differences in parental and extended family backgrounds ■ conflicts around religious practices between parents ■ intrusive maternal grandmother (fails to respect child's privacy) ■ possible abuse (physical and emotional) ■ physical and psychological neglect ■ inconsistent discipline and unpredictability of consequences of behavior ■ psychologically unavailable mother who is incapable of adequate mirroring ■ psychological strain on child who had to take a parental role with the younger sister ■ absence of cultural belongingness because of maternal refusal to allow child to participate in father's religious rituals and cultural beliefs
Precipitating Factors	■ sister's death ■ parental divorce ■ decrease in frequency of contact with father ■ move to new neighborhood ■ custody battle
Reinforcing Factors	■ maternal attention for stomachaches and nightmares ■ paternal attention for accidents (he has medical benefits, thus is called when child needs medical attention) ■ avoidance of visits to maternal grandparents' home due to enuresis ■ attention and intervention at school for deteriorating performance ■ temporary "cease-fire" between parents after accidents and other symptoms ■ maternal discipline that tends to reward acting out behavior

formulation of a case. Whether conceptual work focuses on interpreting belief systems, values, interests, behavioral patterns, development, reinforcement histories, or other facets of the child's psychological being is determined by the theoretical approach of the clinician. The common themes, however, always center on the attempt to gain an understanding of the child from her or his unique personal perspective and an appreciation for how the child has dealt with and adjusted to her or his living situation. For example, behaviorists will look at the child's reinforcement or learning history, assessing how the child has learned various behaviors or symptoms and how well the child is coping. Cognitive-behaviorists will emphasize aspects such as distorted thought patterns exhibited by the child, irrational beliefs she or he endorses, and automatic thoughts that affect the child's moods. Developmental theorists will assess the developmental phase of the child, and the developmental tasks and challenges faced by her or him. Psychodynamic theorists, on the other hand, will assess the child's ego strength, developmental stage, conflicts, defenses, self-development, and similar forces within her or him.

It is impossible to dictate a particular approach to take for this section of the conceptualization, nor would it be prudent to do so. Over the years, research has indicated that there is no *one* theoretical approach that is clearly superior to any other in terms of conceptualization and treatment [though a specific problem may indeed warrant a specific approach; Mash and Barkley, (1998)]. However, it has been established that *having* a firm theoretical background of any type is crucial to the successful completion of treatment. Thus, the clinician who is about to embark upon clinical work with a child needs to take a look at her or his beliefs with regard to human behavior and life and should try to approach the case from a consistent theoretical point of view. Knowledge of various systems of psychotherapy is crucial, and a choice should be made about which theoretical system to ascribe to. Changing this conceptual understanding, and thus the practical approach to treatment, of a child's case midstream is likely to be confusing not only for the therapist and the supervisor, but also and primarily for the child and her or his family. It also tends to indicate that the therapist is floundering and that the treatment does not have a clear sense of direction. Because a child in treatment often is there because her or his life and family do not have consistency and direction, such traits in the therapy are clearly counterproductive.

Careful formulation of the child's intrapsychic processes is thus considered a necessary prerequisite to successful treatment. Using a self-psychological perspective on treatment and the understanding of human behavior, the intrapsychic dynamics of the child presented in the examples in this chapter so far can be summarized as follows:

> This 9-year-old girl appears to have been on the way to a relatively stable adjustment and self-development when the parental divorce and the sudden changes in her environment were imposed upon her. Although she shows definitive slips in her capacity to appraise her own abilities and to maintain her sense of self-esteem in the absence of nurturing others in the environment, she did, until recently, appear capable of taking care of her own needs, in fact, using these skills to parent her younger sister. She has now been left unable to comfort herself, and her moods have become sufficiently severe to feel out of control and to remain unmodulated most of the time. The child appears overwhelmed by the severity of these moods and is no longer able to control them by herself. Several aspects of her developing self, for instance, her vulnerable internalized sense of strength, are being weakened and rendered nonfunctional. Her depression is deepening. In an attempt to make herself feel safer, she has withdrawn from others and has begun evidencing some symptoms that may provide temporary relief, such as stomachaches and accidents. These events result in at least temporary mobilization of potential helpers in her environment and aid her in boosting her internalized sense of strength so that she can continue to face her situation. Her responses to her stressful situation have also resulted in a decrease in her ability to attend and concentrate, with a subsequent deterioration in her academic performance. Lack of adequate nurturance and mirroring from others in her environment have resulted in decreased energy levels and a sense of helplessness and hopelessness that has culminated in the wish to die or at least be hurt. Situational stressors are now extremely difficult for her to face, as her internalized resources to help herself have been taxed to the limit and have been rendered essentially nonfunctional.

Thus, stress now manifests through somatic and physical channels, as evidenced by her stomachaches and enuresis.

Family Dynamics.   As was true for the formulation of intrapsychic processes, all clinicians must and do integrate the family context of a child case to arrive at yet another component of the case conceptualization. Given that children are still firmly embedded in an interpersonal matrix of adults and caretakers, their role can be neither ignored nor underestimated. Thus, their impact on the child's life, their interactions with the child, their effect on the child's behavior, and their own psychological makeup are crucial to understand and place in the context of the child's symptomatic presentation. Family processes can be phrased in terms of a number of theoretical approaches, and again, no one superior approach has emerged in the literature. However, there appears to be much less divergence across clinicians from various systems of psychotherapy in terms of understanding family systems, and most therapists take an interactive approach to this section of the conceptualization. Generally, the focus is on understanding how the behaviors, attitudes, mental health, and interactions of the child's primary caretakers affect the child's current and past psychological adjustment and behavior. Extended family influences are also considered, especially if there is frequent interaction and visitation. The family dynamics, consistent with a self-psychological perspective, of the child presented in the examples in this chapter so far can be summarized as follows:

> It appears that this child's mother has been unable to nurture and enjoy this child from the moment of her birth because of her own needs and psychological deficits. She has relied upon her daughter for her own nurturing and strength, thus significantly overburdening the child and impeding her daughter's psychological growth and self-development. The mother does not have a healthy, integrated self, and she is in great need of others who can help her maintain her sense of balance, esteem, and purpose (e.g., alcohol, this child, her own mother). This has resulted not only in the use of the child as such a helper, but also in the absence of support for the child.
>
> The child's father was quite emotionally distant and unavailable. However, he was a highly successful surgeon who had received much acclaim in the medical community. As a result, apparently the child's father did have some positive influence on her and was an idealizable figure from whom she could glean strength even when he was physically absent. Thus, she was often capable of self regulation, following his role modeling. Further, the child's sister was an important person in her life in the sense that caring for her gave the child a purpose (though it was also a source of distress and feelings of being overburdened).
>
> When her sister died, the child lost her sense of purpose and no doubt experienced feelings of guilt and self-blame that have further undermined her self-esteem. When the father left the family, she also lost her idealized helper and with him her ability to care for herself and to regulate her own affects. This has resulted in a deepening of her depression and sense of hopelessness. Her decreased contact with her father and his extended family have left her feeling more vulnerable and stripped of her most important resource from her earlier childhood years. As she had not completely internalized a permanent sense of strength and self-confidence, this removal from her father may prove detrimental to her continued self development, especially since her mother is not capable of providing adequate nurturance and guidance.
>
> Finally, the child's intrusive grandmother frequently interfered with this child's attempts at nurturing and strengthening herself, for example, by reading her diary and making

fun of her entries, by admonishing her for not taking better care of her mother, by scolding her for trying to be like her father, and by constantly comparing her negatively with her cousins.

Interpersonal Matrix Dynamics.   Family dynamics, as outlined above, are only one aspect of the child's interpersonal matrix. Children interact with other children, baby-sitters, daycare personnel, teachers, and many other individuals every day. All of these people represent potential sources of conflict or aid and must be considered part of the child's overall life. Exploration of the interpersonal matrix is driven by the therapist's theoretical framework and may be considered more important by some than by others. However, most mental health professionals do tend to agree that interpersonal relationships are an important aspect of a child's mental health and day-to-day functioning. After all, ultimately, any gains that are made in therapy are hoped to generalize to the child's interpersonal matrix. This is the final aspect of the case conceptualization, and it leads to a summarizing statement about the child's overall adjustment and driving forces. The dynamics of the interpersonal matrix and the summary of the case of the child presented in the examples in this chapter so far are as follows, again taking a self psychological perspective:

> The move to an unfamiliar neighborhood and the removal from cultural values and religious beliefs that she had just started to accept as her own stripped her from meaningful twinship experiences, leaving her feeling alienated and different from other children. This withdrawal from her peers has initiated a vicious cycle of isolation and self-protection. She is now so fragmented, unsure of herself, and incapable of taking care of her own needs that she maintains an interpersonal distance to protect herself. She avoids interpersonal contacts for fear of being hurt or used again and is withdrawing completely. Simultaneously, she is starved for emotional nurturance and a source of strength. She attempts to meet some of these needs by mobilizing resources in her academic environment.
>
> In summary, this is a child who grew up in an environment in which nurturance needs were not met because of her mother's own psychological needs and her father's emotional distance. Thus, while she did receive some adequate opportunities for learning strength and values from her father, she was overburdened and unable to develop a healthy self. This has left her prone to fragmentation under stress and has resulted in the current symptomatic picture.

Once the case conceptualization has been prepared, clear avenues for intervention should have occurred to the clinician. The conceptualization is a direct precursor to treatment planning. Outlining a therapeutic approach without previously having formulated a case conceptualization is doomed to failure because the plan is bound to be incomplete or haphazard. Further, formulating a case and then using a different approach to treatment is inconsistent and likely to be confusing and replete with mistakes and misunderstandings. However, this does not imply that once a treatment plan has been set, it is written in stone. This is far from the truth. Throughout the work with the child, the therapist will learn new information and gain new insights. She or he is encouraged to modify the conceptualization and the treatment plan as appropriate to these new understandings. However, any reconceptualization should remain consistent with the original theoretical approach that was chosen by the mental health professional. Updating treatment plans does not imply changing direction. Only rarely is the initial conceptualization so inadequate that a major therapeutic shift is necessary.

Treatment Planning

The process of treatment planning occurs upon completion of the thorough assessment phase that has been outlined to this point. It represents the transition between the assessment and the treatment phase of therapy. Thus, treatment never begins before a treatment plan has been formulated, even if the child and her or his family have been seen repeatedly. Any session before the formulation of a treatment plan is considered assessment and has as its purpose the better understanding of the client in the hope of arriving at the best possible treatment plan. Once the treatment plan has been developed, treatment begins, and the focus of the interaction becomes one of behavior change. This behavior change must be mutually agreed upon by the therapist and the client(s); that is, treatment goals must be discussed with the child and her or his family. It is not uncommon or problematic for the clinician and the client to have a slightly different perspective on the goal for treatment. Often, parents are interested in the strict removal of symptoms, whereas the therapist may be interested in changing the child's self-esteem or self-perception. Such differences should be discussed and explained in the context of the presenting symptom to help the parents understand that symptom removal alone is often not enough. It is rarely wise to argue with parents or children about the goals for treatment even if they differ widely. Rather, education and respect are indicated. Thus, the client should be sided with in her or his stated goal, tying this goal in with the larger context of which the clinician is aware. Treatment will be more successful if all parties involved agree on what is being worked on.

Treatment Goals

There are often three sets of treatment goals that can be identified: the therapist's, the child's, and the parents'. There will be significant overlap among these three, but all should be noted and identified in terms of who views a particular goal as most important. Treatment strategies should then be developed in such a manner as to maximize the number of goals that can be accommodated. They should be clear and, for the most part, quantifiable or measurable. They are directly related to the presenting problems and the underlying dynamics that have been identified in the conceptualization. Thus, if a primary presenting problem of depression was indicated, a related treatment goal is the decrease in severity of the depressive symptoms experienced by the child. However, goals can be arranged hierarchically so that larger goals can be broken into component parts that may make treatment progress more obvious, as well as more likely. For example, in decreasing the severity of depression, it is best to have smaller goals that relate to specific symptoms, such as decreased insomnia, increased self-esteem, weight gain, interpersonal involvement, and renewed interests. Further, treatment goals can be divided into two major categories: resolution of the presenting problems and rehabilitation of the underlying case dynamics. Thus, there are various ways in which treatment goals can be dealt with. The most thorough approach will integrate them all and will be demonstrated here.

In this approach, treatment goals will be grouped according to the two broad categories of resolution of presenting problems versus rehabilitation of the underlying case dynamics. Within each category, goals will be arranged according to whether they are global goals or subgoals of an overall symptom. Further, they will be identified with regard to who is most concerned about the particular goals. This results in a hierarchy of goals, an applied example of which is provided in Table 7.4 for the child discussed above. The

TABLE 7.4 Hierarchy of Treatment Goals for a Child Presenting after Parental Divorce

Goal Category Global Goal	Subgoals	Individuals Concerned about This Goal
Resolution of Presenting Problem		
Resolve Depression (Goal 1)		therapist, child, parents
	(1a) increase activity level	child, therapist
	(1b) decrease social isolation	child, therapist
	(1c) weight gain	parents, therapist
	(1d) increase mood	child, parents
	(1e) increase self-esteem	parents, therapist, child
	(1f) enhance concentration	parents, therapist, child
	(1g) decrease crying spells	parents, therapist
	(1h) grieve sister's death	therapist, child, father
Resolve Academic Problems (Goal 2)		therapist, child, parents
	(2a) improve grades	parents, child
	(2b) enhance concentration	therapist, child, parents
	(2c) increase attention span	therapist, child, parents
	(2d) assess for learning disability	parents, therapist
	(2e) enhance achievement overall	child, parents, therapist
Resolve Physical Problems (Goal 3)		therapist, child, parents
	(3a) decrease stomachaches	therapist, child, parents
	(3b) decrease nightmares	therapist, child, parents
	(3c) decrease enuresis	therapist, child, parents
	(3d) increase weight to age appropriate level	therapist, parents
Rehabilitation of Underlying Dynamics		
Enhance Selfobject Environment (Goal 4)		therapist
	(4a) decrease mother's drinking	therapist, father
	(4b) decrease mother's neglect	therapist, child, father
	(4c) monitor and report abuse	therapist, child
	(4d) monitor and report neglect	therapist, child
	(4e) increase visitation with father	therapist, child, father
	(4f) exposure to Asian culture, religion	therapist, child, father
	(4g) increase knowledge about parenting	therapist, child
	(4h) open communication between parents	therapist
	(4i) decrease contact with grandmother	therapist, child, father
	(4j) increase contact with other adults	therapist, child
Promote Healthy Self-Development (Goal 5)		therapist
	(5a) facilitate mirroring pole development	therapist
	(5b) facilitate idealized pole development	therapist
	(5c) facilitate twinship feelings	therapist, parents, child
	(5d) facilitate skill development	therapist, parents, child
	(5e) increase coping ability	therapist, parents, child

format of the table can be used as it is, in the child's treatment plan, but is generally not included in the intake report.

Treatment Strategies

Once goals have been identified, strategies have to be chosen with which to address the specific goals. This process can be quite detailed, as very detailed descriptions can be provided about how the clinician plans to approach each particular problem (e.g., see Table 7.5). However, more often, the strategy choices are global, as it is often difficult to anticipate how a particular problem (and hence its associated) goal will manifest in treatment (e.g., Table 7.5 deleting the specific techniques within each global strategy). Flexibility, in terms of actual in-session interaction with the child, thus, needs to be maintained to enable the clinician to respond according to her or his best judgment. It is likely that each mental health professional has a repertoire of skills that she or he prefers to utilize in varying situations. Again, the actual strategies used by various mental health professionals will vary according to their theoretical orientation.

Although consistency in overall approach and in conceptualization is crucial, flexibility in the use of strategies is paramount. Thus, a psychodynamically oriented therapist may have a rehabilitation goal of helping the child to internalize an idealized pole of the

TABLE 7.5   Treatment Strategies for the Therapy of a Child Presenting after Parental Divorce

Global Strategies Specific Techniques	Treatment Goals Addressed (by numbers)
Play Therapy for Child	1, 1a–1h, 2, 2a–2c, 2e, 3, 3a–3d, 5, 5a–5e
activity therapy	1a, 1d, 1f, 2a, 2b, 2c, 2e, 5a–5e
storytelling	1c, 1d, 1e, 1h, 2e, 3b, 3d, 5a–5e
art therapy	1d, 1e, 1f, 1h, 2a, 2b, 2c, 2e, 5a
mirroring transference	1d, 1e, 1g, 1h, 3a, 3b, 3c, 5a
idealizing transference	1d, 1f, 1g, 2a, 2b, 2c, 2e, 5b, 5e
Group Therapy for Child	1, 1a–1g, 4, 4f, 5, 5a–5e
twinship experience	1b, 4f, 5c, 5d, 5e
activity therapy	1a, 1b, 1d, 1f, 5a, 5c, 5d, 5e
art therapy	1d, 1e, 1f, 1h, 5a, 5d
School Consultation	2, 2a–2e, 3a, 4, 5, 5c–5e
communicate with teacher	2b, 2c, 3a, 4f, 4j, 5c, 5e
academic testing	2d, 2e, 5d
Parent Education and Consultation	4, 4a–4g, 5, 5a–5c (indirectly: 1–3)
Relationship Therapy for Parents	4, 4h–4j, 5, 5a–5c (indirectly: 1–3)
Individual Therapy for Mother	4, 4a–4d, 4i–4j, 5, 5a–5c

self. This aspect of self has to do with self-regulation and requires the knowledge of limits, boundaries, rules, and values. In the process of pursuing this psychodynamically oriented treatment goal, the therapist might utilize behavioral principles that reinforce for the child the necessity and adequacy of certain behaviors, depending upon the setting in which they are displayed. In other words, although a theoretical orientation must be firm with regard to conceptualizing a case, the use of strategies must be adaptable, creative, and flexible. Fortunately, many techniques are available to the child therapist. The remainder of this book is dedicated to the thorough discussion of many of these techniques (e.g., play therapy, art therapy, storytelling, behavior modification) and specific strategies and approaches within them. Strategy choices are noted (though often in abbreviated form) in the child's intake report in the form of recommendations, and are presented in detail in the treatment plan. Table 7.5 exhibits strategy choices as noted in a treatment plan. Table 7.6 shows the corresponding recommendations that would be noted in the intake report.

Expected Treatment Resistances/Hindrances

Another integral part of the treatment plan is the mental health professional's assessment of the possible resistances that may be encountered in the process of the child's treatment. The treatment of children includes a number of people and hence is much more prone to being boycotted or sabotaged in one way or another than therapy with adults. It is often

TABLE 7.6   Treatment Recommendations for Intervention with a Child Presenting after Parental Divorce

Recommendations

1. Offer once weekly 50-minute play therapy sessions for the child.
   (Therapist: Dr. X)
2. Offer attendance of once weekly 75-minute group therapy sessions for the child.
   (Therapist: Dr. A)
3. Consult with school, especially teacher, to open communication and initiate academic assessment; consider intervention in the classroom with teacher.
   (Therapist: Dr. X)
4. Enroll parents in clinic's Parent Education Workshop as space becomes available.
   (Workshop Leaders: Drs. A and F)
5. Offer regular meetings between parents and child's individual therapist to keep parents apprised of child's progress in therapy and to keep communication open.
6. Offer relationship therapy to parents to attempt to resolve their fighting to provide a healthier interpersonal matrix for the child.
   (Therapist: TBA)
7. Offer individual therapy for the mother to help her integrate herself to make her better capable of serving as a healthy parent for the child.
   (Therapist: TBA)
8. Once-monthly consultation of all therapists involved in this case to coordinate treatment.

quite frustrating to recognize that even though the child and therapist are quite committed to the child's therapy, the parents are unwilling to bring the child consistently or on time. Thus, the child's treatment is impeded by a third force over which neither child nor the clinician has much, if any, control. However, parental resistance is not the only potential problem. Several sources of hindrances exist.

A child client might resist treatment because of fear of not being loyal to a parent, fear of the interpersonal setting, inability to trust, and a number of other reasons that are as unique as the specific presentation for treatment. The child's family might resist because they are threatened by the intervention of another adult or for fear of being reported for child abuse or neglect. Often, parents resist not because of malicious intent, but because of their own psychological problems or emotional needs. Thus, they may fail to recognize the severity of their child's symptoms, may downplay their own role in their child's adjustment, or may be offended by a school-initiated referral. As most parents are not entirely certain of their ability to parent "correctly," the challenge of facing a professional might be too great for them to have the strength to deal with this situation effectively and nondefensively.

Resistances do not always come from the child or her or his family. Sometimes, the environment in which the family lives is not conducive to compliance. Perhaps the extended family questions the action by the family who sought the intake consultation, a challenge that can result in the family's failure to follow through with treatment recommendations. Perhaps the particular cultural group to which the child belongs is not convinced of the value of therapy or even attaches a stigma to a person's need for it. Sometimes, socioeconomic factors get in the way, in that families are unwilling to disclose their inability to pay. Occasionally, families make the best attempt at coming for treatment together, but realistic work schedule limitations get in the way. Not often, but yet sometimes, a child's school may negatively influence a family's ability or willingness to follow through with treatment, either by scapegoating the child, not allowing the child to leave school early on a regular basis, making negative comments about the child's progress, or similar interactions.

Finally, there are resistances or hindrances that arise from the therapist or the mental health agency itself. Agencies without sliding fee schedules and with rigid business hours tend not to be conducive to the treatment of children. It is very difficult for families or children to come to treatment between 8 A.M. and 5 P.M., yet many agencies expect parents to do so. Often families who have been identified for referral by an outside agency are not able to cover the cost of treatment. Failure to provide flexible fee schedules will set these families up for failure. Resistances that arise from the clinician can be multifold. They may involve her or his prejudices, stereotypes, expectations, or personality characteristics. It is also possible that a particular child case will result in a very specific countertransference. Resistances due to the therapist are often difficult to note, and are best dealt with through consultation. Some signs of therapist-induced problems in the therapy process include, but are not limited to, failure to make progress even though the child and family have complied with treatment, failure to collect outstanding bills from a family whose fee was set according to ability to pay, dreading the session with the child, avoiding the child's parents, unwillingness to discuss the child's case at staffings, resistance to letting go of the child, or difficulty terminating a case. Anticipating resistances, whether from the clients, the environment, or from the therapist, is the best protection against letting them undermine a child's therapy.

Strengths

In making a treatment plan, the clinician clearly focuses on the problems that the family brought to the intake interview(s). However, it is important to remember in this process that families and children also bring strengths that can facilitate treatment significantly. Noting these strengths and using them in the treatment planning process can improve and speed up interventions significantly. Just as resistances were noted in the child, the family, the environment, the agency, and the therapist, so too are strengths. Thus, a child who is bright and has a good social support network brings two definite strengths to her or his treatment. Parents who are cooperative and concerned can be a great asset to the therapy of a child. A school setting that is supportive of the family's decision to seek services can make a big difference. For instance, one little boy who was referred for treatment had very poor parents who were unable to provide transportation between the agency and his school. As he had been referred by the school because of abuse and neglect in his home, his school made a commitment to bring him to his sessions. He made tremendous strides in treatment, something that would not have been possible without the help of his school. Similarly, teachers who are open to incorporating various strategies used with the child in the classroom often greatly facilitate generalization of progress. Finally, geographic, schedule, and cost compatibility between family and agency is a great asset.

Summary and Concluding Thoughts

This chapter has outlined a careful, step-by-step process for conceptualizing a child therapy case and for making a treatment plan. Emphasis was placed on the comprehensiveness of these documents and processes, as they often hold a critical role in the implementation of treatment. Ignoring any facet of the child's life and adjustment can result in treatment errors that can have grave consequences. Following the guidelines presented in this chapter helps both clinician and child to get well on their way to a successful therapy experience for everyone involved.

8 A Framework for Child Psychotherapy

It is difficult to decide upon a logical progression for a chapter on therapy process, as it superimposes a structure or order that does not exist in exactly the same manner in the therapy room. Treatment in reality is the occurrence of many simultaneous events, and the ordered discussion of these events often gives the false impression that they occur in a predictable manner and sequence in the real-life situation. The reader must understand that this is not so. Instead, therapy process, therapy tools or catalysts, and treatment challenges, all of which will be described and discussed here, are intermingled, facilitate one another, and coexist. In fact, they depend on one another for their existence. There would be no therapeutic goal without a therapy process leading to it. There is no process without the necessary tools; no change without catalysts. Despite the coexistence of these events in the therapy process, they must be addressed individually here to provide the reader with a sufficiently thorough, yet coherent, overview of what happens between a child and therapist when treatment progresses well. The arbitrariness of the orderly approach chosen for this chapter, however, must be borne in mind throughout.

Goals for the Therapeutic Process

The discussion of the therapy process is best begun by a brief overview of goal setting, despite the fact that this is largely within the realm of assessment and intake. Goals for the therapy of each individual child are generally straightforward and well planned out by the time an actual therapy begins. They are listed in detail in the child's treatment plan and are used to monitor progress, as well as to determine when therapy is complete. Goals are very specifically tailored to problems that emerged in the intake interview and through any additional assessment that was conducted. Despite their specificity, goals can be grouped into three categories in a manner appropriate for all child clients. First, there is the category of goals that has to do with resolving the child's presenting problems. Second, there is the category of goals that deals with strengthening the child and her or his psychological and emotional adjustment overall. And third, there is the category of goals that relates to helping a child reenter a healthy point in her or his developmental trajectory with regard to all developmental functions (e.g., self development, language development, motor development, psychosocial development; Russ and Freedheim, 2001). All three sets of goals deserve equal attention and are important in the work with children. However, the latter two are often overlooked even by the most experienced therapists.

The goals pertaining to the resolution of presenting problems are the most measurable and observable goals in a child's therapy and are more commonly used to monitor progress and determine the timing of termination than the other two categories of goals (Brems, 1999). They are couched in terms of behavior that is observable, as well as measurable, as opposed to terms that are global and vague. For instance, two goals that commonly fall into this category of goal setting for children who are depressed are increasing the child's daily intake of food and increasing the child's weight. Both goals can be easily monitored by parents who may track caloric intake and chart weight and height. Even increases in self-esteem fall into this category, as long as they are observed and measured. Thus, if a child were administered a self-esteem inventory and is given the same test at regular intervals throughout treatment, scores can be used to track changes in self-reported well-being.

Goals pertaining to the strengthening of the child's overall psychological adjustment are often more difficult, though not impossible, to measure. These goals are important to add to a list of goals, as they are often forgotten by therapists. They keep the therapist from focusing on details or separate aspects of the child at the expense of monitoring her or his overall improvement and change. Not uncommonly will significant gains have been made in a child's overall psychological health before specific behavior changes are noted. On the other hand, it is possible for a child client to have made progress with regard to several very specific aspects of functioning without having improved her or his overall well-being. Goals that fall into this category reflect the theoretical beliefs of the therapist as to what are important aspects of a child's individual adjustment, a child's family, environment, reinforcement histories, and so forth and where changes need to be facilitated. Specific goals within this category will vary greatly depending upon the theoretical approach of each individual therapist. This is unlike the goals in the first category, which are strictly problem-, not theory-, driven.

For instance, for a cognitive-behaviorist, an overall goal may be the general improvement of a child's ability to use self-talk in a number of situations to avoid depressive or anxiety-provoking thoughts. For a family therapist, an overriding goal may be changing the family structure. A humanistic therapist will use this category of goals to ascertain that a child has developed a way of being that feels genuine or coherent and is free of a false sense of self. A psychodynamic therapist of the Kohutian school may focus on helping the child gain a strong sense of self-confidence, a clear sense of direction, and a set of skills that can support and guide both of these aspects of the child's self. In other words, this set of goals is less directly measurable, but nevertheless just as important as the first set of goals.

The third set of goals, which has to do with the developmental trajectory of the child, refers to the fact that the therapist must help the child master developmental milestones and achieve a certain level of maturity. This maturity is not to be understood in the adult sense of behaving rationally and appropriately, but rather in the sense of "maturity that is relatively appropriate" to the child's age (Spiegel, 1989, p. 24) and developmental level. This set of goals is often left implicit by therapists and is rarely included in writing in a child's treatment plan. Developmental goals can take many different forms. For one child, it might be an appropriate goal to help her or him reach a sense of core self or self-regulation (Stern, 1985). For another child, the focus may be on helping her or him achieve a sense of initiative (Erikson, 1950), while for a third child the most important developmental trajectory may be that of developing appropriate language skills. An overall developmental goal is always the bringing in line with one another all aspects of development. In other words, it is desirable to ascertain that the child's psychosocial development is consistent with her or his cognitive development, that moral development is at the same level of sophistication, that self-development is equally advanced, and so on. Inconsistencies in developmental levels produce problems in and of themselves and always deserve to be included as treatment goals.

Once clear goals have been identified and the therapist has made some preparations for measurement of these goals, therapy is ready to commence. It will remain important throughout the treatment process that the therapist remain aware of all treatment goals and monitor them carefully. This is generally best done by eliciting help from parents and teachers who have daily contact with the child. These individuals can provide the therapist with valuable information about improvements and changes that would be too intrusive for the therapist to monitor herself or himself. For instance, weighing the child during each session would be quite disruptive. Receiving monthly feedback from parents about this issue, on the other hand, can be very helpful.

Phases of Therapy

Once therapy has begun, there are several processes or stages the clinician will become aware of and needs to keep in mind. There are some orderly processes that the therapist needs to recognize to keep treatment focused and on track. Superimposed upon the stages of change that the child is likely to go through in the adjustment to the therapy process is a progression of process behaviors that repeats itself over and over in the course of treatment. This progression is likely to begin once the child has moved beyond the anxious, exploratory stage, and has moved into a stage in which affect is being expressed freely and the relationship with the therapist has become important. This progression of behaviors moves from recollection of events to their reconstruction and reexperience in play and finally to their resolution (Brems, 1999). Although this sequence is likely to occur in this order for any one problem or event, the child may be at different phases of this progression for different problems. In other words, while recollecting one event, the child may already be at the stage of resolving another. Thus, while this progression is easily discussed in an orderly manner, it is less likely to be quite as clear-cut in the actual therapy process. It must also be noted that sometimes entire phases are skipped, with a child moving directly into a reconstruction or resolving a problem without reexperiencing it. Often, reexperience and resolution are closely tied together for minor problems, and the child may progress through these phases in such quick succession that they are no longer distinct. Finally, the four phases, which will be discussed in some detail, are facilitated by the therapist through the use of various therapeutic tools. For ease of presentation, the phases will be discussed first and are displayed in Table 8.1, while specific facilitating tools will be addressed later.

Recollection

In the recollection phase, the child begins to share recollections or memories of issues that are related to the major area of concern with the therapist. Children will exhibit this recollection by presenting their conflict or problem very obviously in play activity and less

TABLE 8.1   The Phases of Therapy Process

Phase	Content of Therapy	Level of Understanding	Strategies
Recollection	sharing of memories provision of information	no tie to presenting problem or etiology	listening questioning probing
Reconstruction	affective involvement in play and memory	still no direct tie to etiology, though affect is recognized as out of proportion	clarifying statements communication of understanding
Reexperience	affective expression in here-and-now with recollection of past event	beginning recognition of a tie between current issues and past events	use of transference explaining strategies projective identification
Resolution	strength confidence coping	tie between presenting problem and other issues is formed	internalization insight

often by sharing it verbally. In this phase of the process, the recollection is often vague, not consciously related to the presenting concern by the child, and rarely endowed with much affect or strong need states. It is a relatively matter-of-fact restating or replaying of events that is generally more meaningful to the therapist than to the child. This phase of a child's treatment is much like the early stage of an adult's treatment, wherein the client gives much information to the therapist about her or his life without making connections between the information that is given and its relevance to the presenting problems. Not uncommonly, adults in this phase of treatment talk about past events, especially from childhood, without being very certain about why these memories are emerging. The connection between the memory and the presenting problem does not occur until a later phase in the process of treatment. Given the fact that no connection has been made by the child or the adult client, interpretation at this time is inappropriate as it would be premature. The therapist best serves the process of treatment by facilitating the recollection through listening, probing, and asking questions, to gain a better understanding of the event's relevance.

An example of a child in this phase of treatment is the interaction with an 8-year-old boy in his third session. He had been referred for aggressive acting out with peers and engaged in a very interesting play activity without much awareness of its revealing and applicable nature.

> Eight-year-old Jason chose to play (for the first time!) with the dollhouse and doll family. He picked up the male adult doll and called him Frank (the child had a live-in grandfather named Francis), the female adult doll and called her Linda (his mother's name was Lisa), and a female child doll named Susan. The threesome ate dinner together, and much focus was placed on Linda serving food to Frank, on Susan having to eat everything on her plate, and then on Linda cleaning up after the meal while Frank smoked a cigarette and had a beer. After cleanup, Susan was put to bed by Linda, who read her a bedtime story and kissed her goodnight. After Susan fell asleep, Linda went to bed and locked her door. Frank tried to

get into her room, banged on her door, and finally climbed through her window. He made a lot of noise, and Susan awoke.

The boy went through this scene quickly and with little affect. After the female child had awakened, he turned to another activity and refused to play with the dollhouse again during this session. However, he did return in his next session and enacted a very similar scene. This scene was understood by the therapist as indicating that the child indeed was witness to abuse of his mother by the grandfather. (This was later confirmed in a session with the mother, who soon thereafter began treatment of her own.) Further, the scene also confirmed in conjunction with previously obtained information that the boy felt quite helpless and unable to protect his mother, yet would have liked to do so. He developed very angry feelings against his grandfather, which found an outlet in the child's aggressive behaviors against peers who were not as powerful as his grandfather. This is an example of a recollection, as the child showed no significant affects in the reenactment of the scene. Further, he had distanced himself from the imparted information by making the child in his play a girl, indicating to the therapist that although he was ready to share this information, he was neither ready to deal with it directly and openly nor able to make a connection between the memory and the presenting concerns of aggressive behavior.

Reconstruction

In the second phase of therapy process, the child has to be able to reconstruct her or his own emotional or psychological state as related to the recollections and memories of phase one. This shift in the process involves the child's affective involvement in play activity and reenactments. It is paralleled in adult treatment by a client who becomes tearful while discussing a painful childhood event without fully recognizing its relevance to the current problem. However, the experience is moved beyond mere recollection in that the client recognizes that the experience continues to evoke affects or need states that are as powerful as they are somehow meaningful. Children will often reconstruct entire relevant scenarios in their play with full expression of affect yet little awareness as to the direct relevance to current problems. The differentiation between a recollection and reconstruction is important, as the therapist's response will vary depending on how the event is understood. As was mentioned earlier, in response to a recollection, the therapist merely gathers more information. However, in response to a reconstruction, the therapist can make a clarifying statement that communicates to the child that the expressed affect or need has been understood. No attempt is made to give an interpretation or to tie the event directly to the current presenting problem.

For instance, reconstruction was at the heart of an event in the therapy of a 3-year-old girl who had been referred because of recent severe night terrors and nightmares that had begun to interfere with her sleep.

Three-year-old Sally liked to retreat to the floor cushions when painful affects emerged related to memories or current events. In one session, she pretended that the cushions were her bed and asked the therapist to go through her bedtime rituals with her. She directed the therapist in what to do, telling her how to tuck her in, how to read a bedtime story, and how to kiss her goodnight. She then would close her eyes and pretend to have gone to sleep. When she "awakened," it was morning and the breakfast routine began. This scene was played out several times, and during the third time, the child began calling the therapist "mommy" and told her not to leave the side of bed while she slept. She became very agitated at this time and indicated that her stepmother and biological father, whom she had to visit every other weekend, refused to tuck her in and read her a story.

This event in this girl's therapy was a reconstruction of both positive and negative bedtime experiences that represented one aspect in the etiology of her nightmares and night terror disorder. It is an example of a reconstruction, as opposed to recollection, as the child became visibly agitated in the absence of the ritual, and was visibly soothed and comforted by the presence of the ritual. Her expressed need to have her "mommy" by her side when she went to sleep was reflected by the therapist who responded to the child's calling her "mommy" by saying, "You really want your mommy when you go to sleep." The relief on her face validated that the therapist had understood her correctly and had correctly identified the event as a reconstruction and the need of the child as one for a nurturing and reliable figure in the child's life.

Reexperience

In the third phase of treatment, the child begins to relate present psychological or emotional states to past ones that may have contributed to the current issue or presenting problem, at least affectively. This type of reexperience is evident in children when they express an affect or need in the present and then spontaneously reenact scenarios from the past that resemble the current situation, or if they respond to a current situation with unwarranted vehemence. Whereas reexperience with adults generally involves making a verbal connection between the relationship of a past event, a particular style of thinking, or a particular way of looking at oneself to the presenting concern, the child does not have to do so verbally. Reexperience in child treatment can occur without conscious or verbal expression of the relationship, as long as nonverbal communication clearly ties present and past, or current problems with a particular style of thinking, and so on.

It is in this phase of treatment that the relationship between the child and the therapist takes on special significance, when rapport is critical, or, in psychodynamic terms, when transferences occur. For instance, in this phase of treatment, the child may respond to actions on the part of the therapist as she or he would respond to similar actions by parents or other significant individuals in the child's life. It is in this phase that the child will endow the relationship with the therapist with a special significance that stems from what the child has learned and experienced over the years. This phase of treatment with adults often involves some irrational behavior on the client's part, some unorthodox interpretations of therapist behavior or verbalization by the client, and other more traditional transference reactions. It involves the expression of ingrained patterns that have developed over the course of a client's life (regardless of age) without regard to their appropriateness in the current context. Thus, a child may express an exceedingly strong affect in response to a here-and-now occurrence that can be explained only by the activation of a related earlier event or the stimulation of a related affect that is not truly relevant in its full force in the current situation.

Reexperience is a powerful occurrence for client and therapist and is easily differentiated from recollection and reconstruction. Most important, recollection and reconstruction are not tied to current happenings in the therapy room or in the therapeutic relationship with the therapist. They are relatively (though obviously not completely) independent of what occurs in the here-and-now. Reexperience, however, by definition always involves a here-and-now component and, because of this, generally results in more potent affective expression and impact. It is during this phase of treatment that interpretation is appropriate, though certainly not required! An example of how reexperience may manifest itself in treatment with a child is the case of a 5-year-old boy who was referred because of fearfulness and inability to make friends.

Five-year-old Mike had become very comfortable in the therapy room and had begun to trust the therapist as evidenced by much spontaneous play and sharing. In one session, he became severely agitated and frightened by the sight of a small moth on the outside of the therapy room window. The following verbal, though metaphorical, exchange took place:
    Mike (panic-stricken, with a high pitched voice): It's going to get me! It will come and get me.
    Therapist: You are afraid the moth will get you.
    Mike: It will come after me. (panicked and almost crying) Make it go away.
    Therapist: You want me to help you be safe.
    Mike (crying): Yes! Kill it…(screaming) kill it.
    Therapist: We can walk up to it and look at it and be safe because it can't come in. We are safe.
    Mike (sobbing less severely): Go up to it…?
    Therapist: Will you come with me and take a closer look at it?
    Mike (no longer crying): Will you carry me?
    Therapist: I will hold your hand and we will be safe.
    They walk up to the moth, and the therapist explains about the moth, shows him its wings, and explains that it cannot come through the glass. This moth flies up, and Mike flinches, then relaxes, though grabbing on the therapist's hand a little harder.
    Mike (forcefully): Steve can't get me now!!
    Therapist (equally forcefully): You feel safe!!

This reexperience process was a powerful moment in this child's therapy. The response of the boy to seeing the moth was a very exaggerated response, yet one that was understandable once its symbolic meaning was understood by the therapist and linked to the child's past experiences. She focused on his need for safety because this had been a recurrent theme in his treatment. Mike had been severely sexually abused by his stepfather, Steve, who was now incarcerated. Nevertheless, Mike continued to have frequent nightmares, was very frightened of men, and generally refused to be with other children. The verbal intervention offered by the therapist was an interpretation despite the fact that it stayed within the child's metaphor, that is, focused on the behavior of the moth, exemplifying that interpretations can be metaphorical rather than direct in the work with children. The mere fact that the child stopped crying could have been used as evidence that he felt understood and at some level not only had heard, but also had accepted the intervention of the therapist. However, he spontaneously made the connection between the current event and his ultimate fear by indicating that he felt safe because he knew his stepfather could not reach him anymore. It must be pointed out that such verbalization of the connection between the here-and-now, the historical development of the problem, and the presenting problem is rare among children. Mike was a very bright and verbal child who had spent several months in treatment by the time this event occurred.

Resolution

Once a child has progressed through the phase of reexperience, resolution is often imminent. In this phase of treatment, the child resolves the presenting problem, often either through gaining understanding of why the problem occurred or through the process of internalization. Internalization means that the child has gained sufficient strength, understanding, and self-confidence that she or he can either cope with the presenting problem or let go of it. With children, this work can be done completely nonverbally and symbolically; insight does not need to be verbalized, as it is not the primary medium of change! Resolution is often much less emotionally powerful than reexperience, as it merely represents the logical conclusion of this earlier phase of treatment. It is often almost an afterthought and not uncommonly occurs immediately after a reexperience. The mark of a child having gained resolution is her or his ability to do the work formerly done by the therapist. In other words, during this phase of treatment, the child can provide her or his own explanations of presenting problems or her or his own strategies for coping. An example, using the case of a 7-year-old girl who was referred because of severe separation anxiety, will clarify how this phase of treatment may manifest in the treatment of children.

> Seven-year-old Janine was seen for her sixteenth session. Despite still engaging in some exploratory behavior, she appeared to become more spontaneous in her affective expression and had begun to trust the therapist. She was moving around the therapy room, which had a large column in one corner that was a remnant of an earlier use for the room. The column was placed such that a child could hide behind it and lose sight of the therapist. Janine moved behind the column and hid for a very brief moment then screamed for the therapist to come and help her. The therapist approached far enough for Janine to see her and said, "You are afraid of what might happen when you can't see me." The child nodded, calmed significantly, and no longer insisted on help. She repeated this behavior several times during the session, each time expressing strong affects. Finally, while approaching the column and the child's field of vision, the therapist said, "I know you are there even when I can't see you. And you know that I am here even when you can't see me." The child came out from behind the column with a big smile and said, "I know."

This interaction exemplifies a resolution immediately following a reexperience. Janine overreacted to the visual separation from the therapist, yet this response was understandable in light of her presenting problem and historical information that had been obtained during the intake. The repeated reexperience, along with the therapist's expression of understanding and then suggestion of reality, led very naturally to the resolution of this particular problem in the therapy. Resolution of the larger problem of separation anxiety had not yet obtained completely, but this small progress had paved the way.

Catalysts for Change

To facilitate the progression through the four phases of therapy process, the therapist relies upon a number of tools, or catalysts, for change. These tools are independent of a therapist's specific theoretical framework (e.g., behavioral, humanistic, psychodynamic) or preferred technique (e.g., group therapy, art therapy, storytelling). They transcend theories and are generally agreed upon as important facilitators of change. Each therapist will develop her or his own repertoire of tools, and their variety and style of use will differ widely from clinician to clinician. However, several catalysts for change appear to be sufficiently universal and important to warrant some discussion here. Nevertheless, it must be remembered that they represent merely a sampling of all the means that are available to therapists to help children change and work in therapy. Often, it is only the therapist's own level of creativity and willingness to take risks that limits the choices of interventions that are being made. The tools presented here are summarized in Table 8.2.

Creation of a Therapeutic Environment

In the early stage of treatment, the therapist must create an environment that communicates to the child that therapy represents a safe setting wherein free emotional expression is valued, never punished, and where trust and confidentiality are fostered. The creation of the therapeutic environment, of course, begins long before the actual treatment with any child commences. Specifically, therapeutic environments are equipped for the safety of the child and the therapist and the conduciveness of self-disclosure and affective expression, as outlined in the chapter concerning the physical environment. However, beyond the actual physical surroundings there is also a psychological environment or atmosphere that must be created for each client anew. This environment involves several components. Most important, it involves physical and psychological safety (see Dodds, 1985; O'Conner, 2000). Second, it involves the facilitation of physical and psychological self-expression (see Axline, 1947; Chethnik, 2000; and Coppolillo, 1987).

Physical and psychological safety are best ascertained through the creation of some psychological structure. This structure refers to the setting of limits and the delineation of therapy rules that protect the child and the therapist and that are clearly stated and presented to the child once treatment begins. Leaving the child guessing about rules, limits, and parameters of the session invites unnecessary limit-testing on the child's part and anxiety about expectations, and it hinders the free flow of creativity and play that is so essential to the work with children. Thus, structuring the environment might appear rigid or inhibiting upon first reading, yet this must not be so. Rigidity and inhibition will emerge only if rules and regulations are unreasonable and go above and beyond their purpose of ensuring safety. Rules that are clearly set only for the purposes of safety will not intrude or hinder. There are only a few general rules. Individual therapists may need to add a few of their own, depending upon their unique environments and clinical settings.

Most commonly, rules that ascertain physical safety are clearly presented to the child in those terms. Specifically, a child client has to be informed that physical aggression in the room is fine as long as it does not result in physical injury of the child or the therapist and

TABLE 8.2 Catalysts for Change

Catalyst Category	Specific Tool
Creation of a Therapeutic Environment	
Physical Safety	■ no physical aggression ■ cleanup rules
Psychological Safety	■ length of session ■ interval of sessions ■ structure of session ■ sameness of setting ■ continuity of therapist presence
Creation of a Therapeutic Relationship	■ exclusive focus on child ■ reassurance and comfort ■ respect ■ physical touch ■ tolerance of nonverbal communication ■ use of metaphor and symbolism ■ transference awareness ■ countertransference awareness
Empathy and Understanding	■ vicarious introspection ■ communication of understanding ■ cross-modal attunement
Methods and Levels of Explaining	■ running commentary ■ reflection ■ pointing out patterns ■ asking clarifying questions ■ identification of feelings ■ identification of sources of feelings ■ catharsis ■ as-if explanation ■ interpretation
Internalization	■ self-assurance and realistic self-appraisal ■ relevant rules or regulations and life-direction

(continued)

TABLE 8.2   Continued

Catalyst Category	Specific Tool
Projective Identification	
	■ projection of affect onto the therapist
	■ acceptance of the affect by the therapist
	■ metabolization of the affect
	■ reintrojection of the affect by the child
	■ projective counteridentification
Use of Defense, Symptoms, and Resistance	
	■ definition as self-protective device
	■ teaching coping skills
	■ environmental modification
	■ teaching parenting skills
	■ effecting familial change

as long as no toys or furniture are broken willfully. Hitting the therapist is generally not allowed. Although the rules are introduced gently as is appropriate to the content and context of the first one or two sessions during which the child is seen, contingencies or enforcement rules are introduced only when a rule is broken by the child. Limit-setting, as was outlined in a previous chapter, should then be used to deal with the individual situation.

Rules for psychological safety are often more difficult to explain to a child than to an adult but are equally important. These rules have to do with informing the child about length of sessions; the general structure of sessions, with a beginning, a middle, and an end; and the intervals between sessions. Further, it may be stressed that the toys in the room will always be available from session to session for the child's use and that they always remain in the room. Some discussion of whether toys may be taken home may follow at this time. These rules have generally already been discussed in the feedback session of the intake interview but need to be repeated in the first treatment session. Providing structure as far as length and process of sessions is concerned is quite important, as it lets the child know that there are limits to how much work has to be done in any one session, and it confirms for the child that there is regularity to therapy that can be counted on. Providing information about the consistency of the room's equipment and the therapist's presence in each session will help some children to transition more easily from one session to the next. Reassurance about the therapist's predictability, consistency, presence, and stability are particularly important in this context. Reiterating psychological safety rules can be as easy as reflected in the following dialogue between a therapist and a 6-year-old boy who had just begun his first session and had been seen for an extensive intake interview two weeks prior by the same therapist:

THERAPIST: Do you remember this room?

TIM: (nods shyly)

This is a good introduction for a child who has been in the playroom before. Most children have been through an intake in the same clinic and will have had some experience with the room in that context. Reminding them of this initial contact subtly points out for the child that the room and toys are stable and consistent across sessions.

THERAPIST: Remember, you may use any of the toys that you want, just like last time you were here.

This reminder is necessary only with timid children, such as Tim in this example. More outgoing or active children not only remember the freedom of the room, but also quickly make use of it upon their return.

TIM: I liked the dollhouse...

THERAPIST: Yes, you did. You very much liked the dollhouse last time you were here!

The therapist's response here communicates to the child that she remembers him and that she noticed his preferences. Although this might not fall into the category of establishing a therapeutic *environment* as defined above, it certainly falls into the next category of catalysts: the therapeutic relationship.

TIM: (walks to the dollhouse) It's still right here!

This comment reaffirms for the therapist that this child has concerns about being left or abandoned and signals for her that a reiteration of the constancy of the therapy environment will be important.

THERAPIST: Yes, all the toys stay in this room, and they will always be here for you when you come each week.

TIM: The paints too?

THERAPIST: Yes, everything stays, including me. I will be here every week for you; always at the same time, always for 50 minutes.

The therapist chooses to stress not only the constancy of the room, but also the constancy of her presence and availability. The stressing of this environmental factor is particularly important for children who have had little stability of relationships in their own home, have experienced abusive parents, or have parents who abuse substances. The latter was the case for this little child.

TIM: (continues to explore the room, a bit more vigorously now) I get to come back every week?!

The new vigor in the boy's behavior at this time confirms for the therapist that the stressing of continuity was heard by the child and relieved some of his fears. His last statement was hesitant but followed by a firm nod of the head. The therapist decided to respond to the hesitation by restating the permanency of her presence.

> **THERAPIST:**   Yes, every Tuesday at 4 o'clock I will be here for you.

The therapist chooses in her restatement to focus on her presence, rather than the child's as she has no control over his presence, only hers. For his presence, she depends on his parents who will have to bring him in, but she wanted the child to know that she would be there for him no matter what. The child turned at this time and began to play with the dollhouse, indicating that for now he felt safe in this new environment. No physical safety rules were approached at this time, as this child was very subdued and the mention of anger and physical aggression would be more likely to intimidate, than relieve, him. A more obviously angry child may therefore receive a slightly differently focused introduction.

Creation of a Therapeutic Relationship

The above example already pointed toward another important set of catalysts for change, namely, the establishment of a therapeutic relationship. The therapeutic relationship is a critical piece in the treatment of any client and care must be taken early in the therapy to facilitate its development, and throughout the therapy to maintain it. There are many traits in a therapist that enhance therapeutic rapport with children and some of the main ingredients that make development and maintenance of a positive relationship possible are quickly listed here.

Child Focus.   Perhaps the most unique component of interaction between a child and a therapist from the child's perspective is the exclusive focus on the child and the child's wishes. There is no self-disclosure on the therapist's part, no imposition of unnecessary rules that would serve merely to enhance the adult's life, complete acceptance of the child and her or his behavior (within the framework provided above), and willingness to let the child lead and choose activities.

Reassurance and Comfort.   In addition to the acceptance that is expressed verbally and nonverbally, the therapist is reassuring and comforting. Especially early in treatment, while the child is still struggling with the concept of therapy and with trust issues, the therapist does not allow anxiety levels to rise out of control and is caring and nurturing. The therapist reassures the child in her or his exploration of the room, in her or his choices of self-disclosure, and in her or his tenuous affective self-expression. The clinician comforts the child when psychological pain mounts but also when physical pain is present. She or he will not ignore pains the child brings to the room, such as cuts and bruises or stomachaches, and takes even minor complaints seriously. Accidents in the play room do occur and also require caring and comforting on the therapist's part. This stance toward the child is often unique in the child's experience and helps her or him learn to trust the therapist quickly and easily.

The therapist's comforting and reassurance are certainly not done to allow the child to shed all responsibility for responsible and moral behavior. Quite to the contrary, therapy introduces responsibility for behavior to children. Cleanup is generally required, and acting out behaviors, while being accepted, are generally discussed with regard to their consequences. However, even in stressing the responsibility, the clinician remains warm and accepting of the child. Above all, the child's needs and desires are respected and responded to with flexibility.

Respect.   Respect for the child can be communicated through silence (Coppolillo, 1987). Often, adults interrupt children's stories or play behavior. The therapist will rarely do so. She or he will often observe the child in silence and will allow the child to complete thoughts and activities before intervening or commenting. Despite, or perhaps because of, this silence, the therapist must remain obviously available for communication and the exchange of information. This may include the tolerance of silence during play, as well as the encouragement of dialogue in the absence of any obvious nonverbal communication. The therapist's availability for communication is often best expressed through simple questions or reflections about the child's activity. For instance, a child who is engrossed in dollhouse play may well be communicating a lot with the therapist on a nonverbal level. However, without a response from the therapist, the child cannot be certain whether the clinician is receiving the communication initiated by the child. Thus, rather than sitting passively, the therapist may choose to accompany the child's behavior with some running commentary that is merely reflective of, and does not intrude into, the child's action. Similarly, simple reflection of the child's overt behaviors and affects are adequate strategies to inform the child that the therapist is paying attention and available for communication.

Physical Touch.   Despite some cautions against this, physical contact can be an important component of establishing rapport. Children like to express affection through physical contact and may feel quite alienated, if not rejected, by refusal of the clinician to reciprocate. Obviously, care has to be taken that physical contact is never sexualized, but the fear of this possibility should not interfere with the occasional hug, tap on the arm, or pat on the back. On the other hand, physical contact must not be overused. Like all strategies used in treatment, it must be well-timed and must have a purpose. It is never a good idea to have a routine of physical contact that is practiced with all children. For one thing, not all children like to be touched. For another, children recognize the difference between a routine touch and a genuine expression. A good rule of thumb is to wait for the child to initiate physical contacts beyond pats on the back. It is not unlikely that a child will change her or his attitude toward physical touch in the course of treatment, moving from shrinking from physical contact to its spontaneous initiation or moving from attempted aggressive contact to caring contact.

One 9-year-old boy, who was being seen because of significant physical aggression, never initiated physical contact with his therapist unless attempting to hit him. Therefore, the therapist was very respectful of the child's boundaries and never touched him. However, in one session, the child's behavior escalated, and the therapist had to restrain him for approximately 10 minutes. After the session, the therapist was quite distraught, as now the only physical contact that had been established by him toward his client was negative. He decided that despite the fact that the child had shrunk from physical touch, he would use some pats on the back and taps on the arm of this boy to begin to introduce positive physical touch. The child responded beautifully. He enjoyed the positive expression of feeling between the clinician and him and reduced the amount of attempted aggressive touching. He soon began to initiate hugs at the beginning of the session and developed a warmth in the relationship with the therapist that was very healing for him.

When physical touch is used with children, their parents should be warned that this is done, to avoid misunderstandings and misinterpretations. In this day and age of sexual and physical abuse, a therapist must protect herself or himself from false accusations. Further, she or he may also model for nontouching parents that the physical expression of caring is appropriate. It is quite sad to see parents, especially fathers, who have stopped touching their children for fear of being falsely accused of inappropriateness with them.

Use of Metaphor and Symbolism.   All children, but especially young children, communicate through metaphor and play, thus requiring the therapist to have some awareness and knowledge of symbolism. Often, children communicate through comments or questions that on the surface appear unrelated to their presenting complaint. However, the therapist must learn to decipher their metacommunication. For example, one girl, who was seen in treatment because of some psychotic symptomatology and who had a very deprived background, once asked the therapist in the course of play whether the cow she was using was going to have enough milk. The therapist, knowing the child's history, immediately understood her concern, which was twofold. First, the child was asking whether the therapist (whom she saw leave the play therapy room prior to her session with another child) would have enough caring and understanding to give to her as well as other children. Second, she was asking whether her own parents were able to provide adequate nurturing and support for her. The therapist, with this understanding in mind, indicated that the cow indeed would have sufficient milk, though occasionally it might appear as though there were not enough to go around. When this concern returned at a later point in this child's therapy, the child learned through mutual storytelling what the calf could do for herself when the cow temporarily runs out of milk. This example demonstrates not only the importance of understanding the metaphor, but also the need for the therapist to respond within the metaphor. Responding to the latent content by making it manifest (e.g., in this example by saying that the mother and father, or the therapist, will indeed attempt to provide for the child as best they can) can be much too threatening to the child. After all, there is often a reason why the child chooses the metaphor, and generally it has to do with the child's attempt at keeping her or his fear under control by addressing the issues indirectly, or unconsciously. It is also important to remain with the child's choice of metaphor or language, and not to introduce the therapist's own metaphor. The child may have difficulty understanding it, or may feel misunderstood by the clinician. Although the novice might feel overwhelmed by the prospect of having to understand symbols and metaphors, this process is generally much easier than it sounds. After all, the therapist never enters treatment with a child blindly. Rather, she or he has in-depth knowledge about the child's dynamics and family situation, information gathered during the intake session (see Chapter Five). Having this context generally provides sufficient information to understand the child's symbolism. Further, children rarely use important symbols or metaphors only once. Thus, even if it is not understood the first time, there will be another chance.

It is important to keep in mind that each child will use symbols and metaphors in unique ways. Thus, what means one thing to one child might have a totally and uniquely different meaning to another. The clinician should never assume that metaphors translate across children. Thus, studying symbolism (there are dictionary-type references that discuss the meanings of various story contents or objects) is generally not useful. It is much more productive to listen to the child's communication with an open mind and to place the play or verbalization in the context of the child's background and presenting concern. The same holds true for nonverbal communication, including body language. Behaviors or gestures are unique to each child and have specific meaning. For one child, lying down on the floor may indicate that she is beginning to trust the therapist, whereas for another child, the same behavior might be a sign of resistance or avoidance. One child who was seen in therapy would take off her shoes at the beginning of the session as a sign that she was ready to get to work; when her session was over, she would put on her shoes as a signal that she was reaching closure and was ready to end. Another child was observed to take off his shoes just like the first child. However, for him, taking off his shoes served a different purpose. He would routinely forget to put his shoes back on at the end of the session, thus having to return to the therapy room after having ended the session. Clearly, he communicated that he was not ready to conform to firm endings and beginnings of each session. Nonverbal communication is a powerful tool used by children of all ages. It must be considered by the aware therapist as a major means of self-expression, as well as a useful avenue for intervention.

Transference. Related to the establishment of a therapeutic relationship is the concept of transference. Transference has many different definitions, ranging from traditional psychoanalytic concepts to very broad interpretations. In the psychoanalytic tradition, transference referred to those needs, feelings, and desires that found expression in the therapy relationship without a here-and-now reason, instead stemming completely from earlier life experiences. These types of transferences were always viewed as inappropriate to the relationship at hand and interpreted in the context of previous, usually parental, relationships. Later, and less traditional, definitions include all needs and feelings brought to the therapy by either the child or the therapist, regardless of how relevant they are to the here-and-now relationship between the two (O'Conner, 2000). It is argued that everyone is affected by all past life experiences, and therefore, all interactions with significant people in one's life are somehow a function of earlier relationships and hence never pure. In this approach, the importance is placed on helping the child become aware of how the past has influenced or patterned the present.

Transference in the context of this book is viewed from a perspective somewhere between these two extremes. It is suggested that transference is never as pure as we suggested traditionally and that there is always a component of the here-and-now relationship that triggers old feelings and needs that are also related to past relationships. Thus, transference is not seen quite as completely independent of what the therapist brings to treatment as in the traditional approaches. It appears much more likely that the personality of the clinician and her or his therapeutic style influences which feelings and needs emerge at any given time in the therapy process. However, in the approach taken here, transference is not seen quite as broadly as suggested by O'Conner (2000), wherein every single component of the child-therapist interaction is viewed as transferential. Instead, the definition of transference as proposed in this book is as follows:

Transference refers to the fact that there are aspects of the child-therapist relationship that are catalyzed by the therapist's overt and intentional behavior and less so by her or his covert or unintentional personality style and that reflect or express a child's unique feelings, needs, and desires, as they were formed through the child's interpersonal environment up to this time in her or his life.

This definition deserves some detailed exploration. It suggests first of all that both child and therapist contribute to the transference. The therapist contributes in two ways. First, she or he contributes through overt and intentional behaviors; behaviors that are designed to facilitate and stimulate certain affects and need states in the child. This is the true definition of a catalyst. The therapist does not create feelings or need states in the child but merely provides a relationship and environment in which previously existing affects and needs can be freely expressed and then understood. Second, the therapist inadvertently contributes characteristics that may further stimulate or hinder the expression of these affects and needs. The inadvertent contribution is generally secondary to personality style, personal feelings, beliefs, and affects and is truly in the spirit of what is generally labeled countertransference. The child contributes in the most important way to the transference relationship with the clinician. Children are not blank slates—not even very young children. They have grown up in unique environments with very individualized interpersonal relationships. These factors, environment and relationships, have affected the child to such a degree as to strongly influence what the child's needs and affects are, particularly in intense interpersonal contexts, such as that presented by psychotherapy. The child responds to her or his therapy environment from that unique historical perspective. The therapist's behavior merely facilitates the expression; it does not alter it in the sense of producing needs or affects that would not otherwise be there. Thus, self-disclosures and affective expressions by the child in the therapy can be confidently understood as arising from the child's unique history and family environment. It is this aspect of the child-therapist relationship that represents the transference between them and can be used to gain further insight into the child's development, environment, needs, and directions for change.

This transference is used to understand the child and to determine where deficits or problems have arisen and how to go about effecting change. This understanding of transference can accommodate various theoretical frameworks as well, as it does not necessarily imply what the content of the expressed affects and needs of the child are, nor their specific interpersonal development. Thus, a cognitive behaviorist may argue that the transference is due to cognitions that the child learned in her or his household, and that certain cognitive patterns were reinforced by the child's family that have led to the child's current feelings and behaviors. A humanist might argue that the needs and feelings are secondary to the lack of genuineness in the child's family that has resulted in the development of a false or incongruous self with which the child is struggling. A family systems theorist might indicate that the feelings and needs are due to family patterns that have resulted in a certain role that is played by the child within the family system. A self psychologist might conclude that the child feels a certain way and expresses specific needs because the needs were not adequately provided for by caretakers in the child's earlier life. However the transference feelings and behaviors are explained, the fact remains that they are present in the child-therapist relationship and that they present the therapist with the unique opportunity to work on these feelings and need states in the therapy room despite the fact that their origin is in a different setting. The following example uses a self psychological conceptual perspective and demonstrates how transference can be used as a catalyst for change.

> Angie, a 7-year-old girl who was referred because of several phobias, developed a very powerful relationship with her male therapist. She expected him to hold her and cuddle her when she felt frightened and overall wanted him to protect her, even from events and interactions outside of the therapy room. She often asked that he tell her mother not to ask her to do certain things and occasionally became upset when he did not comply with her demands. The transference in this case was the child's view of the therapist as all-powerful and her demand that he protect and help her in all possible life circumstances. These demands and perceptions are viewed as transferential because they are not entirely realistic within the therapy relationship, yet their development was certainly facilitated by the warm, nurturing attitude of the therapist, which had stimulated the expression of these needs in the child. She had lost her father 4 years earlier to a drunken-driving accident after one of his binging weekends. Since then, she had been placed in foster care off and on when her mother, who was diagnosed with schizophrenia, had to be hospitalized. Angie had no stability in her life and often felt very unprotected owing to the absence of a father and the inability of her schizophrenic mother to be counted on consistently. Her needs for protection had been re-channeled into various phobias and now found expression in the transference relationship with the therapist. Therapy focused on helping her to recognize her need for protection, on helping her to mobilize her own resources to protect herself, and on building realistic means of protection into her day-to-day life. It had been the powerful transference that revealed the depth of the child's needs and fears and paved the way for change.

Empathy and Understanding

Going hand-in-hand with the establishment of a therapeutic relationship and rapport is the expression of empathy and understanding in the work with children. Empathy is defined here as understanding the child from her or his unique perspective and history, just as the transference is expressed as a result of a child's unique background (Kohut, 1982). This definition requires an experience-near approach, which means understanding the child, as well as her or his presenting symptoms in the here-and-now and in the context of a specific situation as a reflection of how and where the child developed and grew up. Thus, empathy is not merely a warm, fuzzy feeling of caring, but rather an important tool that facilitates insight. This type of empathy has also been referred to as vicarious introspection (Kohut and Wolf, 1978) to indicate that it goes beyond a recognition of how the therapist or other children would feel in a similar situation, but rather is an understanding of how a particular child feels, given her or his unique experiences in life. This type of empathy requires an in-depth understanding of the child, the child's history, and the child's interpersonal environment.

Empathy alone is not enough. The empathic understanding must also be communicated to the child, confirming that empathy is indeed an interpersonal process, not a one-sided one. The cycle of empathy always begins with the self-expression of the child. This self-expression is received by the therapist, who attempts to put the self-expression into the framework of the child's entire life. The therapist interprets or attempts to understand the meaning of the self-expression based on the knowledge of the child's background. Once the therapist is relatively certain to have understood the child correctly, the understanding is communicated back to the child. The communication of understanding can take place either verbally or nonverbally, directly or symbolically. It is never to be confused with an interpretation. In other words, the communication of understanding is an expression of empathy, but not a method of explaining. It is designed merely to tell the child that the clinician understood what the child expressed. Thus, it may consist of the mere labeling of an affect, or it may consist of a behavior on the part of the therapist, such as joining the child's play. This interpersonal cycle of empathy has been described in the social psychology research literature for many years (see Barrett-Lennard, 1981; Brems, 1989a) and certainly appears to apply to the therapy context as well, as demonstrated by the following example:

> Eight-year-old Alex was using clay in her sixth session with her therapist. She created two dogs—one small, the other rather large. The small dog was doing its homework, which was reportedly very difficult and important. It could not finish the task and began calling for help, only to be ignored by the large dog, who was portrayed as watching TV. The small dog became more and more rambunctious and finally tipped over the TV. At this point, the large dog made snoring noises, a way of indicating that it was still not paying attention to the small dog. The small dog then got out of control, as Alex pretended that the dog was tipping over the furniture in the dollhouse. At this point, to avoid further escalation, the therapist decided to communicate that she had understood the child's communication. To do so, she picked up the large dog and, pretending that it was waking up slowly and beginning to watch the small dog, said, "Oh, you are so upset. I think you need my help to calm down."

This is an example of a symbolic communication of understanding, as the therapist remained within the chosen metaphor. It demonstrated that the reflection of understanding is merely that; in other words, no attempt is made to interpret the behavior or activity for the child. In this example, the child was communicating that she did not yet have internalized controls over her behavior and needed external limits to be prevented from acting out aggressively when faced with frustration. This was the understanding that was reflected back to her. It was not yet interpreted for her that the absence of internal controls was directly related to the absence of external controls in her life, as her caretakers were overly permissive and did not care in the least about what the girl was doing.

The ability to empathize and communicate understanding is quite dependent upon or analogous to the process of attunement described by Stern (1985). It requires the therapist to listen carefully, to make inferences about the meaning of a child's behaviors and verbalizations, and to reflect these back to the child in a meaningful, nonredundant manner. Empathy thus serves a similar purpose as attunement, as it helps the child develop self-understanding, self-respect, and self-confidence.

Once the therapist has understood the child and has reflected the understanding either verbally or nonverbally, the therapist begins to help the child develop empathy with herself or himself. The child learns to understand her or his own feelings, and self-expressed needs and affects, and begins to be able to place labels on them. This process of gaining better self-understanding is an important first step in therapeutic change. Just as empathy by the therapist serves to help the child feel better by virtue of letting her or him know that the feelings are real, understandable, and accepted, so does the child's own empathy with herself or himself serve to build up and enhance her or his self-esteem and self-confidence.

Methods and Levels of Explaining

Care was taken in the discussion of the interpersonal cycle of empathy to differentiate the communication of understanding from the process of making interpretations or giving explanations. Explaining the relationship among behavior, affects, thoughts, interpersonal relationships, and environment is an important component of treatment (see Russ and Freedheim, 2001). However, it is generally confined to the later phases of therapy process, as it does not occur during the recollection and reconstruction phases, which are limited to information gathering and empathic understanding, respectively. Explaining can be done in numerous ways, ranging from the simple pointing out of patterns to very direct intervention in the form of direct verbal interpretation. Like the communication of empathic understanding, running commentary and reflection, two commonly used interventions mentioned in the context of establishing a therapeutic relationship (e.g., Landreth, 1991; 2000), are not true forms of explaining, as they merely communicate that the therapist is listening or paying attention. This does not reduce their value as interventions but merely places them in a different category from true explaining strategies.

True explaining strategies have as their purpose much more than the communication of attention and understanding. At their heart is the communication not only of understanding of affects, needs, and behaviors in the here-and-now, but also of their relationship to the child's life as a whole. Explaining strategies are used to communicate transference understanding, as opposed to empathic understanding (Kohut, 1984). They not only reflect what the therapist observes in the child, but also explain it on the basis of the knowledge the clinician has of the child's background and history. Sometimes explaining strategies are aimed merely at the imparting of information. For instance, a child who is expecting a sibling but whose parents are unsure, unable, or unwilling to help her or him understand the biological processes of conception and birth may benefit greatly from learning how babies are conceived and born. Most commonly, however, explaining strategies are less educational and more process-oriented.

Pointing Out Patterns.   The pointing out of patterns is the most basic form of explaining. It requires the clinician to recognize that certain behaviors, needs, affects, and desires are repeated by the child, either in the therapy room or in other settings. The presence of these patterns is then shared with the child, as in the following example:

> Six-year-old Tanya spent several sessions preparing and shopping for food using the anatomical doll family whom she had given names. A pervasive theme in her play was the lack of sufficient food to feed everybody and the running out of money before the shopping trip was completed. As this pattern was once again played out in a session, the therapist decided to make this comment: "Lucy [name of the female child doll] is trying and trying, but it seems like there is never enough food around to fill her up. She keeps asking her mommy and daddy for more, but there is just not enough to go around."

Asking Clarifying Questions.   Sometimes it is necessary to help a child gain better self-understanding by asking questions to clarify thoughts and perceptions for the child (Dodds, 1985; O'Conner, 2000). This is a method of explaining that is slightly more advanced than pointing out patterns, as it is designed to develop cognitive insights. This type of questioning must be differentiated from the information-gathering questions that are used in the recollection phase of treatment. In information gathering, the therapist asks questions for her or his own benefit of clarification, as much as the child's. In the explaining questioning, the questions are designed to lead the child to an insight that the therapist already has. The following example should clarify the difference:

> Twelve-year-old Terrence had been seen for ten sessions when he used two puppets to express himself. He played out a scenario wherein one puppet, a rabbit, was picking on another one, a lion, until the lion kicked the rabbit. The rabbit was terribly hurt by the lion and retreated, crying and whining. The therapist knew that Terrence chronically got into fights with older boys at school, fights that he often provoked by name-calling. As the puppet play was a perfect reenactment of this process that Terrence had denied up to this point, she decided to ask some clarifying questions to help him recognize the contributions he made to the fights. She chose a third puppet, a bear, through which to ask her questions.

> *Bear:* (touching the rabbit carefully) You are hurt. What happened?
>
> *Rabbit:* That stupid lion hit me!
>
> *Bear:* (turning to lion) Is it true that you hit the rabbit??
>
> *Lion:* I sure did. I hate him—he is so stupid, so I hit him!
>
> *Bear:* How come you hate him?
>
> *Lion:* I don't know....
>
> *Bear:* (to rabbit) Why do you think he hates you?
>
> *Rabbit:* Beats me. I didn't do anything!
>
> *Bear:* You didn't pick on the lion or anything?
>
> *Rabbit:* Hell no—he's too big and strong.
>
> *Bear:* (to lion) I saw what happened, and I thought the rabbit picked on you. Didn't he pull your hair and call you a nerd?
>
> *Lion:* Yes, I guess he did.
>
> *Bear:* How do you feel when someone calls you a nerd and pulls your hair?
>
> *Lion:* I don't like it!
>
> *Bear:* Do you sometimes pick on the person back?
>
> *Lion:* Oh yeah—gotta show 'em who's the boss!
>
> *Bear:* (to rabbit) Do you remember picking on the lion?
>
> *Rabbit:* Yeah...I guess I did.
>
> *Bear:* Do you think the lion was just defending himself when he hit you?
>
> *Rabbit:* Yeah, I suppose. I guess I kind of started it.

The child was quite able to play both parts, the rabbit and the lion, throughout this exchange. Through the use of the puppets, he was able to distance enough from the real-life situation to take an objective look at the events and to realize that behaviors have causes and consequences.

Identification of Sources of Feelings. Although the labeling and identification of feelings often fall into the realm of communication of empathic understanding, it can also be an explaining strategy, if it incorporates the identification of the source of the feelings. In this process, the therapist not only is empathically attuned to the feeling that is expressed by the child, but also has made a connection between the feeling and its origin. The child, on the other hand, does not appear to have made this connection, and needs some help in so doing. Helping children recognize the sources of their feelings imparts a sense of control over their affects they did not previously have (Russ and Freedheim, 2001). It also helps them become more altruistic, as they can then recognize that there are sources for other people's feelings as well and these need to be respected.

Following is an example of a therapeutic interaction oriented toward helping a 5-year-old girl recognize why she was mildly school-phobic (well, kindergarten-phobic). This child's mother was severely asthmatic and had almost died on two occasions. One time, she was saved by the girl's brother, who ran to a neighbor, who then alerted emergency medical personnel. The other time, the girl was home alone with the mother and was unable to help her. The mother fortunately recovered on her own.

> Michelle was telling a story in which a little bear cub was afraid to leave the den when summer came. She wanted to stay in the den with her mother and brother and just spend the summer there instead of learning how to fish for salmon and graze in the meadows. The therapist told a story back, designed to label, identify, and explain the little bear's feelings. This was her story: "The little bear cub does not want to leave the den because she would rather stay in for the summer than to learn how to fish and graze. She is afraid of what might happen when she leaves the den because when her little brother left the den the week before, he got hurt by a big grizzly cub who was born last year. The little cub doesn't want to leave because she is afraid she might get hurt too, because her mother is very weak and can't protect her because she is sick. The little cub would rather stay with her mom and take care of her to make sure that she doesn't die. Soon the little cub will learn that she can leave the den and learn how to fish and graze from other mommy bears, and then she can get strong and can eat a lot and feed herself really well. Maybe she can even come back and bring her mom a fish she caught."

The therapist's story identified and labeled the feeling as one of being vulnerable to and unprotected from the world. She proceeded to explain the feeling as the child's fear for her mother's life, and hence her own abandonment. She also identified the child's helplessness and decided to make a suggestion aimed at addressing this feeling therapeutically by explaining that the girl might have to seek alternative sources of support to overcome her vulnerability.

Catharsis. It should be noted in this context that mere catharsis, that is, release of emotion and expression of feeling, is very therapeutic for children (Freedheim and Russ, 2000). Therapists have the responsibility to provide an environment in which even the expression of negative affects feels safe to the child.

As-If Explanations. Sometimes feelings cannot be labeled directly because they might be too threatening for the child to own them. The clinician then best makes these statements using an as-if scenario (O'Conner, 2000). In the as-if situation, an interpretation is stated in general terms to make it more acceptable to the child. Rather than requiring the child to own a feeling or need that she or he expressed in play or symbolically, the therapist may choose to draw the conclusion for children in general. Thus, she or he might say something like "Some girls/boys might feel depressed/angry/anxious if this happened to them."

More direct explanations of obvious feelings or their dynamic sources can be used with children if a process becomes clear within a child's play, indicating that the child has already gained a certain level of awareness of the situational dynamics (O'Conner, 2000). Thus, the child who pretends that a girl doll is very angry because a brother doll got to go to camp might be responded to with a statement such as "This doll says she is very angry at her brother because he got to go to camp. I wonder if she is really angry at her parents because they let *him* go but told *her* she was too young."

Interpretation. Similar to the explaining of sources for feelings is the connection of past experiences and present behaviors or of thoughts and subsequent feelings and actions. This type of explaining is quite sophisticated and requires some cognitive capabilities on the child's part. It requires a level of abstraction and insight that is not necessarily present in all child clients. Thus, it is a strategy that may be less often utilized with children than it is used with adults. Nevertheless, the occasion might may arise when such explaining is quite appropriate. For instance, one 12-year-old girl who had severe nightmares benefitted from learning about the connection between her nightmares and her history of being sexually abused by her father at age 4. Her father used to come to her room late at night after she had gone to sleep and would have intercourse with her. She often pretended to sleep through the entire process and then spent the night trying to stay awake for fear of his return.

This type of explaining is traditionally called an interpretation and, as such, is reserved for the reexperience and resolution phases of treatment. Interpretations can be tailored to children's needs and cognitive development if they can be rendered symbolically or nonverbally. These alterations of the traditional interpretation make it amenable to the work with children. However, it is important to remember that interpretations are most generally oriented toward helping a client achieve some level of insight. However, this might not always be a necessary outcome in the work with children. Children are often very well-served through the internalization of strength, direction, and self-esteem—processes that do not require sophisticated insight (see Kohut, 1984).

Internalization

Internalization is an important catalyst or medium for change in the work with children; in fact, this is perhaps the most important one of all. Internalization is a process as much as a catalyst and thus is not as concrete a strategy as the other catalysts discussed thus far. It permeates therapy and often is involved when other catalysts are used as the more overt or noticeable strategies. Yet despite, or maybe because of, its covert nature, internalization represents an extremely important aspect of child therapy. Internalization is the process of helping a child make certain processes, beliefs, feelings, needs, behaviors, and values her or his own through the use of imitation, modeling, and similar normal developmental occurrences. Children observe their environment very curiously and intently from very early on in life. Much of what they learn, they learn through imitation and modeling. In fact, some clinicians claim that as much as 80 percent of what human beings know and believe is acquired through modeling. Children pay particular attention to models who are important to them in some way or another. A child's earliest models are no doubt her or his primary caretakers during infancy, toddlerhood, and childhood, often the child's biological, adoptive, step-, or foster parents. From these models, children learn many concrete skills. However, these persons or models also serve more subtle purposes related to the child's general self-development. Specifically, there are two major components of a child's self, one having to do with self-esteem and realistic self-appraisal and the other dealing with life direction, values, and self-perceived strength and ability to cope, that are developed through the process of internalization. [The interested reader is referred to Kohut (1984) for more information].

If a child did not internalize certain capabilities or aspects of the self in her or his relationship with prominent figures in her or his life, she or he will be able to use the therapeutic relationship to do so. Thus, interactions with the therapist serve to strengthen the child's internalized self-representations and serve to strengthen the child in many ways without the need for insight or explaining. The child will glean strength from the clinician through the mere interaction with her or him, in much the same way as an infant in a healthy interpersonal environment will learn to do by modeling after, imitating, and internalizing her or his parents' responses, values, and so forth. This process of internalization is crucial to the work with children, as it takes place nonverbally and preverbally, does not rely on cognitive insights, and builds the basis for a strong, goal-directed and self-confident self.

To be able to serve as such a model, the therapist has to recognize where the primary needs of the child lie. Thus, for some children, internalization of self-esteem and realistic self-appraisal may be more important, whereas for others, the internalization of rules and regulations may be paramount. The empathic attunement with the child and communication of empathic understanding will greatly enhance the process of internalization.

An often used example of internalization of rules and regulations is the child who is observed in front of a cookie jar in the absence of a regulating parent. The child will approach the jar and be ambivalent about whether to take a cookie. This child is often observed to mimic a parent's voice to talk herself or himself out of taking a cookie. An example of a therapeutic internalization is presented here by describing an interaction between a female therapist and a 9-year-old girl:

> Sally had been referred by her teacher because of her severe constriction of affect and her inability to play and let herself get dirty. She was always very intent on following rules and could not relax. Sally had been seen for several sessions, during which she had learned some relaxation techniques and had begun to trust the therapist. However, she was still very controlled in her play and had difficulty letting go of her severe approach to life. The therapist had been intent on helping her realize that rules are fine but are there to keep you safe and not to keep you from being playful and explorative. She had modeled on various occasions that getting dirty was okay and safe. For instance, in Sally's play with clay the therapist had purposefully gotten clay in her hair and on her clothes, and reacted with complete unconcern. Often, Sally would get angry or worried about what might happen. She was clearly worried that if she let go just a little bit she would be completely out of control. Thus, she stopped herself from even approaching the limits of a rule for fear of the consequences. Her severe constriction was thus understood as resulting from severe externally imposed rules, as opposed to resulting from a healthily internalized sense of right or wrong. After many sessions, she finally began to relax and explored the room more freely. In one

session, she took the clay and smeared it into her hair, clearly imitating the therapist's earlier actions. Several sessions later, she chose the clay again and this time played without concern. When she got it on her dress, she turned to the therapist and said assertively, "I don't want it in my hair, but it's okay on the dress." The therapist interpreted this behavior as a sign of a beginning internalization of rules. The child could now choose for herself what was appropriate and acceptable for her. She neither followed the strict external rules modeled in her daily interpersonal environment nor completely followed the example of the therapist. Instead, she had internalized her own individualized sense of right and wrong without the need for this ever having been verbalized or discussed directly.

Projective Identification

Internalization was discussed as a catalyst that is of importance because of its nonverbal quality that can be used to influence behavior, attitude, value, or emotional changes. The direct or verbal expression of affect is perhaps the most difficult form of self-expression for many children. Thus, it is useful for the therapist to be aware of a way of understanding and influencing a child's affects without the need for a verbal exchange between clinician and client. Projective identification is such a nonverbal method or therapeutic technique. Projective identification was first described by Melanie Klein as a defense mechanism (1955). She described it as a process wherein an individual splits off negative aspects of the self and projects them onto another person in an attempt to control this person and get her or him to act in accordance with the projector's own needs. Bion (1959) viewed projective identification as a normal developmental process that young children use to explore strong affects while these emotions are safely contained within another person. This process involves projection and reintrojection of strong affects in such a way that there is no threat to the developing self or personality. This definition of projective identification implies that it is an interpersonal process, or a mode of interaction, that is relevant in everyone's development, as well as in the developmental setting of psychotherapies, individual or otherwise (Grotstein, 2000).

Bion's conceptualization of the interpersonal nature of the projective identification process is most closely related to the view of a contemporary writer, Ogden (1993), who views projective identification as serving four functions: defense mechanism, mode of communication, means of object relatedness, and pathway to psychological change. He indicates that as a defense mechanism, projective identification helps the individual to rid herself or himself of undesirable or frightening affects (Klein's definition); as a mode of communication, it helps the individual to feel understood by others by imbuing them with her or his own feelings; as a way of relating to others, it constitutes a relatively safe way of being with others; and finally, as a pathway of psychological change, it makes difficult feelings, that had been projected, available to the individual in altered (i.e., less threatening or frightening) form for reintrojection. It is this latter view of projective identification that makes the concept most relevant in the context of therapeutic catalysts in the work with children (Brems, 1989b; Tansey and Burke, 1995).

As a therapeutic catalyst or technique, projective identification consists of three stages. First, the child will project an unacceptable or frightening affect or self aspect onto the therapist to calm and soothe herself and himself and keep hidden from the developing self-disturbing aspects thereof. Second, the projection of the child must be met by the therapist with acceptance and recognition or understanding, to then be metabolized, that is, altered in some fashion that makes the affect acceptable to the child. Acceptance is communicated nonverbally; recognition of the particular type of feeling is facilitated by the therapist's empathic understanding of the client and by the clinician's exploration of her or his own feelings in the therapy with the child. Metabolization of the affect refers to the therapist's recognition that the affect she or he is experiencing with the child originated from the child, is overwhelming to the child, and must be made less frightening and more acceptable before the child can identify with and own the affect herself or himself again. Third, once thus altered or metabolized, the affect will be identified by the child as her or his own and will be reintegrated into her or his developing self-image or self-definition. This process of reintrojection is critical to the therapeutic impact of projective identification, as without the introjection, no change in the child has occurred.

Without reintrojection, the projective identification would then merely have served as a defense against the affect that was successfully concealed from the developing self of the child by projecting it. Without the metabolization of the projected affect by the therapist, reintrojection would not be possible in a therapeutic way, as the unaltered affect would remain unacceptable or overwhelming to the child, could not be reintegrated into the child's conscious concept of self, and would continue to be rejected by the child. However, if the therapist is successful and accepting, recognizing and altering the affect, it will be acceptable to the child and can be incorporated successfully. Although this process sounds somewhat technical and abstract, it is actually a very experience-near procedure. It always contains some affective involvement on the therapist's part. It is this affective involvement that occasionally causes the cycle to derail and to end unsuccessfully. In other words, if the therapist receives the affect but does not recognize it as the child's, but rather perceives it as her or his own, a projective counteridentification is set in motion. In this scenario, the therapist will feel equally overwhelmed or disturbed by the affect and cannot contain or alter it, and often the therapeutic cycle cannot be closed.

For instance, if a client is utterly confused about life and the direction she or he wants to choose for life, it can occur that the therapist takes on some of the client's projected confusion, only to begin to feel disoriented and ambivalent about the client's treatment. One supervisee was observed to begin to avoid talking about a particular client's case. When this avoidance was addressed, she confessed that she felt very confused and unclear about her treatment goals with this individual. Her therapy had been unfocused, and no themes had begun to emerge across sessions. Upon some exploration with the supervisor, this therapist came to realize that much of her confusion had originated from her client, who was utterly unable to give any focus to his life. When she recognized that the confusion she experienced was not entirely her own, she was able to formulate some treatment goals and was able to begin to direct the sessions.

Projective counteridentification, as described in this example, is most likely to occur around affects that the therapist herself or himself has not mastered completely. Thus, a novice therapist who has not worked with very many children and feels somewhat anxious in sessions with child clients will be particularly vulnerable to projections of anxiety. This occurred in the treatment of one particularly anxious child. This child had experienced life in a household that had little structure or direction, few rules, and little caring. His feelings were similarly unfocused and not governed by the normal rules and moral developmental regulations that would normally be expected of a 10-year-old. Consequently, his behavior was often out of control, destructive toward others, as well as suicidal. Early in his treatment, which occurred early in the therapist's career, he was extremely out of control in the treatment room, often threatening to and actually throwing furniture or climbing on shelves and threatening to jump and hurt himself. The therapist began to dread her sessions with this child and often felt very upset and anxious for half a day before his scheduled appointment. She felt as though she had lost control over the sessions, which indeed she had. In exasperation, she consulted with a supervisor, who recognized the projection of affect and helped the therapist to differentiate between her own level of anxiety and the child's exaggerated projected anxiety, orient her treatment through the setting of definite and revised treatment goals, introduce structure into the therapy environment, and set limits assertively and consistently.

Successful use of projective identification resulted from the above examples of the almost derailed processes. Once the therapists in the examples recognized the origin of the strong affects, they were able to accept the affects and to tolerate them in milder forms. They were able to make environmental and attitudinal changes that rendered the affects manageable and tolerable. Once the affects were thus metabolized, the clients could recognize them in their milder forms as acceptable and tolerable, identified with them, and reintrojected them into their own repertoire of feelings in the milder, more tolerable form. This change in affect was affected entirely through nonverbal interpersonal processes that never had to be discussed or interpreted. A detailed example of the therapeutic use of projective identification with children is presented in Brems (1989b).

Use of Defenses, Symptoms, and Resistance

One final common catalyst for change is the skilled therapeutic use of a child's defenses, symptoms, and resistance that are evidenced in the therapy room. Defense and resistance are always part of treatment and, despite having been dealt with mainly as processes that disturb the therapy, can actually be used as therapeutic aids. To understand defense and resistance as therapy catalysts, they must be redefined, and, some therapists recommend, even relabeled (e.g., Kohut, 1984). The new recommended label for defense or defensive symptom is protective mechanism, a label that suggests the new definition. Defenses are developed by children early on in their lives and generally serve a self-protective purpose. They develop when threats arise either from within or without and represent the child's attempt to deal or cope with this threat as positively and effectively as possible. Thus, all defensive maneuvers ultimately share one trait: They are designed to protect and keep harm away from the developing self. It is irrelevant whether this protection is from intrapsychic processes, as defined by psychodynamic or psychoanalytic theorists; from negative cognitions, as defined by cognitive behaviorists; from family dynamics, as defined by family systems theorists; or even from reinforcement contingencies, as defined by behaviorists. Regardless of how the defense works and why it is viewed to have developed, it always serves to protect or to help the child cope as best as possible.

The child therapist must recognize the need for the defenses or symptoms that developed as means of self-protection. The particular context in which the defense and the symptoms developed must be known for the therapist to understand from what the child is protecting herself or himself. For instance, a young boy who has developed stomachaches as a defense against seeing his parents fight should not be confronted about the defensive nature of his physical complaints, but rather needs to be understood within his dysfunctional family system. His stomachaches are the one thing he can use to control an aversive and difficult situation. In other words, the clinician needs to develop understanding for the defense or the symptom, not confront it with reality testing. To go back to the boy in the example, the therapist would not challenge the reality of the stomachache, arguing that there is no physical cause, but rather would help the child to understand that the stomachache is his way of coping. In this approach, the defensive symptom is not attacked and stripped away. Rather, it is understood and empathically placed into the context wherein it developed.

Stripping away the defense would leave the child vulnerable and without coping strategies. The clinician needs to learn to understand the child's defensive affects and symptoms before unmasking and challenging them; understanding rules and explaining take the backseat (Adams, 1982). Once the child has grown stronger through treatment, familial changes, or environmental modifications and other coping skills have been learned, the symptom or defense can be challenged. Learning alternative problem-solving and coping strategies is thus a critical piece of the therapeutic intervention. It may be facilitated through direct problem solving in the session or via modeling and redirection by the therapist (Russ and Freedheim, 2001). Stripping away the symptom before some other form of coping or strength has been imparted or developed is dangerous and not helpful to the child's continued growth.

This interpretation of defenses and symptoms is very similar to the concept of "going with the resistance." Rather than challenging a child's resistance to treatment, the clinician explores why the resistance has developed to begin with. Most often, the resistance serves the same self-protective purpose as the defense or the symptom. Coming for treatment is frightening, and resisting the process appears to be the only way in which the child can protect herself or himself from further intrusions or pain. Children who come to treatment are there because they have been hurt in more or less direct physical or psychological ways. They have often learned not to trust adults and to protect themselves through withdrawal, acting out, or other behavioral or emotional patterns. To expect them to shed these defenses quickly and easily in the therapy is unrealistic. Allowing the child to bring these patterns into the therapy room, to allow them, observe them, and attempt to understand them, on the other hand, communicates respect and is more likely to result in sufficient trust to help the child give them up. Challenging resistance always results in more resistance. Treatment resistances present unique challenges to treatment. They are addressed further in the next section of this chapter in this context.

Although a number of strategies, or treatment catalysts, have been discussed, many more exist. It is likely that each therapist will develop her or his own preferred means of intervening. However, the strategies presented here are likely to remain in the repertoire of all child therapists, as they are relatively theory-free. The catalysts ultimately help the therapist to help the child address the treatment goals that had been set before therapy began. Additionally, clinicians often observe changes in a child that were not predicted, and new behaviors emerge that were not necessarily targeted by the treatment directly. These outcomes are often quite positive and useful for the child and fall into the category of therapeutic by-products. These by-products tend to involve the resolution of problems that were somewhat related to the presenting problem without being obvious or overt. For instance, as a fearful child improves, she or he may also feel an increase in self-esteem and a decrease in loneliness. Seeing children improve over the course of treatment is a gratifying process. It is the recognition of change and improvement that reinforces the clinician and maintains her or his zeal and enthusiasm for the chosen career. However, the process of change is not always an easy one. There are a few common challenges presented specifically by child clients. These problems and their potential solutions are discussed in the final section of this chapter.

Challenges to the Therapeutic Process

The challenges of child therapy are many (Gabel, Oster, and Pfeffer, 1993). The better prepared the clinician is to face these, the more likely that they will not interfere with treatment, but perhaps will even enhance it. Often, the challenges presented by children are resistances or defensive maneuvers. Thus, as explained above, they must be understood by the therapist as self-protective and be treated as such. They will not be challenged, criticized, or confronted but rather will be understood, used therapeutically, and slowly replaced by more appropriate behaviors. The creativity and sensitivity of the therapist are often the best guides to how the challenges by an individual child should be handled. A few suggestions are provided here. They are by no means exhaustive but are included merely to get novice clinicians prepared to think on their feet.

"NOOOO—I Don't Want to Go in There!!"

For the child with separation anxiety, the first trip to the play room can be fraught with fear and dread. This child will resist leaving the parent and will be full of negative feelings about the interaction with the therapist as it requires the child to leave the caretaker. Mild forms of refusal are best dealt with by reassuring the child that the therapist understands that the child is frightened but that the therapy room is a safe place, and the parent will remain in the waiting room where the child will be greeted after a specified time period. Sometimes it is necessary to allow the child to leave the door to the room open so the child can maintain some visual contact with the person in the waiting room. For extremely anxious children, however, it may be necessary to invite the parent to the room with the child to break the ice and let the child do her or his initial exploration in the parent's presence. If this is the case, the child should be slowly weaned by asking if the child is ready to let the parent go.

Once a child has been weaned or has been to the therapy room once, there is usually no problem in future sessions of getting the child to agree to come to the room. However, the child might have other difficulties reaching the room. For instance, impulsive children may not be able to move along hallways quietly and without disrupting other therapies in rooms along the way. Some children may have some remaining apprehension about going to the room and may attempt to prolong the journey as much as possible. Other children may use the trip to the room to act out and test limits. One 11-year-old child who was seen in a room on a second floor consistently refused the stairs and insisted on riding the elevator. Once in the elevator, he predictably attempted to push the emergency button.

For children with these types of problems, it is best to develop a ritual or firm proce-dure to help them travel to the room. The situation with the 11-year-old child in the above example was solved by the following procedure. He was informed that if he were able to ride the elevator quietly and without pushing the emergency button on the way to the ses-sion, he would be allowed to ride it to the very top of the building before going down to the floor on which the waiting room was located. If he forgot to be quiet on the way to the ses-sion, the stairs had to be taken on the way to the waiting room after the session. In this ex-ample, the therapist chose to reinforce an incompatible behavior (riding the elevator quietly) to eliminate the problem behavior on the way to the session (pressing the emer-gency button). Her reinforcer was the extra-long elevator ride after the session, as she knew this to be a very exciting experience for this child.

For an anxious child, a parent might need to be involved in the transition ritual from the waiting to the therapy room. One 4-year-old girl was allowed to show her mother the way to the room as a means to reduce her anxiety of the trip. Again, the actual procedure chosen by the clinician has to be uniquely adapted to each individual child. The most im-portant thing is not to panic when a child refuses or acts out on the way to the therapy room. There is always a creative solution [refer also to O'Conner (2000)].

"Just One More Time!?"

Often, children enjoy their sessions and have difficulty ending. Sometimes, they refuse to end as a means of testing limits or manipulating the clinician. Occasionally, a child would rather stay because of the real-life situation she or he faces when she or he leaves the safety of the session. No matter what the reason, children generally have excellent excuses why the therapist should allow them to stay just a little bit longer. They may express the need to complete a drawing, the desire to finish a game, or share the sudden memory of some im-portant information. Regardless of what the excuse, the session must end on time. Landreth (1991; 2000) points out that one aspect of treatment is always to help children internalize control and responsible behavior. Ending sessions on time requires them to exercise this self-control and also provides for the consistency and stability of rules that makes therapy so safely predictable. Bending the rules for a child makes the therapist unpredictable and ma-nipulatable. It can create problems of respect in the child-therapist relationship.

The key to ending sessions on time is to warn children and to develop ending rituals. A common procedure is to warn the child that only seven to ten minutes remain of the ses-sion and that cleanup will need to begin soon. This reminder gives the child a chance to finish ongoing business. It also prepares the child for the cleanup time, which represents an excellent ending ritual in and of itself. For some children, a concrete reminder might be necessary, such as an egg timer that is turned 5 minutes before the session's end. For most children, the verbal reminder suffices. Once cleanup begins, the child has a chance to wind down from the session's work and to ready herself or himself to face the world. If cleanup is not enough to prepare the child, an additional ritual might be added. For one child, a trainee had devised a method of taking off and putting on shoes. For this child-clinician dyad, the beginning of a session was signaled by both of them removing their shoes. The ending was ushered in by both of them putting on their shoes. Even then, the child occa-sionally had difficulty transitioning out of the room. She would play helpless, asking the therapist to help her with her shoes. The clinician responded by putting on her own shoes and emphasizing that she knew the child could handle putting on her own shoes. This was an important message, as it told the child several things. First, she would not be able to manipulate the clinician; second, she was reminded that she was capable of putting on her shoes; and third, she was symbolically assured that she could handle the life which was facing her in the waiting room.

In the absence of an established ritual, a child who refuses to leave the room only on occasion might merely need to be reminded that the session must end regardless of the child's wishes. The child should be reassured that she or he will return during the following week and that everything will stay the same. If an issue has remained unresolved, that is, a play activity remained incomplete, the therapist should reassure the child that she or he may complete the activity during the following week. The therapist may also acknowledge that she or he understands that it is difficult for the child to end the session.

"I Want to Go Home…"

Quite to the contrary of the child who refuses to end, is the child who wants to leave early. Therapists appear somewhat split in their opinions about how to handle this issue. For instance, Gardner (1994) believes that it is the child's right to determine when she or he has had enough and therefore advocates allowing an early ending. Ginott (cited in Spiegel, 1996), on the other hand, advocates a rigid refusal to the extent of actually blocking the door if this becomes necessary. A more balanced approach is advocated by Spiegel (1996), who suggests that the therapist attempt to find out why the child wishes to leave and then decide whether the request should be met or refused. It appears that if a therapist is firm about ending on time, this stance should be maintained, whether the limit is tested by the child to extend or shorten the interaction. As such, it appears most sensible to explore why the child wants to leave early but not allow the departure.

Often, children who ask to leave have reached a point in their session that is anxiety-provoking for them. They wish to avoid this anxiety by removing themselves from the stimulus. This is an unrealistic approach to life, in which no one can always escape difficult situations. Therapy can model the appropriate way of handling such difficult situations by helping the child verbalize her or his feelings and dealing with them constructively rather than through avoidance. If the child is extremely anxious and not able to connect with the reasons for her or his anxiety, it may be permissible to let the child visit the parent in the waiting room to refuel and regain some security. However, such visits should be well-structured. They need to be short and infrequent.

One 6-year-old boy who had severe abandonment fears was helped to remain in his sessions by being allowed to visit his parents for a brief 30-second visit when his anxiety threatened to overwhelm him. This practice was allowed for approximately 5 weeks, then he was allowed to visit them only once during the session, while being allowed to look out the door and make visual contact during the other times. The next step in the desensitization process was that no more visits were allowed, only visual contact by opening the door and looking out. The next stage involved allowing him to open the door only once and asking him to imagine his parents sitting on the couch in the waiting room during the other times. Finally, only visualization were allowed. This desensitization and visualization process helped the child to settle into the therapy and also proved a useful strategy for other concerns with which he had presented for treatment.

"Do You Have Kids?"

Questions regarding personal information about the therapist should never lead to an auto-biography. Instead, the clinician must explore the fantasy underlying the question before responding to it. More often than not, the question has a dynamic, or transferential, meaning that must be understood by the clinician. These types of questions tend to occur early in the treatment and often deal with underlying issues of trust and are relevant to rapport-building. For instance, children commonly ask the therapist whether she or he has children of her or his own. This question can have a number of underlying meanings, depending on the specific context of a child's therapy and situation. For instance, it might in reality be a question about whether the therapist can love the child as she or he loves her or his own children; it might be a matter of sibling rivalry; it might be related to the child's concern whether the therapist will have enough concern and caring to go around for everyone and for this child in particular. Sometimes, children will ask the therapist whether she or he loves her or his spouse (parents, children, etc.). This question often really inquires whether the therapist loves the child. Often, children ask about other children the therapist sees in therapy. This is a particularly common question if the child has observed the therapist leave the play therapy room with another child. The concern here is again one of whether the therapist can care for everyone and may often imply some jealousy or competition.

No matter what the content of the personal question is, the therapist must consider its hidden meaning before answering it. If a therapist ever decides to answer a personal question, this response should be very brief and should be directed toward not only the surface issue, but also the deeper meaning. Thus, in response to questions about whether the therapist has children, a self-disclosing yet process-oriented response might be "Yes, and I have enough love and caring for them and all the children I work with." Making such a self-disclosure, however, must be made for a good reason, not because it is the easiest way to respond. In other words, the therapist must have reason to believe that the surface content must be answered before moving to the process issue. This might be true in this example when the therapist is aware that the child lives in the same neighborhood and is likely to see the therapist with her or his family outside of the therapy room. When in doubt, the clinician should refrain from self-disclosure.

"I Have to Go to the Bathroom!"

Questions that have to do with more general process issues tend to occur later in treatment than personal questions about the therapist. They are more commonly oriented toward resistance and defense than toward trust and rapport. For instance, children sometimes express the urge to go to the bathroom. Although on occasion this request might be genuine, it more often than not reflects the child's attempt to leave the therapy room at a moment when difficult affects are being expressed or when overwhelming needs are being mobilized. The first time this request is made, the therapist will generally grant it, as there is no certainty that it is not genuine. For the following sessions, however, the therapist should remember to ask the child to use the bathroom before entering the play room. Thus, requests in such a session can then be explored with the child in the context of the therapy process that is occurring. For instance, one 10-year-old boy had been asked, after the first such occurrence, to use the toilet before entering the next session and nevertheless asked to go to the bathroom during this session as well. The therapist had noticed that the context of the request was very similar to that of the previous session. Specifically, in both sessions, the child had made a self-disclosure about having witnessed abusive behavior on the part of his father in the family home. (Appropriate reports had been made by the therapist about this family.) The child had been struggling for several months with his ability to trust the therapist enough to deal with these issues, and it was therefore very clear that this disclosure, which was made in the context of play with the dollhouse, was extremely anxiety-provoking for the boy. In response to his request, the therapist chose not to address his request at all, but rather responded to what she perceived to be the process issue. Picking up a boy doll in the dollhouse, she said, "I am very scared about talking about what has been happening in my house. But I should remember that my therapist can keep a secret and that she will protect me." The little boy did not repeat his request to go to the bathroom. However, he still chose to turn to less frightening play activities, rechanneling his anxieties within the therapy room.

"I Am Going to Tear This Place Up!"

Although threats of physical aggression and the actual aggressive acting out of children are one of the most frightening prospects for novice clinicians, this need not be so. Aggression can be contained through various processes. Basic limit-setting skills are critical to the management of aggression and knowledge of safe physical restraining techniques are definitely recommended. When aggression is threatened or just beginning, the child needs to be reminded of the physical safety rules that had been introduced. Often, this reminder suffices to end the acting out. If the behavior continues, a contingency must be set up. The child must be informed of what will occur if she or he chooses to continue to escalate the behavior. It is important to remember to set contingencies that are in the therapist's power to enforce and that can have therapeutic value. Thus, a contingency of "You won't get dessert tonight" is clearly inappropriate, as it neither is under the clinician's control nor related to the behavior. Contingencies are best chosen according to logical consequences (Dreikurs and Grey, 1990). If the child does not interrupt the aggression upon hearing the contingency, the therapist must be prepared to enforce it. A last resort contingency can always be the early termination of a session.

If a child escalates despite limit setting and enforcement of contingencies, physical restraint may be necessary. In fact, physical restraint procedures occasionally are also used to keep a child safe from injury to the self. In one group for middle childhood children facing the divorce of their parents, physical restraint was used with two sisters who were becoming extremely aggressive with one another. The constraint served to contain their aggression, as well as to communicate support and guidance to them. The two children were held one each by the two cotherapists after verbal interventions had failed to keep the sisters from hitting one another. They were taken in a loose arm hold with the therapists kneeling and the two girls sitting. As soon as the restraints had been initiated, the girls stopped kicking and hitting, but any loosening of the grips on their arms resulted in escalated behavior. It was interesting to note that the hold that had been placed on both girls did not interfere with kicking, but neither continued to kick as long as they were held. As they were restrained, they began talking to one another, a process that had been extremely difficult for them. They discussed their feelings of jealousy and rivalry. They felt very secure in the hold and remained calm and capable of communication as long as they were held. Slowly, the holds were loosened, but body contact remained necessary for approximately 10 minutes.

This example demonstrates that even if aggression escalates to the point at which it necessitates physical restraint, the actual use of holding does not need to be aversive or countertherapeutic. In fact, it can signal concern and caring and can be a concrete means of helping the child to contain affect.

"Can I Bring My Ice Cream Cone?"

Almost any child who is seen in therapy will at some point arrive with food. Different opinions exist about whether food is appropriate in sessions, with some therapists arguing that it interferes and others claiming that it can be used therapeutically. Thus, the important issue for the novice therapist is to decide beforehand whether she or he will tolerate food in the session. If the clinician decides against food, this limit must be enforced within realistic and therapeutic boundaries. A child who arrives for an after-school session with a half-eaten sandwich might need to be allowed to finish the food in the waiting room to ascertain that she or he is not too hungry to concentrate on her session. However, routine arrival with food might need to be addressed if it appears to have become a means of avoiding the session. Nonnutritious foods can generally wait to be eaten until after the session. However, occasionally, the impact on rapport of forbidding the child to finish an almost-gone candy bar might need to be weighed against the benefits of so doing. If the therapist chooses not to allow the child to finish her or his food or drink before going to the therapy room, she or he should take care to remember to leave the food in a safe place outside the therapy room where the child can predictably retrieve it after the session.

"Can I Take This Home?"

Invariably, children will ask to take home with them an item that they found in the playroom. This request must be explored for its therapeutic meaning as it might represent a longing to extend the therapy, reflect an attachment to something the child made in the therapy, be a way of testing limits that had been set previously, or be a request for a gift. Depending on how the request is interpreted, the therapist may respond in different ways. If the request is meant to prolong treatment by being made at the end of the session, a mere reiteration of the rules of therapy might be sufficient to end the child's behavior. If it is a request for a prolonging of the session by providing the child with a transitional object, different paths may be chosen by the therapist. If the desired object was a project created by the child, such as a painting or small clay figure, the request should be granted. If the object is large and essential to treatment, the request cannot be granted but needs to be discussed with the child. In this instance, the child might be encouraged to create a small object that she or he can take home instead that may function for the same purpose. One thing that works quite well is to make a drawing of the actual desired object. Occasionally, a clinician might choose to allow the child to take home an item as a transitional object if there is a good reason. For instance, one boy who had been seen in therapy for several weeks and who had had large difficulties learning to trust and to make use of the therapy process became particularly attached to a humanlike puppet. During a session that immediately preceded a two-week break in the therapy due to his family's vacation, he requested to take the puppet with him. He was allowed to do so, with the provision that he would return it during the next meeting (which he did).

"It's My Birthday! Do You Have a Present for Me?"

The request for gifts is quite another matter. Often, a child's direct request for a gift has a hidden meaning, such as a request for affection. Opinions vary widely about whether the clinician should or should not give and receive gifts. Some theoreticians claim that the giving of gifts is natural and should be a normal part of treatment. Others believe that no gifts should ever be given. A middle-of-the-road position is presented by Dodds (1985), who advocates that small gifts or edible gifts are fine, especially if they can be justified therapeutically or perhaps are used to communicate special caring to a child who might not otherwise understand this message. As in most cases, it is probably best for a therapist to ask herself or himself why she or he would like to present the child with a gift. If the reason is therapeutic and clearly not countertransferential, the gift may be given. If there is doubt, the clinician should refrain from the temptation of giving until she or he has consulted with a colleague.

The receiving of gifts is equally debatable, but perhaps less so than with adult clients. Children are not likely to make expensive gifts, nor would they understand why a therapist cannot accept a gift. Thus, the acceptance of modest gifts may be warranted. In fact, the rejection of such spontaneous gifts may be more countertherapeutic than beneficial, as long as the gift truly came from the child and not the parent. Food is a common gift presented by children and, if brought for the therapist, is best shared with the child early in the session. One young girl was delighted to bring cookies for her therapist late in the treatment. For her, the process of sharing cookies symbolized her ability to nurture herself and others and her growing affective independence. Rejection of her gift would have communicated that the therapist did not agree with her assessment of her own capabilities and would clearly have been countertherapeutic. It is perhaps possible to conclude that almost anything can be done in the treatment with children, as long as the clinician has thought about the action, has determined it to be therapeutic, and is certain that it did not develop from a countertransferential need on her or his part.

"Guess What This Is?"

The most important thing to recognize about this commonly asked question is that it almost never is intended as it is stated (see Dodds, 1985; Landreth, 1991; 2000). The child usually already has something in mind when asking the therapist about the nature of a drawing or clay model. If the therapist were to answer in this instance and be wrong, the child would be likely to be disappointed, if not disillusioned. It is best for the therapist to lay the responsibility on the child by saying that she or he thinks the child has something in mind and asking the child what the drawing, the model, and so on, represents to her or him.

Often, children also ask the clinician what she or he thinks about a certain project, behavior, action, or affect. Again, responsibility needs to be given back to the child by asking the same question of her or him. Not uncommonly, these questions are not questions to be taken literally but are to be understood as a request for permission by the child to share her or his own thoughts and fantasies. Thus, an answer by the therapist would short-circuit a potential self-disclosure or self-exploration by the child.

Sometimes, these types of questions are also attempts by the child to shirk responsibility and to shift it to the therapist. In these instances, it is best to acknowledge that the child would like to have an answer from the therapist but that she or he will need to figure the answer out herself or himself. The following interaction resulted between a therapist and a 6-year-old girl and serves to demonstrate how to use a child's invitation into a guessing game to help the child self-disclose or grow, without ever answering the original question:

SARA: (TRYING TO COMPLETE A DRAWING SHE HAD BEGUN EARLIER IN THE SESSION)   What color should this be?

THERAPIST: What color would you like it to be?

SARA: It's a big house. It should be white. Do you think I should color it? Or should I leave it white?

THERAPIST: What would you rather do?

SARA: I don't know… It should be white, shouldn't it?

THERAPIST: You are worried to give it the wrong color, and you want me to tell you what to do.

SARA: It has to be just right…

THERAPIST: You are afraid to do the wrong thing. But remember, everything is okay in here. It's all up to you.

SARA: I think I'll make it all black (proceeds to color; as she progresses she continues to talk, more to herself than the clinician)… it's a very sad house. It has to be all black because black is sad…

This example demonstrates that questions and requests are often loaded with unmentioned values, affects, and needs. Direct responses will keep the child from uncovering these needs and affects and are generally not in the best interest of advancing treatment.

"I Didn't Take It…"

Fortunately, it does not occur often that a child will engage in theft. However, it is an incident that is likely to baffle the novice therapist and therefore needs to be addressed. Occasionally, a child, knowing that all therapy toys must remain in the room upon ending the session, will attempt to steal a small toy from the room. She or he might put it in a pocket and "forget" to remove it before leaving the room. If this happens, direct, though gentle, confrontation is necessary. It is not recommended to pretend that the clinician is not aware of the child's action. Rather, a direct approach is preferred (Landreth, 1991; 2000).

Similarly, if the child succeeded in taking an item from the play therapy room, she or he needs to be asked about her or his behavior during the next session and needs to be asked to return the item (Spiegel, 1996). No moralizing is necessary. Children tend to feel very guilty anyhow, and extended scrutiny, moralizing, or perseverating about the incident is counterproductive. One 10-year-old boy was observed by a person in the waiting room to go into another clinician's office while waiting for his father to pick him up. The waiting room person alerted the therapist after the child had already left the center that he had carried a stopwatch when his father arrived. Sure enough, a stopwatch was reported missing from the other clinician's office. When the child returned the following week, the following conversation took place:

> THERAPIST: After you left last week, I noticed that you took a stopwatch that belongs to someone who works here. Please bring it back next week.
>
> TIM: What are you talking about? I didn't take no stopwatch!
>
> THERAPIST: Someone saw you take it, and you need to return it.
>
> TIM: Who saw what?
>
> THERAPIST: I know that you have the stopwatch, and you need to give it back. It is not yours to keep.
>
> TIM: So I took it. Big deal. Why don't you just get a new one?
>
> THERAPIST: I know you don't want to give it back, but it does not belong to you.
>
> TIM: I'd like to keep it.
>
> THERAPIST: You really like the stopwatch.
>
> TIM: Yeah, it's neat. I took it to show-and-tell, and everyone liked it.
>
> THERAPIST: The other kids really admired the watch.
>
> TIM: Yeah, Bill even wanted to borrow it, but I didn't let him.
>
> THERAPIST: You didn't even let anyone borrow it!
>
> TIM: No, they might steal it!
>
> THERAPIST: …Hmm…
>
> TIM: I guess I have to give it back.
>
> THERAPIST: Yes, please bring it with you next week.
>
> TIM: (RETRIEVES THE WATCH FROM HIS POCKET) Here it is.

The example would not be complete without mentioning that the conversation then continued on to explore why Tim liked the watch. It became clear that he often was unable to bring items to show-and-tell and felt embarrassed. The watch had served as his way of ascertaining some attention and recognition from his peers. It is best always to explore why a child took an item as often an important meaning is attached to the theft. Again, this exploration is not focused on a moralizing investigation of the theft, but the emotional significance of the event. It is done directly, not condescendingly.

It must be reemphasized that the examples here are not exhaustive of all the special circumstances that may arise in child therapy. In fact, entire volumes have been written just on this topic (e.g., Gabel, Oster, and Pfeffer, 1993). The above scenarios were included merely to sensitize the novice child therapist to the types of difficulties that may be encountered and to ready her or him to deal with these challenges in a therapeutic and meaningful manner.

Summary and Concluding Thoughts

In this chapter, the reader was introduced to a framework of doing psychotherapy with children. This framework was kept as general as possible to allow for its use with diverse theoretical approaches, as well as with the wide range of specific techniques that can be used in the work with children. The remainder of the book will be devoted to introducing novice clinicians to this diversity of techniques. They will be dealt with individually, but can be and most often are used concurrently. Obviously, not all available techniques can be covered in one volume; only a few of the major techniques will be covered. It is hoped that the interested reader will seek additional guidance from books dedicated to each one of the specific techniques that exist.

The techniques covered in this volume include play therapy, storytelling, behavioral strategies, art therapy, and parent consultation. Other techniques include, but are not limited to, bibliotherapy [Doll and Doll, (1997); Thompson and Rudolph (2000) present an excellent annotated bibliography of therapeutic children's books], cognitive-behavior therapy (Kendall, 2000; and Kratochwill and Morris, 1998), rational-emotive therapy for children (Bernard, 2002), family therapy (Kaslow, Kaslow, Celano, and Farber, 2001; Minuchin, Simon, and Lee, 1996; Satir, 1967), relaxation training (Cautela and Groden, 1982; Pearson, 1998), modeling and social skills therapies (Dowrick, 1986), biofeedback (Finley and Jones, 1992), hypnotherapy (Olness and Kohen, 1996; Wester, 1991), use of metaphor (Olness and Kohen, 1996; Mills and Crowley, 1986), pharmacotherapy (Werry and Aman, 1999), sandtray therapy (Boik and Goodwin, 2000); and many others [for useful summaries of techniques, see Mash and Barkley (1998) or Schaefer, Millman, Sichel, and Zwilling (1986)]. Collections of case examples have been compiled by Roberts and Walker (1997) and Landreth, Homeyer, Glover, and Sweeney (1996).

CHAPTER

9 Play Therapy

Play is perhaps one of the most common techniques utilized by child therapists. Its use for that purpose has been widely documented, described, and supported (O'Conner, 2000; Landreth, 2000; and Schaefer, 1998b; 2000). To understand the importance and relevance of play in the therapeutic work with children, it is first necessary to take a look at the normal, everyday impact that play may have on a child's life and development.

Conceptual Background

The fact that play is guaranteed by the United Nations as an inalienable right of childhood for children all over the world reveals the great importance placed upon play as an important task that facilitates a child's growth and maturation. Play has been described as a child's occupation (Erikson, 1950), and the toys used as the child's tools (Woltman, 1964). However, this definition has been questioned as being merely a way of legitimizing play in adults' eyes (Landreth, 1991), as play is important in and of itself, even if not viewed as a child's work. It is the most "natural medium for self-expression" (Axline, 1947, p. 16), and an excellent means of communication among children, as well as between children and adults. Child's play communicates without words. It is person-dominated, and toys or simple objects are used for the purpose of enhancing the child's growth or helping the child to enact an important life situation (O'Conner, 2000). Play is noninstrumental. In other words, it is the process that is important, not the product or a defined end goal. In fact, there rarely is an end goal in the free play of a child, even when such a goal appears to have been defined by the child. Often an activity is started that appears to lead to a certain outcome, only to be altered in its overt purpose before the child is done. However, despite being thus noninstrumental, play is nevertheless unconsciously purposeful (Landreth, 1991; 2000). Although there might not be an overt goal or end state of play, it nevertheless serves a purpose for the child, even if this purpose is not readily observable or understandable.

The unconscious purposefulness of play is at the crux of play's symbolism. Play is not always only what is seen on the surface. Play has an indirect meaning through which the child may work through everyday problems or may find solutions to problems. The unique meaning of each play activity, both its content and its style, can be understood only over time and through intensive exploration of content, form, associations, accompanying feelings, and fantasies expressed by the child in the activity. Play, understood in this context, serves as an effort at mastery of the environment and often the self, a mastery that is

248

obtained through the planning and experiment (Simmons, 1987) that are inherent in all children's play. This mastery function of play was already recognized by Sigmund Freud, who wrote that "every child at play...creates a world of his [sic] own or, more truly, he [sic] arranges the things in his [sic] world and orders it in a new way that pleases him [sic] better" (1952, p. 174). This definition clearly implies the purposefulness of play. What specifically are the purposes of play? They are multifold, though they may be grouped into three larger categories: namely self-development (or intrapsychic) purposes, maturation (or growth) purposes, and relationship (or interpersonal) purposes. These three functions and their subgoals are summarized in Table 9.1.

The Self-Development Function of Play

Intrapsychic purposes are those which help the child in the task of defining and developing a sense of self. This is a large task of early childhood, and therefore, it is of no surprise that

TABLE 9.1   Purposes of Play in a Child's Everyday Life

Overall Function	Specific Purpose
Self-Development Function	to engage in self-expression
	to define the self
	to express and explore feelings
	to discover likes and dislikes
	to gain a sense of control
	to cope with difficult situations
	to express complexities beyond verbal capacity
	to meet the need to be engaged in an activity
	to feel stimulated
Maturation Function	to explore the environment
	to explore relationships among objects
	to gain a sense of mastery
	to practice language skills
	to practice motor skills
	to practice cognitive skills
	to learn moral judgment
	to learn problem-solving skills
	to organize experiences in meaningful ways
Relationship Function	to communicate with others
	to learn about roles
	to learn about culture and environment
	to learn social skills
	to explore relationships among people
	to work through conflict in relationships
	to feel connected to others
	to use others as models

this is also a major task of play activity. Through play, the child can begin a rudimentary definition of self. Play helps the child to express herself or himself freely and without having to fear any negative consequences. This self-expression always includes a component of self-exploration. Many activities are engaged in. Some will be experienced by the child as more pleasurable than others and will therefore be repeated and will result in an observable pattern of preferences and interests, which the child may later use to define likes and dislikes.

Expression through play is not merely expression of interests, but also expression of affect. Children work out feelings in play. Feelings that might not be allowed expression in a child's family are often tolerated when disguised in play activity. For instance, although the child might not be allowed to shout at her or his mother when angry, she or he is rarely punished or even chastised if she or he allows two dolls to shout at each other. Even if one doll is clearly a child doll and the other an adult doll, parents usually grant children the freedom to engage in doll play freely. This expression of feelings is a very important component of play, as it not only allows for catharsis of emotion, but also teaches the child that affect can be expressed freely, can be controlled through expression, and can be rendered manageable when expressed. Children become aware of nuances of affect through their play, recognizing that there are different levels of the same emotion that may require different levels of expression. Play is important in this regard also, because even if the child wished to express some of these affects and needs verbally, her or his cognitive or language skills might prevent the child from so doing. The nonverbal nature of play allows for the expression of complexities that the child could not master through any other medium or means of communication.

Through the free expression of affect and through the exploration of interests and other aspects of self, the child will also gain a sense of control over herself or himself. Rather than being driven by emotion or need, the child drives or expresses and solves them. The subsequent feeling of control serves to enhance the child's self-confidence and sense of mastery. It ultimately helps the child feel competent to cope with life's difficulties.

Finally, as all living organisms have a need to be stimulated and to feel somehow purposefully engaged in activity, play can serve this function as well. Through play, children remain stimulated, keep boredom from taking over, and experience a sense of meaning in their existence. The importance of this function of play is best demonstrated by observing a child who cannot find a play activity or who is unable to self-initiate a game. This child grows bored, then experiences self-doubts, which may be rechanneled either into internalized feelings, such as anxiety or depression, or externalized feelings, such as anger or hostility.

The Maturation Function of Play

In addition to enhancing self or intrapsychic development, play promotes a child's general growth. Play leads to maturation in a number of developmental arenas, including language skills, motor skills, cognitive skills, problem-solving skills, and moral judgments. Through play, children not only learn new skills in all of these areas, but are also given the opportunity to practice skills in a meaningful and nonthreatening manner. Play can serve as an arena to act out skills modeled after parents or friends. This opportunity not only helps the child to gain a sense of mastery, but also enhances the child's ability to problem solve in general and to cope with new situations. In fact, even modeling in play activity is never done in a truly replicating manner. Instead, the child modifies what she or he has seen to make it fit her or his own unique perspective, needs, and capabilities.

In addition to skills learning and practice, maturation is facilitated for the child through play's exploratory function. Play leads the child to explore the environment, relationships between objects, cause-and-effect relationships, and connections between events. This facilitates the child's meaningful organization of experiences.

The Relationship Function of Play

Closely related to the self-development and maturation functions of play is the relationship function. Through this aspect of play, the child applies what has been learned about the self and what has been mastered and learned through practice to relationships with other people. As the child learns new problem-solving skills in general, she or he can now learn to apply these skills to interpersonal situations. This may initially be done in solitary play that involves a number of puppets, dolls, or other objects that may represent important figures in a child's life. Later, this is done through actual interactive play with playmates in which compromises have to be worked out and conflicts solved.

Play helps a child communicate with others, whether this was an intended component of the activity or not. Thus, communication can take place in solitary play in which an observer becomes the incidental recipient of information or through interactive play in which the playmate is the intended target of communication. The nonverbal nature of play removes the need for language between sender and recipient, thus making communication independent of shared language. Communicating with others helps the child to feel interpersonally connected and enhances her or his feeling of belonging.

Through play with others, the child also learns about roles in relationships and roles that are connected to family rules or cultural and environmental attitudes. Play can be used by the child to practice her or his role in her or his family and friendships and as a participant in her or his culture. Learning about roles is related to learning social skills, as both involve interaction with others that is acceptable and appropriate to the context in which the interaction takes place. In the play with other children, all players have to learn to negotiate and to assert themselves. This has to be done in a manner that is acceptable and well-received by the targets, or it will result in ostracism of the child. However, even as a child creates conflict in her or his play, learning takes place. Conflicts have to be resolved, and there is no better activity to learn conflict resolution than through interactive play. The advantage of interactive over solitary play in the relationship function also stems from the fact that interactive play necessitates the presence of others, who may serve as models. Children not only learn from watching adults, but learn perhaps even more from watching and playing with their peers and friends.

By now, the developmental advantages of play should be quite self-evident. Further, these advantages and functions of play should also be readily apparent as the reasons why play has become an important technique in the work with children. Many of the normal, everyday functions of play are relevant in the therapy context. Thus, play is readily identifiable as relevant to therapy in many ways.

Application to Therapy

As one aspect of the normal function of play is the establishment of relationships, it is easy to see that play can be used to facilitate the relationship between a child and a therapist. Through play, interaction can be easily initiated, can be made to feel familiar to the child, and can introduce a feeling of safety. A second aspect of play's usefulness in therapy is its use for self-disclosure by the child, whether consciously or unconsciously. Specifically, through play, the therapist can learn about the child without having to ask intrusive questions, by observing and becoming a careful recipient of the nonverbal communication sent by the child. Using the symbolism of play, the therapist may receive information that would be too difficult or painful for the child to put into words. Finally, play can be used to help the child to resolve problems and legitimizes nonverbal strategies as a proper or appropriate means of facilitating and understanding the therapy process. These three aspects of play can be labeled the relationship, disclosure, and healing functions of play, in much the same way as the purposes of everyday play were the self-development, maturation, and relationship functions. These functions of play in treatment and their subpurposes are summarized in Table 9.2.

TABLE 9.2   Purposes of Play in Child Therapy

Overall Function	Specific Purpose
Relationship Function	to establish a trusting relationship
	to establish a special relationship
Disclosure Function	to facilitate diagnosis
	to facilitate assessment
	to allow expression of feelings
	to act out unconscious material
	to act out fears
	to allow the expression of forbidden affects
	to allow the expression of forbidden needs
	to allow the expression of conflicts
	to reconstruct conflict
	to reconstruct experiences
Healing Function	to provide an arena for intervention
	to provide a sense of direction
	to deal with defenses
	to resolve resistances
	to relieve tension
	to facilitate catharsis
	to provide corrective emotional experiences
	to teach coping skills
	to experiment with new behaviors

The Relationship Function of Play in Therapy

The most obvious function of play in therapy is that of facilitating the development of a trusting and special relationship between child and clinician. There are not very many places where adults watch children play or engage in play initiated and completely controlled by the child. There is no doubt that this interactive or observing style of play is conducive to the building of trust on the part of the child in the adult. Further, the relationship is, by definition, special because of its differentness in terms of the play activity from other relationships with adults experienced by the child.

The Disclosure Function of Play in Therapy

In addition to facilitating the rapport building between child and clinician, play also aids the clinician in understanding the child and learning about her or him. As was mentioned earlier, in play, emotions, conflicts, problems, and relationship difficulties are reenacted either directly or symbolically. This process of communication and interaction helps the clinician to put together the pieces of the puzzle that is the child's life and presenting problem. It provides information that may be too threatening or frightening for the child to share through any other medium. Obtaining information through play not only helps the clinician to better understand the child, but also facilitates the process of diagnosis, and hence treatment planning.

The disclosure that takes place in play is also healthy for the child in addition to being useful for the clinician. Often, merely having the opportunity to express feelings and conflicts freely is therapeutic for the child. Thus, the disclosure function of play is closely, almost inseparably, linked to its healing function.

The Healing Function of Play in Therapy

In its simplest form, play provides an opportunity for healing merely through the facilitation of catharsis and abreaction. The child is given complete freedom of self- and emotional expression, and this ability to vent is often quite relieving for her or him. Having an adult witness the expression and respond empathically and understandingly further sets the stage for corrective emotional experiences that can help the child to change her or his attitude toward a problem or conflict and greatly relieves any tension experienced by the child.

More important, however, play becomes a technique through which the therapist and child cooperate toward the solution of the presenting, and related, problems. It provides an arena for the therapist for intervention and direction and sets the stage for interpretation and internalization opportunities. With the help of the therapist, the child learns to recognize her or his defenses as self-protective and may choose to substitute new behaviors and more adaptive coping skills. In play, the therapist can model and help the child develop new problem-solving strategies that prepare her or him to cope better with life's problems. The play activities that occur in the therapy allow the child to experiment with new behaviors in a safe setting where failures do not have to hurt or worsen a situation. Play makes it possible for all of these processes to occur nonverbally or symbolically, thus making therapy possible even for very young or low-verbal children (James, 1997).

Finally, one goal of therapy is always generalization of the changes to relevant external settings. Once therapeutic goals have been obtained in the therapy room, a child is encouraged to transfer these gains to other environmental settings and future experiences. Play facilitates this process, as it occurs naturally not only in the therapy room, but also in all types of settings. Thus, it is likely that skills gained through play are more likely to generalize than are skills gained through talking because they will be incorporated into the child's natural repertoire of behaviors in all types of situations.

Variations on the Technique

Although the functions of play in therapy have been discussed somewhat generically so far, theoreticians from different schools of thought have attributed different specific therapeutic roles to the play technique in their style of treatment. The four largest groups of clinicians who utilize play as an important means of facilitating therapeutic change are psychoanalytic/psychodynamic thinkers, relationship-centered or humanistic theorists, behaviorists, and release therapists. All take a slightly different conceptual approach to understanding pathology, and all consequently attribute a slightly different role to the therapist and the use of play. Because all are important, they will be briefly reviewed here.

Psychoanalytic/Psychodynamic Theories

Psychoanalytic and psychodynamic child therapists are often labeled *directive,* because in this school of thought therapists "assume responsibility for guidance or interpretation" (Axline, 1947, p. 9), as opposed to merely following the child's lead and focusing on empathic relating. Two of the most important figures in the psychoanalytic tradition of working with children were Melanie Klein (e.g., Klein, 1975) and Anna Freud (e.g., Freud, 1928). Both adhered to a conflict model of pathology. Simply put, in the conflict model, a clinician assumes that there is a conflicting relationship between one or more aspects of the child's personality. Traditionally, this conflict was seen as arising from the differences between wishes and desires emanating from the person's id versus the needs and direction stemming from the superego. The id was seen as pleasure-seeking and purely hedonistic, whereas the superego was the moralistic aspect of the person's self, which kept behavior and desires under control and within acceptable limits. When conflict between these two aspects of the client's psyche could no longer be mediated by the ego, the reality-oriented aspect of the person's self, it began to create problems for the person. These problems were avoided through the use of defense mechanisms and through the development of symptoms.

For instance, in the conflict model, a boy with a simple phobia of snakes may be viewed as having developed this phobia to avoid awareness of an inner conflict between id wishes and superego guidance. The phobia perhaps served to keep him from situations wherein this conflict might find expression. Thus, if the assumed conflict involves the id wish of sleeping with his little sister, a wish strongly opposed by the incest taboo protected by his superego, his snake phobia may be viewed as having developed to keep him from participating in family camping trips where he might have to sleep in the same tent as his little sister. Similarly, a girl who believes that the world is a hostile place and is unable to trust anyone might simply harbor strong feelings of anger against her father. As anger toward a parent is not an acceptable affect as far as her superego is concerned, direct expression of this emotion is not allowed. Thus, the girl might use a defense of projection, wherein her own anger is projected upon her environment. Perceiving the environment as an angry place certainly explains why she might perceive it as hostile and nontrustworthy.

In the psychoanalytic, or conflict, model of psychopathology, play is used therapeutically in a symbolic fashion and equivalent to free association in the treatment of adults. It is perceived as offering an avenue into the child's psyche, providing a clear look at the conflicts that are hidden or defended against. Play is therefore not to be taken literally, but to be interpreted with its relevance to the conflict of the child. For instance, if the play of the little boy with the snake phobia included play with dolls who are engaging in sexual play, this would be interpreted as a manifestation of his incestuous wishes toward his sister. In addition to being used symbolically, play is also used to establish a therapeutic relationship between the child and the therapist and sets the stage for interpretation. Only through the play activity of the child does the therapist find the opportunity to interpret the child's conflict to her or him, with the assumption that the interpretation will resolve the child's conflict and reduce the symptom and make the defense unnecessary.

Hence, the therapist in the psychoanalytic model is the interpreter—the person solving the riddle behind the symptom and the person who explains the riddle to the child thus relieving conflicts. The goal is insight, and the curative factors are the interpretations made by the therapist and the transference relationship between the therapist and the child. The relationship between child and therapist is perceived as purely transferential, so that whatever feelings emerge in treatment are viewed as by-products of the child's history and personality conflict. The relationship, much as the child's play, is used to corroborate the therapist's theories about the child's inner conflict and is interpreted in the same way as the child's play. Thus, should the boy in the example express love for the therapist, this love would be interpreted as transferential, transferred from the sister onto the therapist. A real relationship between therapist and child would not be acknowledged.

Relationship Theories

Quite opposed to the psychoanalytic therapist, the relationship therapist is nondirective. All direction and responsibility for the therapy session and therapy contacts are left to the child (Axline, 1947; Landreth, 2000). The therapist merely follows the child's lead, reflects the child's feelings, and focuses on the establishment of a warm and empathic relationship with the child. The model of pathology—or, better, the model of recovery from pathology—is a growth model. In this model, the clinician believes that the child has an innate striving for mental health and maturation and, if placed in the correct atmosphere, will rekindle this growth through her or his own resources. Thus, pathology is viewed as developing in an environment in which this natural expression of growth and maturation is somehow stunted, usually owing to the absence of genuine or empathic caretakers who help the child to discover her or his ideal future self. Therapy thus is focused on helping the child to regain this capability.

Play is viewed as the tool through which the child can reacquaint herself or himself with her or his true life direction and desires. Play in child therapy ascertains growth and maturation in the same way that talking is supposed to help the adult client to solve her or his problems. Play is viewed as the way through which the child communicates to herself or himself and to the therapist. Thus, play also facilitates the relationship between the client and the clinician. It is the therapist's role to listen empathically and extract from the child's play the child's true feelings and desires. This understanding is then reflected back to the child in an accepting and understanding manner. The acceptance and understanding confirm for the child that her or his feelings are valid and important and part of her or his self. The permissiveness and respectfulness of the therapist communicate to the child that the child has the answers to problems and has control over her or his life to such an extent as to be able to change it. In other words, the therapist gives the child the responsibility to direct treatment and find a cure.

The goal of this approach to child therapy is not insight, as in the psychoanalytic model, but rather self-actualization and self-acceptance. The child will learn to be who she or he wants to be and will feel accepted for this choice. The curative factor in this type of treatment is the empathic, warm, and secure relationship between the child and the therapist. The relationship is important as it unfolds in the here-and-now, and is not interpreted transferentially only, as in the psychoanalytic model. The structured atmosphere or environment in which this relationship develops also includes supportive limits that are set by the therapist to facilitate safety and feelings of security of the child and to inject the treatment with a dose of realism. However, the prime focus is on the relationship and the empathic, warm, and respectful relating between the two people.

In this model, the boy with the snake phobia would be viewed as being frightened of allowing himself to become who he wants to be. He is viewed as having developed this symptom in response to an environment that has not supported him appropriately for self development. Perhaps, upon his first sight of a snake, he was frightened and this fear was responded to nonempathically. Perhaps his first camping trip was traumatic, yet his fear ridiculed and not accepted. In this therapy, the child would be allowed to explore these feelings and to express them in an environment where they would not only be empathically reflected but accepted as important and valid.

Behavioral Theories

The behavioral therapist has an altogether different approach to the treatment of children. The relationship between the child and the clinician is of little importance, other than to convince the child and her or his parents to comply with the prescribed treatment. Behaviorists can follow a strict conditioning or a social learning model (Bandura, 1999; Patterson, 1977; Skinner, 1976). The boy's snake phobia in this model would be explained as having developed because of the reinforcement or learning history he encountered. For instance, perhaps the first time he saw a snake, he was with his father, who was also frightened of snakes. His father responded with fear and ran from the snake, sweeping up his son in his arms, telling him not to be afraid. Despite the verbal message, the boy recognized the father's fear and learned that snakes are dangerous. His fear might have been further reinforced by a friend who also responded with fear to snakes when the class was on a field trip. By now, the child's fear has become strengthened to a point of complete avoidance of snakes. His fear has nothing to do with internal personality conflicts, as in the psychoanalytic model, nor is it secondary to not having been empathically responded to as in the relationship model. It is plainly understood as a learned response, in fact a socially learned response wherein the child merely models his father's affects.

In the attempt to treat a child, behaviorists view play as a mere by-product, not a focus, of therapy. Play provides a means of establishing rapport and a stage on which reinforcement contingencies or modeling can be implemented that will change the child's behavior. It becomes the therapist's role to dispense reinforcers or to punish, to serve as a model, and to implement relaxation or desensitization programs. The clinician does not need to explain these issues to the child, as insight is not critical; nor does she or he have to treat the child with empathy, warmth, and respect, as this is not critical to the child's change. (This is not to say that behaviorists do not do these things; they are merely not viewed as critical in effecting change.) The goal of treatment is neither to interpret and understand conflicts, nor to help the child feel accepted and self-actualized, but rather to define what maintains, shapes, eliminates, or alters the child's behavior and to gain control over it. The curative factors in the behavioral treatment process are the reinforcers and punishers that are found to be effective in producing behavior change.

For the boy in the example, this might mean that the therapist would embark on a desensitization program with the child. In this process, the child would be taught how to relax. Then, while relaxed, the child would slowly be exposed to the feared stimulus, namely, snakes or snake-related items. The child would be reinforced for remaining calm in the presence of these stimuli until, in the end, the child can tolerate the presence of a snake and remain calm. Obviously, much of this work could theoretically, and often does practically, take place outside the therapy room. Relaxation programs, reinforcement schedules, and so forth can easily be implemented in the child's classroom or at home, making the behavioral treatment method one that creates good generalizability of progress.

Release and Structure Theories

In release and structure therapies, as developed by David Levy (1939, 1979) and Gove Hambridge (1955, 1979), the abreactive effect of treatment is stressed. These clinicians subscribe to a catharsis model. In this model, the expression of affect in a lifelike situation is critical. Play is used to introduce or recreate anxiety-provoking situations that are thought to have precipitated the child's problems. It is the therapist's larger theoretical model that will determine what she or he believes to be the problem's precipitant. Thus, going back to the boy in the example, one release therapist might expose the child to a structured play situation wherein two children engage in incest. Another therapist might create a play scene wherein the child is attacked by a snake. The critical piece that ties these theorists together is the structured play activity that is designed by the therapist to evoke a strong affect in the child.

Some free play is allowed even by these clinicians, primarily for exploration of the problem and for building a relationship with the child. Sometimes, free play is permitted to help the child recover from the intervention of the structured play activity. The role of the therapist consists of introducing the anxiety-provoking play scenes and to set the stage for the child's emotional expression and acting out behavior. There is little, if any, focus on a therapeutic relationship beyond the establishment of sufficient rapport to gain the child's and family's cooperation for treatment. No interpretations are made, and no reinforcement contingencies are planned. The goal of treatment is merely abreaction and catharsis. The curative factors are the structured play scenes introduced by the therapist and the child's emotional responses to them.

This brief overview, summarized in Table 9.3, of these four approaches to the use of play activity with children was provided not to train the reader in these particular theories. Much more time would have to be spent discussing them if that were the purpose. They were presented merely to point out that play can be and has been used in a number of different ways and contexts and can be equally effective in all. The presentation of these models also served to demonstrate that no one of these approaches sufficiently prepares a child clinician to work with the wide range of problems that children present to treatment. Specifically, it is unlikely that very many therapists would treat a child's snake phobia from a traditionally psychoanalytic paradigm. It appears similarly unlikely that a behaviorist would not explore family circumstances in which the child's phobia developed, to intervene not only through reinforce-

TABLE 9.3   Four Conceptual Approaches to Play Therapy

Approach	Model	Role of Play	Role of Therapist	Goal	Curative Factor
Psychoanalytic	Conflict	establish relationship symbolism—like free associations stage for interpretation	interpreter who creates insight transference object	insight	interpretation transference relationship
Relationship	Growth	establish relationship self-exploration means to achieve maturation communication	create a warm, caring environment reflect and accept feelings	self-actualization self-acceptance	here-and-now, warm relationship accepting environment
Behavioral	Conditioning; Social Learning	establish rapport stage to implement treatment	developer of reinforcement, relaxation, and desensitization programs	learn the child's reinforcement contingencies	reinforcers punishers relaxation training desensitization
Release/ Structure	Catharsis	establish relationship means to act out structure medium for abreaction	prepares and directs structured play scenes sets stage for emotional catharsis	catharsis or abreaction	structured play scenes emotional release

ment plans, but to also intervene through the involvement of other family members in the treatment process. Finally, few therapists today disregard the here-and-now relationship that develops between a child and a therapist in the course of play therapy. Consequently, a mixture of the above approaches would appear to provide the most solid conceptual base from which a play therapist might choose to intervene (James, 1997; Webb, 1999).

This eclectic or integrative approach is promoted by many play therapists today (O'Conner, 2000), despite not always being labeled as such, as clinicians prefer to identify themselves with a specific conceptual model. However, if actual treatment dialogues and transcripts are reviewed, significant overlap can be found among the interventions and responses from clinicians of various schools of thoughts. It is the eclectic integration of a number of approaches to play therapy that will be presented in the following pages as the practical implementation of the play technique is discussed. For conceptually pure discussions of play therapy, the reader is referred to the primary references provided above.

Practical Implementation

In the eclectic integrative model of play therapy, the clinician enters the assessment phase of intervention with a conceptually open mind. She or he will explore a number of aspects of the child's life and current presentation and will use all of these factors to develop a conceptualization and treatment plan. Although the case conceptualization is likely to reflect the therapist's preferred theoretical framework, the implementation of strategies to achieve treatment goals is generally flexible and wide-ranging across all four models of play therapy. Thus, an integrative play therapist will not necessarily adhere to one single strategic approach to the child in treatment, but rather will use the techniques that appear most relevant to a specific problem that occurs in the here-and-now in the therapy room. For instance, although a relationship-centered or psychodynamically oriented play therapist will not hand out tangible reinforcers for a positive action by the child, social reinforcers nevertheless are employed constantly. Therapists smile at children after they have accomplished a difficult task, they express pride in a child who has mastered a new skill, and they ignore behaviors that they deem inappropriate. They may even set up specific contingencies in the process of enforcing and implementing limits. Social, as well as coping, skills are often and inadvertently modeled and reinforced by the clinician.

Not uncommonly, the eclectic integrative play therapist will use here-and-now opportunities to help the child develop relaxation strategies, such as breathing exercises, muscle tension–relaxation exercises, visualization, and even some calming self-talk (Kaduson and Schaefer, 1997; 2000; 2001). For instance, one 5-year-old girl was helped to visualize her parents sitting on the couch in the waiting room to help her tolerate separation from her parents. In this process, she was first asked to draw a picture of her parents, then the picture was left in the room for the child to look at whenever she needed the reassurance of her parents' presence. Slowly, the picture was moved to less and less obtrusive places in the therapy room, until the child was able to merely look in the direction of the picture (at this time kept in a closet, completely out of sight!) to reassure herself. This internalization of a vivid picture of her parents also generalized out of the therapy room to help this girl cope better with visitations with her biological father and stepmother every month.

Similarly, the behavioral use of the therapy stage is generally complemented by a solid appreciation of the interpersonal relationship that is developing between the child and the clinician, along with overt to covert interpretations of this relationship as it is relevant in the child's history and present living situation, even by the self-professed behavioral therapist. The eclectic integrative clinician is sensitive to how the child feels in the presence of the therapist and strives to construct an atmosphere of warmth and caring wherein the child feels safe and sufficiently trusting to engage in self-disclosing play activity. This therapist will engage in play with the child when invited to do so, not remaining passively and aloofly uninvolved.

For instance, one 9-year-old girl, who had been referred by her teacher because of her phobic fear to speak out in class, was evaluated for treatment and referred for a desensitization program to deal with this social phobia. In the course of assessment, the clinician was stunned by the amount of trauma that had occurred in this child's life. She had been a victim of repeated sexual abuse by her stepfather after her biological mother had died of a drug overdose. Her biological father had been sentenced to a life term in prison after a drug-related murder shortly after her birth, and she had neither met him nor had any recollection of him or stories about him. She was placed in a number of foster homes after being taken from her stepfather's home, and was desperately wishing to be adopted. With this knowledge, the therapist decided that merely implementing a desensitization program to help this girl deal with her fears was not sufficient. He also attempted to provide a nurturing and supportive environment that conveyed stability and guidance. As such, while in every therapy hour the two worked on her fears, they also engaged in interactive and gentle play. When the girl encountered difficulties in moving from one step in her program to the next, it was not uncommon for her to sit cuddled up to the clinician for support and the warmth of knowing that he cared for her and was prepared to face the difficult task with her.

In addition to using the relationship with the child to provide support and nurturance, it can also be used to explore anger, sadness, isolation, or other interpersonal affects, needs, and desires expressed by a child. The integrative play therapist is open to making interpretations about the current relationship in the context of the child's history. Often, this historic explanation can also be accomplished symbolically through the child's play activity. This symbolic explanation requires that the therapist not be merely a spectator, but participate actively in the child's play.

For instance, the girl described in the previous paragraph often chose to play with the anatomical dolls, without yet having discovered their genitalia. One day, the therapist prepared for the session by laying out a change of clothes for the dolls to encourage exploration by the child (i.e., used a technique that is certainly very related to structured play). The child indeed recognized the invitation and began to undress the girl doll. She evidenced fear and shock upon discovery of the doll's vagina, threw the doll down, and turned to an alternative activity in the room. The therapist, trusting that their relationship was secure enough to endure a challenge, interpreted her behavior for her by indicating that it appeared that the girl was very frightened by the sight of the naked doll. He encouraged her to look closely and to pick up the doll, indicating that he would help her and keep her safe. Together, they picked the doll back up and began to explore. This interaction was very important based on the trusting relationship that had already developed in the girl's treatment. It led to an opportunity for the child to speak through the use of the dolls about her experience of being raped by her stepfather. The opportunity for her to tell of her victimization was not only cathartic, but also extremely valuable, as it helped her process feelings of shame and guilt that had remained with her for several years. These feelings had found their expression in her interpersonal reticence and fearfulness, particularly in the classroom around other children.

In summary, although the eclectic integrative play therapist might well prefer one particular play therapy model for case conceptualization, she or he remains flexible with regard to the implementation of techniques that can facilitate change in the child. The integrative play therapist will adapt her or his strategies of intervention to the specific needs of each individual child, rather than imposing a particular treatment on every child. The flexibility and willingness to try different techniques to meet the child in a place where she or he can work safely and successfully on her or his growth and maturation are critical to play therapy.

Example

The unfolding of play therapy is best experienced by each therapist herself or himself. Recognizing the usefulness of play to help a child enter into a relationship, self-disclose, trust, and ultimately change is an extremely satisfying process. As the novice is not likely to have had this experience, a sample case will be presented here to help her or him gain an appreciation for this development. However, as the reader reviews this case example, she or he must understand the purpose for which it was chosen: It was chosen because of its quick success and its model case quality. Not all cases will unfold this quickly and easily, but it is hoped that all play therapists will have at least one case in their lives that is similar to the one presented here. This case occurred early during the therapist's training, an opportunity that is rare indeed. Perhaps this example can best serve to encourage the novice without suggesting that, if the reader's first few (or even first one hundred cases) are not similarly successful, she or he is not a good play therapist.

The example is based upon the 14-week treatment of a 7-year-old girl who was referred by her foster mother after being placed in her current home following the sudden death of her father and mother in a car accident. The girl had lived with her foster family for 10 weeks by the time she was seen for an intake at the therapist's clinic. The therapist was a psychology trainee doing a one-semester practicum. She anticipated being able to see a child for approximately 15 weeks, the length of the semester. This case was referred to her after the intake interview, as it appeared to be of relatively short-term nature that would allow for a natural termination rather than a transfer.

The intake, which included the foster mother, foster father, and Tracy, the 7-year-old girl, revealed the following information. Tracy was born healthy and developed normally. She was very attached to her biological father and his wife, Tracy's stepmother. Her biological mother had left her husband fifteen months after Tracy's birth and had not been heard from since. Tracy's father always claimed he did not know why his wife had left him and her daughter and knew nothing of her whereabouts. She had no family; she had claimed to have been orphaned at an early age. Tracy's biological mother thus had remained a mystery. Tracy's father met his second wife when Tracy was almost 2 years old and married her after a six-month courtship. This woman was very loving toward Tracy, and Tracy called her "mommy," though she knew the true relationship. Tracy had seen pictures of her biological mother but never had asked many questions about her, being quite happy and content in her nuclear family (father and stepmother). Tracy's father's parents had died before Tracy's birth. They had been in their forties when Tracy's father was conceived, and he himself was 43 when Tracy was born. There was an aunt, who lived in Chicago, and an uncle in Los Angeles, neither of whom felt capable of or was willing to take Tracy in after the accident. Her current foster family was a family with whom she had been familiar, because they attended the same church as Tracy's family. They had decided to take her in when they heard of the tragedy and at the time of the intake were thinking of adopting her. They had no children of their own for unknown reasons.

Tracy's school performance had always been quite good, with special abilities in math. She had several friends, both in her school and in her original neighborhood, where she had lived since birth. She had never presented any problems to the knowledge of her foster parents and her teachers. Immediately after the accident, Tracy moved into her current home. Although there were no problems for the first two weeks in her new home, Tracy then developed severe nightmares, as well as night terrors and wet the bed on three occasions. Her teachers reported that her performance had deteriorated, that she failed to concentrate and attend, and that she had withdrawn from her friends. Everyone in her environment appeared quite concerned about her, yet also indicated that they had believed that her behavior would change spontaneously once she adjusted to the death of her parents and her new surroundings. When her behavior continued to worsen after 8 weeks in her new home, her foster family called to make an appointment at this clinic.

The intake clinicians, after having met with the family and all family holons, diagnosed Tracy as suffering from an adjustment disorder with mixed emotions and academic problems. No diagnosis was made on either Axis II or III. Her stressors were identified as acute, naming the death of her parents, as well as the move to a new neighborhood. Her current GAS level was judged to be 63, compared to a past year level of 95. Treatment goals revolved around helping her to deal with her parents' death and her new living situation, with expected resolution of the current presenting problems if these issues could be resolved. In other words, the clinicians judged that her nightmares, bed-wetting, academic performance, and friendship difficulties were secondary to her life changes and needed no specific treatment at this time. The recommendation was for individual play therapy for Tracy, as no family problems were noted. Tracy was assigned to the trainee therapist, who had also conducted the individual intake interview with the child and thus had already begun to establish a relationship with her.

In her first session, Tracy was shy and refused to do much exploration in the play room. This continued the pattern that had been set in the intake. She was very hesitant to involve herself in conversation with the therapist and did not wish to speak or play. The therapist, believing that the child had been sufficiently challenged by her previous traumata, accepted this stance and chose not to challenge or prod Tracy. For quite a while, the two sat together in silence, with the therapist letting Tracy know that she was there for her and it was up to Tracy to determine how her time would be used. She chose merely to follow Tracy's lead by using the same material used by the child and modeling after her behavior. For instance, Tracy had picked up some clay and was molding various shapes, always destroying one before advancing to the next. The therapist tentatively followed

Tracy's lead by also making shapes with the clay. However, in a slight variation on Tracy's theme, the therapist, Ruth, did not destroy her previous shapes when making new ones. Ruth had decided that Tracy's destruction of the shapes might symbolize her parents' death or the ephemeral nature of relationships in general and did not want to reflect to the child that she held the same belief. Instead, her message was that new shapes (i.e., relationships) can be formed without destroying old ones.

Later in the session, Tracy became more interactive, asking Ruth for permission to use the various toys. She also checked with Ruth on several occasions about the appropriateness of her actions. Ruth interpreted Tracy's inquiries as a means of establishing a relationship with the therapist (not wanting to offend or anger Ruth), but also a reflection of the child's insecurity (not trusting her own judgments and desires). She therefore responded to the child's inquiries with reassurance to communicate that she also wanted to build a relationship with Tracy and with encouragement to communicate that Ruth was certain that Tracy could make good decisions herself. One such interaction was as follows:

TRACY: Is it okay to take my shoes off and walk in the sandbox?

RUTH: In this room we can take our shoes off and feel comfortable because we don't have to worry about getting hurt. Also, in here you can decide for yourself what you would like to do. It's really all up to you because I know that you can decide for yourself.

Although this is a quite lengthy response to a simple question, the therapist justified her response by the importance of the message. It might have been preferable to give the message in chunks, that is, choose the most relevant issue in this case, and wait for a second opportunity to deliver the second message. Children hear messages much more clearly if they are delivered one at a time.

However, Tracy not only appeared to have heard both messages, but also was able to trust their genuineness. When she returned for her second session, she immediately took off her shoes and appeared much more comfortable in the room. She asked the therapist whether she could play with the dollhouse and proceeded to do so without waiting for a response. Using the dolls, Tracy began to tell her story. Here is a description of the play and conversation that followed:

TRACY: This doll should not be in this room, she does not belong there!

RUTH: She should be somewhere else.

TRACY: She left a long time ago. Maybe she died because she sure hasn't been around (throws the doll forcefully over the house, where it landed out of sight).

RUTH (FORCEFULLY):   Now she's gone.

TRACY: ...gone... (grabs two other dolls and puts them in the kitchen).

LARGE FEMALE DOLL: Hello sweetie, good morning, did you sleep well? Did you have any dreams?

SMALL FEMALE DOLL: Oh yes, I dreamed that a little bear came up to our house and chewed up the apple tree. And then dad came and chased it away so we could eat the apples ourselves.

LARGE FEMALE DOLL: Let's eat breakfast. I am very hungry.

SMALL FEMALE DOLL: Me too!!!

(The dolls eat cereal, then clean the dishes and go into the bathroom; the large doll gives the small doll a bath and helps her get dressed; the large male doll comes in.)

LARGE MALE DOLL: Ohhhh! I am still so sleepy. Could you take Teetee to school today?

LARGE FEMALE DOLL: Sure and then we can pick her up together in the afternoon.

(Tracy throws the dolls away and turns to another activity. The therapist does not understand what just happened.)

RUTH: You are done playing with the dollhouse.

TRACY: Yes, it's just fake anyway.

RUTH: What you played wasn't real?

TRACY: No!!! No!!! No!!!

(Ruth backs off, sensing that Tracy is protecting herself.)

Session 2 ended with Tracy painting a picture of Ruth. She wanted to take it home with her. Because the paint was still wet, Ruth promised to keep the picture until the next session and to allow Tracy to take it home after that session. Tracy agreed. Tracy immediately asked for the picture at the beginning of her next session. Ruth retrieved it and Tracy put it back on the easel, adding a few brush strokes in various places. She then turned to the dollhouse. The following dialogue took place:

TRACY (SADLY):   My mommy can't take me to school anymore.

RUTH (TENDERLY):   You are very sad that your mommy can't take you to school.

TRACY: I liked it when she took me to school. Dad took me more than mommy did, but I liked mommy doing it because she always walked to my room with me and looked at my pictures.

RUTH: It was very special when mommy took you because she came in with you.

TRACY: She liked my pictures!

RUTH (REALIZING THAT IT WAS NOT THE COMING IN PER SE, AS MUCH AS THE LOOKING AT HER PICTURES THAT WAS IMPORTANT TO TRACY):   You sure liked showing her your pictures. She thought they were pretty.

TRACY: She even took some home and hanged them up! She had a bunch in the car…

RUTH (VERY TENDERLY, FEARING THE OBVIOUS):   She had pictures in the car with her when she came to pick you up with daddy the day they had the accident. (Ruth now also connects the behavior from Session 2 and reaches out to Tracy to touch her.)

TRACY (WEEPING QUIETLY):   She wanted to hang them in her room!

RUTH: She really liked your pictures and kept them for a long time.

TRACY: Forever!

RUTH: She never got rid of them.

TRACY: Do you want to see my pictures?

RUTH: Yes! I would very much like to see your pictures.

Ruth had stumbled upon a means to connect with Tracy in a meaningful way by having kept Tracy's picture for her from one session to the next. This action revived sad memories in Tracy, who was surprisingly able to deal with the day of her parents' death. Ruth attempted to give support to Tracy by lowering her voice and using some cautious physical touch. Tracy had begun to trust Ruth and was establishing a transference relationship with her, having invited Ruth to care for her pictures much as her stepmother used to do. Tracy failed to take Ruth's picture home with her, and Ruth wondered whether this was test of their relationship.

In session 4, Ruth put Tracy's picture of Ruth back on the easel to communicate her understanding of the importance of pictures in Tracy's life. Tracy saw the picture immediately upon entering the room, ran up to it, and kissed it on Ruth's cheek. She turned to Ruth and then began playing with the dollhouse, going back to the scene of session 2. She replayed the scene almost identically, but this time was able to go further. Here is what happened:

SMALL FEMALE DOLL: I can take the bus. Don't pick me up!

RUTH: She doesn't want her mommy and dad picking her up.

TRACY: No, she wants to ride the bus.

RUTH: Why does she want to ride the bus?

TRACY: All her friends ride the bus, and she is old enough to do it too.

RUTH: She is old enough to get home on her own.

TRACY: But she is such a scaredy-cat. She never wants to ride the bus, always cries and whines! So mommy or dad pick her up every day.

RUTH: Her friends take the bus, but she is too scared, so mommy or dad picks her up.

TRACY (TO SMALL FEMALE DOLL):   Stupid crybaby! Can't you ride the bus? You stupid crybaby.

RUTH: You don't like her much right now…

TRACY: She is such a whiner!

(Tracy turns away from the dollhouse and begins to paint again.)

Ruth had learned important information today. She now knew that the guilt and shame she had suspected in the little girl had a very deep root and would not be easy to break. She clearly had blamed herself for her parents' death and probably was quickly losing the self-confidence and self-esteem that her parents had helped to build so beautifully.

Session 5 began with Tracy asking to play in the sandbox, an activity in which she had not engaged since her first session. She took off her shoes and stepped into the box. She brought several of the dollhouse figures with her, including also several children. She enacted playground play in which several children were happily engaged in interactive play. One doll remained outside the circle. Ruth, being aware of the child's current problems in friendship, chose to comment on the lonely doll.

RUTH: This little girl isn't playing?

TRACY: She is too sad to play…

RUTH: What's making her so sad?

TRACY: She has no one to play with.

RUTH: She feels like she has no one to play with even though there are lots of children in the playground.

TRACY: But these kids don't like to play with her because she is bad.

RUTH (NOT YET SURE WHERE THIS WILL LEAD, CHOOSES MERELY TO REFLECT): She thinks she is a bad girl, and the other kids don't want to play with her.

TRACY: She is bad!

RUTH: What makes her bad?

TRACY: She whines and complains a lot. She is a crybaby. Even her dad tells her that she cries too much and acts like a baby sometimes.

RUTH (AWARE THAT THEY HAVE RETURNED TO A THEME FROM SESSION 4):   She feels she is a crybaby, and because of that people don't like her—sometimes even her dad gets mad at her!

TRACY: He used to want her to ride the bus, but she wouldn't.

RUTH (FEELING IT IS TIME TO BE DIRECT, A QUESTIONABLE DECISION AS THE METAPHOR WAS WORKING):   Your dad used to think you were a crybaby because you wanted mommy to pick you up from school.

Tracy got out of the sandbox and started to paint, ignoring Ruth. Ruth realized her mistake and attempted to reconnect with Tracy by once again following her lead rather than imposing her own need for clarification and directness. Session 5 ended with Ruth and Tracy reconnecting around Ruth's willingness to keep Tracy's paintings for her.

In session 6, Tracy painted for a long time. Ruth allowed her to do so without challenge, still aware of the breach in their relationship. Toward the end of the session, Tracy turned to Ruth, and the following conversation took place:

TRACY: You think I'm a crybaby too!

RUTH: I hurt your feelings, and now you think I don't like the way you act.

TRACY: You think I whine too much.

RUTH: You are worried that I think you whine too much, just like your dad sometimes said you whine too much.

TRACY: He didn't like it that mommy picked me up from school all the time. He told her she spoils me.

RUTH: You liked it that she picked you up from school. That was special.

TRACY: The other kids were mad 'cause they had to ride the bus and I had my mommy pick me up.

RUTH: You were special!

TRACY: Do you think I am a crybaby?

RUTH: I don't think you are a crybaby at all. Sometimes you like for someone to take care of you. You liked your mommy to take care of you, and now you wonder if that was bad.

TRACY: Will you keep my drawings for me?

RUTH: Yes. I will keep them safely in this room till you come back next week.

In session 7, Tracy returned to the dollhouse and finally finished the scene. She reenacted the accident her parents had on the way to work in the morning after they had dropped her off at school. She played out her guilt and her belief that if it were not for her whining, they might still be alive. Ruth attempted to help her understand that nothing she did or could have done would have changed anything and that the event was not her fault. Tracy was hesitant to hear the message. However, at the end of the session she drew a picture. This drawing was of her mommy and daddy in heaven, looking down at Tracy. Tracy was lying in bed having bad dreams. Her parents watched and looked very sad. The following dialogue ensued:

RUTH: They are very sad about your bad dreams every night.

TRACY: Mommy always liked to listen to my dreams. We told our dreams every day! (This explained the story in session 2.)

RUTH: You really miss your mommy in many many ways.

TRACY: My dad too…

RUTH: You love them and they love you, and you wish you could keep telling them about your dreams and show them your drawings and ride home from school with them.

TRACY: I have bad dreams a lot.

RUTH: I would like to hear about your bad dreams, just like your mommy used to listen to your dreams. How about next time you tell me about your dreams?

It is very difficult to end a session when a child has made an important and painful disclosure, but for the sake of continuity and consistency, the boundaries of treatment must be observed. Ruth chose to help Tracy bridge the gap by tying in the events of this session with events that would occur in the next session.

Tracy came to session 8 prepared to tell Ruth her dreams. She had dreamed of a wild bear that was eating up all the berries in an old woman's garden. The old woman could not walk very well, so she was afraid she might have to starve because the bear ate all her berries and she could not walk to the store. Ruth noted several important themes in this dream. First, the bear, which had also inhabited Tracy's first dream in session 2, was again included in this dream but in a more threatening form. Second, food was once again a theme in her dream. However, whereas the dream related in session 2 had a positive ending with her dad protecting the family and ascertaining that they would have enough food, this dream ended on the frightening note of potential starvation. Ruth chose to empathize with the old woman in the dream and told Tracy that she was sure that someone would come to save the old woman and would bring her many berries so she could survive the winter. Tracy at this time turned to the dollhouse and began to set up the kitchen.

> **TRACY:**   It's dinner time, and they are all going to eat together.
>
> **RUTH:**   They are hungry, and they are looking forward to eating dinner together.
>
> **TRACY:**   They always eat dinner together. Eating alone makes the food go bad.
>
> **RUTH:**   They don't like to eat alone.
>
> **TRACY:**   My mommy says the food spoils—you have to eat as a family. Dixie (her foster mother) never eats with Pete (her foster father) and with me because she works late.
>
> **RUTH:**   You are worried about the food with Dixie not eating with you and Pete!
>
> **TRACY:**   Do you think I will die because I eat bad food?
>
> **RUTH:**   The food you eat with Pete is good food, and there is lots of it, so everyone can get enough even though you can't always eat together. (Ruth tried to avoid saying that Tracy's mommy was wrong in saying what she said because she did not want to tarnish Tracy's memory of her mother, nor did she want to engage Tracy in a struggle wherein Tracy would have to convince Ruth that her mommy was right.)
>
> **TRACY (PICKING UP THE SMALL FEMALE AND LARGE MALE DOLL):**   Dinner time. Let's save some food so Dixie can eat when she comes home.

Ruth realized that the food arrangement in the new home was also symbolic of a more basic concern of Tracy's, namely, a fear about whether her foster parents would be able to protect her and nurture her in the same way her parents used to. Ruth's response was designed to address this issue indirectly.

In session 9, Tracy drew another picture, this time of her mommy and dad watching her eating with Pete. She then turned to the dollhouse and enacted bedtime and breakfast themes. These scenes appeared to show that as she was dealing with her parents' death, she was able to begin to draw closer to her foster parents. For instance, in the breakfast scene, it was Dixie who asked her about her dreams, and for the first time, the small female doll had a happy dream to report. Checking with the foster parents, Ruth also uncovered that the number of nightmares had decreased and that there were no more night terrors or bed-wetting. Tracy was still very shy in school, but her academic performance was slowly getting better again.

With the security of building a relationship with her foster parents, Tracy was now able to return to her feelings of guilt and shame surrounding the accident of her parents. In session 10, the accident was reenacted, and Tracy verbalized that if she only were less of a crybaby, her parents would be alive. Ruth helped her work through her painful affects and allowed Tracy to cry freely. Ruth helped the child to allow herself to feel safe in her pain and to feel supported and loved despite her perceived guilt. Later in the session, Tracy returned to the sandbox.

Tracy took several houses and cars and built a complicated road system. She placed several dolls in front of several houses, then took a car that went from house to house picking up dolls. She narrated that this was a mommy picking up children to go to school because the school bus was late and the children needed to get to school on time. For the first time, Tracy revealed she had some recollection of the fact that there had been a reason other than her whining why her parents had taken her to school the day of the accident. There had been an announcement on the radio that the bus was going to be 30 minutes late in their small rural town. Because Tracy's parents had a long commute to a nearby city, they could not wait for her and decided to take her to school themselves. Just before they left, another mother had called to ask them whether they had heard about the announcement and whether they wanted to drop Tracy off at her house so that she would not need to wait alone. The parents had turned down the invitation, indicating they would just drop Tracy at school. Despite the fact that Tracy did not tell this story directly (Ruth had known about it from her foster parents), Ruth was now confident that Tracy recognized that she was not the cause of the accident.

In session 11, Tracy returned to the dollhouse and enacted more breakfast and bedtime scenes. She revealed through her play with the small female and the large male doll that Pete was responsible for taking her to bed, as Dixie worked late. She appeared to enjoy their bedtime ritual, during which Pete read her a story, then tucked her in with a stuffed animal and plugged in her night light. Tracy revealed some ambivalence about enjoying the ritual, as evidenced by this play activity:

TRACY: She likes the storytelling, but maybe she should just go to sleep.

RUTH: She wonders if she shouldn't like the story because it keeps him so busy and he can't do what she thinks he needs to do.

TRACY: Oh, he is so busy. He is a writer, and he works very hard. When he tells her a story, he can't work.

RUTH (KNOWING THAT HER DAD WAS A WRITER, WHEREAS PETE IS AN ENGINEER): Some dads don't have time to read bedtime stories, but other dads do.

TRACY: She knows that, but she worries what he thinks.

RUTH (A BIT LOST, AS SHE DID NOT YET UNDERSTAND THE CHILD'S MESSAGE): She worries what he thinks of her?

TRACY: She likes his story, but he might not like it.

RUTH (STILL WONDERING):   He doesn't like the story, but she does?

TRACY: She likes for him to read to her, but she worries that when he watches he doesn't like him.

RUTH (ACTING ON A HUNCH):   Her dad watches them telling stories, and she is afraid he might be jealous because he couldn't read her stories, but her new dad can and she likes it!

TRACY: Yeah! Maybe he wants to read to her too.

RUTH: I bet he is happy to see her happy because he always wanted to tell her stories but didn't have time. Now she gets her bedtime story, and everyone is happy.

TRACY (CONFIDENTLY AND ASSERTIVELY):   She sure likes it!

It was not surprising for Tracy to feel conflicted over liking her new family. Often, this is perceived as disloyalty to the biological parents and restimulates old guilt feelings about having felt angry at parents, perhaps even having wished them dead. Ruth was very direct in her instruction that Tracy's dad would be happy for her, and Tracy accepted the message easily.

In session 12, Tracy related that she and Dixie and Pete were going on summer vacation together. She appeared excited and happy. Ruth decided that this was a good time to discuss termination, as reports from school and home revealed that Tracy was beginning to adjust quite well. They discussed ending their special time together and that they would both remember one another even after they no longer met every week. Tracy handled the introduction of the topic very well. She demonstrated her general life gains in her play activity during this session. She had returned to the sandbox to build a replica of Dixie's and Pete's house. She related that she had her own room and that Dixie told her they would redecorate it according to Tracy's wishes. Pete had already begun painting the walls and allowed Tracy to help. Tracy then moved to the easel to draw a picture for Ruth of her new room. She asked Ruth to keep the picture at the end of the session, but then changed her mind and asked whether she could take it home to give to Dixie. Ruth, delighted at the shift of the relationship, allowed her to do so.

Session 13 began with Tracy's return to the dollhouse. She reenacted the original breakfast scene and the continuation of the scene according to the real-life occurrence, including the radio announcement, the phone call from her friend's mother, and the actual accident. She was still very sad but able to tolerate this affect. She demonstrated her attachment to Dixie and Pete by staging a funeral during which the three dolls stood so closely that they quite literally supported one another physically. Tracy clearly was able to say goodbye to her parents and welcomed her foster parents. At the end of session 13, Dixie took the therapist aside to inform her that she and Pete had received permission to adopt Tracy. They were planning to tell Tracy that evening and to have a celebration. Dixie wanted to know whether Ruth felt that Tracy was ready for this development. Ruth agreed that it would probably serve to strengthen the family ties, as Tracy had revealed in this session that she had resolved her ambivalence about shifting her attachments.

Session 14 focused on the termination of treatment. Tracy was able to share with Ruth the ways in which she felt better, and Ruth shared with Tracy that she was special and that Ruth would not forget her. The session ended very positively.

Summary and Concluding Thoughts

The example was presented to clarify for the beginning therapist that the treatment with children not only incorporates a number of techniques, but also requires flexibility and the ability to follow a child's play symbolically. This latter ability improves over the course of a child's treatment as the therapist gets to know the child better and begins to understand the child's unique and individualized symbolism. Responding within this symbolism or within a particular metaphor is generally very useful, as it allows the child to deal with difficult matter in an indirect and hence more tolerable manner. Leaving the metaphor or symbolism represents a big step and should only be done if the therapist sees a distinct advantage to dealing with the contents directly. Often, the child will lead the way in leaving the metaphor on her or his own, as was evidenced in Tracy's case. When the therapist left the metaphor prematurely in an early session, the child closed up and withdrew. However, in later sessions, it was Tracy who abandoned the metaphor and spoke directly about her experiences. However, until the very end of her treatment, she returned to the metaphor each time she introduced a new feeling or conflict. Then she moved toward open expression, which generally symbolized resolution of the conflict.

CHAPTER

10 Storytelling Techniques

Storytelling as a formal therapy technique with children was first documented by Richard Gardner in 1971. However, even this author conceded that it was unlikely that he was the first therapist working with children to use this technique. Storytelling appears to be an almost natural means of connecting and communicating with children, whether for therapeutic or other purposes. Children invent stories as part of their development in an attempt to deal with their environment more effectively. To introduce storytelling as a therapeutic technique, first its history, cultural relevance, and developmental importance will be traced. Then its application to and implementation in child therapy will be outlined.

Conceptual Background

Storytelling has been an important means of making sense of the environment and of transmitting information, knowledge, and wisdom from generation to generation among many ethnic groups across the world, including the North American continent. Fables, myths, fairy tales, and legends have been developed for the purposes of transmitting values and knowledge (Pellowski, 1990). Storytelling has also served families to transmit family lore and values from parents or grandparents to children and to help children mature, make sense of their world, and learn about their ancestry and to facilitate parent-child relationships (Godbole, 1982). Children, in turn, use storytelling to reveal information about themselves to family members, friends, teachers, and other significant individuals in their lives; to express affects and needs indirectly; and to engage in problem solving. All three of these uses of storytelling are relevant to storytelling in psychotherapy which combines the purposes of all, namely, the transmission of information and wisdom, the teaching of values and facilitation of relationships, uninhibited self-disclosure, and catharsis that results in psychological growth.

Transmission of Cultural Beliefs, Values, and Knowledge

A number of purposes have been cited for the use of myths, fables, and stories among and within cultures and other groups. Traditional use of stories appears to have been motivated by its facilitation of understanding or making sense of a people's environment (Pellowski, 1990). Storytelling became a coping mechanism that aided people's sense of control over their lives and environments. Relatedly, stories were used to express spiritual or religious beliefs, as well as moral values of a given culture (Pellowski, 1990). Thus, stories were used by elders to guide the actions of younger members of a cultural group and to help them adapt their behaviors according to the codes and values of the group. Through storytelling, human beings expressed and communicated their experiences to others around them, helping them to feel integrated into an understanding group. This self-disclosing and sharing purpose of storytelling may well have been critical to the maintenance of mental health even among the people of early cultures. Traditional stories also served to reflect or illustrate typical situations a person in a given group might face, thus preparing her or him for its occurrence and for adjusting to and coping with it. In summary, stories traditionally have "provide[d] recurring themes which reflect a people's perception of their world, hopes, dreams, values, beliefs, customs, frustrations, humor, and problems as well as solving them" (Greenbaum and Holmes, 1983, p. 415).

By depicting typical situations and problems, listeners can gain an in-depth understanding of problems with which a culture or group of individuals is faced (Greenbaum and Holmes, 1983) and can identify with the individual characters in a story. Individual identification can enhance the listener's sense of belonging to a group and can provide direction and guidance for decision making. Further, stories can be developed to provide the storyteller with an opportunity to express her or his own or the group's psychological and emotional needs, attitudes, and beliefs (Dundes, 1980). This provides great insight into the emotional and psychological atmosphere of a people or an individual and can give the listener a true appreciation of the culture's needs and requirements. Finally, an additional original and continued purpose of storytelling is that of entertainment. Storytelling allowed early cultures, and continues to allow all groups who engage in it, to enjoy the beauty of creation and the aesthetics of expressive language (Pellowski, 1990). Entertainment is likely to draw a group of people together as they recognize their common heritage and their shared psychological and interpersonal climate and can aid in problem solving and growth.

Understanding stories from this perspective render them extremely useful tools, as they become reflections of the culture in which they arose (Miller and Moore, 1989; Schwartz, 1964) and define the meaning of behavior in relation to the culture in which it is expressed. Stories, myths, legends, and other tales thus provide the reader or listener with invaluable information about and understanding of a people's lives, customs, beliefs, and even their sense of humor and psychological preoccupations, facilitating insights into cultural differences and similarities. Similar to the transmission of cultural or group information, stories that are passed on from generation to generation within a family can serve a parallel purpose of educating younger members and can provide listeners and readers with ready insights about a family and its values and traditions.

Transmission of Family Lore, Values, and Wisdom

While cultural storytelling is focused on the sharing of myths, legends, and fairy tales that were developed by the members of a given group, family storytelling involves the sharing of family tales developed and transmitted by parents, grandparents, great-grandparents, and other extended family members. Family narratives are collections of stories made up by family members that are based on either real occurrences, embellished events, or fantasy material. Such family storytelling has been shown to have numerous advantages. Specifically, family narratives help children to develop values through communicating limits, boundaries, and family-endorsed morality (Godbole, 1982). In addition to providing children with a clear sense of right and wrong as perceived by a given family, family stories are also used to pass along parental insights and knowledge. This process of transmitting knowledge may be critical to positive parent-child relationships, as the absence of family stories has been shown to be related to difficulties among parents to establish a caring or meaningful relationship with their children (Sherman, 1990). Similarly, the process of parental storytelling has been related to enhanced parent-child relationships (Godbole, 1982). Family storytelling is also a powerful model for individual storytelling, which serves many purposes that are compatible with the larger purposes of cultural myths, legends, and fables or family narratives.

Communication about the Self

Whereas listening to stories told by parents or to myths and legends developed in one's cultural group is a powerful means to gain new information, glean wisdom, and develop problem-solving skills, personal storytelling provides an excellent medium for children to "[work] through some of the problems of growing up" (Schwartz, 1964, p. 384). Children tell stories to communicate with parents, friends, and teachers and to express meaningful material indirectly when the direct approach appears too frightening or threatening. Stories allow the free expression of feelings, needs, problems, conflicts, and beliefs and, through this self-disclosure, provide opportunities for mastery and maturation. Through their stories, children can symbolically confront problems, test various solutions, and arrive at acceptable alternatives. Stories help children to confront challenges more openly and confidently, facilitate competent problem solving, and therefore result in enhanced self-esteem (Freeman, Epston, and Lobovits, 1997; Smith, 1989). Specific situations that have been hypothesized to be amenable to successful working through with the use of stories are those which involve goal-setting, grieving, dealing with loss, establishing new and close relationships, and becoming a caring individual (Smith, 1989). In summary, personal storytelling is a powerful aid to the socialization process of children (Engel, 1999; Robertson and Barford, 1979). Consequently, storytelling, like play, is an important childhood activity that must be encouraged and fostered and lends itself extremely well to the therapeutic endeavor with children.

Application to Child Therapy

Stories and storytelling in child therapy serve purposes similar to those of stories in a cultural or developmental context (summarized in Table 10.1). Just as stories told by elders of a native people give the listener insights into the functioning of a people and its approach to life and the environment, so does a story told by a child teach the therapist about the child's functioning, approach to life, and beliefs about the family environment. Just as a parent can use stories to inform the child about family values and to enhance rapport with the child and development of values, so can the therapist use stories to facilitate a therapeutic relationship and the internalization of limits and guidelines. Finally, just as a child can use stories to communicate and express herself or himself to family, self, or friends, so can the same child use the story to reveal herself or himself to a therapist. The therapist can respond to the child on the basis of the story, and a dialogue can be established that is based on the child's language.

TABLE 10.1   The Cultural, Familial, and Personal Purposes of Storytelling

Setting	Type of Story	Purpose
Culture	myths legends fairy tales fables	■ understanding of the environment ■ control over the environment ■ coping with the environment ■ expression and transmission of spiritual and religious beliefs ■ transmission of moral values to guide actions ■ self-expression to facilitate identification ■ cultural identification and belongingness ■ preparation for problem situations ■ preparation for and facilitation of coping ■ representation of the psychological and emotional atmosphere of the group ■ entertainment
Family	fantasy narratives true event narratives embellished true events	■ communication of limits, values, and morals ■ fostering of value development ■ teaching of rules and regulations ■ imparting of knowledge and information ■ transmission of wisdom ■ enhancement of parent-child relationships ■ prevention of problems or conflict between parent and child ■ transmission of coping skills
Child	fantasy stories make-believe stories	■ communication ■ expression of feelings, needs, conflicts ■ mastery of feelings, needs, conflicts ■ alternative problem solving ■ meaningful, anxiety-free self-disclosure ■ symbolic working through of conflicts ■ symbolic confrontation of challenges ■ enhancement of self-esteem ■ enhancement of the socialization process

The transmission of values, knowledge, and wisdom that has originally been an important aspect of storytelling in different cultures and families is maintained in the therapy setting. The process is altered somewhat, however. The child relates a story, thus transmitting her or his knowledge and beliefs. The therapist does not merely receive this information, as does a listener in the traditional use of the story, but also responds and provides information, thus becoming a storyteller herself or himself. Thus, in the storytelling technique as applied to therapy, child and therapist switch roles being senders and receivers of information in completing an interaction. In the traditional use of stories, senders do not become receivers in the same interaction, nor do receivers become senders (though they might take on these other roles in a later interaction or in an interaction with another individual).

The Usefulness of Storytelling

There are two primary purposes that make the storytelling technique useful in child therapy, namely, the giving and receiving of information. Both therapist and child give and receive information through the storytelling procedure. Most commonly, children give information first and then receive it (i.e., the child tells the first story). Therapists receive information first and then give it (i.e., the therapist tells her or his own story after having listened to the child's story and only in response to the child's story). This process facilitates not only assessment, but also rapport building and understanding of the child. It provides an environment in which therapeutic intervention can be implemented in a nonthreatening and culturally sensitive manner (Greenbaum and Holmes, 1983).

As was pointed out above, children give information by using stories to express and master feelings, to communicate about themselves and their families, and so forth. Therapists receive information from children's stories by learning about children's problems and frustrations and gaining insight into children's defenses, conflicts, and family dynamics (Gardner, 1995). Stories used in this way are an excellent supplement to other assessment procedures, and can be used to validate hypotheses about the child and her or his family (Brandell, 2000; Mueller and Tingley, 1990; Sherman, 1990). Stories can thus be used to gain a fuller understanding of the child given her or his surroundings, both cultural and familial. The advantage of the story used for this purpose is its nonintrusive and nonobvious nature. Most children are not aware of the vast self-disclosure they engage in while telling a story. In many ways, stories are projective techniques, much like free associations or dreams. They reveal information about the child innocuously, as the child does not need to provide explanations or commentary, does not have to defend or protect self or family, and can share information without needing to feel accountable for it (Close, 1998).

The therapist merely has to listen carefully and has to be able to listen to the underlying message. (This will be addressed fully in the practical implementation section of this chapter.) There is no need to make the child's metacommunication overt or conscious (Kestenbaum, 1985). Instead, the therapist can understand the child on the basis of the metaphor that was used. Further, the therapist can respond using the same metaphor to communicate directly with the child without having to bring the problem up in direct or confrontational language. In Gardner's words, the therapist communicates directly with the child's unconscious and need not worry about making the unconscious conscious for the child (Gardner, 1995; 1997). In this way, the therapist can give something to the child without an overt process of giving or advising. In fact, through the process of responding in the child's metaphor by telling a story back using the same characters and setting, yet a slightly different outcome, the therapist can provide a corrective experience, can suggest solutions and coping strategies, can reinterpret (or reframe) events, and can give advice, without ever doing so overtly (Pearce, 1995; Stiles and Kottman, 1990). This technique of using metacommunication as a therapeutic intervention is very much related, if not equivalent, to the use of metaphor endorsed by Milton Erikson and modified for use with children (Peterson, 1988).

Nature and Themes of Therapy Stories

Above and beyond the general purpose and usefulness of therapy stories in giving and receiving information, there are also certain themes that tend to emerge depending on the stage of therapy that has been reached with a given child. Thus, the nature of the stories of any individual child is expected to change over the course of treatment and can help the therapist to track progress and possibly determine when termination is indicated. Gardner (1971) has highlighted the nature and expectations for five types of stories (summarized in Table 10.2): first stories, early-phase stories, middle-phase stories, late-phase stories, and termination stories.

TABLE 10.2   The Nature and Meaning of Stories

Type of Story	Nature	Meaning or Usefulness
First Story	■ relatively short ■ cautiously provided ■ usually totally uncensored	■ expectations about therapy ■ revelation of the problem from the child's perspective ■ aid to assessment ■ provision of a metaphor that can be used therapeutically
Early-Phase Story	■ still short ■ provided more freely ■ less inhibited or cautious ■ still uncensored	■ provision of insight into the child's and family's dynamics ■ aid to continued assessment ■ adjustment to therapy ■ information about relationship building with therapist ■ expression of affect
Middle-Phase Story	■ longer ■ themes emerge ■ story characters may reemerge ■ more spontaneous	■ facilitation of internalization through repetition of themes ■ desensitization to fears and anxieties connected with the therapy process and therapist ■ internalization of new solutions and alternative responses ■ expression of therapy progress ■ beginning mastery of affect
Late-Phase Story	■ changes in story ■ changes in the moral/lesson ■ incorporation of alternatives ■ more flexibility in story line ■ longer, healthier	■ expression of self-growth ■ expression of improved coping ■ facilitation of exploration of alternatives and options ■ mastery of affect ■ expression of needs in relationships ■ expression of caring in the therapy relationship
Termination Story	■ long, healthy ■ flexible ■ many changes ■ include outside world more	■ mastery of affects and needs ■ reflection upon therapy process and relationship ■ efficient problem solving ■ dealing with saying goodbye

The First Story and the Early-Phase Story.   The first story a child is ever asked to tell in therapy tends to express her or his attitudes toward therapy and, like the early-phase story, represents an excellent projection of processes that the child may not yet be able to share willingly or with full awareness (Gardner, 1995). The first and early-phase stories provide an uninhibited, uncensored look at the child's problem in the child's language and from the child's perspective. Further, they provide the therapist with metaphors that can be used to help the child adapt to the therapy process and build trust and rapport. The first story and the early-phase story of inhibited children, according to Gardner (1971), can still be part of the assessment phase of treatment. They can be used for diagnostic and conceptual purposes, hence can be asked for during the intake process if so desired. An example and discussion of an early-phase story follows:

> Once there was a little horse, and he liked to run on the pasture and chew grass. Sometimes there wasn't a lot of grass. One day a littler horse came along and said, "Go away—it's my pasture and you can't eat my grass." The little horse couldn't eat any more grass, and he got starved. He got very thin. Soon he thought he was gonna die because he couldn't eat. Then came the big horse and said, "Go ahead and eat, but just a little bit." The little horse ate and ate, but then the big horse yelled, "No more!" Then came another horse and said, "You poor horse. I think you need some more food." And then everything was fine. And the moral of the story is "Don't eat too much or the big horse gets mad."

This story is a typical early story, reflecting strong mirroring needs and hope for the therapy process. It was told by a 9-year-old boy who had numerous learning disabilities and health problems. He had been a difficult infant, had spent much time in hospitals, and was placed in a special classroom. His attachment to his mother was questionable, yet he was fond of his father. His father, however, was somewhat unpredictable in his willingness to interact with his son, sometimes initiating or proposing an activity, only to rescind his offer later. The child's parents had decided not to have another child, yet the mother became pregnant again when this child was 7. The brother was a healthy infant who was admired by and received much attention from parents and maternal grandparents. The elder child felt left out and deprived of the kind of caring his brother received.

The child's story very accurately reflected this home situation. His story indicated that he did receive some nurturance before his brother arrived. Yet after the birth of the second child, the boy felt unwelcome and unnurtured (whether this was so is irrelevant; the child's feeling is what counts). Even when his father offered to give him some nurturance as well, the offer lasted only a limited time and could be withdrawn quickly. The moral of the story revealed that the child had learned to ask for little and not to expect consistent nurturance. However, the story did show hope that the therapy process would be helpful. Although this hope was perhaps unrealistically high at this time, it was nevertheless evaluated as positive by the therapist, as it indicated that the child had not given up completely.

The Middle-Phase Story.   Middle-phase stories serve to facilitate therapeutic working through. In this stage of treatment, the child begins to respond to and internalize the changes or alternative solutions suggested in the therapist's stories. Some children will maintain some consistency in story character, whereas other children will invent new characters almost every time. However, all children tend to develop themes that reemerge in most of their stories and are easily recognized by the therapist as relevant to the most pressing or relevant problem or conflict in the child's life. This repetition facilitates the internalization of the therapist's message as many opportunities are provided to reiterate messages in different terms and within different story lines. Themes also serve to decrease children's fears and to help them become desensitized to and deal with anxieties arising in the child-therapist relationship. As the comfort level with the therapist increases, children become more spontaneous and more self-revealing, as well as more open to hearing alternative endings to their stories. Stories can be expected to begin to change slightly in the middle phase, as the child begins to incorporate new learning and the therapy experience into new story lines. However, large changes in the story do not occur until the internalization of change is more firmly embedded and accepted by the child. This occurs in the late phase of treatment as defined by Gardner (1971). An example and discussion of a middle-phase story follows:

> I'm going to tell another story with the rabbit that couldn't run. The rabbit that couldn't run decided that taking lessons was a good idea after all. So she went to the head rabbit and she said, "Can you give me lessons in how to run?" and the head rabbit said "Sure." They started to have lessons, and the rabbit could run. But the next day, the rabbit was at a hill, and she couldn't run up the hill. She cried because she couldn't go up the hill. Then she remembered the head rabbit. She went to the head rabbit and said, "Can you teach me to go uphill?" and the head rabbit said "Sure." So the rabbit learned to run uphill. And the lesson is that if you can't do something, go to the head rabbit to learn it.

The 7-year-old girl who told this story in her tenth session had been referred for treatment because of depression and low self-confidence and self-efficacy. She lived with her biological mother and boyfriend. The mother was severely depressed; the boyfriend alcoholic. There were no other children or adults living in the home, and this girl was extremely shy and withdrawn. Her need for help was identified by her first-grade teacher, who had become a major support for this child.

The girl's story is an example of a very typical middle-phase story. The girl not only repeated a theme that had emerged in other stories that revealed her feelings of incompetence and insecurity, but also reused one of her favorite story characters. Like most middle-phase stories, her story reflected the incorporation of some positive movement and internalization of hope in that the rabbit was able to overcome its problems of not being able to run and to move uphill. This is a significant change from earlier themes in the child's story that were permeated by helplessness and hopelessness about change and the ability to perform or achieve. However, the story is not a late-phase story because the girl had not yet become self-reliant in her attempts to solve her problems. Instead, she relied heavily upon others to give her advice and suggest solutions.

The Late-Phase Story.   Late-phase stories can be recognized by the changes that are beginning to occur in themes and characters. Children begin to incorporate messages heard from the therapist and are beginning to tell stories that suggest solutions, alternatives, and options. Stories at this time become even more spontaneous, longer, and healthier. Child-therapist relationship anxieties tend not to emerge in this stage, as this aspect of therapeutic interaction has been resolved successfully. Instead, stories will include more unrelated characters, as the child's world and coping skills expand. Late-phase stories that are elaborate, healthy, and filled with options suggest that termination may approach and may need to be explored. If other events in treatment and in the child's life point toward the same conclusion, the topic would then be broached with the child's parents and finally with the child herself or himself. (See Chapter Fourteen for specifics about termination decisions and procedures.) Once this has occurred, it is likely that the child's stories will change once again. An example and discussion of a late-phase story follow:

> This is a story about an alien who fell in a hole on earth after his spaceship crashed. When he first fell down, he was very, very scared. He didn't know nobody, and when people came up to his hole, they scared him because they looked different, and they always screamed so loud, and he thought they didn't like him. Then he figured out that the reason they screamed so loud was that they were scared too. Then he figured out that they were scared of him because he looked different. So the next time the people came to where he was, he said, "Don't scream so loud because I am scared too," and they said, "But how can you be scared? You are so green, and green things shouldn't be scared." The alien said that even green things get scared and that they should help him out of his hole so they could find out he wasn't as mean as they thought. Then the people said, "But how can you be scared? You are so big, and big things shouldn't be scared." The alien said that even big things get scared and that they should help him out of his deep hole. The people talked with each other for a while, and then they came down and got him. When they were in the hole, one man said, "You are smaller than I thought you are," one other man said "You are less green than I thought you are," and one other man said "You are scareder than I thought you are." The alien said, "You are nicer than I thought you are, so let's all be glad and let's have a celebration together." The people were happy and carried the alien up out of his hole and invited him for supper. They celebrated and laughed a lot and told stories. And the moral of the story is that when you're scared of something, check it out first because it might be okay, and when you're scared of someone, talk to them because they might be scared too.

This story was told by a 10-year-old boy who was initially referred because of aggressive behavior in the classroom and during break times. Intake revealed severe physical abuse by his mother, a single parent of five boys. The abuse was stopped after involvement of child protection workers and therapy for the mother. The child, in addition to exhibiting aggressive behavior at school, also revealed many fears and anxiety that manifested in frequent nightmares and occasional night terrors. His aggressive behavior quickly diminished once he started therapy and felt protected from his mother's abuse.

His story was an excellent example of a late-phase story. It combined recognition of his previous problems, namely, being afraid of people and making people afraid of him so that they would avoid and withdraw from him; internalization of new and adaptive coping skills, namely, being willing to approach people and to explore possible ways of relating positively with people; and hopeful resolution of interpersonal problems despite differences, namely, the ability to celebrate together despite being different. It reflected his increased level of socialization as the story demonstrated that he was now able to use verbal skills, as opposed to bullying and nightmares, to express his fears. It expressed recognition of the superior quality of verbal skills over impulsive behavior in the moral of the story, which emphasized talking as opposed to quick judgment or giving up of hope. Finally, the alien had appeared in several stories before and was clearly a symbol of himself. Over the course of several stories the alien had made great progress in his self-image and level of self-confidence, revealing the same progress in this child.

The Termination Story. Termination stories are generally healthy stories, much like late-phase stories. However, they also include themes of separation and grieving over the loss of the therapeutic relationship. Termination stories are often used by both child and therapist to test internalizations and coping skills, and they reflect the various emotions that children deal with in separating from their clinician (e.g., denial, anger, depression). However, in addition to these slightly negative emotional themes, there should also be indications of joy over accomplishment and confidence about future problem-solving ability. Occasionally, a very sophisticated termination story may also recapitulate the therapy process as perceived by the child. An example and discussion of a termination story follow:

> Here is the story of the girl who wanted to be an astronaut. She wanted to be an astronaut for a long time. But she never thought she could be an astronaut because her daddy told her she was dumb. Her mommy told her she was dumb too and that she should be a housecleaner, not an astronaut. Then the girl came to school, and her teacher asked what she wanted to be when she grew up and the girl said, "I want to be a housecleaner," and the teacher said, "I think you are too smart to be a housecleaner." And the girl said, "Well, I really want to be an astronaut." So the teacher said, "You'll have to practice real hard, but I think you can be an astronaut if you really, really try." Well, the girl really wanted to be an astronaut, so she tried really hard. She did a lot of math, and she did a lot of drawing, and she did all her homework. But sometimes she still didn't know if she could be an astronaut. She checked with her mommy, and her mommy said, "Well, maybe." So the girl tried some more. Then one day she did really well in her drawing, and then she knew she could be an astronaut because her teacher would show her how. But then the teacher had to go, and then the girl was alone again. But this time she just told her mommy she would be an astronaut, and finally her mommy said, "Yes." Now the girl is an astronaut. And the moral is that, even if your mommy says you can't be an astronaut, maybe you can do it anyway if you try hard and show her how good you can work.

This 11-year-old girl was referred by her maternal grandmother who was concerned that her granddaughter had withdrawn after her biological father remarried and her biological mother moved to a different town. The girl was found to be quite depressed and fearful. She had no goals and felt extremely inadequate. Over the course of therapy, she began to develop several goals and to work toward these with confidence and direction. She needed much guidance, indicating that she was in dire need of an idealizable adult in her life. She responded very well to guidance, ultimately internalizing some structure and direction for herself. Her story was a good example of a termination story because it summarized her treatment process (the teacher represented the therapist), indicated that she had internalized the strength she would need to continue to work toward her goals even if her environment was not always in agreement with these goals, and suggested that she would be able to implement her goals even in the absence of the therapist.

In summary, the storytelling technique can be used to receive and give information, explore behavior and affect patterns in the child, assess treatment progress, and explore readiness for termination. However, it must be pointed out that storytelling should never be the only technique that is used with a child. Storytelling always must be embedded in a larger conceptual and therapeutic context that includes clear goals and other interventions for a given child. Storytelling can be easily incorporated with play therapy techniques, art therapy, and even behavioral strategies. It does not provide a framework for comprehensive treatment and is merely a strategy that increases a therapist's repertoire of skills available to help a child make the best possible use of therapy. Obviously, storytelling is also a highly verbal activity and therefore limited in its usefulness with very young children (below the age of 5) or with children who are not easily verbal.

Variations on the Technique

There are no formalized alternative approaches in the literature to the actual procedure of the storytelling technique as outlined by Gardner (1995). However, clinical use of the procedure suggests and has demonstrated that some variation in implementation is indeed possible depending upon the needs of individual children. For instance, Miller and Boe (1990) have used storytelling in conjunction with sand play to assist children in telling their stories and to teach staff to respond to children through the metaphor. Kottman and Stiles (1990) have applied the technique to Adlerian therapy, outlining stories specific to therapeutic foci inherent in this approach to human behavior. Gabel (1984) has adapted the technique by asking the child to draw, not merely tell, the story in order to solicit assessment information from reticent or oppositional children. Further, while Gardner (1995) suggests that storytelling always involves the telling of a story by the child, and a subsequent retelling of a similar story by the therapist, this procedure can be modified successfully. For instance, for some children, telling a story for the first time can be almost impossible for numerous reasons. Modeling of the storytelling procedure by the therapist in such instances can break the ice and can prepare the child to invent a story of her or his own. Some children prefer to be involved in the retelling of their story, as opposed to allowing the therapist to do the retelling independently. This tends to be the case in the middle and later phases of treatment, when the child is beginning to do her or his own problem solving in collaboration with the therapist. In fact, it can be extremely therapeutic to involve a child in the healthier retelling of the story.

For instance, one 7-year-old girl, who was referred for treatment because of adjustment problems to her parents' marital difficulties and possible impending divorce, told the following story:

> A little bear was lost in the woods without her mommy and her daddy. She looked and looked, but they were nowhere to be found. The little bear was very hungry and scared. There was nothing to eat. She kept looking for her mommy and couldn't find her. The little bear starved to death because there was nothing to eat.

In retelling her story, the therapist had to consider that the child's parents indeed had been extremely neglectful of all three of their children, having been reported for physical neglect by the children's school on numerous occasions. Therefore, a retelling of the story could not falsely encourage the child to rely on her parents' help for nurturance and sustenance, but instead needed to help her learn skills to nurture herself. The therapist decided to retell the story of the bear, beginning as follows:

A little bear was lost in the woods without her mommy and her daddy. She looked and looked, but they were nowhere to be found. The little bear was very hungry and scared. There was nothing to eat. She kept looking for her mommy and couldn't find her. Then she saw some fresh green grass, and she remembered that her big brother used to eat fresh green grass all the time and that it had helped him grow big and strong. So the little bear ate all the grass she could find and felt much better. The next day, all the grass was gone, and she was hungry again. She looked and looked, but her parents were nowhere to be found. The little bear again was very hungry and scared. There was nothing to eat. She kept looking for her mommy and couldn't find her. Then she saw some ripe blueberries on a bush, and she remembered that one of her teachers told her that bears can eat berries when they were ripe. So she ate the berries she could find, and she felt much better.

At this point in the story, the girl interrupted to inform the therapist that the bear can feed herself with raspberries and strawberries as well. The therapist agreed and decided to continue the story in collaboration with the child. Whenever the bear in the story was hungry again, the girl was asked to invent new food sources for the bear. The child became very excited and indicated several times that she had never realized that there were so many ways to find food and get filled up. She then decided to draw each item of food, using paint and the easel. She drew salmon, trout, trees, clams, and small bushes. She became very excited in the process, and it was clear that she had heard the message. Her parents were no longer considered the only source of nurturance, and she realized that there were things she could do to feed herself. At the end of this session, the child asked to keep her food drawing to remind her of the little bear and her ability to fend for herself. The therapist consented gladly.

A therapist may choose to prepare a story beforehand to tell the child if the child cannot think of a story herself or himself. This use of stories is in the spirit of the use of a metaphor. However, unlike the use of a metaphor, the story should contain characters chosen by the child previously. Sometimes, if the child has never told a story, the therapist can use other characters the child has created in play or art to create a story. One of the best ways to construct a story is for the therapist to use the child's answers to the projective questions (e.g., favorite animal and color, desired age, desert island) posed during the intake interview. For instance, one boy who had wished himself to be a turtle and who decided that he would not take anyone to the deserted island with him was subsequently told a story of a turtle who was stranded on an island all by itself. Other variations on the technique are no doubt possible, and the novice therapist is encouraged to follow the child's lead. Flexible use of this technique can lead to ingenious ways of communicating with children through their own metaphors and symbolisms.

Practical Implementation

The verbatim transcripts of the mechanics of the mutual storytelling technique are presented in Gardner (1995), and the novice therapist who is planning to use this strategy for the first time is encouraged to read them in the original reference. However, a thorough summary is presented here according to this author's adaptation and interpretation of the original technique. The guidelines provided here and summarized in Table 10.3 are presented with

TABLE 10.3   Mechanics of the Mutual Storytelling Technique

Step	Purpose	Procedures
Instructions	■ acquaint the child with the procedure ■ relieve any fears or anxieties in the child about the procedure	■ use recording device ■ introduce parts of the story: beginning, middle, end, moral ■ help child overcome anxiety about the procedure ■ help child get started
Child's Story	■ allow the child to express self symbolically ■ learn more about the child and family ■ allow the child to explore options and apply new learning	■ listen carefully ■ ask clarifying questions ■ jot down notes about story line and characters ■ begin to interpret ■ listen for themes, patterns, conflicts, and affects ■ praise the child's effort
Commercial Break	■ interpret the child's story ■ prepare a healthy story in response	■ explore who is represented by the different characters ■ explore feelings and needs ■ explore ambiance ■ assess dynamic meaning
Therapist's Story	■ communicate with the child in the child's metaphor ■ facilitate internalization of change ■ communicate respect and caring ■ communicate alternatives and options	■ recreate the story with identical characters and similar setting and story line ■ incorporate choices, options, and alternatives ■ revise the moral to underscore alternatives ■ make resolution healthier ■ respond to the child's expressions respectfully and therapeutically

the assumption that a child is asked to engage in the process of mutual storytelling for the first time. Obviously, upon reuse of the technique with the same child, the first step in the procedure would be skipped. To implement and capture the stories, Gardner recommends the use of a tape recorder. However, one can equally effectively use a videocamera or other methods (such as a puppet theater) to provide a framework for the technique. A recording device works best, however, as it gives the child the option to listen to the stories a second time.

Instructions

The instructions given to the child include all the necessary information to construct a story. It informs the child that the story must be original, in other words, cannot be a summary of a TV show, book, or comic book that the child may have read or seen in the past. Further, the child is instructed to give the story a beginning, middle, and end, as well as a moral to top off the story. The child is then informed that after she or he has told a story, the clinician will do the same. The possibility of a commercial break between the two stories is also introduced here. After all of these instructions, the child is introduced to an imaginary audience. This introduction serves to help the child overcome any anxiety or embarrassment associated with the procedure. The introduction can be brief or lengthy, depending on the therapist's judgment of how much time the child needs to adjust and prepare. The introduction can consist of asking the child simple questions about herself or himself, such as age, hobbies, and friends. Then the child is asked to proceed with a story.

If the child has difficulty getting started, some help can be given. The therapist can offer to help the child start the story by telling at least the beginning, but also more if necessary, together. In so doing, the therapist makes every attempt to keep her or his part of the story neutral, allowing the child to fill in the critical blanks. For instance, the therapist might start off with the traditional fairy tale beginning, "Once upon a time, there was…," then turning the microphone over to the child, asking her or him to fill in the object or person. This procedure can be continued until the child spontaneously takes over the story line. If the child's first story does not have all the components that were mentioned in the instructions, she or he may be prompted. This includes a prompt for the moral, or lesson, of the story.

The Child's Story

While the child is telling the story, the therapist may want to jot down some notes as she or he will need to tell a second story that needs to closely resemble the child's story. Thus, the main characters and their names need to be remembered as well as the main themes and events. Names of places and order of events also need to be taken down to be reproduced appropriately. In taking notes, the therapist can also begin to formulate questions for the child that will serve to clarify content, process, and meanings of the story. Many children, especially younger children, need such prompts to clarify certain aspects of their story and its characters. Children are not always clear in their differentiation of characters, often referring to them generically. To clarify which character is saying or doing what, the therapist might need to suggest that the child give labels. For instance, if the child introduced two girls in a story and frequently refers to one girl or the other, the clinician might suggest that the child label them Girl One and Girl Two so that the therapist can follow the imaginary dialogue between the two.

If the child alludes to unusual, dangerous, or vague occurrences that give rise to questions in the therapist about such issues as possible delusions or hallucinations and abuse or neglect, these thoughts should be clarified immediately. The therapist might follow up by asking the child whether she or he has had similar experiences. Questioning needs to be done cautiously, not in a challenging manner, to neither offend the child nor create the impression that the child must defend her or his story. Finally, questions can also serve to clarify the meaning of the story and its characters, which the therapist attempts to determine while the child tells the story. If the therapist cannot create a story as quickly as the child ends hers or his, the therapist can create a delay before telling the second story by asking for a "commercial break." The child can do the commercial break herself or himself or with the help of the therapist. However, for the therapist, this time serves to collect her or his thoughts and to formulate an alternative story. The novice therapist is more likely than the skilled clinician to need a commercial break. Also, commercial breaks are more likely early in a child's treatment while the therapist still assesses the child's needs, patterns, and themes. Later in treatment, story themes will repeat themselves and will be more easily interpretable and usable. Similarly, the clinician will have formulated some approaches to alternatives tailored to the needs of a given child.

Commercial Breaks

During the commercial break, the therapist collects her or his thoughts to identify the symbolic meanings of the story figures. Some helpful guidelines for this process exist. First, the clinician needs to determine which story figure represents the child and which of that figure's characteristics are most critical and important to the child's self-definition and presenting problem. Second, other story figures must be evaluated for their representational value as well. In other words, they may represent family members, friends, feared persons, loved individuals, and so on. The therapist must be willing to explore both living creatures and objects according to their symbolic and representational value. It is also important to recognize that sometimes, several aspects of one and the same person may be represented by different figures or characters in the story.

In addition to determining which person in the child's life is represented by which character in the story, it is also necessary to explore the nature and strength of feelings and needs that are being expressed, their origins and targets, and the ease of their expression. Similarly, defenses against the experience and/or expression of needs or feelings need to be assessed, as well as coping strategies employed to help the child deal with difficult content in the story. Once the child's own feelings and needs have been explored, the same process needs to be repeated for the feelings and needs of the other story characters and the real-life people they represent. Once the significance of each figure has been evaluated, the overall atmosphere of the story needs to be attended to. This overall ambiance is very likely to tell the clinician a lot about a child's own emotional state, as well as about the emotional ambiance of the child's home environment. Cold weather in a story might well be reflective of an emotionally cold atmosphere in the home. Lack of liveliness in the child's tale might be a representation of a lack of joy or interaction in the family. Hostile content might reflect the same sentiment in the child and her or his known world.

Finally, the therapist can attempt a dynamic interpretation of the story, in much the same way as an adult client's dream is interpreted. The moral of the story is generally particularly useful in this context, as it tends to synthesize the child's concerns and their origins and meanings. For instance, the moral in the early-phase story above, "Don't eat too much or the big horse gets mad," helps the therapist to recognize the withholding nature of the child's father, represented by the big horse. Similarly, the fact that the little horse in the story was significantly affected by another small horse suggests a theme of sibling rivalry with the infant in the family. Once the therapist believes that she or he understands the meaning of the child's story, the therapist needs to construct an alternative story that addresses the needs, feelings, and defenses expressed in the original tale.

The Therapist's Story

The most important aspect of the therapist's story is the healthy resolution of the conflict or feeling expressed in the child's problem. The therapist uses the same characters as the child, places the story in the same frame of reference, but slightly alters the outcome to include a healthier solution to the child's expressed problem or conflict. This approach serves largely to increase the child's perceived options and alternatives and to suggest alternate coping skills or ways to solutions to problems. It is important that the solutions and coping devices offered to the child are acceptable within the child's family environment. To suggest subtly to a child that a parent should be told about angry feelings when the therapist is not certain that the parent can handle the free expression of negative affects is not only inappropriate, but also dangerous. Therefore, solutions and alternatives need to be tailored not only to the child's needs and emotions, but also to the needs and emotions of the important adults in the child's life. This story also serves to challenge the child to move on to the next level of improvement. Even once a story already incorporates positive rethinking on the child's part, the therapist suggests moving on to the next therapeutic step indicated for the child. For instance, the following story was told in response to the middle-phase story provided above:

> This is another story about the rabbit that couldn't run. The rabbit that couldn't run decided to follow a friend's advice that taking running lessons might help her improve her running skills. She went to the head rabbit and asked her if she would be willing to teach the rabbit how to run so that the rabbit could feel better and do all the things she would like to do. The head rabbit was happy to do so, and they started the lessons right away. Before long, the rabbit could run. But on the next day, the rabbit came to a hill. She had never seen a hill, so she was not sure what to do. She was sure she couldn't run uphill. She almost started to cry because she had just learned how to run and now she was faced with yet another problem. But—then she remembered what the head rabbit had told her: "Whenever you come to a new place, just keep using the same basic steps. Put one foot in front of the other and keep moving forward." So the rabbit decided to try it, and lo and behold, it worked. Soon she was at the top of the hill. And the moral of the story is, when faced with a new problem, just remember what you have already learned, and you can find your own solution.

This story demonstrates the essence of the alternative offered by the therapist. The child was reassured that she would be able to find her own solutions and that she did not need to depend on others to achieve progress in her life. It was suggested that she begin to rely on her own resources, instead of always passively depending upon others.

Example

The example that follows was chosen because of the excellent verbal skills demonstrated by this 9-year-old girl. While the focus of the example is on a few select stories—namely, one story in each category—the reader must keep in mind that other stories were told as well, and many other interventions were applied. Play therapy and drawing were two additional integral techniques; the child's parents were referred for marital therapy, as well as being seen in parent education classes. The parents had refused family therapy, indicating that they thought that it was unnecessary to involve the older child in the treatment process. Although only samples derived through the traditional use of mutual storytelling are included here, often stories in this girl's treatment also were told or shared not following the traditional techniques. In fact, the first story in therapy was told by the therapist. Only after having the process modeled for her was the child able to use this technique herself.

The girl in this example was referred by her parents because she often vomited, yet no physical illness was diagnosable; frequently could not sleep at night, again with no physical cause; and often developed a cough at night that kept other family members awake as well. The intake session revealed a somewhat anxious mother who was very concerned about her daughter, mainly because of others' comments about her. The child's father was very uninvolved with the family and was frequently gone because of his business. He appeared slightly depressed and malcontented with his life. The child's older brother appeared reasonably well adjusted, was a high achiever in school, and had many friends. The family had lived with the maternal grandmother until the second child was born. Both parents worked until that time, and the male child in the family had been largely raised by his maternal grandmother until the family moved to their own apartment upon the birth of the second child. At this point, the mother took charge of the primary care of both children. The daughter's presenting problems were described as chronic, and no one in the family could remember a time when they had not been present. Here is the child's first story:

> Once upon a time, there was a rabbit. This rabbit lived in a mushroom. It was a big mushroom that had many rooms. It was a toadstool mushroom. The rooms had very small windows, and the door was in the back of the mushroom. The little rabbit was very small and couldn't reach the handle of the door, so he had to be in the toadstool a lot. The little rabbit lived in the mushroom with his mommy and daddy and his brother. His brother was very big, and he could use the back door all by himself. Everyone liked his big brother. The little rabbit tried to be just like his brother, but he was too little. His big brother went to have a great adventure, and he saw many things. He was gone for many weeks, and the little rabbit was home all alone with his mommy. His mommy was very sad because the big brother was not home. So the little rabbit asked his mommy to play to make her happy. They played for the whole day, and they had a lot of fun. And the moral of the story is that if someone is unhappy, all you have to do is cheer them up and everything is better.

This first story was somewhat unusual in that it did not appear to incorporate the child's feelings about therapy and the therapist, and it was quite lengthy. There was not a lot of action in this story, and this was interpreted as reflective of the girl's life in general, which did not appear to lead her outside of the family very often. The small rabbit was seen as symbolic of the child herself, despite being clearly male in the child's story. The toadstool house was interpreted to represent the somewhat poisoned home atmosphere in which this child lived. She did not feel loved and sensed a definite preference of her older brother. Indeed, her parents had been very disappointed when this child was born, as they had hoped for another son. The child's mother was very resentful upon the birth of this child, as her own mother refused to take care of a second child, which necessitated that the mother quit her job and take care of her children from now on. As the older child was already in kindergarten by this time, the mother shared her days primarily with her younger child. They rarely left the home and appeared to interact very little.

Thus, the child's story was an excellent metaphor of her home environment, her relationship with her mother, and her jealousy of her older brother. Further, it already pointed toward a major theme that would emerge in future stories, namely, her great need to please her mother at all cost. The following story was told by the therapist in response:

Once upon a time, there was a rabbit. This rabbit lived in a mushroom. It was a big mushroom that had many rooms. It was a toadstool mushroom. The rooms had very small windows, and the door was in the back of the mushroom. The little rabbit was very small and couldn't reach the handle of the door, so he had to be in the toadstool a lot. Now as we know, toadstools are very poisonous. So the little rabbit got very sick from living in the house. The rest of the family didn't get sick because they were big enough to come and go as they pleased and never spent much time in the house. But the little rabbit had to stay there all the time, so he got very sick. Everybody became very worried about the little rabbit because he was so sick. They took him to many doctors, but no one could figure out what was wrong with the rabbit. Finally, they came to a doctor who said, "Oh, well, you live in a toadstool house, and you don't let the little rabbit out very often. No wonder he is sick. Don't you know that toadstool houses are poisonous?" So the family realized that the house had been making the little rabbit sick, and they all learned that they had to make some changes to help the little rabbit get better. The brother was asked to take the little rabbit out to play; the mommy was asked to take the little rabbit out for walks and for good food; and the daddy was told to take the little rabbit out on special adventures. And the little rabbit was taught how to open the back door so that he could let himself out whenever he needed to. So then he made new friends, and he started feeling better. And the moral of the story is, if a little rabbit is sick, you better check that he gets everything he needs to be healthy before blaming him.

In her story, the therapist decided to present her view of the child's presenting problem as a systemic family problem. She also suggested that the child was not to blame for her difficulties and that every family member would have some responsibility in the child's recovery. However, realizing that family change might not occur quickly, she also suggested a strategy for the child to find nurturance elsewhere. From this point, therapy progressed slowly with the child and therapist working on developing a therapeutic relationship. The girl had difficulty establishing trust and often withdrew from the therapy process. However, she discovered several media through which she could uninhibitedly communicate with the therapist. The most important one of these remained storytelling; however, another one was the use of drawing and creating clay models. When the child finally had established a trusting relationship with the therapist, she began to incorporate some of the changes suggested in the therapist's stories. Here is an example of a middle-phase story, approximately 10 weeks into treatment.

Once upon a time, there was a big old camcorder. And this camcorder always took pictures and always worried that every picture had to be just perfect. So one day, she came to a big old house, and it was falling apart, and she was crying and sad because the balcony was falling off and the windows were broken. (Therapist interrupted to ask: "Who was crying?" The child responded: "The house was crying!" The therapist then indicated to the child to go on.) So the camcorder said, "Shape up, I want to take your picture and you are too ugly right now." So the house did everything it could—it polished the windows, it cleaned the floor, it even gave itself new paint and put a new chimney on top. It worked real hard, day and night. Then it called the camcorder and said, "I worked all night and all day and now you can take my picture because I'm really pretty now." The camcorder walked around the house and said, "No, no, no, this is no good. There is still a broken window here and still a little bit of dirt there. I can't take your picture like that! Didn't I tell you to clean up and get pretty. Oh, no, no, no, I just can't take your picture this way" and she left. The house was very disappointed and almost let everything fall apart again. But then she thought, "Well, maybe I'll keep clean and maybe I'll keep fixing me up because who knows, some day another camcorder might come and take my picture for real." And the moral of the story is, even if one camcorder doesn't like you, keep up the good work, because another one might come and like it anyway.

This story was clearly a middle-phase story. It was long and elaborate and had moved on to more meaningful interpersonal issues in the child's life. It also reflected some internalization of change, but not an entirely healthy resolution. In this case, the child was represented by the house, not by the first character introduced in the story. The switch to a feminine pronoun for the house as the story progressed confirmed this interpretation. The camcorder was interpreted as a symbol for the girl's mother, who was exceedingly critical and never quite satisfied with the girl. She often scrutinized the child's appearance and performance. She appeared to measure her own value as a mother according to how well her children performed, placing an awesome burden on this child to do everything she could to please her mother and earn her praise. The healthier aspect of this story is reflected in the fact that the house decides to maintain her own idea of a pretty appearance even after the mother disapproved and in the fact that the house showed hope for someone else to come along and like her. A healthier approach to this latter issue obviously would have been for the house to recognize that it only needed to please itself, no one else. Here is the story that the therapist told in response:

> Once upon a time, there was a big old camcorder. This camcorder always liked to take pictures of pretty things. One day it saw a house, and it thought it was pretty, but not quite good enough. So it told the house, "Why don't you shape up and change so I can take your picture?" The house looked at the camcorder and said, "I am an old house and this is how I look. If you like it, you can take my picture. If you don't, that's too bad because I won't change for you. I like myself the way I am and that's that!" The camcorder thought and thought, and finally decided to take the picture. She was never completely satisfied with it, but she still liked it very much. And the moral of the story is, if you like how you are, don't change yourself for anyone else.

The therapist decided to address the mother's narcissistic need for the child's perfection and to suggest to the child that she would never be able to meet this need for her mother. Instead, the child was asked to focus on her own needs and to learn to like herself as she was and to present that real self to the world. Although this involves some risk, as the world may respond rejectingly, the likelihood is portrayed as greater that ultimately the world will deal with reality. The child's self-acceptance and self-esteem remained critical elements throughout her treatment. Her narcissistic mother and uninvolved father were unable to provide help, and much reliance on the child's own resources had to be stressed.

Ultimately, the child was able to develop healthy self-esteem and strength and to maintain it through the help of others in her life, as well as her own internalized self-acceptance. Here is an example of a late-phase story that demonstrates this process. This story used a similar theme and the same characters developed for the first story. It was told after one year in treatment and suggested not only that great improvements had taken place in the child, but also that the family as a whole unfortunately had not done so.

> Here is our beloved rabbit from the toadstool house again. He was very happy today because he made a new friend. This friend showed her how to plant corn and potatoes and how to water the garden so that lots of fresh vegetables could grow that could help the rabbit grow healthy and strong. The little rabbit ran home very happy and told her mommy and daddy about what she had learned. Her daddy said, "That's nice," and her mommy said, "Oh, but you get so dirty when you work in a garden." The little rabbit was very sad that they did not like her garden. So she decided she would visit her friend and tell her that her mommy and daddy didn't like her garden. Her friend explained that not everyone can have a good garden because it takes a lot of patience and a lot of work, but that the little rabbit could have a good garden even if she had to take care of it without her mommy and daddy. So the little rabbit kept up her garden, and when the carrots came she ate them all up and was proud. And the moral of the story is, even if you live in a toadstool, you can have a garden.

This story revealed that, most important, this child had developed self-esteem and self-confidence that she had not possessed formerly. She referred to the rabbit as "beloved" and was willing to allow the rabbit to act against her parents' wishes or preferences. She was able to set her own goals, to use outside resources to work toward these goals, and finally to implement them and use the fruits of her labor to gratify her own needs for nurturance. Most interestingly, the gender attached to the rabbit had changed early in this story. This was the first time that the child had referred to the rabbit as female, indicating that her level of self-acceptance as a female child had increased along with her self-esteem and strength. The story was interpreted as an excellent indicator of improvement in the child. Unfortunately, the same did not yet appear to hold true for the family, at least from this girl's perspective. The therapist's story follows:

> Here is our beloved rabbit again. She is very happy because she has a new friend and she has learned how to have a garden. She loves to garden because it gives her a chance to be outdoors and to make sure that she has as much food as she needs and wants. She loves her garden very much and plants corn, and potatoes and carrots, and even some flowers. She eats the vegetables, and she uses the flowers to make things around her pretty and enjoyable. She wants very much to share her happiness with her mommy and daddy, and so she tells them all about her garden. But, as it turns out, her mommy and daddy don't like gardening. They prefer to eat other foods and to use other things to make everything look pretty. The little rabbit is a little disappointed, but then she decides that she can like her garden and use it to feed herself, even if her mommy and daddy don't want her to. So she keeps gardening and is very happy. And the moral of the story is, other people don't have to like what you do and it can still make you happy.

The therapist decided to inject the reality that this girl's parents may never be able to enjoy her and her activities in the way she would like them to but that this parental attitude need not interfere with her enjoyment of life. She also suggests that there is more to life than being fed and nurtured and that other activities can create pleasures for this girl. This decision was based on the fact that the girl had become an outstanding student who excelled in many subjects. The therapist communicated to the child that she can pursue her interests regardless of environmental criticisms.

Given the improvements in the child, the therapist decided on the basis of the story that she needed to attempt again to involve the family in family therapy. The child's parents had participated very committedly in marital treatment and were reported to have made good strides in their relationship. However, either their improvements had not translated into the family system, or the girl was unable to recognize the changes in her family. For either instance, family therapy appeared to be the most appropriate route to pursue the question. As the child's parents finally agreed to give family therapy a try, it was decided to terminate the child's individual therapy in one month, at which time the case would be transferred to a family therapist. Hence, the termination process was initiated with the child. The following story was told by the child in her next to last session:

> There was once a poor woman. She thought that she would never have anything in the world, and she was sick to her stomach about it. She worried so much she couldn't sleep. Sometimes she worried so much she cried very loud, and everyone around her noticed how sad she was. She tried and tried to make things better for herself. But no matter what she did, she failed! Then one day along came a rich woman. The rich woman looked at the poor woman and said, "Oh you poor woman, your life is not treating you right. Let me help you." And the rich woman took the poor woman to her house. She taught her how to plant a garden, how to grow her own food, and how to feed herself. Then she taught her how to sew clothes and how to dress herself. Then she showed her how to talk to other people and how to not be all lonely anymore. Then the rich woman said, "I have to go now, but you just keep doing what you're doing without me." And the poor woman thought, "Oh no, I can't do all this alone!" But then she tried anyway. And guess what happened? She learned that she could feed herself, and that she liked herself, and that she even enjoyed to play with other girls besides the rich woman. So she made lots of friends and lived happily ever after. And the moral of the story is, if you believe in yourself, you will be okay even when times are rough or when you're alone.

This story spoke and still speaks for itself. It was a perfect recapitulation of the child's presenting problem and therapeutic journey. It had a sad tone because of the termination but also expressed great hope for the future. The child had learned her lessons, and the therapist saw no need to add a new one. Here is how she responded:

> Once there was a poor woman who was very sad and ill. She had gone from doctor to doctor, but no one could help her, not even her mommy and daddy. Finally she ran into a rich woman who could help. Together they figured out how to keep the poor woman fed and how to keep the poor woman happy. When it came time for the two women to say good-bye, both were sad that they had to say good-bye, but both realized that they each were richer now than they had been before they did all their work together. They will always remember each other!

Summary and Concluding Thoughts

This chapter summarized the procedures for the mutual storytelling technique as developed by Gardner (1971; 1995). It has demonstrated that storytelling provides an excellent means for metacommunication with children. The procedure makes use of the metaphors and symbolisms that are still so natural for young children and can easily be fitted into any child therapy, regardless of the therapist's theoretical background. There is no technique in adult treatment that can quite compare to storytelling. Dream analysis can uncover an adult's unconscious, but the therapist cannot respond on that level. Instead, insight has to be created. Metaphors can rely on other, less obvious, processes to affect change in an adult but generally rely on symbolism created by the therapist, not the client. Thus, storytelling is uniquely applied to child clients and serves an excellent purpose in that realm. It is one of the techniques that is most conducive to the internalization of change without requiring the child to be able to verbalize insights or understanding of how changes occurred. This makes the technique utterly appropriate for the use in child therapy.

11 Graphic and Sculpting Art Techniques

Many philosophers and psychologists believe that human beings have a very basic need and ability to create, to give form to the unformed, to make shapes from the shapeless (Kohut, 1966; Lasch, 1979; Masterson, 1985). This need to create has received various labels, the most concise perhaps being Buber's "originator instinct" (Buber, 1965, p. 85). The need to create arises from the human desire to see oneself reflected in one's surroundings and to imbue one's surroundings with meaning that is relevant to the self. Art, as the term is used in its widest sense, provides a medium for creation and self-expression that may meet this basic human need. Although art is comprised of many disciplines, such as writing, poetry, music, dance, painting, drawing, sculpting, the focus in this chapter is on self-expression through graphic and sculpting art only. This should in no way imply that other forms of art, such as music or dance, might not provide appropriate therapeutic techniques; however, their use with children is less frequently documented than use of graphic and sculpting art.

The term *art* will be used loosely in this chapter. It will include not only the final true art product, or formed expression, that is a symbolic means of self-expression and communication, but also the precursors to this final product. Four precursors to the production of art have been identified: namely, precursory activities, chaotic discharge, stereotype activity, and pictographs (Kramer, 1998). Precursory activities are uses of art media such as paints or clay for the purpose of scribbling, smearing, and other exploration of the medium itself. Chaotic discharge refers to the pounding, splashing, or spilling of art materials that may signal discharge of various affects within the child. Stereotype activity, also referred to as art in the service of defense, includes activities such as copying, tracing, and stereotypic repetition of patterns or themes and is clearly not conducive to the free disclosing self-expression of the child, but rather serves to leave conflicts and affects uncovered through the noncreative use of art media. Finally, pictographs represent the use of pictures or models to replace words. Although this is true for expressive art as well, pictographs are highly idiosyncratic to specific communication between two people that could not be understood by outsiders (e.g., between the client and therapist). Pictographs frequently emerge in a therapy relationship and can be quite meaningful to client and therapist. The final form of art, and often the only one that is considered a true form (Kramer, 1998), is expressive art, which serves not only self-expression, but also communication. All five processes or products are of interest to the therapy process, as they can serve various functions that aid development, growth, and maturation among children. In fact, some theorists suggest that the process through which art is created is more important than the product itself (Creadick, 1985). Hence, all four processes and the product will be implied, as art is discussed with regard to its general conceptual meaning, application to therapy, and actual use in the treatment with children.

Conceptual Background

Art, like play, is viewed as a normal developmental activity among children. However, art, being more goal-directed than play, makes more stringent demands on the child's self, is more lasting and real, is designed to be understood by others, and can seriously affect life decisions (Kramer, 1998). Thus, in contrasting play and art, some theoreticians claim that play's function is to maintain equilibrium or to depict an ideal or fantasized self and outcome. Art, on the other hand, is viewed as bringing out problems and hence as depicting the real self or the realistic outcome of a situation. Art, not play, according to this understanding, makes the human being face reality and seek solutions. Additionally, art gives the growing child the opportunity to relive experiences in an active role, whereas the original role may have been passive, overwhelming, or out of the realm of control for the child. Art creates a completely new and creative process or product out of an old situation, thus ushering in mastery and resolution (Kramer, 1998). Art, in other words, has clear developmental purposes and is encouraged as an important activity for children.

Purposes of Art

The purposes of art are multifold. Art has been referred to as "the purposeful making of symbols" (Kramer, 1998, p. 63), "a child's spontaneous means of [self] expression" (Rambert, 1964, p. 340), the purposeful redirection of unacceptable impulses into acceptable behavior through sublimation (Rubin, 1998), and "a way of bringing order out of chaos" (Ulman, 1971, p. 20 as quoted in Rubin, 1978, p. 254). In a strict developmental or utilitarian sense, art serves a number of additional purposes. It can be used by the child symbolically to gratify wishes, control impulses, express affects and needs, and recreate interpersonal processes and relationships without any fear of consequences or retaliation from the environment (Rubin, 2001). In addition to this function, which appears related to normal mirroring needs of children (Kohut, 1984), art also serves idealizing needs. As such, children can use art to learn control of their environment as they learn to control and use certain art media and their related tools. Additionally, organization can be practiced and self-imposed, as evidenced by the child's developmental movement from free-form scribbles or sculptures to drawings or models that are clearly contained by outline boundaries that set self-imposed limits on the child's activity. Skill development needs are addressed through art by providing a medium for learning and practicing new skills, modeled by others or spontaneously through the child's own desire to create. Such new skills can facilitate the development of new coping behaviors and problem-solving strategies, further aiding the child in self-control and meaningful self-expression. In summary, art is a flexible, normal developmental medium that serves to help children meet the crucial developmental needs for self-exploration, structure, and skill development as they have been outlined by developmental theorists (Kohut, 1984). Given this developmental role of art, the healthy succession of different developmental levels in the production of art needs to be investigated.

Developmental Framework for the Creation of Art

To understand art and the process of its creation, a therapist has to have an understanding of the developmental phases thereof to be able to differentiate normal or healthy expression from regression (Rubin, 2001). Rubin (2001) has outlined nine distinct phases through which a child must pass in learning a new art form or medium. These are outlined in Table 11.1 and briefly discussed here. The first phase is a prephase, referred to as manipulating. It is highly sensory and kinesthetic, serving primarily exploratory purposes. In the

TABLE 11.1   Normal Developmental Levels of the Artistic Process and Product

Level	Characteristic Process	Characteristic Product
Manipulating	exploratory behavior for sensory or kinesthetic stimulation	splashed or smeared paint or splashed, smeared, or crumpled clay or paper
Forming	conscious manipulation of materials as the child gains control over the medium	scribbles, rolled or flattened clay or Play-Doh
Naming	creations begin to stand for something and can be named by the child with encouragement of adults in the environment	child-identified scribbles or molded clay or Play-Doh, products that represent something
Representing	creations take on features, but are still difficult to identify; there are some shape and definite representative value	objects or drawings that have representative value, though it may be difficult to identify (e.g., encephalopod)
Containing	systematic filling in of outlines; staying within boundaries, literally and symbolically	pictures with definite outlines for objects; clay models with definite boundaries that are representative of reality
Experimenting	exploration between and within media; unfolding of creativity; increase in attention to detail	interesting and elaborate pictures or models that capture viewer's attention
Consolidating	preferences for and within media; realistic, though two-dimensional representations; less egocentrism through inclusion of people and objects	picture of others that are elaborate in their inclusion of objects; realistic sculptures
Naturalizing	elaboration and sophistication; attempts at mastery of proportions, shading, and dimensions	three-dimensional and proportioned pictures and sculptures
Personalizing	self-expression and search for personal style; reflection of values, ideas; conflicts are more obvious now	three-dimensional, elaborate, idiosyncratic paintings or sculptures imbued with meaning

next phase, forming, the child begins to gain control over art materials and consciously manipulates the materials to produce different results. This phase may be marked by scribbling, smearing, rolling, or flattening. In phase three, naming, the child's creations begin to stand for something, and with the encouragement of adults in the environment, the child begins to name the creations. Although the child will name the creations, their actual shape might not be at all related to the product or relationship that it is identified to represent. Not until the fourth phase, representing, do creations begin to take on certain features. Actual shapes or representations are still difficult to identify for many adults but do have some shape. These objects or drawings represent and emphasize what the child knows about or focuses in on the object (e.g., the encephalopod drawn by the child that clearly represents a human being despite the omission of critical aspects of the symbolized object).

The fifth phase, containing, reveals a definite shift in the child's approach. Art and its products are no longer a mere mass but become systematic, such as the filling in of an outline. At this point, children learn to stay within boundaries (not just artistically, but also symbolically), demonstrating their ability to control impulses and the self. In phase six, experimenting, the child begins to explore ways through which to express and symbolize the same things in different ways or through various media. The child becomes truly creative, and her or his work becomes more detailed as fine motor control improves, more interesting to the viewer, and more elaborate. In the seventh phase, consolidating, the child begins to express preferences for and within certain art media and creations begin to look very realistic and less egocentric. Drawings are still two-dimensional but include other people and a wider variety of objects, such as trees and houses. Phase eight, naturalizing, evidences the child's increasing elaboration and sophistication. The child in this phase may become frustrated as she or he attempts to master proportions, shading, and dimensionality. It is this stage that can lead the child to a self-critical attitude or even to giving up. This frustration stems from the need to move on to new learning and to give up previous, more comfortable schemata that the child had worked with up to this point. Many children, and hence adults, do not move beyond this stage of artistic development.

The final phase, personalizing, involves the definition of a personal style for artistic self-expression. The child's or adult's art in this phase becomes a reflection of her or his values and ideas. Any conflicts in the individual find their more obvious expression now (though this makes their expression no more meaningful as far as the art's usefulness to the therapeutic process is concerned). Understanding the developmental phase reached by the child in her or his artistic development not only provides an understanding of the child's overall developmental level, but is also relevant to the application of art to child therapy, as it influences the therapist's choices of art media and interpretations of the process and product.

Application to Child Therapy

Art therapy techniques have been successfully applied in numerous settings and for numerous presenting problems, including anticipatory anxiety before surgery (e.g., Geraghty, 1985), nightmares (e.g., Hunyady, 1984), sexual abuse (Murphy, 2001), exposure to violence (Malchiodi, 1997), and dealing with death and dying (Bertoia and Allan, 1988). The use of art techniques in generic child psychotherapy is different from pure art therapy. True art therapy is also focused on artistic eloquence (Kramer, 1998) and gives advice and help with the artistic process and product. If art is used as a technique, however, the psychotherapist uses it somewhat differently. Specifically, the focus in using art techniques in this setting is on the process of creating art and the symbolism of the end product. The correctness or eloquence of the techniques used is not evaluated therapeutically. Hence, art as a technique applied to the work with children does not require artistic capability on the part of the child, but merely her or his willingness to employ art materials for various therapeutic purposes (Landgarten, 1987).

Purpose of the Process and Product of Art in Child Therapy

The purposes of art therapy can be grouped into three major categories: assessment, catharsis, and growth. All three permeate the therapy from beginning to end and will be discussed here.

Assessment.   One use of art for assessment reasons is focused on soliciting diagnostic and dynamic information that aids the therapist in the conceptualization and problem definition of the child's case. As such, art can be used to facilitate for the clinician the recognition of conflicts, needs, and affects, through both the process of creation and the resulting product. Another use of art is focused on determining treatment progress and readiness for termination. In this process, the clinician assesses changes in the artistic process and product to evaluate growth and maturity in the child. Disappearance of certain themes that formerly were interpreted to express conflict or mood disturbances, changes in the process that suggest more patience, increased self-confidence, or greater goal-directness are only a few examples of how art can reflect treatment progress. The primary use of art by the child for assessment purposes then is one of communication and self-disclosure. The primary use of art by the therapist for assessment purposes becomes one of listening to the child's communication and self-disclosure to glean new information.

Numerous formal procedures have been developed to aid therapists with the diagnostic, or initial, component of assessment of using children's art. These include, but are not limited to, the Draw-A-Person Test (Machover, 1952), the House-Tree-Person Drawing (Buck, 1948), the Kinetic House-Tree-Person Drawing (Burns, 1987), and the Kinetic Family Drawing (Burns and Kaufman, 1970). All of these techniques differ significantly in the directions that are provided to the child and the content that is elicited, but their joint purpose is to derive additional information from a child during the assessment phase of treatment. However, the existence of these formal procedures should not imply that unstructured, or free, drawing or scribbling cannot be equally useful in meeting the assessment purpose of art (Kramer, 1998; Naumberg, 1966). This is particularly true, as interpretation (discussed in detail below) proceeds along the same lines regardless of how the art product was solicited.

Catharsis.   If art is used for the purpose of catharsis, the expression and mastery of feelings are emphasized. In the cathartic experience, the child is allowed once again to process past occurrences, through either the process or product of the artistic self-expression. For example, a child might pound clay vigorously in recalling an anger-provoking event or may sculpt an erupting volcano. The expression of current events and their associated affects is also in the spirit of allowing catharsis or a free expression of feelings and needs. The primary use of art by the child for the purpose of catharsis then is self-expression to release and master affect and conflict. The primary use of art by the clinician for the purpose of catharsis then is the encouragement and facilitation of the child's uninhibited experience of affects and needs and their expression.

Growth.   Finally, art as a growth-promoting medium may be used to facilitate the establishment of rapport or therapeutic relationships. It is designed to help the child learn alternative means of problem solving and to foster creativity in this regard. The exploration of alternatives and the creative multifold use of various media are particularly helpful in this regard. Various solutions can be attempted by the child and can stress for the child that flexibility and alternative approaches are critical to the growth process. Use of art materials will enhance skill learning and encourage talent development. This, in turn, serves to increase self-confidence, as does product completion in and of itself. In fact, the unfolding of the creative process in art therapy has been compared to the unfolding, or development, of a cohesive and vigorous self in clients, especially children (Sanville, 1987). Finally, through enhancing self-esteem and through encouraging problem solving and the searching for alternatives, art promotes the working through of conflicts. The child is free to express conflicts through the process and product of her or his creative activity and thus is more likely to experience resolution and mastery. The most important use of art for both child and therapist for the purpose of growth is the interpretation of meaning and subsequent resolution. Art in this context becomes a catalyst for change.

To be able to help the therapeutic purposes of art (summarized in Table 11.2) to emerge in the child-therapist interaction, the therapist must have an understanding of the meaning of the creative process and artistic product. In other words, the ability to interpret what the child's behaviors and creations reveal is critical to the useful application and implementation of art as a therapy technique. The novice clinician therefore must spend some time to familiarize herself or himself with the symbolism of art products, the meaning of the process through which a product is created, and the form of the end result. However, it must be noted that, as is true for play and metaphors, identical process, form, or product can have different meanings for different children and in different situations. Therefore, although a few general guidelines for interpretation will be provided here, it is crucial to approach a child's artistic process with an open mind, to fully recognize its meaning and importance on an individual and idiosyncratic basis. Further, while it is critical for the clinician to understand the child's drawing, and to be able to interpret it, this same rule does not hold for the child. In other words, the child may benefit from the process of creating art without any insight or verbalizations whatsoever, merely through internalization of what was spontaneously expressed and felt, as well as symbolically mastered (Oster and Gould, 1987).

Interpretation of the Process and Product of Art in Child Therapy

The interpretation of the artistic process and product has been described as a process of listening with one's eyes (Landgarten, 1987). This appears to be a particularly apt definition of the essence of using art as a therapeutic strategy for two reasons. First, the use of art can

TABLE 11.2   The Therapeutic Purposes of Art

Overall Purpose	Specific Subpurposes
Assessment	diagnostic information that aids conceptualization
	diagnostic information that aids treatment planning
	dynamic and interpersonal information
	recognition of conflicts and problems
	recognition of affects and needs
	determination of change that implies progress
	determination of readiness for termination
Catharsis	free expression of affects and needs
	uninhibited processing of past occurrences
	expression and recreation of current events
	expression and recreation of anticipated events
	release and mastery of affects and conflicts
Growth	establishment of therapeutic rapport
	exploration of alternative problem solving
	fostering of creative problem solving
	fostering of creativity in approach and solutions to problem situations
	skill learning and talent development
	increased self-esteem and self-confidence
	increased goal-directedness

help a client to recognize feelings or needs that she or he did not formerly acknowledge or have awareness of. As such, the creation becomes a visual reminder for the child of problems, feelings, needs, and, most important, solutions and alternatives. This visual reminder might not need to be interpreted out loud by the therapist to have a profound impact on the child's therapeutic growth. Second, the use of art can focus a therapist's attention on issues that the child has not verbalized for one reason or another. Thus, art may literally open the clinician's eyes to new information or processes within the child and her or his family and environment. This helps the clinician to revise treatment plans and plan interventions that can lead to the resolution of such unspoken issues. To facilitate the process of listening with one's eyes, the therapist must be familiar with the three dimensions through which art can be interpreted: process, form, and content (also presented in Table 11.3). In all three areas, interpretations must be viewed merely as hypotheses to be corroborated by other materials and data. It would be a mistake to believe that art process and products are definitive in their meaning. Hence, the following discussion of interpretation must be understood in the context of hypothesizing to avoid arbitrary inferences and illusory correlations between a child's art production and reality.

Process Interpretation.   Process interpretation refers to the therapist's exploration of the child's approach to the use of art materials. The clinician observes how the child responds to the presentation of materials, which materials are selected, how they are han-

TABLE 11.3   Approaches to the Interpretation of the Artistic Process and Product

Type	Definition	Behaviors/Products Observed	Example
Process	exploration of the child's approach to the creative process and art media	■ response to presentation of media ■ selection of specific media ■ handling and use of media ■ attitude toward the media	Refusal to use clay as the artistic medium because of fear of getting dirty may imply obsessive or compulsive traits.
Form	meaning extracted from the overall shape and impression of the creation	■ degree of organization such as in placement, completeness, and symmetry ■ clarity, movement, color ■ size and relative size	A family drawing in which the child is significantly smaller than all others may reveal a child's perceived importance.
Manifest Content	evaluation of the actual content	■ actual objects ■ actual figures ■ actual portrayed relationships	A drawing of a happy scene may reflect happy feelings.
Associative Content	evaluation of titles, stories, etc., as related to the artistic product	■ spontaneous verbalizations about the creation ■ response to questions about the creation ■ spontaneous/requested titles	A sculpture that represents a first school day titled "My worst day," hints at school problems.
Latent Content	analysis of the symbolism of the artistic product	■ all objects (e.g., kites, keys) ■ all human and humanlike figures ■ all other items (e.g., a sun, rain, wind)	Inclusion of knives or other aggressive objects may indicate hostility, aggression, or history of abuse.

dled, and how they are put together. Further, the child's attitude toward the creative process is observed carefully to note hesitation, enjoyment, spontaneity, inhibition, and similar reactions. This aspect of interpretation is particularly useful in forming hypotheses about preferred defenses or coping mechanisms. For instance, a child who frequently uses a defense of undoing might create several figures or objects from clay or Play-Doh, only to hide or destroy them immediately after they are completed. Similarly, in using drawing or painting, the child might paint a dark color over the picture to hide it after it has been created, that is, revealed. Restrictive defenses, such as isolation or restriction of affect, intellectualization, or constriction, can result in a very controlled approach in which the child shows no spontaneity or creativity. She or he might adhere to a very rigid outline and might fail to use color in preparing drawings or paintings. Relatedly, such a child might refuse clay altogether because of fear of soiling hands. Process interpretations have to be made in a developmental context. Certain behaviors are appropriate at some ages or developmental levels, but not at others. Thus, a 10-year-old who merely uses art media to smear or pound might evidence regression; however, a 3-year-old engaging in the same behavior might demonstrate age-appropriate use.

Observation of the process can also provide hypotheses about the content of conflicts or situations that present problems. For this purpose, the therapist needs to watch where and when the child appears anxious, disorganized, fearful, saddened, or otherwise emotionally affected. For instance, a child who is drawing a family picture might suddenly become very angry. Upon closer inspection, it might be noted that this anger emerges consistently in the context of drawing a particular sibling. Significant problems in the relationship with this brother or sister can be inferred and should be subsequently investigated. Similarly, a child who was constructing a pleasant scene with clay figurines, yet suddenly became disorganized and began to destroy figures, could be communicating to the therapist that this scene that had been produced is anxiety-producing and currently overwhelming for the child.

All of these interpretations must be made against a backdrop of carefully completed assessment that helps the clinician to gain confidence in her or his interpretations. Further, they cannot be taken at face value, but rather must be confirmed by later and additional observations and data collection. Nevertheless, some commonalities (however tentative) in the meaning of behaviors have been documented. For instance, excessive concern about staying within outlines appears to signal concern with impulse control, whereas excessive erasing appears to be related to anxiety or uncertainty or may reflect a timid request for help (Ogden, 1979). Process information is extremely valuable but can still be enhanced by supplementing the information gleaned from it with hypotheses based on the form and content of the art activity and product (Malchiodi, 1998).

Form Interpretation.   Form interpretation refers to the meaning extracted from the overall shape and impression of a creation. The degree of organization, as expressed in a picture's or sculpture's placement, completeness, and symmetry is one critical form component. Additionally, clarity, movement, and color need to be assessed and evaluated (Ogden, 1979). Size of objects and their relative size as compared to one another add another important dimension to be interpreted. For instance, placement of a drawing on the right side of a page tends to be related to intellectualization, introversion, and an orientation toward the future, whereas placement low on a page may signal insecurity and depression (Ogden, 1979). Edge placement may imply insecurity, as well as searching for externally imposed boundaries in the absence of internalized structure (Burns, 1982). Excessively light pressure has been associated with timidity, fearfulness, and low energy levels (Ogden, 1979), whereas excessively heavy pressure is sometimes related to aggression or organicity (Burns, 1982). Excessively large figures tend to be created by expansive, grandiose clients (Ogden, 1979); excessively small figures by insecure individuals with depression or withdrawal tendencies (Burns, 1982). However, the relative size of objects in the same drawing may also reflect their respective emotional saliency for the child (Burns, 1987). Excessive shading is not uncommonly associated with anxiety and occasionally with agitated depression (Burns, 1987).

Although the above interpretations have been documented in the research literature, they must be neither overutilized nor treated in any other way than as hypotheses. In other words, as was true for process interpretation, specific meanings of a form may emerge highly idiosyncratically for an individual child. As such, the therapist is always encouraged to attempt to ascertain that her or his hypotheses are not arbitrarily imposed upon the child and her or his actions and products. Instead, hypotheses must be confirmed through other sources of information and data collection. Nevertheless, the books and manuals that do exist to guide the clinician in assessing the form of children's drawings can be extremely helpful to the novice clinician who is still struggling with a wealth of new information (e.g., Burns, 1982, 1987; Ogden, 1979).

Finally, form interpretations, as is true with process interpretations, have to be placed into the developmental context of the child. A very young child's activity cannot be scrutinized for its absence of boundaries, as this use of art is not expected until school age. Similarly, a child who has just discovered boundaries and outlines should not be viewed as constricted or defensive if she or he uses this approach repeatedly. It is more likely that she or he is merely experimenting with a new and developmentally fitting use of the art medium. Another very useful component of assessing developmental levels in form interpretation is the comparison of a single child's performance across various projects, or even within the same project. For instance, if a child is capable of drawing at an experimenting level of art development, in other words, can draw meaningful and elaborate figures in general, it is expected that all drawings express this level of elaboration and maturation. However, if this same child reverts to creating encephalopods each time she or he draws or sculpts a figure representative of the self, this may be interpreted as a regression and a meaningful statement about self-esteem and self-image.

Content Interpretation.   Content interpretation refers to the use of the picture's or sculpture's actual end product (Levick, 1998). There are three levels of content interpretations that must be paid attention to, to glean the maximum amount of information from the final product. First, the manifest (or surface) topic or subject matter must be explored. This level of analysis is comparable to the interpretation of manifest contents in dream analyses with adult clients. As such, the actual content of a picture may be evaluated. For instance, one girl chose to draw two houses within close vicinity of one another. She then connected them with a sky bridge and labeled one house with her own name and the other with her therapist's name. This manifest content alone suggested to the therapist that this girl still felt a very strong need to remain connected with her clinician. Because this drawing was prepared in a session before the child was scheduled to go on a four-week vacation, this interpretation guided the therapist's interventions for the remainder of the session, as it appeared important to reassure the child that even through the separation, a tie (though merely mental; the sky bridge) indeed could be maintained between the two.

Second, the associative content derived from titles to or stories about drawings or clay models can be explored to form additional hypotheses, especially if the manifest content is not easily understood. The child whose case example was presented in Chapter Ten drew a picture that preceded and paralleled the early-phase story she had told. Namely, she drew an unelaborated toadstool devoid of other objects. Although the manifest content was already somewhat informative (e.g., little elaboration; questionable home atmosphere as evidenced by the choice of a poisonous mushroom as a house), the child's commentary while she was drawing the picture was even more illuminating. She indicated that the rabbits living in the house could not run very fast and were not allowed to go far from the home. She related that they would like to go far away but were quickly reined in by their mother whenever they attempted to do so. This commentary suggested that in addition to providing a poisoned environment, the children's mother prevented them from seeking nurturance elsewhere, forbidding them to interact with other adults who might potentially meet these children's needs for nurturance.

Associative content interpretation becomes even more important when a drawing or sculpture has no recognizable content. Many children begin their experience with art media by producing shapes that reflect a very low developmental level and hence are not obvious to the therapist. Encouraging commentary about such creations will provide access to their meaning, which mere inspection of content would have denied. For instance, one child drew a picture that had two halves that were solidly separated from one another by a heavy black line. On one side, the child used cheerful colors, wavy lines, and free brush strokes. The other side of the painting was dominated by dark colors and rigid contours. Certainly, content was somewhat useful here in helping the therapist recognize the possibility of a splitting defense or black-or-white thinking. However, it was the associative content that provided the meaningful information. When asked for a title for the painting, the boy indicated that this was a self-portrait based on how he thought his father viewed him. Upon a request for elaboration, he revealed that sometimes his father heaped praise upon the child, especially after the boy had mastered a new skill or was honored for some type of achievement by his teacher. However, at other times, the father deprecated the child, destroying his confidence and self-esteem. Clearly, although splitting did occur in this child's life, it was his father who engaged in the defense, not the child.

Finally, the implied (or latent) content of the product needs to be analyzed. This analysis considers the symbolisms of the drawing or model. There are some symbols that are common within a given culture, community, or even just one child (Rubin, 2001). The therapist has the responsibility to learn about these symbols and recognize their latent meanings in each individual child's presentations. As is true for process and form, a few common meanings that can be used with caution have been identified by the research literature. For instance, houses are often symbols of mothers or family life in general, whereas the sun is more likely to represent a father figure. Witches can represent hostility or self-deprecation. Cars or other vehicles can symbolize independence and striving for autonomy (Ogden, 1979). Animals in a treehole often signal dependency needs [a return to the womb perhaps (Burns, 1987)]. Knots or other wounds or scars in a tree trunk might symbolize the experience of a trauma (Ogden, 1979), the specific placement of the scar indicating the time period in the child's life when the trauma occurred. For instance, a scar halfway up a tree implies that the timing of the trauma was halfway through the child's life (if the child is 10 years old, the trauma would be hypothesized to have occurred at age 5). A kite might signal escapism from a restrictive home environment, whereas a ladder might reflect tension (Burns, 1987). Water is often considered a symbol of the unconscious (Ogden, 1979).

Many other symbolisms have been suggested, and the reader is referred to other sources for more information (e.g., Burns, 1982, 1987; Ogden, 1979).

In assessing latent content, it has also been suggested to approach the child's drawings from two perspectives. First, the clinician views the picture's content while ignoring all human figures; then the figures are viewed, ignoring all other content (Burns, 1982). This helps the clinician to refocus attention on specific details of the picture and may lead to questions that can be asked to illuminate additional meanings. For instance, while looking at a drawing, a therapist might recognize, by ignoring all other content, that all the human figures are shown merely from the waist up. Other objects were used to block the view of humans from the waist down. Once this fact is noticed, the therapist can ask herself or himself or the child directly why only pieces of the human figures were visible. Similarly, in another drawing, the therapist might recognize, upon ignoring all human figures, that the picture is devoid of any other objects. This recognition needs to be explored to assess why the child cannot recognize other things in her or his surroundings.

Finally, in assessing latent content, the clinician must take care to note themes that repeat themselves across a number of creations. Such themes might provide additional hypotheses that would have remained elusive had the pattern only occurred once or was not recognized as repetitive. For instance, a child who always includes clouds in her or his picture may certainly have a different approach to or experience with life than a child who always includes sunshine. A child who has an even balance of rain and sunshine across numerous drawings, on the other hand, might have the most realistic perception of her or his world of the three children. A child who never sculpts human figures, but rather focuses on mechanical objects, might have a highly disrupted interpersonal environment. Once themes have been identified, the therapist must also note if sudden or gradual changes occur. Thus, if the child who has never sculpted a human figure suddenly places one inside a sculpture she or he creates, this is a noteworthy occasion and may well signal therapeutic progress or growth.

In summary, facilitation and careful observation of the artistic or creative process and the end result provide the clinician with a wealth of information and provide the child with rich opportunities for self-expression, catharsis, and problem solving (Malchiodi, 1998). Awareness of the basic purposes of art, namely, assessment, catharsis, and growth, provides a framework for interpretation. The extraction of meaning from the child's behaviors and creations must be carefully conducted along at least three dimensions, specifically, process, form, and content analysis. Knowledge of and experience with these dimensions of using art techniques in the general therapy of children and being able to place them in a general developmental framework prepare the clinician to implement this strategy in her or his work with child clients (Levick, 1998).

Variations on the Technique

Although the stated purposes and overall procedures for interpretation of the artistic process and product are relatively stable across therapists and theoretical approaches, there are a number of variations on the actual use of art media. The two largest schools of thought are represented by Naumberg (1966) and Kramer (1998). These two theorists, although both being credited with developing critical art therapy techniques and both utilizing its interpretation and expressive force, differ significantly in their emphases. Naumberg (1966), developing art therapy out of a fairly traditional psychoanalytical model, stresses interpretation and the creation of insight in the client. She believes that expressive media are yet another road to the unconscious. Kramer (1998), by contrast, believes that art therapy can be extremely useful even without the use of dynamic or latent content interpretations. She explains that expressive media provide useful and therapeutic intervention strategies in and of themselves. They are viewed as means to rechannel, or sublimate, unacceptable impulses into acceptable activities, thus helping the child to solve problems and find solutions without conscious awareness or insight. Regardless of which approach a novice therapist prefers upon reading both descriptions, it is most likely that art techniques are ultimately used in both manners. It does appear that with some children, the expressive use of art leads to meaningful internalizations and therapeutic changes, without need for overt interpretation. However, other children prefer to talk about their creations and to assess their meaning in collaboration with the therapist. Thus, flexibility and willingness to tailor the approach to individual children's needs appear proper.

Kramer and Naumberg agree on the use of free art and therefore tend not to prescribe specific projects, but merely provide a framework for self-expression. Other art therapists, however, use either formal assessment procedures [see discussion by Oster and Gould (1987)] or specific instructions tailored to lead to very specific goals (Landgarten, 1987). For instance, Landgarten (1987) might ask specific tasks of different family members in the context of family art therapy. Parents might be asked to draw themselves at their children's current ages to assess the possibility of projections of feelings or roles. To help a child process an anticipated stressful event, such as a hospitalization, Landgarten might ask her or him to draw the hospital, then to draw a picture that expresses the child's feelings about the hospital, and finally to create a drawing that shows both the good and bad components of having to go to the hospital. These pictures can subsequently be used to problem-solve or process feelings around the anticipated event. Another example presented by Landgarten (1987), using sculpting, is that of a child who suffered from terrible nightmares. She asked the boy to sculpt a monster and then to use it to show her what happened in his dreams. Then she instructed him to sculpt the figure of a sheriff. She used the latter figure to frighten the monster, thus removing the fearful connotation of this sculpture. Ultimately, she encouraged the child to play both roles himself.

This brief presentation of various approaches to the use of art should demonstrate that there are an almost infinite number of approaches to working with expressive media in therapy with children. Whereas pure art therapists will exclusively use art techniques to facilitate assessment, growth, and catharsis, the generalist can choose art techniques in addition to play, stories, behavioral interventions, and so forth. Regardless of whether art is used exclusively or in combination with other strategies, it provides a powerful approach to working with children that tends to decrease resistance and increase cooperation and trust. Implementation of art can vary as widely as variations on the technique exist. For the remainder of this chapter, the focus will be on the implementation of art techniques within a general therapy framework, using it flexibly to incorporate all of the variations discussed above.

Practical Implementation

The practical implementation of art techniques is quite spontaneous and generally adapted flexibly to the child's needs and preferences. Thus, art techniques may sometimes be used interpretatively and sometimes expressively only. Freestyle may be most appropriate with some children and in some situations, whereas others may call for the prescription of certain drawings or sculptures. This flexible and nonexclusive approach is chosen as it tends to be particularly useful with resistant or involuntary clients such as children presented by parents, families mandated for treatment by the courts, and referred adolescents (Riley, 1987).

The function of the therapist who chooses to use art as a technique is somewhat different from the function of a pure art therapist. "[A]rt therapists [serve] children in many capacities: as their auxiliary muscles, as sources of factual information, as instructors in artistic technique, as providers of sanctuary for beneficial regression and for experimenting with new attitudes toward the self and the environment, as recipients of confidences and fantasies, and last but not least, as objects of identification" (Kramer, 1998, p. 158). However, the generalist psychotherapist does not generally address the first three functions of the art therapist. Further, according to Rubin (2001), art therapists are artists themselves. This makes them able not only to focus on treatment, but also on teaching the technique or the medium. This is very much unlike the therapist who merely uses art as a technique. This generalist neither needs to be an artist, nor has to worry about teaching anything (in fact, should not teach).

Despite these differences between art therapists and general psychotherapists, they agree that the clinician is responsible for creating an environment that provides a frame or a structure within which the child can self-express freely and uninhibitedly through the use of art media. The environment must provide enough structure to provide boundaries, limits, and safety rules without being controlling or imposing unnecessary restrictions. The generalist tends to remain passive while observing the child's artistic process and creation, so as not to imply correct versus incorrect use of materials or evaluation of the product. She or he encourages spontaneity and fantasy to promote self-disclosure, catharsis, and growth. Critical to the ability to provide such an environment is the correct choice of art materials that should be available in the room or offered to the child directly.

The selection of materials has to meet several criteria to assure the therapist that fitting use will result. First, the materials or media present have to be age appropriate. Not all materials are equally useful with children of differing ages. Finger paints tend to be excellent for use with very young children, who do not have sufficient motor coordination to work with a paint brush or felt-tip marker. The latter, however, might be a more relevant choice for an older child. Similarly, clay has been identified as an excellent material to be used with developmentally delayed or very young children because the sensory stimulation it provides is ideally suited to help a child to develop a sense of boundaries and object relations (Henley, 1991). Enough materials should be available that the child truly has a choice, but not so many that decisions are too difficult to make. Media should not be anxiety-provoking for the child. A child who is clearly fearful of clay or Play-Doh should not be unduly encouraged to use this medium. Perhaps as the child grows through the use of other techniques, she or he might change her or his approach to this medium; however, the choice should be left up to the child. The coordination and fine motor control of the child must be considered. For instance, a very uncoordinated child might not be able to handle scissors to assemble a collage. This also exemplifies the fact that special needs of children must be considered in presenting materials to them. Finally, another influencing factor may be the child's prior experience with certain art media. Some media might be more comfortable for the child because they have been encountered before. Others might be less comfortable because a prior encounter was negative and unsuccessful. Thus, while the therapist needs to keep a wide range of materials for drawing, painting, modeling, and constructing available, the encouragement of their use needs to be considered carefully and in the context of each individual child's needs, talents, interests, and other variables.

Once a medium has been chosen by the child, either alone or in collaboration with the therapist, the clinician begins to observe the creative process to see what emerges. If the child has difficulty getting started but clearly is attracted to the art medium by having expressed a preference for it over free play activity, storytelling, or other strategies, the clinician can use a number of techniques to help the child overcome this initial hesitation. For instance, the child might be instructed to swing her or his arm freely to relax it and then to make a free scribble on the paper. This scribble can subsequently be explored for potential objects or meanings that emerge spontaneously or can be elaborated upon until such an object or meaning emerges (Rubin, 2001). In another approach, the child might be asked to make a few blots or scribbles and then to connect them to see whether an image emerges (Rubin, 2001). In fact, if an extremely reticent child cannot begin with simple blots or squiggles, the therapist can produce these, and the child can connect them. This procedure is similar to the approach in the Draw-a-Story Game (Gabel, 1984), in which the child is encouraged to tell a story about an image that was created on the basis of a simple line or scribble provided by the clinician.

Once the child is immersed in the creative process, the therapist helps it along through cautiously commenting on the child's emerging creation to indicate interest, caring, and understanding. These comments are not to be evaluative in nature. Some interpreting may be appropriate as specific themes emerge. However, the communication of understanding and empathy is more critical than the creation of insight. Failed attempts at creation must be responded to empathically, not condescendingly or chastisingly. The child should never be forced to finish an incomplete creation. Instead, the therapist should ask why the project was abandoned. Examples of good impulse control may be reinforced and the child may be helped to rechannel negative affects or impulses into creative art activity.

Once the process is complete and has resulted in a product, attention is shifted to this outcome. The therapist can encourage the child to talk about what was created (Rubin, 2001). Questions may be asked about the drawings to elicit associations and to corroborate hypotheses the clinician has forged so far. Sometimes, a story to accompany the creation can shed new light on the creation and can provide useful insight. Additional information may be solicited by asking specific questions about different aspects of the product or about its title and accompanying story line.

Occasionally, a clinician might want to assign a particular art project to help the child explore a particular affect or meaning or to help the child prepare for an anticipated event (Landgarten 1987). Once the process is set in motion, the procedure and interpretation that are followed are identical to what has been described already. One event that can be greatly facilitated by a directed, perhaps even a joint, project is termination of treatment. Client and therapist might attempt a project together that symbolizes or represents the process of therapy or the changes the child has made. This project can result in a tangible product that can not only be used to verbally review the treatment process together, but can also serve as a farewell gift for the child. Similar interventions may be used at critical points in a therapy, such as before a vacation or other breaks in treatment. The creation of a joint project that the child can take home can result in excellent transitional objects. Art projects can also be used to underscore other therapeutic activities, such as stories or play. In the chapter dealing with storytelling, such an example was provided. It introduced a girl who chose to paint the food items in the story about a hungry bear. She then asked to take home the drawing as a tangible reminder of what she had learned in her session.

An example of the implementation of art techniques in a general therapy setting is provided below. This particular example was chosen because the child whose case is presented often spontaneously chose to introduce certain art activities corollary to play and storytelling. He was a very talented boy who received a lot of satisfaction from the creative process in and of itself. He also began to generalize the use of art to his life outside of treatment, where it became an excellent coping strategy for him.

Example

This 7-year-old boy was presented for treatment by his mother and her partner, who had recently moved in with mother and son. The boy's biological parents had divorced when he was 3 years old because of incompatibility. They had remained on friendly terms, and the child's visits with his father had been very regular. He had maintained a caring relationship with both parents and had always appeared to enjoy his visits. However, approximately two years previously, he had begun to refuse visits, often cried before having to leave, and was sullen when he returned. His mother investigated changes in the father's life, but he denied any. She also explored with her son why he had a change of heart, yet he refused to talk. Although this mother was greatly concerned about her child, she was not directly aware of the possibility of treatment and therefore had never initiated it. It was not until her partner moved into the home and witnessed the child's behavior that she (the partner) recommended therapy for the child to the mother.

The boy was very reticent during the intake interview, and his mother was unable to give much information surrounding the presenting concern. The partner described the child's affect as increasingly depressed. Both women agreed that he had failed to show age-appropriate weight gains, had become shy and withdrawn, had little self-esteem and self-confidence, and did not appear able to get much enjoyment from play. His visits with his father were still a cause of great distress for the child but continued on a regular basis. An additional interview with the father revealed that he also had noted the changes in his child but indicated that he had no idea why they were occurring. The father described the son as withdrawn and shy and tended to blame this affect on the lesbian relationship of the boy's mother. However, the onset of the child's depression clearly had preceded this relationship. Further, the boy and his mother's partner appeared to have a very positive relationship. The boy's father denied any intimate relationships since the time of the divorce.

The clinician suspected a form of abuse, but direct questioning about physical and sexual abuse of all parents led to denials. Questions to the child were met with silence and refusal to speak. His response indicated to the therapist that the possibility of abuse could not be ruled out at this time. On the basis of the intake information, the child received preliminary diagnoses of dysthymia and major depression. A recommendation for individual treatment was made, as no specific family systemic problems emerged during assessment. Further, the therapist believed that crucial information was still missing and was perhaps known only by the child. Therefore, individual time with the child was deemed most appropriate. The goal was to continue assessment while treating his depression through play, storytelling, and art. All parental figures had also agreed to participate in a parent education course. However, this intervention did not appear critical as all three showed good parenting skills and were on positive terms with one another.

During assessment, the boy was asked for three routine drawings: the Draw-A-Person Test (DAP), Kinetic House-Tree-Person Drawing (K-HTP), and the Kinetic Family Drawing (KFD). All three drawings comprised stick figures only, remained very unelaborated, and evidenced stereotypic activity, revealing the child's high level of defense at intake. Over the course of his first month of treatment, primary focus was placed on building trust and fostering self-disclosure. Play and stories were the most important media. In his fifth session, the boy spontaneously asked to draw. Using colored pencils and crayons, he drew the head of a woman, once in front view, once in side view. Under the drawing (Figure 11.1), he wrote "Wanted: Liza—You can trust her." His therapist's name was Lisa, and his drawing was his first clear indication that he had begun to trust her. He gave the drawing to his therapist, asking her to keep it safe. She posted it on the wall for the remainder of the current session and during subsequent sessions.

In his next session, he immediately recognized the picture on the wall and proudly pointed out that he had created it. He then asked to draw again. This time, he indicated he would redo one of the drawings the therapist had asked for in his first session. He proceeded to draw a K-HTP. This drawing appeared to confirm the therapist's suspicions of sexual abuse of the child. As can be seen in Figure 11.2, all objects were highly phallic in nature. Given her suspicions, the clinician asked the child to tell a story about his drawing. Despite his prior willingness to tell stories, he refused. However, he did indicate that he would tell her more later. As he spoke, he proceeded toward the sandtray. He staged a furious war between several monsters and small nontraditional male figures. (The room was equipped with two sets of very alternative male and female figurines; the children were shown in very nongender-traditional activities, with girls lifting weights and boys holding dolls; many figures were pudgy, some had special disabilities.) In his war, the monsters subdued and frightened the boy figures over and over. The child built strong forts of sand for the boys, yet nothing kept out the monsters. He built caves to hide them, but they were found. The clinician initiated the following conversation at this time:

LISA: No matter what they do, the monsters keep coming!

KEN: There is no getting away for these kids.

LISA: They are very afraid, but they don't know what to do because everything they try fails.

FIGURE 11.1   Ken's First Spontaneous Use of Graphic Art: Mugshot Drawing of the Therapist *+

*Pencil tracing of the original drawing which was done in colored pencils and crayons.

+All illustrations are pencil or felt pen tracings of the original artwork. All were slightly altered as need to protect the identity of the child and therapist. For instance, "Liza" was not the same name on the drawing in Figure 11.1. However, there was a slight error in the spelling of the therapist's actual name, and this error was reflected in the incorrect spelling of the fictitious name. Similar modifications that neither altered the essence of the drawings nor changed their interpretive value were made on all illustrations.

KEN: And nobody, nobody knows what's happening…

LISA: They aren't telling anyone?

KEN: They can't!!!

LISA: They can't tell anyone because the monsters told them not to?!

(Lisa is trying to confirm her hypothesis of abuse by suggesting a common theme to the child, i.e., the abuser's warning not to tell.)

KEN (SURPRISED):   Yeah!! They told them not to or terrible things would happen. He would slash them open and cook them up for dinner.

(Lisa notes that the monsters had now been identified as one male person by the use of the pronoun "he.")

FIGURE 11.2 Ken's Second Attempt at the K-HTP: The Emergence of a Phallic Theme*+

*Felt pen tracing of the original drawing which was done in pencil.

+All illustrations are pencil or felt pen tracings of the original artwork. All were slightly altered as need to protect the identity of the child and therapist. Modifications that neither altered the essence of the drawings nor changed their interpretive value were made on all illustrations.

LISA: He threatened to hurt them if they told. In fact, he was gonna slash and cook them. So now they are scared to tell, and they can't get help.

KEN: They would like to tell… They are really afraid.

LISA: They have to tell to feel better. If they don't tell, nobody can help, and things won't get better. There are some secrets that cannot be kept. Monsters have a habit of threatening kids, when really they can't hurt them if the kids tell!

(Again Lisa decides to pursue the abuse topic directly.)

KEN: They don't know what to do!

LISA (VERY GENTLY):   They are so afraid! But they have to tell. It really will help!

KEN (THROWING THE DOLLS IN THE SAND AND TURNING AWAY FROM THE SANDTRAY):   Let's play with the blocks!

(Lisa decides not to allow the child to redirect.)

LISA: You don't want to talk about what is hurting you. But we need to talk about it. It's too big for you to deal with alone. Let me help you!

KEN (CRYING):   The monsters make the little boy do things....

Lisa continued to prod Ken along and uncovered his story of sexual abuse by the father. The abuse did not occur during every visit. However, Ken feared it every time he went. His father had asked him to promise not to tell because then Ken would no longer be allowed to come for his visits. As Ken was deeply connected to his father, he did not want to be barred from visitation. The therapist had to prepare Ken for what would happen next, namely, that his father would be reported and that Ken's fear and his father's threat indeed would become reality. Ken's visitation with his father would stop, at least for a while.

The revelation of abuse and the subsequent events were very difficult for Ken, yet also resulted in an immediate improvement in many of his depressive symptoms. However, he now began the difficult task of working through his feelings of anger and betrayal against his father, whom he truly had trusted and loved. His drawings became more expressive at this time, and he used them to express his feelings vividly. He used many dark colors, such as dark blue, purple, and brown. He often drew furiously, not creating any specific shape, but rather throwing paint on the paper in a very cathartic manner. This regression from using representing and forming art to using paint to smear and release revealed his strong feelings very clearly. He also enjoyed using clay to pound and smash. He often created a number of small clay balls, then smashed them with his hand until they were flat. This became a very repetitive activity for him, and he released a lot of emotion. His mother reported that he engaged in the same art activities at home as well. She was extremely concerned about this, as before his drawing had been very contained and he had seldom used Play-Doh because he thought it was too messy. The mother was helped to understand what the child was doing, to ascertain that she would continue to allow him to engage in the activity both at home and in therapy. Slowly, Ken progressed beyond the angry use of art media and started to contain his affect. As he and the clinician dealt with his anger and betrayal (also at the therapist for having made the report!), and as these feelings were resolved, his art became more contained.

He once again used clay to create meaningful shapes, but now the content of his shapes reflected his anger and betrayal. He often created biting dogs and spewing volcanoes. However, the specific shapes of the materials revealed that although his anger was still present, it was contained and had become more manageable for the child. His drawings also began to take shape again, both in therapy and at home. An example of the types of drawings he created at this stage in treatment is reproduced in Figure 11.3. In this drawing, he revealed his great ambivalence toward his father, who appears to be symbolically represented by the sun in the upper right-hand corner of the picture. Although this sun certainly provides light and brightness for the entire scene, it also has big teeth that look quite

FIGURE 11.3   A Sample of Ken's Middle-Phase Drawings: Integrating Nurturance and Aggression*+

*Pencil tracing of the original drawing which was done with colored felt-tip markers.

+All illustrations are pencil or felt pen tracings of the original artwork. All were slightly altered as needed to protect the identity of the child and therapist. Modifications that neither altered the essence of the drawings nor changed their interpretive value were made on all illustrations.

menacing. The child in the sandbox is thought to be representative of Ken, who had first revealed the abuse by his father while playing in the sand in the therapy room. Also, the use of a sandbox indicates some containment and protection. This impression is further supported by the rainbow, which provides a barrier between the child and the sun. He can enjoy the sunshine without having to fear the teeth (supervised visitations with his father had been implemented by this time).

Art remained an important medium in this child's therapy and work at home. As he was removed from the abusive situation and as his father received treatment, Ken improved and became more involved with his peers at school. Therapy was terminated after 33 sessions, and a cooperative drawing was used to symbolize the ending and to produce a transitional object that Ken could take with him. The drawing was a recapitulation of many drawings and sculptures that had been of importance in his treatment progress. For instance, the therapist began her contribution by drawing the mugshot that Ken had created of her in the first month of treatment. Ken drew the sun with teeth and the child in the sandbox. Other figures and images were included and led to a reprocessing of what had occurred in the 10 months of therapy. Because Ken was allowed to take this picture home, it is not available for reproduction here.

Summary and Concluding Thoughts

This chapter introduced the novice therapist to the use of graphic and sculpting art as a therapeutic technique. It emphasized the use of these media in a general therapeutic setting, rather than discussing art therapy per se. The practical implementation of art techniques in that context allows for a variety of uses of the medium. It is always marked by sensitivity, flexibility, respect, and an open mind on the clinician's part. It can be uniquely adapted to the individual needs of the child and can be used as a supplementary strategy to play or storytelling. It can help to overcome resistances and can serve to introduce and discuss difficult topics or affects. Art is an excellent intervention with children and fits well with the other strategies introduced in this text. The clinician interested in the use of art is encouraged to read as many of the sources cited in this chapter as possible, as the interpretation of art must be conducted skillfully and responsibly. Art therapy is a specialized discipline with its own unique training programs and requirements. It was not the purpose of this chapter to create art therapists, but merely to introduce the generalist to yet one more technique that is uniquely adaptable to the work with children, individually and in groups.

12 Behavioral Techniques

Behavioral techniques are widely used and endorsed by child therapists. Although there are numerous strategies that are included within this category of intervention, all are based on the premise that most behavior and many fears are learned and can be changed through the application of various learning principles. Behavioral techniques have been submitted to intense scrutiny in the research literature and have survived this process with excellence. There is much empirical evidence that points toward the success of behavioral techniques in creating change in children's behavior (Gresham and Watson, 1997; Slavenburg, Kendall, and Van Bilsen, 1995). This change is not ephemeral or situational, but rather has been shown to generalize to alternative situations and settings and to be maintained across the years. To provide the therapist in training with a thorough introduction to behavioral interventions in child therapy, the conceptual background of these techniques will need to be explored first. Then the techniques will be briefly discussed with regard to their relevance to child therapy and finally will be defined in some detail. An implementation example follows. Excellent additional information can be found in Martin and Pear (1998) and Kazdin (2000).

Conceptual Background

Behavioral interventions are based on the conceptual premise that most behavior and some affects or fears are learned. Unconscious motivations, social interest motivations, drives, and other concepts that are deemed important in other approaches to human behavior are considered nonessential and uneconomic, though not necessarily nonexistent. The traditional, or radical, behavioral perspective emphasizes the interaction or relationship between behavior and environmental responses or events that elicit, maintain, or extinguish certain behaviors. All human beings are viewed as directly affected by their environment in a manner that shapes and determines their reactions and future behavior. Children are perceived as neutral at birth, in other words, as neither endowed with internal drives or needs nor predisposed for certain reactions through temperament or personality. Children learn behaviors strictly through their interaction with the environment and slowly increase the number of skills and behaviors they exhibit as a function of environmental feedback. They are responders not shapers, products of conditioning not agents of environmental change. As behaviors are learned, they are stored in memory and then used as needed and appropriate on the basis of environmental cues. More recently, some behaviorists have also begun to concentrate on cognitions. Such cognitive-behavioral perspectives focus not only on interactions between the child and the environment, but also on the child's thoughts or cognitions during a given learning process or response. However, even in exploring cognition, these behavior theorists still view behavior as the primary focal point and end result of learning. There are three primary approaches to learning that are considered the basis of the major behavioral therapy interventions in use today. These are respondent conditioning, based on Ivan Pavlov's (1927) and Joseph Wolpe's (1958) work; operant conditioning, based on B. F. Skinner's (e.g., 1971; 1976) investigations; and social learning theory based on Albert Bandura's (1999) achievements. The former two are identified with the more traditional behavioral schools of thought, whereas the latter is identified with the cognitive-behavioral tradition.

Respondent Conditioning Model

In respondent (or classical) conditioning, learning takes place through the inadvertent or planned pairing of two events. One of these events is considered neutral because it does not in and of itself result in an immediate response in the child. The other is considered a stimulus, as it results in a specific behavior or feeling on the child's part. As this reaction of the child is indeed predictable, given the nature of this stimulus and the child's learning history, the event is labeled the unconditioned stimulus. As the other event does not elicit a response, it is labeled a neutral stimulus. The response of the child to the unconditioned stimulus is labeled an unconditioned response, as it occurs naturally or predictably. If the unconditioned stimulus and the neutral stimulus are paired in such a way that the unconditioned response occurs immediately after both events, the child may begin to associate the neutral stimulus with the response that was originally tied only to the unconditioned stimulus. If this learning is sufficiently strong, future occurrence of the neutral stimulus may result in the same response that was before exhibited only after the unconditioned stimulus. While the response is identical in this situation, it is now labeled a conditioned response as it did not naturally or predictably occur after the neutral stimulus.

Respondent conditioning is often implicated in the development of fears in children. Following is an example of how such a fear developed according to this classical conditioning model of learning. Usually, children are not afraid of being outside playing in a sandbox (a neutral stimulus). However, many young children are naturally afraid of loud noises (an unconditioned stimulus). On a pretty spring day, a baby-sitter decided to allow a 1-year-old boy to go outside to play in the sandbox. She had just taken him outside when a neighbor began drilling in his back yard. The child began to scream and was almost inconsolably distressed. The baby-sitter quickly picked him up and brought him back inside the house. When the neighbor had finished his task, she decided to take the child back outside. She no sooner had approached the sandbox with the child than he began to cry. It had taken only one pairing of a neutral stimulus (the sandbox) with an unconditioned stimulus (the noise from the drill) for this child to develop a conditioned response (the crying in response to being placed in the sandbox). Whereas formerly only the noise had produced the screaming (then an unconditioned response), it was now also produced by the sandbox (now the conditioned stimulus). This example, depicted in Figure 12.1, demonstrates the powerful impact the pairing of unconditioned and neutral stimuli can have on children's behaviors and emotional responses.

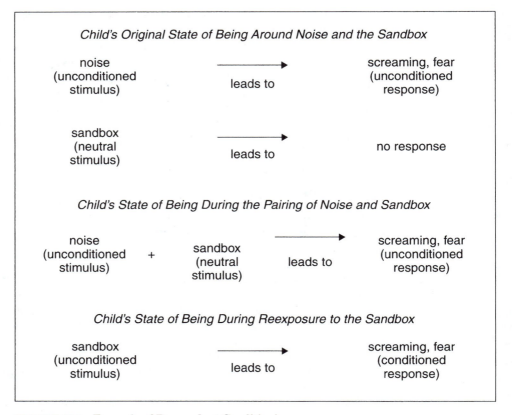

FIGURE 12.1   Example of Respondent Conditioning

Operant Conditioning Model

In operant (or instrumental) conditioning, learning takes place through the experience of environmental consequences or contingencies that either develop, maintain, eliminate, decrease, or increase a certain behavior. The original behavior that resulted in such an environmental consequence is labeled an *operant*, as it operates upon the environment to create a particular situation that, in turn, is likely to affect the rate of the original behavior. The environmental consequence is a stimulus that affects whether the child's behavior recurs or disappears. As such, a stimulus-response chain is set in motion, wherein the environmental intervention becomes a stimulus for the child's behavior, the response. Some environmental consequences are perceived by the child as positive and can be used to maintain, increase, or develop behaviors. Others are perceived as aversive or undesirable and thus result in a decrease or the elimination of a given behavior or operant. Positive and negative reinforcement fall into the former category; extinction and punishment into the latter.

Positive Reinforcement.   Positive reinforcement is the presentation of a desirable consequence after the demonstration of a behavior to increase its frequency. For instance, a parent might give praise to a child for having cleaned up the play area in the living room without having been asked to do so. This praise is likely to result in repetition of the child's cleaning behavior, as the behavior was followed by a pleasant interaction with the parent. A most critical component of the success of positive reinforcement is the appropriateness of the environmental consequence for the child's behavior. The environmental stimulus in a positive reinforcement situation is called a reinforcer. A reinforcer has to be perceived as such by the child. In other words, a reinforcer will not work unless the child perceives it as a positive or desirable event. For instance, one father decided to use positive reinforcement to increase the number of times his son brushed his teeth. Every time the son brushed his teeth, his father gave him a Matchbox car. The son's tooth-brushing behavior failed to increase; in fact, it decreased. The father could not understand this. He had collected Matchbox cars when he was a child and believed them to be quite reinforcing. When he discussed his distress about the failure of his positive reinforcement plan with his therapist, the clinician was quick to recognize that this father had made a very common mistake. Assuming that an object or event that is reinforcing to him would also be reinforcing to his son, he used it in his program. He never checked with his child whether he liked Matchbox cars as well. When he asked his son whether he liked these toys, he found out that he did not. He then explored what might be reinforcing for his son and realized that his son liked Pokémon cards. When he began to use these stickers as reinforcers, his son's tooth-brushing behavior began to increase in frequency.

In addition to being appropriate to the child's desires, the reinforcer must also be delivered immediately and consistently (with predictable frequency, not necessarily each time). If a reinforcer is not delivered right after the desired behavior has occurred, the child might not be able to connect the behavior to the reinforcer. For instance, one mother was attempting to increase her 4-year-old daughter's dressing behavior. She decided to tell the child a bedtime story on each day when she dressed herself alone in the morning. The daughter loved bedtime stories, yet her dressing behavior did not increase. In troubleshooting the mother's approach, it became clear that the two events, the dressing and the delivery of the reinforcer, were spaced too far apart in time for the daughter to be able to make a stable and reinforcing connection between them.

A reinforcer is also only effective if it is not so abundant that the child does not need any more of it, and if it is not otherwise easily accessible to the child. Even if a child loves cookies, the use of another cookie to reinforce the child for having played by herself or himself quietly for a while will not be effective if the child feels too full to eat another thing. Similarly, using stickers loses its reinforcing quality if the child has accumulated so many stickers that she or he no longer knows what to do with them. This abundance of a reinforcer, referred to as satiation, is a particular problem with young children and in reinforcement programs that rely on food items as reinforcers. Finally, a reinforcer is not a reinforcer if the child can gain easy access to it through other means. For instance, one mother decided to use orange juice as a reinforcer for her son's homework behavior. Every time he completed his math problems without having to be prompted, he was allowed to have a glass of orange juice. This child loved orange juice, yet he failed to increase the frequency with which he made his math homework spontaneously. It was discovered that he was allowed to drink orange juice freely most times of the day. Thus, he failed to see why he should have to work for it through doing his homework if he could have the juice almost any time anyhow.

In determining a reinforcer for a particular child, nontangibles should not be forgotten. Although small toys, stickers, foods, and other tangible goods are easily recognized as reinforcers, human interactions and social interactions can also be powerful reinforcers. In fact, for many children, time alone with a parent, a hug, public praise, a smile, and so forth may be more powerfully reinforcing and meaningful than yet another sticker or piece of gum. Children often are very willing to work hard for attention. In fact, it is not unlikely that the source of their misbehavior is their way of searching for attention from a parent who will not otherwise interact with the child freely.

To summarize, positive reinforcement is used primarily to increase existing behaviors. It can also be used to slowly shape new behaviors in children. For the positive reinforcement process to work, the reinforcer must be appropriate, delivered immediately and predictably, not freely available to the child anyhow, and not so abundant as to lose its reinforcing quality. It can be a tangible object or a nontangible, such as praise, attention, or time spent together.

Negative Reinforcement.   Negative reinforcement, much like positive reinforcement, is used to increase the occurrence of behavior. However, in this instance, the child is not presented with a reinforcer, but rather is allowed reprieve from an undesirable or aversive event that is already present in the environment. For instance, a parent might tell the child that she or he will turn off her or his (the parent's) favorite record, which the child despises, each time the child completes cleaning her or his room. In this case, an aversive event, the record, was removed to increase the child's cleaning behavior. Negative reinforcement is also used by car manufacturers who are attempting to increase the use of seat belts. A buzzer sounds when the ignition is turned on and does not end unless the seat belt buckle is inserted into its slot. As soon as the seat belt is buckled, the aversive event is removed, increasing the likelihood that every person will buckle up. Removal of the stimulus must follow the same guidelines that were presented for the use of reinforcers. In other words, it must be appropriate, not freely possible, not abundantly available, and not too far removed in time.

Punishment.   Punishment is a procedure designed to decrease the occurrence of behavior, that is, to deal with behaviors that the parent wants to eliminate from the child's repertoire. Punishment is achieved through the presentation of an undesirable or aversive consequence when the inappropriate behavior occurs. A common punisher used by parents is spanking. Society uses incarceration as a punisher for people who commit crimes in the attempt to decrease criminal behavior. Obviously, the punisher must be appropriate, presented in a timely and consistent manner, and more undesirable than the behavior itself is reinforcing. For instance, incarceration is not an effective punisher if it is not consistently applied each time a person engages in a criminal act. The problem becomes obvious: If the behavior is not noticed, the punisher cannot be applied effectively. There are several additional problems associated with the use of punishment (Kazdin, 2000). For instance, although it may be effective in the short term, its long-term effectiveness is questionable. Further, the presentation of an aversive or undesirable event may instill conflicts and aversive behaviors or fears in the child. Punishment may actually increase inappropriate behavior by serving as a model for aggressive behavior or as a reinforcer. (For some children, punishing attention may be more desirable than no attention at all.) The use of punishment is therefore not generally endorsed unless other behavioral strategies have failed and the behavior is dangerous to the child. For instance, some punishment procedures may be used with severely developmentally disabled children who engage in self-destructive behaviors such as eye-gouging or head-banging. In these cases, the injuries that result from the behavior are greater than the risks presented by punishment.

Extinction.   Extinction, like punishment, is used to decrease undesirable or inappropriate behaviors. However, unlike punishment, it involves not the presentation of a noxious stimulus, but rather the removal of a positive stimulus present in the environment as the child engages in the undesirable behavior. As such, it is the inverse of punishment, in the same way as negative reinforcement is the inverse of positive reinforcement. For instance, a child who likes to hear music might be told that each time she or he throws a temper tantrum, the music will be turned off. The music (the positive stimulus in the environment), present when the child began tantruming, is thus removed to decrease the frequency of the tantruming behavior. A commonly used strategy is the removal of attention. If a child acts out in the presence of a parent, clearly to gain additional attention, the parent might remove herself or himself from the situation, making it impossible for the child to get further attention unless the child stops the acting out behavior. Again, as with all stimuli discussed so far, the removed stimulus must be appropriate (i.e., must have had reinforcing quality); must be removed immediately, predictably, and consistently; and must not be freely available or overly abundant (e.g., reattainable without the decrease in the inappropriate behavior).

The four operant strategies, summarized in Table 12.1, can be combined in various ways to develop more sophisticated therapeutic programs for children. This application of operant conditioning will be addressed in detail later in this chapter.

Social Learning Theory

In social (or observational) learning theory, learning is hypothesized to take place through the observation and subsequent imitation of direct or symbolic models. In other words, a child might learn a new behavior by watching another individual, the model, engage in it. The imitation of the behavior does not have to be immediate, though the behavior must

TABLE 12.1   The Four Strategies of Operant Conditioning

Strategy	Type of Stimulus	Action	Example
Positive Reinforcement	positive stimulus (reinforcer)	presentation	presenting a cookie each time the child does homework alone
Negative Reinforcement	negative stimulus (undesirable event)	removal	turning off a loud noise in the classroom as soon as all children are sitting still
Punishment	negative stimulus (punisher)	presentation	yelling at the child each time she or he forgets to take out the garbage
Extinction	positive stimulus (desirable event)	removal	no longer reading a bedtime story if the child tries to delay bedtime

have been encoded in the child's memory to be imitated or used at a later time. In place of a live model, a symbolic model may be used, such as a videotape, movie, or picture. Children learn many new behaviors through modeling, including behaviors needed for adaptive living such as tying shoes, washing hands, and so forth. For the modeling process to be successful, the child has to be capable of engaging in four distinct processes, which are displayed and exemplified in Table 12.2. First, she or he must have a sufficient attention span, as well as attentional ability or motivation, to observe the model's behavior in detail. Second, the child must have sufficient memory ability to be able to retain a cognitive representation of the behavior, even in the absence of the model. Third, the child must have the motor skills necessary to reproduce the behavior at least somewhat successfully, though correction of the attempted imitation is often not only appropriate, but also desirable. Fourth, and finally, the child must have sufficient external or internal motivation to engage in the modeled behavior. Although the imitation of a model may be immediate, as in the deliberate teaching of a new skill, it also may be delayed in time, as in the inadvertent imitation of a behavior witnessed previously. In other words, the acquisition and performance of the behavior do not have to be concurrent.

Application to Child Therapy

Just as learning principles serve to explain the acquisition of adaptive behaviors and new skills, so can they serve to explain maladaptive, or problem, behavior (Gelfand and Hartmann, 1992). Hence, behavioral theorists argue that no behavior, regardless of how maladaptive it appears, is abnormal or pathological. Instead, the behavior is viewed with regard to its learning history in the child's life, as well as the reinforcement history that is

TABLE 12.2   The Four Processes of Modeling or Observational Learning

Process	Example
Attention	A boy watches very intently as an older boy builds a paper airplane—The older boy is someone this child admires and has often attempted to emulate.
Retention	The boy is too shy to interact with the older boy and has no paper; hence, as he watches carefully, he tries to remember each step of the airplane-folding process the older child models.
Reproduction	After returning home later in the day, the boy asks for a piece of paper and begins to construct an airplane; his mother is watching with interest, wondering where her son had picked up this new skill; she also helps him along with several helpful hints when the boy appears uncertain about the next step in the process.
Motivation	The boy is obviously pleased with himself upon completion of the product (internal positive feedback), enjoys flying the airplane around the house (external positive feedback), and receives praise for his accomplishment from his mother (more positive external feedback).

maintaining it. Problem behaviors are viewed as no more than bad habits or faulty learning patterns (Johnson, Rasbury, and Siegel, 1997). This approach to misbehavior or presenting problems of children ascertains that children are not viewed as pathological or abnormal. Regardless of theoretical background, it behooves every novice therapist to borrow this attitude toward children's behavior from behavioral theorists. Children are shaped by their environment in many ways, regardless of the degree to which a theorist believes in other motivational factors, such as innate personality styles, genetic factors, or biological processes. All behavior must be explored in its context in the child's family and larger cultural and social environment.

Some child clinicians may perceive behavioral approaches to explaining human behavior as incompatible with principles of free will, as all children, in fact all people, are viewed merely as "victims" of, or responders to, their environment. However, it is an indisputable reality that environmental factors do influence behavior in many ways. Behaviorists, particularly Skinner (1971), suggest that becoming aware of how the environment shapes and determines behavior and using that knowledge will provide true freedom. Thus, the reader is encouraged not to perceive behavioral interventions as restrictive or authoritarian. Although this point may be and is disputed ardently, it is important to recognize the usefulness of behavioral principles in many realms of life and learning. Behavioral techniques can be very instrumental in helping a clinician effect change in a child client, without interfering with other beliefs about human behavior that the therapist may hold. Although behavioral theory might not be accepted by all clinicians as accounting for the entire spectrum of human behavior, affects, motivations, and so forth, the principles that have been based upon behavioral theories can be successfully incorporated into a child therapy intervention nevertheless.

Behavioral techniques used in that manner become strategies that increase the clinician's general repertoire of clinical skills without having to become the theoretical framework used by the clinician to conceptualize the entire case. Although this approach certainly is prone to some attack by purely behavioral therapists, it will be endorsed in this chapter. As such, behavioral interventions are discussed as extremely useful means of intervening in child therapy without suggesting that they must provide the entire framework for the work with the child. As were play therapy, storytelling, or art therapy techniques, behavioral strategies are viewed as strategies that are taught to novice child clinicians and employed by seasoned child therapists in the attempt to ascertain that a sufficiently wide spectrum of skills is available to the mental health service provider to maximize the likelihood of success in a child's treatment.

Another advantage of the use of behavioral strategies is the fact that it lends itself well to the assessment of change in the child and of treatment effectiveness (Bergan and Kratochwill, 1990). To use behavioral principles, a therapist must do two things: First, she or he has to obtain an accurate and extensive history and baseline count of the behavior that is presented as a problem; second, she or he must set clear behavioral goals for the treatment process. This strict focus on observable and quantifiable behavior guides the therapist carefully in the treatment process and the measurement of movement toward treatment goals. In other words, behaviorally oriented treatment involves the clear definition, measurement, and quantification of original behavior, as well as behavior throughout therapy until termination. For instance, if a child is presented to treatment because of her or his tendency to speak out of turn in the classroom, the therapist's first step would be to define the behavior and assess the frequency of its occurrence. This could be done either through a classroom observation or through the collaboration with the child's teacher. Then the behavioral treatment process would be implemented. The child's behavior would continue to be observed and counted during predetermined intervals to assess whether an improvement in the number of disruptions in the classroom is occurring. When the frequency of behaviors has dropped to the desired level, treatment focused specifically on this behavior could be terminated. Many therapists could benefit from the incorporation of clearly defined behavioral changes that can be measured and observed in the treatment of children. Such measurement can be an objective indication of the child's improvement and can also be used to praise the child and motivate the parents to continue treatment or to view treatment as a helpful process.

Finally, the use of behavioral strategies usually necessitates the involvement of parents and/or teachers, as well as the cooperation and consultation of the child. Thus, it may enhance the willingness of parents and teachers to cooperate with treatment as they feel more ownership of the therapy process. As the implementation also usually occurs not in the therapy room exclusively (in fact, it may never occur in that setting at all), but instead in the environment in which the behavior tends to be problematic, generalization is excellent and virtually built into the treatment program. Behavioral strategies can also continue to be used by cooperative and willing parents, teachers, and children once treatment has been completed, as they can be diversely adapted to numerous problem behaviors (Barkley, 1997; 1998). Thus, in addition to helping a child solve a presenting problem, the therapist provides the child and her or his significant others with tools that can be adapted for future use.

Given their diverse applicability, behavioral strategies have a permanent place in child treatment (Mash and Barkley, 1998). Although they may not always be the only strategies utilized with a particular child, some of them are almost ubiquitously used with all children. Two excellent examples of such ubiquitousness are positive reinforcement and extinction, both of which tend to be utilized by all therapists many times in the course of treatment (whether inadvertently or purposely so). Behavioral strategies consequently can be carefully woven into the network of interventions planned by the therapist for a particular child regardless of the underlying conceptual framework of the clinician. They can be taught to parents and teachers in an educative manner for later use with the child, for use with other children, and for prevention purposes. Although the clinical application will be detailed here, the preventive application will be discussed in some detail in the chapter on parent education.

Variations on the Technique

Behavioral methods have excellent support in the literature with regard to their usefulness for a great variety of behavior problems among children [for brief reviews of this literature refer to Powers (2001); Spiegler and Guevrement (1997); also see journals such as the *Journal of Applied Behavior Analysis, Behavior-Therapist, Behavior Therapy, Behavior Research and Therapy,* and *Cognitive and Behavioral Practice*]. Although the methods of intervention can be as simple as the basic reinforcement or extinction procedures outlined earlier, more complex programs have been developed specifically for therapeutic purposes. Sophisticated behavioral programs that have been found highly useful and successful in the treatment of childhood problems can be based in either respondent, operant, or social learning theory and will be discussed in detail individually.

Strategies Based Upon Respondent Conditioning

Strategies in this category are based on the pairing of two stimuli that are not naturally paired in the child's environment. [For more information about these strategies also refer to Morris and Kratochwill (1998)]. Through the pairing of stimuli, new responses can be produced in the child that will take the place of the maladaptive behavior. Although only two approaches are covered here, namely, systematic desensitization and aversive conditioning, others exist, such as the bell-and-pad procedure used for functional enuresis (Walker, 1998) and flooding used for phobias (Spiegler and Guevremont, 1997).

Systematic Desensitization.   This procedure is most commonly used with children who have severe anxieties or phobias. It relies not only on respondent conditioning, but also on the concept of reciprocal inhibition. Reciprocal inhibition indicates that a person cannot have two conflicting physiological responses at the same time, for example, cannot feel relaxed and fearful simultaneously. In using systematic desensitization, the clinician approaches the child's anxiety by pairing relaxation exercises or visual imagery that result in a relaxed response with the feared stimulus until the feared stimulus produces the same relaxed response as the relaxation. In other words, the relaxation training or visualization process is the unconditioned stimulus that results in the unconditioned physiological response of relaxation and peaceful feelings. This unconditioned stimulus is paired with a feared stimulus (the neutral stimulus in the classical conditioning paradigm) until the neutral stimulus becomes a conditioned stimulus that results in the conditioned response of relaxation. Reciprocal inhibition aids this process of conditioning, in that it ascertains that the fearful response to the slow and careful presentation of the feared (neutral) stimulus cannot override the feeling of relaxation and peacefulness produced by the relaxation or imagery.

The first step in a systematic desensitization program always involves teaching the child a method of relaxation that results in relaxed and peaceful feelings for the child. Two commonly used methods are progressive muscle tension–relaxation procedures and visual imagery. Relaxation programs developed for children are available and highly recommended for use (Cautela and Groden, 1982; Koeppen, 1974). Once the child has mastered a system of relaxation and is able to relax quickly and reliably, she or he is ready to move on to the next step of the program: the pairing of the unconditioned and neutral stimuli. This pairing is conducted in a carefully paced manner so that the child is not exposed to the most feared stimulus immediately. Instead, a hierarchy of feared stimuli is constructed in collaboration with the child so that the therapist may expose her or him to anxiety-producing events step by step. The creation of a hierarchy of fearful events must be done carefully. The first item in the hierarchy should not result in a fearful emotional response whatsoever. Each successive item should have a slightly larger negative emotional impact on the child than the previous one. The number of items in a hierarchy is dependent upon the strength of the child's phobic reaction to the feared stimulus. The more fearful the child, the longer the hierarchy may need to be, as more items may be needed for the child to manage her or his fear successfully. Some hierarchies are developed in such a manner as to make each progressive item merely quantitatively larger than the previous one; others incorporate items that vary qualitatively while all being related to the feared stimulus.

For instance, the hierarchy for a child who fears cats might consist of a first item that requires a 1-second imagined exposure to the animal, slowly increasing the length of the exposure time to several minutes. Another child with the same fear might develop an entirely different hierarchy. In this case, the first item on the hierarchy may be for the child to imagine the house of a friend who owns a cat, without any reference to the animal. Subsequent items might include visualizations of the friend's room with the cat hiding out of sight under the bed. A later item might involve the friend holding the cat, and the final item might require the child to visualize herself or himself holding the cat.

Both quantitative and qualitative hierarchies are likely to work; they merely approach the problem from two slightly different perspectives. In using a qualitative approach, the therapist must take care to order items correctly to prevent premature exposure of the child to an item that might prove overwhelming and break through the relaxed response, resulting in the experience of anxiety. Further, in presenting the progressive items to the child, the therapist must be very much attuned to the child's emotional response. If the child is perceived to become less relaxed, the clinician should back up, reverting to an earlier item in the hierarchy until the child is once again fully relaxed. At times, if a response appears to approach anxiety, the relaxation procedure might need to be repeated. Systematic desensitization programs can also be carried out in the actual presence of the fear-producing stimulus. This procedure is called in vivo desensitization. It can be used in conjunction with the traditional process as well, generally being used after several sessions of imagined exposure to the feared stimulus, or may be a corollary to the systematic desensitization process in the therapy room. In vivo procedures can be very powerful and have to be implemented carefully. They often require the involvement and cooperation of other people in the child's life, such as teachers, trainers, parents, or friends.

For instance, a child with a public speaking phobia that is sufficiently severe to result in the child's attempts to skip school on the day of speech class may be involved in a traditional imagined desensitization program at the same time as participating in an in vivo procedure. The first step in the in vivo procedure might require the child to go to school on the day of speech class. The second step might require the child to remain in speech class for 10 minutes. This time frame could then be expanded until the child can attend speech class without experiencing anxiety. Then the child might be asked to speak publicly for 20 seconds, slowly increasing this time frame to several minutes. All along, the same child may also be working through a similar hierarchy in the therapy room with the therapist.

An applied example of systematic desensitization is presented in the case example at the end of this chapter. The hierarchies developed for the systematic and in vivo desensitization programs for this child are presented on pages 338 and 339.

Aversive Conditioning.   Another commonly used respondent conditioning strategy is aversive conditioning. In this procedure, an aversive stimulus is paired with a maladaptive, yet somehow intrinsically rewarding, behavior to decrease the amount of pleasure felt in response to the problem behavior. For instance, a child who frequently doodles during class lectures might be told to snap a rubber band she or he was asked to wear on her or his wrist. In this example, the doodling behavior is the neutral stimulus that is paired with a conditioned stimulus (the snap of the rubber band) that leads to an unpleasant unconditioned response (pain on the wrist). After a sufficiently large number of pairings, the doodling behavior itself will result in a conditioned aversive response (anticipation of pain) and therefore will decrease in frequency. It must be noted that although this procedure has some merits in reducing undesirable behavior, it is negatively focused. It should not be used in isolation, but rather should be part of a larger behavioral (or other therapeutic) program that contains positive interactions with the child as well.

Strategies Based Upon Operant Conditioning

Strategies in this category are based on the principle that behaviors are either maintained or reduced on the basis of environmental feedback and stimuli. [For thorough discussions of these strategies, also refer to Kazdin (2000) and Martin and Pear (1998).] Operant conditioning programs are designed to decrease or increase behaviors and teach or eliminate behaviors or emotional responses by manipulating a child's environment in such a way as to reinforce appropriate behaviors, while ignoring inappropriate ones (punishment is rarely used). Numerous operant conditioning strategies exist, and new ones can be invented by each therapist or parent. Indeed, the number of applications and variations of operant strategies is limited only by the creativity of the clinician. Presented here are four of the most commonly used operant procedures: shaping, reinforcement of incompatible behaviors, time out, and token economies.

Shaping. The shaping process is used to develop new behaviors. Shaping of new behaviors is accomplished by analyzing a behavior according to its component parts and beginning to reinforce the child for the rudiments of the behavior. The child is not expected to be able to engage in the entire or final desired behavior in one large step, but rather is allowed and reinforced for developing the behavior in small steps that increasingly approximate the target behavior. The steps leading toward the desired behavior are called successive approximations, and care has to be taken that the child is appropriately reinforced for each successive approximation. Once the child has mastered a step, the reinforcement for that successive approximation is phased out, and reinforcers are not provided until the next step in the behavior chain is demonstrated. This necessitates watching the child carefully and focusing on positive behavior.

The positive focus of shaping makes the procedure an excellent corollary to more aversive behavioral procedures, such as the respondent conditioning procedure of aversive conditioning. Using the same disruptive child as in the example for aversive conditioning, a shaping program could be added to the rubber band intervention for disruptive behavior, to begin to reinforce the child step by step for more appropriate classroom behavior. A target behavior would be defined along with successive approximation toward that target. A reinforcer would be delivered by the teacher each time an approximation of the behavior occurred. Immediate and appropriate delivery and careful selection of an effective reinforcer would be critical. For example, the target behavior might be defined as active participation in class discussion as evidenced by making at least three relevant comments during each lesson. Successive approximations might involve behaviors such as taking relevant notes that indicate that the child is following the lecture, raising a hand to indicate that the child would like to make a comment, actually making one relevant comment in the course of a lecture, making two relevant comments, and finally making three relevant comments.

Shaping can also be applied to one single behavior that is broken into component parts. For instance, if the child needs to learn how to make her or his own bed alone, reinforceable successive approximations may be defined in small steps. The first step might consist of the child pulling up the covers as she or he gets out of bed. The second step may involve fluffing the pillow in addition to pulling up the covers. The third step might add the requirement that the child tuck in the sheet. Steps would be added in such an additive manner until the target behavior is reached.

Reinforcement of Incompatible Behaviors.   Another procedure that is positively focused and easily added to aversive procedures is the positive reinforcement of incompatible behaviors. This procedure, using positive reinforcement, has two emphases: the elimination or decrease of an undesired behavior and the development or increase of a desired behavior. The desired behavior that will be positively reinforced either in its entirety (as in simple positive reinforcement) or in its component steps (as in shaping) is selected on the basis of its incompatibility with the undesirable behavior. In other words, the desired and undesired behaviors cannot humanly be engaged in at the same time. Thus, increasing the desired behavior results in an automatic decrease of the undesirable behavior. The latter would be treated with extinction if it were to occur.

For example, if a girl were presented for treatment because of her chronic tendency to be late for dinner, an incompatible behavior might be to make her responsible for setting the dinner table and sounding the bell to let the rest of the family know that dinner is being served. In this case, the girl would be positively reinforced for setting the table and sounding the bell. (Probably a shaping procedure would be best utilized, as it may be unreasonable for the child to know the entire process of setting a table from the beginning; modeling may be used as well, as may a token economy.) Increasing her table-setting and bell-sounding behavior will automatically reduce her lateness to dinner, as she is the person responsible for letting everyone else know when dinner is served. If the child were to forget to set the table and sound the bell and were late to dinner, her behavior would be ignored (extinction, as no attention would be given to the undesired behavior), and she would also automatically lose out on receiving the reinforcer that she could have earned through the appropriate behavior.

Time Out and Response Cost Procedures.   Time out and response cost procedures both are designed to decrease or eliminate undesirable behaviors by removing reinforcing events from the child's environment. As is true for all strategies that are negatively focused, alternative positive programs (e.g., reinforcement of an incompatible behavior) should be attempted first. Only if positively focused programs remain unsuccessful are negatively focused programs implemented. Even then, they are best complemented by another behavioral program that uses reinforcers to increase the frequency of an existing positive behavior or to develop additional desirable behaviors.

The time out procedure is essentially a carefully designed extinction procedure that is frequently used by parents and teachers but only occasionally used in the therapy room. It can be used for an individual behavior or for several behaviors that have the same reinforcement history. The first step in designing a time out procedure is to investigate which events in the child's environment are maintaining or reinforcing the child's inappropriate behavior. In implementing the time out procedure, the clinician, parent, or teacher removes the child from these events for a certain period of time. The time out area must be designed such that it has no reinforcing qualities in and of itself. For instance, the use of a child's room or a bathroom (both common choices among parents) is inappropriate because of the child's access to many rewarding objects and activities. Relatedly, the use of a broom closet or attic (also choices that have been reported by parents) is extremely inappropriate because of the fearful stimuli associated with such settings for many children. Time out is neither to be reinforcing nor to be punishing. The best time out area is one that is specifically designated for that purpose, for instance, a corner in a dining room that is well lighted but very unstimulating, as the child has access to neither sounds of radio, television, or family members nor to toys or books. Sitting on a staircase also works if the stairs are inside the home or apartment, not outside or separate from the family's living quarters. In a classroom, a certain corner or table might be specified as the time out area, and all children know not to interact with the child placed in this area. In a therapy room, time out can be implemented by using a corner or chair. Time out in the therapy room should be used only in extreme circumstances, since it is easily interpreted as nonacceptance of the child and places the therapist in an adversary role with the child.

The timing of time out can be approached in numerous ways. Some therapists endorse the specification of a certain number of minutes, after which the child is allowed to return from the time out area. Other clinicians suggest that the child be given the responsibility to determine when she or he is ready to return from time out and behave appropriately. Yet others believe that the child should be given permission to return from time out by the person who implemented it when the child appears ready. Any of these approaches can be either suitable or abused. Leaving a child in time out for 30 minutes is punitive and not in the spirit of time out. Leaving the child in time out for 2 minutes and allowing her or him to return from time out while she or he is still tantruming defeats the purpose of the procedure. Not letting the child know how long she or he will need to be in time out leaves the child wondering and fearful. Allowing a child to set her or his own time out period is possible only if the child is responsible and understands the purpose of the procedure. Therefore, thought has to be given to the determination of the length of the procedure. Perhaps the best guideline is to use time out with a regulated interval initially, moving to a child-determined interval only when the child recognizes the utility of the procedure.

Response cost programs take extinction programs one step further by not only removing the child from reinforcers in the environment, but also adding a penalty or fine. For instance, children might lose privileges or tokens earned in a token economy program (see below). Response cost thus can essentially be defined as a punishment procedure yet avoids some of the common disadvantages of punishment proper, such as the modeling or reinforcement of inappropriate behavior and the conditioning of fearful responses or withdrawal in the child.

Token Economies.   Token economies can be as simple as positive reinforcement or as complex as a complicated contingency program that combines a number of operant strategies such as shaping, reinforcement of incompatible behaviors, and response cost. The underlying similarity of all is the use of tokens as reinforcers. Tokens are items such as stars, points, or chips that are not inherently reinforcing but have gained reinforcing quality by being paired with a powerful reinforcer (i.e., they are essentially conditioned reinforcers, in the same way as neutral stimuli become conditioned stimuli that produce a conditioned response in the classical conditioning model!). Using tangible (or unconditioned) reinforcers such as the ones discussed so far is not always practical. Some problems have already been alluded to. Foods and similar small items do not maintain their reinforcing quality for extended periods of time owing to satiation. Social reinforcers, such as praise or attention, might not work right away with all children. Some reinforcers might be too expensive to be provided each time the appropriate behavior occurs, and some reinforcers might not be possible to administer in all situations. When any of these problems is at issue, tokens can be used as backup reinforcers that can be exchanged for primary reinforcers.

There are literally hundreds of ways in which token economies can be implemented. A few examples will be provided here, not to imply that these are the best ways to use tokens, and certainly not the only ways, but rather to stimulate the novice clinician to look at the process of setting up contingency plans with creativity and an open mind. An example of a simple positive reinforcement token economy is the use of stars to increase a child's handwashing behavior. Each time the child washes her or his hands before a meal or snack without having to be prompted to do so, she or he receives a star on a chart that is mounted by the sink. When the child has earned five stars, she or he may exchange them for a tangible reinforcer from a prespecified shopping list. If the child does not exchange the five stars, but prefers to keep on earning stars, she or he may exchange ten stars from another shopping list of even more desirable items or twenty stars from yet another menu.

A token economy for the same child that combines positive reinforcement and response cost not only provides the child with stars for appropriate behavior, but also has a contingency for what happens if the child does not wash hands before a meal or snack. Rather than merely using extinction or reminders, in this case one star would be wiped off the chart each time the child has to be prompted to wash her or his hands. The star chart and reinforcement menus would remain the same, but the response cost contingency would be added.

A complex token economy may combine positive reinforcement, reinforcement of incompatible behaviors, and response cost. For instance, if parents presented a boy for treatment who frequently hits his younger sister, breaks toys, and refuses to play by himself, a token economy could be developed that ties together the behavioral interventions for all of these target problems. The child would be allowed to earn one point for each 10-minute interval during which he plays quietly by himself without hitting his sister and without breaking a toy (positive reinforcement of a desirable behavior). He may receive an additional point for each toy he played with during a given day that was not broken (positive reinforcement of an incompatible behavior, i.e., of not breaking toys). Bonus points can be earned for days when he does not hit his sister at all. Each time he hits his sister, two points are subtracted from his chart (response cost for an inappropriate behavior). The points are backed up by a graded system of tangible reinforcers that allow the boy to self-reinforce in either short (exchange as few as five points for a reinforcer) or long (collect as many as 50 points for a large reinforcer) intervals. This boy's (Billy's) point chart and associated reinforcement menus are presented in Figure 12.2.

FIGURE 12.2   Point Chart for Billy

How to Earn Points

- 10 minutes playing alone and quietly = 1 point earned
- each toy played with and not broken   = 1 point earned
- not hitting sister all day long   = 3 bonus points earned

How to Lose Points

- hitting sister = 2 points lost

	Monday	Tuesday	Wednesday	Thursday	Friday	Saturday	Sunday
Week One							
Week Two							
Week Three							
Week Four							
Week Five							

Billy's Reinforcement Menus

5 points may be exchanged for one of the following:

- 10 minutes of play with mom
- 10 minutes of play with dad
- one short bedtime story
- one board game with mom and/or dad
- one Pokémon card
- one new magic marker

(continued)

FIGURE 12.2   Continued

- one sheet of colored cardboard
- one 10-minute phone call to a friend in town
- one candy bar (may only choose this item once per day)
- one can of soda (may only choose this item once per day)

10 points may be exchanged for one of the following:

- half hour of mom's **undivided** attention
- half hour of dad's **undivided** attention
- may stay up half an hour later
- extra half hour of TV watching
- a new book
- one extra trip to the library
- one extra serving of dessert
- two 15-minute phone calls to one or two friends in town
- may ask mom or dad to take the garbage out for him once
- one long bedtime story

20 points may be exchanged for one of the following:

- a 2-hour trip to the park with mom
- a 2-hour trip to the park with dad
- may stay up till 10 p.m. on Friday or Saturday
- may watch cartoons on Saturday morning
- may ask mom or dad to make his bed for him one morning
- may ask mom or dad to take the garbage out for him three times
- may make one 15-minute long-distance phone call
- may invite a friend for a sleepover
- may choose a new toy at the store for up to $5
- may choose the destination for a family outing

50 points may be exchanged for one of the following:

- a 1/2-day trip to the park with mom
- a 1/2-day trip to the park with dad
- may choose a new toy at the store for up to $20
- may make one big wish come true

To summarize, token economies have numerous advantages over the use of tangible reinforcers (Kazdin, 1977). They can be administered immediately and every time the desired behavior occurs. They neither result in satiation nor are impossible to administer in certain situations. The tangible reinforcers that back up the tokens can be individualized for each child, even if used in a group setting such as a classroom. This property of token economies makes them highly applicable in group settings, including classrooms, hospital units, residential settings, or homes that have several children. Again, the actual implementation and combination of strategies is limited only by the creativity of the person developing and implementing the program and can take into consideration changing needs and preferences of the child.

Strategies Based Upon Social Learning

The strategies in this category are based on observational learning principles that suggest that children learn many behaviors, as well as emotional responses, from watching others in their environment and incorporating the observed actions in a meaningful way into their own behavioral repertoire. The process of observational learning varies primarily according to the type of model used. Caring and powerful models of the same gender tend to be more successfully imitated than other models (Bandura, 1999). Three types of models that may meet these criteria and/or have been used successfully in the treatment of children are other human beings, videotaped or filmed models, and videotaped or filmed self (Powers, 2000). The use of other human beings is referred to as live modeling, the use of filmed other models as symbolic modeling, and the use of the filmed child as self modeling. A fourth procedure that combines several features of the previous three modeling processes is called participant modeling.

Live Modeling.   In live modeling, the child watches another human being perform a behavior the child is to learn. This may involve a new skill acquisition or the modeling of not fearing a stimulus that is currently feared by a child. A live modeling approach to a snake phobia would thus be to ask the child to watch another person handle a snake. The child would not be expected to touch the snake herself or himself.

A live modeling approach to skills acquisition would be to ask the child to watch a model who engages in a desirable behavior, such as, for instance, prosocial behavior for a withdrawn child. A live model does not always have to be selected by the therapist. The child can be asked about idealized others in her or his environment who might serve as models. For instance, a child who has to learn social skills might be asked if there is another child in the same school who possesses the skills the child would like to learn. If there is such a live model, the child could then be asked to observe this child and to identify a number of behaviors in which this other child engages that the client would like to learn and imitate.

Symbolic Modeling.   In symbolic modeling, rather than watching a live model, the child is exposed to a film or video of relevant models. The snake phobic child might watch a video showing several fearless children handling a snake and talking about snakes without anxiety. The withdrawn child might watch a film of children interacting positively or of a social skills training program in progress. An excellent example of symbolic modeling is provided by a film developed by the Department of Pediatrics at the University of Oklahoma Health Sciences Center designed to ready children for a spinal tap procedure. The film depicts a young girl who has been taught numerous relaxation and breathing techniques to cope successfully with this invasive medical procedure. Symbolic modeling can also involve asking the client to visualize herself or himself engaging in the desired behavior or facing the feared stimulus. However, this procedure has not yet been frequently applied to children.

Self Modeling.   In the self modeling procedure, originally developed by Hosford (1980), successful incidents of the desired behavior engaged in by the child are captured on video and then shown to the child in the attempt to increase their frequency of occurrence. If the behavior is very complex, the child may be taped engaged in behaviors that represent successive approximations for the target behavior. The child, in viewing her or his own videotape, serves as her or his own model. This is a powerful application of modeling theory and has been found to be very versatile and successful (Dowrick, 1991).

Participant Modeling.   In participant modeling, the child is exposed to a live, symbolic, or self model and then is asked to imitate the behavior in the presence of the therapist. Feedback is provided about the child's performance as the behavior occurs. If the desired behavior is a very difficult one, the model will break the process into its component steps and will model these steps one at a time. The child imitates each individual step and practices it to an acceptable criterion level before moving on to the next step. Whereas the therapist provides much feedback and reinforcement early in the process, or early on in the mastery of each step, this external feedback is slowly phased out toward the point of mastery to let the successful completion of the behavior serve as its own reinforcer for the child. Participant modeling has been reported to be one of the most successful and powerful modeling procedures for children (Gelfand and Hartmann, 1992).

Practical Implementation

The proper implementation of behavioral strategies requires thorough assessment, goal-setting, treatment planning, and data collection during implementation of interventions. As such, it is a far cry from being the superficial strategy that opponents of behavioral interventions make it out to be. In fact, behavioral assessment is extremely thorough and takes into account numerous and complex familial and environmental factors. The intake information outlined in previous chapters is as critical to behavioral interventions as any other treatment.

Once assessment of the child has been completed, the problem behaviors have to be identified and defined carefully, and their baseline rate has to be established. This procedure requires that the therapist, parents, teachers, or other caregivers in the child's life must observe the child and record the child's behavior to obtain an exact understanding of when, where, and how often the problem behavior occurs. As such, a teacher may be asked to count the number of disruptions during a given lesson and to note the circumstances of the occurrence. Similarly, a parent may be instructed to count how often the child acts out aggressively, by noting specific behaviors and circumstances. The child may be asked to rate a fear or phobia on a scale from 1 to 10, depending on different settings and occurrences. These measurements then serve as a basis for assessing treatment effectiveness. Only if the therapist knows where the child started out can she or he assess whether an intervention has been successful in reducing an undesired behavior or increasing a target behavior that has to be taught (Kazdin, 2000).

Once a baseline has been established, goal setting can be more realistic. For instance, a child who is observed to engage in an attention-seeking action at least once in every 30-minute interval cannot be expected to show no attention-seeking behaviors within the first month of treatment. A more appropriate goal for this child might be to reduce attention seeking to no more than five occurrences in one day during the first month of treatment, three occurrences a day during the second month of treatment, and so forth. Similarly, a child whose undesirable behavior occurs only while she or he is visiting with a particular friend might not be sufficiently challenged by a treatment goal that does not specify the environment wherein the change is to take place. Goals for behaviors that are to be addressed through the use of behavioral strategies are clearly defined. They specify the exact number of occurrences in specific environments or around certain individuals.

Behavioral goals are rarely set by the therapist exclusively. Instead, child, parents, teachers, or any other relevant individual may be consulted about the desired treatment outcome. This involvement of child and others is likely to increase cooperation with and investment in the treatment process by all parties involved. The involvement also continues beyond the goal-setting stage, as many behavioral strategies are not only applied in the treatment room, but also in relevant settings in the child's life. As such, environments outside the therapy room have to be prepared for the implementation of treatment interventions. Parents and teachers have to be taught to implement programs that were selected by the therapist. In fact, teachers, parents, and children are critical to the determination of appropriate reinforcers as they have more extended knowledge of the child than the therapist who just made the child's acquaintance. While the therapist provides the theoretical knowledge and framework for the intervention, family members have to provide the specifics of the child's behavior and reinforcement history to make treatment work. This is particularly true for operant conditioning strategies. Respondent conditioning strategies are more likely to be implemented by the therapist in the therapy room.

Although reinforcers are most commonly disbursed by a parent or teacher, it is not impossible to make the child responsible for her or his own reinforcer. This is particularly true for token economies, in which the child may be asked to record points on the chart or to track the number of tokens earned in other ways. If token economies are used, it is best to have charts and menus highly visible in the child's room to provide a good visual reminder of the program for the child. If the child is too young to read, contingencies can be displayed not in written but pictorial form. Magazine pictures of children or photographs of the child herself or himself can be used to display an appropriate behavior and the number of stars earned by this behavior may be pasted next to the picture as a visual reminder for the child that different behaviors may earn different numbers of points. Similarly, pictures of undesirable behaviors may be posted on the board with a heavy red line drawn through them.

All throughout the implementation of the behavioral strategy, records must be kept of the child's behavior to monitor progress. It is not unusual for baseline behaviors to worsen during the initial stage of treatment, as the child is likely to test the limits of the person responsible for the disbursement or withholding of reinforcers. However, after the initial testing of limits, improvements in the child's behavior should emerge rather quickly. As most of the operant treatment strategies and in vivo desensitization programs are best implemented in the actual environment, generalization of progress is built into treatment.

Behavioral strategies and interventions are best used to supplement other treatment strategies. A therapist can set up token economies in the child's home and classroom, can conduct relaxation training and a desensitization program in the therapy room, and can use play therapy, storytelling, art therapy, and other strategies to interact therapeutically with the child. Such a comprehensive approach is most likely not only to reduce undesired and to increase desired behaviors, but also to address issues that are not purely behavioral in nature, such as the child's awareness and playing out of family roles, affective awareness and expression, recognition of needs, teaching of coping skills, and so forth. The example provided below reflects the case of a child who was treated using such a comprehensive approach.

Example

The boy whose case will be presented here was seen once weekly by the therapist for over a year. His parents were seen by the same therapist once weekly for three months and then on an as-needed basis for parent education training, which was to aid them in the implementation of a token economy in the home. One of the child's teachers was involved in the third week of treatment to implement a token economy in the classroom and an in vivo desensitization program in gym class as an extension of the systematic desensitization that was used by the therapist in the individual therapy sessions. The therapist used storytelling to explore family problems and to help the child develop new coping skills. Play was used to facilitate the development of a therapeutic relationship, and art therapy facilitated the child's self-expression, as well as additional monitoring of treatment progress. As the focus of this chapter is on behavioral intervention, only that aspect of the child's therapy will be highlighted here. However, it is exceedingly important to remember that this behavioral intervention was firmly embedded in a larger conceptual context and child-therapist interaction, and would not be endorsed in and of itself.

This 10-year-old boy was presented for treatment by his parents, who had just been contacted by his teacher and informed that Michael had skipped school twice in one week. When his parents attempted to talk to Michael about the situation, he cried but could not verbalize why he was so distraught. When they further explored the situation with his teachers, they found out that Michael had been very withdrawn and fearful in the past three months. One teacher believed that Michael's mood was particularly depressed on days when the class was scheduled for physical education. Michael routinely attempted to avoid physical education, claiming stomachaches or headaches. Both days of school he had skipped recently were days with physical education class in the morning. During the intake, Michael revealed that he hated gym class because he felt inadequate and had often been made fun of by several larger boys. Michael was slight in build and somewhat younger than most of his classmates. He indicated that he hated having to race against other boys because he always lost. Further, he felt very panicky in these situations and one time fell and hurt himself badly.

Michael's father was very upset by his son's failure in gym class. He was a former bodybuilder and still conscious about physical appearance and exercise. He ran several miles daily and often entered races, winning occasionally. Michael's mother was hurt that her son had not confided in her. She revealed that Michael was not very close to her and had withdrawn even more since the birth of his younger sister six months earlier. Also present for the intake was Michael's older brother Steven, a 16-year-old who indicated that he was bored by the intake and wanted to get out of it as soon as possible. Michael adored his older brother, but he rarely allowed Michael to play or interact with him. Steven was athletic and had recently received his driver's license, which frequently removed him from the family. He had a 10 P.M. curfew and rarely arrived home before that time.

Michael was diagnosed with a simple phobia, and the feared stimulus was identified as gym class. He also was assessed for depression and showed several signs, though not enough to diagnose dysthymia. He did appear unusually withdrawn and shy, and his self-esteem appeared compromised. When asked how he rated himself with regard to how positively he felt about himself on a 1 (low) to 10 (high) point scale, he said 3. Michael's teacher volunteered to do some ratings of Michael's withdrawal behavior in the school setting and reported that he refused interactions with children who approached him four out of five times, stayed by himself during breaks the entire time, complained of stomachaches during every gym class, and reported headaches approximately twice per week. On the basis of this information, Michael, his parents, and the therapist set four primary treatment goals. The first goal was to keep Michael from avoiding gym class by reducing the fear and physical pain responses he had developed in connection with this activity. The second goal was to involve Michael more actively with other children by increasing the number of offers to play that he accepted to three out of five offers, by increasing the amount of time spent with children during break to 10 of the 15 minutes, and by increasing his involvement with other children in after-school activities. The third goal was to help Michael increase his self-rated self-esteem to at least a 7 on a 10-point scale. The fourth goal was to continue to work on assessing the family relationships, especially the relationship between father and son and the role change for Michael since the birth of the baby. Parent education was recommended for the parents to help them implement behavior programs in the home, to prevent future difficulties with the other children, and to explore their own psychological needs. Family therapy was recommended as a follow-up to Michael's individual treatment.

Behavioral interventions were chosen to address the first two treatment goals. Play therapy was chosen to address the third and fourth goals. Only the behavioral strategies will be elaborated upon here. To reduce Michael's fear and physical response to gym class, a two-pronged approach was developed. First, a systematic desensitization program was started in the therapy sessions in which a hierarchy was developed. Second, an in vivo program was designed in collaboration with the gym teacher and implemented once Michael had mastered the relaxation techniques. To reduce Michael's withdrawal behavior in school and at home, two token economy programs were implemented, reinforcing him for interacting with other children. A response cost program was also part of this token economy.

The therapist and Michael developed a hierarchy of anxiety-producing situations connected to his fear of gym class. Michael was taught progressive muscle tension–relaxation, using Koeppen's (1974) procedure. Once he mastered basic relaxation, the in-session desensitization program began. In the third week of treatment, an in vivo component was added in collaboration with the gym teacher. Michael progressed through the systematic desensitization hierarchy over the course of 18 weeks, indicating just how strong his fear of gym class was. He was able to move to the second item of his in vivo hierarchy in week 6 and required three additional weeks before moving to item three. He progressed to the items graded 22 and higher after an additional six weeks and was not able to do the final item until week 24 (his next semester). The hierarchies for the two desensitization programs are presented in Tables 12.3 and 12.4.

The therapist, Michael, his brother Steven, and his parents developed a token economy for home and school. Michael's teacher agreed to cooperate with the school component of the program. The program combined positive reinforcement, reinforcement of

TABLE 12.3   **Michael's Systematic Desensitization Hierarchy**

0	Going to school on a day without gym class
3	Wearing gym clothes at home without any intent to exercise
5	Being in the gym alone without any intent to exercise
6	Going to school on a day with gym class, knowing you won't have to go to gym at all
7	Going to school on a day with gym class, knowing you won't have to participate at all, but you'll have to sit and watch
9	Going to school on a day with gym class, knowing you won't have to participate at all, but you'll have to sit and watch while wearing gym clothes
12	Sitting in gym class in street clothes, just watching the other kids
14	Sitting in gym class in gym clothes, just watching the other kids
16	Going to gym class, but only participating in warm-ups
19	Going to gym class, but only participating in warm-ups and cool-downs
21	Going to gym class, but only participating in warm-ups and cool-downs, and 10 minutes of noncompetitive exercise of your choice
22	Going to gym class, but only participating in warm-ups and cool-downs, and 20 minutes of noncompetitive exercise of your choice
23	Going to gym class, but only participating in warm-ups and cool-downs, 20 minutes of noncompetitive exercise of your choice, and 5 minutes of competitive exercise of your choice
24	Going to gym class, but only participating in warm-ups and cool-downs, all noncompetitive exercise, and 5 minutes of competitive exercise of your choice
24	Going to gym class, but only participating in warm-ups and cool-downs, all noncompetitive exercise, and 10 minutes of competitive exercise of your choice
25	Going to gym class, but only participating in warm-ups and cool-downs, all noncompetitive exercise, and 10 minutes of competitive exercise of your choice, and having to perform a task individually in front of the other kids and doing fine
25	Going to gym class, but only participating in warm-ups and cool-downs, all noncompetitive exercise, and 10 minutes of competitive exercise of your choice, and having to perform a task individually in front of the other kids and messing up
25	Going to gym class, but only participating in warm-ups and cool-downs, all noncompetitive exercise, and 10 minutes of competitive exercise of your choice, and having to perform a task individually in front of the other kids and messing up so badly everyone laughs

Note 1: The steps will be presented and imagined one after the other as they can be tolerated without experiencing a fear or physical response while Michael is fully relaxed.

Note 2: The steps are graduated from zero (no fear or physical response) to 25 (extreme fear and strong physical response) on the basis of how strongly Michael would respond without relaxation.

incompatible behaviors, and response cost for undesirable behavior. Specifically, Michael had a daily reinforcement chart at school and a weekly chart at home. At school, Michael's teacher was responsible for delivery of the tokens, in this case stars, that were placed on the daily chart. Michael received one star for each observed positive interaction with another

TABLE 12.4 Michael's In Vivo Desensitization Hierarchy

5	Going to school on a day with gym class but knowing that he will not have to go to that class
10	Going to gym class but knowing that he will not have to participate in the class; he will sit and watch
15	Going to gym class but knowing that he will only participate in the warm-up exercises, which last 5 minutes and are noncompetitive; then he will only sit and watch
18	Going to gym class but knowing that he will only participate in the warm-up exercises, which last 5 minutes and are noncompetitive; then he will be allowed to sit and watch until closing exercises which are for cool-down purposes and are noncompetitive
20	Going to gym class but knowing that he will participate only in the warm-up exercises, which last 5 minutes and are noncompetitive; then he will be allowed to sit and watch all competitive exercises; he will participate in 10 minutes of noncompetitive exercises of his choice and will join cool-down
22	Going to gym class but knowing that he will participate only in the warm-up exercises, which last 5 minutes and are noncompetitive; then he will be allowed to sit and watch all competitive exercises; he will participate in 20 minutes of noncompetitive exercises of his choice and will join cool-down
23	Going to gym class but knowing that he will participate only in the warm-up exercises, which last 5 minutes and are noncompetitive; then he will be allowed to sit and watch all competitive exercises; he will participate in 20 minutes of noncompetitive exercises of his choice; he will participate in 5 minutes of competitive exercises of his choice and will join cool-down
25	Going to gym class but knowing that he will participate in the entire gym class, including warm-up, noncompetitive exercises, competitive exercises (never more than 10 minutes), and cool-down

Note 1: The steps will be implemented in real life one after the other as they can be tolerated without experiencing a fear or physical response while Michael is fully relaxed.

Note 2: The steps are graduated from zero (no fear or physical response) to 25 (extreme fear and strong physical response) based on how strongly Michael would respond without relaxation.

child during break time (positive reinforcement). He also received a star for each time he was observed to respond positively to being approached by another child (reinforcement of an incompatible behavior). He received two stars for each break time during which he spent less time alone than he spent with other children (reinforcement of an incompatible behavior). At home, he received a star for each time he initiated an interaction with another child, whether in person or over the telephone. He received a star for every 30-minute period during which he interacted with another child. In both settings, Michael lost a star each if he did not interact with any children during all breaks (at school) or free time (at home). Exchange of stars for tangible reinforcers was possible based on a graded menu to allow Michael to determine intervals between receipt of a tangible reinforcer. Simplified copies of Michael's charts and reinforcement menus are displayed in Figures 12.3 and 12.4. His original charts and menus were prepared by him and his older brother in a collaborative activity

FIGURE 12.3 Michael's School Reinforcement Chart

How to Earn Stars

- any positive interaction with another child   =   1 star
- positive response to another child inviting to play =   1 star
- less time alone during break than with children   =   2 stars

How to Lose Stars

- no interaction with another child during the entire break =   1 star

---

Stars Earned Today

Michael interacted positively with another child   _____ stars

    Description of what he did: _____

    _____

    _____

    _____

Michael responded positively to a child
who invited him to play or join an activity   _____ stars

Description of what he did: _____

    _____

    _____

    _____

Michael spent less time alone than with others   _____ stars

How much did he spend with other children during

Break One _____

Break Two _____

Break Three _____

Break Four _____

Michael did not interact with another child during   _____ stars

Break One _____

Break Two _____

Break Three _____

Break Four _____

Total Stars Earned in School Today: **_____ STARS**

FIGURE 12.4   Michael's Home Reinforcement Chart

How to Earn Stars

- initiate an interaction with another child   =   1 star
- interaction with another child in a 30-minute period =   1 star

How to Lose Stars

- no interaction with another child all afternoon   =   lose 1 star
- no interaction all Saturday morning   =   lose 1 star

Day + Stars	Initiated Interaction —description of interaction	Interacted in 30-minute period —description of interaction
Monday		
Tuesday		
Wednesday		
Thursday		
Friday		
Saturday		
TOTAL STARS EARNED THIS WEEK: _____	(note: stars lost need to be subtracted for total)	

(continued)

FIGURE 12.4   Continued

Reinforcement Menus for Michael

Level One Rewards (worth 10 stars)

- spend half hour alone indoors any way he wants to
- spend half hour alone outside any way he wants to
- spend 15 minutes daytime with older brother Steven
- two large cookies (may choose no more than once per day)
- a pack of chewing gum
- one can of Dr. Pepper (may choose no more than once per day)
- allowed to read a new comic book
- have a short story read to him by mom or dad
- play a board game with mom or dad
- may listen to a favorite CD on the family stereo system

Level Two Rewards (worth 20 stars)

- spend half a daytime hour with brother Steven
- spend an extra afternoon at the library
- spend an extra Saturday afternoon at the museum
- spend one hour alone indoors
- spend one hour alone outdoors
- have a long bedtime story read to him by mom or dad
- have a short story read to him by mom or dad any time
- have two helpings of dessert, even if he didn't finish dinner
- may buy one new container of Play-Doh
- may buy a new notebook
- allowed to buy a new comic book
- a new T-shirt
- may listen to three favorite CDs on the family stereo system

Level Three Rewards (worth 40 stars)

- spend one daytime hour with brother Steven
- spend one afternoon after school alone indoors
- spend one afternoon after school alone outdoors
- spend one afternoon with dad
- spend one afternoon with mom
- one new set of magic markers
- one new science book
- one new Pokémon figure
- determine the destination of a family outing
- have unlimited access to the family stereo for one afternoon
- have a long bedtime story read by brother Steven

Level Four Rewards (worth 100 stars)

- spend one afternoon with brother Steven
- spend a day at the museum with dad
- spend one Saturday alone indoors and/or outdoors
- buy one new toy for up to $25
- buy new clothes for up to $25
- cash in on one big wish

and were quite sophisticated, with pictures of Michael interacting with friends in various settings and activities. The brother had agreed to be involved in this activity after the therapist had met with him and explained his potentially influential role with Michael as a model.

Summary and Concluding Thoughts

This chapter served to familiarize the novice clinician with behavioral strategies to be used either within a strictly behavioral, or more eclectic, framework. A differentiation was made among respondent (or classical) conditioning, operant (or instrumental) conditioning, and social learning theory. Use of these strategies has a number of advantages, including the thorough assessment of baseline behavior, accurate assessment of treatment progress, involvement of the child and significant others in the goal-setting and treatment implementation processes, excellent generalization, and a nonpathological approach to behavior. In addition to these advantages, it should be noted that behavioral therapists do not neglect the child-therapist relationship and understand its importance to the successful outcome of treatment. Thus, rapport building and empathy, though not focused on in this chapter, are not inherently incompatible with a behavioral approach. Nevertheless, in this chapter, it was recommended to use behavioral strategies exactly as such, and not as the exclusive framework of conceptualization of a child therapy case. Instead, a more comprehensive system, such as the one outlined in Chapter Eight, was recommended for this purpose.

13 Parent Education

Being a parent is perhaps the most difficult job held by most adults (and even many adolescents) without any prior training or education whatsoever. It is no big wonder that mistakes are made, unrealistic expectations set, feelings hurt, and families broken. Somehow, adults are expected to know what is needed for good parenting just from having grown up around their own parents, adoptive parents, foster parents, and so on. They are considered experts on child development and communication; teachers of affective expression and morality; helpers with homework and heartbreaks; and mediators of quarrels and conflicts. All of these expectations would be difficult for a trained mental health professional to meet, yet that same professional is often quick to blame a parent who failed in one of these many roles. Parents cannot be perfect; neither can children. Helping parents acknowledge and accept their children's imperfections, and acknowledging and accepting the parents' own imperfections, is the task of a good clinician (Mahoney et al., 1999).

It does not suffice to teach basic parenting strategies. Parents must feel understood, valued, and cared for by their child's therapist or their cooperation in treatment will leave much to be desired and their minds will be closed to new learning. As such, each parent education program should include some basic interventions such as rapport building, reflection, empathy, modeling, and similar strategies. Some of the existing programs include these components, many do not. This chapter will provide a review of several traditional programs that have been presented in the literature and used in clinical practice for decades. Then, drawing from these traditional approaches, an innovative, practically applied program will be discussed that includes sensitivity to parents' needs, as well as basic education.

Three cautions must be addressed about this chapter. First, the chapter focuses on parent education, that is, the training of parenting skills. It does not propose to teach the beginning child clinician to conduct parent therapy groups or individual parental therapy. In fact, child therapists generally avoid conducting therapy with the parents of a child client, as such an intervention would represent a dual relationship. If therapy is indicated for the parents (and it often is), they are best served with a referral to another clinician, preferably in the same clinic or private practice group. The two therapists may then communicate (with appropriate releases of information) to coordinate treatment and assess the child's and parents' progress and its generalization to the family setting.

Second, for the purposes of this chapter, "parents" are any adults in a caretaking role vis-à-vis a child. There is no need for a blood relationship, or even a legal relationship. In fact, parent education is as appropriate for baby-sitters and day-care personnel, as for parents who live with the child on a day-to-day basis. Thus, while the term "parent" was chosen to discuss child training strategies in this chapter, the reader must transcend the label and apply it loosely to any adult in a caretaking role with a child.

Third, it is not the purpose of this chapter to review the literature with regard to which strategies are best for which types of families and presenting problems. This literature is complex and often not very straightforward. Instead, this chapter attempts only to familiarize the child therapist with the basic building blocks of parent education upon which she or he can build as she or he gains more experience in the field. The strategies presented here tend to be useful to all parents, though they will work most effectively with parents who are cooperative and willing to participate in their children's treatment. Parents who are resistant, or whose children are extremely aggressive or hostile, may be in need of more specialized services such as behavioral parent groups or psychotherapy.

Conceptual Background

There are three primary schools of thought that have resulted in parent education programs: Adlerian individual psychology, Rogerian humanism, and Skinnerian behaviorism. Individual psychology was the basis for the concept of natural and logical consequences as developed by Dreikurs (Dreikurs and Grey, 1990; Dreikurs and Soltz, 1964), and later expanded upon by Dinkmeyer and McKay (1976). Alfred Adler (1956), a German-born psychiatrist who early in his career adhered to Freudian principles, believed that all behavior has a purpose or a goal, and that the psychological and behavioral movement of individuals, including children, is always toward a higher goal or more advanced level of functioning. The nature of this higher goal is largely, if not entirely, determined by the fundamental human need for belongingness. Thus, all individuals' striving is for the better of society, or in the social interest of the group to which the individual attempts to belong. Factors within and outside of each person help determine whether this socially appropriate goal is maintained or whether an inappropriate goal is substituted that leads to maladaptive behavior. In other words, people are viewed as actively interacting with the environment rather than passively responding to it and as molding their behavior according to the feedback they receive. Thus, actual environmental factors, as well as individual interpretations thereof, help to determine behavior and responses.

Applied to children, these principles of individual psychology suggest that children inherently strive for growth and improvement and that this improvement is generally determined by the child's need to belong to a group of people, to feel connected to a social group, the earliest of which is the child's family. If the environment and the child's interpretation thereof are healthy and accurate, this striving will result in actions that are in the social interest and to the benefit of all. However, if the child misinterprets the environment, or if the environment is nonresponsive or inappropriately responsive, the child's striving will be derailed in a negative way. It is then up to a clinician to help parents redirect the child and to help her or him reenter the healthier, socially oriented developmental trajectory. This can be done through the use of natural and logical consequences, encouragement, and democratic family functioning (Dreikurs and Grey, 1990), all of which are parenting strategies taught through parent education according to this model of human behavior.

Humanism, the second school of thought to result in a parent education program, led to the development of Parent Effectiveness Training (Gordon, 1970; Gordon and Sands, 1978), which was later expanded to include Teacher Effectiveness Training as well. Carl Rogers (1961), an American-born theorist who grew up in a strictly fundamentally religious family environment, had a deep faith in the tendency of humans to develop in a positive and constructive manner, as long as respect and trust are developed and provided in their lives. He perceived people as basically rational, socialized, forward-moving, and realistic. He believed that behavior is motivated either by urges within the person, or by the environment which strengthens or weakens certain actions. The disagreement between personal urges and socially condoned behaviors, affects, and needs is viewed as the root of all conflict for humans. Specifically, behavior that is designed to help the person move toward self-actualization as she or he has defined it for herself or himself at times clashes with environmental sanctions and results in changes in behavior that prevent the person from being the way she or he really would like to be. This results in the formation of a false sense of self, or a self that is not congruent with the person's ideal self or way of being. Hence, it is Rogers's belief that for people to be able to self-actualize, and thus be emotionally and psychologically healthy, they need an environment that is accepting of them, interacts with genuineness, and allows for the free and uncensored expression of affect. Empathic responsiveness of the environment to the individual is perceived as critical to the development of a healthy self.

Applying these humanistic principles to children means that as children grow up and interact with their environment, they are viewed as striving to self-actualize and to achieve their definition of their ideal self. Infants, hypothesized by humanist theorists to be unaware of environmental feedback, will follow their organismic urges freely, not experiencing any conflict. However, as children grow up, feedback from the environment increases in meaning and soon is used to determine the appropriateness of behaviors and affects. If the environment is accepting of and empathic with the child's expressed urges, a healthy self can develop that is congruent with the child's ideal self. However, if the environment is nonaccepting, rejecting, or indifferent, a self will develop that is not congruent with the child's own urges, but rather with the perception of the self created by the environment. This results in an incongruence between what the child does and wants to do, what the child really feels and actually expresses, and what the child needs and asks for. This incongruence is perceived by Rogers as the source of all psychological and emotional problems. It can be dealt with through therapy for the child, as well as through educating parents about the importance of becoming more aware of their child's genuine needs, desires, and affects, and stressing the importance of being accepting of and empathic with these manifestations of the child's developing self. Two primary strategies developed for parents for this purpose are active listening and I-messages (Gordon, 1970), both taught in parent education programs based on this model.

Finally, behaviorism has been used by a number of parent educators, including Krumboltz and Krumboltz (1972) and Becker (1971). B. F. Skinner (1971; 1976) firmly believed that theories such as Adler's and Rogers's were unnecessary and not very economical. He proposed instead that all behavior is learned strictly as a result of the events or consequences that follow it. This operant conditioning approach implies that behavior is not intrinsically determined, but rather a response to environmental contingencies. Thus,

No Way

behaviors can be easily changed, taught, and eliminated by applying the correct environmental response. All behaviors are acquired in the same manner, and hence, there is no such thing as normal versus abnormal behavior. Instead, behavior is seen merely as more or less functional or dysfunctional. Both functional and dysfunctional behaviors are learned and can be changed through the application of four principles. These principles, or primary responses, outlined by behaviorists are positive reinforcement, negative reinforcement, punishment, and extinction. All four were covered in Chapter Twelve and do not need to be explained again.

Applied to parent education, behavioral principles imply that if the therapist can only teach the parent how to correctly apply the four responses, the child's behavior can be modified as desired by the parent. This approach clearly implies much more control and direction on the parents' part than the other approaches to parent education, which are more concerned with the child's self-expression and acceptance. Primary parenting strategies according to this behavioral model are outlined in detail by Krumboltz and Krumboltz (1972) and are identical to those applied by a clinician (see Chapter Twelve). Thus, the information imparted to a child's parents in a behaviorally informed parent education program is the same as the information used in therapy by the behaviorally informed clinician.

Exploring the three schools of thought that have become foundations for parent education demonstrates that there are numerous opinions about and approaches to human behavior and mental health. It is likely that no single approach can account for the complexity of the human phenomenon in and of itself. Thus, it appears most appropriate to be familiar with as many approaches as possible in order to be able to pick and choose among a number of strategies when faced with a particular situation or client. Having an overall framework of integration for such an eclectic approach would certainly appear to be advantageous and is the purpose of the practical implementation section of this chapter.

Application to Child Therapy

Although parent education is obviously not a child therapy technique per se, as it is not applied to the child client, but rather to the parent, there are numerous reasons for including these strategies in the comprehensive training of a child clinician. First, parent education provides a means for the child therapist to interact with a child client's parents without engaging in a therapeutic endeavor that may constitute a dual relationship. In other words, although attempts at conducting therapy with a child and her or his parents at the same time may lead to difficult situations and potential ethical dilemmas, the concurrent contact with parents of a child client in a parent educator role is less likely to cause dual relationship conflicts. Most writers agree that parent education is not equivalent to the conduct of therapy in that its primary focus is academic, not therapeutic [see Brim (1959) who was one of the first authors to write about this distinction].

Another conceptual reason for including parent education training for the child clinician is that keeping parents involved with the clinician will give them additional reasons to maintain contact with the clinic, thus reducing the risk of premature termination of the child's treatment. Further, it has been hypothesized that parents are under increasing amounts of stress due to many factors, including single parenting, shrinking nuclear families, frequent moves of families leaving them without a support network, and dual profession parents. For these parents, the support from a clinician who engages in parent education may prove invaluable. Finally, parent education has been viewed as a means of prevention, not just remediation. Thus, while parent education as discussed in this text is focused on helping parents who have children already in treatment, it is also likely to contribute to the prevention of future problems with the same child and her or his siblings.

Research has lent further support to justify parent education (Jackson and Leonetti, 2001). Specifically, a number of studies have shown that parent education indeed can have positive effects for children and their parents in a number of realms (Nicholson, Janz, and Fox, 1998). Reviews of existing literature have suggested that there are few quantifiable differences among the different types of parenting programs that exist with regard to produced outcome or improvement. In other words, whether the program is focused on logical consequences, parent effectiveness training, behavior modification, or combinations thereof, does not appear to affect outcome as far as the child's improvement is concerned (Tramontana, Sherrets, and Authier, 1980). However, there are some program components that have been identified as particularly important, relevant, or conducive to program effectiveness. These include, but may not be limited to, active participation of the parents with the children (Coleman and Ganong, 1983), assessment of parental needs along with the incorporation of strategies that address these needs (Kroth and Otteni, 1983), parental support (Pfannenstiel and Seltzer, 1989), and individualized tailoring of programs to parents (Powell, 1983).

The short-term effectiveness of parent education has been well documented (Abikoff, 1991; Anastopoulos, DuPaul, and Barkley, 1991; Dickinson and Cudaback, 1992; Graziano and Diament, 1992; Wright, Stroud, and Kennan, 1993), despite several clear methodological problems in this literature (cf. Todres and Bunston, 1993). Long-term benefits have been less successfully documented, in part owing to flaws in the evaluation process (Todres and Bunston, 1993). Nevertheless, there is agreement that parent education helps parents to develop more realistic and positive attitudes about parenting and assists them in becoming better, more confident parents, regardless of the type or model of parenting education that is presented (Barber, 1992; Pehrson and Robinson, 1990). Participation in parent education programs may help parents to become more positively involved with their children and in child-rearing activities (McBride, 1991) and can have direct positive effects on children's behavior (Morgan, Nu'Man-Sheppard, and Allin, 1990).

One potential problem with parent education programs is that they may be too abstract for some parents to understand and apply to their own situations. Insensitive programs leave parents feeling not only confused and misled, but even less secure and more anxious about their parenting skills than before participation (Rodd, 1990; Todres and Bunston, 1993). This finding may explain why dropout rates are higher for lower socioeconomic status (SES) parents (e.g., Jackson and Leonetti, 2001) and why lower SES parents actually experience negative effects from participation in parent education programs [e.g., lowered self-efficacy; Brems (1994)].

Lack of cultural sensitivity has also been cited as a reason for unsuccessful parent education interventions (Glanville and Tiller, 1991). It has been argued that there has to be a goodness of fit between the parents and the program's content; that is, parenting education classes must be adapted to the specific needs of the population that is being served. Lack of goodness of fit may explain why parenting education programs have found to be less effective with parents of nondominant cultural backgrounds (Heffer and Kelly, 1987). Ethnocultural considerations must be made and culturally aware, and sensitive interventions must be part of the program (Short and Johnston, 1994). For example, parent education programs have to be sensitive of and adapted to different perspectives of different cultural groups on family structures and identities, parent-child interactions, and style of communication between adults and children and among adults (Harry, 1992) to be effective and to meet the criterion of goodness of fit.

One of the most destructive criticisms of traditional parent education programs has been that they aid only parents who do not have very many problems with their children to begin with, whereas they tend to decrease the self-confidence of parents who already have problems with their children, or who come from lower socioeconomic strata (Jackson and Leonetti, 2001). Although these research data may be used by some to argue against the use of parenting education programs, they may also be used to design alternative programs that are more sensitive to parental needs. Thus, although some questions remain with regard to the effectiveness of parent education, ranging from questions about the appropriateness of various intervention programs to the adequacy of the research designs that have been implemented to assess treatment outcome (Todres and Bunston, 1993), clinicians continue to use parent education as an important intervention strategy. Therefore, it is safe to assume that despite some questions in the research literature, clinical relevance is judged sufficiently high to render parent education important to the training of children's mental health service providers for years to come. Traditional programs, however, must consider and incorporate the findings of research studies, and should therefore become more conceptually comprehensive, procedurally interactive, and topically relevant to parental backgrounds and needs (Schroeder and Gordon, 1991). The application of any one particular "canned" approach no longer appears warranted; instead, an integration of strategies seems necessary (Mahoney et al., 1999).

For the novice clinician to be able to apply such an integrative approach, she or he must receive some training in and have familiarity with all major approaches that have been used effectively and consistently. Therefore, in the remainder of this chapter, three distinct approaches to parent education will be presented: programs based on logical consequences, parent effectiveness training, and behavior modification. These approaches will be discussed individually first and then will be integrated within an overriding conceptual framework that not only allows for tailored parent interventions that adhere to the research-based recommendations outlined above, but also has been shown equally effective in imparting information as traditional programs (Brems, Baldwin, and Baxter, 1993). While other theorists have attempted such integrations (Green, 1975; Popkin, 1983a, 1983b), no system has done so either sufficiently comprehensively or with an empathic and individually tailored focus on the parent.

Variations on the Technique

Natural and Logical Consequences

Natural and logical consequences are the two primary strategies taught to parents by Adlerian parent educators. They are based on the underlying assumptions that children have an inherent capacity to develop in healthy, effective ways and that they develop and mature and want to find acceptance within their family system. To that end, children observe and attempt to pattern their behavior according to their observations and perceived approval or disapproval. However, despite children thus being expert observers, they misinterpret messages and events at times and then respond inappropriately or in a manner that appears out of context. For instance, a child might act out aggressively after the birth of a sibling because of the child's misinterpretation of the event as a rejection of her or him by the parent. Another child, perceiving a mother's business trip as punishment, might become depressed and withdrawn.

puts the burden on the child !

What ties both examples together, however, is the child's desire to belong and to be loved, which drives the resultant reaction to the external event. According to Dreikurs and Grey (1990), if the parent does not recognize the source of the child's behavior, namely, the need and desire to belong, and responds in a rejecting or otherwise less than optimal manner, the child may develop mistaken goals that result in prolonged or repetitive misbehaviors. The four mistaken goals outlined by Adlerian parent educators, and presented in Table 13.1, are exaggerated needs for attention, power struggles, retaliation and revenge, and demonstration of inadequacy or deficiency (discouragement). A child who has developed a goal of attempting to gain as much attention as possible might throw temper tantrums in public. The tantrums might have resulted in attention by the parents, thus maintaining the inappropriate behavior.

TABLE 13.1   The Four Mistaken Goals of Children's Misbehavior

Mistaken Goal	Purpose	Examples
Attention Getting	■ child misbehaves to get attention from people in the environment, especially parents and teachers	■ clowning at school ■ fighting with siblings ■ not following through with chores
Struggle for Power	■ child refuses to comply to control a situation or the parent despite having already gained attention from the parent; victory means having avoided a command from the parent	■ acting out at bedtime that results in getting to stay up later ■ delaying a chore until someone else does it
Revenge	■ child wants to get back at adults by whom child felt mistreated; usually follows a series of battles with the parent in which the child has been unable to gain attention or power	■ running away from home ■ refusing to participate in family affairs ■ secretly breaking rules after a quarrel with parent
Excuse or Inadequacy	■ child gives up trying to do anything right and is very discouraged and hopeless; regression occurs often	■ doing no homework ■ refusing to learn new skills ■ blaming inability for not doing chore

A child who is struggling for power might refuse to go to bed at night and might prolong bedtime rituals or may ask for things until late in the evening, keeping the parent preoccupied with her or him. The parent who finally gives in to the child and allows the child to stay up late has lost the struggle. Getting into repeated severe power struggles with a child, in which the child is left feeling punished, hopeless, and helpless, might result in the child's goal to obtain revenge or to retaliate. This child, after an attempt to prolong the bedtime ritual, might finally have been punished and have been locked into her or his room after a spanking. The child, now feeling rather enraged, seeks revenge. She or he might proceed to get out some crayons and draw pictures on the room's carefully painted walls. The parent, discovering the damage in the morning is upset, and the child has successfully retaliated.

A child who is discouraged will have a goal of proving to everyone that she or he is inadequate, never good enough. This child might get into a lot of trouble at school for severe acting out, which results in a label of the child that she or he is a problem and not to be trusted. Alternatively, the child might develop many learning problems, show a deterioration in grades, and fail to complete homework, proving inadequacy. These behaviors of the child, though obviously misguided by a mistaken goal, are nevertheless the child's manner of using her or his own intelligence and "hereditary endowments" (Dreikurs and Soltz, 1964, p. 17) to create solutions to problems. Parent educators of this tradition firmly believe that if the child's goal can be detected and subsequently corrected, the child's solutions to problems will result in healthy and appropriate behavior, guided by the child's goal to belong and to contribute in a positive manner to the family or environment. To help children maintain or learn appropriate goals, Dreikurs recommends a very specific family environment for children.

Environment. The environment in which a child can be expected to grow and behave in a healthy and appropriate manner is one that provides the child with a sense of self-respect and a sense of accomplishment. The family environment exudes enjoyment in the child, expresses pride in the child's attempts at growing and creating, and treats the child with empathy in the presence of failure. The household would be run very democratically, and rather than criticizing children for their behavior, parents would attempt to analyze why the child responded as she or he did and would then respond to the motivation of the child. If the motivation is derived from a mistaken goal, the parent would redirect the child's goals instead of being critical or getting caught up in the child's motivation. For instance, the attention-seeking child who throws temper tantrums might be told that she or he either may spend time with the parents and have their full attention or may choose to continue the tantrum. The parents would then remove themselves from the situation if the child chose to continue the tantrum to avoid providing more attention to the child's inappropriate behavior.

Further, the environment is designed in such a manner as to be sensitive to the Adlerian hypothesis that a child is affected by the family atmosphere and family constellation. For instance, if the family atmosphere is angry or hostile, the child is likely to show angry, hostile behavior. If parents fight, children fight. Family constellation, that is, birth order, is considered critical in helping to shape a child's behavior (Adler, 1956). Adler believed that a child's position within the family and the evolution of that position contribute to the child's behavior and goals. For example, an eldest child would be expected to show particular behaviors that one would not expect a youngest child to exhibit and vice versa. Given recent research in the area of birth order, it is best to reconceptualize this aspect of Adlerian parent education principles as referring to the child's role in the family. In other words, children do play certain roles in their families; some children are mediators between parents, others are distractors from systemic problems. Regardless of the role, it is critical for the environment to be aware that some of the child's behavior is best understood in the context of her or his role in the family. Thus, some change is best created through changes in the environment that would result in a new role for the child.

Finally, Adlerian parent educators believe that the parental method of training strongly affects the child's reactions and goals for behavior. Dreikurs and his coauthors (Dreikurs and Grey, 1990; Dreikurs and Soltz, 1964) do not endorse the use of punishment, indicating that it tends to result in power struggles and retaliation or revenge. Reward systems are perceived as bribes that result in a child's undue expectations to have things given to her or him and hence decrease the child's willingness for cooperation. The use of force is considered inappropriate, as it is neither democratic nor respectful and provides poor modeling. Excessive criticism is perceived as harmful for the child's self-esteem and self-respect and is viewed as leading the child to mistaken goals. As Dreikurs and Soltz point out, "We cannot build on weaknesses—only on strength" (1964, p. 107). Overprotection of the child is deemed equally inappropriate, as it fails to model reality for the child and may lead to false expectations. Further, it does not allow the child to use and strengthen her or his own resources in the attempt to solve problems, thus not preparing her or him for adult life. Instead of these methods, the use of Adlerian strategies is suggested.

Strategies. The two most important strategies of this school of thought are natural and logical consequences. Parents who use these strategies of training children rely on using naturally occurring or parentally predetermined consequences to the child's behavior to modify actions on the child's part. Specifically, natural consequences are the experiences or events that follow a child's behavior or action in the absence of parental intervention, that is, events that follow a child's action naturally and that affect the child's future behavior. For instance, the natural consequence of touching a hot stove is a painful burn that will teach the child not to touch a hot stove. Obviously, although natural consequences are powerful teaching tools, they are not always acceptable. Specifically, they are not appropriate in situations in which the child could be harmed, in which the natural consequence might be so far in the future that the child cannot make a logical connection between the behavior and the consequence, and in situations that do not have a natural consequence. In other words, using a natural consequence with a child who cannot swim but insists on playing closely by the river is not an appropriate parenting choice, as the child might fall into the water and drown. Using a natural consequence with a child who refuses to brush teeth is not appropriate, as the development of cavities might occur too late for the child to connect it to the refusal. Finally, if a parent does not find it appropriate for a child to read at the dinner table, the use of natural consequences is impossible as there is no inherent consequence to the behavior.

When the use of natural consequences is either not possible or not appropriate, logical consequences are designed to take their place. Logical consequences are the experiences or events that follow a child's behavior or action as determined previously by a parental decision to affect the child's behavior in a certain way. They are events designed by parents to make the child's actions safer or more acceptable to family or social values. For example, a mother who does not tolerate lateness for dinner might set up a logical consequence wherein the child who is late for dinner must eat the leftovers alone and must clean up the dishes afterward. Logical consequences are presented as choices that the child is allowed to make and are presented in *either-or* or *when-then* format. In other words, the parent presents the consequences in a manner that implies neither a restriction nor a punishment.

For instance, if a child is supposed to clean her or his room before being allowed to watch TV, this consequence would be presented as follows: "*When* you have cleaned your room, *then* you may watch TV." The parent would neither say, "You cannot watch TV until you have cleaned your room," as this would imply a restriction, nor say, "If you don't clean your room, there is no TV for you today," as this would imply a punishment. Instead, the focus is placed on giving the child a choice. A child with a new kitten who has been very rough with it might be told, "You may *either* pet the kitten gently *or* put it back in the box. You decide" (a logical consequence and choice), but not "Don't be so rough with the kitten, or I'll take it away from you and put it back in the box" (a punishment).

Logical consequences work only if they can be enforced and if they are used consistently. If the child does not follow through, the parent must be prepared to enforce the rule. Thus, if the child in the above example still plays roughly with the kitten, an appropriate parental response would be to say, "I see you decided not to be gentle with the kitten. I guess that means you decided that you don't want to play with it right now. Please take it back to its box." Then the parent sees to it that child takes the kitten to the box. Similarly, if the child in the TV example fails to clean the room, the parental response would be "I see you decided not to make your bed. I guess that means you decided that you don't want to watch TV." In both examples, it is important to note that as the parent enforces the consequence, she or he also points out again that the child has made a choice. A bargain had been made between child and parent, and when the child failed to follow through, the parent responded according to the terms that were set up beforehand. The parent does not respond to the child angrily, nor does the parent give nonverbal cues of misgivings or disrespect. Instead, the consequences are merely reiterated and enforced respectfully yet firmly.

To summarize, in setting up consequences, the parent has to be firm but respectful and must follow through consistently. Setting consequences and not following through firmly leaves the child doubtful about the parent's authority and ability to provide strength and guidance. This firmness, however, must be accompanied by encouragement to help the child discover her or his strengths and competencies. This encouragement may not just be verbal, but rather is also reflected in the parents' voice, body posture, and other nonverbal cues. Consequences are best set up in such a way as to be appropriate in most instances to provide the child with routine and predictability. Yet parents need to remain flexible within appropriate limits. It is best to use consequences to avoid giving attention inappropriately (i.e., without reinforcing the wrong behavior), to avoid power struggles, to avoid conflict that results in retaliation and revenge, and to avoid discouragement of the child that leads to feelings of inadequacy and incompetence.

Consequences can be decided upon by the parents in collaboration with the child, rendering decisions and choices even more democratic and meaningful. Consequences are best set up before a problem behavior recurs in order to anticipate and prepare—to be proactive, not reactive. This approach to parenting is designed to teach the child independence and respects the child's privacy, which will help the child recognize not only her or his own rights, but also the rights of others. Thus, it is the goal of Adlerian parent education to help the child function in and contribute to the family in a manner that is respectful and democratic, and enhances the self-esteem and free affective self-expression of the child and the entire family.

Parent Effectiveness Training

In the spirit of Rogers's humanistic theory, parent effectiveness trainers (Gordon, 1970) perceive children as competent problem solvers and believe that children can contribute to solutions to problems with their own helpful suggestions. These theorists believe that before a parent intervenes with a child, she or he must explore who owns the problem. There are three possibilities in this regard: the problem is owned by the child, the problem is owned by the parent, or there is no ownership of a problem by either the child or the parent.

If the child owns the problem, the parent is not directly affected, though she or he may be vicariously upset because of the caring the parent feels for the child. However, the issue is one that is more important and upsetting for the child. For instance, a child who is depressed because she or he has no one to play with is the owner of this particular problem. The parent might be indirectly affected by this problem and might feel compassion for the child, but the parent is not the owner of the problem. Similarly, if a parent is upset by the fact that the child does not keep her or his room tidy, the parent owns the problem. Generally, the child is not bothered by the messy room and hence is not affected by this issue, except vicariously by noting the parent's affect. Finally, if the child exhibits a behavior that satisfies a need for the child and is viewed by the child as fulfilling a purpose and this same behavior does not interfere with the parent's life, then there is no problem in the relationship, even if a third person does take offense.

Depending upon who is identified as the owner of the problem, parents will intervene in different manners. They will be advised by parent effectiveness trainers to use active listening skills if the problem is owned by the child and I-messages if the problem is owned by the parent. However, regardless of who owns a given problem, there are certain issues that a parent must be aware of when dealing with children. Most important, these theorists suggest that acceptance, understanding, and empathy must permeate the relationship between parent and child to foster an environment in which the child can mature and grow uninterruptedly according to her or his own needs and desires. The free unfolding of the child's ideal self and striving toward self-actualization must be accepted by the parent, as must the hypothesis that only the child can know what she or he ultimately needs to do to solve a problem. This requires a very specific family environment.

Environment.   Parental acceptance, honesty, and openness are critical factors in a family environment that allows the free unfolding of the child's self. They must be accompanied by open communication that helps the child to explore her or his own needs, desires, and, most important, affects. The parent must create an environment that is flexible and supportive of the child and in which the child feels supported, accepted, and understood. Such an environment includes the parent's willingness to meet the child in compromise by making changes in the environment and in the self that can foster the child's growth without impeding or hindering the parent in her or his own process of self-actualization. Thus, in an environment created by parents trained by humanist parent educators, the willingness on parents' parts to engage in environmental modification and parental change is a critical component in dealing with children. Further, parents who are trying to develop a supportive environment will avoid belittling the child and her or his perceived problems.

There are a large number of strategies that can interfere with open communication, despite the fact that they may appear to be designed to enhance it (Gordon, 1970; Popkin, 1983a, 1983b). For instance, some parents might use open communication as an excuse to interfere, meddle, or give advice. They might fail to grant the child her or his right to privacy and might offer solutions to problems. Some parents might attempt to moralize or threaten the child into changing behavior; others might imply that the child is never wrong. Other parents might attempt to distract the child from the problem, implying that it is not serious enough to be discussed or considered, whereas other parents might analyze the child and try to sway the child's decision by indicating that they (the parents) have more experience and know the best solutions. These examples of misguided ways of interacting with children that interfere with open communication are outlined and expanded upon in Table 13.2.

Strategies.   The misguided interventions that are part of a nonresponsive environment need to be replaced by more appropriate strategies for children to be able to mature and grow positively. The two most important parent effectiveness strategies that were devised by Gordon (1970) for that purpose are active listening and I-messages.

TABLE 13.2   Parental Interventions That Interfere with Open Communication

---

1. Attempting to manipulate the child into thinking like the parent
2. Using moralizing to convince the child to do things the parent's way
3. Parroting the child instead of listening for the underlying feelings or messages
4. Listening without acknowledging the child's feelings and without responding to the child's affect
5. Giving commands to keep situations or behaviors under control
6. Giving advice to convince the child or influencing the child with arguments and opinions
7. Distracting or placating the child to protect her or him from problems
8. Analyzing the child and trying to explain motives to her or him
9. Using sarcasm or ridicule to make the child see the folly of an attitude, belief, or feeling
10. Pretending or lecturing that greater experience gives the parent the right to decide how to solve a child's problems
11. Interrogating or questioning the child that distracts from the child's feeling
12. Withdrawing or diverting from the child's problem in the hope that the child will forget about it
13. Blaming or judging the child and giving the message that the child is at fault
14. Ignoring the child who expresses the need to talk or interact
15. Overidentifying with the child when the child needs the parent to be strong and not similarly hurt or confused
16. Counterattacking the child by pointing out how the child has been wrong in the past
17. Threatening the child with negative consequences for actions or feelings

Active Listening. Active listening is a five-step process designed to help parents understand their children better, especially in situations in which the child has identified that she or he has a problem. It is a process through which the parent expresses caring and concern, as well as acceptance and the genuine attempt to understand the child and to help the child arrive at a solution to the problem. It is done without advice giving and without lecturing; the problems outlined in Table 13.2 are avoided. The first step in the process of active listening is attentive listening. Parents are taught to open conversations and not only to listen to the actual content of the child's verbalization, but also to watch the child to listen for her or his feelings that may be expressed more readily through nonverbal communications. Parents keep their own talking to a minimum and, instead, give their child their full attention. Their own verbalizations are strictly designed to let the child know that the parent is indeed listening to and hearing the child.

The second step of active listening is the listening for feelings. The parent is encouraged to listen for the child's expression of affect and is reminded that feelings can never be wrong or inappropriate. In addition to listening to the feelings, the parent must also acknowledge to the child that the feelings were heard, understood, and, most important, accepted. The parent must express interest in finding out more about the child and her or his feelings and needs to communicate full acceptance to the child.

In the third step, the parent reflects the child's feelings back to the child in an attempt to connect the child's feeling to the content of the situation or problem that the child is describing. This step is often difficult for parents, as many are not used to talking about feelings, much less identifying them. Therefore, parents often need help in learning labels for feelings and in learning how to reflect these feelings back to their children. Learning to connect feelings to a context or to the content of the problem situation also presents a challenge for many parents. Much practice is often necessary with a clinician before a parent is ready to listen to a child's affect acceptingly and understandingly. Once the parent has understood the affect, has reflected it back to the child, and has placed it in a context for the child, problem solving can begin.

Looking for alternatives and predicting consequences are the problem-solving, and the fourth, step in the active listening process. This is not to imply that parents give advice or commands at this time. Quite to the contrary, in this step, parents help the child learn to problem-solve by helping her or him see alternatives or consequences for herself or himself. The child is not told what to do but is encouraged to develop her or his own course of action. This is best done by asking the child questions about what she or he thinks or would like to do, how she or he might have tackled similar problems in the past, what potential consequences might occur, and what could be done to change a given situation. The child is asked these questions to stimulate her or his own problem solving and creativity, not steer her or him toward a specific solution. This step is not to be misused as a manipulation to get the child to see the situation through the parent's eyes so that the child will respond the way the parent might want the child to respond.

The final step of active listening, and the one that is most frequently forgotten, is follow-up. The previous step of the active listening process had served to help the child devise a solution to a problem, and then the child was encouraged to attempt to implement the solution. To round out the active listening process, the parents must follow up with the child to investigate whether the child successfully implemented the solution and whether the implementation led to the desired results. Regardless of the success of the intervention, praise and encouragement are critical components of the follow-up stage. If the solution was unsuccessful and the child's problem was not solved, the active listening process can begin anew at this time.

Active listening takes much practice on parents' parts and is not easy to learn. Parents will need much encouragement while learning this new skill, and it is often possible to help them learn the skill through modeling it for them in the process of teaching it. Active listening, to reiterate, is most appropriate when the problem is owned by the child and when the parent is not directly, yet perhaps vicariously, affected by the problem. If the problem is owned by the parent, not by the child, active listening will not result in any solutions. Instead, I-messages will need to be used by the parent, as the child is not necessarily aware of the parents' affective state or response.

I-Messages. I-messages serve to inform the child about the parent's feelings and thus are the inverse of active listening, which served to help the parent understand the child's feelings. Whereas active listening was a five-step process, an I-message is delivered in one statement. However, this statement has four components, all of which have to be included at all times when I-messages are used. The first component of an I-message is designed to describe to the child the behavior or situation that causes the parent a problem without making a judgment about the behavior or situation. This part of the I-message usually begins with "When you...."

The second component explains to the child how the parent feels when faced with the behavior or situation outlined in the first component of the message. It always begins with "I feel...." The third component informs the child of the reason why this feeling occurs and how it interferes with the parent's well-being or peace of mind. As it is the explanatory section of the I-message, it always begins with "because...." The fourth, and final, section of the I-message describes an alternative behavior or situation for the child that the parent would prefer and that in the parent's opinion would solve her or his problem. This component is necessary, as a child needs to know how she or he can change or what is expected of her or him. Merely telling the child that she or he is doing something wrong without suggesting an alternative can leave the child struggling with what to do next. If at all possible, a choice should be given to the child with regard to what can be done to take care of the problem. This gives the child a level of control and helps the child to feel more included in the decision-making and problem-solving process. This section of the I-message often begins with "I would like you to...or...."

For instance, if a parent is bothered by the fact that, despite having made an agreement that the child will take out the garbage every evening, the child fails to do so, the parent may give the following message: "*When you* don't take out the garbage as you agreed to, *I feel* upset and treated unfairly *because* it leaves me working around smelly garbage in the kitchen. *I would like for you to* stick to our agreement and take out the garbage every evening *or* very early the next morning." Thus, the I-message serves to help the child learn to understand and respect others' feelings, as well as to give parents an avenue for communicating their feelings and reactions without anger and conflict. The I-message facilitates a courteous interaction between parent and child that respects the needs of both. Sometimes, however, it is unreasonable or impossible for the child to change. In this instance, it may be time for an environmental or a parental change.

→ Does it work?

Environmental Modification and Parental Change.   The use of the environmental modification technique implies that the identified problem of either the child or the parent may have been inherent in an environmental condition that is amenable to change. In this instance, a problem may occur neither because of the child's or the parent's direct behavior nor because of a parent's response to a child's behavior, but rather owing to environmental factors that are less than positive. The best strategy in such a case is to change a variable in the environment to take care of or remove the problem. For instance, in one family, two daughters had to share a bedroom, and the dresser and closet in it. Both children had been complaining for some time that the other child intruded into the sister's section of the dresser and closet. The parents had tried active listening with both children to find out whether the children could arrive at a solution, without success. Finally, the parents chose to modify the sisters' environment. They painted two of the four dresser drawers green and two of them red, assigning one daughter the green drawers and the other the red ones. Then they put a divider inside the closet, assigning one daughter the right side and the other the left. Both children were satisfied with this solution that clearly demarcated each child's territory.

It is also possible that occasionally, parents respond negatively to a child's behavior, attempt to change the child's behavior through an I-message, but recognize that the child's behavior is not changing. It is important for parents to evaluate whether the child's behavior truly needs to change or whether the parent is creating a problem that does not exist. In other words, humanistic parent educators recognize that parents make unreasonable requests of their children at times and that children do not always need to be the individuals to change their behaviors or attitudes. In such instances, it is best for the parent to change. For example, one mother was quite upset about her 14-year-old son's messy room. She had given numerous I-messages, had listened to his perspective on the problem, and finally realized that her son's room was his private space and should be under his direction. She therefore decided to change her own attitude about his room and to view his room as his private domain that had nothing to do with her need for cleanliness. She decided to let him keep his room as he wanted to keep it and distanced herself from the problem by not entering the room, something her son had suggested repeatedly. Further, as she was also bothered by what company might think if they caught a glimpse of the messy room, she decided to modify the environment as well, by keeping the door to his room shut, whenever guests were expected.

The strategies employed by parent effectiveness trainers clearly have as their goal effective and creative problem-solving ability, on both the child's and the parent's part. They further emphasize that children and parents deserve respect and acceptance, and that mutual understanding and caring are conducive to growth and maturation for all family members. Affective expression is valued and encouraged in this system of parenting and hence supplements the more behavioral-oriented approach of logical and natural consequences.

Behavior Modification

Parent educators of the behavior modification tradition are focused on behavior, as the label suggests. Affective expression and awareness are not the primary goals for these theorists. Behaviorally oriented parent educators, such as Krumboltz and Krumboltz (1972) and Patterson and Gullion (1974), believe that children are born helpless but learn to adapt to their environment through interaction with it. They explain that most behavior is learned from others and can therefore be retrained and changed through the learning principles outlined by behavior modification and social learning theory. Because the emphasis is on the learned nature of most behavior, this implies that not only children's responses are learned in the interaction with their environment, but also the parents'. In other words, these theorists acknowledge that, just as parental behavior can shape and influence a child's behavior, the child's behavior can shape and influence the parents' behavior. Thus, the parent educator, while focusing on modifying the child's behavior, must also pay attention to how the parents' behavior is reinforced and punished by the child's actions. For instance, this educator would point out for the parent that the parent's frequent use of spanking is reinforced by the child's subsequent quietness and withdrawal which gives the parent some time to herself or himself. Recognizing the interaction of reinforcement and punishment between parent and child can be critical to understanding behavior sequences that occur repeatedly. Nevertheless, the greatest focus of this type of parent education is on the modification of children's behavior. This modification is best accomplished in an environment designed from a behaviorist's or social learning theorist's perspective.

Environment. In a behavioral environment, parents are viewed as authorities and as the persons responsible for maximizing the opportunity for learning in the environment. Parents set up rewards and punishments to steer children's behavior and are ultimately responsible for the child's actions. Parents have to decide for themselves what may be desirable and undesirable behaviors for their children, and it is in this sense that parental values enter into the equation. However, once the desirability and timing of behaviors have been decided upon by a parent, the direction of the behavior can be achieved easily through setting up specific contingencies and conditions in the child's life. To be successful in this endeavor, parents must be organized and must have a clear understanding of the child's behavior and its frequency and location of occurrence. Vagueness is not tolerated well in a behavioral approach to parent education. Instead, in a behavioral environment, rules and expectations are clear, as are the contingencies for breaking the rules or violating the expectations. Therefore, it is important for parents to establish how they want their child to behave, in which circumstances, and at what times.

Finally, in a behavioral or social learning environment, parents are well aware of the power of modeling, recognizing that all of their behaviors are likely to be repeated by the child. Thus, to prevent certain behaviors in a child, the parent should not engage in that behavior herself or himself. For instance, if a parent has decided that physical aggression is not a value that is acceptable in her or his home, the use of physical aggression cannot only be forbidden to the child, but must also not be modeled by the parent. Thus, the use of corporal punishment in such a household would be a contradiction as it provides a model for physical acting out to the child. Social learning theorists agree that inconsistencies between parental values and behaviors are recognized by children and that the child will model after the more obvious event, which is the parent's behavior. Although modeling and other behavioral principles can thus work inadvertently, they can also be applied systematically and efficiently to control children's behavior.

Strategies. A number of sophisticated strategies have been developed to develop, maintain, eliminate, and modify behaviors and emotional responses and can be taught to parents by behavioral parent educators for use in the child's home. These strategies are identical to the strategies used by behaviorally oriented child clinicians and have been covered in detail in Chapter Twelve. Their application to parent education should be clear from this prior discussion. Just as reinforcement can be used in a therapy room to increase the frequency of a desired behavior, so too can a parent be taught to use a similar reinforcer in the home to modify the child's response in that environment. Parents can be taught to help children develop new behaviors through the processes of modeling or shaping and can be taught to recognize and appropriately reinforce successive approximations to a new behavior. Parents can be taught how to use alternative strategies to punishment to eliminate undesirable behaviors, such as extinction and reinforcement of incompatible behaviors. Parents can be instructed in the use of reinforcement schedules and in the appropriate timing and nature of reinforcers. They can be made aware of the powerful uses of modeling and of how their own children may control the parents' behaviors.

Although the teaching of behavioral principles to parents sounds relatively easy and straightforward, parents often need close supervision and monitoring in the early stages of using behavioral principles, as they tend not to have sufficient patience to allow the procedures to take hold. Warning parents of potential increases in the child's misbehavior in the early phases of the implementation of behavior programs serves to keep parents cooperative and patient. The behavioral parent educator will spend much time monitoring the parent's implementation of behavioral programs to ascertain that reinforcement is done correctly.

During all the time spent with parents, it remains the goal of all behavioral parent educators to teach parents the skills necessary to aid in the development, maintenance, and elimination of behaviors, as well as to facilitate the modification of behaviors and emotional responses. The focus remains on external control mechanisms of children's responses and not the development of inherent problem-solving potential or psychological growth. Empathy, self-actualization, acceptance, and other constructs endorsed by Adlerian or Rogerian parent educators are not generally primary considerations of behaviorally oriented theorists.

Practical Implementation

The overview of the three primary approaches to parent education served to introduce the novice therapist to a number of parenting strategies that can be effective in creating behavioral and affective change in children. The programs discussed so far are each individually focused on particular goals while ignoring some of the benefits other programs may offer. For instance, behavioral strategies focus primarily on behavior changes, while parent effectiveness training is more concerned with the expression and acceptance of affects and needs. In reality, parents are faced with a variety of situations with their children, and thus need a variety of possible responses. Exclusive focus on one arena or another is not sufficient for the well-rounded therapist or parent.

Using a self psychological model to parent education results in the use of an integrative approach to teaching parenting skills. This model (Brems, 1990, 1996; Brems and Sohl, 1995), based on Kohut's (see Kohut, 1984; Kohut and Wolf, 1978) theory of development and psychotherapy, integrates behavioral, humanistic, and Adlerian strategies into a developmental framework that is responsive to children's and parents' needs when they present for treatment. This responsiveness to all individuals involved ascertains that the parents are not only cognitively, but also emotionally, capable to apply the parenting strategies taught to them by parent educators.

Self Psychological Principles

According to self psychological principles, development of the self is facilitated by three primary processes between the child and the caretaker: mirroring, idealization, and twinship (Kohut, 1984). Mirroring is the process through which a child learns self-confidence and a healthy self-appraisal of her or his own skills and capabilities. An infant is not born with this innate sense of self-respect, self-esteem, or realistic self-appraisal. These are characteristics and skills that need to be learned. This process of learning occurs through interaction with the environment and important people within it. The interactions that facilitate the development of self-esteem and realistic self-appraisal, that is, the mirroring pole of the self, are referred to as mirroring. Mirroring affirms the child's separateness, value or worthwhileness, and realistic limitations. This happens in the interaction with caretakers who show spontaneous pride and joy over the infant, who label feelings and respond to affect, who participate with the infant, and who provide developmentally appropriate feedback. The mirroring caretaker does not routinely exhibit hostility, indifference, or excessive criticism toward the child. As the child is exposed to these behaviors on the caretaker's part, she or he slowly begins to internalize these beliefs about herself or himself. As parents demonstrate for the child that she or he is worthwhile by expressing pride in the child, the child slowly learns to feel proud of herself or himself. This process of internalization is enhanced by the occasional failure of the parent to be available for mirroring. It is in the absence of the mirroring caretaker that the child has to learn to depend on her or his own internal resources to maintain self-esteem and to continue to decide realistically what she or he can and cannot do. *Continued* absence of a mirroring other, however, results in the failure of the child to develop an internalized sense of self-esteem and ability to appraise her or his own abilities, leaving the child dependent upon external sources of this type of feedback. Because these are not always available, the child is left feeling unsure and unable to evaluate her or his own value and capabilities.

Similarly, the process of idealization is critical to the child's development of a sense of direction and strength. The infant is not born with an innate sense of strength or values that can direct her or his life, that is, an idealized pole of the self. Children need to learn about their own strength to survive, as well as about rules, values, and limits through interactions with the environment. They need consistent contact with a caretaker who has the strength to support and reassure the child, even in difficult situations; a caretaker who can model values and enforce rules without being threatening or menacing; a caretaker who regulates internal tension for the infant by limit-setting and by providing external structure and stability upon which the infant can come to rely. As the child is embedded in this type of relationship, she or he will slowly internalize these values and strengths into the developing self. As with the mirroring pole of the self, the development of an internalized sense of strength and values is greatly facilitated by the occasional failure of the caretaker. Again, it is in the absence of the caretaker that the child learns to rely on her or his own resources to comfort herself or himself and to make her or his own decisions about what is right and wrong. *Consistent* failure, however, leaves the child without an internalized structure and sense of ability to cope and to determine values and rules, leaving her or him floundering with regard to how to behave and how to direct her or his own life.

Finally, through the process of twinship, the child recognizes that she or he is like other human beings and can feel part of humanity. The infant is not born with an innate sense of belonging, nor does the young child know clearly where her or his interests and talents lie. Instead, the child has to learn about skills and interests and has to feel a sense of belongingness through her or his interaction with the environment. Children need a caretaker who is willing to allow them to imitate and model after the parent, who feels sufficiently secure to allow the child to develop peer relationships that can foster positive skill and talent development, and who does not strive to isolate the child. In the process of modeling after a significant figure in their lives, children begin to feel a likeness with others and kinship with humanity as a whole. Further, by striving to be like others who are important to the child, she or he also learns new skills and talents and can learn to recognize where her or his strengths and interests lie. For instance, a young boy who watches his father shave is often observed to imitate the father's behavior in an attempt to be more like him. In this process, the child learns a new skill in addition to feeling part of the male half of the human race. The process of twinship is also critical for the child in the context of peer relationships and in the school environment, where the child's desire to belong and to fit in with others leads to new learning and the mastery of new skills and talents.

This process of internalizing a sense of belonging and a sense of what is inherently interesting for the child is greatly facilitated by the occasional failure of the caretaker. As in acquiring mirroring and idealizing skills, the child acquires a continuous sense of belonging in the absence of the twinship caretaker. Further, it is in the absence of an immediate model that the child will need to rely on memory to attempt new skills and may alter behaviors slightly to fit her or his own needs. The child will then develop an acceptance of differentness that does not threaten her or his overall sense of belonging. During this time, the child may recognize new interests and talents that would have remained unexplored had there always been a model for the child. The development of skills is of particular importance, as it provides the bridge (called the tension arc of the self) between the child's sense of self-esteem (mirroring pole of the self) and the child's ideals and values (idealizing pole of the self). In other words, only if the child has developed the skills to pursue her or his goals and values, will her or his self-esteem remain intact.

As all three of these growth-facilitating interpersonal processes are initiated in the child's first few days or weeks of life, it is critical that parents understand them well and can facilitate or provide them. As Stern (1985) has demonstrated through numerous research projects, most parents intuitively make themselves available as mirroring, idealizable, and twinship objects. In the first function, they provide nurturance, both physiological and psychological, and use attunement to understand the child's affects and to help the child learn the labels for these affects. Parents inadvertently provide guidance and strength to their children and teach them about rules and values. Finally, through early shared play activity and through allowing the child to partake in the parents' as well as friends' lives, children learn new skills and feel part of a family or larger group. However, not all parents understand the importance of these processes, nor do all parents engage in the appropriate behaviors that foster a child's growth and self development. Some parents have to be taught how to provide mirroring, idealization, and twinship for their children. Because these somewhat abstract self psychological labels have very concrete behavioral translations, they lend themselves well to being taught to parents in the attempt to make parents better able to facilitate their child's development. Thus, self psychology is inherently relevant to parent education.

Application to Parent Education

As self psychology is a developmental model of human behavior, its application to parent education also contains a strong developmental focus. A self psychologically oriented parent educator begins the training with a thorough overview and discussion of child development. Specifically, she or he will help parents to understand the milestones and tasks children go through at different ages and will help parents to understand what can be expected of children of different ages with regard to cognition, moral behavior, physical ability, emotional awareness and expression, language, and social adjustment and interaction. Although this information is initially delivered generically, it is then directly applied to the parents' child. In other words, the theoretical information is translated into actual behaviors that the parent can observe in her or his own child, as well as into behaviors that the parent can expect or can steer the child toward in interactions with her or him. A thorough understanding of children's development, especially with regard to cognitive and language skills, is thus critical to a self psychological parent education program. Because this information was covered in Chapter Three, it will not be repeated here.

In applying the self psychological processes that are hypothesized to facilitate a child's development, it is necessary to look at the contribution of each mirroring, idealization, and twinship. The most critical component of mirroring between parent and child is the communication of empathy, acceptance, and openness that facilitates the expression of affect and the unfolding of the developing self. This sense of acceptance was also appropriately emphasized by humanistic parent educators such as Gordon (1970), who incorporated active listening for the purpose of communication of affect as a primary component of effective parenting. The empathic and affectively permissive interaction between parents and children is critical not only to the child's internalization of self-esteem, but also to the child's realistic recognition of what she or he is and is not capable of. This feedback best takes the form of nurturing behaviors or verbalizations that are not critically but constructively relevant to the child and that assist the child in making decisions about what she or he can and cannot do. For example, an empathically attuned parent would not encourage a 2-year-old child to attempt to use a pair of scissors, whereas that same encouragement not only would be appropriate for a 5-year-old, but would also challenge this child to stretch beyond current skills. If the parent were to challenge the young child into attempting skills clearly beyond the child's capacity, this child is likely to become self-conscious, cautious, and fearful of learning new skills as she or he would not have many experiences of success. On the other hand, never challenging a child to try new behaviors leaves a child dependent, unable to care for the self, and with low self-confidence. Teaching parents how enhancing self-esteem through praise and pride interacts with challenging the child to try new tasks at a developmentally appropriate rate is the primary purpose of teaching parents to serve as mirroring others for their child.

Because nurturance is a critical component in this process and happens to be a label that can be understood by most parents, mirroring parenting strategies are labeled *nurturing parenting strategies* for the purposes of parent education.

The two most critical components of idealization between parent and child are the parent's ability to provide strength and guidance and the parent's willingness to allow the child to look up to the parent for direction and focus. A parent who is unable to allow a child to idealize her or him will not be able to provide enough stability and direction for the child to feel safe and supported. The feedback given to children by parents not only is critical to the child's sense of direction, but also serves to help the child assess which behaviors and values are and are not acceptable in her or his environment, both familial and cultural. A sense of stability and direction is provided through several parenting techniques developed by behaviorists who very much favor the role of authority for parents, as well as by Adlerians who stress that rules and consequences must be clearly spelled out for children to know what is expected of them. Parents who cannot be strong for their children often leave their children feeling weak as well. Who has not observed several toddlers comparing and bragging about the strength of their fathers! These children need a strong other to identify with to convince themselves of their own strength. Idealization also brings with it the need to teach children rules and regulations. As such, parents must communicate to the child what is acceptable behavior in the family or larger context. It is through the process of idealization that children are acculturated. In other words, ethnicity, religious beliefs, socioeconomic status, and so forth may play a large role in which values and rules a parent teaches a child. Thus, teaching parents that setting rules and boundaries and being a strong role model for their children is important to the child's development of a sense of direction and strength and is critical to helping them become able to serve as an idealized other. As the strategies in this category of parenting are largely focused on guidance, and as this is an understandable term for most parents, it was adopted to reflect this aspect of parenting. Idealizing parenting strategies are hence labeled *guidance strategies* for the purposes of parent education.

The most critical component of twinship between parent and child is the facilitation of a sense of kinship or belonging. Belongingness is an important component of many Adlerian parenting strategies and is considered an important motivator for human behavior. It is through the wish for companionship and sameness that the child strives to imitate and model after others, thus learning skills and new behaviors. Behavioral parent educators of the social learning school have long recognized that modeling is a powerful means of teaching children new behaviors. Although twinship begins in the family, parents also have to understand that twinship needs are extremely relevant in the child's world outside the home. Children model after teachers when they first enter school, then switch their attention to same-gender peers and finally to a mixed-gender peer group in adolescence. Parents who do not allow their child to participate in group activities or friendships outside the home deprive their child of important sources of twinship. It is through the maximization of the number of models available in a child's life that she or he maximizes the number of skills attempted and imitated. A child may well realize a talent in an area in which parents never performed, through imitating a teacher or peer. As most parents can relate to and understand the need for belonging and companionship, the twinship parenting strategies are labeled *companionship strategies* for the purposes of parent education.

Mirroring, idealization, and twinship are needs that not only facilitate maturation and growth in children, but also maintain levels of adaptation and render individuals increasingly skilled and sophisticated in adulthood. Every human being, regardless of age, enjoys and needs nurturance, guidance, and companionship. In fact, many parents are very needy of these same interactions in their own lives and often strive to find them wherever they can. Unfortunately, many parents whose children are presented for treatment grew up without appropriate nurturance, guidance, and companionship as children themselves and are still searching for these interactions in their current adult life with a zeal that is appropriate only in childhood. These parents not infrequently turn to their own children to have these needs met, thus overburdening them in a developmentally inappropriate fashion (Miller and Ward, 1996). Specifically, although parents can be expected to serve as mirroring, idealizable, twinship caretakers for their children, their children cannot be expected to do the same for their parents (though they may occasionally and inadvertently do so).

The ability to recognize parents who are depleted themselves and who have not completed their own self development is critical to the good parent educator and to the individual tailoring of parent education interventions. Parents who have many of the same needs as their children will need to be approached with more patience than parents who are developmentally mature and capable of providing for their children's basic psychological needs. Thus, parents in the former category should always be referred for therapy themselves to help them strengthen their own self while the child's clinician teaches them how to interact more appropriately with their children. Parents who can take care of their own psychological needs and have appropriate external sources to help them do so in times of stress are ready to learn about self psychologically oriented parenting strategies from their child's clinician. They can be taught how to nurture and guide a child and to help her or him feel as though she belongs, without the need for supportive therapeutic intervention for themselves from another therapist. Nevertheless, even with these more mature parents, parent educators who follow the self psychological model will apply to the parents themselves many of the very skills they are teaching for use with children. This is even more critical, however, with the depleted parents who are in treatment themselves.

As parent educators help parents recognize a child's needs and identify appropriate parenting strategies from the nurturance, guidance, and companionship categories, they also apply the same techniques to the parents. This approach serves several purposes. First, most skills are best learned through observation of a model and through imitation. Thus, if a parent educator models active listening with the parent, this same parent can then better apply the skill to the child. Further, parents who feel supported and guided themselves are more likely to be able to provide strength and guidance for their children. Parents who are taught what to expect developmentally from their child will be better able to challenge and praise their child in developmentally appropriate ways. Parents who feel understood and accepted, as opposed to blamed and scrutinized, will be more likely to extend the same acceptance to others in their own lives. While the application of self psychologically driven parenting strategies is possible in any type of therapy setting, group settings are particularly amenable to this approach. In a group setting, parents not only deal with the parent educator, but can also learn vicariously through the problems presented by other parents. They can model after other group participants and can learn to apply their new skills with other adults in the group before testing them in their home with their children. The supportiveness that develops in parent education groups informed by self psychology is often an extremely up-lifting experience for parents who have struggled alone to help themselves and their child (Brems, Baldwin, and Baxter, 1993).

Environment

The environment endorsed by self psychological parent educators is one that contains nurturing and strong caretakers who can provide for the basic psychological needs of their children. These adults can provide limits and direction to children, share responsibility for problem solving, and respect and accept all individuals involved. They create an atmosphere of affective availability and mutual support. They are neither afraid to provide realistic feedback and structure in a child's life, nor are they afraid to listen to a child's concerns and alter their own behavior based upon this feedback. They are flexible, yet have standards; they are supportive, yet have limits; they are willing to include their children in their lives, yet also have a life of their own. Such an environment will foster healthy self development in the child and will result in a child who is realistically self-confident, aware, and responsive to appropriate rules and values and who feels part of a secure and caring family. To create such an environment, parents have to know about nurturance, guidance, and companionship strategies and must apply them consistently and predictably. Their occasional failures will not lead to disaster; in fact, they are likely to foster more independence and growth in the child as they encourage internalization of skills.

Strategies

Self psychologically informed parenting techniques are virtually limitless; can be designed creatively and independently by parents, teachers, and clinicians; are flexibly adapted to individual, familial, or environmental needs; and can be drawn from numerous sources, including the three parenting models presented in this chapter. All specific techniques, however, can be grouped into the three overriding categories of nurturance strategies, guidance strategies, and companionship strategies. These three groupings of strategies are used to outline children's specific needs and provide parents with a framework for responding to their children. Although specific techniques will be mentioned as each category of strategies is discussed, this is not to imply that these specific interventions are the only ones available. Parents and clinicians will find that they will develop their own additional techniques as new situations and behaviors arise.

Nurturing Strategies.   Nurturing strategies are all directed toward helping the child internalize a sense of self-esteem, self-respect, and realistic self-appraisal. They share numerous characteristics that are critical to all of them. Specifically, nurturance strategies ascertain that the parent exhibits spontaneous pride, joy, and pleasure in the child and that the child feels that the parent accepts, enjoys, and confirms the child's accomplishments and achievements. These strategies are effective only if the parent is developmentally appropriate in the behavior she or he rewards in the child. For instance, a 1-year-old may be responded to with pride for rolling a ball in the parent's direction, as this is truly an achievement for this infant. However, the same behavior by a 5-year-old child would not result in the same expression of pride, but rather in a challenge for the child to move beyond this skill, perhaps by encouraging the child to throw the ball to the parent.

Nurturing strategies also require that parents label feelings, respond to affects they observe in the child, and never disavow a child's feelings. In fact, nurturing the child means accepting the child's feelings, even if the parent disagrees with them or does not understand them entirely. Hostility, indifference, and nonconstructive criticism are directly opposed to nurturing and do not fit in a self psychologically informed parent education program. Given the developmental necessity of nurturing interventions on a parent's part, these strategies cannot be overused. In fact, they should be used often and regularly as they confirm for the child the parent's willingness to be involved with the child, to enjoy the child, and to help the child identify and express feelings.

Examples of nurturance parenting strategies can be as straightforward as cuddling, touching, expressing loving feelings toward the child, encouraging the child, and caring for the child physically. However, also in this category are positive reinforcement (Krumboltz and Krumboltz, 1972) and active listening (Gordon, 1970), two skills borrowed from other parent education programs that must be trained and taught to parents by a skilled parent educator to ascertain their correct use. Both positive reinforcement and active listening meet the criteria of nurturing skills as they set up a positive interaction between parent and child. The use of positive reinforcement is particularly useful if applied not only while trying to develop a new behavior, but also to maintain an existing one. For instance, praising the child for having behaved well is an important nurturing use of positive reinforcement that is often overlooked by parents who tend to focus on the child's negative behaviors. Active listening is particularly useful in helping the child identify and express affects. It is most truly in the spirit of nurturance if the parent is able to help the child clarify feelings for herself or himself without interfering with them and without attempting to change them or solve the problem to which they are connected. I-messages can also fall into the category of nurturance strategies if they serve to help clarify feelings and model the expression of affect. However, they also fit some of the criteria for guidance strategies and hence overlap these two categories of self psychologically oriented parenting strategies.

Guidance Strategies.   Guidance strategies are all directed toward helping the child learn the rules and values of the family and larger environment and to provide the child with a sense of strength and direction. Although there are many strategies that can lead to these goals, all share numerous characteristics. Specifically, guidance strategies ensure that parents spontaneously respond in a way that provides security, reassurance, and guidance and that parents provide uplifting care that allows the child to glean a sense of strength from the interaction with the caretaker. They require the caretaker to regulate tension for the child by setting limits and providing external structure and stability upon which the child can rely before the child has developed these limits and boundaries for herself or himself. Parents who use guidance strategies successfully are also self-confident enough to allow the child to idealize them. For instance, if a child openly admires a skill the parent is engaged in, the parent would respond with pride and confidence, not by belittling the skill or by indicating that she or he was only able to perform the skill by chance. In other words, parents who are able to guide and can allow idealization for the purpose of modeling strength for their child respond to the child with strength, confidence, and caring.

As children have a developmental need for guidance, these strategies can be used often. However, as they also have a strong component of limit-setting and boundary enforcement, they can be, but should not be, overused. Finding a balance to the use of guidance strategies is often a challenge for parents who first learn these skills. However, this problem is generally easily solved by ascertaining that the parent also uses nurturance strategies freely. Parents should never be frightened to use these strategies when the child obviously asks for them or needs them, that is, when the child clearly flounders, feels weak, or is incapable of finding a solution alone.

Guidance strategies range from simply being with the child in difficult situations, hugging the child to communicate confidence, or waving to a child who is separating from the parent physically and appears unsure to the sophisticated use of several behavioral and Adlerian parenting strategies. Behavioral strategies that fall into this category are extinction, time out, and the reinforcement of incompatible behaviors. Through the use of all of these procedures, the parent sets rules and places limits on the child's behavior. Although these rules might not always be explicit, the strategies are still in the spirit of guidance. Similarly, logical and natural consequences guide a child's behavior and demonstrate that the parent is ultimately in charge and is strong enough to enforce contingencies. However, these strategies are always very explicit and as such very clear in their teaching value. Finally, I-messages can be guidance strategies in that the parent identifies acceptable behaviors for the child. By giving the child a choice of acceptable behaviors, the parent models for the child that the child is capable of setting limits and boundaries herself or himself and facilitates the internalization of rules and values tremendously. Further, I-messages often have a nurturing component (as pointed out previously) and thus are a very safe guidance strategy that can be used often and with confidence.

Companionship Strategies.   Companionship strategies are all directed toward helping the child feel a sense of belonging and kinship, facilitating the learning of skills, and identifying talents. Although there are numerous strategies in this category as well, they too share a number of common characteristics. Specifically, companionship strategies ensure that parents provide activities in which the child can share and that result in opportunities for imitation and modeling. They stress that parents must allow the child relationships with people outside the family that can foster positive skill and talent development that would not be available for imitation within the family. In other words, isolation of a child is inappropriate and never recommended. In fact, it is this component of a child's development that suggests that daycare and baby-sitters even early in a child's life can be used very appropriately toward the child's growth and maturation. Companionship strategies also can be used to point out to parents that children are more likely to imitate what they see being done, as opposed to what they hear being endorsed. This difference in attitudes or values versus behaviors is critical for parents to understand as it can be used to explain why some strategies, such as the use of corporal punishment, are not effective, as they may merely serve to model inappropriate behavior.

Companionship strategies are often focused positively, much like nurturance strategies, and hence can be used freely and as often as possible. Obviously, a child should not be forced to participate in an activity under the guise that it would provide an opportunity for modeling. Strategies in this category can be as simple as frequent parent–child play, allowing the child to share in activities (such as watching and helping a father bake cookies or watching and helping a mother washing a car), allowing sleepovers and parties, facilitating child–friend and child–teacher contacts, enrolling the child in extracurricular activities, to sophisticated strategies adapted from behavioral, Adlerian, and humanistic parent educators. For instance, parental change and environmental modification (Gordon, 1970) are in the spirit of companionship as they model flexibility for the child and give the child input into difficult decisions. Modeling is obviously a much-used behavioral strategy that can be employed not only inadvertently or without planning, but also deliberately to teach or change behavior (Patterson and Gullion, 1974).

All self psychologically informed parenting strategies (summarized in Table 13.3) in unison will aid the parent and the child in the journey toward the ultimate goal which is the development of a cohesive, vigorous, and orderly self for the child. The cohesiveness of the self helps the child maintain her or his self-confidence and realistic self-appraisal during challenging times. The vigor of the self provides the child with adequate strength and direction to remain focused and safe even in difficult circumstances. Order of the self facilitates coping and self-identity for the child even when circumstances are trying and likely to threaten the child's sense of belonging and ability. The child who is raised by a parent informed by a self psychological model of parent training will have direction with

TABLE 13.3   Self Psychological Parenting Strategies

Strategy	Needs for	Specific Techniques
Nurturing Strategies	■ acceptance ■ labeling of feelings ■ feedback about performance	■ cuddling ■ touching ■ loving ■ providing for physical needs ■ positive reinforcement ■ active listening ■ I-messages
Guidance Strategies	■ guidance ■ strength ■ limit setting ■ structure	■ supporting the child ■ comforting the child ■ natural consequences ■ logical consequences ■ reinforcement of incompatible behavior ■ extinction ■ time out ■ I-messages
Companionship Strategies	■ belongingness ■ companionship ■ skill acquisition ■ interest exploration	■ parent-and-child play ■ allowing sleepovers ■ encouraging exchanges with nonfamily members ■ parental change ■ environmental modification ■ modeling

healthy goals, self-esteem, and the capacity to differentiate and communicate feelings effectively. Further, this child will be empathic and respectful of others' needs.

Summary and Concluding Thoughts

This chapter provided an overview of the primary parent education strategies that therapists tend to use. It also provided a conceptual framework that integrates these strategies in a meaningful and comprehensive manner to facilitate the well-rounded development of children. The material in this chapter, summarized in Table 13.4, hopefully has clarified for the therapist in training that parent education often is a critical component of a child's treatment as it is the therapist's best way to create changes in the child's home environment. Although parent education is not supposed to provide therapy for the adults in the

TABLE 13.4 Comparison of the Three Primary Parenting Education Programs with the Self Psychological Program

Program	Assumptions	Environment	Strategies	Goals
Adlerian Logical Consequences	■ inherent capacity to develop in healthy, effective ways ■ grow within the family system ■ want acceptance ■ want the common good	■ encouragement that fosters self-respect ■ democratic process ■ joint work toward common goals	■ natural consequences ■ logical consequences ■ encouragement	■ foster competence to function in and contribute to family ■ communicate openly
Humanistic Parent Effectiveness Training	■ children as competent problem solvers ■ children need acceptance	■ parental honesty, acceptance, and openness ■ open communication	■ active listening ■ I-messages ■ environmental modification ■ parental change	■ effective, creative problem-solving ■ mutual acceptance
Behavior Modification Training	■ children learn to adapt to environment ■ all behavior is learned ■ feelings are of secondary importance	■ parents as authority ■ maximization of learning opportunity ■ parents control behavior through setting contingencies	■ reinforcement ■ shaping ■ modeling ■ extinction ■ time out ■ satiation	■ develop, maintain, eliminate behaviors and emotional reponses
Self Psychological Parent Education	■ need for strength, nurturance, and companionship ■ use of interaction with the environment to develop a self	■ nurturing, strong caretakers who are available for modeling ■ shared responsibility for problem solving ■ availability of support and empathy ■ acceptance	■ nurturance strategies ■ guidance strategies ■ companionship strategies	■ cohesive, orderly, strong self ■ awareness of affect ■ empathy with and caring for others

child's life, it does provide empathy and understanding for them. It is hoped this support will make them better able to provide the same understanding and empathy for their children. Knowledge is power, and nowhere is imparting knowledge more important than with parents who are struggling to help a child improve and feel better.

In addition to interacting with parents around educational issues, the therapist will also consult with parents on numerous issues over the course of a child's therapy. Although parent consultation includes a wide variety of therapist-parent interactions, it never includes therapy for the parent. The relationship between parent and clinician remains clearly defined as consultative or educational, never therapeutic. This guideline prevents the clinician from entering into a dual relationship with the child or the parent.

Parent consultation implies meetings with parents to keep them up to date on treatment developments of the child's therapy, to answer questions, to assess the child's behavior in contexts other than the therapy room, to help parents recognize the value of treatment for the child, and to make termination decisions. Through consultations, the therapist keeps parents involved in a child's treatment and may prevent premature terminations. The more involved parents are willing to be, the better. Consultation often involves the teaching of parenting strategies and may open the door to such an intervention even with resistant parents.

CHAPTER

14 Endings

*T*ermination is the unfortunate word that has been chosen to describe the process of ending treatment and of saying good-bye. This choice of terminology appears so unfortunate because of the pictures a mind's eye will conjure upon hearing the word termination: Some think of death, others think of the cessation of any link between client and clinician, others even link the term with killing. In truth, termination is merely the ending of the relationship between the client and the therapist as it existed up to date. However, in reality, the bond between the two people who worked toward the growth of one of them can never be broken completely. Nothing will ever undo the work these people have done together or the special feeling they developed for each other. The memories of their joint efforts and the benefits reaped from their work will remain with both individuals for a lifetime.

Nevertheless, ending therapy is a bittersweet event, for both the child and the clinician. It is bitter because it means severing a relationship that has come to be of great importance to the child, and often also to the therapist. It is sweet because of what it implies: the elimination of symptoms and establishment of emotional stability and health of the client. The ending or termination of treatment is, after all, the universal goal of all therapies, regardless of the client's symptoms and the therapist's theoretical and practical approach to treatment. As such, ending is not only inevitable, but also desirable. Nevertheless, therapists and clients alike often dread endings and turn terminations into sad occurrences that sometimes overshadow the joyousness of the event. In this chapter, termination will be explored from various angles. Some terminations are indeed sad because they were agreed upon neither by the client nor by the therapist, but forced by external factors. Other terminations are indeed happy because they signal arrival and growth. Regardless of how an ending has come about, the therapist is responsible for making it as productive and positive for the child as possible. Termination need not be unpleasant, but rather can be seen as a cause for celebration, as a reaffirmation of the relationship as one that is oriented toward growth, and as an integral part of the complete therapy process (O'Conner, 2000). In fact, Sigmund Freud himself is often quoted as seeing therapy from the second session on as a termination process, that is, a process of learning to say good-bye to important people in one's life without feeling overwhelmed, abandoned, alone, or rejected. It will be in this more positive light that termination will be discussed in this chapter.

Types of Endings

There are numerous ways in which treatment can be ended or interrupted (Cangelosi, 1997). The most desirable reason for ending is certainly the natural termination that occurs because treatment goals have been reached and both individuals agree that the client is ready to face her or his life on her or his own. Such mutually agreed upon terminations are, if not rare, at least much less frequent than premature terminations. In fact, although exact figures vary quite a bit in the literature, attrition rates due to premature terminations range from approximately 30 to 70 percent (e.g., Novick, Benson, and Rembar, 1981). Reasons for premature terminations vary almost as widely as the prevalence figures, but some patterns have emerged. A study by Novick, Benson, and Rembar (1981) revealed a number of important factors that appeared related to premature terminations. All of these factors seem to hold up well clinically and hence are worth mentioning here. For instance, Novick, Benson, and Rembar (1981) reported that the age of a child appears to have an effect, with older children and older adolescents being more likely to drop out of treatment prematurely than young children and young adolescents. A child who lives with her or his single or married mother is more likely to remain in treatment than a child living with a single father or with neither biological parent. The closer a family lives to the clinic at which the child is being seen for treatment, the more likely that a natural termination will be allowed to occur. As a parent's, especially a mother's, socioeconomic status and level of education increase, the likelihood of the child being taken out of therapy prematurely decreases. Further, privately sought therapy is less likely to end before the child is ready to end than is therapy that was initiated because of legal action.

Reasons for premature terminations can be grouped into three categories: therapist-initiated reasons [also called forced terminations (Novick, 1982)], client-initiated reasons [also called unilateral terminations (Novick, 1982)], and externally initiated reasons (e.g., Coppolillo, 1987). Therapist-initiated reasons include such factors as the ending of a practicum or internship for a trainee, illness or geographic relocation of the therapist, countertransference, or inability to establish a working relationship with a child. Client-initiated reasons for children include not only the child's, but also the parents' or family's actions. Thus, these factors may include a geographic relocation of the family, sudden illness of a child or a parent responsible for the child's transportation to and from the clinic, and a family's or parent's arbitrary reason to quit therapy, perhaps for reasons that are attributable to resistance to treatment. Finally, externally initiated reasons, which, of the three categories, are least likely to occur, may include the closure of a clinic because of lack of funding, incompatible clinic and family schedules, or interference by schools or other agencies in the child's treatment.

Obviously, some of these reasons are quite genuine and are not necessarily under a person's (either therapist, child, or parent) control. For instance, a family move may not be realistically delayed because of a child's therapy needs. However, other reasons are less concrete and justifiable. Parental resistance to a child's therapy is an unfortunately common cause of premature endings for children's treatment. Yet, often these resistances could have been dealt with or avoided. Therapist countertransference could have been addressed through supervision or consultation, in much the same way as a therapist's inability to establish a working relationship. Because of these less concrete and justifiable reasons, many clinicians believe that these types of factors seldom work in isolation (e.g., Coppolillo, 1987). For instance, if a family withdraws a child because they believe that no progress has been made and this withdrawal occurs suddenly and without preparation, chances are that the therapist has somehow failed to work sufficiently with the parents to have overcome their resistance or the therapist has indeed mismanaged the case and the child has not improved because of the therapist's failure to seek consultation. Similarly, a therapist who fails to establish a relationship with a parent might be the victim of her or his own countertransferences which might have prevented her or him from dealing effectively with an abusive parent. This parent, in turn, is more likely to withdraw the child because the parent himself or herself feels neglected, uncared for, or even attacked by the clinician. Thus, although consultation and supervision certainly are no panacea for premature endings, they may well serve to prevent a good number of them. Similarly, although regular meetings with parents for consultation or involvement of parents in their own therapy might be similarly unsuccessful at avoiding all premature endings, they may reduce their likelihood of occurrence.

Natural Termination

Premature terminations obviously imply that the child's therapy was not complete when the ending occurred and that further work remains to be done. Sometimes, premature terminations result in transfers; more commonly, they truly are the end of the child's work in therapy. Some children, however, are lucky enough to complete treatment and become part of a natural termination. Such natural terminations can be ushered in in a variety of ways and the clinician has to learn to identify the time in treatment when the ending is near and must be approached with the child. In other words, there have to be reasons to justify endings, as well as signals from both child and therapist that the timing is right for termination.

Reasons for a Natural Termination

Just as there are many reasons for premature terminations, there are a number of reasons for natural terminations. Different theorists may use slightly different guidelines, but some consensus does emerge. Specifically, there is agreement that foremost, there must be resolution of the presenting problems and a decrease in or disappearance of symptoms evidenced by the child (Adams, 1982; Brems, 1999; Dodds, 1996; Horney, 1939; Spiegel, 1996). Further, the child must have become more developmentally appropriate in a number of realms, including cognition, experience of affect, expression of affect, morality, self development, and interpersonal relating (Ablon, 1988; Kohut, 1984; O'Conner, 2000; Spiegel, 1996). The child must have evidenced increased problem-solving ability and cognitive flexibility, allowing her or him to generalize skills and adapt skills to new situations, as well as to recognize options and alternatives (Adams, 1982; Coppolillo, 1987; Hutchins and Vaught, 1997). This increased capacity to cope and use adequate defenses (Ablon, 1988) should be accompanied by increased spontaneity in behavior, as well as in need and affect expression (Adams, 1982; Horney, 1939). Further, the child should feel greater capacity for enjoyment, increased self-confidence and self-value, and an integrated sense of self (Horney, 1939; Kohut, 1984; Landreth, 2000). There should be evidence that the child has become more independent and is now ready to progress and grow on her or his own (Adams, 1982; Coppolillo, 1987; Dodds, 1985). Finally, the amount of conflict experienced by the child, either intrapsychically, interpersonally, familially, or elsewise, should be greatly reduced and manageable, and the child should be capable of setting her or his own limits and boundaries for behavior and affect (Ablon, 1988; Landreth, 1991, 2000).

Although this might appear to be a rather long list of changes that a therapist must look for to be able to end treatment, it is unlikely that most of them do not automatically develop and become evident in unison, as these improvements are intimately tied to one another. For instance, it is unlikely that the reduction of symptoms would not result in increased spontaneity and self-esteem. Similarly, getting back on track developmentally usually implies that the child becomes more independent and sufficiently cognitively complex to do her or his own problem solving and limit setting. It is noteworthy in examining this list of changes, however, that nowhere in the literature is there any suggestion that the child must be completely free of problems or conflicts to end therapy. The emphasis for all theorists remains on *decreasing* problems and conflicts and *increasing* coping ability. Cure, in the traditional sense of removing all symptoms and problems in the present and the future, is never a goal in child treatment. In fact, Freud, speaking about adult treatment, even acknowledged that cure is unrealistic. He believed that "above all, don't try to cure, just learn and earn some money" (Sigmund Freud in a letter to C. G. Jung, as quoted by Ablon, 1988, p. 98). Spiegel echoes this sentiment in the context of work with children, by writing that "the task, at least with children, is to repair, not to remake" (Spiegel, 1996, p. 195). This approach to treatment frees both child and therapist from having to attempt to achieve the unattainable: perpetual happiness and freedom from conflict.

If a therapist believes that there are sufficient reasons (summarized in Table 14.1) for a natural termination to be initiated, there is one final means of double-checking this decision. Teyber (2000) suggests that there be verification of the reasons for termination from

TABLE 14.1   Reasons for a Natural Termination

- resolution of presenting problems
- reduction or disappearance of symptoms
- developmentally appropriate cognitions
- developmentally appropriate expressions of affect
- developmentally appropriate experiences of affect
- developmentally appropriate morality
- developmentally appropriate self development
- developmentally appropriate interpersonal relationships
- increased problem-solving ability
- increased cognitive flexibility
- ability to generalize and adapt skills to new situations
- ability to see and explore options and alternatives

- better coping ability
- increased spontaneity in behavior
- increased spontaneity in affect expression
- increased spontaneity in need expression
- greater capacity for enjoyment
- increased self-confidence
- increased self-esteem or self-value
- increasingly clear self-definition
- increased independence
- internalized ability to set limits and boundaries
- decreased experience of intrapsychic conflict
- decreased experience of interpersonal conflict
- decreased experience of familial conflict

three sources: the therapist, the client, and one external source. Obviously, by this time, the first source has been established, that is, the therapist has decided that enough evidence exists to suggest sufficient improvement in the child to warrant ending. Ideally, this evidence is corroborated by the child, who might begin to tell enough stories about change outside the therapy room to imply that she or he also believes that progress has been made. The third source is often a parent or a teacher. In fact, getting corroboration from a third source is much easier in the work with a child than in the work with an adult. In the latter, this evidence is generally secondhand, delivered by the client as a statement about what other people are beginning to say about her or him. In child treatment, however, there is always some level of involvement of a parent, caretaker, guardian, or teacher who can be interviewed to assess the child's behavioral change outside the therapy room. Finally, in addition to corroborating the evidence pointing toward the need for termination through other sources, the clinician can also begin to look for signs and signals above and beyond concrete improvement or symptom resolution.

Signals of an Impending Natural Termination

There are many signals, from both the child and the therapist, that indicate that an ending of therapy may be at hand and that the timing is right to terminate treatment. Some of these signs might occur even before the therapist has identified the reasons for termination outlined. In this case, the signals might have to be analyzed to make a decision as to whether the signs are occurring because of resistance or other untherapeutic reasons, or because the reasons for ending have been reached, but were overlooked by the therapist. It is indeed not uncommon for a therapist to rationalize the continuation of therapy even after presenting problems have been resolved, under the guise of working on underlying problems or personality restructuring. Such continued work may indeed be justified in some cases; however, if signals arise from the child that indicate that it is time to end, the therapist may need to explore her or his own countertransferences about why continuation is deemed important.

Signs experienced by the therapist that the end may have come are quite varied in nature but are always related to the relationship that has been established with the child. An important signal is given when the therapist begins to note that she or he is growing increasingly fond of the child and is having fewer and fewer ambiguous feelings about her or him. At the same time, the therapist might consider the child increasingly interesting and, while having high hopes for the child's achievement and health outside of the therapy room, feels less responsible for making these things happen. The therapist feels less burdened by the work with the child, less protective, and less in need to provide continuous support to the child. In other words, the child is perceived as more capable, stronger, and more of an equal partner in the client-therapist relationship. Thus, when the ending is near, the therapist might note that she or he has to work less hard in sessions and is perhaps even bored on occasion by the work that is being done. In fact, if the therapist finds herself or himself feeling less responsible and justifies lateness or cancellations, it might well be time to reiterate the child's treatment goals and assess whether the reasons for a natural termination have perhaps been reached.

Similarly, the child who is ready for termination will begin to spend more and more time talking about issues that concern her or his future that are not directly relevant to treatment. The child will begin to engage in behaviors that are new or unusual—that are "firsts" (Landreth, 1991, p. 323). For example, a child who has never used the finger paints available in the room might now choose them; a child who was never hostile toward the therapist might now be so; a child who always used to take off her or his shoes after entering the room might now fail to do so; an adolescent who always chose to sit in a particular chair might suddenly switch to a different one. Although children are seldom responsible for their own transportation, thus making coming late for treatment rarely a termination sign (it is for adults!), they might be less interested in getting started right away upon entering the room. Perhaps the child will ask to end sessions early or just runs out of things to do or say. Sometimes, a parent begins to cancel sessions for the child, picking up on the child's decreased need for sessions and giving in to requests to let other activities take precedence.

All of these signs can obviously also communicate resistance to treatment. However, their context, timing, and novelty usually help the therapist to recognize them for what they are. In other words, if a child had been in treatment for only a brief period of time, had not yet shown a significant attachment to the therapist or the therapy process, and started running out of things to say, this child's behavior could be confidently interpreted as resistance (or self-protection). However, if the same behavior occurred in a child who had been in treatment for several months, had built a meaningful relationship with the therapist, and had repeatedly evidenced her or his belief in the importance of the therapy, it could be confidently interpreted as a termination signal. None of the signals (also displayed in Table 14.2) is foolproof; none can be used in isolation. It is best to view them in their context, to

TABLE 14.2   Signals for a Natural Termination

Therapist Signals
- becomes increasingly fond of the child
- finds the child increasingly more interesting
- has high hopes for the child's achievement without feeling responsible for helping the child reach these goals
- feels less protective of the child
- feels less burdened with the responsibility for the child
- feels less need to support the child continuously
- works less hard in session
- may occasionally become bored in session
- may become less responsible about not being late for sessions
- may become less responsible about not canceling sessions

Client Signals
- engages in "firsts"
- is less interested in starting sessions on time or right away
- asks to end sessions early
- runs out of things to say or do before session is over
- convinces parent to cancel sessions
- gives other activities precedence
- spends more time talking about things outside the therapy
- spends more time talking about plans for the future

look for additional signals, and to explore whether the reasons for termination are obvious as well. If all of these factors are answered affirmatively, it is time to consider termination.

Preparation for Termination

Preparation for termination begins with the therapist who has to come to terms with the fact that the therapy is coming to an end. She or he must have correctly evaluated all reasons and correctly read her or his own as well as the child's signs. Once convinced that the end of treatment has indeed been reached, the therapist must explore her or his own feelings about the impending break with the child. It is unrealistic to expect that no feelings would surface. To have seen a child through to the termination of treatment means having traveled with the child down a road that may have been difficult at times, joyous at times, but most of all, goal-directed and intense. It is not always countertransferential to have feelings and to be ambivalent about ending. Countertransference becomes an issue only if the therapist has recognized the reasons and signs, yet chooses to continue treatment. Acceptance of feelings is paramount at this stage, as it will be important to model this process for the child once the actual process of ending treatment begins in the work with the child.

Next, the child's parents should be consulted and dealt with. In this meeting, the parents need to be warned about the impending termination, need to be prepared for the behaviors and feelings that may emerge in the child during the process, and need to be consulted about a date for the final session. However, despite the discussion of the topic with parents at this point in time, the child must be informed of the ending by the therapist, not the parents. Thus, the meeting with the parents ideally takes place directly before a session with the child, and the topic of termination would be broached with both parties on the same day, requiring no secrecy on the parents' part. However, if such a schedule cannot be arranged, the parents must commit not to disclose the information to the child until it has been shared with the child by the therapist. If the therapist is uncertain about the parents' willingness or ability to cooperate in this endeavor, she or he may choose to address the topic with the child first and the parents last.

Addressing the topic of ending with a child client is often easier than anticipated. As has been pointed out, there usually have been signals from both the child and the therapist about the impending ending. Therefore, an easy way to approach the topic is to begin to interpret the child's hints directly during the session. For instance, one 12-year-old boy who had been seen for 34 sessions began to do many firsts, missed two sessions in one month, and began to talk about his summer vacation plans, despite summer being two months away. The therapist recognized the signals, explored the reasons, and decided that it was time to end. She approached the topic with the boy's parents, who corroborated that he had improved significantly in several realms. They agreed to allow the therapist to introduce the topic to the child and helped her to set a firm ending date, which was to coincide with the beginning of summer vacation. In the next session, the therapist asked the child what he thought it meant that he was spending less and less time talking about his problems at school and more and more time about his summer vacation. He responded that there were few problems left to work on and that he was ready to start a new phase in his life. The therapist probed the "new phase of life," only to find out that the boy himself had recognized that he no longer felt he needed to see the therapist as often.

In addition to showing how a child's behavior can be used to open the door for termination, this example also introduced the idea that what would be a natural break in treatment anyway can be conveniently used as a termination point. In this case, treatment would have been interrupted by the child's visit with his father at the beginning of summer vacation. This natural break was used to specify a logical ending point. Further, the example points toward the importance of setting a firm date for the last session. Although some therapists (e.g., Spiegel, 1996) argue that children might not need this structure as much as adults do, as they often do not yet have a good sense of time, most child clinicians (e.g., Landreth, 2000; O'Conner, 2000) agree that it is good practice to set a date. Not only is setting a date critical, but also weekly reminders should be given to the child about the number of sessions left.

To summarize, the easiest sequence of preparing for termination is for the therapist to recognize the signals and reasons, to process her or his own feelings about ending, to introduce the idea to the parents, and then to broach the topic with the child in the context of interpreting signals given by the child. However, signals are not always obvious and children not always sufficiently verbal to hear and process interpretations. In such cases, the therapist, after having met with the parents, might address termination by asking the child gently how long she or he thought treatment might continue on (Dodds, 1985). Often, children at this point will express their fantasy which is that therapy will never end. This fantasy needs to be redirected to a realistic time frame. If the child responds well, a date may then be announced. If the child appears distraught, the topic may be reintroduced again and again over a few sessions before an actual ending date is specified. Most therapists suggest that a child be given ample time to process the ending of the therapeutic relationship, suggesting that two to four months be given. During this time, reminders are given, and feelings are discussed. The actual content and process of this last phase of treatment will be discussed below. However, first one comment remains to be made about the child who has obvious difficulties with the decision to end.

If a child has difficulty ending or if a parent is concerned about the process, two procedures may be considered to prepare them better. The child and parent may be weaned from treatment, or they may be allowed time to practice termination by using natural breaks to prepare them for saying their final good-bye. In the first procedure, rather than ending therapy from one session to the next, sessions are spaced farther and farther apart to give child, parent, and therapist a chance to evaluate how the child is coping with the decreased contact with the clinician. This spacing can be very individually tailored to the needs of the child. Often, spacing begins by meeting every other week and then continues to meetings once per month for two to three months. However, there is no rule about how to set the weaning schedule, and this should be negotiated with the child or the parent. Sometimes, if the spacing between sessions is too long, the child never returns for a session that was formally defined as the last session. This represents an avoidance of the termination that should not be allowed. Thus, if an appointment is missed during the weaning phase, it is critical for the therapist to call and make an appointment for what is specified as the final session.

In the second procedure, the child and parent are helped with termination by introducing vacation breaks that can be used to practice saying good-bye. This procedure obviously carries with it a component of weaning in that it also results in sessions that are spaced farther apart. However, in the weaning procedure, the emphasis is on whether and how the child will tolerate the longer breaks between sessions. In the practicing procedure, the emphasis is on saying good-bye and slowly letting go of the therapist. A combination of both procedures is obviously easy to design and often used.

Once the child, the family, and the therapist have prepared for termination by discussing the ending and setting a date, the actual process of termination has been set in motion. This phase of treatment has some features that are quite distinct from the therapy process in general. Hence, it warrants some discussion.

The Process of Termination

The process of termination is ushered in and is almost inseparable from the preparation for ending. It is a gradual process that helps the child (and the clinician) adapt to the idea that the relationship will end. If plenty of warning is possible (two to four months), the early stages of the termination process are quite innocuous. During these first few weeks, the therapist might merely remind the child of the termination date and will count down the weeks for the child. Thus, up to about the fourth to the last session, not much actual processing of separation might need to be done directly, though it is likely to be expressed in the child's play, stories, art, or behavior (Cangelosi, 1997).

General Guidelines

When in the last month of treatment, the therapist gently forces the child to confront the ending. Not only are the final date and number of sessions remaining mentioned at the beginning of each session, the child is also asked to express feelings about this ending. A variety of feelings tend to emerge in this phase of termination and these will be discussed in detail and context below. In general, regardless of the type of feeling that emerges, the child is encouraged to own the feeling and to express it. The therapist also owns her or his feelings, in a significant change from how she or he used to relate to the child. Specifically, although most therapists will have chosen not to self-disclose to the child up to this point in treatment, most will now disclose their own reactions to ending therapy (Dodds, 1985). They will speak to their sadness and disappointment, but also to their excitement about what being ready for ending implies. This self-disclosure paves the way for exploring what termination means, namely, for the exploration of what has been accomplished in treatment thus far. This shifts the focus to a more positive one, as the positives tend to outweigh the negatives in a natural termination. Thus, the child and the clinician might discuss the growth they have seen together in the child; they might address the child's increased ability to cope, set limits, and solve problems; they will discuss how the child's problems have decreased and how her or his general emotional well-being has improved. In this process, they work toward a true appreciation and enjoyment of the child's improvement, thus placing termination in a much more positive light.

This process of exploring gains is not to imply that there is not some sadness about ending the special relationship between child and therapist. This sadder aspect of termination must be acknowledged. The two individuals might talk about how they will miss one another, what they have enjoyed and endeavored together, and how it will feel not to meet anymore. Also, often some work is left to be done for the child, and this is the time to talk about this work and encourage the child to do it and to feel confident to do it alone, without the therapist. This review of the therapy process and preparation for the future are done over several sessions and represent an ending ritual in and of themselves (O'Conner, 2000). However, the clinician and child might choose to add an official ending ceremony to their last session. Perhaps they will paint a picture together that the child will keep that shows the changes in the child; perhaps they will share food for the first time; or perhaps they will choose a toy from the therapy room that the child may keep as a memento of the therapy. Most therapists agree that a gift at the end of the last session given to the child may be an appropriate way to provide a transition and to symbolize that the child will take something away from therapy even if she or he will never see the clinician again (e.g., Spiegel, 1996).

Some therapists endorse leaving the door open and letting the child know that she or he can return for further sessions if the need arises. For instance, O'Conner (2000) suggests giving the child a business card at the end of the last session to signal that she or he may return and may contact the therapist again. In leaving the door open, it is important to do so in such way as not to suggest to the child that this termination is not really an ending. Termination should be final. Termination with the expectation to meet again is never clean and often fails. Thus, if the door is left open, it should be left open as a generic invitation to seek services again if large problems arise, and it should be mentioned that services can be sought from any, not just this, therapist.

In the process of reviewing therapy progress, anticipating future challenges, and engaging in self-exploration and mutual affective self-disclosure, many feelings and behaviors will emerge in the child that need to be dealt with as they occur. Further, to prevent parental overreaction, parents need to be warned that some of these feelings or actions may spill over into the child's day-to-day life. Helping parents anticipate a child's potential regression and return to previously conquered symptoms during the termination process will make them accomplices who will help to facilitate the process as opposed to turning them into critics who begin to doubt the timing of termination or the entire value of treatment. In other words, as the therapist and parents are faced with the child's termination feelings, they must remain aware of the context and the ephemeral nature of these expressed affects.

The types and strength of expressed termination affects are somewhat unpredictable and vary greatly from child to child (Landreth, 1991; 2000). They may range from easy acceptance to anger, in all kinds of gradations. Common feelings include fear and anger expressed toward the therapist. Sadness may be expressed at the anticipated loss of the relationships, and feelings of "unloveworthiness" (Dodds, 1985, p. 153) might surface. However, the child might also express pride or excitement over the accomplishments of therapy and may be quite delighted to end treatment, viewing it as a milestone of great positive significance. Often, symptoms reappear in children during the last weeks of treatment, and the child may be found less able to cope. It is critical to see this regression in the context of termination and not overreact to it. Instead, the behavior should be interpreted to the child as an attempt to prevent the ending, and the child should be reminded that a termination date has been set and will not be altered. Again, keeping parents apprised of this process and involving them in it will greatly facilitate it.

Stages of Termination

The behaviors and affects children tend to show during the termination phase can best be understood if they are placed into a comprehensive framework of how human beings tend to deal with loss. One framework that has been developed in the past for exploring and understanding people's reactions to loss is that of the stages of adaptation to death and dying outlined by Kübler-Ross (1971, 1975). Kübler-Ross observed in her work with terminal patients and their families that the patient, as well as the family members, passed through distinct phases of affect in the process of adapting to the thought of death or the loss of a loved one. Specifically, people facing death or the loss of a loved one tended to respond with initial denial, followed by anger, which tended to result in the attempt to bargain with a higher power to prevent the loss, which was followed by depression when bargaining did not result in a change of the situation and finally by acceptance of the inevitability of the situation. While the stages tended to occur most commonly in this order, Kübler-Ross also conceded that for some individuals, stages overlapped, may have been skipped, or may have occurred in a different order. However, the overwhelming evidence showed that this stage model could describe the affects and behaviors often noted in the dying patient and the family facing the loss of a member.

Although Kübler-Ross developed these stages, or reactions, specifically with death and dying in mind, they can be applied to numerous situations involving significant losses in people's lives. The loss of a friend can be equally tragic and can result in the same sequence of feelings and behaviors, whether the friend is lost to death, a geographic relocation, or some other ending. Thus, in further discussing children's termination behaviors and affects, Kübler-Ross's stage theory will be applied as a framework for the conceptual understanding of what is occurring between child and clinician in the termination phase of therapy. As is true in the original theory, the stages may occur in any order, though acceptance is always last if it does occur. Further, some children may skip a particular stage or may go through more than one stage at once. For ease of presentation, however, Kübler-Ross's (1971) original order is maintained in the following discussion and in the overview of the stages in Table 14.3, as applied to termination of treatment.

Denial.   The first introduction of termination with children is not uncommonly met with the same type of denial that is encountered in family members of a dying patient or in the person facing death herself or himself. In an attempt to deny the inevitability of the ending of the special relationship, the child might ignore the therapist when the subject is broached or might make light of the subject in such a manner as to deny the potential impact of the ending of the relationship. This denial is one of the major reasons why the topic of termination needs to be introduced with sufficient advance warning so that it may be reintroduced repeatedly, each repetition making the child's denial more difficult. Sometimes, the denial is so pronounced that special care might need to be taken to ascertain that the client has heard the therapist and has registered the meaning of the message. For instance, one child, upon being asked how long he thought he would keep coming to see the

TABLE 14.3   **Stages of a Natural Termination**

Stage	Child's Behavior	Therapist's Intervention
Denial	■ ignores the therapist ■ avoids the topic of ending ■ represses the information ■ pretends not to have heard the therapist	■ works to get the child's attention ■ brings up the topic repeatedly ■ discusses the topic until convinced the child heard it
Anger	■ behaves aggressively ■ plays out aggressive, seemingly unrelated scenes ■ blames the therapist ■ behaves with anger or hostility toward the clinician	■ recognizes child's affect and behavior in the context of ending ■ interprets child's behavior and affect ■ helps child express anger, frustration
Bargaining	■ reports return of symptoms ■ reports appearance of new problems ■ openly tries to negotiate an extension of therapy ■ finds reasons why not to end therapy	■ recognizes old symptoms and new problems in context of ending ■ interprets child's symptoms, problems ■ holds firmly to the original ending date
Depression	■ expresses sadness over the loss of the relationship ■ may evidence mild symptoms of depression ■ fears loss of therapeutic progress without the therapist ■ grieves the loss of the relationship and the therapy process	■ recognizes any symptoms of depression in context of ending ■ interprets child's symptoms and fears ■ expresses own feeling of loss and sadness ■ models grieving process for child ■ acknowledges/validates feelings
Acceptance	■ accepts the inevitability of ending ■ reviews therapy process ■ reviews and recognizes own progress ■ makes plans for future ■ says farewell to the therapist ■ has bittersweet feelings	■ models acceptance ■ helps review the therapy process ■ helps review child's progress ■ models leave-taking ■ delights in child's progress ■ shares own feelings

therapist, indicated his belief that therapy would last forever. The therapist proceeded to explain the realistic time limits of treatment and tried to negotiate an ending time with the child. The boy turned away from the therapist and ignored her quite effectively, engaging in a number of activities such as hammering and pounding that made hearing her extraordinarily difficult. The clinician decided to interpret his behavior for him, explaining that she understood his wish to continue forever and that it was difficult and sad for him to imagine not coming back to see her. The child did stop his hammering but never acknowledged the communication of the clinician during this session. His denial made it extremely important for the therapist to continue bringing up the topic in ensuing sessions. The child finally conceded that he understood he needed to end but also explained that it was not time for him to do so because he had started wetting his bed again. This return of symptoms signaled to the therapist that the boy now indeed had received the message of having to terminate. Moving on to a later stage in the process of adjusting to ending, he was now bargaining for at least an extension of the experience.

Sometimes denial is well veiled under a cover of easy acceptance. This form of denial may be operating when a client denies the potential impact of ending and responds without affect. For instance, one adult client, when presented with ending the therapy relationship, indicated that she of course had thought of the fact that therapy needed to end and that she was prepared to face this termination when it came. She showed no significant affect or concern, and the therapist proceeded to set a date with the client. Because she accepted the date easily, he assumed that he did not need to remind her carefully and failed to bring up termination during several subsequent sessions. Finally, in the last month of treatment, he reminded her that only four sessions were left remaining for the two of them to say good-bye. The client feigned shock and surprise, indicating that she had no idea that treatment needed to be ended. When the therapist reminded her of their prior conversation, she denied any recollection of it and, even when shown progress notes from that session, insisted that the therapist may have meant to bring the issue up to her but failed to. She then proceeded to get angry, signaling that she had moved onto the next stage of dealing with her impending loss.

Anger.   Denial is most commonly followed by anger, as in the adult example above. Anger can be expressed by the child client in a number of ways and needs to be understood in the context of ending, rather than as a reemergence of original anger and hostility. The better prepared the therapist is for the child's anger, the easier it will be for her or him to refrain from personalizing the child's anger and from feeling guilty about abandoning the child. Guilt feelings for the therapist are a possible occurrence at this time because the child's anger often will target the therapist as the reason for the destruction of a beautiful relationship, the source of a felt rejection or abandonment, and the harbinger of unnecessary and unfeeling news. Sometimes, the anger is also externalized, blame being directed toward parents or schools, which serve as reasons the child conjures up to maintain a positive image of the therapist. In either event, the clinician must refrain from letting the object of the child's anger become the focus of the interpretation or the anger, keeping firmly in mind that the child is angry at the process of having to end. It is also important to realize that the anger might not be expressed immediately after termination is discussed, but may become an issue later in the same session or even not until a subsequent session.

For instance, when termination was discussed with a 10-year-old girl, she proceeded to cooperate in setting a date and expressed her agreement with the therapist that she indeed had improved significantly. When the topic felt settled to both child and clinician for the time being, the girl turned to her usual play with puppets. However, her puppet play had an unusual flavor during this session and became increasing aggressive and hostile. Soon two of her favorite puppets (often interpreted by the therapist as a representation of the child and the therapist or the child and her ideal self) engaged in a particularly vicious argument, then began a physical fight. They were quarreling quite vehemently over preparing a guest list for a birthday party and could not agree upon whom to invite. Rather than settling the problem rationally and calmly, as the child had clearly learned over the course of treatment, the puppets decide to engage in a fist fight and let the winner decide the guest list. The puppet that usually represented the child won the fight and proceeded to tell the other puppet that everyone she knew would be invited except the other puppet (the puppet often representing the therapist). She explained her decision by indicating that the (therapist) puppet had been very mean to her and did not deserve to see her ever again. The clinician easily understood the message delivered by the child so eloquently: She (the clinician) had disappointed the girl by severing the relationship, and she needed to be punished. The therapist allowed the child her anger and did not attempt to intervene in the puppet play. She decided instead to wait and see whether the girl would be able to resolve her anger on her own, which she indeed was able to in her next session. Only after having evidence that the child felt less angry and had resolved some of her feelings of rejection and abandonment did the therapist introduce the idea that some of the child's strong feelings might be related to ending treatment. The girl began to cry and revealed that she was very afraid of saying good-bye, fearing that she would once again feel as poorly about herself as she had when treatment began. She had moved to a more advanced stage in the termination process.

Bargaining. Often, facing the inevitability of ending and having expressed anger about it results in a final attempt on the child's part to change the situation. This attempt, called bargaining, is directed either toward never ending therapy or toward at least extending it for a while. Whereas dying patients are reported to do much of their bargaining with a higher power in the attempt to extend their lives, children bargain with the therapist to stay in therapy just a little bit longer. Bargaining is not necessarily a conscious endeavor, though it may be. Conscious bargaining may be reflected in the child's attempt to negotiate a later ending date or in promises to make certain changes the parents or therapist have implied as desirable in exchange for additional sessions. However, unconscious bargaining is much more common among children (and adults, for that matter). The return of symptoms or the emergence of new problems represents a child's attempt to bargain for extra therapy time. After all, if one therapy goal was for the child to stop having bad dreams, the return of such dreams may result in renewed efforts on the therapist's part, which may lead to a postponement of the termination date. Or if a child indeed improved in all areas targeted by treatment, perhaps the emergence of a new problem, such as acting out at school, may convince parents and clinician to continue treatment a while longer.

Return of symptoms and sudden new problems after having negotiated an ending date must be understood in the context of bargaining and cannot be given in to. Instead, the therapist needs to help the child understand what is occurring, pointing out that there is a hope connected with the problem that has to do with extending treatment. It is critical not to extend the termination date at this time, but rather to stress to the child that she or he will indeed be ready to end when the agreed-upon time comes, regardless of the current crisis. Consultation with, and preparation of, parents is critical at this phase of termination, as they might otherwise become unknowing accomplices of their child. In other words, parents need to be warned about the possible reemergence of problems and need to be helped to understand these in the context of bargaining. This prevents overreaction to the behavior, and thus reinforcement of it, by well-meaning parents.

For instance, in the above example of the boy who once again began bed-wetting, his foster parents had been warned that some return of symptoms could occur during the ending phase of treatment. Therefore, when the bed indeed was wet, in the morning, they responded matter-of-factly, asked him to help remove and launder the sheets, and encouraged him not to worry too much about the problem. Because they had been warned by the therapist, they were able to keep from panicking and reinforcing the child's bargaining position by joining his effort to convince the therapist that therapy must go on. The boy wet his bed twice in one week, then never wet his bed again as he began to accept termination and began to realize the continuity of the success of his work with the therapist would be maintained even without weekly contacts.

Depression.   Depression is also a common affect expressed by children in the ending phase. It can range from rather severe-appearing dysphoria with decreased psychomotor movement, self-disparaging comments, slight insomnia, or temporary loss of appetite to relatively mild feelings of sadness. Fortunately, the latter is much more common than the former in natural terminations (though this is not necessarily the case in forced terminations). The expression of sadness about ending the relationship with the therapist is often a most important component of working through termination. It helps the child to express her or his attachment to the therapist and the sadness of loss. The healthy aspect of this expression is that it usually leads to a recognition of the positive aspects of the relationship that will not be lost even after termination, thus leading to acceptance, and, in fact, to a joyous and proud ending of treatment. Sadness is also often felt by the therapist, and this appears to be accepted as an appropriate time for self-disclosure, even among therapists who do not usually do so. The clinician might share with the child that she or he also feels sad about not seeing the child any longer and then proceeds to model for the child that this sadness can be part of saying good-bye without overshadowing the positive implications of therapy.

For instance, in the example of the girl with the puppets, her anger had given way to expressed sadness. This sadness was not just the grieving of the loss of the therapist, but also an expression of her fear that losing the therapist implied a loss of her progress in treatment up to date. Addressing the fear of losing ground is an important feature of the depression phase of adjusting to loss. The therapist must help the child to recognize that progress is independent of continued meetings and will be maintained even without weekly meetings. Generally, if the child was indeed ready for a natural termination, sufficient self-esteem has been internalized by this time in treatment that the child will be able to hear the therapist's message. The stage of depression is therefore critical to helping the child not only recognize the sadness yet survivability of loss, but also the continuity of change and general strengthening of the self.

Acceptance.   Once the child has understood the inevitability of ending, has expressed anger at it, has attempted to bargain an extension, and has expressed sadness over the loss, acceptance of the termination follows naturally. By progressing through the prior stages, the child has explored all possibilities to extend treatment and has processed all important feelings connected with the loss of the therapy relationship. The child and clinician have come to the realization that there is continuity in the change that has occurred, that the child has been strengthened, and that the child is capable of saying good-bye in a productive way. Having dealt with these possibilities and affects, the child and therapist are now ready to explore the positives of their relationship and their work up to this point and to move to an acceptance that is full of joy and pride, despite the sadness over the loss of a relationship. The phase of acceptance, in other words, is the phase in which child and therapist review treatment progress together, explore in retrospect the change the child has made, take a look at the specialness of their relationship, and let themselves become aware of the positive implications their ending has for the child. Both acknowledge the importance of the relationship, and both may choose to reveal that they will always keep alive a memory of the other person, even if they should never see one another again. The exchange of a gift or the sharing of a closing ritual can become the symbol of the two people's acceptance that their relationship in its present form has come to an end. An example of a last session that was beautifully executed and reflected this level of acceptance follows:

> Michelle, a 10-year-old girl who had been in treatment with Kate for 24 sessions appeared for her final session with a small book she had prepared for the therapist as a parting gift. The book was her depiction of her treatment process as she understood it. Therapist and child had discussed the child's progress in treatment over the last three to four sessions in preparation of the last session and had agreed in the previous session that their last time together would be spent briefly recapping major milestones in treatment and preparing a picture together that would symbolize their work and relationship. The book Michelle brought had been prepared to help the two individuals look at the therapy milestones through the child's eyes and was a beautiful collection of pictures and stories that had been developed in treatment. After having read the book, therapist and child went to work on their picture. Michelle drew a very small heart in blue and black, then a very large heart in shades of orange and red. While preparing her picture, she revealed that when she came for treatment, she felt as though she had a very small heart when she first met the therapist—a heart that had no room for other people and that she used to protect herself. (Michelle had been passed from foster home to foster home while her parents were abusing drugs; after 5 years they relinquished parental rights, and Michelle was adopted by her mother's brother and his partner; she was referred to treatment at the same time she moved in with this couple.) The large heart represented her at termination, when she felt open to people and felt loved by her world around her. The therapist drew a number of people who all looked quite confused and circled around a little child who sat in the middle crying. She explained that when Michelle first came to therapy, that is how her world looked to the therapist. Then Kate drew a man, a woman, and Michelle in a house with large windows and an open door. Outside were numerous children and adults, whom she identified by names as some of Michelle's friends and herself. She explained that now Michelle's world looked much more orderly and inviting and that Michelle was now able to accept friends into her world without being frightened. The picture was then given to Michelle as a parting gift. Both therapist and child reiterated how important their work had become to both of them and that they would never forget each other. The therapist did not deem it important to let Michelle know that she could always return to treatment if the need arose, as Michelle was quite strong and had very supportive parents who had been reminded of this fact earlier. At the end of the session, the following dialogue occurred:

> *Michelle:* I know I will miss you, but I have our picture, and if I forget that I am strong now, I can look at it and then I'll remember. But I think I'll still miss you a lot!

Kate: I will miss you too because you are very special. But I can always look at your book, and then you are with me all over again. That way I can be with you without having to see you.

Michelle: Just like I can do with the picture...

Kate: Yes, and even if you ever lost the picture, you could just close your eyes and remember all the hard work you did, and that will help you make it through tough times!

Michelle: Yes, I can just close my eyes and see this room and Trudy [the name for one of her favorite puppets].

Kate: Goodbye, Michelle. I'll miss you, and I am a little sad, but I'm mainly proud and happy for you. Goodbye [hugs the child].

Michelle: Bye-bye, Kate. I love you. [They stop their embrace, and the child goes to meet her adoptive parents in the waiting room; this time the therapist does not accompany her out of the room.]

Premature Terminations

Not all children are lucky enough to experience a natural termination. Perhaps many more are forced out of treatment for a number of reasons. However, the process of ending may not be neglected, even if it does arrive prematurely and quickly. If the ending is forced (i.e., therapist-initiated), it tends to be more easily dealt with than if it is unilateral (i.e., client-initiated), because the therapist will have taken care to have left a sufficient number of sessions to make the termination process as natural as possible. In this case, the process outlined for a natural termination is almost entirely applicable, only to be modified to include a discussion of work that is left to be done. If the ending is arranged suddenly by client or external factors, the therapist must insist on a few sessions to say good-bye to the child (Coppolillo, 1987; Spiegel, 1996). In these few sessions, the therapist must attempt to deal with the child's anger, bargaining, depression, and other feelings to help the child and herself or himself arrive at a point of acceptance and readiness to seek services elsewhere. Meetings with parents are critical to review with them the progress of their child while also pointing out the work that is left to be done. If the termination resulted from resistance, this may be difficult to do but must be attempted nevertheless. If external factors forced the termination, parents are often grateful for these meetings and want help in setting up continued treatment for their child. The therapist can then help facilitate a transfer.

One feeling that is common in child and therapist in a premature termination that does not generally arise during the natural termination process is the feeling of helplessness. Regardless of how a premature termination takes place, the child generally feels as though she or he had no control over the decision (unless of course it is the child who refuses to return to treatment, in which case the therapist must explore for herself or himself what went wrong in the treatment process). This sense of helplessness must be dealt with, just as the anger and hurt of a natural termination are dealt with. However, this is difficult to do, especially if the therapist feels a sense of helplessness as well. For instance, one child was forced to terminate prematurely by external circumstances. Her custodial arrangement between her biological mother and father had suddenly and arbitrarily been changed by a court decision. This change resulted in the child's geographic relocation to a distant city in the same state. The child and her biological father had long opposed and fought this court decision, and both now felt extremely helpless and frightened. They looked toward the therapist to feel more empowered, but the clinician herself felt extremely helpless and unable to exert any control over the situation. Nevertheless, she was very aware that she needed to control her experience of helplessness and must not let it show during sessions to be able to help her clients cope. Therefore, the therapist herself initiated consultation with a colleague to help her deal with her sense of helplessness and anger at a judicial system that allowed this situation to occur. This consultation made her better able to face the parent and child, yet still did not suffice to make termination a positive or happy one.

Fortunately, the therapist does not always feel as helpless as the child and can usually help the child deal with her or his sense of helplessness in a more efficient and therapeutic manner. For instance, in one case, an 8-year-old boy was quite angry, hurt, and helpless about his single mother's decision to leave the state and start a new career. This move was doubly difficult for the boy, as it meant not only leaving treatment prematurely, but also leaving friends and, most important, his biological father, whom he visited regularly. The boy felt very betrayed by his mother and believed that there was nothing he could do to change his fate. In addressing his sense of helplessness in treatment, it became clear that he had never told his often-absent mother how important his visits with his father were to him. He was encouraged to do so and to explore the possibility of maintaining contact. The child did indeed talk to his mother (as did the clinician) and received permission to initiate a phone call once a week, receive unlimited phone calls, initiate one visit a month, and accept an unlimited number of invitations for visits. The mother also agreed to allow the boy to visit his father for three months in the summer and to recontact the therapist during those times. These solutions were extremely effective in helping this child not only to overcome his sense of helplessness in this situation, but also to increase his self-confidence in shaping his own fate in general.

No doubt, not all cases of helplessness have a solution that is as obvious or easy. However, all generally have some way in which the child can be helped to feel more a part of the decision or to be able to at least confront parents about their imposition. The therapist needs to help the child see these opportunities and should not be shy about scheduling meetings with parents to help them gain some empathy with their child's plight, as well as their child's right for self-determination.

Special Issues

There are a number of other issues related to termination. Two of these will be briefly discussed here because they occur commonly. These are therapy transfers and therapy contracts for therapies that are time-limited from the outset. Therapy transfers are very common when the premature termination is initiated by the therapist and somewhat likely if the client-initiated termination is not due to resistance but other mitigating circumstances. When a therapy transfer is necessary, it is best if the termination process for a natural termination is followed with an eye toward special feelings that tend to emerge in the premature termination. However, all along in the process, focus is not on ending a relationship and a process, but only on ending the relationship without ending the process of therapy. This procedure is shorter than a strict termination, as the child only needs to say good-bye to the therapist, not the therapy. Although this might appear to make the process easier, this is not necessarily the case. Some therapists have to face their own countertransferences at this time. It is not uncommon to hear therapists discuss with consultants or trainees with supervisors the question of to whom to refer their clients. There is often an underlying fantasy that the client will never be as well served by a new therapist. It is important for the therapist to realize that is not necessarily true so that the child is not indirectly set up to reject the new clinician.

Some therapists recommend that a new therapist be introduced in the last few sessions with the current therapist to let the child and new therapist become acquainted in the presence of the trusted clinician. It is possible, however, that such an arrangement will interfere with the process of saying good-bye to the "old" therapist as the child may be encouraged merely to switch her or his attachment to the new person without facing feelings about ending an important relationship. This procedure may also set up the new therapist to be directly compared with the previous therapist, and he or she may easily become the target of the anger that could not be freely expressed in an individual interaction with the therapist who is leaving the child. Thus, before inviting a second clinician into the session, the therapist should explore whether this procedure will indeed serve to enhance the leave-taking or whether it merely serves to make a difficult situation easier by cloaking or avoiding it.

If at all possible, the transfer should take place at a natural break in treatment, so that the child has time to process the absence of the previous therapist before entering into a new therapy relationship. Some clinicians (Sandler, Kennedy, and Tyson 1980) suggest that the transfer therapist be more experienced than the original therapist, owing to the special needs of a client in beginning work with a new therapist. This may be a justifiable position therapeutically but is often neither possible nor completely free of countertransference issues. In other words, most commonly, transfers occur because a trainee has finished a practical experience in a clinic. Usually, the child is then picked up by the trainee replacing the original therapist. It is rare that the child is transferred to a regular staff clinician. In some circumstances, the child might be transferred to the child's supervisor. This appears to be one of the most successful ways of conducting a transfer, as it will provide continuity in the approach to treatment and the theoretical orientation favored by the clinician and would meet the criterion of replacing the old with a more experienced therapist.

Some treatments are begun with the knowledge that the relationship between the child and the clinician will be shorter than the course of therapy will require. This is again most commonly true for therapy cases involving a trainee therapist. Planning for termination and transfer is critical in these cases, as is preparing child and family from the very first session. The child and family have a right to be informed that the therapist will be available for only a certain number of weeks and that this might not be long enough for treatment to be completed. This inevitability of a transfer must be introduced from the beginning in the service of ethics and professionalism.

Summary and Concluding Thoughts

Terminations are difficult for both therapist and child, yet are critical for the continued success of the therapy in the child's life without the therapist. Through a successful termination process, the child is able to leave the therapy situation and the clinician with minimal difficulty and is able to consolidate and continue the change and growth she or he has attained. One major effect of termination is the aspect of practicing leave taking and saying good-bye to important relationships in the child's life. As such, termination can prepare the child for the task of separating from parents in adolescence and from taking leave from other important people in her or his life. Further, and importantly, the child's perception of termination might well affect her or his perception of the entire therapy process. With a successful termination, the child will be more likely to have positive memories of therapy; a negative termination experience might well flavor the entire therapy experience in an unfortunate manner. Termination can be difficult also for the therapist who has developed a close relationship with the child. The difficulty enters when the therapist is torn between wanting to continue the relationship and being aware that the child must go off on her or his own to complete the therapeutic growth. Whether symbolically or verbally, all of these issues need to be addressed in the last few sessions of therapy, as discussed above. The *ending* of treatment is indeed as important as its beginning!

BIBLIOGRAPHY

Abikoff, H. (1991). Cognitive training in ADHD children: Less to it than meets the eye. *Journal of Learning Disabilities, 24,* 205–209.

Ablon, S. L. (1988). Developmental forces and termination in child analysis. *International Journal of Psychoanalysis, 69,* 97–104.

Achenbach, T. M. (1991a). *Manual for the Youth Self-Report & 1991 Profile.* Burlington, VT: ASEBA, Department of Psychiatry, University of Vermont.

Achenbach, T. M. (1991b). *Manual for the Child Behavior Checklist/4–18 & 1991 Profile.* Burlington, VT: ASEBA, Department of Psychiatry, University of Vermont.

Achenbach, T. M. (1991c). *Manual for the Teacher's Report Form & 1991 Profile.* Burlington, VT: ASEBA, Department of Psychiatry, University of Vermont.

Achenbach, T. M. (1991d). *Integrative Guide for the 1991 CBCL/4–18, YSR, & TRF Profiles.* Burlington, VT: ASEBA, Department of Psychiatry, University of Vermont.

Achenbach, T. M. (1997). *Manual for the Young Adult Self-Report & Young Adult Behavior Checklist.* Burlington, VT: ASEBA, Department of Psychiatry, University of Vermont.

Achenbach, T. M., and McConaughy, S. H. (1996). *Empirically Based Assessment of Child & Adolescent Psychopathology Practical Applications.* Thousand Oaks, CA: Sage.

Achenbach, T. M., and Rescorla, L. A. (2000). *Manual for the ASEBA Preschool Forms & Profiles.* Burlington, VT: ASEBA, Department of Psychiatry, University of Vermont.

Adams, P. L. (1982). *A Primer of Child Psychotherapy* (2nd ed.). Boston: Little, Brown, & Company.

Adler, A. (1956). *The Individual Psychology of Alfred Adler* (Ansbacher, H. L., and Ansbacher, R. R., Eds.). New York: Basic Books.

Ahia, C. E., and Martin, D. (1993). *The Danger-to-Self-or-Others Exception to Confidentiality* (ACA Legal Series, Vol. 8). Alexandria, VA: American Counseling Association.

Alarcon, R. D., and Foulks, E. F. (1995). Personality disorders and culture: Contemporary clinical views (Part A). *Cultural Diversity and Mental Health, 1,* 3–17.

American Academy of Child and Adolescent Psychiatry. (1997). Practice parameters for the assessment and treatment of children and adolescents with bipolar disorder. *Journal of American Academy of Child and Adolescent Psychiatry, 36,* 138–157.

American Counseling Association. (1995). *Code of Ethics and Standards of Practice.* Alexandria, VA: Author.

American Psychiatric Association. (1987). *Diagnostic and Statistical Manual of Mental Disorders* (3rd ed., Rev.). Washington, DC: Author.

American Psychiatric Association. (1994). *Diagnostic and Statistical Manual of Mental Disorders* (4th ed.). Washington, DC: Author.

American Psychiatric Association. (2000). *Diagnostic and Statistical Manual of Mental Disorders* (4th ed., text rev.). Washington, DC: Author.

American Psychological Association. (1987a). Model act for state licensure of psychologists. *American Psychologist, 42,* 696–703.

American Psychological Association. (1987b). Resolutions approved by the National Conference on Graduate Education in Psychology. *American Psychologist, 42,* 1070–1084.

American Psychological Association. (1992). Ethical principles of psychologists and code of conduct. *American Psychologist, 42,* 1597–1611.

American School Counselor Association. (1998). *Ethical Standards for School Counselors.* Alexandria, VA: Author.

Anastasi, A. (1997). *Psychological Testing* (7th ed). New York: Prentice-Hall.

Anastopoulos, A. D., DuPaul, G. J., and Barkley, R. (1991). Stimulant medication and parent training therapies for attention deficit hyperactivity disorder. *Journal of Learning Disabilities, 24,* 210–218.

Anderson, B. S. (1996). *The Counselor and the Law* (4th ed.). Alexandria, VA: American Counseling Association.

Armour-Thomas, E., and Gopaul-McNicol, S. A. (1998). *Assessing Intelligence: Applying a Biocultural Model.* Thousand Oaks, CA: Sage.

Atkinson, D. R., Morten, G., and Sue, D. W. (2002). *Counseling American Minorities: A Cross Cultural Perspective* (6th ed.). Dubuque, IA: William C. Brown.

Autti-Raemoe, I. (2000). Twelve-year follow-up of children exposed to alcohol in utero. *Developmental Medicine & Child Neurology, 42,* 406–411

Axline, V. (1947). *Play Therapy.* New York: Ballantine.

Azar, S. T. (1992). Legal issues in the assessment of family violence involving children. In R. T. Ammerman and M. Hersen (Eds.). *Assessment of Family Violence* (pp. 47–70). New York: Wiley.

Bandura, A. (1999). Social cognitive theory of personality. In L. A. Pervin and O. P. John (Eds.), *Handbook of Personality: Theory and Research* (2nd ed., pp. 154–196). New York: Guilford.

Barber, J. G. (1992). Evaluating parent education groups: Effects on sense of competence and social isolation. *Research on Social Work Practice, 2,* 28–38.

Barkley, R. A. (1997). *Defiant Children: A Clinician's Manual for Parent Training* (2nd ed). New York: Guilford.

Barkley, R. A. (1998). *Attention Deficit Hyperactivity Disorder: A Handbook for Diagnosis and Treatment* (2nd ed.). New York: Guilford.

Barnett, O. W., Miller-Perrin, C. L., and Perrin, R. D. (1997). *Family Violence across the Lifespan: An Introduction.* Thousand Oaks, CA: Sage.

Barnouw, V. (1985). *Culture and Personality.* Chicago: Dorsey.

Barrett-Lennard, G. (1981). The empathy cycle: Refinement of a nuclear concept. *Journal of Counseling Psychology, 28,* 91–100.

Barrios, B. A., and O'Dell, S. L. (1998). Fears and anxiety. In E. J. Mash and R. A. Barkley (Eds.), *Treatment of Childhood Disorders* (2nd ed., pp. 249–337). New York: Guilford.

Baumrind, D. (1973). The development of instrumental competence through socialization. In A. D. Pick (Ed.), *Minnesota Symposia on Child Psychology* (Vol. 7, pp. 3–46). Minneapolis: University of Minnesota Press.

Beck, J. S., Beck, A. T., and Jolly, J. (2001). *Manual for the Beck Youth Inventories.* San Antonio, TX: Psychological Corporation.

Becker, W. C. (1971). *Parents Are Teachers: A Child Management Program.* Champaign, IL: Research Press.

Beckham, E. E. and Leber, W. R. (1995). *Handbook of Depression* (2nd ed.). New York: Guilford.

Bellak, L. (1943). *The Thematic Apperception Test.* Cambridge, MA: Harvard University Press.

Bellak, L. (1997). *The TAT, CAT, and SAT in Clinical Use* (6th ed.). New York: Grune & Stratton.

Bellak, L., and Bellak, S. S. (1949). *Children's Apperception Test.* Larchmont, NY: CPS.

Bellak, L., and Bellak, S. S. (1965). *Children's Apperception Test—Human Figures.* Larchmont, NY: CPS.

Bergan, J. R., and Kratochwill, T. R. (1990). *Behavioral Consultation and Therapy.* New York: Plenum.

Bernard, M. E. (2002). *Rational-Emotive Therapy with Children and Adolescents: Theory, Preventative Methods, Treatment Strategies* (2nd ed.). New York: Wiley.

Bertoia, J., and Allan, J. (1988). Counseling seriously ill children: Use of spontaneous drawings. *Elementary School Guidance and Counseling, 22,* 206–221.

Bion, W. R. (1959). Attacks on linking. *International Journal of Pychoanalysis, 40,* 308–315.

Birmaher, B., Ryan, N. D., Williamson, D. E., Brent, D. A., Kaufman, J., Dahl, R. E., Perel, J., and Nelson, B. (1996). Childhood and adolescent depression: A review of the past 10 years. *Journal of the American Academy of Child & Adolescent Psychiatry, 35,* 1427–1439.

Bjorklund, D. F. (1999). *Children's Thinking: Developmental Function and Individual Differences* (3rd ed). Pacific Grove, CA: Brooks/Cole.

Blomquist, G. M., and Blomquist, P. B. (1990). *Zachary's New Home: A Story for Foster and Adopted Children.* New York: Magination.

Boik, B. L., and Goodwin, E. A. (2000). *Sandplay Therapy: A Step-By-Step Manual for Psychotherapists of Diverse Orientations.* New York: Norton.

Bourg, W., Broderick, R., Flagor, R., Kelly, D. M., Ervin, D. L., and Butler, J. (1999). *A Child Interviewer's Guidebook.* Thousand Oaks, CA: Sage.

Bowlby, J. (1999). *Separation Anxiety and Anger* (Vol. 2). New York: Basic

Brandell, J. R. (2000). *Of Mice and Metaphors: Therapeutic Storytelling with Children.* New York: Basic.

Brems, C. (1989a). Dimensionality of empathy and its correlates. *Journal of Psychology, 123,* 329–337.

Brems, C. (1989b). Projective identification as a self psychological change agent in the psychotherapy of a child. *American Journal of Psychotherapy, 43,* 598–607.

Brems, C. (1990). *Manual for a Self-Psychologically Oriented Parent Education Program.* Anchorage, AK: University of Alaska Anchorage.

Brems, C. (1994). *The Child Therapist: Personal Traits and Markers of Effectiveness.* Boston: Allyn & Bacon.

Brems, C. (1995). Women and depression: A comprehensive analysis. In E. E. Beckham and W. Leber (Eds.), *Handbook of Depression* (2nd ed., pp. 539–566). New York: Guilford.

Brems, C. (1996). A model for working with parents in child clinical practice. *Journal of Psychological Practice, 2,* 11–22.

Brems, C. (1998a). Implications of Daniel Stern's model of self development for child psychotherapy. *Journal of Psychological Practice, 3,* 141–159.

Brems, C. (1998b). Cultural issues in psychological assessment: Problems and possible solutions. *Journal of Psychological Practice, 4,* 88–117.

Brems, C. (1999). *Psychotherapy: Processes and Techniques.* Boston: Allyn & Bacon.

Brems, C. (2000). *Dealing with Challenges in Psychotherapy and Counseling.* Pacific Grove, CA: Brooks/Cole.

Brems, C. (2001). *Basic Skills in Psychotherapy and Counseling.* Pacific Grove, CA: Brooks/Cole.

Brems, C., Baldwin, M., and Baxter, S. (1993). Empirical evaluation of a self-psychologically oriented parent education program. *Family Relations, 42,* 26–30.

Brems, C., and Sohl, M. A. (1995). The role of empathy in parenting strategy choices. *Family Relations, 44,* 189–194.

Brim, O. G. (1959). *Education for Child-Rearing.* New York: Free Press.

Brislin, R. (1993). *Understanding Culture's Influence on Behavior.* Fort Worth, TX: Harcourt Brace College.

Brooks, J. B. (1999). *The Process of Parenting* (5th ed.). Mountain View, CA: Mayfield.

Buber, M. (1965). *Between Man and Man.* New York: Macmillan.

Buck, J. N. (1948). The H-T-P test. *Journal of Clinical Psychology, 4,* 151–159.

Buck, J. W., and Hammer, E. F. (1969). *Advances in House-Tree-Person Techniques: Variations and Applications.* Los Angeles: Western Psychological Services.

Bulkley, J. (1988). Legal proceedings, reform and emerging issues in child sexual abuse cases. *Behavioral Sciences and the Law, 6,* 153–180.

Bulkley, J. A., Feller, J. N., Stern, P., and Roe, R. (1996). Child abuse and neglect laws and legal proceedings. In J. Briere, L. Berliner, J. A. Bulkley, C. Jenny, and T. Reid (Eds.), *The APSAC Handbook on Child Maltreatment* (pp. 271–296). Thousand Oaks, CA: Sage.

Burkhardt, S. A., and Rotatori, A. F. (1995). *Treatment and Prevention of Childhood Sexual Abuse: A Child-Generated Model.* Washington, DC: Taylor & Francis.

Burks, H. F. (1978). *Psychological Meanings of the Imagine! Game.* Huntington Beach, CA: Arden.

Burns, R. C. (1982). *Self-Growth in Families: Kinetic-Family-Drawings Research and Applications.* New York: Brunner/Mazel.

Burns, R. C. (1987). *Kinetic House-Tree-Person Drawings (K-HTP).* New York: Brunner/Mazel.

Burns, R. C., and Kaufman, S. H. (1970). *Kinetic Family Drawings (K-F-D): An Introduction to Understanding Children Through Kinetic Drawing.* New York: Brunner/Mazel.

Burns, R. C., and Kaufman, S. H. (1972). *Actions, Styles, and Symbols in Kinetic Family Drawings (KFD): A Manual.* New York: Brunner/Mazel.

Cain, J. (2000). *The Way I Feel.* Seattle: Parenting Press.

Cangelosi, D. M. (1997). *Using Play to Say Goodbye: Planned, Unplanned, and Premature Endings in Child Psychotherapy.* Northvale, NJ: Jason Aronson.

Canino, I. A., and Spurlock, J. (2000). *Culturally Diverse Children and Adolescents: Assessment, Diagnosis, and Treatment.* New York: Guilford.

Carter, R. T., and Helms, J. E. (1993). White racial identity attitudes and cultural values. In J. E. Helms (Ed.), *Black and White Racial Identity: Theory, Research, and Practice* (pp. 145–163). New York: Greenwood.

Castillo, R. J. (1997). *Culture and Mental Illness: A Client-Centered Approach.* Pacific Grove, CA: Brooks/Cole.

Cautela, J., and Groden, J. (1982). *Relaxation: A Comprehensive Manual for Adults, Children, and Children with Special Needs.* Champaign, IL: Research Press.

Chess, S., and Hertzig, M. E. (1990). *Annual Progress in Child Psychiatry and Child Development.* New York: Brunner/Mazel.

Chethnik, M. (2000). *Techniques of Child Therapy: Psychodynamic Strategies* (2nd ed.). New York: Guilford.

Christophersen, E. R., and Purvis P. C. (2001). Toileting problems in children. In C. E. Walker & M. C. Roberts (Eds.), *Handbook of Clinical Child Psychology* (3rd ed., pp. 453–469). New York: Wiley.

Close, H. T. (1998). *Metaphor in Psychotherapy: Clinical Applications of Stories and Allegories.* Atascadero, CA: Impact.

Cohen, C. P., and Naimark, H. (1991). United Nations Convention on the Rights of the Child: Individual rights concepts and their significance for social science students. *American Psychologist, 46,* 60–65.

Cohen, D. J., and Volkmar, F. R. (1997). *Handbook of Autism and Pervasive Developmental Disorders* (2nd ed.). New York: Wiley.

Coleman, M., and Ganong, L. H. (1983). Parent-child interaction: A prototype for parent education. *Home Economics Research Journal, 11,* 235–244.

Conners, C. K. (1997). *Manual for the Conners' Rating Scales.* North Tonawanda, NY: Multi-Health Systems.

Coppolillo, H. P. (1987). *Psychodynamic Psychotherapy of Children.* Madison, CT: International Universities Press.

Corey, G., Corey, M., and Callanan, P. (1998). *Issues and Ethics in the Helping Professions* (5th ed). Pacific Grove, CA: Brooks/Cole.

Crary, E., Katayama, M., and Steelsmith, S. (1996). *When You're Happy and You Know It.* Seattle: Parenting Press.

Creadick, T. A. (1985). The role of the expressive arts in therapy. *Journal of Reading, Writing, and Learning Disabilities International, 1,* 55–60.

Cross, W. E., Jr. (1971). The Negro-to-Black conversion experience: Toward a psychology of Black liberation. *Black World, 20,* 13–17.

Crowther, J. H., Bond, L. A., and Rolf, J. E. (1981). The incidence, prevalence, and severity of behavior disorders among preschool-age children in daycare. *Journal of Abnormal Child Psychology, 9,* 23–42.

D'Andrea, M., and Daniels, J. (1991). Exploring the different levels of multicultural counseling training in counselor education. *Journal of Counseling and Development, 70,* 78–85.

D'Andrea, M., Daniels, J., and Heck, R. (1991). Evaluating the impact of multicultural counseling training. *Journal of Counseling and Development, 70,* 143–150.

Dana, R. H. (1993). *Multicultural Assessment Perspectives for Professional Psychology.* Needham Heights, MA: Allyn & Bacon.

Dana, R. H. (1996). Thematic Apperception Test (TAT). In C. S. Newmark (Ed.), *Major Psychological Assessment Instruments* (2nd ed., pp. 166–205). Boston: Allyn & Bacon.

DeKraii, M. B., Sales, B., and Hall, S. R. (1998). Informed consent, confidentiality, and duty to report laws in the conduct of child therapy. In R. J. Morris and T. R. Kratochwill (Eds.), *The Practice of Child Therapy* (3rd ed., pp. 540–559). Boston: Allyn & Bacon.

Dickinson, N. S., and Cudaback, D. J. (1992). Parent education for adolescent mothers. *Journal of Primary Prevention, 13,* 23–35.

Dillard, J. M. (1983). *Multicultural Counseling: Toward Ethnic and Cultural Relevance in Human Encounters.* Chicago: Nelson-Hall.

Dinkmeyer, D., and McKay, G. D. (1976). *The Parent's Handbook.* Circle Pines, MN: American Guidance Service.

Dodds, J. B. (1985). *A Child Psychotherapy Primer.* New York: Human Sciences.

Doll, B., and Doll, C. A. (1997). *Bibliotherapy with Young People: Librarians and Mental Health Professionals Working Together.* Englewood, CO: Libraries Unlimited.

Doll, E. A. (1953). *The measurement of social competence.* Circle Pines, MN: American Guidance Service.

Donaldson, M. (1987). *Children's Minds.* London: Fontana.

Dougherty, E. H. and Schinka, J. A. (1989). *Mental Status Checklist for Children.* Odessa, FL: Psychological Assessment Resources.

Dowrick, P. W. (1986). *Social Survival for Children: A Trainer's Resource Book.* New York: Brunner/Mazel.

Dowrick, P. W. (1991). *Practical Guide to Using Video in the Behavioral Sciences.* New York: Wiley.

Dreikurs, R., and Grey, L. (1990). Logical Consequences: A New Approach to Discipline. New York: Dutton/Plume.

Dreikurs, R., and Soltz, V. (1964). *Children: The Challenge.* New York: Hawthorne Books.

Dundes, A. (1980). *Interpreting Folklore.* Bloomington, IN: Indiana University Press.

Dunn, L. M., and Dunn, L. M. (1997). *Peabody Picture Vocabulary Test—Third Edition.* Circle Pines, MN: American Guidance Service.

Durfee, M. B. (1979). Use of ordinary office equipment. In C. Schaefer (Ed.), *The Therapeutic Use of Child's Play* pp. 401–411), Northvale, NJ: Jason Aronson.

Elbert, J. C. (1999). Learning and motor skills disorders. In S. D. D. Netherton, D. Holmes, and C. E. Walker, C. E. (Eds), *Child and Adolescent Psychological Disorders: A Comprehensive Textbook* (pp. 24–50). Oxford, England: Oxford University Press.

Eliot, L. (1999). *What's Going on in There? How the Brain and Mind Develop in the First Five Years of Life.* New York: Bantam.

Engel, S. (1999). *The Stories Children Tell: Making Sense of the Narratives of Childhood.* New York: W. H. Freeman.

Erikson, E. (1950). *Childhood and Society.* New York: Norton.

Exner, J. E. (1993). *The Rorschach: A Comprehensive System: Vol. I. Basic Foundations* (3rd ed.). New York: Wiley.

Exner, J. E. (1994). *The Rorschach: A Comprehensive System: Vol. 3. Assessment of Children and Adolescents* (2nd ed). New York: Wiley.

Fine, M. J., and Gardner, P. A. (1991). Counseling and education services for families: An empowerment perspective. *Elementary School Guidance and Counseling, 26,* 33–44.

Finley, W. W., and Jones, L. C. (1992). Biofeedback with children. In C. E. Walker and M. C. Roberts (Eds.), *Handbook of Clinical Child Psychology* (3rd ed). New York: Wiley.

Firestone, R. W. (1997). *Suicide and the Inner Voice: Risk Assessment, Treatment, and Case Management.* Thousand Oaks, CA: Sage.

Flavell, J. H., Shipstead, S. G., and Croft, K. (1978). Young children's knowledge about visual perception: Hiding objects from others. *Child Development, 49,* 1208–1211.

Francis, G., and Gragg, R. A. (1996). *Childhood Obsessive Compulsive Disorder.* Thousand Oaks, CA: Sage.

Freeman, J., Epston, D., and Lobovits, D. (1997). *Playful Approaches to Serious Problems: Narrative Therapy with Children and Their Families.* New York: Norton.

Freud, A. (1928). *Introduction to the Technique of Child Analysis.* New York: Ayer.

Freud, A. (1946). *The Ego and the Mechanisms of Defense.* New York: International Universities Press.

Freud, S. (1952). *A General Introduction to Psychoanalysis*. New York: Pocket Books.

Gabel, S. (1984). The Draw-a-Story game: An aid in understanding and working with children. *Arts in Psychotherapy, 11,* 187–196.

Gabel, S., Oster, G., and Pfeffer, C. R., (1993). *Difficult Moments in Child Psychotherapy*. Northvale, NJ: Jason Aronson.

Gallahue, D. L., and Ozmun, J. C. (2002). *Understanding Motor Development: Health and Human Performance* (5th ed.). McGraw-Hill.

Gardner, R. A. (1971). *Therapeutic Communication with Children: The Mutual Storytelling Technique*. Northvale, NJ: Jason Aronson.

Gardner, R. A. (1973). *The Talking, Feeling, Doing Game*. Cresskill, NJ: Creative Therapeutics.

Gardner, R. A. (1993*). Child Psychotherapy: The Initial Screening and the Intensive Diagnostic Evaluation*. Northvale, NJ: Jason Aronson.

Gardner, R. A. (1994). *Understanding Children*. Northvale, NJ: Jason Aronson.

Gardner, R. A. (1995). *Storytelling in Psychotherapy with Children*. Northvale, NJ: Jason Aronson.

Gardner, R. A. (1997). *Understanding Children*. Northvale, NJ: Jason Aronson.

Garner, D. M., and Garfinkel, P. E. (Eds.). (1997). *Handbook of Treatment for Eating Disorders* (2nd ed.). New York: Guilford.

Gasta, C. (1976). *Assertive training in a highschool setting*. University of Alaska, Unpublished Master's Thesis.

Gelfand, D. M., and Hartmann, D. P. (1992). *Child Behavior Analysis and Therapy* (2nd ed.). Boston: Allyn & Bacon.

Geraghty, B. (1985). Case study: Art therapy with a Native Alaskan girl on a pediatric ward. *American Journal of Art Therapy, 23,* 126–128.

Gesell, A., Ilg, F. L., and Ames, L. B. (1995). *Infant and Child in the Culture of Today* (rev. ed.). Northvale, NJ: Jason Aronson.

Gibbs, J. T., and Huang, L. N. (Eds.). (1998). *Children of Color: Psychological Interventions With Minority Youth* (rev. ed.). San Francisco: Jossey-Bass.

Gil, E. (1991). *The Healing Power of Play*. New York: Guilford.

Ginott, H. G. (1960). A rationale for selecting toys in play therapy. *Journal of Consulting and Clinical Psychology, 24,* 243–246.

Ginott, H. G. (1964). Problems in the playroom. In M. R. Haworth (Ed.), *Child Psychotherapy* (pp. 125–130). New York: Basic Books.

Ginott, H. G. (1999). Play group therapy: A theoretical framework. In D. Sweeney and L. Homeyer (Eds.), *The Handbook of Group Play Therapy: Whom It's Best For, How It Works, How To Do It* (pp. 15–23). San Francisco: Jossey-Bass.

Gitlin-Weiner, K., Sandgrund, A., and Schaefer, C., (Eds.). (2000). *Play Diagnosis and Assessment* (2nd ed). New York: Wiley.

Glanville, C. L., and Tiller, C. M. (1991). Implementing and evaluating a parent education program for minority mothers. *Evaluation and Program Planning, 14,* 241–245.

Godbole, A. Y. (1982). Dyad as a technique of behavioral change. *Psycho Lingua, 12,* 95–110.

Goldstein, J. H. (Ed.). (1994). *Toys, Play, and Child Development*. Cambridge, England: Cambridge University Press.

Goodenough, F. L. (1926). *Measurement of Intelligence by Drawings*. New York: World Book.

Gordon, R. A. (2000). *Eating Disorders: Anatomy of a Social Epidemic* (2nd ed.). Malden, MA: Blackwell.

Gordon, T. (1970). *PET: Parent Effectiveness Training*. New York: Wyden.

Gordon, T., and Sands, J. (1978). *P. E. T. in Action*. New York: Bantam.

Graziano, A. M., and Diament, D. M. (1992). Parent behavioral training: An examination of the paradigm. *Behavior Modification, 16,* 3–38.

Green, K. A. (1975). *Positive Parenting: Parent's Guide*. Menlo Park, CA: Family Communication Skills Center.

Greenbaum, L., and Holmes, I. H. (1983). The use of folktales in social work practice. *Social Casework, 64,* 414–418.

Greenspan, S. I., and Greenspan, N. T. (1991). *The Clinical Interview of the Child* (2nd. ed.). Washington, DC: American Psychiatric Press.

Gresham, F. M., and Watson, T. S. (Eds.). (1997). *Handbook of Child Behavior Therapy*. Boulder, CO: Perseus.

Grinder, R., and Bandler, J. (1975). *The Structure of Magic* (Vols. 1 and 2). Palo Alto, CA: Science Behavior Books.

Grotstein, J. S. (2000). *Splitting & Projective Identification*. Northvale, NJ: Jason Aronson.

Gustafson, K. E., and McNamara, J. R. (1987). Confidentiality with minor clients: Issues and guidelines for therapists. *Professional Psychology: Research and Practice, 18,* 503–508.

Hambridge, G. (1955). Structured play therapy. *American Journal of Orthopsychiatry, 25,* 601–617.

Hambridge, G. (1979). Structured play therapy. In C. E. Schaefer (Ed.), *The Therapeutic Use of Child's Play* (pp. 187–205). Northvale, NJ: Jason Aronson.

Hammer, E. F. (1997). *Advances in Projective Drawing Interpretation* Springfield, IL: Charles C. Thomas.

Handen, B. L. (1998). Mental retardation. In E. J. Mash and R. A. Barkley (Eds.), *Treatment of Childhood Disorders* (2nd ed., pp. 369–415). New York: Guilford.

Handler, L. (1996). The clinical use of figure drawings. In C. S. Newmark (Ed.), *Major Psychological Assessment Instruments* (2nd ed., pp. 206–293). Boston: Allyn & Bacon.

Harry, B. (1992). Developing cultural self awareness: The first step in values clarification for early interventionists. *Topics in Early Childhood Education, 12,* 333–350.

Hart, B. M., and Risley, T. R. (1995). *Meaningful Differences in the Everyday Experience of Young American Children.* Baltimore: Brookes.

Hart, B. M., and Risley, T. R. (1999). *The Social World of Children Learning to Talk.* Baltimore: Brookes.

Hart, S. N. (1991). From property status to person status: Historical perspective on children's rights. *American Psychologist, 46,* 53–59.

Harter, S. (1985). *The Self Perception Profile for Children: Revision of the Perceived Competence Scale for Children.* Manual, University of Denver.

Harter, S. (1988). *The Self Perception Profile for Adolescents.* Unpublished Manual, University of Denver.

Harter, S. (1990). Issues in the assessment of the self-concept of children and adolescents. In A. M. LaGreca (Ed.), *Through the Eyes of the Child* (pp. 292–325). Boston, MA: Allyn and Bacon.

Harter, S., and Pike, R. (1984). The Pictorial Perceived Competence Scale for Young Children. *Child Development, 55,* 1969–1982.

Hawkes, L. (1979). Puppets in child psychotherapy. In C. Schaefer (Ed.), *The Therapeutic Use of Child's Play* (pp. 359–372). Northvale, NJ.

Haworth, M. R., and Keller, M. J. (1964). The use of food in therapy. In M. R. Haworth (Ed.), *Child Psychotherapy.* New York: Basic

Haywood, K., and Getchell, N. (2001). *Life Span Motor Development* (3rd ed.). Human Kinetics.

Heffer, R. W., and Kelly, M. L. (1987). Mothers' acceptability of behavioral interventions for children: The influence of parent race and income. *Behavior Therapy, 18,* 153–163.

Helfer, M. E., Kempe, R. S., and Krugman, R. D. (1997). *The Battered Child* (5th ed.). Chicago: University of Chicago Press.

Helms, J. E., and Carter, R. T. (1993). Development of the White Racial Identity Inventory. In J. E. Helms (Ed.), *Black and White Racial Identity: Theory, Research, and Practice* (pp. 67–80). New York: Greenwood.

Henley, D. R. (1991). Facilitating the development of object relations through the use of clay in art therapy. *Journal of Art Therapy, 29,* 69–84.

Hodgkinson, H. L. (1985). *All One System: Demographics of Education, Kindergarten through Graduate School.* Washington, DC: Institute for Educational Leadership.

Hogan-Garcia, M. (1999). *The Four Skills of Cultural Diversity Competence.* Pacific Grove, CA: Brooks/Cole.

Horney, K. (1939). *New Ways in Psychoanalysis.* New York: W. W. Norton.

Hosford, R. E. (1980). Self-as-a-model: A cognitive social learning technique. *The Counseling Psychologist, 9,* 45–62.

Howell, R. J., and Ogles, B. M. (1989). Psychologist-client privileged communication laws for the fifty states: Duty to report, duty to warn. *American Journal of Forensic Psychology, 7,* 5–24.

Hughes, H. M. (1984). Measures of self-concept and self-esteem for children ages 3 to 12 years: A review and recommendations. *Clinical Psychology Review, 4,* 657–692.

Hunyady, H. (1984). A report on a drawing therapy for children's nightmares. *Journal of Evolutionary Psychology, 5,* 129–130.

Hutchins, D. E., and Vaught, C. C. (1997). *Helping Relationships and Strategies* (3rd ed.). Pacific Grove, CA: Brooks/Cole.

Iijima Hall, C. C. (1997). Cultural malpractice: The growing obsolescence of psychology with the changing U.S. population. *American Psychologist, 52,* 642–651.

Ivey, A. E. (1995). Psychotherapy as liberation: Toward specific skills and strategies in multicultural counseling and therapy. In J. G. Ponterotto, J. M. Casas, L. A. Suzuki, and C. M. Alexander (1995). *Handbook of Multicultural Counseling* (pp. 53–72). Thousand Oaks, CA: Sage.

Iwaniec, D. (1995). *The Emotionally Abused and Neglected Child: Identification, Assessment, and Intervention.* New York: Wiley.

Jackson, B. (1975). Black identity development. ME-FORM. *Journal of Educational Diversity and Innovation, 2,* 19–25.

Jackson, R. H., and Leonetti, J. (2001). Parenting. In C. E. Walker and M. C. Roberts (Eds.), *Handbook of Clinical Child Psychology* (3rd ed., pp. 807–824). New York: Wiley.

Jacobson, J. W., and Mulick, J. A. (Eds.). (1996). *Manual of Diagnosis and Professional Practice in Mental Retardation.* Washington, DC: American Psychological Association.

James, O. O. (1997). *Play Therapy: A Comprehensive Guide.* Northvale, NJ: Jason Aronson.

Johnson, J. E., Christie, C. F., and Yawkey, T. D. (1998). *Play and Early Childhood Development* (2nd ed.). New York: Longman.

Johnson, J. H., Rasbury, W. C., and Siegel, L. J. (1997). *Approaches to Child Treatment* (2nd ed). Boston: Allyn & Bacon.

Kaduson, H. G., and Schaefer, C. E. (1997). *101 Favorite Play Therapy Techniques.* Northvale, NJ: Jason Aronson.

Kaduson, H. G., and Schaefer, C. E. (Eds.). (2000). *Short-Term Play Therapy for Children.* New York: Guilford.

Kaduson, H. G., and Schaefer, C. E. (Eds.). (2001). *101 More Favorite Play Therapy Techniques* Vol. 2. Northvale, NJ: Jason Aronson.

Kagan, J., and Lamb, S. (1990). *The Emergence of Morality in Young Children.* Chicago: University of Chicago Press.

Kail, R. V. (2001). *Children and their Development* (2nd ed.). New York: Prentice-Hall.

Kalichman, S. C., Craig, M. E., and Follingstad, D. R. (1990). Professionals' adherence to mandatory child abuse reporting laws: Effects of responsibility attribution, confidence ratings and situational factors. *Child Abuse and Neglect, 14,* 69–77.

Kaslow, N. J., Kaslow, F. W., Celano, M., and Farber, E. W. (2001). *Textbook of Family Theory and Therapy.* New York: Wiley.

Kaufman, A. S., and Kaufman, N. L. (1983). *K-ABC: Kaufman Assessment Battery for Children.* Circle Pines, MN: American Guidance Service.

Kaufman, A. S., and Kaufman, N. L. (1985). *Kaufman Test of Educational Achievement.* Circle Pines, MN: American Guidance Service.

Kaufman, A. S., and Kaufman, N. L. (1990). *Manual for the Kaufman Brief Intelligence Test.* Circle Pines, MN: American Guidance Service.

Kazdin, A. E. (1977). *The Token Economy: A Review and Evaluation.* New York: Plenum.

Kazdin, A. E. (1990). Conduct disorders. In A. S. Bellack, M. Hersen, A. E. Kazdin (Eds.), *International Handbook of Behavior Modification and Therapy* (2nd ed.). New York: Plenum.

Kazdin, A. E., and Marciano, P. L. (1998). Childhood and adolescent depression. In E. J. Mash and R. A. Barkley (Eds.), *Treatment of Childhood Disorders* (2nd ed., pp. 211–248). New York: Guilford.

Kazdin, A. E. (2000). *Behavior Modification in Applied Settings* (6th ed.). Pacific Grove, CA: Brooks/Cole.

Kedesdy, J. H., and Budd, K. S. (1998). *Childhood Feeding Disorders: Biobehavioral Assessment and Intervention.* Baltimore: Paul H. Brookes.

Kendall, P. C. (2000). *Child and Adolescent Therapy: Cognitive-Behavioral Procedures* (2nd ed.). New York: Guilford.

Kestenbaum, C. J. (1985). The creative process in child psychotherapy. *American Journal of Psychotherapy, 39,* 479–489.

Kestenbaum, C. J., and Williams, D. T. (1992). *Handbook of Clinical Assessment of Children and Adolescents* Vol. 1. New York: New York University Press.

Killen, M., and Hart, D. (Eds.). (2000). *Morality in Everyday Life: Developmental Perspectives.* Cambridge, England: Cambridge University Press.

Kim, M. S. (1994). Cross-cultural comparisons of the perceived importance of conversational constraints. *Human Communication Research, 21,* 128–151.

Klein, M. (1955). On identification. In M. Klein, *Envy and Gratitude and Other Works, 1946–1963* (pp. 141–175). New York: Delacorte Press/Seymour Laurence.

Klein, M. (1975). *The Psychoanalysis of Children* (A. Strachey, Trans.). New York: Delacorte.

Klin, A., Volkmar, F. R., and Sparrow, S. S. (2000). *Asperger Syndrome.* New York: Guilford.

Koeppen, A. S. (1974). Relaxation training for children. *Elementary School Guidance and Counseling, 9,* 14–21.

Kohut, H. (1966). Forms and transformations of narcissism. *Journal of the American Psychoanalytic Association, 14,* 243–272.

Kohut, H. (1982). Introspection, empathy, and the semicircle of mental health. *International Journal of Psychoanalysis, 63,* 359–407.

Kohut, H. (1984). *How Does Analysis Cure?* Chicago: International Universities Press.

Kohut, H., and Wolf, E. (1978). Disorders of the self and their treatment. *International Journal of Psychoanalysis, 59,* 413–425.

Kottman, T. (1995). *Partners in Play.* Alexandria, VA: American Counseling Association.

Kottman, T., and Stiles, K. (1990). The mutual storytelling technique: An Adlerian application in child therapy. *Individual Psychology Journal of Adlerian Theory: Research and Practice, 46,* 148–156.

Kramer, E. (1998). *Childhood and Art Therapy* (2nd ed). Chicago: Magnolia Street.

Kratochwill, T. R., and Morris, R. J. (1998). *Treating Children's Fears and Phobias* (2nd ed). New York: Prentice-Hall.

Kreilkamp, T. (1989). *Time-limited, Interactive, Short-term Therapy With Families and Children.* New York: Brunner/Mazel.

Kronenberger, W. G., and Meyer, R. G. (2001). *The Child Clinician's Handbook* (2nd ed.). Boston: Allyn & Bacon.

Kroth, R., and Otteni, H. (1983). Parent education programs that work: A model. *Focus on Exceptional Children, 15,* 2–16.

Krumboltz, J. D., and Krumboltz, H. B. (1972). *Changing Children's Behavior.* Englewood Cliffs, NJ: Prentice Hall.

Kübler-Ross, E. (1971). The five stages of dying. *Encyclopedia Science Supplement,* 92–97. New York: Grolier.

Kübler-Ross, E. (1975). *Death: The Final Stage of Growth.* Englewood Cliffs, NJ: Prentice Hall.

Kurlan, R. (Ed.). (1993). *Handbook of Tourette's Syndrome and Related Tic and Behavioral Disorders.* New York: Marcel Dekker,

Lachar, D. (1982). *Personality Inventory for Children (PIC): Revised Format Manual Supplement.* Los Angeles: Western Psychological Services.

Lachar, D., and Gruber, C. P. (1995). *Manual for the Personality Inventory for Youth.* Los Angeles: Western Psychological Services.

Lachar, D., and Gruber, C. P. (2001). *Manual for the Personality Inventory for Children—Second Edition.* Los Angeles: Western Psychological Services.

Lachar, D., Wingenfeld, S. A., Kline, R. B., and Gruber, C. P. (2000). *Manual for the Student Behavior Survey.* Los Angeles: Western Psychological Services.

LaFramboise, T. D., Coleman, H. L., and Hernandez, A. (1991). Development and factor structure of the Cross-Cultural Counseling Inventory—Revised. *Professional Psychology: Research and Practice, 22,* 380–388.

LaFramboise, T. D., and Foster, S. L. (1996). Ethics in multicultural counseling. In P. B. Pedersen, W. J. Lonner, J. G. Draguns, and J. E. Trimble, (Eds.), *Counseling Across Cultures* (4th ed., pp. 47–72). Honolulu: University of Hawaii Press.

LaGreca, A. M. (1990). *Through the Eyes of the Child.* Boston: Allyn and Bacon.

Lampe, R., and Johnson, R. P. (1988). School counselors and ethical dilemmas. *TACD Journal, 16,* 121–124.

Landgarten, H. B. (1987). *Clinical Art Therapy: A Comprehensive Guide.* New York: Brunner/Mazel.

Landreth, G. L. (1991). *Play Therapy: The Art of the Relationship.* Muncie, IN: Accelerated Development, Inc.

Landreth, G. L. (2000). *Innovations in Play Therapy: Issues, Process, and Special Populations.* Philadelphia: Taylor & Francis.

Landreth, G. L., Homeyer, L., Glover, G., and Sweeney, D. S. (1996). *Play Therapy Interventions with Children's Problems: Case Studies with DSM-IV Diagnoses for Practicing Play Therapists.* Northvale, NJ: Jason Aronson.

Lane, R. D., and Schwartz, G. E. (1986). Levels of emotional awareness: A cognitive-developmental theory and its applications to psychopathology. *American Journal of Psychiatry, 144,* 133–143.

Lasch, C. (1979). *Culture of Narcissism.* New York: Warner Books.

Laughlin, H. P. (1983). *The Ego and Its Defenses* (rev. ed.). New York: Jason Aronson.

Lebo, D. (1979). Toys for non-directive play therapy. In C. Schaefer (Ed.), *The Therapeutic Use of Child's Play.* Northvale, NJ.

Lee, C. C. (Ed.) (1997). *Multicultural Issues in Counseling: New Approaches to Diversity* (2nd ed., rev.). Alexandria, VA: American Counseling Association.

Lerner, R. M., Skinner, E. A., and Sorrell, G. T. (1980). Methodological implications of contextual/dialectic theories of development. *Human Development, 23,* 225–235.

Levick, M. (1998). *See What I'm Saying: What Children Tell Us through Their Art.* Dubuque, IA: Islewest.

Levy, D. (1939). Release therapy. *American Journal of Orthopsychiatry, 9,* 713–736.

Levy, D. (1979). Release therapy. In C. E. Schaefer, *The Therapeutic Use of Child's Play.* Northvale, NJ: Jason Aronson.

Levy, T. M., and Orlans, M. (1998). *Attachment, Trauma, and Healing: Understanding and Treating Attachment Disorder in Children and Families.* Washington, DC: Child Welfare League of America.

Lezak, M. D. (1995). *Neuropsychological Assessment* (3rd ed.). New York: Oxford University Press.

Lichtenberg, J. D. (1990). Einige Parallelen zwischen den Ergebnissen der Saeuglingsbeobachtung und klinischen Beobachtungen an Erwachsenen, besonders Borderline-Patienten und Patienten mit narzisstischer Persoenlichkeitsstoerung. *Psyche, 10,* 871–901.

Lichtenberg, J. D. (1991). *Psychoanalysis and Infant Research.* Hillsdale, NJ: Analytic Press.

Lodhi, S., and Greer, D. (1989). The speaker as listener. *Journal of the Experimental Analysis of Behavior, 51,* 353–359.

Lovinger, S. L. (1998). *Child Psychotherapy: From Initial Therapeutic Contact to Termination.* Northvale, NJ: Jason Aronson.

Lum, D. (1999). *Culturally Competent Practice.* Pacific Grove, CA: Brooks/Cole.

Luxem, M. C., and Christophersen, E. R. (1999). Elimination disorders. In S. D. D. Netherton, D. Homes, and C. E. Walker (Eds.), *Child and Adolescent Psychological Disorders: A Comprehensive Textbook* (pp. 195–223). Oxford, England: Oxford University Press.

Macciocchi, S. N., and Barth, J. T., (1996). The Halstead-Reitan Neuropsychological Test Battery. In C. S. Newmark (Ed.), *Major Psychological Assessment Instruments* (2nd ed., pp. 431–459). Boston: Allyn & Bacon.

Machover, K. (1952). *Personality Projection in the Drawing of the Human Figure.* Springfield, IL: Charles C. Thomas.

Mahoney, G., Kaiser, A., Girolametto, L., MacDonald, J., Robinson, C., Safford, P., and Spiker, D. (1999). Parent education in early intervention: A call for a renewed focus. *Topics in Early Childhood Special Education, 19,* 131–142.

Malchiodi, C. A. (1997). *Breaking the Silence: Art Therapy with Children from Violent Homes.* New York: Brunner/Mazel.

Malchiodi, C. A. (1998). *Understanding Children's Drawings.* New York: Guilford.

March, J. S. (Ed.). (1995). *Anxiety Disorders in Children and Adolescents.* New York: Guilford

Marcus, I. W., and Marcus, P. (1990). *Scary Night Visitors: A Story for Children with Bedtime Fears.* New York: Magination.

Markwardt, F. C. (1989). *Manual for the Peabody Individual Achievement Test-Revised (PIAT-R).* Circle Pines, MN: American Guidance Service.

Martin, G., and Pear, J. (1998). *Behavior Modification: What It Is and How To Do It* (6th ed). Englewood Cliffs, NJ: Prentice Hall.

Mash, E. J., and Barkley, R. A. (1996). *Child psychopathology.* New York: Guilford.

Mash, E. J., and Barkley, R. A. (Eds.) (1998). *Treatment of Childhood Disorders* (2nd ed.). New York: Guilford.

Masterson, J. F. (1985). *The Real Self: A Developmental, Self and Object Relations Approach.* New York: Brunner/Mazel.

Matsumoto, D. (1994). *Cultural Influences on Research Methods and Statistics.* Pacific Grove, CA: Brooks/Cole.

McBride, B. A. (1991). Parent education and support programs for fathers: Outcome effects on paternal involvement. *Early Childhood Development and Care, 67,* 73–85.

McConaughy, S. H., and Achenbach, T. M. (1994). *Manual for the Semistructured Clinical Interview for Children and Adolescents.* Burlington, VT: ASEBA, Department of Psychiatry, University of Vermont.

McGoldrick, M., and Gerson, R. (1999). *Genograms: Assessment and Intervention* (2nd ed). New York: W. W. Norton.

McGoldrick, M., Pearce, J. K., and Giordano, J. (Eds.). (1996). *Ethnicity and Family Therapy* (2nd ed.). New York: Guilford.

McGrath, P., and Axelson, J. A. (1993). *Accessing Awareness and Developing Knowledge: Foundations for Skill in a Multicultural Society.* Pacific Grove, CA: Brooks/Cole.

McKenna, K., Gordon, C. T., and Rapoport, J. L. (1994). Childhood-onset schizophrenia: Timely neurobiological research. *Journal of the American Academy of Child & Adolescent Psychiatry, 33,* 771–781.

Melton, G. B. (1991). Socialization in the global community: Respect for the dignity of children. *American Psychologist, 46,* 66–71.

Melton, G. B., Ehrenreich, N. S., and Lyons, P. M. (2001). Ethical and legal issues in mental health services for children. In C. E. Walker and M. C. Roberts (Eds.), *Handbook of Clinical Child Psychology* (3rd ed., pp. 1074–1093), New York: Wiley.

Miller, A., and Ward, R. (1996). *The Drama of the Gifted Child: The Search for the True Self* (3rd ed.). New York: Basic Books.

Miller, C., and Boe, J. (1990). Tears into diamonds: Transformation of child psychic trauma through sandplay and storytelling. *Arts in Psychotherapy, 17,* 247–257.

Miller, P. J., and Moore, B. B. (1989). Narrative conjunction of caregiver and child: A comparative perspective in socialization through stories. *Ethos, 17,* 429–449.

Mills, J. C., and Crowley, R. A. (1986). *Therapeutic Metaphors for Children.* New York: Brunner/Mazel.

Minuchin, S., Simon, G. M., and Lee, W-Y. (1996). *Mastering Family Therapy: Journeys of Growth and Transformation.* New York: Wiley.

Monges, M. M. (1998). Beyond the melting pot: A values clarification exercise for teachers and human service professionals. In T. M. Singelis (Ed.), *Teaching about Culture, Ethnicity, and Diversity: Exercises and Planned Activities* (pp. 3–8). Thousand Oaks, CA: Sage.

Morgan, J. R., Nu'Man-Sheppard, J., and Allin, D. W. (1990). Prevention through parent training: Three preventive parent education programs. *Journal of Primary Prevention, 10,* 321–332.

Morris, R. J. and Kratochwill, T. R. (Eds.). (1998). *The Practice of Child Therapy* (3rd ed.). Boston: Allyn & Bacon.

Morrison, J., and Anders, T. F. (1999). *Interviewing Children and Adolescents: Skills and Strategies for Effective DSM-IV-IV Diagnosis.* New York: Guilford.

Mueller, E., and Tingley, E. (1990). The Bear's Picnic: Children's representations of themselves and their families. *New Directions for Child Development, 48,* 47–65.

Murphy, J. (2001). *Art Therapy with Young Survivors of Sexual Abuse: Lost for Words.* New York: Brunner/Mazel.

Namyniuk, L. (1996, November). *Cultural considerations in substance abuse treatment.* Paper presented at the 3rd Biennial Conference of the Alaska Psychological Association, Anchorage, AK.

Namyniuk, L., Brems, C., and Clarson, S. (1997). Dena A Coy: A model program for the treatment of pregnant substance-abusing women. *Journal of Substance Abuse Treatment, 14,* 285–298.

National Association of School Psychologists. (1997). *Principles for Professional Practice.* Bethesda, MD: Author.

Naumberg, M. (1966). *Dynamically Oriented Art Therapy: Its Principles and Practice.* New York: Grune and Stratton.

Nemiroff, M. A., and Annunziata, J. (1990). *A Child's First Book about Play Therapy.* Washington, DC: American Psychological Association.

Netherton, S. D. D., Holmes, D., and Walker, C. E. (Eds.). (1999). *Child and Adolescent Psychological Disorders: A Comprehensive Textbook.* Oxford, England: Oxford University Press.

Newman, B. M., and Newman, P. R. (1998). *Development Through Life: A Psychosocial Approach* (7th ed.). Pacific Grove, CA: Brooks/Cole.

Nichols, M. P., Schwartz, R. C., and Minuchin, S. (1994). *Family Therapy: Concepts & Methods* (3rd ed.). Boston: Allyn & Bacon.

Nicholson, B. C., Janz, P. C., and Fox, R. A. (1998). Evaluating a brief parental-education program for parents of young children. *Psychological Reports, 82,* 1107–1113

Novick, J. (1982). Termination: Themes and issues. *Psychoanalytic Inquiry, 2,* 329–365.

Novick, J., Benson, R., and Rembar, J. (1981). Patterns of termination in an outpatient clinic for children and adolescents. *Journal of the American Academy for Child Psychiatry, 20,* 834–844.

Oates, R. K. (1996). *The Spectrum of Child Abuse.* New York: Brunner/Mazel

O'Conner, K. J. (2000). *The Play Therapy Primer* (2nd ed.). New York: Wiley.

Ogden, D. (1979). *Psychodiagnostics and Personality Assessment: A Handbook* (2nd ed.). Los Angeles: Western Psychological Corporation.

Ogden, T. H. (1993). *Projective Identification and Psychotherapeutic Technique.* (2nd ed.). Northvale, NJ: Jason Aronson.

Ollendick, T. H., and Hersen, M. (1997). *Handbook of Child Psychopathology* (3rd ed.). Norwell, MA: Kluwer Academic.

Olness, K., and Kohen, D. P. (1996). *Hypnosis and Hypnotherapy with Children* (3rd ed.). New York: Guilford.

One-Third of a Nation. (1988). *A Report of the Commission on Minority Participation in Education and American Life.* Washington, DC: American Council on Education.

Oster, G. D., and Gould, P. (1987). *Using Drawings in Assessment and Therapy: A Guide for Mental Health Professionals.* New York: Brunner/Mazel.

Overstreet, S., Nelson, C. C., and Holden E. W. (1999). Adjustment disorders in children and adolescents, In S. D. D. Netherton, D. Holmes and C. E. Walker, C. E. (Eds), *Child and Adolescent Psychological Disorders: A Comprehensive Textbook* (pp. 464–476). Oxford, England: Oxford University Press.

Owens, R. E., Jr. (2001). *Language Development: An Introduction* (5th ed.). Boston: Allyn & Bacon.

Papay, J. J., and Spielberger, C. D. (1986). Assessment of anxiety and achievement in kindergarten and first- and second-grade children. *Journal of Abnormal Child Psychology, 14,* 279–286.

Patterson, G. R. (1977). *Living With Children: New Methods for Parents and Teachers* (rev. ed.). Champaign, IL: Research Press.

Patterson, G. R., and Gullion, M. E. (1974). *Living with Children: New Methods for Parents and Teachers (rev. ed.).* Champaign, IL: Research Press.

Pavlov, I. P. (1927). *Conditioned Reflexes.* London: Oxford University Press.

Pearce, S. S. (1995). *Flash of Insight: Metaphor and Narrative in Therapy.* Boston: Allyn & Bacon.

Pearson, M. (1998). *Emotional Healing and Self-Esteem: Inner-Life Skills of Relaxation, Visualisation and Meditation for Children and Adolescents.* Sterling, VA: Stylus.

Pedersen, P. (2000). *A Handbook for Developing Multicultural Awareness* (3rd ed.). Alexandria, VA: American Counseling Association.

Pedersen, P. B., Lonner, W. J., Draguns, J. G., and Trimble, J. E. (Eds.). (1996). *Counseling Across Cultures* (4th ed.). Honolulu: University of Hawaii Press.

Pehrson, K. L., and Robinson, C. C. (1990). Parent education: Does it make a difference? *Child Study Journal, 20,* 221–236.

Pellowski, A. (1990). *The World of Storytelling.* Bronx, NY: H. W. Wilson.

Peterson, R. W. (1988). The collaborative metaphor technique: Using Eriksonian techniques and principles in child, family, and youth care work. *Journal of Child Care, 3,* 11–27.

Pfannenstiel, J. C., and Seltzer, D. A. (1989). New parents and teachers: Evaluation of an early parent education program. *Early Childhood Research Quarterly, 4,* 1–18.

Phinney, J. S. (1990). Ethnic identity in adolescents and adults: Review of research. *Psychological Bulletin, 108,* 499–514.

Phinney, J. S. (1996). When we talk about American ethnic groups, what do we mean? *American Psychologist, 51,* 918–927.

Piaget, J. (1967). Genesis and structure in the psychology of intelligence. *Six Psychological Studies by Piaget.* Chicago: Random House.

Piers, E. V. (1984). *Revised Manual for the Piers-Harris Children's Self-Concept Scale.* Los Angeles, CA: Western Psychological Services.

Pietrofesa, J. J., Pietrofesa, C. J., and Pietrofesa, J. D. (1990). The mental health counselor and duty to warn. *Journal of Mental Health Counseling, 12,* 129–137.

Ponterotto, J. G., and Alexander, C. M. (1996). Assessing the multicultural competence of counselors and clinicians. In L. A. Suzuki, P. J. Meller, and J. G. Ponterotto (Eds.), *Handbook of Multicultural Assessment* (pp. 651–672). New York: Jossey-Bass.

Ponterotto, J. G., and Casas, J. M. (1991). *Handbook of Racial/Ethnic Minority Counseling Research.* Springfield, IL: Charles C. Thomas.

Ponterotto, J. G., Casas, J. M., Suzuki, L. A., and Alexander, C. M. (2001). *Handbook of Multicultural Counseling* (2nd ed.). Thousand Oaks, CA: Sage.

Popkin, M. H. (1983a). *Active Parenting Handbook.* Atlanta: Active Parenting.

Popkin, M. H. (1983b). *Active Parenting Action Guide.* Atlanta: Active Parenting, Inc.

Porter, R. B., and Cattell, R. B. (1985). *Handbook for the Children's Personality Questionnaire (CPQ).* Champaign, IL: Institute for Personality and Ability Testing.

Powell, D. R. (1983). Evaluating parent education programs: Problems and prospects. *Studies in Educational Evaluation, 8,* 253–259.

Powers, S. W. (2001). Behavior therapy with children. In C. E. Walker and M. C. Roberts (Eds.), *Handbook of Clinical Child Psychology* (3rd ed., pp. 825–839). New York: Wiley.

Putnam, F. W. (1996). Posttraumatic stress disorder in children and adolescents. *American Psychiatric Press Review of Psychiatry, 15,* 447–467.

Rabin, A. I. (1974). *Assessment with Projective Techniques.* New York: Springer.

Rambert, M. L. (1964). The use of drawings as a method of child pychoanalysis. In M. R. Haworth (Ed.), *Child Psychotherapy* (pp. 340–349). New York: Basic Books.

Rapoport, J. L., and Ismond, D. R. (1996). *DSM-IV Training Guide for Diagnosis of Childhood Disorders.* Levittown, PA: Brunner/Mazel.

Reid, W. H. (1997). *The Treatment of Psychiatric Disorders: Revised for DSM-IV* (3rd ed.). New York: Brunner/Mazel.

Reinherz, H. Z., Giaconia, R. M., Paradis, A. D., Wasserman, M. S., and Hauf, A. M. C. (2000). General and specific childhood risk factors for depression and drug disorders by early adulthood. *Journal of the American Academy of Child & Adolescent Psychiatry, 39,* 223–231.

Reynolds, C. R., and Kamphaus, R. W. (1992). *Manual for the Behavior Assessment System for Children.* Circle Pines, MN: American Guidance Service.

Reynolds, W. M. (1989). *Reynolds Child Depression Scale: Professional Manual.* Odessa, FL: Psychological Assessment Resources.

Reynolds, W. M., and Richmond, B. O. (1978). What I Think and Feel: A revised measure of children's manifest anxiety. *Journal of Abnormal Child Psychology, 6,* 271–280.

Richardson, T. Q., and Molinaro, K. L. (1996). White counselor self-awareness: A prerequisite for developing multicultural competence. *Journal of Counseling and Development, 74,* 238–242.

Richman, L. C., and Wood, K. M. (1999). Psychological assessment and treatment of communication disorders: Childhood language subtypes. In S. D. D. Netherton, D. Holmes, and C. E. Walker, C. E. (Eds), *Child and Adolescent Psychological Disorders: A Comprehensive Textbook* (pp. 51–75). Oxford, England: Oxford University Press.

Riley, S. (1987). The advantages of art therapy in an outpatient clinic. American Journal of Art Therapy, 26, 21–29.

Roberts, M. C., and Walker, C. E. (1997). *Casebook of Child and Pediatric Psychology.* New York: Guilford.

Robertson, M., and Barford, F. (1979). Story making in the psychotherapy with a chronically ill child. In C. Schaefer (Ed.), *The Therapeutic Use of Child's Play.* Northvale, NJ.

Rodd, J. (1990). Some training considerations for leaders of parent education groups. *Australian Journal of Sex, Marriage & Family, 11,* 100–108.

Rogers, C. R. (1961) *On becoming a person.* Boston: Houghton Mifflin.

Rorschach, H. (1942). *Psychodiagnostics: A Diagnostic Test Based on Perception.* Bern: Huber, 1942 (1st German Edition, 1921; U. S. distributor: Grune and Strutton).

Rothbaum, F., and Weisz, J. R. (1989). *Child Psychopathology and the Quest for Control.* Newbury Park, CA: Sage Publications.

Rothstein, A., Benjamin, L., Crosby, M., and Eisenstadt, K. (1999). *Learning Disorders: An Integration of Neuropsychological and Psychoanalytic Considerations.* Madison, CT: International Universities Press.

Rubin, J. A. (1998). *Art Therapy: An Introduction.* Philadelphia: Taylor & Francis.

Rubin, J. A. (2001). *Approaches to Art Therapy: Theory and Technique.* Philadelphia: Psychology Press.

Rubin, R. (1978). *Bibliotherapy sourcebook.* Phoenix, AZ: Oryz Press.

Russ, S. R., and Freedheim, D. K. (2001). Psychotherapy with children. In C. E. Walker and M. C. Roberts (Eds.), *Handbook of Clinical Child Psychology* (3rd ed). New York: Wiley.

Samuda, R. J. (1998). *Psychological Testing of American Minorities* (2nd ed.). Thousand Oaks, CA: Sage.

Sandler, J., Kennedy, H., and Tyson, R. (1980). *The Technique of Child Psychoanalysis.* Cambridge, MA: Harvard University Press.

Sanville, J. (1987). Creativity and the constructing of the self. *Psychoanalytic Review, 74,* 263–279.

Satir, V. (1967). *Conjoint Family Therapy: A Guide to Theory and Technique.* Palo Alto, CA: Science and Behavior Books.

Sattler, J. M. (1992). *Assessment of Children* (3rd ed.). La Mesa, CA: Author.

Scarf, M. (1987). *Intimate Partners.* New York: Random House.

Schaefer, C. E. (Ed.). (1995). *Clinical Handbook of Sleep Disorders in Children.* Northvale, NJ: Jason Aronson.

Schaefer, C. E. (1998a). *Childhood Encopresis and Enuresis: Causes and Therapy.* Northvale, NJ: Jason Aronson.

Schaefer, C. E. (1998b). *The Therapeutic Powers of Play.* Northvale, NJ: Jason Aronson.

Schaefer, C. E. (2000). *The Therapeutic Use of Child's Play.* Northvale, NJ: Jason Aronson.

Schaefer, C. E., Millman, H. L., Sichel, S. M., and Zwilling, J. R. (1986). *Advances in Therapies for Children.* San Francisco: Jossey-Bass.

Schaefer, C. E., and Reid, S. E. (2000). *Game Play: Therapeutic Use of Childhood Games.* New York: Wiley.

Schickedanz, J. A., Schickedanz, D. I., Forsyth, P. D., and Forsyth, G. A. (2000). *Understanding Children and Adolescents.* Boston: Allyn & Bacon.

Schinka, J. A. (1988). *Student Referral Checklist for Grades K–6.* Odessa, FL: Psychological Assessment Resources.

Schroeder, C. S., and Gordon, B. N. (1991). *Assessment and Treatment of Childhood Problems.* New York: Guilford.

Schwartz, E. K. (1964). A psychoanalytic study of the fairy tale. In M. R. Haworth (Ed.), *Child Psychotherapy* (pp. 383–395). New York: Basic Books.

Sedlak, A. J. (1990). *Technical Amendment to the Study Findings—National Incidence and Prevalence of Child Abuse and Neglect: 1988.* Rockville, MD: Westat.

Seifer, R. (2000). Temperament and goodness of fit: Implications for developmental psychopathology. In A. J. Sameroff, M. Lewis, and S. M. Miller (Eds.), *Handbook of Developmental Psychopathology* (2nd ed., pp. 257–276). New York: Plenum

Shadle, C., and Graham, J. (1981). *The Talking/Listening Game.* San Luis Obispo, CA: Dandy Lion.

Shaffer, D. R. (2000). *Social and Personality Development* (4th ed.). Pacific Grove, CA: Brooks/Cole.

Shaffer, D., Lucas, C. P., and Richters, J. E. (Eds.). (1999). *Diagnostic Assessment in Child and Adolescent Psychopathology.* New York: Guilford.

Shapiro, E. S., and Kratochwill, T. R. (Eds.). (2000). *Conducting School-Based Assessments of Child and Adolescent Behavior.* New York: Guilford.

Sharma, P., and Lucero-Miller. D. (1998). Beyond political correctness. In T. M. Singelis (Ed.), *Teaching about Culture, Ethnicity, and Diversity: Exercises and Planned Activities* (pp. 191–194). Thousand Oaks, CA: Sage.

Sherman, M. H. (1990). Family narratives: Internal representations of family relationships and affective themes. *Infant Mental Health Journal, 11,* 253–258.

Short, K. H., and Johnston, C. (1994). Ethnocultural parent education in Canada: Current status and directions. *Canadian Journal of Community Mental Health, 13,* 43–54.

Simmons, J. E. (1987). *Psychiatric Examination of Children* (4th ed.). Philadelphia: Lea and Febinger.

Sinason, V. (1988). Dolls and bears: From symbolic equation to symbol. *British Journal of Psychotherapy, 4,* 349–363.

Singelis, T. M. (Ed.) (1998). *Teaching about Culture, Ethnicity, and Diversity: Exercises and Planned Activities.* Thousand Oaks, CA: Sage.

Singelis, T. M., and Brown, W. J. (1995). Culture, self, and collectivist communication: Linking culture to individual behavior. *Human Communications Research, 21,* 354–389.

Singelis, T. M., Triandis, H. C., Bhawuk, D. S., and Gelfand, M. J. (1995). Horizontal and vertical dimensions of individualism and collectivism: A theoretical and measurement refinement. *Cross-Cultural Research, 29,* 240–275.

Skinner, B. F. (1971). *Beyond Freedom and Dignity.* New York: Knopf.

Skinner, B. F. (1976). *About Behaviorism.* New York: Random House.

Slavenburg, J. H., Kendall, P. C., and Van Bilsen, H. P. (Eds.). (1995). *Behavioral Approaches for Children and Adolescents: Challenges for the Next Century.* Boulder, CO: Perseus.

Smith, C. A. (1989). *From Wonder to Wisdom: Using Stories to Help Children Grow.* New York: New American Library.

Sodowsky, G. R., Taffe, R. C., Gutkin, T., and Wise, C. L. (1994). Development of the Multicultural Counseling Inventory: A self-report measure of multicultural competencies. *Journal of Counseling Psychology, 41,* 137–148.

Sparrow, S. S., Balla, D. A., and Cicchetti, D. V. (1984). *Vineland Adaptive Behavior Scales.* Circle Pines: American Guidance Service.

Speier, P. L., Sherak, D. L., Hirsch, S., and Cantwell, D. P. (1995). Depression in children and adolescents. In E. E. Beckham and W. Leber (Eds.), *Handbook of Depression* (2nd ed., pp. 467–493). New York: Guilford.

Spiegel, S. (1961). The use of puppets as a therapeutic tool with children. *Virginia Medical Monthly, 88,* 272–275.

Spiegel, S. (1989). *An interpersonal approach to child therapy.* New York: Columbia University Press.

Spiegel, S. (1996). *An Interpersonal Approach to Child & Adolescent Psychotherapy.* Northvale, NJ: Jason Aronson.

Spiegler, M. D., and Guevremont, D. C. (1997). *Contemporary Behavior Therapy* (3rd ed.). Pacific Grove, CA: Brooks/Cole.

Spielberger, C. D. (1973). *Preliminary Manual for the State-Trait Anxiety Inventory for Children ("How I*

Feel Questionnaire"). Palo Alto, CA: Consulting Psychologists.

Spitzer, R. L., Gibbon, M., Skodol, A. E., Williams, J. B. W. and First, M. B. (1994). *DSM-IV Casebook.* Washington, DC: American Psychiatric Press.

Stern, D. N. (1977). *The First Relationship: Infant and Mother.* Cambridge, MA: Harvard University Press.

Stern, D. N. (1985). *The Interpersonal World of the Infant.* New York: Basic Books.

Stern, D. N. (1989). The representation of relational patterns. In A. J. Sameroff and R. N. Emde (Eds.), *Relationships and Relationship Disorders.* New York: Basic Books.

Stiles, K., and Kottman, T. (1990). Mutual storytelling: An intervention for depressed and suicidal children. *School Counselor, 37,* 337–342.

Straus, M. B. (1999). *No-Talk Therapy for Children and Adolescents.* New York: Norton.

Sue, D. W., and Sue, D. (1999). *Counseling the Culturally Different: Theory and Practice* (3rd ed.). New York Wiley.

Sue, S., Allen, D. B., and Conaway, L. (1978). The responsiveness and equality of mental health care to Chicanos and Native Americans. *American Journal of Community Psychology, 6,* 137–146.

Sullivan, A., and Brems, C. (1997). The psychological repercussions of the sociocultural oppression of Alaska Native peoples. *Genetic, Social, and General Psychology Monographs, 123,* 411–440.

Suzuki, L. A., Meller, P. J., and Ponterotto, J. G. (2000). *Handbook of Multicultural Assessment: Clinical, Psychological, and Educational Applications* (2nd ed.). New York: Jossey-Bass.

Swenson, L. C. (1997). *Psychology and the Law* (2nd ed.). Pacific Grove, CA: Brooks/Cole.

Tansey, M. J., and Burke, W. F. (1995). *Understanding Countertransference:From Projective Identification to Empathy.* Hillsdale, NJ: Analytic Press.

Tataki, R. T. (1993). *A Different Mirror: A History of Multicultural America.* Boston: Little, Brown.

Teyber, E. (2000). *Interpersonal Process in Psychotherapy* (4th ed). Pacific Grove, CA: Brooks/Cole.

Thomas, R. M. (2000). *Comparing Theories of Child Development* (5th ed.). Belmont, CA: Wadsworth.

Thompson, C. L. and Rudolf, L. B. (2000). *Counseling Children* (5th ed.). Pacific Grove, CA: Brooks/Cole.

Thorndike, R. L., Hagan, E. P., and Sattler, J. M. (1986). *Guide for Administering and Scoring the Stanford-Binet Intelligence Scale: Fourth Edition.* Chicago: Riverside Publishing.

Todres, R., and Bunston, T. (1993). Parent education program evaluation: A review of the literature. *Canadian Journal of Community Mental Health, 12,* 225–257.

Tramontana, M. G., Sherrets, S. D., and Authier, K. J. (1980). Evaluation of parent education programs. *Journal of Child Clinical Psychology, 9,* 40–43.

Triandis, H. C. (1989). The self and social behavior in differing cultural contexts. *Psychological Review, 96,* 506–520.

United Nations General Assembly. (1989). *Adoption of a Convention on the Rights of the Child.* New York: Author.

U. S. Census Bureau. (1980). *Population Profile of the United States: 1980. Population Characteristics* (Series P-25, No. 952). Washington, DC: U.S. Government Printing Office.

U.S. Census Bureau. (2001). *Census 2000 Redistricting Data (P.L. 94-171).* Washington, DC: U.S. Government Printing Office.

Volkmar, F. R. (1996). Childhood and adolescent psychosis: A review of the past ten years. *Journal of the American Academy of Child and Adolescent Psychiatry, 35,* 843–851.

Walker, A. J., Noble, C. A., and Self, P. A. (2001). Cross-cultural research with children and families. In C. E. Walker and M. C. Roberts (Eds.), *Handbook of Clinical Child Psychology* (3rd ed.). New York: John Wiley and Sons.

Walker, C. E. (1998). Elimination disorders: Enuresis and encopresis. In M. C. Roberts (Ed.), *Handbook of Pediatric Psychology* (2nd ed., pp. 537–557). New York: Guilford.

Walker, C. E., Bonner, B. L., and Kaufman, K. L. (1988). *The Physically and Sexually Abused Child: Evaluation and Treatment.* New York: Pergamon.

Walker, N. E., Brooks, C. M., and Wrightsman, L. S. (1999). *Children's Rights in the United States: In Search of a National Policy.* Thousand Oaks, CA: Sage.

Webb, N. B. (1999). *Play Therapy with Children in Crisis: Individual, Group, and Family Treatment.* New York: Guilford.

Wechsler, D. (1967). *Manual for the Wechsler Preschool and Primary Scale of Intelligence.* San Antonio: The Psychological Corporation.

Wechsler, D. (1974). *Manual for the Wechsler Intelligence Scale for Children—Revised.* San Antonio: The Psychological Corporation.

Wechsler, D. (1989). *Manual for the Wechsler Preschool and Primary Scale of Intelligence—Revised.* San Antonio: The Psychological Corporation.

Wechsler, D. (1991). *Manual for the Wechsler Intelligence Scale for Children—Three.* San Antonio: The Psychological Corporation.

Wechsler, D. (1999). *Manual for the Wechsler Abbreviated Scale of Intelligence.* San Antonio, TX: Psychological Corporation.

Wechsler, D. (2001). *Manual for the Wechsler Individual Achievement Test—Second ed.* San Antonio, TX: Psychological Corporation.

Weeks, W. H., Pedersen, P. B., and Brislin, R. W. (1986). *A Manual of Structured Experiences for Cross-cultural Learning.* Yarmouth, ME: Intercultural.

Wenar, C. (1982). Developmental psychopathology: Its nature and models. *Journal of Clinical Child Psychology, 11,* 192–201.

Wenar, C., and Kerig, P. (1999). *Developmental Psychopathology* (4th ed.). New York: McGraw-Hill.

Werry, J. S. and Aman, M. G. (1999). *Practitioner's Guide to Psychoactive Drugs for Children and Adolescents.* New York: Plenum.

Westen, D., Klepser, J., Ruffins, S. A., Silverman, M., Lifton, N., and Boekamp, J. (1991). Object relations in childhood and adolescence: The development of working representations. *Journal of Consulting and Clinical Psychology, 59,* 400–409.

Wester, J. (1991). *Clinical Hypnosis with Children.* New York: Brunner/Mazel.

Whitehurst, G. J. (1982). Language development. In B. B. Wolman (Ed.), *Handbook of Developmental Psychology* (pp. 367–386). Englewood Cliffs, NJ: Prentice Hall.

Whitmore, K., Willems, G., and Hart, H. (2000). *A Neurodevelopmental Approach to Specific Learning Disorders.* Cambridge, England: Cambridge University Press.

Wicks-Nelson, R., and Israel, A. C. (1999). *Behavior Disorders of Childhood* (4th ed.). New York: Prentice-Hall.

Wilcox, B. L., and Naimark, H. (1991). The Rights of the Child: Progress toward human dignity. *American Psychologist, 46,* 49–52.

Wilkinson, G. S. (1993). *Manual for the Wide Range Achievement Test—Third Edition.* Lutz, FL: Psychological Assessment Resources.

Wimbarti, S., and Self, P. A. (1992). Developmental psychology for the clinical child psychologist. In C. E. Walker and M. C. Roberts (Eds.), *Handbook of Clinical Child Psychology* (2nd ed., pp. 33–46). New York: John Wiley.

Wirt, R. D., Lachar, D., Klinedinst, J. K., and Seat, P. D. (1977). *Multidimensional Description of Child Personality: A Manual for the Personality Inventory for Children.* Los Angeles: Western Psychological Services.

Wirth, L. (1945). The problem of minority groups. In R. Linton (Ed.), *The Science of Man in the World Crisis* (pp. 347–372). New York: Columbia University Press.

Wolpe, J. (1958). *Psychotherapy by Reciprocal Inhibition.* Stanford, CA: Stanford University Press.

Woltman, A. G. (1964). Concepts of play therapy techniques. In M. R. Haworth (Ed.), *Child Psychotherapy.* New York: Basic Books.

Woodcock, R. W., and Johnson, M. B. (1989). *Woodcock-Johnson Psycho-Educational Battery—Revised.* Allen, TX: DLM Teaching Resources.

Woodcock, R. W., McGrew, K. S., and Mather, N. (2000). *Manual for the Woodcock Johnson Complete Battery.* Itasca, IL: Riverside.

Wright, L., Stroud, R., and Kennan, M. (1993). Indirect treatment of children via parent training: A burgeoning form of secondary prevention. *Applied and Preventative Psychology, 2,* 191–200.

Zakich, R. (1975). *The Ungame.* Placentia, CA: The Ungame Company.

Zakich, R., and Monroe, S. (1979). *Reunion.* Placentia, CA: The Ungame Company.

Zeanah, C. H., Anders, T. F., Seifer, R., and Stern, D. N. (1991). Implications of research on infant development for psychodynamic theory and practice. In S. Chess and M. E. Hertzig (Eds.). *Annual Progress in Child Psychiatry and Child Development* (pp. 5–34). New York: Brunner/Mazel.

Zellman, G. L. (1990). Child abuse reporting and failure to report among mandated reporters. *Journal of Interpersonal Violence, 5,* 3–22.

Zinn, H. (1995). *A People's History of the United States.* New York: Harper.

Zucker, K. J., and Bradley, S. J. (1999). Gender identity disorders and transvestic fetishes. In S. D. D. Netherton, D. Holmes and C. E. Walker, C. E. (Eds), *Child and Adolescent Psychological Disorders: A Comprehensive Textbook* (pp. 367–396). Oxford, England: Oxford University Press.

Zwiers, M. L., and Morrissette, P. J. (1999). *Effective Interviewing of Children: A Comprehensive Guide for Counselors and Human Service Workers.* Philadelphia: Accelerated Development.

AUTHOR INDEX

SUBJECT INDEX